Lecture Notes in Computer Scie

Edited by G. Goos, J. Hartmanis and J. van

Springer
Berlin
Heidelberg
New York
Barcelona
Hong Kong
London
Milan
Paris
Singapore
Tokyo

Michael Kerckhove (Ed.)

Scale-Space and Morphology in Computer Vision

Third International Conference, Scale-Space 2001
Vancouver, Canada, July 7-8, 2001
Proceedings

Springer

Series Editors

Gerhard Goos, Karlsruhe University, Germany
Juris Hartmanis, Cornell University, NY, USA
Jan van Leeuwen, Utrecht University, The Netherlands

Volume Editor

Michael Kerckhove
University of Richmond, Dept. of Mathematics & Computer Science
Richmond, VA 23173, USA
E-mail: mkerckho@richmond.edu

Cataloging-in-Publication Data applied for

Die Deutsche Bibliothek - CIP-Einheitsaufnahme

Scale space and morphology in computer vision : third international
conference, scale space 2001, Vancouver, Canada, July, 7 - 8, 2001 ;
proceedings / Michael Kerckhove (ed.). - Berlin ; Heidelberg ; New York ;
Barcelona ; Hong Kong ; London ; Milan ; Paris ; Singapore ; Tokyo :
Springer, 2001
    (Lecture notes in computer science ; Vol. 2106)
    ISBN 3-540-42317-6

CR Subject Classification (1998): I.4, I.3.5, I.5, I.2.10

ISSN 0302-9743
ISBN 3-540-42317-6 Springer-Verlag Berlin Heidelberg New York

Springer-Verlag Berlin Heidelberg New York
a member of BertelsmannSpringer Science+Business Media GmbH

http://www.springer.de

© Springer-Verlag Berlin Heidelberg
jointly with IEEE Computer Society Los Alamitos, CA
Printed in Germany

Typesetting: Camera-ready by author, data conversion by Christian Grosche, Hamburg
Printed on acid-free paper   SPIN: 10839532   06/3142   5 4 3 2 1 0

Preface

The scale-space conference series dates back to the NSF/ESPRIT transatlantic collaboration on "geometry-driven diffusion" (1993–1996). This collaboration led to a series of very successful workshops followed by a PhD summer school on Gaussian Scale-Space Theory in Copenhagen, in the spring of 1996. The following year, the First International Conference on Scale-Space Theory in Computer Vision (Utrecht, July, 1997) was held. The series of international conferences has now grown to three. As was the case for the Second International Conference (Corfu, September 1999), the 2001 conference was affiliated with the ICCV as one of its several workshops. Entitled the "Workshop on Scale-Space and Morphology", the purpose of the conference was to encourage the exchange of information and to foster interactions among researchers in scale-space theory in computer vision and mathematical morphology. With the publication of these proceedings, we feel that our purposes have been accomplished.

The conference was held for the first time in North America, and succeeded in attracting participants from the western hemisphere and the pacific rim. A concerted effort was also made to make the workshop attractive to and affordable for graduate students. Of 60 high-quality submissions (including many papers in the subject areas that were accepted at ICCV or the overlapping Workshop on Variational and Level Set Methods), 18 papers were selected for oral presentations. They form Part I of this volume. Part 2 of the volume consists of 23 papers accepted for poster presentations. Invited talks were given by Professor Jitendra Malik, of the Computer Vision Group at the University of California at Berkeley, and by Professor Amiram Grinvald, of the Weizmann Institute of Science in Rehovot, Israel.

On behalf of the Program Board, I would like to thank the authors for their excellent presentations and written work; the referees for their time and valuable comments (each paper was reviewed by 3 referees); and the members of the General Board for their guidance in putting the conference together. We are grateful to the IEEE Computer Society (especially to Keith Price and Tom Fink for their assistance), to the ICCV Workshops Chair Jim Clark, and to Jim Little and David Lowe, the local organizers for ICCV in Vancouver. On a personal note I would like to thank the members of the Program Board, who kept me on course and encouraged me toward the finish line in preparing this volume, and to thank Libbie Geiger at the University of Richmond for her secretarial assistance. Finally, the conference participants deserve recognition for making the event both enjoyable and worthwhile.

May 2001   Michael Kerckhove

Organizers

General Board

Michael Kerckhove (University of Richmond, USA)
Pietro Perona (California Institute of Technology, University of Padua, Italy)
Bart ter Haar Romeny (Image Sciences Institute, Utrecht University, The Netherlands)
Stephen Pizer (University of North Carolina - Chapel Hill, USA)
Guillermo Sapiro (University of Minnesota, USA)

Program Board

Michael Kerckhove (University of Richmond, USA)
Frederic Guichard (Poseidon / Vision IQ, Paris, France)
Ron Kimmel (Technion Israel Institute of Technology, Israel)
Tony Lindeberg (KTH, Stockholm, Sweden)
Petros Maragos (National Technical University of Athens, Greece)
Nir Sochen (Tel Aviv University, Israel)

Program Committee

Luis Alvarez, Universidad de Las Palmas de Gran Canaria
Junior Barrera, Universidade de São Paulo
Rein van den Boomgaard, University of Amsterdam
Alfred M. Bruckstein, Technion Israel Institute of Technology
Frederic Cao, CMLA ENS-Cachan
James L. Crowley, INRIA Rhone-Alpes
Rachid Deriche, INRIA Sophia Antipolis
Olivier Faugeras, INRIA Sophia Antipolis
Luc Florack, University of Utrecht
John Goutsias, Johns Hopkins University
Lewis Griffin, King's College London
Henk Heijmans, Centre for Mathematics and Computer Science (CWI)
Peter Johansen, University of Copenhagen
Renato Keshet, Hewlett-Packard Laboratories, Israel
Ben Kimia, Brown University
Jan Koenderink, University of Utrecht
Ferran Marques, Universitat Politecnica de Catalunya
Fernand Meyer, Centre de Morphologie Mathématique
Farzin Mokhtarian, University of Surrey

Mads Nielsen, IT University of Copenhagen
Wiro Niessen, Image Science Institute, Utrecht
Ole Fogh Olsen, IT University of Copenhagen
Eric Pauwels, Centre for Mathematics and Computer Science (CWI)
Joachim Rieger, Martin-Luther-Universität Halle
Jos Roerdink, University of Groningen
Philippe Salembier, Universitat Politecnica de Catalunya
Christoph Schnoerr, University of Mannheim
Jayant Shah, Northeastern University
Pierre Soille, EC Joint Research Centre, Space Applications Institute, Italy
Jon Sporring, University of Copenhagen
Luc Vincent, LizardTech Inc, USA
Joachim Weickert, University of Mannheim

Invited Adresses

Jitendra Malik (Computer Vision Group, University of California at Berkeley)
"Ecological Statistics of Grouping Cues in Natural Images"

Amiram Grinvald (Weizmann Institute of Science in Rehovot, Israel)
"Real Time Visualization of Cortical Dynamics; Linking Single Neurons to Neuronal Assemblies."

Sponsoring Institutions

IEEE Computer Society
Technical Committee on Pattern Analysis and Machine Intelligence (PAMI)

Table of Contents

Oral Presentations

Poster Presentations

Using the Vector Distance Functions to Evolve Manifolds of Arbitrary Codimension

José Gomes[1] and Olivier Faugeras[2]

[1] I.B.M Watson Research Center, Yorktown, New York, U.S.A
[2] I.N.R.I.A Sophia Antipolis, France and M.I.T, Boston, U.S.A

Abstract. We present a novel method for representing and evolving objects of arbitrary dimension. The method, called the Vector Distance Function (VDF) method, uses the vector that connects any point in space to its closest point on the object. It can deal with smooth manifolds with and without boundaries and with shapes of different dimensions. It can be used to evolve such objects according to a variety of motions, including mean curvature. If discontinuous velocity fields are allowed the dimension of the objects can change. The evolution method that we propose guarantees that we stay in the class of VDF's and therefore that the intrinsic properties of the underlying shapes such as their dimension, curvatures can be read off easily from the VDF and its spatial derivatives at each time instant. The main disadvantage of the method is its redundancy: the size of the representation is always that of the ambient space even though the object we are representing may be of a much lower dimension. This disadvantage is also one of its strengths since it buys us flexibility.

1   Introduction and History

In this paper we present a general method for representing objects of arbitrary dimension embedded in spaces of arbitrary dimension. The representation method is also the basis for evolving such objects according to a variety of motions, including mean-curvature. We are not limited to objects of constant dimension, for example we can cope with open curves or surfaces, or even with objects such as the one shown in figure 1 which is the union of an open curve, an open surface, and a volume.

The history of curves and surfaces in Computer Vision can be traced back to the early work on snakes by Kass, Witkins and Terzopoulos [14]. This pioneering work was reformulated by Caselles, Kimmel and Sapiro [6] and by Kichenassamy *et al.* [15] in the context of PDE-driven curves and surfaces. There is an extensive literature that addresses the theoretical aspects of these PDE's and offers geometrical interpretations as well as results of uniqueness and existence [10,12,7].

The level set methods were introduced by Osher and Sethian in [16] and provide both a nice theoretical framework and efficient practical tools for solving such PDE's. In these methods, the time evolution is achieved by means of a time-dependant implicit representation of the curve or surface.

M. Kerckhove (Ed.): Scale-Space 2001, LNCS 2106, pp. 1–13, 2001.

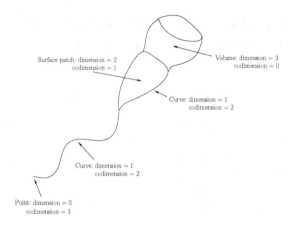

Surface patch: dimension = 2
codimension = 1

Volume: dimension = 3
codimension = 0

Curve: dimension = 1
codimension = 2

Curve: dimension = 1
codimension = 2

Point: dimension = 0
codimension = 3

Fig. 1.

But the level set methods were developed in the framework of the evolution of closed manifolds of codimension one and the case of higher codimension has been less investigated. Some recent contributions in this direction are the following.

In 1996, Ambrosio and Soner, inspired by ideas of De Giorgi, published a paper [2] in which they showed that the level-set method could be extended to the case of arbitrary codimension. Their idea is to replace the evolution of the smooth manifold under mean curvature motion by that of a tubular neighborhood of the manifold, in effect a hypersurface. They show that the evolution of this tube is related to that of the manifold in a simple way and that it is not the mean curvature motion of the hypersurface. A different approach, closer to what we propose in the present paper, has also been proposed by Sapiro and collaborators in a preliminary paper on tracking curves on a surface [4].

There are a number of problems with Ambrosio and Soner's approach, the main one being that it sweeps in some sense the dust under the rug: even though it does evolve correctly the manifold of interest, it turns out that recovering this manifold is in itself a major problem since it is not explicitly represented.

It is therefore natural to turn to a different approach and to attempt to represent an arbitrary smooth manifold $\mathcal{M}$ of dimension k as the intersection of $n - k$ hypersurfaces; the evolution of the hypersurfaces is computed in order to guarantee that their intersection evolves as required for $\mathcal{M}$ and that they remain transverse. This approach is natural since it is based on the definition of the dimension (or the codimension). It was suggested by Ambrosio and Soner in [2] but not pursued because it was thought to be too difficult. The corresponding program can nonetheless be studied, as described in [5,11]. We shall not pursue it here because it is not easy to deal with such objects as the one represented in figure 1 and to deal with changes in the dimension of the manifold during the evolution.

In 1998, Ruuth, Merriman, Xin and Osher [17], considering the particular features of the complex Ginzburg-Landau equation, introduced another method for evolving space curves according to the mean curvature motion. The curve is represented by means of a (two-dimensional) complex function of unit magnitude defined on $\mathbb{R}^3$ whose phase angle "winds" around the curve. The time evolution is "diffusion-generated", *i.e.* it is the consequence of a diffusion-renormalization loop. Very convincing results are shown demonstrating in particular the possibility for the curve to have its topology altered during the evolution. Nevertheless, this function is not defined at points of the curve of interest and it is a serious disadvantage in the context of sampled functions.

Alternatively, we shall follow a slightly counterintuitive idea that was proposed by Ruuth, Merriman and Osher in a discrete setting [18] and whose roots are in a work by Steinhoff, Fan and Wang [20]. We were inspired by the last section of this technical report and our paper elaborates on some of the suggestions of these authors and generalizes them in a variety of directions. The idea is to introduce redundancy in the representation of the manifold $\mathcal{M}$: instead of representing it as the intersection of k hypersurfaces, we propose to represent it as the intersection of n hypersurfaces. These hypersurfaces are related in a natural manner to the distance of the points of $\mathbb{R}^n$ to $\mathcal{M}$ and evolve in such a way as to guarantee that their intersection evolves according to the desired evolution for $\mathcal{M}$. Introducing this redundancy allows for more flexibility in the representation: manifolds with non constant dimensions (in space) and boundaries such as the one in figure 1 can now be represented and evolved. Their dimension can even change in time, *i.e.* increase or decrease.

The plan of the paper is as follows. In section 2 we introduce our redundant representation, called the Vector Distance Function (VDF), for arbitrary smooth manifolds of dimension k. In section 3 we study some of its differential properties. In section 4 we start looking at the problem of evolving a manifold by evolving its VDF instead: we show that this problem has a very simple solution that guarantees that the VDF remains a VDF at all times. In section 5 we discuss the problem of manifolds with a boundary and we show that it is closely related to changes in the dimension. We conclude and show a preliminary result in section 6.

2   The Vector Distance Function (VDF) to a Smooth Manifold

Let $\mathcal{M}$ be a closed subset of $\mathbb{R}^n$. For every point x we note $\delta(x)$ the distance $dist(\mathbf{x}, \mathcal{M})$ of $\mathbf{x}$ to $\mathcal{M}$. This function is Lipschitz continuous and therefore almost everywhere differentiable [9]. The same holds for the function $\eta(\mathbf{x}) = \frac{1}{2}\delta^2(\mathbf{x})$. We note $\mathbf{u}(\mathbf{x})$ its derivative, defined almost everywhere:

$$\mathbf{u}(\mathbf{x}) = D\eta(\mathbf{x}) = \delta(\mathbf{x})D\delta(\mathbf{x}).$$

This equation shows that, since $\delta(\mathbf{x})$ satisfies *a.e.* the eikonal equation,

$$\|D\delta\| = 1, \tag{1}$$

$\mathbf{u}(\mathbf{x})$ is a vector of length $\delta(\mathbf{x})$. Moreover, at a point $\mathbf{x}$ where δ is differentiable, let $\mathbf{y} = P_{\mathcal{M}}(\mathbf{x})$ be the unique projection of $\mathbf{x}$ onto $\mathcal{M}$. This point is such that

$$\delta(\mathbf{x}) = \|\mathbf{x} - \mathbf{y}\|.$$

Besides, if $\mathcal{M}$ is smooth at $\mathbf{y}$, the vector $\mathbf{x} - \mathbf{y}$ is normal to $\mathcal{M}$ at $\mathbf{y}$ and parallel to $D\delta(\mathbf{x})$:

$$\mathbf{u}(\mathbf{x}) = \mathbf{x} - \mathbf{y} \equiv \mathbf{x} - P_{\mathcal{M}}(\mathbf{x}).$$

The vectors such as $\mathbf{x} - \mathbf{y}$, normal at $\mathbf{y}$ to $\mathcal{M}$, define the *characteristics* of the distance function δ. Starting from a point $\mathbf{y}$ of $\mathcal{M}$ and following a characteristic, *i.e.* a direction in the normal space $N_{\mathbf{y}}\mathcal{M}$, we either go to infinity or reach a point $\mathbf{z}$ at finite distance where δ is not differentiable and therefore $\mathbf{u}$ is not defined. Such a point belongs to the skeleton of $\mathcal{M}$. Because of the previous properties of the function $\mathbf{u}$, we have the following proposition

Proposition 1. *Let $\mathbf{x}$ be a point of $\mathbb{R}^n$ where $\mathbf{u}$ is defined. The following relation*

$$\mathbf{u}(\mathbf{x} + \alpha\mathbf{u}(\mathbf{x})) = (1 + \alpha)\mathbf{u}(\mathbf{x}) \tag{2}$$

holds true for all values of $+\infty \geq \alpha_m > \alpha \geq -1$ such that $\mathbf{x} + \alpha_m\mathbf{u}(\mathbf{x})$ is the first point on the characteristic where $\mathbf{u}$ is not defined.

Proof. Use the equation $\mathbf{u}(\mathbf{x}) = \mathbf{x} - P_{\mathcal{M}}(\mathbf{x})$ and the fact that $P_{\mathcal{M}}(\mathbf{x} + \alpha\mathbf{u}(\mathbf{x})) = P_{\mathcal{M}}(\mathbf{x})$ for all α's such that $\alpha_m > \alpha \geq -1$.

It may be interesting to pause here and make the remark that the VDF to a smooth manifold $\mathcal{M}$ is an implicit representation of this manifold:

Proposition 2. *Let $\mathcal{M}$ be a smooth closed manifold and $\mathbf{u}$ its VDF, defined a.e.. Then*

$$\mathcal{M} = \mathbf{u}^{-1}(\mathbf{0}). \tag{3}$$

In effect, $\mathcal{M}$ is the intersection of the n hypersurfaces of equations $u_i(\mathbf{x}) = 0$, $i = 1, \cdots, n$. Since $\mathbf{u}$ represents implicitly $\mathcal{M}$, the rank of the differential $D\mathbf{u}$ of $\mathbf{u}$ which is defined *a.e.* if $\mathcal{M}$ is smooth provides some interesting information about the dimension of $\mathcal{M}$. Indeed, we have

Lemma 1. *The codimension of $\mathcal{M} = \mathbf{u}^{-1}(\mathbf{0})$ is equal to the rank of the differential $D\mathbf{u}(\mathbf{x})$ at points of $\mathcal{M}$.*

Proof. This is a particular case of the implicit function theorem. *cf* [13] for details.

This latter fact is not particular to VDF's but, as we shall see in the next section, the relation between $D\mathbf{u}$ and the codimension of $\mathcal{M}$ is even more remarkable in the case of VDF's since the codimension of $\mathcal{M}$ can be determined by the value of $D\mathbf{u}$ at points *off* $\mathcal{M}$.

Because we are interested in evolving the manifold $\mathcal{M}$ through the evolution of $\mathbf{u}$, while keeping $\mathbf{u}$ a VDF, we are interested in finding a characterization of the VDF's analogous to the one for distance functions, (1). This will be our first step in the exploration of the differential properties of the function $\mathbf{u}$ that will be pursued in the next section.

Proposition 3. *Let* $\mathbf{u} : \mathbb{R}^n \longrightarrow \mathbb{R}^n$ *be such that*

$$(D\mathbf{u})^T \mathbf{u} = \mathbf{u} \quad a.e. \tag{4}$$

and $\mathbf{u}$ *is continuous at all points of the set* $\mathcal{M} = \mathbf{u}^{-1}(\mathbf{0})$. *Then* $\mathbf{u}(\mathbf{x}) = D\eta(\mathbf{x})$ *a.e., where* $\eta(\mathbf{x})$ *is the function* $\frac{1}{2}dist^2(\mathbf{x}, \mathcal{M})$ *to the set* $\mathcal{M}$.

Proof. Define $\phi(\mathbf{x}) = \|\mathbf{u}(\mathbf{x})\|$ and compute its first order derivative with respect to $\mathbf{x}$

$$\nabla\phi = \frac{D\mathbf{u}^T \mathbf{u}}{\|\mathbf{u}\|} = \frac{\mathbf{u}}{\|\mathbf{u}\|}.$$

Hence $\|\nabla\phi\| = 1$ *a.e.*, which means that ϕ is equal to the distance function to the set $\mathcal{M}$ plus a constant: $\phi = \delta + C$. In addition, the combination of $\phi = \delta + C$ and $\phi = \|\mathbf{u}\|$ shows that $\mathbf{u} = (\delta + C)\nabla\delta$. The continuity of $\mathbf{u}$ on $\mathbf{u}^{-1}(0)$ implies that $C = 0$. Indeed, let $\mathbf{x}_0$ be a point of $\mathcal{M}$ and $\mathbf{n}$ be a unit vector of $N_{\mathbf{x}_0}\mathcal{M}$, the normal space of $\mathcal{M}$ at $\mathbf{x}_0$. We consider the line $\lambda : \mathbf{x}_0 + \lambda\mathbf{n}$ and the variations of δ and $\nabla\delta$ along this line. The product $\delta\nabla\delta$ is continuous on $\mathcal{M}$ but $\nabla\delta$ is not. Finally $\mathbf{u} = \phi\nabla\phi = \nabla\left(\frac{\delta^2}{2}\right)$.

Equation (4) is the characteristic equation of the class of Vector Distance Functions.

The previous proposition says nothing about the regularity of the set $\mathcal{M}$. In fact, the proof of proposition 3 assumes that $\mathcal{M}$ is smooth enough to have a normal space at every point. This is explained later in the paper. If we want that set to be a smooth manifold, then it is likely that $\mathbf{u}$ must satisfy some extra regularity conditions. We have not pursued this direction but a clue can be found in the paper [1] where it is shown that, given a smooth manifold $\mathcal{M}$, the first and second fundamental forms of $\mathcal{M}$ can be recovered from the *third* order derivatives of the distance function δ to $\mathcal{M}$ at all points where it is differentiable.

To provide the reader with some intuition, we show in figure 2 the VDF of a smooth manifold of dimension 1, a circle, embedded in $\mathbb{R}^2$.

3   Properties of VDF's

We now study some differential properties of the VDF $\mathbf{u}$. Most of them can be found in [2] and the others are proved in [13].

Equation (2) yields, for $\alpha = -1$ the (almost obvious) equation

$$\mathbf{u}(\mathbf{x} - \mathbf{u}(\mathbf{x})) = \mathbf{0}. \tag{5}$$

We use this equation to show the following propositions.

Proposition 4. *The derivative of a VDF satisfies the following relation at each point of* $\mathcal{M}$:

$$D\mathbf{u} = (D\mathbf{u})^2. \tag{6}$$

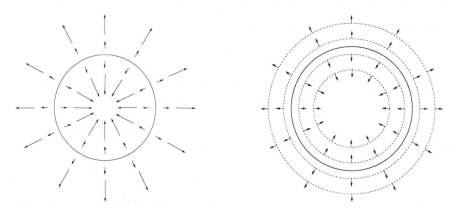

Fig. 2. The left figure shows that the VDF of a circle is a radial field equal to **0** on the circle and undefined at the center. The right figure proposes an alternate visualization of VDF's: since VDF's are vector fields, it might be useful to visualize separately the direction and the magnitude fields. In this figure, the direction field of the VDF of a circle is represented by unit vectors and its magnitude is visualized by some of its level-sets (dashed lines). Any vector function can be represented in that way but in the case of VDF's, the dashed lines are parallel to the represented curve and the unit vectors are normal to the dashed lines.

Therefore it is a projector on a vector subspace and we have the following proposition.

Proposition 5. *When evaluated at* $\mathbf{x}$ *on* $\mathcal{M}$, $D\mathbf{u}(\mathbf{x})$ *is the projector on the normal space* $N_{\mathbf{x}}\mathcal{M}$. *This implies that* $D\mathbf{u}(\mathbf{x})$ *has* $n-k$ *(the dimension of* $N_{\mathbf{x}}\mathcal{M}$*) eigenvalues equal to 1 and* k *(the dimension of* $T_{\mathbf{x}}\mathcal{M}$*) eigenvalues equal to 0. In particular, the rank of* $D\mathbf{u}$ *is equal to* $n-k$ *on* $\mathcal{M}$.

We now come to the study of the eigenvalues and eigendirections of $D\mathbf{u}$ outside $\mathcal{M}$. The results are quite simple if we consider the line defined by the two points $\mathbf{x}$ and $P_{\mathcal{M}}(\mathbf{x})$: let $\mathbf{n}$ be the unit vector parallel to $\mathbf{x} - P_{\mathcal{M}}(\mathbf{x})$ and consider the line $s \longrightarrow P_{\mathcal{M}}(\mathbf{x}) + s\mathbf{n} \equiv \mathbf{x}(s)$; such a line is called a *characteristic line*. Consider further the values $s_{min} < 0$ and $s_{max} > 0$ (possibly infinite) such that $D\mathbf{u}(\mathbf{x}(s))$ is defined on the open interval $I =]s_{min}, s_{max}[$; the eigendirections of $D\mathbf{u}(\mathbf{x}(s))$ are constant and $n-k$ eigenvalues are equal to 1 for all s in I. Such an open segment is called a *characteristic* segment. More precisely, we have the following proposition

Proposition 6. *The eigendirections of the symmetric matrix* $D\mathbf{u}$ *are constant along each characteristic segment.*
Moreover, if a ray is parameterized by its arc-length s, *starting at* $P_{\mathcal{M}}(\mathbf{x})$, *then*

each one of the eigenvalues of $D\mathbf{u}$ has one of the three following forms:

$$\lambda(s) = 1, \quad or$$
$$\lambda(s) = 0, \quad or$$
$$\lambda(s) = \frac{s}{s \pm c}, \ c > 0, \tag{7}$$
$$\forall s \in I,$$

where c depends on the particular eigendirection. The first form corresponds to the eigenvectors of $D\mathbf{u}$ which are elements of the normal space to $\mathcal{M}$ at $P_{\mathcal{M}}(\mathbf{x})$; there are $n - k$ such eigenvalues. The second and third forms (the second form is obtained from the third form by taking $c = \infty$) correspond to eigenvectors of $D\mathbf{u}$ which are elements of the tangent space to $\mathcal{M}$ at $P_{\mathcal{M}}(\mathbf{x})$. There are k such eigenvalues.

There is also a remarkable relation between the second order spacial derivative of $\mathbf{u}$ and the mean curvature of $\mathcal{M}$.

Proposition 7. *The mean-curvature vector of $\mathcal{M}$, of dimension k, at $\mathbf{x}$ is equal, up to a scale factor, to the Laplacian $\Delta\mathbf{u}(\mathbf{x})$ of $\mathbf{u}$ at the same point:*

$$\mathcal{H}(\mathbf{x}) = -\frac{1}{k}(\Delta\mathbf{u}(\mathbf{x})), \quad \forall \mathbf{x} \in \mathcal{M}.$$

4   How to Evolve a Smooth Manifold by Evolving Its VDF

Let us consider a family $\mathcal{M}(\mathbf{p}, t)$ of smooth manifolds of dimension k, where $\mathbf{p}$ is a k-dimensional vector parameterizing $\mathcal{M}$ at each time instant t. We assume the initial conditions

$$\mathcal{M}(\cdot, 0) = \mathcal{M}_0(\cdot),$$

where $\mathcal{M}_0$ is a smooth manifold of dimension k. Furthermore the evolution of the family $\mathcal{M}$ is governed by the following PDE

$$\mathcal{M}_t(\mathbf{p}, t) = \mathcal{H}(\mathcal{M}(\mathbf{p}, t), t) + \Pi^N_{\mathcal{M}(\mathbf{p},t)}(\mathcal{D}(\mathcal{M}(\mathbf{p}, t), t)) \overset{def}{=} \mathbf{V}(\mathcal{M}(\mathbf{p}, t), t), \tag{8}$$

where $\mathcal{H}(\mathcal{M}(\mathbf{p}, t), t)$ is the mean curvature vector at the point $\mathcal{M}(\mathbf{p}, t)$ of the manifold $\mathcal{M}$ and $\mathcal{D}(\mathbf{x}, t)$ is a vector field defined on $\mathbb{R}^n \times \mathbb{R}^+$ representing a velocity induced on $\mathcal{M}$ by some data. $\Pi^N_{\mathcal{M}(\mathbf{p},t)}$ is the projection operator on the normal space $N\mathcal{M}_{\mathcal{M}(\mathbf{p},t)}$ to $\mathcal{M}$ at the point $\mathcal{M}(\mathbf{p}, t)$. The goal of this section is to explore a way of evolving $\mathbf{u}$, the VDF to $\mathcal{M}$, instead of $\mathcal{M}$ while guaranteeing three conditions:

i) That **u** remains a VDF at all time instants.
ii) That $\mathbf{u}^{-1}(\mathbf{0}) = \mathcal{M}$ at all times where $\mathcal{M}$ is defined.
iii) That the manifold $\mathcal{M}$ evolves according to (8).

Since the value of the field $\mathbf{b} = \mathbf{u}_t$ is needed in order to evolve **u**, we shall develop now the idea that **b** is itself the solution to a certain PDE which can be solved numerically.
It is not too difficult, from (4), to find a characterization of **b**.

Proposition 8. *The velocity field* **b** *of the VDF* **u** *is characterized by the first order, quasi-linear Partial Differential Equation*

$$D\mathbf{b}\mathbf{u} = (\mathbf{I} - D\mathbf{u})\mathbf{b}, \tag{9}$$

with initial conditions

$$\mathbf{b}(\mathcal{M}(\mathbf{p}, t), t) = -\mathbf{V}(\mathcal{M}(\mathbf{p}, t), t), \tag{10}$$

wherever **u** *is defined and differentiable.*

Proof. Take the time derivative of equation (4).

We propose to solve numerically (9) with the initial condition (10): this provides us with the value of the field $\mathbf{u}_t$ needed to evolve (*i.e.* update) **u** and is therefore a practical way of evolving the VDF.
A geometrical interpretation of this is the following.

Proposition 9. *At all points* **x** *where* **b** *is defined, its component in the normal space* $N_{P_{\mathcal{M}}(\mathbf{x})}\mathcal{M}$ *to* $\mathcal{M}$ *at the point* $P_{\mathcal{M}}(\mathbf{x})$ *is equal to minus the normal velocity* $\mathbf{V}(P_{\mathcal{M}}(\mathbf{x}), t)$ *of the point* $P_{\mathcal{M}}(\mathbf{x})$:

$$\mathbf{b}(\mathbf{x}, t)_{|N_{P_{\mathcal{M}}(\mathbf{x})}\mathcal{M}} = \mathbf{b}(\mathbf{x} - \mathbf{u}(\mathbf{x}, t))_{|N_{P_{\mathcal{M}}(\mathbf{x})}\mathcal{M}} \equiv \mathbf{b}(P_{\mathcal{M}}(\mathbf{x}))_{|N_{P_{\mathcal{M}}(\mathbf{x})}\mathcal{M}}$$
$$\equiv -\mathbf{V}(P_{\mathcal{M}}(\mathbf{x}), t). \tag{11}$$

Proof. We use the method of characteristics (see e.g. [3]) and rewrite (9) along the characteristics of **b** so that a set of ODE's are obtained (*cf* [13] for a detailed and instructive proof).

As far as the tangential components are concerned, their variation along the characteristic lines can be related to the coefficients of proposition 6 (*cf* [13]).

5   Smooth Manifolds with a Boundary and Changes in Dimension

A simple example will introduce the new issues of this section. In the plane $\mathbb{R}^2$, we consider the time dependent segment $[A(t), B(t)]$ whose endpoints have respectively the velocities $\boldsymbol{v}_A(t) = \alpha\boldsymbol{i}$ and $\boldsymbol{v}_B(t) = \beta\boldsymbol{i}$ with $\alpha < 0 < \beta$ and with initial condition $A(0) = B(0) = O$. This situation describes a point transforming into a segment with increasing length: it is a prototype of a change of dimension followed by the evolution of a smooth manifold with boundary. We note $\mathbf{x} = [x, y]^T$ the coordinates of a point of $\mathbb{R}^2$. The VDF to this object is easily shown to satisfy

$$\mathbf{u}_t(x, y, t) + Du\mathbf{V} = \mathbf{0} \quad \text{with} \quad \mathbf{V}(x, y, t) = \begin{cases} \boldsymbol{v}_A & \text{if } x < \alpha t, \\ \mathbf{0} & \text{if } \alpha t < x < \beta t, \\ \boldsymbol{v}_B & \text{if } x > \beta t. \end{cases} \quad (12)$$

This equation is a variant of a well-known class of PDE's called the *transport equations* [9]. One of its solution is readily shown to be

$$\begin{cases} \mathbf{u}_0(\mathbf{x} - \mathbf{A}) & \text{if } x < \alpha t, \\ \mathbf{u}_0(x, 0) & \text{if } \alpha t < x < \beta t, \\ \mathbf{u}_0(\mathbf{x} - \mathbf{B}) & \text{if } x > \beta t. \end{cases}$$

At first glance (see figure 4), the vector field $\mathbf{b} = -Du\mathbf{V}$ is not of the form presented in the previous section because it is only piecewise-smooth, $\mathbf{b}$ being discontinuous on the lines of equations $x = \alpha t$ and $x = \beta t$. But, as shown in the figure, the evolution of the point O is quite remarkable: it is a smooth manifold of dimension 0 which is turned into a smooth manifold with boundary (the segment AB). The velocity field $\mathbf{b}$ is discontinuous on the vertical axis at time $t = 0$ which has the effect of allowing the point to "spread" to a line segment. At time $t > 0$ the velocity field $\mathbf{b}(., t)$ is of the form $\mathbf{V}(P_{AB}(.))$ everywhere except on the previous two lines. We note that the *normal* component of $\mathbf{V}$ is continuous across these two lines, being equal to 0 everywhere, while its *tangential* component is discontinuous over them. This last point is the reason why the segment $[AB]$ can grow in time.

The situation we have just described is archetypal of all cases in higher dimensions and codimensions and reveals an undesirable lack of generality in the analysis of the previous section and suggests that *non-continuous* $\mathbf{b}$'s may also be interesting since they can account for changes of dimension and tangent velocities at the boundary of a manifold (both are intimately related as it can be learned from the segment example).

In order to deal with these new issues, it is necessary in the first place to provide ourselves with a model for the intuitive but vague notion of "changing dimension". We shall say that an initial smooth manifold $\mathcal{W}$ of dimension $m < n$ at $t = 0$ increases its dimension if it "spreads" out in the direction of some privileged normal directions and becomes another manifold $\mathcal{M}(t)$, $t > 0$, of higher dimension $k \in \{m+1, \cdots, n\}$ with a smooth boundary $\partial\mathcal{M}$ of dimension $k-1$. The increment in dimension is equal to the number of linearly independent orthogonal normal directions where this filling occurs. The modeling of a decrease in dimension is obtained by reversing the direction of time. This spreading follows the path of some geodesic curves of the ambient space that are thrown in all of the chosen normal directions[1], starting from $\mathcal{W}$. For instance, in the example above,

---

[1] See [19,8] for important results concerning the exponential map and its use in the study of neighborhoods.

the initial manifold $\mathcal{W}$ is the point O, the target manifold $\mathcal{M}$ is the segment $[AB]$, the geodesic paths followed to spread the point O are the segments $[OA]$ and $[OB]$ (of course, depending on the chosen metric, the geodesic paths may not be straight lines so that O could have been spread to a "curved" curve as well) and the boundary $\partial\mathcal{M}$ of the target manifold is made of the two end points A and B. These simple notions generalize naturally in any dimension.

In this model, there is a special manifold, noted $R_{\partial\mathcal{M}}$, which plays a singular role. Indeed, consider the ruled [8] hypersurface whose generatrix is $\partial\mathcal{M}$ and whose rulings directions are *all* the normal directions of $\mathcal{M}$. In the above example, $R_{\partial\mathcal{M}}$ is made of the two lines of equations $x = \alpha t$ and $x = \beta t$ since they are "ruled" hypersurfaces starting at A and B (which both form $\partial\mathcal{M}$) and directed to the normal to $[AB]$ (which plays the role of $\mathcal{M}$). Then we have the two following propositions (*cf* [13] for proofs) generalizing the observations made on the example above.

Proposition 10. *The spatial derivative D$\mathbf{u}$, of the VDF to the smooth manifold $\mathcal{M}$ with boundary $\partial\mathcal{M}$ is discontinuous on the special ruled hypersurface $R_{\partial\mathcal{M}}$ defined above, generated by $\partial\mathcal{M}$ and the normal space to $\mathcal{M}$ at points of $\partial\mathcal{M}$.*

Proposition 11. *The tangential component of the time derivative $\mathbf{u}_t$, of the VDF to the smooth manifold $\mathcal{M}$ with boundary $\partial\mathcal{M}$ can be discontinuous on the hypersurface $R_{\partial\mathcal{M}}$ generated by $\partial\mathcal{M}$ and the normal space to $\mathcal{M}$ at points of $\partial\mathcal{M}$. The normal component is continuous.*

We have characterized the singularities of the VDF to a manifold which has a boundary. It is also possible to go a little further and see what singularities exist at the very moment of the change of dimension (*i.e.* at $t = 0$ in our simple example). It suffices to study $\lim_{t \to 0} R_{\partial\mathcal{M}}$ and it is done in [13]. These two propositions will hopefully be used to design appropriate numerical schemes that would deal with these singularities.

6   Some Remarks and Conclusion

The method of the VDF's for representing arbitrary smooth manifolds with or without a boundary finds its roots in the work of Ambrosio and Soner [2] where we found inspiration and some of the technical results that we needed, and in the work of Ruuth, Merriman, Xin and Osher [18] that inspired us the idea of the VDF representation. Our contributions are the development of a) a method for evolving a VDF instead of a smooth closed manifold while guaranteeing that it stays a VDF over time and that the manifold evolves correctly, b) a theory that describes changes of dimension by a generalized transport equation and c) a theory that extends a) to deal seamlessly with smooth manifolds with boundaries. Moreover, in our approach, the function we evolve is regular on the manifold of interest unlike for example the method presented in [17].

These theoretical developments are being implemented. Let us make two remarks concerning this implementation. The first remark is related to the computation of the velocity field $\mathbf{b}$. Even though proposition 9 provides a characterization of $\mathbf{b}(\mathbf{x})$ in terms of $\mathbf{V}(\mathbf{x} - \mathbf{u}(\mathbf{x}))$, our method is to compute $\mathbf{b}$ by applying proposition 8 and solving the quasi-linear PDE (9) with initial conditions (10).

The second remark is that because of the accumulation of numerical errors, the function $\mathbf{u}$ may drift away from the class of VDF's. In order to correct for this drift, we suggest that it may be a good idea to combine the solution of $\mathbf{u}_t = \mathbf{b}$ with that of

$$\mathbf{u}_t = ((D\mathbf{u})^T + (\alpha - 1)\mathbf{I})\mathbf{u}, \tag{13}$$

where

$$\alpha = Trace(D\mathbf{u}(D\mathbf{u})^T) + \mathbf{u} \cdot \Delta\mathbf{u} - div\mathbf{u}.$$

Equation (13) is the Euler-Lagrange equation of the following functional

$$\frac{1}{2} \int_{\Omega} \|(D\mathbf{u})^T \mathbf{u} - \mathbf{u}\|^2 \ d\mathbf{x},$$

where Ω is some neighborhood of $\mathcal{M}$. This functional arises naturally from proposition 3.

We have implemented this VDF reprojection and the numerical results are very good (*cf* figure 3).

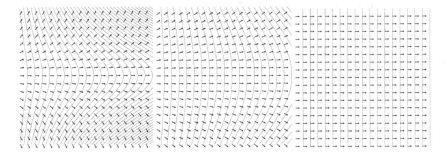

Fig. 3. The VDF to the vertical line of equation $x = 0$, *i.e.* the left border of the grid, is exagerately perturbated (on the left image) and the obtained function is used as the initial condition for equation (13) which is solved using a regular forward differences scheme. After a few iterations (in the center and right images), the function is retransformed into the correct VDF to the line of equation $x = 0$. See figure 2 to understand the visualization.

To conclude, we think that the VDF method for representing and evolving shapes has the following advantages: it can deal with smooth manifolds with and without boundaries, with shapes of different dimensions; if discontinuous velocity fields are allowed dimension can change; the evolution method that we propose guarantees that we stay in the class of VDF's and therefore that the intrinsic properties of the underlying shapes such as their dimension, curvatures can be read off easily from the VDF and its spatial derivatives. The main disadvantage is its redundancy: the size of the representation is always that of the ambient space even though the object we are representing is of a much lower dimension. This disadvantage is also one of its strengths since it buys us flexibility.

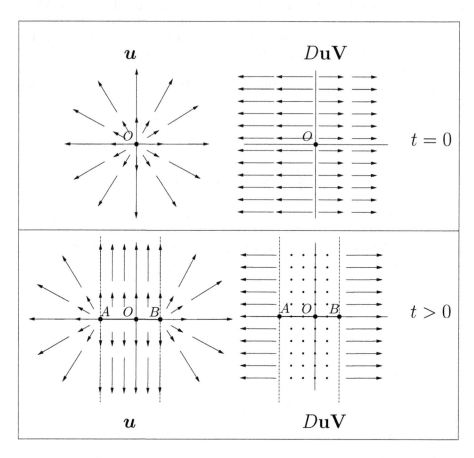

Fig. 4. Changing dimension: If we allow the velocity field **b** to be discontinuous, we can induce changes in the dimension of the manifold. The example shows the simplest of all manifolds, a single point O in the plane and its VDF (upper left-hand corner), the velocity field $\mathbf{b}(.,0) = -D\mathbf{u}\mathbf{V}$ is discontinuous on the vertical axis (upper right-hand corner). At a later time $t > 0$ the point O has become the line segment $[AB]$ (its VDF is shown in the lower left-hand corner); the new velocity $\mathbf{V}(.,t)$ is shown in the lower right-hand corner. The initial point, a smooth manifold without boundary of dimension 0 is turned into a closed (in the topological sense) open (in the usual sense) curve, a smooth manifold with boundary (the two endpoints A and B) of dimension 1.

References

1. L. Ambrosio and C. Mantegazza. Curvature and distance function from a manifold. *J. Geom. Anal.*, 1996. To appear.
2. Luigi Ambrosio and Halil M. Soner. Level set approach to mean curvature flow in arbitrary codimension. *J. of Diff. Geom.*, 43:693–737, 1996.
3. V.I. Arnold. *Geometrical Methods in the Theory of Ordinary Differential Equations*. Springer-Verlag New York Inc., 1983.
4. M. Bertalmio, G. Sapiro, and G. Randall. Region Tacking on Surfaces Deforming via Level-Sets Methods. In Mads Nielsen, P. Johansen, O.F. Olsen, and J. Weickert, editors, *Scale-Space Theories in Computer Vision*, volume 1682 of *Lecture Notes in Computer Science*, pages 58–69. Springer, September 1999.
5. Paul Burchard, Li-Tien Cheng, Barry Merriman, and Stanley Osher. Motion of curves in three spatial dimensions using a level set approach. Technical report, Department of Mathematics, University of California Los Angeles, September 2000.
6. V. Caselles, R. Kimmel, and G. Sapiro. Geodesic active contours. In *Proceedings of the 5th International Conference on Computer Vision*, pages 694–699, Boston, MA, June 1995. IEEE Computer Society, IEEE Computer Society Press.
7. Y.G. Chen, Y. Giga, and S. Goto. Uniqueness and existence of viscosity solutions of generalized mean curvature flow equations. *J. Differential Geometry*, 33:749–786, 1991.
8. M.P. DoCarmo. *Riemannian Geometry*. Birkhäuser, 1992.
9. L.C. Evans. *Partial Differential Equations*, volume 19 of *Graduate Studies in Mathematics*. American Mathematical Society, 1998.
10. M. Gage and R.S. Hamilton. The heat equation shrinking convex plane curves. *J. of Differential Geometry*, 23:69–96, 1986.
11. J. Gomes and O. Faugeras. Shape representation as the intersection of $n - k$ hypersurfaces. Technical Report 4011, INRIA, 2000.
12. M. Grayson. The heat equation shrinks embedded plane curves to round points. *J. of Differential Geometry*, 26:285–314, 1987.
13. Authors hidden. Representing and evolving smooth manifolds of arbitrary dimension embedded in R^n as the intersection of n hypersurfaces: The vector distance functions. Technical Report 4012, Institution name is hidden, 2000.
14. M. Kass, A. Witkin, and D. Terzopoulos. SNAKES: Active contour models. *The International Journal of Computer Vision*, 1:321–332, January 1988.
15. S. Kichenassamy, A. Kumar, P. Olver, A. Tannenbaum, and A. Yezzi. Gradient flows and geometric active contour models. In *Proceedings of the 5th International Conference on Computer Vision*, Boston, MA, June 1995. IEEE Computer Society, IEEE Computer Society Press.
16. S. Osher and J. Sethian. Fronts propagating with curvature dependent speed : algorithms based on the Hamilton-Jacobi formulation. *Journal of Computational Physics*, 79:12–49, 1988.
17. S.J. Ruuth, B. Merriman, J. Xin, and S. Osher. Diffusion-Generated Motion by Mean Curvature for filaments. Technical Report 98-47, UCLA Computational and Applied Mathematics Reports, November 1998.
18. S.J. Ruuth, B. Merriman, and S. Osher. A fixed grid method for capturing the motion of self-intersecting interfaces and related pdes. Technical Report 99-22, UCLA Computational and Applied Mathematics Reports, July 1999.
19. Michael Spivak. *A Comprehensive Introduction to Differential Geometry*, volume I–V. Publish or Perish, Berkeley, CA, 1979. Second edition.
20. J. Steinhoff, M. Fan, and L. Wang. A new eulerian method for the computation of propagating short acoustic and electromagnetic pulses. *Journal of Computational Physics*, 157:683–706, 2000.

Computing Optic Flow by Scale-Space Integration of Normal Flow

Kim S. Pedersen[1] and Mads Nielsen[2]

[1] DIKU, University of Copenhagen
Universitetsparken 1, DK-2100 Copenhagen Ø, Denmark
[2] IT University of Copenhagen
Glentevej 67-69, DK-2400 Copenhagen, Denmark

Abstract In this paper we will present a least committed multi-scale method for computation of optic flow fields. We extract optic flow fields from normal flow, by fitting the normal components of a local polynomial model of the optic flow to the normal flow. This fitting is based on an analytically solvable optimization problem, in which an integration scale-space over the normal flow field regularizes the solution. An automatic local scale selection mechanism is used in order to adapt to the local structure of the flow field. The performance profile of the method is compared with that of existing optic flow techniques and we show that the proposed method performs at least as well as the leading algorithms on the benchmark image sequences proposed by Barron et al. [3]. We also do a performance comparison on a synthetic fire particle sequence and apply our method to a real sequence of smoke circulation in a pigsty. Both consist of highly complex non-rigid motion.

1 Introduction

Motion analysis is a large topic within computer vision and image analysis, because knowledge of motion, as perceivable in image sequences, is necessary for various tasks such as object tracking, time-to-contact, structure from motion, etc. Motion analysis is conducted by associating a vector field of velocities to the image sequence, which describes the rate and direction of change of the intensity values. We define the *optic flow* as the velocity field, which describes the temporal changes of the intensity values of the sequence. Optic flow is not equivalent to a projection of the true physical motion onto the image plane, among other things, because of changing intensity values caused by reflections and varying lighting conditions. But the main reason for this is the *aperture problem* as coined by Marr [15]. The aperture problem is the fact that we can only deduce the motion that results in a change in the intensity patterns of the captured image sequence. The problem of determining the motion along image isophotes (i.e. iso-intensity curves) is inherently ambiguous. By introduction of assumptions about the flow we can obtain various types of realizations of optic flow. Usual assumptions used in other methods are local or global rigidity or affinity. The only unbiased local motion we can obtain is the motion orthogonal

M. Kerckhove (Ed.): Scale-Space 2001, LNCS 2106, pp. 14–25, 2001.

to the isophotes of the image. This type of velocity field is called the *normal flow*.

A large variety of methods exist for estimation of optic flow [1,2,4,8,12,19] (which is far from an exhaustive list). See also Barron et al. [3] for a discussion and evaluation of various methods.

We wish to develop an algorithm, which can be used for doing motion analysis in experimental fluid dynamics (see [20]). For that reason it is important that it is least committed, in order to reduce possible biases in the approximated flow. Since normal flow is the only unbiased or least committed realization of optic flow, we will use it as a basis for obtaining an estimate of the full flow. We believe that a least committed estimate can be obtained by locally modeling the full optic flow on top of the normal flow. Ideally we seek to estimate the optic flow field which at each point has the corresponding normal flow vector as its normal component[1]. This constraint only fix one degree of freedom (d.o.f.), which means that an infinite number of solutions exist. In order to circumvent this problem, we introduce a polynomial model of the local optic flow. We use a linear Gaussian scale-space to formalize the concept of local validity or the integration scale of our model. This integration scale-space regularizes the problem and lets us fix the missing tangential d.o.f. by estimating, in a least squares sense, the parameters of our local model constrained by the normal flow found at the integration scale or in the region of model validity. The solution to this constrained minimization problem can be stated in closed form and it is expressed in terms of a Taylor expansion of the normalized structure tensor. In order to take full advantage of this multi-scale approach we use an automatic local scale selection mechanism, based on a method by Niessen et al. [18], to select the scale of model validity.

In this paper we compute the normal flow by using the method proposed by Florack et al. [4]. It is an incorporation of the so-called *Optic Flow Constraint Equation* (OFCE), originally proposed by Horn and Schunck [8], into the linear Gaussian scale-space formalism. In this method the normal flow is in general modeled by an M'th order polynomial, but we choose the somewhat restrictive zeroth order model. This choice is based on the assumption that locally this model is a good approximation of the normal flow. Other choices of model order and normal flow methods are possible.

We believe that scale-space integration of normal flow and modeling locally the optic flow in this scale-space is different from other methods. The conscious inclusion of measurement scale lets us select the appropriate neighborhood in which our local model is valid. Other authors [2,4,12,19] have introduced polynomial models of the flow structure directly into the OFCE, contrary to modeling the optic flow on top of the normal flow as we propose. The use of an integration neighborhood for the approximation of optic flow and in the related stereo matching problem has been used by several authors [1,4,9,12,19].

We evaluate the performance of our algorithm by using the methods proposed by Barron et al. [3] in their survey of performance of optic flow methods. Our performance results will be compared with the results for other optic flow

---

[1] By normal component we mean the projection of the sought optic flow onto the direction orthogonal to the local isophote.

techniques on among other a synthetic fire sequence. In order to show a possible application of this least committed approach, we also apply our method to a real sequence of smoke circulation in a pigsty.

The organization of this paper is the following: In Sec. 2 we describe our scale-space representation as well as some notation. Sec. 3 is a brief introduction to the theory of normal flow. The proposed method for computation of optic flow is presented in Sec. 4 and finally, the performance of the presented algorithm is discussed in Sec. 5.

2 Spatiotemporal Gaussian Scale-Space

Both Koenderink [11] and Lindeberg [13] have proposed temporal causal scale-space representations. In this paper we choose simply to disregard temporal causality, since we are not interested in real-time applications. It is our opinion that a generalization of our method to one of the above mentioned temporal causal representations is possible. We choose to use the linear Gaussian scale-space representation, introduced among others by Koenderink [10].

We use the spatiotemporal scale-space representation $L(\boldsymbol{x};\sigma,\tau) : \mathbb{R}^{N+1} \times \mathbb{R}_+ \times \mathbb{R}_+ \mapsto \mathbb{R}$ of the spatiotemporal image $f(\boldsymbol{x}) : \mathbb{R}^{N+1} \mapsto \mathbb{R}$ defined by the convolution of the image with the *scale-space aperture function* $G(\boldsymbol{x};\sigma,\tau) : \mathbb{R}^{N+1} \times \mathbb{R}_+ \times \mathbb{R}_+ \mapsto \mathbb{R}$,

$$L(\boldsymbol{x};\sigma,\tau) = f(\boldsymbol{x}) * G(\boldsymbol{x};\sigma,\tau). \tag{1}$$

The aperture function is the spatiotemporal Gaussian

$$G(\boldsymbol{x};\sigma,\tau) = \frac{1}{\sqrt{2\pi\tau^2}(2\pi\sigma^2)^{N/2}} \exp\left(-\frac{x^i x^i}{2\sigma^2} - \frac{(x^t)^2}{2\tau^2}\right) \tag{2}$$

where σ and τ are called the *spatiotemporal scale parameters*. Throughout this paper, we will use the index notation where x^i denotes the i'th spatial component of the vector $\boldsymbol{x}$, and x^t denotes the temporal component. When we are talking about both spatial and temporal components we write the component index with a Greek letter, e.g. x^μ. We will also sometimes make use of Einstein's summation convention, i.e. repeated lower and upper indices indicates summation over these, $x^i x^i \equiv \sum_i x^i x^i$.

3 Theory of Normal Flow

We will in this paper assume that we can compute the normal flow of an image sequence. We choose to use the scale-space OFCE proposed by Florack et al. [4] as a method for computation of normal flow. We will briefly outline this method in order to establish some necessary notation.

Horn and Schunck [8] proposes an optic flow method which is based on the local assumption that the image intensities are preserved at points moving along the flow. Furthermore, it is assumed that the temporal velocity component is constant, $v^t(\boldsymbol{x}) \equiv 1$. This assumption expresses that the flow is everywhere non-vanishing and temporal causal. These assumptions lead to the well-known optic flow constraint equation (OFCE). It is interesting to notice that the later assumption breaks down generically in a countable set of points ([17]). In this paper we will assume that this assumption is valid at every point in the image.

Florack et al. [4] incorporates the ideas of Horn and Schunck into the scale-space paradigm, by defining the optic flow constraint equation under the spatiotemporal scale-space aperture. For a 2-dimensional image sequence $f(\boldsymbol{x})$, the OFCE can be written as the Lie derivative[2] under the scale-space aperture $G(\boldsymbol{x}; \sigma, \tau)$ of the intensity function of the sequence along the flow $\boldsymbol{v}(\boldsymbol{x})$. We have

$$\mathcal{L}_{\boldsymbol{v}} L(\boldsymbol{x}; \sigma, \tau) = \int_{\boldsymbol{x} \in \mathrm{IR}^3} (f_t + v^x f_x + v^y f_y) G \, d\boldsymbol{x} \equiv 0 \tag{3}$$

where $f_\mu = \partial f / \partial x^\mu$.

Normal flow is defined by the so-called *normal flow constraint*. Florack et al. define the normal flow constraint under the scale-space aperture function as

$$\int_{\boldsymbol{x} \in \mathrm{IR}^3} (v^x f_y - v^y f_x) G \, d\boldsymbol{x} \equiv 0 \,. \tag{4}$$

Florack et al. introduce a polynomial model of the flow $\boldsymbol{v}$ into (3) and (4). This lets them state the problem of normal flow estimation in terms of a system of linear equations. Each term of these equations can be expressed as a linear combination of scale-space image derivatives, due to the definition of Hermite polynomials in terms of Gaussian derivatives. As mentioned, we will only use the zeroth order model for approximation of normal flow, but we will use the M'th order polynomial model proposed by Florack et al. as our local model of the optic flow. We define the M'th order polynomial model $\boldsymbol{v}_M(\boldsymbol{x})$ of the vector field $\boldsymbol{v}(\boldsymbol{x})$ at $\boldsymbol{x} = \boldsymbol{0}$ as

$$v_M^\mu(\boldsymbol{x}) = \sum_{l=0}^{M} \frac{1}{l!} \tilde{v}_{\rho_1 \ldots \rho_l}^\mu x^{\rho_1} \cdots x^{\rho_l} \,. \tag{5}$$

Here x^ρ, v^μ denote the components of the spatiotemporal vectors $\boldsymbol{x}, \boldsymbol{v} \in \mathrm{IR}^{N+1}$ and $\tilde{v}_{\rho_1 \ldots \rho_l}^\mu$ are the model coefficients approximating the partial derivatives of $\boldsymbol{v}(\boldsymbol{x} = \boldsymbol{0})$ at the origin.

4 Least Committed Optic Flow

Ideally we want to obtain an optic flow field which has a normal component that is equal to the normal flow. This is an ill-posed problem, because an infinite number of solutions exist, due to our lack of knowledge about the tangential component. We intend to regularize this problem by locally modeling the tangential

---

[2] The Lie derivative of a scalar function $f(\boldsymbol{x})$ is the derivative of $f(\boldsymbol{x})$ along the direction of a specified vector field $\boldsymbol{v}$, $\mathcal{L}_{\boldsymbol{v}} f = f_\mu v^\mu$.

component of the optic flow field by a polynomial model, under the constraint that the normal component of the model should be close to the normal flow. We use a spatiotemporal integration scale-space to define the scale of validity of our local model.

This constrained optimization problem can be formalized by a functional $E(v(x; \varpi))$ of the optic flow field $v(x; \varpi)$ at integration scale ϖ, describing the degree of discrepancy between the normal flow field $u(x)$ and the normal component of the sought optic flow field under the Gaussian integration aperture[3] $G(x; \varpi)$. We define the discrepancy as the least squares difference, thus we can write the functional as

$$E(v(x; \varpi)) = \int_{x \in \mathbb{R}^{N+1}} w(x) \| \eta(v \cdot \eta) - u \|^2 G(x; \varpi) \, dx \,, \qquad (6)$$

where $\eta(x) = \frac{u}{\|u\|}$ is the normalized direction of the normal flow $u(x)$. The term $w(x)$ is a function of the uncertainty of the underlying normal flow estimates and acts as a weight, which penalizes poorly estimated normal flow vectors. In Sec. 5 we choose to use the numerical uncertainty of the normal flow as the penalty function $w(x)$, but other choices are of course possible.

We introduce the M'th order polynomial model v_M, defined in (5), into the functional $E(v(x; \varpi))$. The model parameters $\tilde{v}^\mu_{\rho_1 \dots \rho_l}$ can be obtained by minimizing the functional $E(v_M(x; \varpi))$, that is

$$\hat{v}^\mu_{\rho_1 \dots \rho_l} = \arg \min_{\tilde{v}^\mu_{\rho_1 \dots \rho_l}} E(v_M) \,, \quad l = 0, \dots, M \,. \qquad (7)$$

The integrand of the functional $E(v_M)$ is quadratic, which trivially means that one minimum exists and that this minimum $\hat{v}^\mu_{\rho_1 \dots \rho_l}$ is the solution to the system of differential equations given by $\partial E / \partial \tilde{v}^\mu_{\rho_1 \dots \rho_l} = 0$. We therefore arrive at:

Result 1 (M'th Order Optic Flow). *The M'th order optic flow approximation $v_M(x; \varpi)$ is given by (5), where the model parameters $\tilde{v}^\beta_{\nu_1 \dots \nu_i}$ are obtained by solving the minimization problem of (7). The solution is given by the following set of linear equations*

$$\frac{\partial E}{\partial \tilde{v}^\mu_{\rho_1 \dots \rho_l}} = \sum_{i=0}^M \frac{1}{i!} \tilde{v}^\beta_{\nu_1 \dots \nu_i} \int_{x \in \mathbb{R}^{N+1}} w(x) \eta^\mu \eta^\beta \mathcal{M}_{\nu_1 \dots \nu_i \rho_1 \dots \rho_l}(x; \varpi) \, dx$$

$$- \int_{x \in \mathbb{R}^{N+1}} w(x) u^\mu \mathcal{M}_{\rho_1 \dots \rho_l}(x; \varpi) \, dx = 0 \,, \quad (8)$$

where $\mathcal{M}_{\rho_1 \dots \rho_l}(x; \varpi) = x^{\rho_1} \cdots x^{\rho_l} G(x, \varpi)$ is the l'th order mixed Gaussian monomials at integration scale ϖ.

Proof. We seek the solution of

$$\frac{\partial E}{\partial \tilde{v}^\mu_{\rho_1 \dots \rho_l}} = 0 \,. \qquad (9)$$

---

[3] For the sake of simplicity we choose to use a scale-space representation with only one integration scale parameter ϖ. The spatiotemporal scale-space aperture function of (2) can readily be interchanged with the aperture function $G(x; \varpi)$.

By using the chain rule $\partial E/\partial \tilde{v}^{\mu}_{\rho_1...\rho_l} = \int \partial q/\partial \tilde{v}^{\mu}_{\rho_1...\rho_l} \partial F/\partial q \, d\boldsymbol{x}$, where $F(\boldsymbol{v}_M)$ is the integrand of $E(\boldsymbol{v}_M)$ and $q = \boldsymbol{v}_M \cdot \boldsymbol{\eta}$, we get

$$\frac{\partial E}{\partial \tilde{v}^{\mu}_{\rho_1...\rho_l}} = \int_{\boldsymbol{x} \in \mathbb{R}^{N+1}} \frac{2w(\boldsymbol{x})}{l!} \cdot \left(\eta^{(\alpha)^2} \eta^{\mu} \eta^{\beta} \left(\sum_{i=0}^{M} \frac{1}{i!} \tilde{v}^{\beta}_{\nu_1...\nu_i} x^{\nu_1} \cdots x^{\nu_i} \right) \right.$$
$$\left. - \eta^{\mu}(\boldsymbol{\eta} \cdot \boldsymbol{u}) \right) \cdot x^{\rho_1} \cdots x^{\rho_l} G(\boldsymbol{x}; \varpi) \, d\boldsymbol{x} = 0 \, . \quad (10)$$

Notice that $\eta^{(\alpha)^2} = 1$, $\eta^{\mu}(\boldsymbol{\eta} \cdot \boldsymbol{u}) = u^{\mu}$, and that the constant $2/l!$ can be removed. If we introduce the notation $\mathcal{M}_{\rho_1...\rho_l}(\boldsymbol{x}; \varpi) = x^{\rho_1} \cdots x^{\rho_l} G(\boldsymbol{x}, \varpi)$, this system of linear equations can be written as

$$\frac{\partial E}{\partial \tilde{v}^{\mu}_{\rho_1...\rho_l}} = \sum_{i=0}^{M} \frac{1}{i!} \tilde{v}^{\beta}_{\nu_1...\nu_i} \int_{\boldsymbol{x} \in \mathbb{R}^{N+1}} w(\boldsymbol{x}) \left(\eta^{\mu} \eta^{\beta} \mathcal{M}_{\nu_1...\nu_i \rho_1...\rho_l}(\boldsymbol{x}; \varpi) \right.$$
$$\left. - u^{\mu} \mathcal{M}_{\rho_1...\rho_l}(\boldsymbol{x}; \varpi) \right) d\boldsymbol{x} = 0 \, . \quad (11)$$

$\square$

We developed our method at the origin of the vector field $\boldsymbol{v}(\boldsymbol{x} = \boldsymbol{0})$, which means that in general a translation to the point of interest should be introduced, which in turn transforms the integrals of Result 1 into convolution integrals.

The l'th order mixed Gaussian monomials $\mathcal{M}_{\rho_1...\rho_l}(\boldsymbol{x}; \varpi)$ can be expressed in terms of linear combinations of the partial derivatives of the Gaussian by using the definition of Hermite polynomials and the separability of the Gaussian (see e.g. [4]). This lets us interpret the two integrals of Result 1 as a set of scale-space derivatives of the normal flow $\boldsymbol{u}$ and the matrix $\eta^{\mu} \eta^{\beta}$.

Since the normal flow is defined to be parallel to the gradient direction, the matrix $(w \eta^{\mu} \eta^{\beta}) * G(\boldsymbol{x}; \varpi)$ of Result 1 can be interpreted as the normalized spatiotemporal structure tensor (see e.g. [23]). For the Florack et al. [4] method the normal flow is only parallel to the gradient in the zeroth order case. This gives another possible interpretation of Result 1, namely that we are seeking the flow field which, by the product with the normalized structure tensor, is equal to the normal flow. The introduction of our flow model corresponds to a Taylor expansion of the normalized structure tensor. Other authors have used the structure tensor as the basis of methods among other things for doing motion analysis [7].

In Result 1, we assume that the Gaussian derivatives are scale normalized and furthermore we use natural coordinates, $\frac{x}{\sigma}$. We use the standard method of scale normalization which is based on dimensional analysis, [5], and can be stated as

$$\left[\frac{\partial^n L}{\partial x^{\mu^n}} \right]_{norm} = \sigma^n \frac{\partial^n L}{\partial x^{\mu^n}} \, . \quad (12)$$

In the context of feature detection Lindeberg [14] has proposed a method in which the structure of the raw image controls the normalization factor. Pedersen and Nielsen [21] has augmented this method by introducing the fractal dimension of the underlying image structure as a control parameter of the normalization factor. In this paper, We have chosen to use the standard normalization method instead of the more advanced normalization procedures, but for future work, it could be interesting to examine the use of image structure as a control parameter for normalization of derivatives in the context of optic flow field estimation.

The structures of image sequences exist on different scales and consequently the optimal measurement scale will vary between different regions in an image sequence. In conjunction with optic flow and the related stereo vision problem different approaches to the problem of scale selection has been taken; Kanade and Okutomi [9], Weber and Malik [22], Gårding and Lindeberg [6], Niessen et al. [18], and Nielsen et al. [16].

In this paper an automatic local scale selection method will be used similar to the one proposed by Niessen et al. [18]. They propose to use the numerical stability as a criteria for scale selection. As a measure of numerical stability they use the Frobenius norm $\|\mathbf{A}^{-1}\|_F^2$ of the system of linear equations $\mathbf{A}v = b$ used in the method by Florack et al. [4]. The Frobenius norm of a matrix is the sum of the singular values of that matrix. Since we use the Florack et al. multi-scale normal flow method, the outcome of Result 1 is a spatiotemporal integration scale-space of the vector field $v_M(x; \sigma, \tau, \varpi)$. An automatic scale selection mechanism can therefore be stated as the selection of the spatiotemporal integration scale triplet (σ, τ, ϖ) at each point in space-time, for which $\|\mathbf{\Psi}^{-1}\|_F^2$ is minimal. Here $\Psi_{\nu_1...\nu_i\rho_1...\rho_l}^{\mu\beta}(x; \sigma, \tau, \varpi) = (w(x)\eta^\mu\eta^\beta) * \mathcal{M}_{\nu_1...\nu_i\rho_1...\rho_l}$ represent the matrix part of the system of linear equations described in Result 1.

The algorithm proposed in this paper is clearly a sequential process of the computation of normal flow followed by the computation of the optic flow. The computations of the different scale-space derivatives in the normal flow and optic flow steps can readily be parallelized. The sequential structure of the process lets us implement the proposed algorithm in a highly modular fashion.

5   Discussion of Performance

We compute the zeroth and first order optic flow for different benchmark image sequences and compare the results with the findings of other authors. We use the angular error measure used by Barron et al. [3] as well as three of their synthetic benchmark image sequences with known ground truth: The translating trees (TTS), diverging trees (DTS), and Yosemite sequences. We also do a comparison on a synthetic fire particle sequence[4] (see Fig. 1). In order to show that our method can handle complex non-rigid motion, we compute the optic flow of a real sequence of smoke circulation in a pigsty (see Fig. 2). The angular error $\epsilon = \arccos(\hat{v}_c \cdot \hat{v}_e)$ is defined as the angle between the measured vector v_e and the correct vector v_c, where $v = (1, v^x, v^y)$ and $\hat{v} = v/\|v\|$.

---

[4] Available through anonymous FTP,
`ftp://ftp.diku.dk/diku/users/kimstp/fire.tar.gz`.

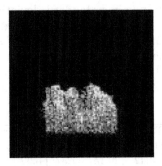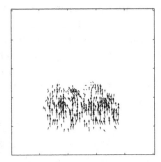

Figure 1. The middle image from the synthetic fire particle sequence (left) and the corresponding correct flow field (right). The sequence consists of 32 images of 256×256 gray value pixels with velocities between 0 and 3.79. We show every fourth vector for the middle image scaled by a factor of 3.

In the following we use the abbreviations

$$
\begin{aligned}
\Psi_{kl}^{ij}(\boldsymbol{x}; \sigma, \tau, \varpi) &= (w(\boldsymbol{x})\eta^i(\boldsymbol{x}; \sigma, \tau)\eta^j(\boldsymbol{x}; \sigma, \tau)) * \mathcal{M}_{kl}(\boldsymbol{x}; \varpi) \\
\Phi_{kl}^i(\boldsymbol{x}; \sigma, \tau, \varpi) &= (w(\boldsymbol{x})u^i(\boldsymbol{x}; \sigma, \tau)) * \mathcal{M}_{kl}(\boldsymbol{x}; \varpi) .
\end{aligned}
\tag{13}
$$

In order to keep the notation simple we assume that each partial derivative of the Gaussians in $\mathcal{M}_{kl}(\boldsymbol{x}; \varpi)$ is scale normalized by (12). When using scale normalization of the derivatives it is important to remember that this effectively corresponds to changing the measurement units, hence the computed flow vectors are expressed in units of the scale. As an uncertainty measure of the normal flow, we use $w(\boldsymbol{x}) = 1/\|\mathbf{A}^{-1}\|_F^2$, where the matrix $\mathbf{A}$ is given by the linear equations $\mathbf{A}\boldsymbol{u} = \boldsymbol{b}$ defining the normal flow ((3) and (4)).

We use the zeroth and first order spatial model for the optic flow even though our method in general lets us use spatiotemporal models. This means that we purely base our approximation of optic flow on a spatial analysis of the underlying spatiotemporal normal flow field. According to Result 1 the optic flow approximated by the zeroth order spatial model $v_0^i = \tilde{v}^i$ is given by the solution to

$$
\begin{aligned}
\Psi^{xx}\tilde{v}^x + \Psi^{xy}\tilde{v}^y &= \Phi^x \\
\Psi^{xy}\tilde{v}^x + \Psi^{yy}\tilde{v}^y &= \Phi^y .
\end{aligned}
\tag{14}
$$

The optic flow modeled by the first order spatial model $v_1^i = \tilde{v}^i + \tilde{v}_x^i x + \tilde{v}_y^i y$ is given by the solution to the system of linear equations given by the partial derivatives of the functional $E(\boldsymbol{v}_1)$ with respect to the six model parameters $\tilde{v}_j^i = (\tilde{v}^x, \tilde{v}^y, \tilde{v}_x^x, \tilde{v}_x^y, \tilde{v}_y^x, \tilde{v}_y^y)^T$,

$$
\begin{aligned}
\frac{\partial E}{\partial \tilde{v}_j^x} &= \Psi_j^{xx}\tilde{v}^x + \Psi_j^{xy}\tilde{v}^y + \Psi_{xj}^{xx}\tilde{v}_x^x + \Psi_{xj}^{xy}\tilde{v}_x^y + \Psi_{yj}^{xx}\tilde{v}_y^x + \Psi_{yj}^{xy}\tilde{v}_y^y - \Phi_j^x = 0 \\
\frac{\partial E}{\partial \tilde{v}_j^y} &= \Psi_j^{xy}\tilde{v}^x + \Psi_j^{yy}\tilde{v}^y + \Psi_{xj}^{xy}\tilde{v}_x^x + \Psi_{xj}^{yy}\tilde{v}_x^y + \Psi_{yj}^{xy}\tilde{v}_y^x + \Psi_{yj}^{yy}\tilde{v}_y^y - \Phi_j^y = 0 .
\end{aligned}
\tag{15}
$$

In order to solve these linear equations we have used the pseudo inverse of the matrix Ψ_{kl}^{ij}, since it can be close to singular.

Table 1. Mean angular errors and corresponding standard deviations of approximated zeroth ($M = 0$) and first ($M = 1$) order optic flow based on zeroth order normal. The results have been computed at different sets of spatiotemporal and integration scales (σ, τ, ϖ). The last two rows show results produced with the automatic scale selection method discussed in Sec. 4. The scales was selected from the sets $\sigma \in \{1.0, 1.414, 2.0, 2.828, 4.0, 5.656, 8.0\}$, $\tau \in \{1.0, 2.0, 3.0\}$, $\varpi \in \{1.0, 2.0, 4.0, 8.0\}$.

Parameters	TTS		DTS		Yosemite		Fire	
	Mean	St. dev.	Mean	St. dev.	Mean	St. dev.	Mean	St. dev.
M=0, $(1, 2, 2)$	0.99	4.50	2.43	3.42	20.15	17.37	5.92	14.61
M=1, $(1, 2, 2)$	0.87	1.76	1.17	1.74	21.83	19.00	5.78	14.79
M=0, $(2, 2, 4)$	0.42	0.87	3.41	2.64	17.16	13.89	7.88	14.60
M=1, $(2, 2, 4)$	0.52	1.23	1.49	1.88	16.94	13.45	7.42	14.78
M=0, $(4, 2, 8)$	0.31	0.19	5.19	3.10	18.42	11.95	12.88	16.62
M=1, $(4, 2, 8)$	0.25	0.25	1.49	0.88	17.30	10.69	11.71	17.75
M=0, multi-scale	0.34	0.23	5.02	3.86	11.50	15.66	7.85	15.57
M=1, multi-scale	0.15	0.11	0.80	0.47	8.51	12.57	7.55	15.65

We have computed the optic flow for the four synthetic benchmark sequences using fixed scales and automatic scale selection (Table 1). We see that for some types of sequences the automatic scale selection improves the results. This is not true for the fire sequence and zeroth order results for all but the Yosemite sequence. This indicates that scale selection based on numerical stability might not be the best solution. We believe that a way to improve this would be to incorporate information of the structure of the normal flow into the scale selection mechanism. Furthermore, for certain fixed fine scales we find that the first order model does not produce better results than the zeroth order model. The reason for this is that at fine scales the accuracy of the higher order partial derivatives needed in the first order model reduces. Note as well that the zeroth order optic flow model does not handle the sequences consisting of non-translational motion well; this concerns the DTS, Yosemite, and fire sequences. This is not surprising considering that these sequences consist of a type of motion which is poorly modeled by this type of model.

In Table 2 we show some of the results from Table 1 together with the best results of other optic flow techniques. Unfortunately we could only get results for the Yosemite sequence for the Alvarez et al. [1] method. We see that both the zeroth and first order scale selected optic flow models perform as well as, and in some cases better than, other methods for most benchmark sequences. For the diverging trees and Yosemite sequences the results of the zeroth order optic flow are mediocre. The reason for this is, as mentioned above, that the zero order model is a poor model of this type of flow. We expect that the first order result for the Yosemite sequence is mediocre, because of the apparent limitations of the scale selection method and our limiting choice of spatial models of the optic flow. Our method delivers good results for the fire sequence, which shows that it works well on sequences consisting of complex non-rigid motion.

Table 2. Mean angular errors and standard deviations for different optic flow techniques obtained from Barron et al. [3] (the best results for different methods), Alvarez et al. [1], and Florack et al. [4] (first order multi-scale results). The last three rows are results obtained with our method. The fire results for other methods were computed by using the implementations by Barron et al. [3].

Techniques	TTS		DTS		Yosemite		Fire	
	Mean	St. dev.	Mean	St. dev.	Mean	St. dev.	Mean	St. dev.
Horn & Schunck	2.02	2.27	2.55	3.67	9.78	16.19	9.08	18.97
Uras et al.	0.62	0.52	4.64	3.48	8.94	15.61	14.68	25.64
Nagel	2.44	3.06	2.94	3.23	10.22	16.51	10.84	21.75
Anandan	4.54	3.10	7.64	4.96	13.36	15.64	14.38	22.77
Singh (step 2)	1.25	3.29	8.60	5.60	10.44	13.94	9.94	19.71
Alvarez et al.	–	–	–	–	5.53	7.40	–	–
Florack et al.	0.49	1.92	1.15	3.32	–	–	–	–
$M=1, (1,2,2)$	0.87	1.76	1.17	1.74	21.83	19.00	5.78	14.79
$M=0$, multi-scale	0.34	0.23	5.02	3.86	11.50	15.66	7.85	15.57
$M=1$, multi-scale	0.15	0.11	0.80	0.47	8.51	12.57	7.55	15.65

In Fig. 2 we show the zeroth and first order optic flow for a real complex sequence of smoke circulation in a pigsty[5]. Notice that our method captures the circular motion in the sequence and that the produced fields follow the structure of the smoke. It is clear that the zeroth order model breaks down at several points contrary to the first order model which seems to do a good job at almost all image points. We would expect that higher order models would improve the results to some extend, but it is also well-known that too complex models would lead to over-fitting to the data and it is therefore important to choose the model order carefully.

6 Conclusion

In this paper we have presented an algorithm for approximation of optic flow based on a polynomial model of the local flow and regularized by a Gaussian integration scale-space. The method fits the normal component of the model to the underlying normal flow, which we presume is given, and the tangential component is extracted by integration of the local structure of the normal flow. In order to take full advantage of the multi-scale property of the method, we have suggested the use of an automatic local scale selection mechanism proposed by Niessen et al. [18]. We have compared the performance of the proposed method based on zeroth and first order models with that of other optic flow methods, [1,3,4]. We thereby show that the method with these models performs as well as, and in some cases outperforms, other optic flow methods.

The optic flow method proposed in this paper is least committed in the sense that we model the local variation of the optic flow by a polynomial model

---

[5] See http://www.diku.dk/users/kimstp/demos/ for more details.

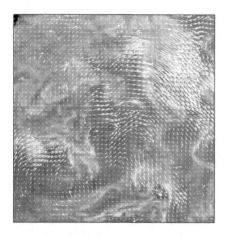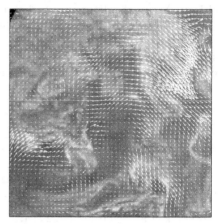

Figure 2. Smoke circulation in a pigsty. The sequence consists of 16 images of 256×256 gray value pixels. Here we only show a part of the middle image of the sequence with the corresponding zeroth (left) and first (right) order scale selected optic flow. We plot every fourth vector scaled by a factor of 5. In the top of the image there is a circular motion from left to right and in the bottom there is a slow motion from right to left.

for which the range of validity is determined by the choice of local integration scale. This makes the proposed algorithm a useful tool in e.g. experimental fluid dynamics ([20]), which we illustrated with an analysis of a sequence of smoke circulation in a pigsty. We measured the performance of our and other methods on a complex synthetic fire particle sequence consisting of non-rigid motion, thereby showing that our method is able to handle this type of motion better than other methods.

When using this as well as other methods, it is important to choose the model order carefully, because the actual number of d.o.f. will vary across the image. In regions with non or little local flow structure we would expect that zeroth order flow would give us accurate measurements, because of the low number of d.o.f. Regions with a large amount of local flow structure leads to a large number of d.o.f. and therefore higher order models are necessary. We therefore believe that a local order selection mechanism, like the minimum description length principle, would be a valuable tool combined with the optic flow method proposed in this paper.

Acknowledgments

Thanks to Theo Engell-Nielsen for producing the synthetic fire particle image sequence.

References

1. L. Alvarez, J. Weickert, and J. Sanchez. Reliable estimation of dense optical flow fields with large displacements. *IJCV*, 39(1):41 – 56, 2000.
2. J. Arnspang. Optic acceleration. In *Proc. of 2nd ICCV*, pages 364–373, 1988.
3. J.L. Barron, D.J. Fleet, and S.S. Beauchemin. Performance of optical flow techniques. *IJCV*, 12(1):43–77, 1994.
4. L. Florack, W. Niessen, and M. Nielsen. The intrinsic structure of optic flow incorporating measurement duality. *IJCV*, 27(3):263–286, 1998.
5. L. Florack, B. ter Haar Romeny, J. Koenderink, and M. Viergever. Linear scalespace. *JMIV*, 4(4):325–351, 1994.
6. J. Gårding and T. Lindeberg. Direct computation of shape cues using scale-adapted spatial derivative operators. *IJCV*, 17(2):163 – 191, 1996.
7. G.H. Granlund and H. Knutsson. *Signal Processing for Computer Vision*. Kluwer, Dordrecht, 1995.
8. B.K.P. Horn and B.G. Schunck. Determining optical flow. *Artificial Intelligence*, 17:185–203, 1981.
9. T. Kanade and M. Okutomi. A stereo matching algorithm with an adaptive window: Theory and experiment. *IEEE Trans. PAMI*, 16(9):920–932, 1994.
10. J. Koenderink. The structure of images. *Biol. Cyber.*, 50:363–370, 1984.
11. J. Koenderink. Scale-time. *Biol. Cyber.*, 58:159–162, 1988.
12. T. Lindeberg. Direct estimation of affine image deformations using visual front-end operations with automatic scale selection. In *Proc. of ICCV'95*. Springer, 1995.
13. T. Lindeberg. Linear spatio-temporal scale-space. In *Proc. of Scale-Space'97*, LNCS. Springer, 1997.
14. T. Lindeberg. Edge detection and ridge detection with automatic scale selection. *IJCV*, 30(2):117–154, 1998.
15. D. Marr. *Vision*. W. H. Freeman & Co., San Francisco, 1982.
16. M. Nielsen, R. Maas, W. Niessen, L. Florack, and B. ter Haar Romeny. Binocular stereo from grey-scale images. *JMIV*, 10(2):103–122, 1999.
17. M. Nielsen and O.F. Olsen. The structure of the optic flow field. In *Proc. of ECCV'98*, LNCS. Springer, 1998.
18. W. Niessen and R. Maas. Optic flow and stereo. In J. Sporring et al., editor, *Gaussian Scale-Space Theory*, pages 31–42. Kluwer, 1997.
19. M. Otte and H.-H. Nagel. Optical flow estimation: Advances and comparisons. In *Proc. of ECCV'94*, LNCS. Springer, 1994.
20. K.S. Pedersen. Turbulence in optical flow fields. Technical Report DIKU-00-3, DIKU, 2000.
21. K.S. Pedersen and M. Nielsen. The hausdorff dimension and scale-space normalisation of natural images. *JVCIR*, 11(2):266 – 277, 2000.
22. J. Weber and J. Malik. Robust computation of optical flow in a multi-scale differential framework. *IJCV*, 14:67–81, 1995.
23. J. Weickert. *Anisotropic Diffusion in Image Processing*. Teubner, 1998.

Image Registration, Optical Flow, and Local Rigidity

Martin Lefébure[1] and Laurent D. Cohen[2]

[1] Current address: 69 rue Perronet, 92200 Neuilly Sur Seine, France,
was with Poseidon Technologies
`mlefebure@compaqnet.fr`
[2] CEREMADE, Université Paris-Dauphine, 75775 Paris cedex 16, France
`cohen@ceremade.dauphine.fr`

Abstract. We address the theoretical problems of optical flow estimation and image registration in a multi-scale framework in any dimension. We start by showing, in the translation case, that convergence to the global minimum is made easier by applying a low pass filter to the images hence making the energy "convex enough". In order to keep convergence to the global minimum in the general case, we introduce a local rigidity hypothesis on the unknown deformation. We then deduce a new natural motion constraint equation (MCE) at each scale using the Dirichlet low pass operator. This allows us to derive sufficient conditions for convergence of a new multi-scale and iterative motion estimation/registration scheme towards a global minimum of the usual nonlinear energy instead of a local minimum as did all previous methods. We then use an implicit numerical approach. We illustrate our method on synthetic and real examples (Motion, Registration, Morphing).

1 Introduction

Registration and motion estimation are one of the most challenging problems in computer vision, having uncountable applications in various domains [13,14,6,4], [10,23]. These problems occur in many applications like medical image analysis, recognition, visual servoing, stereoscopic vision, satellite imagery or indexation. Hence they have constantly been addressed in the literature throughout the development of image processing techniques. As a first example (Figure 1) consider the problem of finding the motion in a two-dimensional images sequence. We then look for a displacement $(h_1(x_1, x_2), h_2(x_1, x_2))$ that minimizes an energy functional:

$$\int \int |I_1(x, y) - I_2(x + h_1(x, y), y + h_2(x, y))|^2 dx dy.$$

Next consider the problem of finding a rigid or non rigid deformation $(f_1(x_1, x_2), f_2(x_1, x_2))$ between two images (Figure 1), minimizing an energy functional:

$$\int \int |I_1(x, y) - I_2(f_1(x, y), f_2(x, y))|^2 dx dy.$$

M. Kerckhove (Ed.): Scale-Space 2001, LNCS 2106, pp. 26–38, 2001.

Fig. 1. Two images on the left: Finding the motion in a two-dimensional images sequence. Two images on the right: Finding a non rigid deformation.

At last consider the stereoscopic matching problem: given a stereo pair, the epipolar constraint allows to split the two-dimensional matching problem into a series of line by line one-dimensional matching problems. One has just to find, for every line, the disparity $h(x)$ minimizing:

$$\int |I_1(x) - I_2(x + h(x))|^2 dx.$$

Although most papers deal only with motion estimation or matching depending on the application in view, both problems can be formulated the same way and be solved with the same algorithm. Thus the work we present can be applied both to registration for a pair of images to match (stereo, medical or morphing) or motion field / optical flow for a sequence of images. In this paper we will focus our attention on these problems assuming grey level conservation between both signals or images to be matched. Let us denote by $I_1(x)$ and $I_2(x)$ respectively the study and target signals or images to be matched, where $x \in D = [-M, M]^d \subset \mathbb{R}^d$, and $d \geq 1$. In the following I_1 and I_2 are supposed to belong to the space $C_0^1(D)$ of continuously differentiable functions vanishing on the domain boundary ∂D. We will then assume there exists a homeomorphism f^* of D which represents the deformation such that:

$$I_1(x) = I_2 \circ f^*(x), \forall x \in D.$$

In the context of optical flow estimation, let us denote by h^* its associated motion field defined by $h^* = f^* - Id$ on D. We thus have:

$$I_1(x) = I_2(x + h^*(x)). \tag{1}$$

h^* is obviously a global minimum of the nonlinear functional

$$E_{NL}(h) = \frac{1}{2} \int_D |I_1(x) - I_2(x + h(x))|^2 dx. \tag{2}$$

We can deduce from (1) the well known Motion Constraint Equation (also called Optical Flow Constraint):

$$I_1(x) - I_2(x) \simeq < \nabla I_2(x), h^*(x) > , \forall x \in D. \tag{3}$$

E_{NL} is classically replaced in the literature by its quadratic version substituting the integrand with the squared difference between both left and right terms of the MCE, yielding the classical energy for the optical flow problem:

$$E_L(h) = \frac{1}{2} \int_D |I_1(x) - I_2(x) - <\nabla I_2(x), h(x)>|^2 dx.$$

Here ∇ denotes the gradient operator. Since the work of Horn and Schunk [13], MCE (3) has been widely used as a first order differential model in motion estimation and registration algorithms. In order to overcome the too low spatio-temporal sampling problem which causes numerical algorithms to converge to the closest local minimum of the energy E_{NL} instead of a global one, Terzopoulos et al. [18,23] and Adelson and Bergen [8,22] proposed to consider it at different scales. This led to the popular coarse-to-fine minimizing technique [14,9,10,19,11]. It is based on the remark that MCE (3) is a first order expansion which is generally no longer valid with h^* searched for. The idea is then to consider signals or images at a coarse resolution and to refine iteratively the estimation process. Since then many authors pointed out convergence properties of such algorithms towards a dominant motion in the case of motion estimation [7,9,12], or an acceptable deformation in the case of registration [10,19,20], even if the initial motion were large. Let us mention that many authors assume that deformation fields have some continuity or regularity properties, leading to the addition of some particular regularizing terms to the quadratic functional [13,5,23,3,2]. This very short state-of-the-art is far from being exhaustive but it allows to raise four common features shared by all most effective differential techniques:

1. a motion constraint equation,
2. a regularity hypothesis on the deformation,
3. a multi-scale approach,
4. an iterative scheme.

However, most of the multi-scale approaches assume that the MCE is more "valid" at lower resolutions. But to our knowledge and despite the huge literature, no theoretical analysis can confirm this. It may come from the fact that blurred signals or images are always "more similar". Choosing a particular low pass operator Π_σ (here $\sigma \geq 0$ is proportional to the number of considered harmonics in the Fourier decomposition) and some deformation $f^* = Id + h^*$ satisfying a local rigidity hypothesis with respect to a signal or image I_1, we shall find a linear operator $P_\sigma^{I_1}$ depending on I_1 such that:

$$\Pi_\sigma \left(I_1 - I_2 \right) \simeq P_\sigma^{I_1}(h^*), \tag{4}$$

the sharpness of this approximation being decreasing with respect to both h norm and resolution parameter σ. We are faced with the following motion size/structure hypothesis trade-off: for some fixed estimation reliability, the larger the motion, the poorer its structure. This transforms the problem to solving the energy minimization in a finite dimensional subspace of approximation obtained through Fourier Decomposition. In this context we are led to consider the new energy to be minimized:

$$E_L(h) = \frac{1}{2} \int_D |\Pi_\sigma(I_1 - I_2) - P_\sigma^{I_1}(h)|^2 dx.$$

Considering general linear parametric motion models for h^*, we give sufficient conditions for asymptotic convergence of the sequence of combined motion estimations towards h^* together with the numerical convergence of the sequence of deformed templates towards the target I_2. Roughly speaking, the shape of the theorem will be the following:

Theorem: If

1. at each step the residual deformation is "locally rigid", and the associated motion can be linearly decomposed onto an "acceptable" set of functions the cardinal of which is not too large with respect to the scale,
2. the initial motion norm is not too large, and the systems conditionings do not decrease "too rapidly" when iterating,
3. the estimated deformations $Id + \hat{h}_i$ are invertible and "locally rigid",

Then the scheme "converges" towards a global minimum of the energy E_{NL}.

The outline of the paper is as follows. In Section 2 we recall the energy convexifying properties of multi-scale approaches together with fast convergence in case of purely translational motion. In Section 3 we turn to the general motion case and introduce a new local rigidity hypothesis and a low pass filter in order to derive a new MCE of the type of equation (4). In Section 4 we design an iterative motion estimation/registration scheme based on the MCE introduced in Section 3 and prove a convergence theorem. In order to avoid the a priori motion representation problem, we adopt an implicit approach and constrain each estimated deformation to be at least invertible. We show numerical results for some signals and the stereo problem in dimension 1, and for large deformations problems in dimension 2. Section 6 gives a general conclusion to the paper.

2 Purely Translational Motion Estimation

In this section we assume the motion to be found is only translational. This simple case will allow us to show the energy convexifying properties of multi-scale approaches together with fast convergence of iterative algorithms.

2.1 Synthetic 1D Energy Convexifying Example

Consider a test signal (Figure 2) and its purely translated copies. The energy given by the mean quadratic error between shifted test signals and considered as a function of the translational parameter can be convexified using signals at a poorer resolution. Indeed we show the energy as a function of the translation parameter calculated with original test signals (Figure 2) and with same signal at a poorer resolution (Figure 2), namely signals reconstructed with only 5 and 3 first harmonics of the Fourier base. This readily yields more and more convexified energies as the resolution is lower. Based on this convexifying property, a generic algorithm for estimating the translational parameter is as follows:

1. Find the finest resolution j for which the energy is convex enough.
2. Minimize the MCE-based energy with signals at resolution j.
3. Refine the result by increasing the resolution and minimizing the new energy.

2.2   Convergence Conditions

In [16] we prove that this iterative process can converge to the solution provided the initial motion norm is not too important with respect to the chosen signal or image resolution. This one-dimensional result was easily extended to dimension $d > 1$ (see [17]).

3   General Motion Multiresolution Estimation

In Section 2 we have considered only purely translational motion estimation and registration. Our purpose here is to take over the general case for the motion. Our approach is based on the fact that the motion is hidden in the difference between both functions to be matched. This will lead us to analyze this difference at some particular resolution. Making some assumptions on the structure and local behaviour of the motion and the type of scale-space, we will find a new MCE and show that we can control the sharpness of it, which has not been taken care of previously.

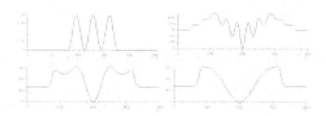

Fig. 2. Test Signal. First line: On the left, the second signal is the same shifted by 200; on the right: Energy as a function of shift parameter. There are numerous local minima around the global minimum at $x = 200$ at scale 7.. Second line: same energy with signals reconstructed with only 5 harmonics (left) and 3 harmonics (right) using the multiresolution pyramid spanned by the first elements of the Fourier base.

3.1 Controlling the Residuals when Mixing Differential and Scale-Space Techniques

Using a regularizing kernel G_σ at scale σ, Terzopoulos et al. [18,23] and Adelson and Bergen [8] were led to consider the following modified MCE:

$$G_\sigma * (I_1 - I_2)(x) \simeq < G_\sigma * \nabla I_2(x), h^*(x) >$$

To our knowledge and despite the huge literature on these approaches, no theoretical error analysis can be found when such approximations are done. However it has been reported from numerical experiments that the modified MCE was not performing well at very coarse scales, thus betraying its progressive lack of sharpness. Assuming a local rigidity hypothesis and adopting the Dirichlet operator Π_σ, we will find a different right hand side featuring a "natural" and unique linear operator $P_\sigma^{I_1}$ in the sense that:

$$\Pi_\sigma(I_1 - I_2)(x) \simeq P_\sigma^{I_1}(h^*)(x), \tag{5}$$

with remainder of the order of $\|h^*\|^2$ for some particular norm and vanishing as the scale is coarser.

3.2 Local Rigidity Property

In this paragraph we introduce our local rigidity property of deformations.

Definition 1. $f \in Hom(D)$ is ξ-rigid for $I_1 \in C^1(D)$ iff:

$$Jac(f)^t.\nabla I_1 = det(Jac(f))\nabla I_1, \tag{6}$$

where $Jac(f)$ denotes the Jacobian matrix of f and $det(A)$ the determinant of matrix A, and $Hom(D)$ the space of continuously differentiable and invertible functions from D to D (homeomorphisms).

All ξ-rigid deformations have the following properties (see [15] for the proofs). Assume f^* is ξ-rigid for $I_1 \in C_0^1(D)$ and $I_1 = I_2 \circ f^*$. Then,

1. equation (6) is always true if dimension d is 1;
2. suppose $d = 2$: then,
3. if $Jac(f^*)$ is symmetric, then (6) means that if $|\nabla I_1| \neq 0$,
    - direction $\eta = \frac{\nabla I_1}{|\nabla I_1|}$ is eigenvector ($\lambda = det(Jac(f))$ is an eigenvalue);
    - direction $\xi = \frac{\nabla I_1^\perp}{|\nabla I_1|}$ is "rigid" ($\lambda = 1$ is an eigenvalue);
    then for all $x \in D$ where I_1 is not locally constant we have $h(x) = h^*(x)$.

3.3 The Dirichlet Operator

Let $D = [-M, M]^d$; $S_\sigma = \{k \in Z^d, \forall i \in [1, d], |k_i| \leq M\sigma^2\}$; $c_k(I)$ denotes the Fourier coefficient of I defined by: $c_k(I) = \frac{1}{(2M)^{\frac{d}{2}}} \int_D I(x) e^{-\frac{i\pi<k,x>}{M}} dx$. Then the Dirichlet operator Π_σ is the linear mapping associating to each function $I \in C_0^1(D)$ the function $\Pi_\sigma(I) = G_\sigma * I$, where the convolution kernel G_σ is defined by its Fourier coefficients as follows:

$$c_k(G_\sigma) = \begin{cases} 1 \text{ if } k \in S_\sigma \\ 0 \text{ elsewhere} \end{cases}$$

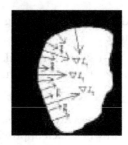

Fig. 3. An example of motion $h = f - Id$ of a ξ-rigid deformation f for image I_1. We show a level set of image I_1, and the fields ∇I_1 and h along its boundary. h varies only along the direction of ∇I_1.

3.4   New MCE by Linearization for the Dirichlet Projection

Now that we have introduced our rigidity property of deformations and the Dirichlet projection, we obtain the

Theorem 1. *If $f^* = Id + h^*$ is ξ-rigid for $I_1 = I_2 \circ f^* \in C_0^1(D)$, then we have:*

$$\|\Pi_\sigma(I_1 - I_2) - P_\sigma^{I_1}(h^*)\|_{L^2} \leq \frac{\pi}{2}\sigma^{d+2}\|h^*|\nabla I_1|^{\frac{1}{2}}\|_{L^2}^2.$$

This inequality is nothing but the sharpness of MCE (5): $\Pi_\sigma(I_1 - I_2)(x) \simeq P_\sigma^{I_1}(h^*)(x)$, at scale σ. It clearly expresses the fact that measuring the motion (e.g perceiving the optical flow) h^* is not relevant outside of the support of $|\nabla I_1|$. *Proof.* See [17]   ■

4   Theoretical Iterative Scheme and Convergence Theorem

In section 3 we found a new MCE and showed that we can control the sharpness of it. In this section we will make a rather general assumption on the motion in the sense that it should belong to some linear parametric motion model without being more specific on the model basis functions. Though it is somewhat restrictive to have motion fields in a finite dimensional functional space, this structural hypothesis will be a key to bounding the residual motion norm after registration in order to iterate the process. This makes it possible to consider a constraint on motion when there is a priori knowledge (like for rigid motion) or consider multi-scale decomposition of motion for an iterative scheme.

4.1   Linear Parametric Motion Models and Least Square Estimation

Let us assume the motion h^* has to be in a finite dimensional space of deformation generated by basis functions $\Psi(x) = (\psi_i(x))_{i=1..n}$. Thus h^* can be decomposed in the basis: $\exists\ \Theta^* = (\theta_i^*)_{i=1..n}$ unique, such that:

$$h^*(x) = <\Psi(x), \Theta^*> = \sum_{i=1..n} \theta_i^* \psi_i(x), \ \forall x \in Supp(|\nabla I_1|).$$

MCE (5) viewed as a linear model writes: $\Pi_\sigma(I_1 - I_2) = <P_\sigma^{I_1}(\Psi), \Theta^*>$. Now set, for σ s.t. the $P_\sigma^{I_1}(\psi_i)$ be mutually linearly independent in L^2:

$$M_\sigma = P_\sigma^{I_1}(\Psi) \otimes P_\sigma^{I_1}(\Psi), \quad Y_\sigma = \Pi_\sigma(I_1 - I_2),$$

where $\otimes$ stands for the tensorial product in L^2. Then applying basic results from the classical theory of linear models yields: $\hat{h} = <\Psi, \hat{\Theta}> = <\Psi, M_\sigma^{-1} B_\sigma>$, where column B_σ's components are defined by $(B_\sigma)_i = <P_\sigma^{I_1}(\psi_i), Y_\sigma>$.

4.2 Estimation Error and Residual Motion

Given the least square estimation of the motion of last paragraph, we have

Lemma 1. *In this framework the motion estimation error is bounded by inequality* $\||(\hat{h} - h^*)|\nabla I_1|^{\frac{1}{2}}\|_{L^2} \leq \frac{\pi}{2}\sigma^{d+2}\left(Tr(M_\sigma^{-1})\right)^{\frac{1}{2}}\|h^*|\nabla I_1|^{\frac{1}{2}}\|_{L^2}^2.$

Proof. See [17]   ∎

If $Id + \hat{h}$ is invertible, we can define:

$$I_{1,1} = I_1 \circ \left(Id + \hat{h}\right)^{-1}. \tag{7}$$

Letting r_1 denote the residual motion such that $I_{1,1} = I_2 \circ (Id + r_1)$, if $Id + \hat{h}$ is ξ-rigid for I_1 then a variable change yields equality $\||(\hat{h} - h^*)|\nabla I_1|^{\frac{1}{2}}\|_{L^2} = \|r_1|\nabla I_{1,1}|^{\frac{1}{2}}\|_{L^2}$, thus giving by Lemma 1 the following bound on the residual motion norm:

$$\|r_1|\nabla I_{1,1}|^{\frac{1}{2}}\|_{L^2} \leq \frac{\pi}{2}\sigma^{d+2}\left(Tr(M_\sigma^{-1})\right)^{\frac{1}{2}}\|h^*|\nabla I_1|^{\frac{1}{2}}\|_{L^2}^2. \tag{8}$$

In view of equality (7) and inequality (8), iterating the motion estimation/registration process looks completely natural and allows for pointing out sufficient conditions for convergence of such a process. Indeed, provided the same assumptions are made at each step, relations (7) and (8) can be seen as recurrence ones, yielding both r_p and $I_{1,p}$ sequences.

4.3 Theoretical Iterative Scheme

Having control on the residual motion after one registration step, we deduce the following theoretical iterative motion estimation / registration scheme:

1. Initialization: Enter accuracy $\epsilon > 0$ and the maximal number of iterations N. Set $p = 0$, and $I_{1,0} = I_1$.
2. Iterate while $(\|I_{1,p} - I_2\| \geq \epsilon\ \&\ p \leq N)$
   (a) Enter the set of basis functions $\Psi_p = (\psi_{p,i})_{i=1..n_p}$ that linearly and uniquely decompose r_p on the support of $|\nabla I_{1,p}|$.
   (b) Enter scale σ_p and compute: $\hat{h}_p = <\Psi_p, M_{p,\sigma_p}^{-1} B_{\sigma_p}>$.
   (c) Set $I_{1,p+1} = I_{1,p} \circ (Id + \hat{h}_p)^{-1}$.

4.4 Convergence Theorem

Now that we have designed an iterative motion estimation / registration scheme, let us infer sufficient conditions for the residual motion to vanish. This leads us to state our following main result:

Theorem 2. *If:*

1. *$\forall p \geq 0$, $I_{1,p} \sim I_2$ (as defined in Section 3.2), and residual motion r_p can be linearly and uniquely decomposed on a set of basis functions $\{\psi_{p,i}, i = 1..n_p\}$;*
2. *$\forall p \geq 0$, there exists a scale $\sigma_p > 0$ such that the set of functions $\{P_{\sigma_p}^{I_{1,p}}(\psi_{p,i}),$ $i = 1..n_p\}$ be free in L^2 and, for $p = 0$, we assume that :*

$$\||h^*|\nabla I_1|^{\frac{1}{2}}\|_{L^2} < \left(\frac{\pi}{2}\sigma_0^{d+2}Tr(M_{0,\sigma_0})^{\frac{1}{2}}\right)^{-1};$$

Set $C_0 = \left(\frac{\pi}{2}\sigma_0^{d+2}Tr(M_{0,\sigma_0})^{\frac{1}{2}}\||h^*|\nabla I_1|^{\frac{1}{2}}\|_{L^2}\right)^{-1};$

3. *The sequence of conditioning ratios satisfy criteria: $\forall p \geq 0$,*

$$\frac{\sigma_{p+1}^{d+2}Tr(M_{p+1,\sigma_{p+1}})^{\frac{1}{2}}}{\sigma_p^{d+2}Tr(M_{p,\sigma_p})^{\frac{1}{2}}} \leq C_0;$$

4. *$\forall p \geq 0$, estimated deformations $Id + \hat{h}_p \in Hom(D)$ and are ξ-rigid for $I_{1,p}$;*

Then, $\lim_{p \to \infty} \|r_p|\nabla I_{1,p}|^{1/2}\|_{L^2} = 0$.

Proof. See [17]   ∎

4.5 Numerical Algorithm Requirements

Firstly, due to the fact that h^* is unknown we have to make an arbitrary choice for the scale at each step. Secondly we at least have to ensure that $Id + \hat{h}$ be invertible at each step. Finally we are faced with the motion basis functions choice.

Multi-scale Strategy . The scale choice expresses both a priori knowledge on the motion range and its structure complexity. Here we assume that $(\sigma_p)_p$ is an increasing sequence, starting from $\sigma_0 > 0$ such that:

$$\#S_{\sigma_0} \geq \#\{\text{expected independent motions}\}. \tag{9}$$

Then let $\alpha \in]0, 1[$. In order to justify the minimization problem at new scale $\sigma_{p+1} > \sigma_p$, we will choose it such that:

$$\|(\Pi_{\sigma_{p+1}} - \Pi_{\sigma_p})(I_{1,p+1} - I_2)\|_{L^2} > \alpha\|I_{1,p+1} - I_2\|_{L^2}, \tag{10}$$

Invertibility of $Id + \hat{h}_p$. Let $\beta > 0$. We will apply to $I_{1,p}$ the inverse of the maximal invertible linear part of the computed deformation e.g. $\left(Id + t^*.\hat{h}_p\right)^{-1}$, where

$$t^* = \sup_{t \in [0,1]} \{t \ / \ det(Jac(Id + t.\hat{h}_p)) \geq \beta\}. \tag{11}$$

Choosing the Set of Basis Functions . A major difficulty arising in the theoretical scheme comes from the lack of a priori knowledge on the finite set of basis functions to be entered at each step. In Section 5 we will use an implicit approach via the optimal step gradient algorithm when minimizing the quadratic energy associated to MCE (5).

5   Implicit Approach of Basis Functions and Results

We now use the optimal step gradient algorithm for the minimization of the quadratic functional associated to MCE (5). There are at least two good reasons for doing this:

- the choice of base functions is implicit: it depends on the signals or images I_1 and I_2, and the scale space.
- we can control and stop the quadratic minimization if the associated operator is no longer positive definite.

The general algorithm does not guaranty that the resulting matrix M_{p,σ_p} be invertible. Hence we suggest to systematically use a stopping criteria to control the quadratic minimization, based on the descent speed or simply a maximum number of iterations N_G. In that case our final algorithm writes:

1. Initialization: Enter accuracy $\epsilon > 0$ and the maximal number of iterations N. Set $p = 0$, $I_{1,0} = I_1$, and choose first scale σ_0 according to (9).
2. Iterate while ($\|I_{1,p} - I_2\| \geq \epsilon$ & $p \leq N$ & $\sigma_p \leq 1$)

   (a) Choose σ_p satisfying (10).
   (b) Apply N_G iterations of the optimal step gradient algorithm for the minimization of $E_p(h) = \|\Pi_{\sigma_p}(I_{1,p} - I_2) - P_{\sigma_p}^{I_{1,p}}(h)\|_{L^2}^2$.
   (c) Compute $I_{1,p+1} = I_{1,p} \circ (Id + t^*.\hat{h}_p)^{-1}$ with t^* defined by (11) and increment p.

In the following experiments we have set $\alpha = 2.5\%$, $N_G = 5$, $\beta = 0.1$. In [17], we show results on one-dimensional synthetic and real signals, and with all intensity lines of a stereo pair. Recall that ξ-rigidity is not a constraint when $d = 1$ and thus $\hat{h}_\infty$ is relevant only when $|I'_1(x)| \neq 0$.
We illustrate the algorithm on pairs of images with large deformation for registration applications and movies for motion estimation applications.

Registration Problems Involving Large Deformation : In figure 4 we show the different steps of the algorithm performing the registration between the first and last images. In Figure 5, we show the study and target images, and the deformed study image after applying the estimated motion.

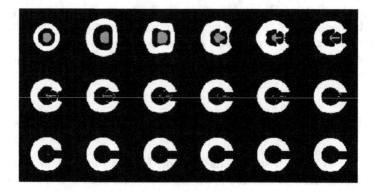

Fig. 4. Registration movie of a target to a 'C' letter. Again, each image corresponds to a step in the iterative scheme.

Fig. 5. Scene registration example: Study image (left), deformed Study image onto Target image (center), and Target image (right).

Optical Flow Estimation Examples : In Figure 6 we show the sequence of the registered images of the original Cronkite sequence onto first image using the sequence of computed backward motions. The result is expected to be motionless. On top of Figure 6, we show the complete movie obtained by deforming iteratively only the first image of Cronkite movie. For that we use the sequence of computed motions between each pair of consecutive images of the original movie. In Figure 6 on the bottom, we see the error images.

6   Conclusion

We have addressed the theoretical problems of motion estimation and registration of signals or images in any dimension. We have used the main features of previous works on the subject to formalize them in a framework allowing a rigorous mathematical analysis. More specifically we wrote a new ridigity hypothesis that we used to infer a unique Motion Constraint Equation with small remainder at coarse scales. We then showed that upon hypotheses on the motion norm and structure/scale tradeoff, an iterative motion estimation/registration scheme could converge towards the expected solution of the problem e.g. the

Fig. 6. On the left, registered sequence of the original sequence onto first image using the computed backward motions. On the right, movie obtained by deforming only the first image of Cronkite movie using the sequence of computed motions

global minimum of the nonlinear least square problem energy. Since each step of the theoretical scheme needs a set of motion basis functions which are not known, we have designed an implicit algorithm and illustrated the method in dimension one and two, including large deformation examples.

References

1. L. Alvarez, J. Esclarin, M. Lefébure, J. Sanchez. A PDE model for computing the optical flow. *Proc. XVI Congresso de Ecuaciones Diferenciales y Aplicaciones*, Las Palmas, pp. 1349–1356, 1999.
2. L. Alvarez, J. Weickert, J. Sanchez, Reliable estimation of dense optical flow fields with large displacements. TR 2, Universidad de Las Palmas, November 1999.
3. G. Aubert, R. Deriche and P. Kornprobst. Computing optical flow via variational techniques. *SIAM J. Appl. Math.*, Vol. 60 (1), pp. 156–182, 1999.
4. N. Ayache. Medical computer vision, virtual reality and robotics. IVC (13), No 4, May 1995, pp 295-313.
5. Ruzena Bajcsy and Stane Kovacic. Multiresolution elastic matching. CVGIP, (46), No 1, pp. 1–21, 1989.
6. J.L. Barron, D.J. Fleet, and S.S. Beauchemin. Performance of optical flow. IJCV, 12(1):43–77, 1994.
7. M. Ben-Ezra, B. Rousso, and S. Peleg. Motion segmentation using convergence properties. In *ARPA Im. Unders. Workshop*, pp II 1233-1235, 1994.
8. J.R. Bergen and E.H. Adelson. Hierarchical, computationally efficient motion estimation algorithm. *J. of the Optical Society Am.*, 4(35), 1987.
9. P. Bouthemy and J.M. Odobez. Robust multiresolution estimation of parametric motion models. *J. of Vis. Comm. and Image Repres.*, 6(4):348–365, 1995.
10. G. Christensen, R.D. Rabbitt, and M.I. Miller. 3D brain mapping using a deformable neuroanatomy. *Physics in Med and Biol*, (39), March :609–618, 1994.

11. D. Fleet, M. Black, Y. Yacoob and A. Jepson. Design and use of linear models for image motion analysis. *IJCV*, 36(3), 2000.
12. P.R. Giaccone, D. Greenhill, G.A. Jones. Recovering very large visual motion fields. *SCIA97*, pp 917-922.
13. B.K.P. Horn and Brian Schunck. Determining optical flow. *Artificial Intelligence*, (17) (1-3) :185–204, 1981.
14. M. Irani, B. Rousso, and S. Peleg. Detecting and tracking multiple moving objects using temporal integration. In *ECCV92*, pp 282–287, 1992.
15. M. Lefébure Estimation de Mouvement et Recalage de Signaux et d'Images: Formalisation et Analyse. PhD Thesis, Université Paris-Dauphine, 1998.
16. Martin Lefébure and Laurent D. Cohen. A multiresolution algorithm for signal and image registration. In *In Proc. ICIP'97*, Santa Barbara, California, Oct. 1997.
17. M. Lefébure and L. D. Cohen. Motion estimation and registration of signals and images: formalization and analysis. CEREMADE Technical Report, 0102, January 2001. To appear in Journal of Mathematical Imaging and Vision.
18. D. Terzopoulos. Multiresolution algorithms in computational vision. *Image Understanding*. S. Ullman, W. Richards, 1986.
19. J.P. Thirion. Fast non-rigid matching of 3D medical images. TR 2547, INRIA, 1995.
20. A. Trouvé. Diffeomorphisms groups and pattern matching in image analysis. IJCV, 28(3), 1998.
21. J. Weickert. On discontinuity-preserving optic flow. *Proc. Computer Vision and Mobile Robotics Workshop*, Santorini, pp. 115–122, Sept. 1998.
22. G. Whitten. A framework for adaptive scale space tracking solutions to problems in computational vision. In *ICCV'90, Osaka*, pp 210–220, Dec 1990.
23. A. Witkin, D. Terzopoulos, M. Kass. Signal matching through scale space. IJCV, 1(2):133–144, 1987.

What Do Features Tell about Images?

Mads Nielsen and Martin Lillholm

IT University of Copenhagen, Glentevej 67
DK – 2400 Copenhagen NV, Denmark
{malte,grumse}@itu.dk

Abstract. According to the Marr paradigm [10], visual processing is performed by low-level feature detection followed by higher level task dependent processing. In this case, any two images exhibiting identical features will yield the same result of the visual processing. The set of images exhibiting identical features form an equivalence class: a *metameric class* [7]. We choose from this class the (in some precise sense) simplest image as a representative. The complexity of this simplest image may in turn be used for analyzing the information content of features. We show examples of images reconstructed from various scale-space features, and show that a low number of simple differential features carries sufficient information for reconstructing images close to identical to the human observer. The paper presents direct methods for reconstruction of minimal variance representatives, and variational methods for computation of maximum entropy and maximum a posteriori representatives based on priors for natural images. Finally, conclusions on the information content in blobs and edges are indicated.

1   Introduction

An image is often perceived as the graph of an intensity function over the spatial domain. Not every characteristics of this graph is of interest to the observer. An observer only interested in image edges, will consider two images having the same edges as being per definition identical, since all observables (edges) are identical. This leads us to the conclusion that the most appropriate operational definition of *image structure* is a *collection of operationally defined image features*. The set of image features is not fixed for all observers/tasks, thus two images of identical structure for one task may have deviating structure for another task (set of features). Since the number of possible different operationally defined features is infinite, we may attribute an infinite number of different structures to a given image.

We will only investigate a small subset of all possible operationally defined features, namely those that can be expressed solely in terms of local scale-space derivatives. Particularly, we address blobs and edges. We adapt the approach of Gaussian scale-space [14,6] so that multi-local features may be expressed as features at a finite scale [8]. The features of an image change as a function of the free scale parameter, and this total scale-space behavior of features in general describes the image graph to a very high degree. As examples, it has been proven

M. Kerckhove (Ed.): Scale-Space 2001, LNCS 2106, pp. 39–50, 2001.

that one may reconstruct the image from the multi-scale zero-crossings of the Laplacian [4] or alone from the scale-space top-points in the analytical case [5].

In this paper, we will not investigate the case where the image may be uniquely reconstructed from the features. We investigate the case where the detected features define a metameric class of images. As a representative of this class we chose the simplest image in the class. Simplicity is defined relative to an expectation (prior), and we suggest the use of different priors. Among these we propose Gaussian intensity distribution, photon distribution entropy, and a Brownian motion model for natural images [2].

In the case of using the maximum of photon distribution [13] our work resemble the work of Zhu, Wu, and Mumford [16,15] in their *constructive image processing*. They use outcomes of filters for building a stochastic model of a class of images or textures. They approximate the distribution of images as the maximum entropy distribution yielding the same feature statistics. In our work, we do not look at an ensemble of images, and a distribution of features, but at one given set of features detected in an image and the class of images having these features.

The present work may be used for image representation (compression). We show that few features are sufficient to describe an image to a very high degree. Furthermore, the present work yields an easy way to grasp the intuition of which information a feature actually carries about the image. In this way we see the major contribution of this paper, not a matter of efficient image coding, but as to describe the actual information contents in features and combinations hereof. We wish to gain insight into features, their selection, and importance.

Elder and Zucker [1] presented work on reconstructing images from scale-space edges. However, they did not reconstruct images that exhibit the same features, but merely use the scale of an edge to indicate the slope of the edge in the image and then reconstructed the image as a minimal surface. We wish to emphasize that the present image representation scheme is a projection: The reconstructed image exhibits observables identical to those measured in the original image.

In the following we briefly describe the features of choice and the computation of the representative of the metameric class. In terms of image coding or image representation, we will denote this the *reconstruction* of the image from the features. Finally, we give examples and draw conclusions.

2   Scale-Space Feature Detection

The scale-space image $L(x, \sigma)$ is constructed by convolving the original image I with a Gaussian of standard deviation *sigma*, and derivatives hereof by convolution with scale-normalized Gaussian derivatives so that

$$\partial_{\tilde{x}} L(x, \sigma) = \sigma^\gamma \partial_x L(x, \sigma)$$

where the σ-term gives the scale normalization and γ is a free parameter for feature-dependent tuning of the scale selection [8,9]. Normally $\gamma = 1$ but for some features a better scale selection is obtained by choosing a different γ. This is related to the local Hausdorff dimension of the image graph close to the feature [11].

Feature detectors can now be created as non-linear combinations of scale-space derivatives:

Feature	Strength	Spatial	Scale	γ
Blob	$\triangle L$	$\max_x(\triangle L)$	$\max_\sigma(\triangle L)$	1
Edge	L_w	$L_{ww} = 0$	$\max_\sigma(L_w)$	1/2
Corner	$L_w^2 L_{vv}$	$\max_x(L_w^2 L_{vv})$	$\max_\sigma(L_w^2 L_{vv})$	1
Ridge	L_{vv}	$L_{vw} = 0$	$\max_\sigma(L_{vv})$	3/4

Here v is along the isophote direction and w along the gradient direction. $\max_\sigma$ denotes maximum over scale and $\max_x$ denotes a spatial maximum.

These feature detectors select a number of points of interest or attention in the image, and their corresponding scale. In principle, we could choose any measurement of the image as representation of the image. However, we believe that the abovementioned feature points are special points, and in the following we will investigate their information contents.

3 Selection of a Representative of a Metameric Class

Assume a set of point features are given. They are each given in terms of a number of localized linear filters, and the corresponding filter value. That is, we know that the image $I(x)$ satisfy the constraints:

$$\int_\Omega I(x) f_i(x) dx = c_i, i = 1 \ldots K \tag{1}$$

Many images $I : \mathbb{R}^N \mapsto \mathbb{R}_+$ may fulfill Eq. 1; the metameric class. We are interested in one representative of this class. We select this representative as the image minimizing one of the three different complexity measures:

$$V = \int_\Omega (I(x) - \mu)^2 dx \tag{2}$$

$$H = -\int_\Omega I_n(x) \log I_n(x) dx \tag{3}$$

$$B = \int_\Omega |\nabla I|^2 dx \tag{4}$$

where $I_n = \frac{I}{\int_\Omega I(x) dx}$.

The **intensity variance** (V) corresponds to assuming a Gaussian prior of intensities. In this way the simplest image is the maximum a posteriori estimate of the image given the features. The measure must be minimized to yield this.

This measure is very simple, but has the drawback that the complexity is defined globally and thereby not takes the concept of homogeneous regions into account (see Fig. 1).

The photon distribution entropy (H) is the stochastic complexity of the distribution of the position of a photon hitting the image. That is, the distribution corresponds to an image normalized in intensity to unity. A reconstruction of maximum entropy is thus as close as possible to the uniform distribution (uniform image). This measure nicely takes into account the fact that image intensities are positive values. It is a measure of the global variance. Like the above variance measure, it does not take homogeneous regions into account.

The local variation (B) measures how much the image varies locally. The reconstruction according to this measure will *locally* be as homogeneous as possible. The reconstruction may be derived as the maximum a posteriori estimate according to a prior for natural images. The prior is a Gaussian Brownian motion in intensity:

$$P(J) \propto \prod_\Omega e^{-\frac{I_x^2+I_y^2}{2s^2}}$$

This has been shown to approximate the distribution of natural images [2]. However, more refined analysis show that the distribution of the local variation in natural images is not exactly Gaussian, and the spatial correlation pattern in images in e.g. a forest show a little less correlation than the classical Brownian motion model [12]. However, we will use the Brownian motion model since it is simple and has the property of non of the above, that homogeneous regions are taken into account (see Fig. 1).

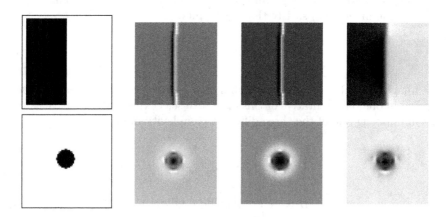

Fig. 1. Reconstruction of iconic images(64x64) from the various priors using only very sparse information. From left to right are original image, minimum variance reconstruction, maximum entropy reconstruction, and Brownian motion model reconstruction. 32 edge points are used for the edge image and 9 blobs for the blob image.

4 Linear Reconstruction

In this section we show how the variance measure leads to a very simple, direct, and linear computation of the reconstruction.

Using standard techniques of calculus of variation and Lagrange multipliers, the distribution satisfying Eq. 1 and having minimal variance satisfies

$$\frac{\delta}{\delta J}\left[\int_{\Omega}(J-\mu)^2 + \sum_{i=0}^{K}\lambda_i f_i J dx\right] = 0,$$

where J is the reconstruction and we have identified f_0 as the unit function over Ω to ensure that $\int_{\Omega} J dx = c_0$. Since the variance is a convex functional and the constraints are linear, the solution is unique:

$$J = \sum_i \lambda_i f_i. \tag{5}$$

The "only" remaining problem is to identify the values of the Lagrange multipliers λ_i so that J satisfies Eq. 1. In general, this may be a hard problem. However, in the case above, everything is linear, and we may construct a simple linear solution:

The reconstructed image must exhibit the same features as the original so that

$$c_i = \int_{\Omega} f_i \sum_j \lambda_j f_j dx = \sum_j \lambda_j \int_{\Omega} f_i f_j dx$$

Hence we identify

$$\lambda_j = \sum_i (\int_{\Omega} f_i f_j dx)^{-1} c_i$$

where the inverse is computed as the matrix inversion of $a_{ij} = \int_{\Omega} f_i f_j dx$. Finally, we find the reconstructed image J as

$$J = \sum_{ij} f_j (\int_{\Omega} f_i f_j dx)^{-1} c_i \tag{6}$$

where one may recognize the terms in front of c_i as the *pseudo inverse* of a matrix F containing columns of values of the filters f_i defined on a discrete domain. Above, we kept the continuous formulation all way through the reasoning in order to demonstrate that the resulting image J is defined on a continuous domain, if the filters are too. However, in the experiments below we use the discrete formulation and the pseudo inverse for computations:

$$J = F(F^T F)^{-1} c \tag{7}$$

For examples of actual reconstructions see Fig. 2.

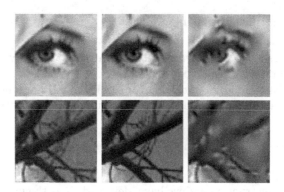

Fig. 2. Minimum variance reconstruction of Lena's left eye and tree image. From left to right: reconstructions on basis of 200 blobs and 200 edge points, original images, and reconstructions based on 40 blobs and 40 edge points.

5   Variational Reconstruction

Above, we gave a linear closed form solution for reconstructing the image of minimum variance. However, in general, we would like to be able to use alternative priors. This may be the maximum entropy criterion on photon position or on basis of other empirically verified priors on natural images [2,12,3]. Below we outline a variational approach as a standard constrained gradient descend. For general image functionals it yields a local maximum. For convex functionals this is obviously also the global maximum.

Assume an energy functional $E[J]$ to optimize under the feature constraints (Eq. 1). Assume also a suboptimal representative J^0 of the metameric class satisfying Eq. 1. In practice we compute this as the minimal variance solution above. A gradient descend in energy reads

$$\partial_t J = -\gamma E_J$$

where $E_J \equiv \frac{\delta E}{\delta J}$. This makes the solution depart from the metameric class. We construct an evolution equation constrained to the metameric class by projecting the solution back onto the metameric class. We may then talk about an *observation-constrained evolution*.

Since the constraints of Eq. 1 are linear we obtain:

$$\partial_t J = -\gamma(E_J[J] - E_J[J]\bot M) \tag{8}$$

where $E_J \bot M_c$ is defined as the part of E_J orthogonal to the metameric class:

$$E_J[J]\bot M = \sum_{ij} f_j \left(\int_\Omega f_i f_j dx \right)^{-1} \int_\Omega f_i E_J[J] dx$$

This is derived as the reconstruction (Eq. 6) based upon the filter measurements of the variation E_J. The corresponding discrete formulation (Eq. 7) reads:

$$E_J[J]\bot M_c = F(F^T F)^{-1} F^T E_J[J]$$

Minimizing Eq. 3 yields the maximum entropy reconstruction. Starting by the minimum variance solution (Eq. 6) a variational solution is reached by Eq. 8, where

$$E_J[J] = 1 + \log J.$$

This scheme is guaranteed to converge as the entropy is convex and the constraints linear.

Likewise, for the local variation functional based on the Brownian motion prior:

$$E_J[J] = -\triangle J.$$

In this case the complexity minimization is a standard image diffusion process creating a Gaussian scale-space. The evolution preserving observations (Eq. 8) may then be denoted *observation-constrained diffusion* of images. This functional derived from a Brownian motion model of natural images is convex, hence the evolution is ceased to converge towards the global optimum.

6 Experiments

In this section we give some simple examples to approach the information contents of edges and blobs. We examine the suitability of the various priors to create visually appealing reconstructions from blobs and edges. We examine how to represent the features; by their feature strength or by the fact that they are features (local maxima of feature strength). We discuss and show experiments of how to select features, and finally we show that feature points are better for representing images than random points.

Priors and Features. The lower the probability of an event is, the more information it carries. Thus, optimally we choose features representing unlikely events with respect to the image prior. Intuitively, the Brownian motion model wants to create images that are as smooth as possible. Edges indicate the local "unsmoothness" of the image. This suggests that the interplay of edges and the Brownian prior is optimal. Blobs contain information on the dark and light regions of the image. This suggests that blobs are well suited for the global measures, especially the variance measure. These points are illustrated in Fig. 1.

Feature Representation. Having selected a feature type for representing an image, the question is how to represent or "code" this feature . To our mind, two natural choices exist: A feature point may be represented by the fact that it is a feature or by the values of the corresponding feature measure. In the latter case, there is no guarantee that the reconstruction will exhibit the same feature (have a local maximum in feature strength), but it exhibits the same feature strength. In the first case there is no guarantee that the feature in the reconstruction will have same feature strength. In Fig. 3 we compare the variance of blob and edge reconstructions based on different orders of derivatives. The first order image structure codes the edge strength and the edge orientation. The second order image structure codes either edge presence (plus one directional second order derivative) or blob strength (plus the orientation and elongation, see below). The third order image structure indicate the presence of a blob (plus two more directional third order derivatives).

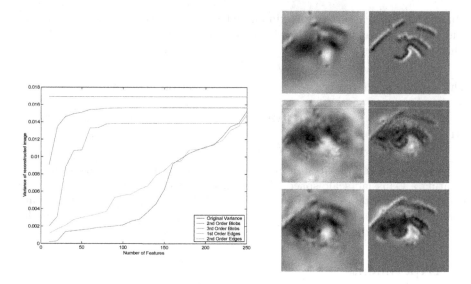

Fig. 3. Information carried by presence and strength of blobs and edges. The graph shows the minimal variance for a reconstruction given the selected features. The features have been selected ordered by their individual feature strength. Topmost line is the theoretical largest variance: the variance of the input image. Image (left column, middle) shows a reconstruction based on 80 blobs represented by 3rd order structure. Above and below are blob representations using 2nd order structure. Above is equally much variance, below is equally many blobs. Right columns are reconstruction based on edges. Middle: reconstruction based on 160 edge points represented by 2nd order structure. Below: same edges but width 1st order structure. Above: same variance is obtained by 80 edge points using 1st order structure.

It is evident from Fig. 3 that blob structure (the total 2nd order structure in blobs) carries much more information (variance) than the edge structure. It is also evident that the feature strength measures carry more information than the feature presence measures. This is due to the lower order of differentiation of the information. The second order structure is invariant to addition of an affine intensity function, whereas the third order structure is invariant to addition of a second order polynomial.

Feature Type. Intuitively edges and blobs carry different information on images. In Fig. 4 reconstructions of equal variance are compared. These experiments show what one could expect: Edges carry information on the rapid transitions whereas blobs carry information on the global structure.

Blob Representation. The blobs where shown above to carry much information in their full second order structure. Actually, the feature strength measure is the Laplacian. In Fig. 5, reconstructions based on the full structure and only the Laplacian are compared. It is evident that the elongation and orientation

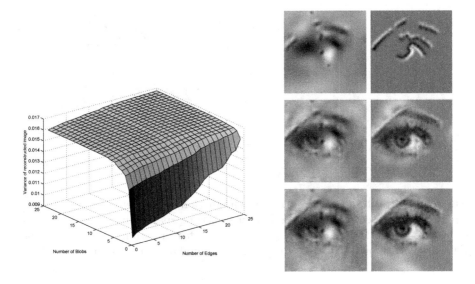

Fig. 4. Comparison on the structure in edges and blobs. The graph shows the variance as function of number of edges (1st order rep.) and blobs (2nd order rep.). First column of images shows reconstructions based on blobs (20, 80, 250 from above). Last column shows reconstructions based on edge points (80, 230 250 from above). 80 or 230 edge points and 20 blobs contain approximately equally much variance. 250 edge points and 80 or 250 blobs contain equally much variance.

of the blobs carried by the full second order structure reveal much information. Furthermore, the figure shows that blob presence carries as much information as blob strength, but only when many blobs are selected. Few blob strengths carry more information than the presence of the same few blobs.

Selection of Features. Given a set of image observations in terms of measurements in feature positions, we wish to select a subset of maximum information. This is a hard problem. Instead, we look at how much each observation carries individually, as if it were used alone for reconstruction. In this the minimum variance reconstruction J is $\lambda f = F^T(FF^T)^{-1}c$, and thereby (zero mean images)

$$Var[J] = J^T J = c(FF^T)^{-1^T} FF^T(FF^T)^{-1}c = c(FF^T)^{-1}c$$

This is for simplicity given in the discrete notation, but the result also holds in the continuous formulation. Indicated below is the information of a scale-normalized ($\gamma = 1$) derivative of value c at scale σ:

J	J_x	J_{xx}	J_{xy}	J_{xxx}	J_{xxy}
$\frac{8}{32\pi}c^2$	$\frac{4}{32\pi}c^2$	$\frac{6}{32\pi}c^2$	$\frac{2}{32\pi}c^2$	$\frac{15}{32\pi}c^2$	$\frac{3}{32\pi}c^2$

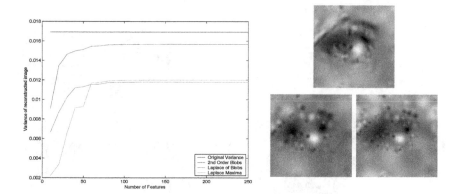

Fig. 5. The graph shows the variance as a function of number of blobs for 3 different blob representations: full 2nd order structure, spatial and scale derivatives of feature strength $((\triangle L)_x, (\triangle L)_y, (\triangle L)_t)$, and feature strength $(\triangle L)$. To the right are corresponding images for 80 blobs from above and left to right below.

The information is dependent on the derivation but *independent* of scale. This shows that as long as features do not overlap they should be chosen directly from their scale-normalized feature strength. It should be noticed however, that edges used scale-normalized derivatives with respect to $\sqrt{\sigma}$ and thereby actually carries information proportional to $c^2\sigma$ for first order and $c^2\sigma^2$ for second order. We propose a greedy algorithm for selection of features, choosing feature in descend filter value. This algorithm does not take into account the interplay of features, and is thereby not optimal, but extremely simple as all features may be judged independently. This strategy was used in all of the above experiments.

In Fig. 6 we compare different strategies for selection of features. Firstly, we choose the strategy mentioned above, selection based on largest feature strength first. Secondly, we choose a strategy of randomly selecting blobs. Finally, we select random points in scale-space. The random points are uniformly distributed over scale-space taking the natural scale-space metric into account $(\Delta x \propto \sigma, \Delta y \propto \sigma, \Delta\sigma \propto \sigma)$. We conclude from the figure, that blobs selected by feature strength carry more information than randomly selected blobs, and that blobs carry more information than blob strength in random points.

7   Discussion

Based on the experiments above, we make the following comments on how much information different types of features and their representation carry:
– Images may be reconstructed to a very high degree of visual precision based upon edge strength and blob strength in a number of detected feature points.
– Using only blob strength does not carry sufficient information for visually pleasing reconstructions.
– Taking the total blob structure (all 3 second derivatives) into account yields

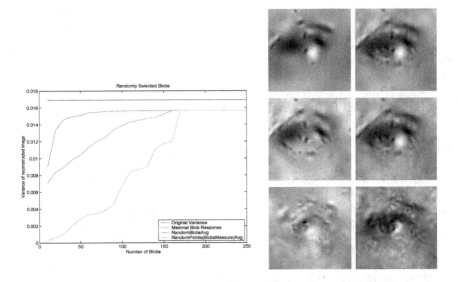

Fig. 6. The graph shows the variance of the reconstruction based on 2nd order structure as a function of number of points for three different point selection strategies: Blobs by feature strength (top row, 20 and 80 blobs), random blobs (middle row, 80 and 160 blobs), and random points (80 and 160 points). Selection by strength of 20 blobs has same variance as random selection of 80 blobs and random selection of 160 points.

potentially much more visually appealing reconstructions, but still not all information in the image has been collected.
– Edge strength and orientation alone carries more information about images than blob strength, but not as much as the total blob structure in blobs.
– As it was also predicted theoretically by looking at independent features, feature strength carries more information than feature presence.
– In order to create truly visually appealing reconstructions, blob strength and edge strength is not sufficient independently, they are both needed.

Tony Lindeberg's scheme of selecting features based upon feature strength [9] computed as normalized scale-space derivatives corresponds to selecting points of maximal information under the minimal variance prior. We see this as an underpinning of his conceptually simple but effective scale selection mechanism.

We have seen that the choice of prior is important when only very sparse information on the image has been sampled. However, when information sufficient for creating reconstructions of high visual accuracy has been sampled, the change of prior does not visually change the reconstruction. This is very natural. One way to put this is: For very little information sampled, the metameric class is large, and the different priors may choose representatives far from each other. When much information has been collected, the metameric class is small, and any sensible prior will essentially point to the same image.

The conclusion (that feature strength carries sufficient information to visually reproduce an image) shows, that feature detection is not necessarily a matter of information reduction, but merely a matter of changing into a representation that may easier subserve computation of visual tasks. Is only feature position taken into account, we see a true reduction of information. As long as this is the relevant information which has been extracted, feature detection communicating only the position of features is then a sorting of information.

References

1. J.H. Elder and S.W. Zucker. Scale space localization, blur, and contour-based image coding. In *CVPR96*, pages 27–34, 1996.
2. D.J. Field. Relations between the statistics of natural images and the response proporties of cortical cells. *J. Optic. Soc. Am.*, 4(12):2379–2394, Dec 1987.
3. J. Huang, A.B. Lee, and D. Mumford. Statistics of range images. In *CVPR00*, pages I:324–331, 2000.
4. R.A. Hummel and R. Moniot. Reconstructions from zero-crossings in scale-space. *ASSP*, 37(12):2111–2130, December 1989.
5. Peter Johansen, Mads Nielsen, and Ole F Olsen. Branch points in one-dimensional gaussian scale-space. *JMIV*, 2000. To appear.
6. J.J. Koenderink. The structure of images. *BioCyber*, 50:363–370, 1984.
7. J.J. Koenderink and A.J. van Doorn. Metamerism in complete sets of image operators. In *AIU96*, pages 113–129, 1996.
8. T. Lindeberg. On scale selection for differential operators. In *ISRN KTH*, 1993.
9. T. Lindeberg. Feature detection with automatic scale selection. *IJCV*, 30(2):79–116, November 1998.
10. D. Marr. Vision: A computational investigation into the human representation and processing of visual information. In *W.H. Freeman*, 1982.
11. K.S. Pedersen and M. Nielsen. The hausdorff dimension and scale-space normalization of natural images. *JVCIR*, 11(2):266–277, June 2000.
12. D.L. Ruderman and W. Bialek. Statistics of natural images: Scaling in the woods. *Physical Review Letters*, 73(6):100–105, August 1994.
13. S.J. Wernecke and L.R. d'Addario. Maximum entropy image reconstruction. *TC*, 26(4):351–364, April 1977.
14. A.P. Witkin. Scale space filtering: A new approach to multi-scale descriptions. In *IU84*, pages 79–95, 1984.
15. Y.N. Wu, S.C. Zhu, and X.W. Liu. Equivalence of julesz and gibbs texture ensembles. In *ICCV99*, pages 1025–1032, 2000.
16. S.C. Zhu, Y. Wu, and D. Mumford. Minimax entorpy principles and its application to texture modeling. *NeurComp*, 9(8):1627–1660, 1997.

Features in Scale Space:
Progress on the 2D 2nd Order Jet

Elena Tagliati and Lewis D. Griffin

Div. of Radiological Sciences and Medical Engineering
The Guy's King's and St'Thomas' Medical and Dental School
King's College London, London SE1 9RT, UK
elena.tagliati@kcl.ac.uk

Abstract. We present theoretical and computational results that develop Koenderink's theory of feature analysis in human vision [1,7]. Employing a scale space framework, the method aims to classify image points into one of a limited number of feature categories on the basis of local derivative measurements up to some order. At the heart of the method is the use of a family of functions, members of which can be used to account for any set of image measurements. We will show how certain families of simple functions naturally induce a categorical structure onto the space of possible measurements. We present two such families suitable for 1D images measured up to 2nd order, and various results relevant to similar analysis of 2D images.

1   Introduction

This paper is concerned with the analysis of models of feature detection in 2D within the framework of scale space theory [1,2,7,12].

The visual system has the task of measuring the retinal illuminance distribution. Since this is a continuous physical function, the space of possible illuminance distributions is infinite dimensional. The visual system, however, can only perform a finite number of measurements. And so, in contrast, the space of possible measurements is only finite dimensional.

The measurements that the visual system performs are physical operations which thus have certain limitations upon them; in particular, they cannot sample the illuminance at a zero-sized point of the visual field, but only over some aperture of non-zero size (or scale). This has been formalized in the idea of scale space [8,9,11].

Scale space allows many types of analysis: within scale, between scale and so on. Here we are concerned with "local analysis", i.e. at a single scale and location. This is often referred to as feature analysis.

Koenderink's insight into the problem of feature analysis is that the concept of metamerism is key [1,7]. Metamerism is a phenomenon common to many measurement systems - certainly imaging systems - whereby a finite number of measurements is insufficient to completely determine the physical reality, and thus there can be distinct physical inputs which are observationally equivalent.

M. Kerckhove (Ed.): Scale-Space 2001, LNCS 2106, pp. 51–62, 2001.

In the remainder of the introduction we further review the background concepts of scale space and metamerism. In the body of the paper we will introduce our approach by presenting results on feature detection in 1D images and then report progress on understanding feature detection in 2D images.

1.1   Scale Space

Arguments have been made [1,7,12] that the visual system should sample retinal irradiance with Gaussian apertures of a range of scales. This leads to a scale space representation of a signal $I(x, y)$ by $I : \mathbf{R}^2 \times \mathbf{R}^+ \to \mathbf{R}$, where the parameter $t \in \mathbf{R}^+$ describes the current level of scale [1,2,3,4,12,13,9,11]:

$$I(\,\cdot\,;t) = G_t(\,\cdot\,) * I(\,\cdot\,) \tag{1}$$

and

$$G_t(x, y) = \frac{1}{4\pi t}\, e^{-\frac{x^2+y^2}{4t}} \tag{2}$$

This formalization also provides a solution to the problem of how to differentiate physical functions [10,8]: convolution with a scaled Gaussian derivative kernel does both observation and differentiation in a single step, as it is shown from the following relationship:

$$(-1)^n \partial^n G_t * I = G_t * \partial^n I. \tag{3}$$

We write $\boldsymbol{o}_{mn}$ for the observation that results from measuring the $\frac{\partial^{m+n}}{\partial x^m \partial y^n}$ derivative at a point (2D example). Thus,

$$\boldsymbol{o}_{mn} = (-1)^{m+n} G_t^{(m,n)} * I \tag{4}$$

Hence *observations* ($\boldsymbol{o}_{mn}$) are the numbers that result from performing *measurements* by application of *operators* ($G_t^{(m,n)}$) to illuminance *distributions*. For example, $\boldsymbol{o}_{00}$ will be the observation resulting from measurement with the undifferentiated isotropic Gaussian kernel.

1.2   Truncated Taylor Series

While the primate visual system may use operators up to the 4th or to the 5th order [15], in contemporary image processing one typically uses operators up to the 2nd order, producing the six observations $\boldsymbol{o}_{ij}$, where $0 \le i + j \le 2$. Such an ordered set of observations resulting from measurement with operators up to some order we will refer to as an *observation vector*. The dimensionality of the image space will thus be a function of the maximum order of measurement. For 1D images, we will have the $(n+1) -$ tuple $(\boldsymbol{o}_0, \boldsymbol{o}_1, ... \boldsymbol{o}_n)$ and for 2D images the $\frac{1}{2}(n+1)(n+2) -$ tuple $(\boldsymbol{o}_{00}, \boldsymbol{o}_{10}, ... \boldsymbol{o}_{0n})$.

1.3   Jets and Metamery Classes

In standard mathematical usage the nth order jet is defined to be the equivalence class of functions that have the same n −truncated Taylor expansion at a given point [18], i.e. when measured produce the same observation vector. Thus observation vectors uniquely index jets[1], and so while different observation vectors are necessarily due to different distributions, there are distinct illuminance distributions which do correspond to one and the same observation vector. Such indistinguishable pairs of patterns are referred to as "metamers", which is analogous to colour vision [16], where distinct spectra of light can give rise to the same colour sensation.

The phenomenon of metamerism is pervasive [14] and important, not least because by characterizing what aspects of stimuli a measurement is blind to one better understands what is actually being measured.

1.4   Representative Functions

The problem now is to characterize these equivalence classes (the jets) of the visual system and to classify them into distinct "feature types", as categories are not obvious in space of observation vectors. Koenderink [7,1] suggests to look at functions associated with the observation vectors to find categories there. The idea is to select a function from each jet to stand for the jet. For this strategy to succeed one needs a selection rule that is guaranteed to pick one and only one function from each jet. Koenderink builds upon work by Schrödinger [17] on colour vision to outline an elegant solution to this problem. The solution involves selecting a representative function that takes on only two values and has a transition locus between the two values that is particularly simple.

Koenderink then goes on to suggest that these particular representative functions can be subdivided into qualitatively distinct ("feature") classes. While it is clear how to do this for 1D images and for 2D images measured up to 2nd order, it is less clear how to proceed for higher dimensions and orders.

1.5   Constraints on the Illuminance

If there are constraints on the measured illuminance distribution, then they may result in constraints on the observations. For example, if illuminance is constrained to be non-negative, then the observation o_{00} will always be non-negative. One can use constraints to guide the selection of the function that will be the representative of the jet.

Koenderink [7,1] uses upper- and lower-bound limits on illuminance, which he motivates by physical considerations. We, in contrast, do not enforce any such constraints as we regard representative functions not as candidate explanations, but merely as indices of jets. This decision arose from our study of the 1D - 2nd

---

[1] Koenderink uses the following terminology: "picture" for physical irradiance distribution, "image" for observation vector, and "icon" for jet.

order jet case; we noticed that if we consider a limited illuminance range then the model found surprising metamers of the signal - especially near certain features such as extrema, which were narrow relative to the scale of measurement. When we do not enforce these constraints, we observe that metamers match the local contrast better.

2   Notes on 1D, 2nd Order Jet

In this section, we report on our analysis of feature detection in 1D images before discussion of the more difficult case of 2D images. In 1D (2nd order jet), an observation vector is the triple (o_0, o_1, o_2).

For any observation vector, we consider the jet consistent with it; with the intention of choosing a representative function from the jet. For this to be possible unambiguosly, we need to identify an entire family of representative functions with the property that one and only one member of the family is contained in each possible jet. This will only be possible if the family has the same dimensionality as the observation vectors. So for the 1D, 2nd order jet considered here, the family needs to be three-dimensional.

Koenderink proposed several alternative families of representative functions [1,7]. In all of his suggested solutions, the members of the families are functions that attain at most two values and have at most two locations were they change discontinuously between the two values. The locations of these transitions provide two of the requisite three degrees of freedom of the family. The remaining degree of freedom comes from choosing the values that the functions attain. Despite there being two values to choose, only one degree of freedom comes from this choice because in Koenderink's solutions either (i) one of the values is forced to be zero, (ii) one of the values is forced to be illuminance$_{max}$, or (iii) the sum of the two values is forced to be illuminance$_{max}$.

We have implemented these solutions and found them to produce unexpected representative functions for observation vectors with 0th order terms near 0 or illuminance$_{max}$. The unexpected representative functions were of much greater contrast than the local structure that they were accounting for. We trace the problem to the use of illuminance constraints, and so have experimented with two alternative families of solutions without such constraints. We find that the representative functions obtained with these alternative families are always well matched in contrast to the local structures that they explain. The two solutions we have experimented with are:

- Only one transition point (1 d.o.f), but both values of the function unconstrained (2 d.o.f.).
- Two transition points but with a constraining relationship between them (1 d.o.f.) and both values of the function unconstrained (2 d.o.f.).

We will develop these two models in the following two subsections.

2.1   Edge Representation

Our first model employs as representative functions a family of step functions. The family has three degrees of freedom, one degree of freedom (ξ) specifies the location of the step while the other two degrees of freedom (l, r) specify the values of the function either side of the step. Hence a member of the family is given by $f_{\xi,l,r}(x) = l + \frac{1}{2}(r - l)\, sgn(x - \xi)$. The 2nd order observation vector resulting from measurement of $f_{\xi,l,r}$ is:

$$\left(\int_{\mathbf{R}} G_t(x) f_{\xi,l,r}(x)\, dx \;, \; -\int_{\mathbf{R}} G_t'(x) f_{\xi,l,r}(x)\, dx \;, \; \int_{\mathbf{R}} G_t''(x) f_{\xi,l,r}(x)\, dx \right). \quad (5)$$

To apply this model to the analysis of actual data, one first measures the data at some location to produce a particular observation vector and then one finds ξ, l, r so that eqn.(5) equals the measured observation vector. Although such a triple ξ, l, r is guaranteed to exist and be unique, finding them is non-trivial as we lack a closed form expression for them in terms of the observation vector; instead we use a gradient descent routine. Results are presented in Fig.1.

2.2   Full Bar and Gap Representation

In the previous section we noted that using Koenderink's suggested families of representative functions sometimes resulted in local approximations with surprisingly high contrast. Although we (in the main) cured this problem by using an alternative family of representative functions, we found the observation suggestive and wondered whether we could find even lower contrast approximations with a different family of functions.

We have achieved this goal by considering functions with at most two transitions and two values. This gives a four d.o.f. family, one more than is needed or acceptable. This extra d.o.f. means that for any given observation vector, there will be a one parameter family of functions that when measured produce the observation vector. One can then ask the question, of this one parameter family, which function is of the lowest contrast [2,3], i.e. which has its two values closest together? This problem is easily solved using the method of Lagrange multipliers, and produces a pleasingly simple result: if the two transition points of the lowest contrast solution are at $x = \alpha$ and $x = \beta$, then $\alpha\beta = -2t$ (where t is the scale of the measurements producing the observation vector). This condition is already

---

[2] A standard definition of contrast is $C = (I_{max} - I_{min})/(I_{max} + I_{min})$ (Michelson contrast), where I_{max} and I_{min} are the limits of the intensity in the image . Instead, we use the simple definition $C = I_{max} - I_{min}$.

[3] As Koenderink has observed [1,4], there are many criteria one could choose. We make no claim, at this stage, for any special advantages to the minimum contrast condition. Further work considering the effects of different conditions will be necessary to settle this.

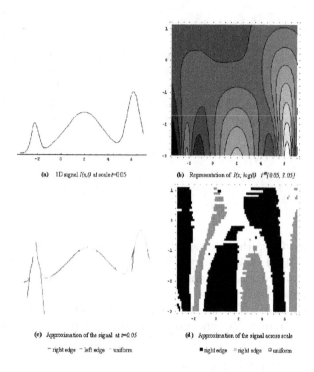

(a) 1D signal $I(x,t)$ at scale t=0.05

(b) Representation of $I(x; \log(t))$ t^{*}[0.05, 3.05]

(c) Approximation of the signal at t=0.05

  right edge – left edge – uniform

(d) Approximation of the signal across scale

  ■ right edge ■ right edge □ uniform

Fig. 1. *1D (2nd Order Jet): Edge Representation.* In the top row is shown the original 1D signal at a particular scale (a) and its scale space representation (b). In (c) we have the representation that follows from the application of the model to the signal in (a). The algorithm approximates the signal at each point by using a right or left step edge, or a uniform function as indicated by the varying greylevel of the thick curve. The strongly marked curve segments are the locus of the step edge height midpoints and so give some clue as to where the step edges are located. Uniform functions have been chosen as the local model whenever the transition of the step edge found by the algorithm is too distant from the point being analysed. If uniform functions are not used and instead all points are modelled as left or right step edges, the characteristic 'tick' formation at the end of many of the strongly marked curves would be even more pronounced. In (d) the same approximation is applied across scale.

familiar to us from Koenderink's work on colour and spatial vision; in particular Ostwald's theory of semi-chromes [6]. Following Koenderink's nomenclature, we will refer to the condition $\alpha\beta = -2t$ as the "full pattern" condition[4].

Having understood how (at least for the 1D, 2nd order jet) the "minimum contrast" criterion leads to the "full pattern" condition we can now propose a novel

---

[4] Again some terms come from the analogy with color theory[16]; in this case "full patterns" remind Schrödinger "full colors", i.e. the one with the maximum of monochromatic content.

three-dimensional family of functions suitable for indexing the 1D, 2nd order jet. Such functions attain at most two unconstrained values (two d.o.f.) and they have at most two points of transition that must satisfy the full condition (one d.o.f.). We illustrate the use of this family of functions in Fig.2.

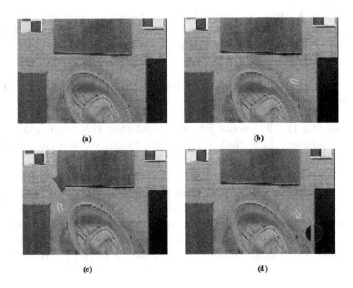

Fig. 2. *1D (2nd Order Jet): Full Bar and Gap Representation.* Shows the 1D 2nd order technique of section 2.2) applied to a 2D image. We apply it by measuring the 0th, 1st and 2nd derivatives only in the gradient direction. These three numbers then form the input to our 1D analysis. The original image is shown in (a). The other three images (b, c, d) show results of the application of the algorithm to a selected point. The radius of the circle, that encloses the neighborhood of the selected point, is proportional to the square root of the measurement scale ($t = 4$) at which the analysis is performed. The signal is approximated by a gap (b) or a bar (d). Although the approximating function in (c) is a bar, it appears to be an edge because the second transition falls outside of the circle.

3 Notes on 2D, 2nd Order Jet

We now consider the case of 2D images (2nd order jet), for which an observation vector is six-dimensional: $(o_{00}, o_{10}, o_{01}, o_{20}, o_{11}, o_{02})$.

Koenderink has suggested [1] that adequate candidates to be representative functions are the binary-valued functions with a transition locus that is a conic curve. This is an attractive suggestion as it produces categorical feature classes as desired. Each conic type corresponds to a different feature type: ellipses to blobs, parabolas to corners and hyperbolas to necks or gaps.

The family of such functions has seven degrees of freedom, five coming from the conic transition locus and two from the function values. The observation space is six-dimensional, so we have an extra degree of freedom. As we did in 1D, we can use a minimum contrast condition to eliminate the extra degree of freedom.

In 1D (2nd order jet), we found that the minimum contrast condition led to the "full pattern" condition. Our guess is that something similar is true for conics and we explore this in the following subsections.

3.1 Relatedness of "Complementary" - "Scale Relation" - "Full Patterns" Conditions

In the case of the 1D, 2nd order jet, we found that the "minimum contrast" condition is equivalent to a "full pattern" condition. We want to clarify what this "full pattern" condition means in 2D; in order to do this, we start by defining a "complementary" condition , we then introduce the concept of a "scale relationship" and finally we show that all these conditions are related.

These concepts we are going to introduce apply either to set of points or to algebraic curves; we want to define them and study their inter-relationships and equivalence. We begin with the definition of "complementary" condition.

Let us introduce a vector of Gaussian derivatives up to the 2nd order[5]:

$$
\boldsymbol{g}_t(x,y) =
\begin{pmatrix}
G_t^{(1,0)}(x,y) \\
G_t^{(0,1)}(x,y) \\
G_t^{(2,0)}(x,y) \\
G_t^{(1,1)}(x,y) \\
G_t^{(0,2)}(x,y)
\end{pmatrix}
\tag{6}
$$

Complementary Condition. A set of 5 points[6] $P_i = (x_i, y_i)$ (in the domain of the image) is complementary if and only if one can put weighted delta functions at those points that when measured give the achromatic axis, a vector with zero entries in all the slots but the first one, corresponding to the 0th order element[7]; i.e. $\exists w_i$ such that:

$$
\sum_{i=1}^{5} w_i\, \boldsymbol{o}[\delta(P_i)] = \boldsymbol{0}
\tag{7}
$$

---

[5] We do not consider the element corresponding to the 0th order.

[6] In an Ω- dimensional observation system ($\Omega = 6$ for the case of 2D, 2nd order jet), we consider a set of $(\Omega - 1)$ points.

[7] In our case it is the 5-dimensional null vector, as we do not consider the 0th order.

where $o[\delta(P_i)] \equiv g_t(P_i)$. Calling w the vector of weights and M the matrix with $o[\delta(P_i)]$ as columns, we can rewrite eqn.(7) as:

$$M \cdot w = 0 \qquad (8)$$

which admits solutions if and only if $|M| = 0$. Using elementary properties of determinants together with the fact that Gaussian derivatives are Hermite polynomials multiplied by the original Gaussian, the complementary condition expressed in (8) becomes:

$$
\begin{vmatrix}
-x_1 & -x_2 & -x_3 & -x_4 & -x_5 \\
-y_1 & -y_2 & -y_3 & -y_4 & -y_5 \\
\frac{x_1^2}{2t}-1 & \frac{x_2^2}{2t}-1 & \frac{x_3^2}{2t}-1 & \frac{x_4^2}{2t}-1 & \frac{x_5^2}{2t}-1 \\
\frac{x_1 y_1}{2t} & \frac{x_2 y_2}{2t} & \frac{x_3 y_3}{2t} & \frac{x_4 y_4}{2t} & \frac{x_5 y_5}{2t} \\
\frac{y_1^2}{2t}-1 & \frac{y_2^2}{2t}-1 & \frac{y_3^2}{2t}-1 & \frac{y_4^2}{2t}-1 & \frac{y_5^2}{2t}-1
\end{vmatrix}
= 0 \qquad (9)
$$

On the other hand, five points uniquely identify a conic; a good question is if there is anything special about the conic corresponding to points in complementary position. Firstly, we have found that if there exists five points of a conic which are in complementary position, then all other five points of that conic are in complementary position. That is what we call a "complementary" conic. A conic is described also by five parameters, and we have found that the parameters of a "complementary" conic satisfy a specific condition, the "scale relationship", which we are going to define in the next subsection.

Scale Relationship. Let us consider a conic χ of the form $a_{00} + a_{10}x + a_{01}y + a_{20}x^2 + a_{11}xy + a_{02}y^2 = 0$. If it is a "complementary conic", it is easy to show[8] that the eqn.(9) referred to any five points of χ is equivalent to the following equation for the conic parameters:

$$2t(a_{20} + a_{02}) + a_{00} = 0 \qquad (10)$$

which we call the "scale relationship". In the case of 1D, 2nd order jet it corresponds to $\alpha\beta = -2t$ (see sect.(2.2); but there we used transition point coordinates instead of curve parameters).

We want to show the equation (10) is also true for "full patterns", a term coined by Koenderink [1,4] in analogy with a concept from color science.

---

[8] We just sketch the proof here; considering properties of determinants, we multiply each row by the suitable conic parameter (different from zero!) and then we replace one row by the linear combination of all the others. This turns out to be the equation of the conic, which is zero for all the points, plus the extra terms: $2t(a_{20} + a_{02}) + a_{00}$, which are the same in all the columns. So, if this last part is zero we have an entire row of zeros, and the determinant will be zero.

Full Pattern Condition. We have been considering binary-valued functions with conic transitions. When measured, these produce an observation vector (o). As the conic parameters are varied while holding the two function values constant, the observation vector varies, sweeping out a 5-dimensional submanifold.

A conic is full when the tangent space to the submanifold contains the achromatic axis, i.e. $\exists w_i$ such that:

$$\sum_{i=1}^{5} w_i \frac{\partial o}{\partial a_i} = 0 \qquad (11)$$

where the a_i are conic parameters[9]. If we introduce a matrix T, the columns of which are the derivatives of the observation vector[10] with respect to each conic parameter, we can rewrite eqn.(11) as[11]:

$$T \cdot w = 0 \qquad (12)$$

and this is true if and only if $|T| = 0$. If we notice the similarity between derivatives of conics with respect to the parameters and Hermite polynomials in Gaussian derivatives, we can then follow a procedure similar to what we have done for the complementary condition (the difference is that we have still double integrals as matrix elements). We obtain that also $|T| = 0$ is equivalent to the "scale relationship".

We have found that both the "complementary" condition and the "full pattern" condition are equivalent to eqn.(10). We will use this fact in the next section, where we are going to show that minimum contrast - amongst conic patterns - leads to full patterns.

3.2   Minimum Contrast and Full Patterns

Let χ be the conic function and r, s be the two values of the binary-valued function we will select as representative of the jet; ignoring the 0th order term the observation vector of our model is defined as:

$$o[\chi(x,y)] = (s - r) \iint_{\mathbf{R}^2} g_t(x,y) \cdot \Delta[\chi(x,y)] dx dy \qquad (13)$$

and it has to be equal to the five-dimensional vector of measurements m. Now we want to impose the minimum contrast condition; we use the method of lagrange multipliers, which gives the following system of equations:

$$\frac{\partial}{\partial \alpha_j}((r - s)^2 + \boldsymbol{\lambda} \cdot \boldsymbol{m}) = 0 \qquad j = 1, 2, ..., 7 \qquad (14)$$

---

[9] $i = 10, 01, 20, 11, 02$

[10]   The derivatives of the observation vector respect to conic parameters factor out conic variables and delta function. For example, $\frac{\partial o}{\partial a_{10}} = \iint_{\mathbf{R}^2} g_t(x,y) \cdot x\, \delta[\chi(x,y)]\, dx dy$

[11] $T = \iint_{\mathbf{R}^2} c \cdot g_t^{\mathrm{T}}(x,y) dx dy$ and $c = (x, y, x^2, xy, y^2)$.

where $\alpha_j = r, s, a_{10}, ..., a_{02}$. If we focus on the case $\alpha_j \neq r, s$ and we replace the measurement vector with the observation vector, we can reduce the system (14) to:

$$\lambda \cdot \frac{\partial o}{\partial a_i} = 0 \qquad \forall i, \ i = 10, 01, ..., 02 \tag{15}$$

But they are the same as the "full" equations (11), being in fact the five 'a_i' the parameters of the conic; it follows also they are equivalent to the "complementary" condition and to the "scale relationship".

4   Conclusions and Discussions

In this paper, we presented methods for feature analysis of the 2nd order jet, either for 1D or 2D images. Using a scale space framework, we considered derivative measurements up to a certain order at any given point of an image (and at a particular scale). We aimed to classify on the basis of such measurements image points into one of a small number of feature categories. From Koenderink's theory, based on an analogy with colour vision [1,7], the key concept is to identify a family of functions, elements of which are natural candidates to account for any set of image measurements. These functions are characterized by being binary-valued with constrained transition loci between the two values. the constraints are such that in 1D the functions have at most two points of transition; in 2D the transition locus is defined by a conic. As a criterion is needed to select a representative among the family of functions, we chose the "minimum contrast" condition, for both the 1D and the 2D case. We proved that the solutions picked out by it also satisfy the "full pattern" condition and the "scale relationship". In 1D this is expressed by the fact that the product of the values of the transition points is equal to $-2t$, where t is the measurement scale. This allows us to implement in a simple way our feature analysis, and the results are shown in Fig.(2). In 2D the scale relationship is $2t(a_{20} + a_{02}) + a_{00} = 0$, a simple relation between the conic parameters.

References

1. Koenderink, J.J., van Doorn, A. Receptive Field Assembly Specificity. *J. Vis. Comm. and Im. Process*, Vol.**3**, No. **1**, (1992) 1–12
2. Koenderink, J.J., van Doorn, A. The Structure of Images. *Biol. Cybern.*, Vol.**50**, (1984) 363–370
3. Koenderink, J.J., van Doorn, A. Representation of Local Geometry in the Visual System. *Biol. Cybern.*, Vol.**55**, (1987) 367–375
4. Koenderink, J.J., van Doorn, A. Generic Neighborhood Operators. *IEEE Trans. on Pattern An. Mach. Intell.*, Vol.**14**, No. **6**, (1992) 597–605
5. Koenderink, J.J., van Doorn, A.: Illuminance Critical Points On Generic Smooth Surfaces. *J.Opt.Soc.Am. A*, Vol.**10**, No. **5**(19923) 844–854
6. Koenderink, J.J., van Doorn, A. Mensurating the Colour Circle: Ostwald's "Principle of Internal Symmetry". ECVP(2000)
7. Koenderink, J.J. What is a Feature?. *J. Intell. Syst.*, Vol.**3**, No. **1**, (1993) 49–82

8. ter Haar Romeny, B.M., Florack, L.M.J., Koenderink, J.J., Viergever M.A. Scale Space: Its Natural Operators and Differential Invariants. In: Information Process. in Medical Imag., LCNS, Vol.**511**, (1991) 239–255

9. Weickert, J., Ishikawa, S., and Imiya A. On the History of Gaussian Scale Space Axiomatics. In: Gaussian Scale-Space Theory, Kluwer, Dordrecht, (1997) 45–59

10. ter Haar Romeny, B. Applications of Scale Space Theory. In: Gaussian Scale-Space Theory, Kluwer, Dordrecht, (1997) 3–19

11. Nielsen, M. Scale Space Generators and Functionals. In: Gaussian Scale-Space Theory, Kluwer, Dordrecht, (1997) 99–114

12. Lindeberg, T. Scale Space Theory in Computer Vision. Kluwer, Boston, MA, (1994)

13. Lindeberg, T.: On the Axiomatic Foundations of Linear Scale Space. In: Gaussian Scale-Space Theory, Kluwer, Dordrecht, (1997) 75–97

14. Richards, W.: Quantifying Sensory Channels - Generalizing Colorimetry To Orientation And Texture, Touch, And Tones. *Sensory Processes*, Vol.**3**, No. **3**, (1979) 207–229

15. Young, R.A. The Gaussian Derivative Theory of Spatial Vision: Analysis of Cortical Cell Receptive Field Line-Weighting Profiles. Gen.Motors Res.Tech.Rep. GMR-4920, (1985)

16. Schrödinger, E.: Theorie der Pigmente von größter Leuchtkraft, Ann. Physik, Vol.**62**, (1920) 603

17. Schrödinger, E.: Grundlinien einer Theorie der Farbenmetrik im Tagessehen I, II, Ann. Physik, Vol.**63**, (1920) 397–427

18. Majthay, A.: Foundations of Catastrophe Theory, Pitman Adv. Publ. Progr., (1985) 137–146

Tracking of Multi-state Hand Models Using Particle Filtering and a Hierarchy of Multi-scale Image Features[*]

Ivan Laptev and Tony Lindeberg

Computational Vision and Active Perception Laboratory (CVAP)
Department of Numerical Analysis and Computer Science
KTH, S-100 44 Stockholm, Sweden
{laptev,tony}@nada.kth.se

Abstract. This paper presents an approach for simultaneous tracking and recognition of hierarchical object representations in terms of multi-scale image features. A scale-invariant dissimilarity measure is proposed for comparing scale-space features at different positions and scales. Based on this measure, the likelihood of hierarchical, parameterized models can be evaluated in such a way that maximization of the measure over different models and their parameters allows for both model selection and parameter estimation. Then, within the framework of particle filtering, we consider the area of hand gesture analysis, and present a method for simultaneous tracking and recognition of hand models under variations in the position, orientation, size and posture of the hand. In this way, qualitative hand states and quantitative hand motions can be captured, and be used for controlling different types of computerised equipment.

1 Introduction

When representing real-world objects, an important constraint originates from the fact that different types of image features will usually be visible depending on the scale of observation. Thus, when building object models for recognition, it is natural to consider hierarchical object models that explicitly encode features at different scales as well as hierarchical relations over scales between these.

The purpose of this paper is to address the problem of how to evaluate such hierarchical object models with respect to image data. Specifically, we will be concerned with graph-like and qualitative image representations in terms of multi-scale image features (Crowley and Sanderson 1987, Lindeberg 1993, Pizer et al. 1994, Triesch and von der Malsburg 1996, Shokoufandeh et al. 1999, Bretzner and Lindeberg 1999), which are expressed within a context of feature detection with automatic scale selection. A dissimilarity measure will be proposed

---

[*] The support from the Swedish Research Council for Engineering Sciences, TFR, the Royal Swedish Academy of Sciences and the Knut and Alice Wallenberg Foundation is gratefully acknowledged. We also thank Lars Bretzner for many valuable suggestions concerning this work and for his help in setting up the experiments.

M. Kerckhove (Ed.): Scale-Space 2001, LNCS 2106, pp. 63–74, 2001.

for comparing such model features to image data, and we will use this measure for evaluating the likelihood of object models.

Then, within the paradigm of stochastic particle filtering (Isard and Blake 1996, Black and Jepson 1998, MacCormick and Isard 2000), we will show how this approach allows us to simultaneously align, track and recognise hand models in multiple states. The approach will be applied to hand gesture analysis, and we will demonstrate how a combination of qualitative hand states and quantitative hand motions captured in this way allows us to control computerised equipment.

2   Hand Model and Image Features

Given an image of a hand, we can expect to detect a blob feature at a coarse scale corresponding to the palm, while fingers and finger tips may appear as ridge and blob features, respectively, at finer scales. Here, we follow the approach of feature detection with automatic scale selection (Lindeberg 1998), and detect image features from local extrema over scales of normalized differential invariants.

2.1   Detection of Image Features

Given an image f with scale-space representations $L(\cdot;\ t) = g(\cdot;\ t) * f(\cdot)$, constructed by convolution with Gaussian kernels $g(\cdot;\ t)$ with variance t, a scale-space maximum of a normalized differential entity $\mathcal{D}_{norm}L$ is a point $(x;\ t)$ where $\mathcal{D}_{norm}L(x;\ t)$ assumes a local maximum with respect to space x and scale t. To detect multi-scale blobs, we search for points $(x;\ t)$ that are local maxima in scale-space of the normalized squared Laplacian

$$\mathcal{B}_{\gamma-norm}L = (t\,\nabla^2 L)^2 = \sum t^2\,(\partial_{xx}L + \partial_{yy}L)^2 \tag{1}$$

while multi-scale ridges are detected as scale-space extrema of the following normalized measure of ridge strength

$$\mathcal{R}_{\gamma-norm}L = t^{2\gamma}((\partial_{xx}L - \partial_{yy}L)^2 + 4(\partial_{xy}L)^2), \tag{2}$$

where $\gamma = 3/4$. Each feature detected at a point $(x,\ t)$ in scale-space indicates the presence of a corresponding image structure at position x having size t. To represent the spatial extent of such image structures, we evaluate a second moment matrix in the neighborhood of $(x;\ t)$

$$\nu = \int_{\eta \in \mathbb{R}^2} \begin{pmatrix} (\partial_x L)^2 & (\partial_x L)(\partial_y L) \\ (\partial_x L)(\partial_y L) & (\partial_y L)^2 \end{pmatrix} g(\eta; s_{int})\,d\eta \tag{3}$$

at integration scale s_{int} proportional to the scale of detected features. Graphically, this image descriptor is then represented by an ellipse centered at x and with covariance matrix $\Sigma = t\nu_{norm}$, where $\nu_{norm} = \nu/\lambda_{min}$ and λ_{min} is the smallest eigenvalue of ν. Figures 1(a)-(b) show such descriptors obtained from an image of a hand.

An extension of this approach to colour feature detection is presented in (Sjöbergh and Lindeberg 2001).

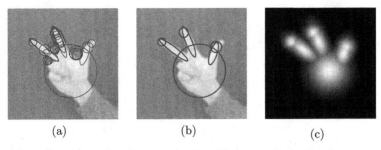

(a)   (b)   (c)

Fig. 1. Blob and ridge features for a hand: (a) circles and ellipses corresponding to the significant blob and ridge features extracted from an image of a hand; (b) selected image features corresponding to the palm, the fingers and the finger tips of a hand; (c) a mixture of Gaussian kernels associated with the blob and ridge features, which illustrate how the selected image features capture the essential structure of a hand.

2.2   Hierarchical and Graph-Like Hand Models

One idea that we shall explore here is to consider relations in space and over scales between such image features as an important cue for recognition. To model such relations, we shall consider graph-like object representations, where the vertices in the graph correspond to features and the edges define relations between different features. This approach continues along the works by (Crowley and Sanderson 1987) who extracted peaks from a Laplacian pyramid of an image and linked them into a tree structure with respect to resolution, (Lindeberg 1993) who constructed a scale-space primal sketch with an explicit encoding of blob-like structures in scale-space as well as the relations between these, (Triesch and von der Malsburg 1996) who used elastic graphs to represent hands in different postures with local jets of Gabor filters computed at each vertex, (Shokoufandeh et al. 1999) who detected maxima in a multi-scale wavelet transform, as well as (Bretzner and Lindeberg 1999), who computed multi-scale blob and ridge features and defined explicit qualitative relations between these features.

Specifically, we will make use of quantitative relations between features to define hierarchical, probabilistic models of objects in different states. For a hand, the feature hierarchy will contain three levels of detail; a blob corresponding to a palm at the top level, ridges corresponding to the fingers at the intermediate level and blobs corresponding to the finger-tips at the bottom level (see figure 2). While a more general approach for modelling the internal state of a hand consists of modelling the probability distribution of the parameters over all object features, we will here simplify this task by approximating the relative scales between all features by constant ratios and by fixing the relative positions between the ridges corresponding to the fingers and the blobs corresponding to the finger-tips. Thus, we model the global position (x, y) of the hand, its overall size s and orientation α. Moreover, we have a state parameter $l = 1 \ldots 5$ describing the number of open fingers present in the hand posture (see figure 2b). In this way, a hand model can be parameterised by X, where $X = (x, y, s, \alpha, l)$.

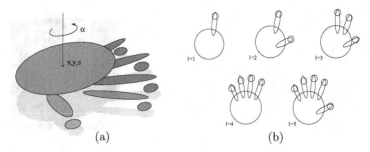

Fig. 2. Model of a hand in different states: (a) hierarchical configuration of model features and their relations; (b) model states corresponding to different hand postures.

3   Evaluation of Object Model

To recognize and track hands in images, we will use a maximum-likelihood estimate and search for the model hypothesis X_0 that given an image $\mathcal{I}$ maximizes the likelihood $p(\mathcal{I}|X_0)$. There are several ways to define such a likelihood. One approach could be to relate the model features directly to local image patches. Here, we will measure the dissimilarity between the features in the model and the features extracted from image data.

3.1   Dissimilarity between Two Features

Consider an image feature F (either a blob or a ridge), defined in terms of a position μ and a covariance matrix Σ according to section 2.1. The dissimilarity between two such features must take into account the difference in their position, size, orientation and anisotropy. To measure the joint dissimilarity of these features, we propose to model each such image feature by a two-dimensional Gaussian function having the same mean and covariance as the original feature

$$\bar{g}(x,\mu,\Sigma) = h(\Sigma)\,g(x,\mu,\Sigma), = \frac{h(\Sigma)}{2\pi\sqrt{\det(\Sigma)}}e^{-\frac{1}{2}(x-\mu)'\Sigma^{-1}(x-\mu)}, \qquad (4)$$

and compute the integrated square difference between two such representations

$$\phi(F_1,F_2) = \int_{\mathbb{R}^2} (\bar{g}(x,\mu_1,\Sigma_1) - \bar{g}(x,\mu_2,\Sigma_2))^2\,dx \qquad (5)$$

given a normalising factor $h(\Sigma)$, which will be determined later so as to give a scale-invariant dissimilarity measure. The choice of a Gaussian function is natural here, since it is the function that minimizes the entropy of a random variable given its mean and covariance. The Gaussian function at each image point can also be thought of as measuring the contribution of this point to the image feature. Figure 1(c) illustrates features of a hand represented in this way.

Using the fact that the product of two Gaussian functions is another amplified Gaussian function with covariance $\hat{\Sigma} = (\Sigma_1^{-1} + \Sigma_2^{-1})^{-1}$ and mean $\hat{\mu} =$

$\hat{\Sigma}(\Sigma_1^{-1}\mu_1 + \Sigma_2^{-1}\mu_2)$, the integral in (5) can be evaluated in closed form:

$$\phi(F_1, F_2) = \frac{h^2(\Sigma_1)}{4\pi\sqrt{\det(\Sigma_1)}} + \frac{h^2(\Sigma_2)}{4\pi\sqrt{\det(\Sigma_2)}} - C\frac{h(\Sigma_1)h(\Sigma_2)\sqrt{\det(\Sigma_1^{-1})\det(\Sigma_2^{-1})}}{\pi\sqrt{\det(\Sigma_1^{-1} + \Sigma_2^{-1})}}$$

(6)

where

$$C = \exp\left(-\tfrac{1}{2}(\mu_1'\Sigma_1^{-1}\mu_1 + \mu_2'\Sigma_2^{-1}\mu_2 - (\mu_1'\Sigma_1^{-1} + \mu_2'\Sigma_2^{-1})\hat{\mu})\right)$$

To be useful in practice, ϕ should be invariant to the joint translations, rotations and size variations of both features. From (6), it can be seen that $\phi(F_1, F_2)$ will be scale-invariant if and only if we choose $h(\Sigma) = \sqrt[4]{\det(\Sigma)}$. Thus, we obtain

$$\phi(F_1, F_2) = \frac{1}{2\pi} - C\frac{\sqrt[4]{\det(\Sigma_1^{-1})\det(\Sigma_2^{-1})}}{\pi\sqrt{\det(\Sigma_1^{-1} + \Sigma_2^{-1})}}.$$

(7)

It is easy to prove that the dissimilarity measure ϕ in (7) is invariant to joint rescalings of both features, i.e. $\phi(F_1, F_2) = \phi(\tilde{F}_1, \tilde{F}_2)$, where $\tilde{F}(\mu, \Sigma) = F(\kappa\mu, \kappa^2\Sigma)$ for some scaling factor κ. Moreover, ϕ is invariant to simultaneous translations and rotations of both features. As illustrated in figure 3, the dissimilarity measure ϕ assumes its minimum value zero only when the features are equal, while its value increases when the features start to deviate in position, size or shape.

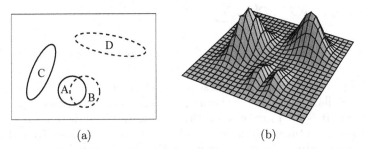

(a) (b)

Fig. 3. Two model features (solid ellipses) and two data features (dashed ellipses) in (a) are compared by evaluating the square difference of associated Gaussian functions. While the overlapping model (A) and the data (B) features cancel each other, the mismatched features (C and D) increase the square difference in (b).

3.2 Dissimilarity of Model and Data Features

Given two sets $\mathcal{F}^m, \mathcal{F}^d$ with N^m model and N^d data features respectively, we consider the model and the data as two mixtures of Gaussian distributions

$$G^m = \sum_i^{N^m} \bar{g}(x, \mu_i^m, \Sigma_i^m), \quad G^d = \sum_i^{N^d} \bar{g}(x, \mu_i^d, \Sigma_i^d),$$

where $\bar{g}(x, \mu_i^m, \Sigma_i^m)$ and $\bar{g}(x, \mu_i^d, \Sigma_i^d)$ are normalized Gaussian functions associated with model and data features as defined in (4). In analogy with the dissimilarity between two features, we define the dissimilarity between the model and the data by integrating the square difference of their associated functions:

$$\Phi(\mathcal{F}^m, \mathcal{F}^d) = \int_{\mathbb{R}^2} (G^m - G^d)^2 \, dx. \tag{8}$$

By expanding (8) we get

$$\Phi(\mathcal{F}^m, \mathcal{F}^d) = \underbrace{\sum_i^{N^m} \sum_j^{N^m} \int_{\mathbb{R}^2} \bar{g}_i^m \bar{g}_j^m \, dx}_{Q_1} + \underbrace{\sum_i^{N^d} \sum_j^{N^d} \int_{\mathbb{R}^2} \bar{g}_i^d \bar{g}_j^d \, dx}_{Q_2} - \underbrace{2 \sum_i^{N^m} \sum_j^{N^d} \int_{\mathbb{R}^2} \bar{g}_i^m \bar{g}_j^d \, dx}_{Q_3}$$

whose computation requires comparisons of all feature pairs. We can note, however, that overlap between the features within a model will be rare, as will overlaps be between features in the data. Therefore, we do the approximations

$$Q_1 \approx \sum_i^{N^m} \int_{\mathbb{R}^2} (\bar{g}_i^m)^2 \, dx, \quad Q_2 \approx \sum_i^{N^d} \int_{\mathbb{R}^2} (\bar{g}_i^d)^2 \, dx, \quad Q_3 \approx 2 \sum_i^{N^m} \int_{\mathbb{R}^2} \bar{g}_i^m \bar{g}_{k_i}^d \, dx, \tag{9}$$

where $\bar{g}_{k_i}^d$ corresponds to the data feature $F_{k_i}^d$ closest to the model feature F_i^m with regard to the dissimilarity measure ϕ. In summary, we approximate Φ by

$$\Phi(\mathcal{F}^m, \mathcal{F}^d) \approx \sum_{i=1}^{N^m} \phi(F_i^m, F_{k_i}^d) + \frac{N^d - N^m}{4\pi}, \tag{10}$$

where ϕ is the dissimilarity measure between a couple of features according to (7), F_i^m, $i = 1..N^m$ are the features of the model and $F_{k_i}^d$, $i = 1..N^m$ are the data features, where $F_{k_i}^d$ matches best with F_i^m among the other data features.

The dissimilarity measure Φ characterizes the deviation between model and data features. It is dual in the sense that it considers the distance from model features to data features (*offset criterion*) as well as the distance from data features to model features (*outlier criterion*). The simultaneous optimization with respect to these two criteria is important for locating an object and recognizing it among the others. To illustrate this, consider the matching of a hand model in states with one, two and three open fingers $l = 1, 2, 3$ (see figure 2(b)) to an image of a hand as shown in figure 1(a). If we match according to an offset criterion only, hypotheses with one and two open fingers ($l = 1, 2$) will have the same fitting error as a hypothesis with three open fingers ($l = 3$). Thus, the offset criterion alone is not sufficient for the correct selection of a hand state. To solve the problem, we must require the best hypothesis to also explain as much of the data as possible by minimizing the number of mismatched data features (outlier criterion). This will result in a hypothesis that best *fits* and *explains* the data, i.e. the hypothesis with the correct state $l = 3$.

3.3   Likelihood

To find the best hypothesis of a hand X_0, we will search for the minimum of the dissimilarity measure Φ in (10) over X. For the purpose of tracking (using particle filtering as will be described in section 4), it is more convenient, however, to maximize a likelihood measure $p(\mathcal{I}|X) = p(\mathcal{F}^d|\mathcal{F}^m)$ instead. Thus, we define a likelihood function as

$$p(\mathcal{F}^d|\mathcal{F}^m) = e^{-\Phi(\mathcal{F}^m,\mathcal{F}^d)/2\sigma^2}, \tag{11}$$

where the parameter $\sigma = 10^{-2}$ controls the sharpness of the likelihood function.

4   Tracking and Recognition

Tracking and recognition of a set of object models in time-dependent images can be formulated as the maximization of a posterior probability distribution over model parameters given a sequence of input images. To estimate the states of object models in this respect, we will follow the approach of particle filtering to propagate object hypotheses over time, where the likelihood of each particle is computed from the proposed likelihood and dissimilarity measures (10) and (11).

To a major extent, we will follow traditional approaches for particle filtering as presented by (Isard and Blake 1996, Black and Jepson 1998, Sidenbladh et al. 2000, Deutscher et al. 2000) and others. Using the hierarchical multi-scale structure of the hand models, however, an adaptation of the layered sampling approach (Sullivan et al. 1999) will be presented, in which a coarse-to-fine search strategy is used to improve the computational efficiency, here, by a factor of two. Moreover, it will be demonstrated how the proposed dissimilarity measure makes it possible to perform simultaneous hand tracking and hand posture recognition.

4.1   Particle Filtering

Particle filters aim at estimating and propagating the posterior probability distribution $p(X_t, Y_t|\tilde{\mathcal{I}}_t)$ over time, where X_t and Y_t are static and dynamic model parameters and $\tilde{\mathcal{I}}_t$ denotes the observations up to time t. Using Bayes rule, the posterior at time t can be evaluated according to

$$p(X_t, Y_t|\tilde{\mathcal{I}}_t) = k\, p(\mathcal{I}_t|X_t, Y_t)\, p(X_t, Y_t|\tilde{\mathcal{I}}_{t-1}), \tag{12}$$

where k is a normalization constant that does not depend on variables X_t, Y_t. The term $p(\mathcal{I}_t|X_t, Y_t)$ denotes the likelihood that a model configuration X_t, Y_t gives rise to the image $\mathcal{I}_t$. Using a first-order Markov assumption, the dependence on observations before time $t-1$ can be removed and the model prior $p(X_t, Y_t|\tilde{\mathcal{I}}_{t-1})$ can be evaluated using a posterior from a previous time step and the distribution for model dynamics according to

$$p(X_t, Y_t|\tilde{\mathcal{I}}_{t-1}) = \int p(X_t, Y_t|X_{t-1}, Y_{t-1})\, p(X_{t-1}, Y_{t-1}|\tilde{\mathcal{I}}_{t-1})\, dX_{t-1}\, dY_{t-1}. \tag{13}$$

Since the likelihood function is usually multi-modal and cannot be expressed in closed form, the approach of particle filtering is to approximate the posterior distribution using N particles, weighted according to their likelihoods $p(\mathcal{I}_t|X_t, Y_t)$. The posterior for a new time moment is then computed by populating the particles with high weights and predicting them according to their dynamic model $p(X_t, Y_t|X_{t-1}, Y_{t-1})$.

4.2   Hand Tracking and Recognition

To use particle filtering for tracking and recognition of hierarchical hand models as described in section 2, we let the state variable X denote the position (x, y), the size s, the orientation α and the posture l of the hand model, i.e., $X = (x, y, s, \alpha, l)$, while Y denotes the time derivatives of the first four variables, i.e., $Y_t = (\dot{x}, \dot{y}, \dot{s}, \dot{\alpha})$. Then, we assume that the likelihood $p(\mathcal{I}_t|X_t, Y_t)$ does not explicitly depend on Y_t, and approximate $p(\mathcal{I}_t|X_t)$ by evaluating $p(\mathcal{F}^d|\mathcal{F}^m)$ for each particle according to (11). Concerning the dynamics $p(X_t, Y_t|X_{t-1}, Y_{t-1})$ of the hand model, a constant velocity model is adopted, where deviations from the constant velocity assumption are modelled by additive Brownian motion, from which the distribution $p(X_t, Y_t|X_{t-1}, Y_{t-1})$ is computed. To capture changes in hand postures, the state parameter l is allowed to vary randomly for 30 % of the particles at each time step.

When the tracking is started, all particles are first distributed uniformly over the parameter spaces X and Y. After each time step of particle filtering, the best hypothesis of a hand is estimated, by first choosing the most likely hand posture and then computing the mean of $p(X_t, Y_t|\tilde{\mathcal{I}}_t)$ for that posture. Hand posture number i is chosen if $w_i = \max_j(w_j)$, $j = 1, \ldots, 5$, where w_j is the sum of the weights of all particles with state j. Then, the continuous parameters are estimated by computing a weighted mean of all the particles in state i.

4.3   Hierarchical Layered Sampling

The number of particles used for representing a distribution determines the speed and the accuracy of the particle filter. Usually, however, most of the particles represent false object hypotheses and serve as to compensate for uncertainties in the estimated distribution. To reduce the number of such particles, and thus improve the computational efficiency, one approach is to divide the evaluation of the particles into several steps, and to eliminate unlikely particles already at the earliest stages of evaluation. This idea has been used previously in works on partitioned sampling (MacCormick and Isard 2000) and layered sampling (Sullivan et al. 1999).

The layered sampling implies that the likelihood function $p(\mathcal{I}_t|X_t)$ is decomposed as $p = p_1\, p_2 \ldots p_n$ and that false hypotheses are eliminated by re-sampling the set of particles after a likelihood $p_i(\mathcal{I}_t|X_t)$ has been evaluated at each layer $i = 1 \ldots n$. The idea is to use a coarse-to-fine evaluation strategy, where p_1 evaluates models at their coarsest scale, while p_n performs the evaluation at the finest scale.

In the context of hierarchical multi-scale feature models, the layered sampling approach can be modified such as to evaluate the likelihoods $p_i(\mathcal{I}_t|X_t)$ independently for each level in the hierarchy of features. Hence, for the hand model described in section 2, the likelihood evaluation is decomposed into three layers $p = p_1 p_2 p_3$, where p_1 evaluates the coarse scale blob corresponding to the palm of a hand, p_2 evaluates the ridges corresponding to the fingers, and p_3 evaluates the fine scale blobs corresponding to the finger tips.

Experimentally, we have found that the hierarchical layered sampling approach improves the computational efficiency of the tracker by a factor two, compared to the standard sampling method in particle filtering. Figure 4 illustrates a comparison between these two approaches concerning the performance of hand posture recognition step of the tracker – see (Laptev and Lindeberg 2000) for a more extensive description.

Hierarchical layered sampling   *Standard sampling*

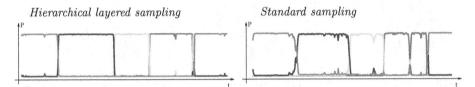

Fig. 4. Curves representing probabilities of model states $l = 1, ..., 5$ while tracking a hand with changing postures. The results are shown for the hierarchical vs. the standard sampling technique, using the same number of particles.

5   Hand Gesture Analysis

An application we are interested in is to track hands in office and home environments, in order to provide the user with a convenient human-machine interface for expressing commands to different types of computerized devices using hand gestures. The idea is to associate the recognised hand states with actions, while using the estimated continuous parameters of the hand model to control the actions in a quantitative way.

The problem of hand gesture analysis has received increased attention in recent years. Early work of using hand gestures for television control was presented by (Freeman and Weissman 1995) using normalised correlation. Some approaches consider elaborated 3-D hand models (Regh and Kanade 1995), while others use colour markers to simplify feature detection (Cipolla et al. 1993). Appearance-based models for hand tracking and sign recognition were used by (Cui and Weng 1996), while (Heap and Hogg 1998, MacCormick and Isard 2000) used silhouettes of hands. Graph-like and feature-based hand models have been proposed by (Triesch and von der Malsburg 1996) for sign recognition and in (Bretzner and Lindeberg 1998) for tracking and estimating 3-D rotations of a hand.

The proposed approach is based on these works and is novel in the respect that it combines a hierarchical object model with image features at multiple scales and particle filtering for robust tracking and recognition.

5.1 Multi-state Hand Tracking

To investigate the proposed approach, an experiment was performed of tracking hands in different states in an office environment with natural illumination. The particle filtering was performed with $N = 1000$ particles, which were evaluated on the $N^d = 200$ strongest scale-space features extracted from each image. Figures 5(a)-(c) show a few results from this experiment. As can be seen, the combination of particle filtering with the dissimilarity measure for hierarchical object models correctly captures changes in the position, scale and orientation of the hand. Moreover, changes in hand postures are captured.

| *Size variations* | *Rotations* | *State change* |

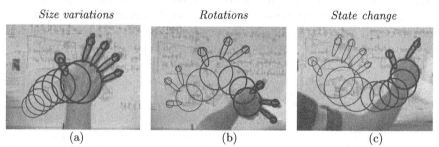

| (a) | (b) | (c) |

Fig. 5. Result of applying the proposed framework for tracking a hand in an office environment. (a): size variations; (b) rotations; (c): a change in hand state $l : 5 \to 2$.

As a test of the stability of the hand tracker, we developed a prototype of a drawing tool called DrawBoard, where hand motions are used for controlling a visual drawing in a multi-functional way. In this application, the cursor on the screen was controlled by the position of the hand, and depending on the state of the hand, different actions could be performed. A hand posture with two fingers implied that DrawBoard was in a drawing state, while a posture with one finger meant that the cursor moved without drawing. With three fingers present, the shape of the brush could be changed, while a hand posture with five fingers was used for translating, rotating and scaling the drawing. Figure 6 shows a few snapshots from such a drawing session.[1] As can be seen from the results, the performance of the tracker is sufficient for producing a reasonable drawing.

A necessary pre-requisite for this purely intensity-based system to give satisfactory results is that there is a clear contrast in intensity between the object and the background. In on-going work, it is shown that the sensitivity to the choice of background can be reduced substantially by (i) performing colour-based feature detection, and by (ii) including a complementary prior on skin colour. In a project for computer-vision-based human-computer-interaction, this extended system is used for capturing hand gestures controlling different types of computerized equipment (Bretzner et al. 2001).

The integrated algorithm currently runs at about 10Hz frame rate on a modest dual processor PC with two 550MHz Pentium III processors. An important component in reaching real-time performance is an efficient pyramid implementation of the multi-scale feature detection step (Lindeberg and Niemenmaa 2001).

---

[1] A longer movie clip is available from http://www.nada.kth.se/cvap/gvmdi/.

Drawing with a pencil of varying size   *Changing the shape of the pencil*

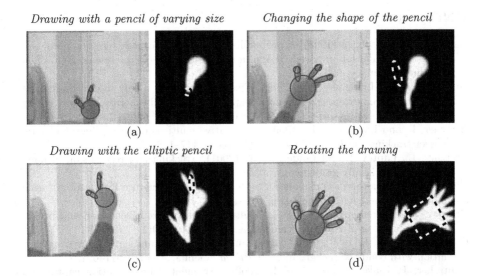

Drawing with the elliptic pencil   *Rotating the drawing*

Fig. 6. DrawBoard. The hand is used as a drawing device where the position, the size and the orientation of a pencil are controlled by the corresponding parameters of a hand in the image (a),(c). In (b) the user is able to change the elliptic shape of a pencil by rotating a hand in a state with three open fingers. In (d) the drawing is scaled and rotated with a hand in a state with five open fingers.

6 Summary and Discussion

We have demonstrated how a view-based object representation in terms of a hierarchy of multi-scale image features can be used for tracking and recognition in combination with particle filtering, based on a scale-invariant dissimilarity measures, which relates features in the object representation to image data and enables discrimination between different spatial configurations. The combination of this measure with multi-scale features makes the approach truly scale-invariant and allows for object tracking and recognition under large size variations.

In an application to hand gesture analysis, we have shown how qualitative states and quantitative motions of a hand can be captured. In this context, the use of a hierarchical multi-scale model allows us to perform hierarchical layered sampling, which improves the computational efficiency by reducing the number of particles.

In combination with a pyramid implementation of the feature detection stage, real-time performance has been obtained, and the system has been tested in application scenarios with human-computer interaction based on hand gestures. In this context, the qualitative hand states were used for selecting between different actions, while the continuous parameters were used for controlling these actions in a quantitative way.

Although a main emphasis here has been on hand models, we believe that the proposed framework can be extended for tracking and recognizing broader classes of objects consisting of qualitatively different structures at different scales.

References

Black, M. and Jepson, A. (1998). A probabilistic framework for matching temporal trajectories: Condensation-based recognition of gestures and expressions, *ECCV'98*, Freiburg, Germany, 909–924.

Bretzner, L. and Lindeberg, T. (1998). Use your hand as a 3-D mouse or relative orientation from extended sequences of sparse point and line correspondences using the affine trifocal tensor, *ECCV'96*, Freiburg, Germany, 141–157.

Bretzner, L. and Lindeberg, T. (1999). Qualitative multi-scale feature hierarchies for object tracking, *Scale-Space'99*, Corfu, Greece, 117–128.

Bretzner, L., Laptev, I. and Lindeberg, T. (2001). Tracking and recognition of hand postures for visually guided control. *In preparation*.

Cipolla, R., Okamoto, Y. and Kuno, Y. (1993). Robust structure from motion using motion parallax, *ICCV'93*, Berlin, Germany, 374–382.

Crowley, J. and Sanderson, A. (1987). Multiple resolution representation and probabilistic matching of 2-d gray-scale shape, *IEEE-PAMI*, **9**(1): 113–121.

Cui, Y. and Weng, J. (1996). View-based hand segmentation and hand-sequence recognition with complex backgrounds, *ICPR'96*, Vienna, Austria, 617–621.

Deutscher, J., Blake, A. and Reid, I. (2000). Articulated body motion capture by annealed particle filtering, *CVPR'00*, Hilton Head, SC, II:126–133.

Freeman, W. T. and Weissman, C. D. (1995) , Television control by hand gestures, *Face and Gesture'95*, Zurich, Switzerland.

Heap, T. and Hogg, D. (1998). Wormholes in shape space: Tracking through discontinuous changes in shape, *ICCV'98*, Bombay, India, 344–349.

Isard, M. and Blake, A. (1996). Contour tracking by stochastic propagation of conditional density, *ECCV'96*, Cambridge, UK, I:343–356.

Laptev, I and Lindeberg, T. (2000) Tracking of multi-state hand models using particle filtering and a hierarchy of multi-scale image features, Technical report ISRN KTH/NA/P–00/12–SE.
`http://www.nada.kth.se/cvap/abstracts/cvap245.html`.

Lindeberg, T. (1993). Detecting salient blob-like image structures and their scales with a scale-space primal sketch: A method for focus-of-attention, *IJCV*, **11**: 283–318.

Lindeberg, T. (1998). Feature detection with automatic scale selection, *IJCV*, **30**(2): 77–116.

Lindeberg, T. and Niemenmaa, J. (2001). Scale selection in hybrid multi-scale representations, *in preparation*.

MacCormick, J. and Isard, M. (2000). Partitioned sampling, articulated objects, and interface-quality hand tracking, *ECCV'00*, Dublin, Ireland, II:3–19.

Pizer, S. M., Burbeck, C. A., Coggins, J. M., Fritsch, D. S. and Morse, B. S. (1994). Object shape before boundary shape: Scale-space medial axis, *JMIV* **4**: 303–313.

Regh, J. M. and Kanade, T. (1995). Model-based tracking of self-occluding articulated objects, *ICCV'95*, Cambridge, MA, 612–617.

Shokoufandeh, A., Marsic, I. and Dickinson, S. (1999). View-based object recognition using saliency maps, *IVC*, **17**(5/6): 445–460.

Sidenbladh, H., Black, M. and Fleet, D. (2000). Stochastic tracking of 3-D human figures using 2-D image motion, *ECCV'00*, Dublin, Ireland, II:702–718.

Sjöbergh, J. and Lindeberg, T. (2001). *In preparation*.

Sullivan, J., Blake, A., Isard, M. and MacCormick, J. (1999). Object localization by Bayesian correlation, *ICCV'99*, Corfu, Greece, 1068–1075.

Triesch, J. and von der Malsburg, C. (1996). Robust classification of hand postures against complex background, *Face and Gesture'96*, Killington, Vermont, 170–175.

A Note on Two Classical Shock Filters and Their Asymptotics

Frédéric Guichard[1] and Jean-Michel Morel[2]

[1] Poseidon-Technologies, 3 rue Nationale
92100 Boulogne-Billancourt, France
fguichard@poseidon.fr
[2] CMLA, ENS Cachan, Avenue Président Wilson
91235 Cachan cedex, France
morel@cmla.ens-cachan.fr

Abstract. We establish in 2D, the PDE associated with a classical de-bluring filter, the Kramer operator and compare it with another classical shock filter.

1   Introduction

Gabor remarked in 1960 that the difference between the original u_0 and a blurred version image of it $k * u_0$ is roughly proportional to its Laplacian. In order to formalize this remark, we have to notice that k is spatially concentrated, and that we may introduce a scale parameter for k, namely $k_h(\mathbf{x}) = \frac{1}{h} k(\frac{\mathbf{x}}{h^{\frac{1}{2}}})$. Then

$$\frac{u_0 * k_h(\mathbf{x}) - u_0(\mathbf{x})}{h} \to \Delta u_0(\mathbf{x}),$$

so that when h gets smaller, the blur process looks more and more like the heat equation

$$\frac{\partial u}{\partial t} = \Delta u, \quad u(0) = u_0.$$

Conversely, Gabor deduced that we can, in some extent, deblur an image by reversing time in the heat equation :

$$\frac{\partial u}{\partial t} = -\Delta u, \quad u(0) = u_{observed}.$$

Numerically, this amounts to iterating substraction of its Laplacian from the observed image :

$$u_{restored} = u_{observed} - h\Delta u_{observed}.$$

$$u_{observed} \leftarrow u_{restored}$$

This operation can be repeated several times with some small values of h, until it... blows up. Indeed, the reverse heat equation is extremely ill-posed. All the same, this Gabor method is efficient and can be applied with some success to most digital images obtained from an optical device. See also [5] for other information about Gabor image enhancement.

M. Kerckhove (Ed.): Scale-Space 2001, LNCS 2106, pp. 75–84, 2001.

Some attempts to improve the time-reverse heat equation are:

The Osher–Rudin Equation of Shock Filter. Osher and Rudin [11] proposed to shapen a blurred image u_0 by applying the following equation:

$$\frac{\partial u}{\partial t} = -sign(\Delta u)|Du|, \text{ with } u(0, \mathbf{x}) = u_0(\mathbf{x})$$

This can be seen as a pseudo inverse of the Heat equation, where the propagation term Du is tuned by the sign of the Laplacian. We will call in the following TR_t the operator that associates to $u_0(.)$ the function $u(t, .)$.

The Kramer Algorithm. In [4], Kramer defines a filter for sharpening blurred images. The filter replaces the gray level value at a point by either the minimum or the maximum of the gray level values in a neighborhood. This choice depending on which is the closest to the current value. This filter is then localized and iterated on the image. Let us call TK this filter. Kramer's filter can be interpreted as a partial differential equation, by the same kind of heuristic arguments which Gabor developed to derive the heat equation. In [12] the authors proposed a finer version of the Kramer filter by ponderating the minimum or the maximum by a parabolic function (see following).

It was proved, in [12], that the Kramer and the Osher–Rudin filters share the same asymptotic behavior for regular 1D signal. That is they are infinitesimally identical in 1D! However, as we will see this is not true in 2D that is in the case of images. As we shall see, this equation is

$$\frac{\partial u}{\partial t} = -sign(D^2u(Du, Du))|Du|.$$

Thus, the Laplacian is replaced by a directional second derivative of the image, $D^2u(Du, Du)$.

The general aim of this paper is to prove this result and to establish existing links and differences between the two filters in 2D. It is organized as follow:

In Section 2, we recall or establish some mathematical statements on scaled general monotone operators and their asymptotic. In Section 3 we establish the asymptotic of the Kramer filter in 2D and, conversely, we propose an algorithm similar to Kramer that simulates the Osher–Rudin equation. At last in Section 4, we underline a link between these filters and two very classical edge detectors : the Canny and the zero-crossings of the Laplacian. Most of the statements with complete proofs can be found in the manuscript notes [3]

Before entering the cope of this note, let us point that several methods for improving the time-reverse heat equation have been proposed. Some are similar to the two ones we are going to study, as contrast enhancement filters as e.g. in [9]. Another class of such attempts covers so called "restoration" methods. Roughly, the main idea is to search for a function $u_{restored}$, so that once blurred with the heat equation $u_restored$ gives the original image $u_{observed}$. Since applying the heat equation is equivalent to the convolution with an appropriate Gaussian function G_σ, one searches for $u_{restored}$, so that $u_{restored} * G_\sigma = u_{observed} \pm$ noise. This last equation does not yield a unique solution. So, among possible solutions $u_{restored}$ is chosen as the most regular one. The regularity is then measured by a energy / norm, like the Total Variation in [10]. The "restoration" methods seem to give the most promising debluring results. This note will definitely not cover these techniques, however we will at the end give an example for comparison with the shock filters.

2 General Form of Scaled Monotone Operator and Mathematical Tools

2.1 Scaled Monotone Operators

We consider a family $\mathcal{F}$ of functions from $\mathbb{R}^2$ into $\mathbb{R}$ representing a class of images. We define an image operator on $\mathcal{F}$ as a operator from $\mathcal{F}$ into $\mathcal{F}$. An operator T is said monotone if $(\forall \mathbf{x} \in \mathbb{R}^2, u(\mathbf{x}) \geq v(\mathbf{x})) \to (\forall \mathbf{x}, Tu(\mathbf{x}) \geq Tv(\mathbf{x}))$. The following theorem gives us a general form for any monotone and translation invariant operator:

Theorem 1 (Matheron [8], Serra [13], Maragos [7]). *Let T be a monotone function operator defined of $\mathcal{F}$, invariant by translation and commuting with the addition of constant. There exists a family $\mathbb{F}$ of functions such that*

$$Tu(\mathbf{x}) = \sup_{f \in \mathcal{F}} \inf_{\mathbf{y} \in \mathbb{R}} u(\mathbf{y}) - f(\mathbf{x} - \mathbf{y}).$$

Note: It is a general property of the monotone and translation invariant filter to preserve Lipschitz property of any Lipschitz function. As consequence, the choice $\mathcal{F}$ can be by default made by considering the set of the Lipschitz functions.

Definition 2. *We define a β-scaled operator T_h associated to T by*

$$T_h(u)(\mathbf{x}) = \inf_{f \in \mathbb{F}} \sup_{\mathbf{y} \in \mathbb{R}^N} (u(\mathbf{x} + \mathbf{y}) - h^\beta f(\mathbf{y}/h)). \tag{1}$$

2.2 Asymptotic Theorem

The utility of the Legendre transform in the study of the monotone operators has been noticed in e.g. [6]. Let us recall it:

Legendre Fenchel Transform.

Definition 3. *Let f be a function from $\mathbb{R}^N$ into $\bar{\mathbb{R}}$, we denote the Legendre transform of f by $f^* : \mathbb{R}^N \to \bar{\mathbb{R}}$ defined by*

$$f^*(p) = \sup_{\mathbf{x} \in \mathbb{R}} (p.\mathbf{x} - f(\mathbf{x})).$$

Let us note that if f is convex then the Legendre transform is finite for every p.

First Order Asymptotic.

Lemma 4. *Let f be a function satisfying the following conditions:*

$$\exists C > 0 \text{ and } \alpha > \max(\beta, 1) \text{ such that } \liminf_{|\mathbf{x}| \to \infty} \frac{f(\mathbf{x})}{|\mathbf{x}|^\alpha} \geq C \text{ and } f(0) \leq 0 \quad (2)$$

Then, for any C^1 and bounded function u, if $\beta < 2$:

$$\sup_{\mathbf{y} \in \mathbb{R}^N} (u(\mathbf{x} + \mathbf{y}) - h^\beta f(\mathbf{y}/h)) - u(\mathbf{x}) = h^\beta f^*(h^{1-\beta} Du(\mathbf{x})) + O(h^{2(1-\frac{\beta-1}{\alpha-1})})$$

A interesting particular case is when $\beta = 1$:

$$\sup_{\mathbf{y} \in \mathbb{R}^N} (u(\mathbf{x} + \mathbf{y}) - h f(\mathbf{y}/h)) - u(\mathbf{x}) = h f^*(Du(\mathbf{x})) + O(h^2)$$

Proof. Without loss of generality we can choose $\mathbf{x} = 0$ and $u(\mathbf{x}) = 0$ so that we are looking for an estimate of

$$\sup_{\mathbf{z} \in \mathbb{R}^N} (u(\mathbf{z}) - h^\beta f(\mathbf{z}/h))$$

when h tends to 0. Setting $\mathbf{y} = \mathbf{z}/h$, we have,

$$\sup_{\mathbf{z} \in \mathbb{R}^N} (u(\mathbf{z}) - h^\beta f(\mathbf{z}/h)) = \sup_{\mathbf{y} \in \mathbb{R}^N} (u(h\mathbf{y}) - h^\beta f(\mathbf{y})).$$

Let us first prove that we can discard from the preceding sup the $\mathbf{y}$ that goes too fast toward ∞ as h tends to 0. We consider the subset S_h of $\mathbb{R}^N$ of the $\mathbf{y}$ such that

$$u(h\mathbf{y}) - h^\beta f(\mathbf{y}) \geq u(0) - h^\beta f(0) \geq 0.$$

We obviously have

$$\sup_{\mathbf{y} \in \mathbb{R}^N} (u(h\mathbf{y}) - h^\beta f(\mathbf{y})) = \sup_{\mathbf{y} \in S_h} (u(h\mathbf{y}) - h^\beta f(\mathbf{y})).$$

Since u is bounded, we have $\forall \mathbf{y} \in S_h$, $f(\mathbf{y}) \leq C_1 h^{-\beta}$ for some constant C_1 depending only on $\|u\|_\infty$. Assume that there exists $\mathbf{y}_h \in S_h$ tending to ∞ as h tends to zero. For h small enough, condition (2) gives $f(\mathbf{y}_h) \geq C|\mathbf{y}_h|^\alpha$, which combined with the preceding inequality yields $|\mathbf{y}_h| \leq C_2 h^{-\beta/\alpha}$. Such a bound holds if $\mathbf{y}_h \in S_h$ is bounded, so that we have

$$\forall y \in S_h, |\mathbf{y}| \leq C_2 h^{-\beta/\alpha}$$

As consequence, $\forall y \in S_h$ we have $|h\mathbf{y}| = o(1)$ and we can do an expansion of u around 0, so that

$$\sup_{\mathbf{y} \in \mathbb{R}^N} (u(h\mathbf{y}) - h^\beta f(\mathbf{y})) = \sup_{\mathbf{y} \in S_h} (hDu(0).\mathbf{y} - h^\beta f(\mathbf{y}) + O(h^2|\mathbf{y}|^2))$$

We can now find finer bound for the set S_h repeating the same argument. $\forall \mathbf{y} \in S_h$ we have,

$$hp.\mathbf{y} - h^\beta f(\mathbf{y}) + O(h^2\mathbf{y}^2) \geq 0$$

which yields

$$|p| \geq h^{\beta-1} f(\mathbf{y})/|\mathbf{y}| + O(h|\mathbf{y}|)$$

Assume that $\mathbf{y}_h \in S_h$, satisfying the preceding inequation, tends to ∞ when h tends to 0, then by (2), we obtain $|\mathbf{y}_h| = O(h^{-\frac{\beta-1}{\alpha-1}})$. Once again, if $\mathbf{y}_h$ is bounded this estimate holds. So we have

$$\sup_{\mathbf{y}\in\mathbb{R}^N} (u(h\mathbf{y}) - h^\beta f(\mathbf{y})) = h^\beta (\sup_{\mathbf{y}\in S_h} (h^{1-\beta} p.\mathbf{y} - f(\mathbf{y}) + O(h^{2(1-\frac{\beta-1}{\alpha-1})-\beta})))$$

$$= h^\beta (\sup_{\mathbf{y}\in\mathbb{R}^N} (h^{1-\beta} p.\mathbf{y} - f(\mathbf{y})) + O(h^{2(1-\frac{\beta-1}{\alpha-1})})) = h^\beta (f^*(h^{1-\beta}p)) + O(h^{2(1-\frac{\beta-1}{\alpha-1})})$$

It is easily checked that $O(h^{2(1-\frac{\beta-1}{\alpha-1})}) = o(h^\beta)$ for all $\beta < 2$.   ○

Theorem 5. *Let $\mathbb{F}$ be a family of functions, all satisfying the condition (2) with a constant C not depending on the choice of a function within the family. Let T_h be the β-scaled operator associated with the family $\mathbb{F}$ and with a rescaling parameter β equal to 1. Then for all C^1 and bounded function u we have:*

$$\frac{(T_h(u) - u)(\mathbf{x})}{h} = H_1(Du(\mathbf{x})) + o(1)$$

where

$$H_1(p) = \inf_{f\in\mathbb{F}} f^*(p).$$

This theorem is an immediate consequence of the preceding lemma applied with $\beta = 1$.

Second Order Case - Some Heuristics, See [2]. Theorem 5 gives the first order possible behavior of a non-flat monotone operator. Question occurs on what happens if this first order term is 0, that is if $H_1(p) = 0$ for all p. In that case, it is necessary to push the expansion to the second order :

We have with $p = Du(0)$ and $A = D^2u(0)/2$,

$$\sup_{\mathbf{y}\in\mathbb{R}^N} u(h\mathbf{y}) - h^\beta f(\mathbf{y}) = \sup_{\mathbf{y}\in\mathbb{R}^N} hp.\mathbf{y} + h^2 A\mathbf{y}.\mathbf{y} - h^\beta f(\mathbf{y}) + O(|h\mathbf{y}|^3)$$

Since this last expression is increasing with respect to A it is then expected that the left side of the equality converges when h tends to 0, to some function $F(A, p)$ where F is non decreasing with respect to A. As consequence, among second order operator only elliptic operator can be obtained as the asymptotical limit of a general localized monotone operator [1].

Example: *The Heat Equation as the asymptotic of a non-flat morphological operator (in N-D).*

Lemma 6. *We set for $p \in I\!R^N$, $Q \in SM(I\!R^N)$ (symmetric matrix), and $h > 0$,*

$$f_{p,Q,h}(\mathbf{x}) = p\mathbf{x} + Q(\mathbf{x},\mathbf{x}) \quad if \ \mathbf{x} \in B(0,h)$$
$$= -\infty \qquad\qquad otherwise$$

We then set $I\!F_h = \{f_{p,Q,h}; with \ Q \in SM(I\!R^N); Tr(Q) = 0 \ and \ p \in I\!R^N\}$ which is to say that $I\!F_h$ is made of the truncature around zero of all quadratic forms whose trace is zero. With $T_h(u)(\mathbf{x}) = \inf_{f \in I\!F_h} \sup_{\mathbf{y} \in I\!R^N} u(\mathbf{x}+\mathbf{y}) - f(\mathbf{y})$, one has for any $u \in C^3$,

$$T_h(u)(\mathbf{x}) - u(\mathbf{x}) = \frac{1}{2N}h^2 \Delta u(\mathbf{x}) + o(h^2)$$

Proof is just made of simple algebraic computations. Complete proof can be found in [3].

3 Application to Image Enhancement: Kramer's Operators and the Osher–Rudin Shock Filter

3.1 The Kramer Operator

Let us now set mathematically the Kramer filter and its variant proposed in [12]. The asymptotic of the Kramer or its variant are similar while not strictly identical. But, proofs of asymptotic are the same for both. They can be defined as follow:

For Kramer operator set $q(\mathbf{x}) = 0$ if $|\mathbf{x}| < 1$ and $q(\mathbf{x}) = +\infty$ otherwise. For its variant [12] simply set $q(\mathbf{x}) = \mathbf{x}^2/2$. Then for both set $I\!F^+ = \{q\}$. Set T_h^+ the rescaled, (with $\beta = 1$), non-flat operator associated with the structuring elements set $I\!F^+$ and T_h^- its dual operator. That is

$$(T_h^+ u)(\mathbf{x}) = \sup_{\mathbf{y} \in I\!R^N} u(\mathbf{y}) - hq((\mathbf{x} - \mathbf{y})/h),$$

$$(T_h^- u)(\mathbf{x}) = \inf_{\mathbf{y} \in I\!R^N} u(\mathbf{y}) + hq((\mathbf{x} - \mathbf{y})/h).$$

The shock filter TK_h is then defined by

$$(TK_h u)(\mathbf{x}) = \begin{cases} (T_h^+ u)(\mathbf{x}) & if \ (T_h^+ u)(\mathbf{x}) - u(\mathbf{x}) < u(\mathbf{x}) - (T_h^- u)(\mathbf{x}), \\ (T_h^- u)(\mathbf{x}) & if \ (T_h^+ u)(\mathbf{x}) - u(\mathbf{x}) > u(\mathbf{x}) - (T_h^- u)(\mathbf{x}), \qquad (3) \\ u(\mathbf{x}) & otherwise. \end{cases}$$

It is important to note that TK is NOT a monotone operator but that T^+ and T^- are monotone. TK can be seen as an conditional filter made of two monotone operators.

Lemma 7. *First order asymptotic of the Kramer Filter.*

$$(T_h^+ u)(\mathbf{x}) - u(\mathbf{x}) = hH(|Du(\mathbf{x})|) + O(h^2) \ \ and$$

$$(T_h^- u)(\mathbf{x}) - u(\mathbf{x}) = -hH(|Du(\mathbf{x})|) + O(h^2)$$

So that

$$\lim_{h \to 0} \frac{(TK_h u)(\mathbf{x}) - u(\mathbf{x})}{h} = \pm H(|Du(\mathbf{x})|) \ \ or \ 0$$

where $H(p) = |p|$ in the case of the Kramer filter, and $H(p) = |p|^2/2$ for its variant.

This lemma is an immediate consequence of Theorem 5. At this step, we remark that the differences $(T_h^+ u)(\mathbf{x}) - u(\mathbf{x})$ and $u(\mathbf{x}) - (T_h^- u)$ are equal at the first order, and therefore the choice will be made based on second order derivatives of u.

Proposition 8. *One has for any function $u \in C^3$ around $\mathbf{x}$,*

$$\lim_{h \to 0} \frac{(TK_h u) - u}{h}(\mathbf{x}) = -sign(D^2 u(Du, Du)) \, H(|Du(\mathbf{x})|)$$

where $H(p) = |p|$ in the case of the Kramer filter, and $H(p) = |p|^2/2$ for its variant.

Proof. One has to push the asymptotic of T_h^+ and T_h^- to the second order. We only do here the case of variant filter. We have

$$T_h^+(u)(\mathbf{x}) = \sup_{\mathbf{y} \in \mathbb{R}^N} u(\mathbf{y}) - \frac{(\mathbf{x} - \mathbf{y})^2}{2h} \quad and \quad T_h^-(u)(\mathbf{x}) = \inf_{\mathbf{y} \in \mathbb{R}^N} u(\mathbf{y}) + \frac{(\mathbf{x} - \mathbf{y})^2}{2h}$$

Since T_h^+ and T_h^- are translation invariant, we can limit our study at $\mathbf{x} = 0$. Moreover, since u is bounded, we can limit the sup to the $\mathbf{y} \in B(0, h)$. If u is C^3 at point 0, we can set $u(\mathbf{y}) = u(0) + \mathbf{p}.\mathbf{y} + A(\mathbf{y}, \mathbf{y}) + o(\mathbf{y})^2$ So that,

$$T_h^+(u)(0) - u(0) = \sup_{\mathbf{y} \in B(0,h)} u(\mathbf{y}) - \frac{|\mathbf{y}|^2}{2h} - u(0) = \sup_{\mathbf{y} \in B(0,h)} (\mathbf{p}.\mathbf{y} + A(\mathbf{y}, \mathbf{y}) - \frac{|\mathbf{y}|^2}{2h} + o(h)^2$$

Set $Q_h(\mathbf{y}) = 2h\mathbf{p}.\mathbf{y} + (2hA - Id)(\mathbf{y}, \mathbf{y})$, so that we have

$$T_h = \sup_{\mathbf{y} \in B(0,h)} (Q_h(\mathbf{y})/(2h)) + o(h)^2$$

For h small enough $B_h = Id - 2hA$ is positive and invertible. Therefore, the sup of Q_h over the $\mathbf{y}$ exists, and is achieved for $\mathbf{y}_h$ such that

$$2h\mathbf{p} + 2B\mathbf{y}_h = 0 \Rightarrow \mathbf{y}_h = -hB^{-1}(\mathbf{p})$$

Thus,

$$T_h^+(u)(0) - u(0) = \frac{h}{2}(Id - 2hA)^{-1}(\mathbf{p}, \mathbf{p}) + o(h^2) = \frac{h}{2}(Id + 2hA)(\mathbf{p}, \mathbf{p}) + o(h^2)$$

We conclude that

$$T_h^+(u)(0) - u(0) = \frac{h}{2}|\mathbf{p}|^2 + h^2 A(\mathbf{p}, \mathbf{p}) + o(h^2) \tag{4}$$

Similarly,

$$T_h^-(u)(0) - u(0) = \frac{h}{2}|\mathbf{p}|^2 - h^2 A(\mathbf{p}, \mathbf{p}) + o(h^2) \tag{5}$$

From these two last equalities and translation invariance we deduce that, for $\forall \mathbf{x}$:

$$((T_h^+ u)(\mathbf{x}) - u(\mathbf{x})) - (u(\mathbf{x}) - (T_h^- u)(\mathbf{x})) = 2h^2(D^2 u(\mathbf{x}))(Du(\mathbf{x}), Du(\mathbf{x})) + o(h^2) \tag{6}$$

We therefore have

$$T_h(u)(\mathbf{x}) - u(\mathbf{x}) = -h^2|Du(\mathbf{x})|^2 \ sgn(\ D^2 u(\mathbf{x})\ (Du(\mathbf{x}), Du(\mathbf{x}))\ )/2 + o(h^2)$$

○

Let us remark that if u is a 1D function, then $sign(D^2 u(Du, Du))$ coincides with the sign of the Laplacian. That is that the Kramer operator corresponds, in 1D, asymptotically to the Osher–Rudin shock filter. However they differ in 2D.

3.2   The Osher–Rudin Shock Filter

The Osher–Rudin Shock Filter has been proposed by the authors directly in its asymptotic way, that is by a PDE. The question occurs on the existence of a scheme similar to the Kramer one, but that would simulate the Osher–Rudin shock filter. Such a scheme can be defined as follow:

Let B_h be a disk of radius h centered at 0. Let $Mean_h$ be the mean value on the disk B_h. We define the operator T_h by:

$$
\begin{aligned}
T_h u(\mathbf{x}) &= min_{\mathbf{y} \in B_h} u(\mathbf{x} + \mathbf{y}) \quad \text{if } Mean_h(u)(\mathbf{x}) > u(\mathbf{x}) \\
&= max_{\mathbf{y} \in B_h} u(\mathbf{x} + \mathbf{y}) \quad \text{if } Mean_h(u)(\mathbf{x}) < u(\mathbf{x}) \\
&= \qquad u(\mathbf{x}) \qquad\qquad\quad \text{otherwise}
\end{aligned}
$$

Proposition 9. *One has*

$$\lim_{h \to 0} \frac{T_h u - u}{h} = -sign(\Delta u)|Du|$$

The proof follows from the fact that $Mean_h(u)(\mathbf{x}) - u(\mathbf{x}) = \Delta u(\mathbf{x}) + o(h^2)$.

4   Conclusion

The preceding study permits to establish the following diagram. It makes clearer the relationships between the various kinds of edge detectors and debluring filters.

In 2D:	Kramer Filter	Osher–Rudin Filter
$\frac{\partial u}{\partial t} =$	$- \|Du\| sgn(D^2 u(Du, Du))$	$- \|Du\| sgn(\Delta u)$
replace u by	min or max of u in a neighborhood	min or max of u in a neighborhood
depending	on which of the two is the nearest to u	on whether the mean of u in a neighborhood is above or below u.

Associated edge detector	Canny edge detector $D^2 u(Du, Du) = 0$	Zero-Crossing of Laplacian $\Delta u = 0$

In particular, by the same arguments as Osher–Rudin [11], we can claim that Kramer's operator enhances Canny edges. Osher and Rudin proved that their operator enhanced Hildreth-Marr edges.

The figure 1 illustrates the effect of both operators. Left, an original blurred image, next the Osher and Rudin shock filter (steady state), next improved Krammer operator (steady state) and at last for comparison purpose the Rudin-Osher-Fatemi debluring method [10]. This last, in contrary to the two studied in this paper, makes an explicit used of knowledge about blurring kernel and noise statistic.

References

1. L. Alvarez, F. Guichard, P.L. Lions, and J.M. Morel. Axioms and fundamental equations of image processing. *Archive for Rational Mechanics and Analysis.*, 16(9):200–257, 1993.
2. F. Cao. Partial differential equation and mathemetical morphology. *Journal de Mathematiques Pures et Appliquees*, 77(9):909–941, 1998.
3. F. Guichard and J.-M. Morel. *Image Iterative Smoothing and PDE's.* downloadable manuscript : please write email to fguichard@poseidon.fr, 2000.
4. H.P. Kramer and J.B. Bruckner. Iterations of a non-linear transformation for enhancement of digital images. *Pattern Recognition*, 7, 1975.
5. M. Lindenbaum, M. Fischer, and A.M. Bruckstein. On gabor contribution to image-enhancement. *PR*, 27(1):1–8, January 1994.
6. P. Maragos. Slope transfroms: Theory and application to nonlinear signal processing. *IEEE Transactions on signal processing*, 43:864–877, 1995.
7. P. Maragos and R.W. Schafer. Morphological filters. part II: Their relations to median, order-statistic, and stack filters. *ASSP*, 35:1170–1184, 1987.
8. G. Matheron. *Random Sets and Integral Geometry.* John Wiley, N.Y., 1975.
9. F. Meyer and J. Serra. Contrasts and activity lattice. *Signal Processing*, 16:303–317, 1989.
10. Leonid I. Rudin, Stanley Osher, and Emad Fatemi. Nonlinear total variation based noise removal algorithms. *Physica D 60, No.1-4, 259-268. [ISSN 0167-2789]*, 1992.
11. Osher, Stanley and Leonid I. Rudin. Feature-oriented image enhancement using shock filters. *SIAM J. Numer. Anal. 27, No.4, 919-940. [ISSN 0036-1429]*, 1990.

Fig. 1. Image deblurring by shock filters and by a variational method. Top-left: blurred image, Top-right: Osher–Rudin shock filter [11] which is a pseudoinverse of the heat equation attaining a steady state, Bottom-left: Kramer's improved shock filter [12], Bottom-right: also attaining a steady state and the Rudin, Osher, Fatemi restoration method [10], obtained by deblurring with a controlled image total variation and using explicit knowledge of the blurring kernel.

12. J.G.M Schavemaker, M.J.T Reinders, J.J. Gerbrands, and E. Backer. Image sharpening by morphological filtering. *submitted to Pattern Recognition*, 1999.
13. J. Serra. *Image Analysis and Mathematical Morphology*. Academic Press, 1982.

Bayesian Object Detection through Level Curves Selection

Charles Kervrann

INRA - Biométrie, Domaine de Vilvert
78352 Jouy-en-Josas, France
ck@jouy.inra.fr

Abstract. Bayesian statistical theory is a convenient way of taking *a priori* information into consideration when inference is made from images. In Bayesian image detection, the *a priori* distribution should capture the knowledge about objects. Taking inspiration from [1], we design a prior density that penalizes the area of homogeneous parts in images. The detection problem is further formulated as the estimation of the set of curves that maximizes the posterior distribution. In this paper, we explore a posterior distribution model for which its maximal mode is given by a subset of level curves, that is the boundaries of image level sets. For the completeness of the paper, we present a stepwise greedy algorithm for computing partitions with connected components.

1 Introduction

In most problems of image analysis, incorporation of prior knowledge is important for making inference based on the images. Bayesian object detection is the problem of how to estimate the number of simply connected objects and their location in a non-ideal environment. Bayesian approaches specify ways for segmenting the entire image using global energy criteria. Indeed, it is usually straightforward to transfer a Bayesian criterion into an energy minimization criterion. In addition, additivity is desirable in models which must be analyzing by Markov Chains Monte Carlo sampling. Thereby, the discrete [8,2] or continuous [18,17] energy functional is traditionally designed as a combination of several terms, each of them corresponding to a precise property which must be satisfied. While this modeling offers a powerful theoretical framework and minimizers exist [17,25], they have several disadvantages. First, these models lead to very difficult optimization problems that are notoriously slow to converge [2]. Second, the weight parameters which are key ingredients of a wide range of segmentation energies, are usually not correctly estimated, yielding to supervised segmentation methods. Third, sampling from a Markov Random Fields distribution does not always produce patterns that look like images.

Object detection belongs to the field of high-level imaging, in which the image modeling is on a more global scale compared to low-level imaging which deals with (smoothing) prior models on a pixel level. In particular, more global prior

M. Kerckhove (Ed.): Scale-Space 2001, LNCS 2106, pp. 85–97, 2001.

models for the simply connected objects can be applied. There has been a growing interest in this field, particularly along the guidelines of Grenander's general pattern theory using deformable templates [9]. Moreover, Zhu *et al.* attempted to unify snakes [12], balloons [5] and region growing methods within a general energy/Bayes framework [25]. These prior models are generally realistic and incorporate prior information about the outline of objects in a Bayesian image analysis framework. In other respects, both approaches estimate the curves that maximally separate unknown statistics inside and outside the curves [25,9]. The *maximum a posteriori* (MAP) estimate is generally determined by prohibitive stochastic search procedures [9] or other variants of steepest ascent algorithms [25]. Thereby, additional *a priori* knowledge may be specified to ease the segmentation task: statistics inside region boundaries are assumed to be known [9,4] or estimated using *ad-hoc* methods [20,24]. The global energy functional may be then optimized, for instance, within a level set framework [19,22] which provides the advantages of numerical stability and topological flexibility [4,20,24]. In practical imaging, these methods may suffer from the problem of initialization of curves [25], off-line estimation of the mixture model of Gaussians approximating the probability density function of the image [20], or selection of hyperparameters weighting the contribution of energy terms [25,20,4].

In this paper, we address these problems and follow the Bayesian approach for recovering simply connected objects in the plane. The prior model focuses on how the area and number of objects can varied in images (Section 2). It allows to partition the image into few regions, though in a more restrictive manner than previous approaches [25,20] since it can generate irregular boundaries. Unlike other approaches [25,9], we shall see that maximizing the posterior distribution is herein equivalent to select a subset of connected components of image bilevel sets (Section 3). Section 4 presents the numerical implementation of our model and the computation of the image segmentation. In Section 5, we illustrate this approach with some experiments on satellite images. Conclusions and perspectives are presented in Section 6.

2   The Bayesian Framework

Let S be an open subset of $\mathbb{R}^2$ and f a grey-scale image treated as a function defined on S. In practical imaging, S is a collection of pixels within a discretized rectangle, and possible values of f are given by integers $[0, 256[\cap\mathbb{N}$. Below we will work in the continuous setup, where S is a subset of a Euclidian space and $f : S \to \mathbb{R}^+$ represents the observed data function. The continuous setup allows us to refer to analytic tools, while leaving always a possibility to "discretize" the problem. We use the terminology "site" or "pixel" to denote a point of the image, even in the continuous case. Each point $x \in S$ is assigned a grey value $f(x)$. According to Matheron [15], we interpret the image f as a family of sets defined by $L_\gamma(f) = \{x \in S : f(x) \geq \gamma\}$, $\gamma \in \mathbb{R}^+$. Each level sets $L_\gamma(f)$ is assumed to be of finite perimeter. Therefore, f will belong to the bounded variation (noted BV) space [1].

Let $\{\Omega_i \subset S\}$ be a set of disjoint and non-empty image domains or objects, and $\{\partial\Omega_i\}$ their boundaries. A partition of the space S consists in finding a set $\{\Omega_i\}_{i=1}^P$ and a background $\overline{\Omega}$ defined as the complementary subset of the union of objects $\overline{\Omega} = S \setminus \cup_{i=1}^P \Omega_i$, $\Omega_i \cap_{i \neq j} \Omega_j = \emptyset$ and $\Omega_i \cap_i \overline{\Omega} = \emptyset$.

We assume that the observed image f has been produced by the model $f = f_{\mathrm{true}} + \varepsilon$, where ε is a zero-mean Gaussian white noise: $\varepsilon(x) \overset{iid}{\sim} \mathcal{N}(0, \sigma^2)$, $x \in S$. The true image $f_{\mathrm{true}}(x) = \sum_{i=1}^P \overline{f}_{\Omega_i} 1_{x \in \Omega_i} + \overline{f}_{\overline{\Omega}} 1_{x \in \overline{\Omega}}$ is supposed piecewise constant, where $\overline{f}_{\Omega_i}$ and $\overline{f}_{\overline{\Omega}}$ denote respectively the unknown average values of f over Ω_i and $\overline{\Omega}$, and $1_{x \in E}$ is the set indicator function of the set E. The variance σ^2 is assumed to be known and constant over the entire image [25]. So, the likelihood for the data f given $\{\Omega_1, \cdots, \Omega_P\}$ is specified by

$$p(f \mid \Omega_1, \cdots, \Omega_P) \propto \exp -\frac{1}{2\sigma^2} \left\{ \sum_{i=1}^P \int_{\Omega_i} (f(x) - \overline{f}_{\Omega_i})^2 dx + \int_{\overline{\Omega}} (f(x) - \overline{f}_{\overline{\Omega}})^2 dx \right\}. \quad (1)$$

We seek a partition of the rectangle S into a finite set of objects Ω_i, each of which corresponding to a part of the image where f is constant. Therefore, we define the following collection $\mathcal{C}_P$ of $P \geq 0$ admissible, closed and connected objects

$$\mathcal{C}_P = \{\{\Omega_1, \ldots, \Omega_P\} \subset S \; ; \; S \setminus \overline{\Omega} = \bigcup_{i=1}^P \Omega_i \; ; \; \Omega_i \bigcap_{1 \leq i \neq j \leq P} \Omega_j = \emptyset \}.$$

When $P = 0$, there is no object in the image. Following the Bayesian approach, we use some functional of the posterior distribution of $\{\Omega_1, \cdots, \Omega_P\}$:

$$p(\Omega_1, \cdots, \Omega_P \mid f) \propto p(f \mid \Omega_1, \cdots, \Omega_P) \pi(\Omega_1, \cdots, \Omega_P) \quad (2)$$

where $p(f \mid \Omega_1, \cdots, \Omega_P)$ is the likelihood given by (1) and $\pi(\Omega_1, \cdots, \Omega_P)$ is the prior distribution of objects. The posterior distribution is used in a further inferential issue concerning the objects within the Bayesian paradigm. The a priori distribution should capture the knowledge about $\{\Omega_1, \cdots, \Omega_P\}$. We define a density that penalizes the area $|\Omega_i|$ of objects. Additionally, the variables $\{|\Omega_i|\}$ may be considered as independent random variables with density $g(|\Omega_i|)$. Hence, the prior distribution is of the form $\pi(\Omega_1, \cdots, \Omega_P) = Z_p^{-1} \prod_{i=1}^P g(|\Omega_i|)^a$ where Z_P is a normalization constant and a a real positive value. The density $g(|\Omega_i|)$ is chosen to be a non-negative monotically decreasing function of the object area $|\Omega_i|$. For instance, Alvarez et al. [1] have realized experimentally that the area distribution of homogeneous parts in images follows a power law $\beta|\Omega_i|^{-\gamma}$. The parameters β and γ (close to 1, 2 for values of $|\Omega_i|$ in a certain range) give the intensity of the model. In what follows, we shall consider this model for the density $g(|\Omega_i|)$. There are other possible choices of $g(|\Omega_i|)$; the case of $g(|\Omega_i|) \propto \exp -\beta|\Omega_i|^\gamma$ has been already discussed in [13,1]. This model is related to the Markov connected components fields [16].

3   Bayesian Inference

All kinds of inference are made from $p(\Omega_1, \cdots, \Omega_P \mid f)$. Finding the *maximum a posteriori* (MAP) estimate is herein our choice of inference. As a consequence, the MAP estimation of objects comes to the minimization of a global energy function $E_\lambda(f, \Omega_1, \ldots, \Omega_P)$ defined as

$$\underbrace{\sum_{i=1}^{P} \int_{\Omega_i} (f(x) - \overline{f}_{\Omega_i})^2 \, dx + \int_{\overline{\Omega}} (f(x) - \overline{f}_{\overline{\Omega}})^2 \, dx}_{E_d(f, \Omega_1, \ldots, \Omega_P)} + \lambda \underbrace{\sum_{i=1}^{P} (\gamma \log(|\Omega_i|) - A)}_{E_p(\Omega_1, \ldots, \Omega_P)} \quad (3)$$

where $E_p(\Omega_1, \ldots, \Omega_P)$ is the penalty functional, $E_d(f, \Omega_1, \ldots, \Omega_P)$ the data model, $\lambda = 2a\,\sigma^2 > 0$ the regularization parameter and $A = \log(\beta)$. The penalty functional tends to regulate the emergence of objects Ω_i in the image and gives no control on the smoothness of boundaries. The regularization parameter λ can be then interpreted as a scale parameter that only tunes the number of regions [17,14,13]. If $\lambda = 0$, each point is potentially a region and $\overline{\Omega} = \emptyset$; the global minimum coincides with zero and this segmentation is called the "*trivial segmentation*" [17,14].

Our MAP estimator is defined by (when exists)

$$(\widehat{\Omega}_1, \ldots, \widehat{\Omega}_{\widehat{P}}) = \text{argmin}_{0 \le P \le T}\, \text{argmin}_{\{\Omega_1, \ldots, \Omega_P\} \in \mathcal{C}_P}\, E_\lambda(f, \Omega_1, \ldots, \Omega_P) \quad (4)$$

where $\mathcal{C}_P \subseteq \mathcal{C}_T, \forall P \le T$, and T is the maximum number of admissible objects registered in a bank $\mathcal{C}_T$. We recall that $\widehat{\overline{\Omega}} = S \setminus \cup_{i=1}^{\widehat{P}} \widehat{\Omega}_i$ is the complementary subset of estimated objects $\{\widehat{\Omega}_1, \ldots, \widehat{\Omega}_{\widehat{P}}\}$. By using classical arguments on lower semi-continuous functionals on the BV space, we assume here existence of minimizers of $E_\lambda(f, \Omega_1, \cdots, \Omega_P)$ among functions of sets finite perimeter (or of bounded variation) [17,25]. However, a direct minimization with respect to all unknown domains Ω_i and parameters $\overline{f}_{\Omega_i}$ is a very intricate problem, even if T is low since objects are not designed. In what follows (Lemma 1), we prove that the object boundaries that minimize $E_\lambda(f, \Omega_1, \ldots, \Omega_P)$ are level lines of the function f, which makes the problem tractable.

LEMMA 1. *If there exists minimizers and no pathological minimum exists, then the energy minimizing set of curves is a subset of level lines of f:*

$$f_{|\partial \widehat{\Omega}_i} \equiv \mu_i, \qquad i = 1, \ldots, \widehat{P}.$$

i.e. the border $\partial \widehat{\Omega}_i$ of each $\widehat{\Omega}_i$ is a boundary of a connected component of a level set of f.

Proof of Lemma 1   Let Ω_δ be a variation of a set Ω, i.e. the Hausdorff distance $d_\infty(\Omega_\delta, \Omega) \le \delta$. To prove Lemma 1, we assume that, for any connected perturbation of Ω such $d_\infty(\Omega_\delta, \Omega) \le \delta$, two neighboring sets Ω and Ω' do not merge into one single set $\Omega \cup \Omega'$ and, for any connected perturbation of Ω such $d_\infty(\Omega_\delta, \Omega) \le \delta$, Ω does not split into two new sets. This corresponds to prohibited topological changes. Without loss of generality, we prove Lemma 1 for one object Ω and a background $\overline{\Omega}$, that is the closure of the complementary set of Ω. For two sets A and B, denote $\int_{A \backslash B} f \overset{\text{def}}{=} \int_A f - \int_B f$. Then, we have

$$\int_{\Omega_\delta \backslash \Omega} 1 \overset{\text{def}}{=} |\Omega_\delta| - |\Omega| \quad \text{and} \quad \left(\int_{\Omega_\delta} f \right)^2 - \left(\int_\Omega f \right)^2 = 2 \int_\Omega f \int_{\Omega_\delta \backslash \Omega} f + \left(\int_{\Omega_\delta \backslash \Omega} f \right)^2. \tag{5}$$

The difference between the involved energies is defined as $\Delta E_\lambda(f, \Omega) = E_\lambda(f, \Omega_\delta) - E_\lambda(f, \Omega) = T_1 + T_2 + T_3 + T_4 + T_5$ where

$$T_1 = \int_{\Omega_\delta} f^2 - \int_\Omega f^2, \quad T_2 = \frac{1}{|\Omega|} \int_{\Omega_\delta \backslash \Omega} \lambda \gamma, \quad T_3 = -\frac{1}{|\Omega_\delta|} \left(\int_{\Omega_\delta} f \right)^2 + \frac{1}{|\Omega|} \left(\int_\Omega f \right)^2,$$

$$T_4 = \int_{S \backslash \Omega_\delta} f^2 - \int_{S \backslash \Omega} f^2, \quad T_5 = -\frac{1}{|S| - |\Omega_\delta|} \left(\int_{S \backslash \Omega_\delta} f \right)^2 + \frac{1}{|S| - |\Omega|} \left(\int_{S \backslash \Omega} f \right)^2. \tag{6}$$

Denote $\Delta |\Omega| = |\Omega_\delta| - |\Omega|$. Using (5), and passing to the limit $\Delta |\Omega| \to 0$, i.e. $|\Omega_\delta| \simeq |\Omega|$, we obtain (higher order terms are neglected)

$$T_1 = -T_4 = \int_{\Omega_\delta \backslash \Omega} f^2, \quad T_2 = \frac{\lambda \gamma}{|\Omega|} \int_{\Omega_\delta \backslash \Omega} 1,$$

$$T_3 = -\frac{2}{|\Omega|} \int_{\Omega_\delta \backslash \Omega} f \int_\Omega f - \frac{1}{|\Omega|} \left(\int_{\Omega_\delta \backslash \Omega} f \right)^2 + \frac{1}{|\Omega|^2} \int_{\Omega_\delta \backslash \Omega} 1 \left(\int_\Omega f \right)^2, \tag{7}$$

$$T_5 = \frac{1}{|S| - |\Omega|} \left\{ 2 \int_{\Omega_\delta \backslash \Omega} f \int_{S \backslash \Omega} f - \left(\int_{\Omega_\delta \backslash \Omega} f \right)^2 - \frac{1}{|S| - |\Omega|} \int_{\Omega_\delta \backslash \Omega} 1 \left(\int_{S \backslash \Omega} f \right)^2 \right\}.$$

We define the following image moments $m_0 = \int_\Omega 1$, $m_1 = \int_\Omega f$, $K_0 = \int_S 1$, $K_1 = \int_S f$. Using the *mean value theorem for double integral*, which states that if f is continuous and a connected subset E is bounded by a simple curve, then for some point x_0 in E we have $\int_E f(x) dE = f(x_0) \cdot |E|$ where $|E|$ denotes the area of E, it follows that

$$\Delta E_\lambda(f, \Omega) = \left\{ \overbrace{\left[\frac{m_1^2}{m_0^2} - \frac{(K_1 - m_1)^2}{(K_0 - m_0)^2} + \frac{\lambda \gamma}{m_0} \right]}^{M_0} + \overbrace{\left[\frac{2(K_1 - m_1)}{K_0 - m_0} - \frac{2 m_1}{m_0} \right]}^{M_1} f(x_0) \right.$$
$$\left. - \left[\frac{1}{m_0} + \frac{1}{K_0 - m_0} \right] f(x_0)^2 \int_{\Omega_\delta \backslash \Omega} 1 \right\} \int_{\Omega_\delta \backslash \Omega} 1. \tag{8}$$

Let x_b be a fixed point of the border $\partial \Omega$. Choose Ω_δ such that $\partial \Omega_\delta = \partial \Omega$ except on a small neighborhood of x_b. The energy having a minimum for Ω, $f(x_b)$ needs to be solution of the following equation

$$\lim_{\Delta |\Omega| \to 0} \frac{\Delta E_\lambda(f, \Omega)}{\Delta |\Omega|} = [M_0 + M_1 f(x_b)] + O(\Delta |\Omega|) = 0. \tag{9}$$

By passing to the limit $\Delta|\Omega| \to 0$, we obtain $M_0 + M_1 f(x_b) = 0$. This equation has one single solution. The coefficients M_0 and M_1 do depend on neither x_b nor $f(x_b)$, and $M_0 \neq 0$. The function f is continuous and $\partial\Omega$ is a connected curve. Therefore $f(x_b)$ is constant when x_b covers $\partial\Omega$. This completes the proof. □

We have proved Lemma 1 with a connected perturbation including the situation when $|\Omega_\delta| - |\Omega| = |\partial\Omega|$ where $|\partial\Omega|$ is the boundary length of Ω. Equation 9 states a *necessary condition* which is essential to prove that a subset of level lines globally minimizes the energy.

If f is of bounded variation, the connected components of level sets can be characterized by their boundaries, that is the so-called *level lines* of f [3]. In consequence of Lemma 1, those curves constitute the borders $\{\partial\Omega_i\}$ of objects $\{\Omega_i\}$.

4   A Stepwise Greedy Algorithm for Image Segmentation

This section describes our algorithmic procedure for object boundaries estimation. Our recommendations for the concrete choice of the input parameters are collected in this section. The algorithm we propose does require neither the number of regions nor any initial mean gray values for regions and background.

4.1   Level Sets and Object Boundaries

The key ingredient of the procedure is the construction of objects whose boundaries are image level lines [3]. In practical imaging, we can associate with an image 255 level sets $\{L_\gamma(f)\}$, $0 \leq \gamma \leq 255$. We consider the scenario where a point x belongs to one single connected component at once within the image level sets. We take into account this fact and define the bilevel sets of f as the set of pixels $x \in S$ such that $v \leq f(x) \leq w$, $0 \leq v \leq w$. Instead of computing all the 255 level sets, we restrict only this computation to a small number of $K(< 255)$ level sets and adaptively quantize the image histogram using an entropy method [11]. For $l \in \mathbb{N}$ varying from 1 to K, let b_l be the binary image with $b_l(x) = 1$ if $f(x) \in [t_{l-1}, t_l)$ and $b_l(x) = 0$ otherwise, where t_l is a threshold. We call those images the K-bilevel sets of $f \in [f_{\min}, f_{\max}]$ [1]. In general, each bilevel set is made up of $n(t_l)$ disjoint connected components, where $n(t_l)$ is a function of the threshold t_l and $S = \cup_{l=1}^{l=K} [\Omega_{t_l,1} \cup \Omega_{t_l,2} \cup \cdots \cup \Omega_{t_l,n(t_l)}]$. A crude way to build pixels sets corresponding to objects would be to proceed to a connected components labeling of binary images $\{b_l\}$, $1 \leq l \leq K$, and to associate each label with an object Ω_i.

If f is bounded, the connected components of level sets can be characterized by their surrounding curves, that is the level lines [3,1]. If we map these level lines for a given set of K levels, we get a segmentation of the image also called *topographic map* [3,7]. More generally, one can consider a segmentation achieved using only some connected components of level sets, which is the philosophy of our approach. The most perceptible level lines can be determined by an isoperimetric criterion [7] or the detection of T-junctions of level lines [3]. Both criteria are strong indicators of region boundaries. Instead, we use herein a simpler criterion where perceptually significant level lines are the level sets boundaries of an quantized image by using K quantizers and an entropy method [11]. Entropy methods seek to maximize the information content between objects and background pixels of an image. The method due to Kapur *et al.* chooses the thresholds $\{t_l\}$ to be the values at which the information is maximum. As a consequence, the detection of meaningful level lines will depend on the quantization parameter K. Unlike previous criteria [3,7], this quantization operation is not invariant to contrast changes. Nevertheless, we shall see that, in practice, $K = \{4, \ldots, 8\}$ seems sufficient to detect physically meaningful objects in the image.

4.2   The Segmentation Procedure

The proposed algorithm is not a region growing algorithm as described in [14,17] since all objects are built once and for all. Although our work is related to morphological approaches based on connected operators [21,6,10], it is an independent approach since we seek minimizers of a global objective functional. In addition, it differs from the watershed approach since regions that emerge from the watershed segmentation are not necessarily connected components within the image level sets [23].

We post-process the connected components to remove any components whose surface area $|\Omega_i|$ is less than some threshold $|\Omega_{\min}|$ (a parameter of the method) to eliminate regions corresponding to noise and artifacts in the original image [21,6,10]. To implement our level set image segmentation based on energy minimization, a four step method is used. Let K, λ, $|\Omega_{\min}|$ be the input parameters set by the user.

1. Bilevel Set Construction. The first step completes a crude mapping of each image pixel on a given bilevel set. At present, we quantize the function $f \in [f_{\min}, f_{\max}]$ in $K = \{4, \cdots, 8\}$ non-equal-sized and non-overlapping intervals $[t_{l-1}, t_l)$, $l = \{1, \cdots, K\}$. Given this set of intervals estimated using the maximum entropy sum method [11], let b_l be the bilevel set image with $b_l(x) = 1$ if $f(x) \in [t_{l-1}, t_l)$ and $b_l(x) = 0$ otherwise.

2. Object Extraction. A crude way to build pixels sets corresponding to objects is to proceed to a connected components labeling of images $\{b_l\}$ and to associate each label with an object Ω_i. Though this process may work in the noise-free case, in general we would also need some smoothing effect of the connected components labeling. So we consider a size-oriented morphological operator acting on sets that consists in keeping all connected components of the output of area larger than a limit $|\Omega_{\min}|$. This *connected operator* in mathematical morphology will never introduce new features or edges and boundaries of remained connected components are preserved [21,6,10]. The list of connected components then forms the bank $\mathcal{C}_T$ of admissible objects $\{\Omega_1, \ldots \Omega_T\}$ with $|\Omega_i| \geq |\Omega_{\min}|$.

3. Configuration Determination. The connected components are then combined during the third step to form object configurations. For instance, these configurations can be built by enumeration of all possible object combinations, i.e. 2^T configurations. Each configuration is made of a subset of objects taken in the bank $\{\Omega_1, \ldots \Omega_T\}$. The background $\overline{\Omega}$ corresponds to the complementary set of objects selected for each configuration.

4. Energy Computation and Object Configuration Selection. Energy calculations take the image intensities of the original (not quantized) image to establish piecewise-constant approximation errors. Energies of the form $\{\int_{\Omega_i}(f(x) - \overline{f}_{\Omega_i})^2\, dx\}$ are computed once and stored on a RAM memory. The energy term $\int_{\overline{\Omega}}(f(x) - \overline{f}_{\overline{\Omega}})^2\, dx$ is efficiently updated for each configuration since $\overline{\Omega}$ is the complementary subset of the union of objects $\{\Omega_i\}_{i=1}^P$. The configuration that globally minimizes the energy functional corresponds to the MAP segmentation. The time necessary to perform image segmentation essentially depends on the size of the object bank $\mathcal{C}_T$.

4.3   Computational Issues

Now we discuss how some parameters of the procedure can be selected and indicate one possible choice used in our experimental results. On the discrete domain S, the neighborhoods of a pixel x are typically defined via 4-connectivity or 8-connectivity.

Number of Bilevel Sets. The value of K is mainly determined by the number of meaningful objects that one wishes to extract and the computational effort one is able to spend. Decreasing K allows to reduce the number of connected component. In our approach, we determine the optimal configuration of objects by supervising a small set of levels. In practice, our approach successfully segmented various images into only 4 or 8 levels.

Minimal Area of Objects. The area-oriented operator affects the image by remaining connected components within the image level sets that do not satisfy the minimum criterion [21,6,10]. Boundaries of connected components are not distorted by this operator as occurs with other types of image filters (such as openings and closings using structuring elements). Our default choice is $|\Omega_{\min}| \in [0.0001, 0.001] \times |S|$.

Prior Parameters A and γ. For fixed K, we consider the sets of observations $\{\log(|\Omega_i|), \log(g(|\Omega_i|)), 1 \le i \le T\}$. We perform a linear regression on this set so as to find the straight line (in the log-log coordinates) $\log(g(|\Omega_i|)) = A - \gamma \log(|\Omega_i|)$ the closest to the data in the least squares sense [1].

Hyperparameter λ. The choice of this parameter determines mostly the properties of the segmentation result. Increasing this parameter reduces the final number of objects to be extracted. If f is a function from S to $[0, 255]$, a default choice for the hyperparameter is $\lambda \in [0.1, 1.] \times 255^2$. Of course larger values of λ lead to even extraction of only one object. In practice, it's possible for us to to tune this parameter according to image contents.

Energy Minimization. For a fixed bank $\mathcal{C}_T = \{\Omega_1, \cdots, \Omega_T\}$ of T objects, one way to choose the optimal set of of objects $\{\widehat{\Omega}_1, \cdots, \widehat{\Omega}_{\widehat{P}}\}$, $\widehat{P} \leq T$, is to search for all possible combinations of P objects and compute the corresponding energy $E_\lambda(f, \Omega_1, \cdots, \Omega_P)$. Enumerating all possible sets of objects in the object bank and comparing their energies is computationally too expensive if T is large (typically, it is infeasible if $T > 32$). Instead of a such brute force search, we propose the following stepwise greedy algorithm for minimizing $E_\lambda(f, \Omega_1, \cdots, \Omega_P)$.

We start from $P = 0$ and introduce one object Ω_j at a time. Energies of all objects are assumed to be already stored in a RAM memory. At the first step, we compute the T energies with one single object Ω_j at once against the complementary subset $\overline{\Omega} = S \setminus \cup_{j \neq i=1}^T \Omega_i$. Let $\widehat{\Omega}_1$ be the estimated object that best lowers E_λ. This object is stored on a RAM memory as an object of the optimal configuration. It is removed from the initial bank $\mathcal{C}_T$. At any steps of the algorithm, a new object is chosen to maximally decrease the energy E_λ.

Suppose that at the P-th step, $\widehat{P}$ and $\widehat{\overline{\Omega}}$ are not known but we have estimated P objects $\{\widehat{\Omega}_1, \cdots, \widehat{\Omega}_P\}$ and a current background $\overline{\Omega} = S \setminus \{\widehat{\Omega}_1, \cdots, \widehat{\Omega}_P\}$. Let $E_\lambda(f, \widehat{\Omega}_1, \cdots, \widehat{\Omega}_P)$ be the current computed energy. Then at the $(P+1)$-th step, we choose the object $\Omega_j \in \mathcal{C}_T \setminus \{\widehat{\Omega}_1, \cdots, \widehat{\Omega}_P\}$ which has the maximal difference, i.e.

$$\widehat{\Omega}_{P+1} = \arg \max_{\Omega_j \in \mathcal{C}_T \setminus \{\widehat{\Omega}_1, \cdots, \widehat{\Omega}_P\}} E_\lambda(f, \widehat{\Omega}_1, \cdots, \widehat{\Omega}_P) - E_\lambda(f, \widehat{\Omega}_1, \cdots, \widehat{\Omega}_P, \Omega_j) \quad (10)$$

The algorithm stops at P-th step when the adding of any object does not decrease E_λ. This means that the optimal number of objects is $\widehat{P} = P$ and the remained objects of the bank are a part of the estimated background, i.e. $\widehat{\overline{\Omega}} = S \setminus \{\widehat{\Omega}_1, \cdots, \widehat{\Omega}_{\widehat{P}}\}$.

This fast algorithm selects a suboptimal configuration of objects corresponding to a local minima of the energy functional. Using this algorithm, $\frac{T \times (T+1)}{2}$ object configurations are examined at the most, whereas the supervision of all the configurations corresponds to 2^T global energy computations.

5 Experimental Results in Image Segmentation

Experiments were conducted on satellite and meteorological images to evaluate the performance of the algorithm. Recall that obtaining the most meaningful objects is the goal of this work. For this reason, K was set fairly low in the experiments ($K = 4$ or $K = 8$) to obtain large regions and to improve robustness to noise and artifacts in the image. Regions which areas $|\Omega_i| < [0.0001, 0.001] \times |S|$ are discarded. For our method, λ varies across the images depending on the image contents. It is set empirically and values that gave visually better results were chosen. Most segmentations took approximately about 1-15 seconds on a 296MHz workstation.

Figure 1a shows an aerial 256×256 image (in the visual spectrum) depicting the region of Saint-Louis during the rising of the Mississippi and Missouri rivers in July 1993. We are interested in extracting the rivers and a background

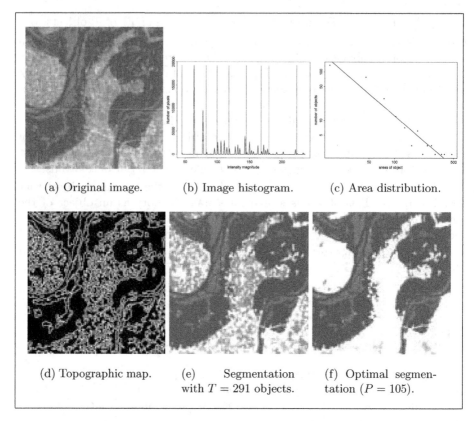

(a) Original image.   (b) Image histogram.   (c) Area distribution.

(d) Topographic map.   (e)   Segmentation   (f) Optimal segmen-
                         with $T = 291$ objects.   tation ($P = 105$).

Fig. 1. *Satellite image ($K = 8$, $|\Omega_{min}| = 0.00025 \times |S|$, $\lambda = 0.25 \times 255^2$).*

corresponding to textured urban areas. Figure 1 shows the segmentation results
when $K = 8$, $|\Omega_{\min}| = 0.00025 \times |S|$ and $\lambda = 0.25 \times 255^2$. In this experiment, the
maximum number of significant components is $T = 291$ (Fig. 1d-e). The con-
nected components that do not satisfy the minimum area criterion are labeled in
"white" in Fig. 1e. The image histogram has been quantized with $K = 8$ quantizers and an entropic method (Fig. 1b). We estimated the values of $A = 3.727$
and $\gamma = 1.486$ by fitting a straight line $\log(g(|\Omega_i|) = A - \gamma \log(|\Omega_i|)$ to the ob-
served data by linear regression. In that case, the least squares error is 2.007 and
$17 \leq |\Omega_i| \leq 2.886 \, 10^4$ pixels. Figure 1f displays the crudely piecewise-constant
approximation results by setting $\lambda = 0.25 \times 255^2$. It takes about 15 seconds
($25095 < \frac{T \times (T+1)}{2} = 42486$ iterations) of computing time for building $\mathcal{C}_T$ and
selecting the best configuration ($P = 105$ objects) using the stepwise greedy
algorithm. Enumerating all the configurations is infeasible since $2^T = 3.9810^{87}$
iterations ! The non-connected background is labeled in "white" in Fig. 1f and
the objects are filled with their mean gray values $\{\overline{f}_{\Omega_i}\}$.

The performance of the segmentation procedure is demonstrated for a satellite (210×148) image shown in Fig. 2. For the set of parameters $K = 4$,

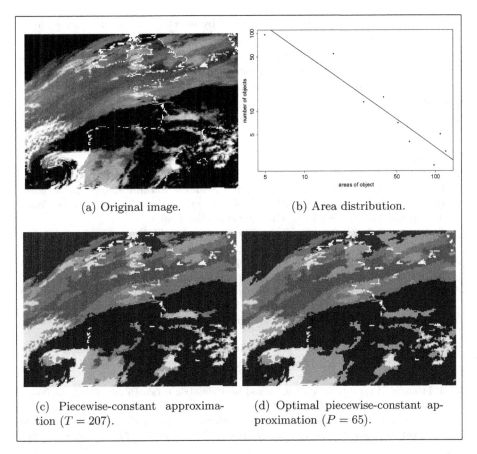

(a) Original image.   (b) Area distribution.

(c) Piecewise-constant approxima-   (d) Optimal piecewise-constant ap-
tion ($T = 207$).   proximation ($P = 65$).

Fig. 2. *Meteorological image* ($K = 4$, $|\Omega_{min}| = 0.00015 \times |S|$, $\lambda = 0.75 \times 255^2$).

$\lambda = 0.75 \times 255^2$ and $|\Omega_{\min}| = 0.00015 \times |S|$, the algorithm selected $P = 65$ objects from the bank which contains $T = 213$ objects (Fig. 2d). The piecewise-constant approximation of the image using $T = 213$ objects is shown in Fig. 2c. The algorithm stopped at the $11765\,th$ iteration (2s of CPU time), i.e. before the maximal iteration $\frac{T \times (T+1)}{2} = 22791$. We performed a linear regression to estimate the values of A and γ ($5 \leq |\Omega_i| \leq 1.159\,10^4$): $A = 1.482$, $\gamma = 1.202$. This corresponds to a least squares error of 1.34.

6   Conclusion and Perspectives

In this paper, we have presented a Bayesian approach for extracting structures in images. The prior model penalizes the area of the homogeneous parts of the image. Morphological approaches based on connected operators have already applied a such criterion but the filtering/segmentation process is not generally based on the optimization of a global objective functional. In addition, we proved that our MAP estimator can be determined by selecting a subset of image level lines. A total CPU time of a few seconds using a suboptimal stepwise greedy algorithm for partitioning a 256×256 image into meaningful regions makes the method attractive for many time-critical applications. In terms of future directions for research, we propose to create a non-linear scale-space by successive applications of an area morphology operator to select most meaningful regions in the image.

References

1. L. Alvarez, Y. Gousseau, and J.M. Morel. Scales in natural images and a consequence on their bounded variation. In *Int. Conf. on Scale-Space Theories Comp. Vis.*, pages 247–258, Kerkyra, Greece, September 1999.
2. A. Blake and A. Zisserman. *Visual Reconstruction.* MIT Press, Cambridge, Mass, 1987.
3. V. Caselles, B. Coll, and J.M. Morel. Topographic maps and local contrast changes in natural images. *Int J. Computer Vision*, 33(1):5–27, 1999.
4. T. Chan and L. Vese. Active contour model without edges. In *Int. Conf. on Scale-Space Theories Comp. Vis.*, pages 141–151, Kerkyra, Greece, September 1999.
5. L.D. Cohen. On active contour models and balloons. *CVGIP: Image Understanding*, 53(2):211–218, 1991.
6. J. Crespo, R. Schafer, J. Serra, C. Gratin, and F. Meyer. The flat zone approach: a general low-level region merging segmentation method. *Signal Processing*, 62(1):37–60, 1997.
7. J. Froment. Perceptible level lines and isoperimetric ratio. In *Int. Conf. on Image Processing*, Vancouver, Canada, 2000.
8. S. Geman and D. Geman. Stochastic relaxation, gibbs distributions, and the bayesian restoration of images. *IEEE Trans. Patt. Anal. and Mach. Int.*, 6(6):721–741, 1984.
9. U. Grenander and M.I. Miller. Representations of knowledge in complex systems. *J. Royal Statistical Society, series B*, 56(4):549–603, April 1994.
10. R. Jones. Connecting filtering and segmentation using component trees. *Computer Vision and Image Understanding*, 75(3):215–228, 1999.
11. J.N. Kapur, P.K. Sahoo, and A.K.C. Wong. A new method for gray-level picture thresholding using the entropy of the histogram. *Comp. Vis. Graphics and Image Proc.*, 29:273–285, 1985.
12. M. Kass, A. Witkin, and D. Terzopoulos. Snakes: active contour models. *Int J. Computer Vision*, 12(1):321–331, 1987.
13. C. Kervrann, M. Hoebeke, and A. Trubuil. Level lines as global minimizers of energy functionals in image segmentation. In *Euro. Conf. on Comp. Vis.*, pages 241–256, Dublin, Ireland, June 2000.
14. G. Koepfler, C. Lopez, and J.M. Morel. A multiscale algorithm for image segmentation by variational method. *SIAM J. Numerical Analysis*, 31(1):282–299, 1994.
15. G. Matheron. *Random Sets and Integral Geometry.* John Wiley, New York, 1975.
16. J. Møller and R.P. Waagepertersen. Markov connected component fields. *Adv. in Applied Probability*, pages 1–35, 1998.
17. J.M. Morel and S. Solimini. *Variational methods in image segmentation.* Birkhauser, 1994.

18. D. Mumford and J. Shah. Optimal approximations by piecewise smooth functions and variational problems. *Communication on Pure and applied Mathematics*, 42(5):577–685, 1989.

19. S. Osher and J. Sethian. Fronts propagating with curvature dependent speed: algorithms based on the hamilton-jacobi formulation. *J. Computational Physics*, 79:12–49, 1988.

20. N. Paragios and R. Deriche. Coupled geodesic active regions for image segmentation: a level set approach. In *Euro. Conf. on Comp. Vis.*, pages 224–240, Dublin, Ireland, June 2000.

21. P. Salembier and J. Serra. Flat zones filtering, connected operators, and filters by reconstruction. *IEEE Trans. Image Processing*, 4(8):1153–1160, 1995.

22. J. Sethian. *Level Sets Methods: Evolving Interfaces in Geometry, Fluid Mechanics, Computer Vision, and Material Science*. Cambridges University Press, 1996.

23. L. Vincent and P. Soille. Watershed in digital spaces: an efficient algorithm based on immersion simulations. *IEEE Trans. Patt. Anal. and Mach. Int.*, 13(6):583–598, 1991.

24. A. Yezzi, A. Tsai, and A. Willsky. A statistical approach to snakes for bimodal and trimodal imagery. In *Int. Conf. on Comp. Vis.*, pages 898–903, Kerkyra, Greece, September 1999.

25. S.C Zhu and A. Yuille. Region competition: unifying snakes, region growing, and bayes/mdl for multiband image segmentation. *IEEE Trans. Patt. Anal. and Mach. Int.*, 18(9):884–900, 1996.

A Multi-scale Feature Likelihood Map for Direct Evaluation of Object Hypotheses*

Ivan Laptev and Tony Lindeberg

Computational Vision and Active Perception Laboratory (CVAP)
Dept. of Numerical Analysis and Computing Science
KTH, S-100 44 Stockholm, Sweden

Abstract. This paper develops and investigates a new approach for evaluating feature based object hypotheses in a *direct* way. The idea is to compute a feature likelihood map (FLM), which is a function normalized to the interval $[0, 1]$, and which approximates the likelihood of image features at all points in scale-space. In our case, the FLM is defined from Gaussian derivative operators and in such a way that it assumes its strongest responses near the centers of symmetric blob-like or elongated ridge-like structures and at scales that reflect the size of these structures in the image domain. While the FLM inherits several advantages of feature based image representations, it also (i) avoids the need for explicit search when matching features in object models to image data, and (ii) eliminates the need for thresholds present in most traditional feature based approaches. In an application presented in this paper, the FLM is applied to simultaneous tracking and recognition of hand models based on particle filtering. The experiments demonstrate the feasibility of the approach, and that real time performance can be obtained by a pyramid implementation of the proposed concept.

1 Introduction

When interpreting image data, the purpose of filtering is to emphasize and abstract relevant properties in the data while suppressing others. Common approaches for computing image descriptors involve either (i) the computation of sparse sets of image features (feature detection) or (ii) the computation of dense maps of filter responses (direct methods).

In this respect, a main strength of feature based approaches is that they provide an abstracted and compact description of the local image shape. Image features are usually invariant to absolute intensity values and can selectively represent characteristic visual properties of image patterns. In particular, using multi-scale feature detection it is possible to estimate the size of image structures and to represent image patterns in a scale-invariant manner. Relations between

---

* The support from the Swedish Research Council for Engineering Sciences, TFR, and from the Royal Swedish Academy of Sciences as well as the Knut and Alice Wallenberg Foundation is gratefully acknowledged.

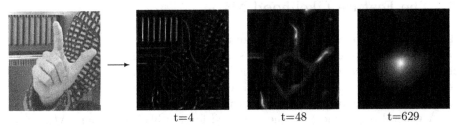

t=4   t=48   t=629

Fig. 1. The result of computing the proposed feature likelihood map on an image of a hand. At any point (x, y, t) in scale-space, this function approximates the likelihood of symmetric blob-like or ridge-like image structures. In this figure, the feature likelihood map is shown for three scale levels $t = 4$, 48, 629, which (here) are characteristic scales for the background, the fingers and the palm of a hand, respectively. Note that the response of the map is well localized in space and scale and that the response is invariant to the local amplitude of the image structures.

features in terms of positions, scales, types and other attributes may then be effectively used for recognizing objects and image patterns.

The use of features for image representation, however, also has drawbacks. One is that image features may depend on thresholds used for separating relevant image structures from noise. This may make the results unstable for patterns with low contrast. Another disadvantage is that algorithms involving matching of sparse points in image space usually lead to combinatorial complexity.

The aim of this paper is to develop a *dense* image representation, which preserves the advantages of feature-based representation, while avoiding the problems of local thresholding and selection of sparse image features for matching. The idea is to compute a function on a multi-scale feature space, which is normalized to the interval [0, 1] and thus independent of the local contrast of the grey-level pattern. Moreover, the function will be defined in such a way that its response is localized in space and scale, with the strongest responses near the centers of blob-like and ridge-like structures. The proposed function, referred to as a *feature likelihood map*, can be used for approximating the likelihood of image features. Figure 1 illustrates this concept for an image of a hand.

A main reason behind this construction is to provide means for *direct* verification of feature-based object hypotheses. Given a hypothesis, the verification on such a map does not require explicit search and will therefore be highly efficient. In particular, this approach is convenient for object tracking and object recognition based on the recently developed approach of particle filtering. In this paper, the feature likelihood map will indeed be used for *simultaneous* hand tracking and hand recognition. The viability of the approach will be demonstrated with a pyramid implementation, which gives real time performance.

2   The Feature Likelihood Map

The aim of the proposed likelihood map is to emphasize specific structures in the image domain, and to localize them in space and scale. To study this problem, we initially restrict ourselves to symmetric blob-like and elongated ridge-like image features. The general ideas behind this construction, however, are more general and apply to many other aspects of local image structures.

A general requirement on the proposed feature likelihood map, $\mathcal{M} : \mathbb{R}^2 \times \mathbb{R}_+ \mapsto \mathbb{R}$, is that for a blob of size t_0 located at a point (x_0, y_0) in space, $\mathcal{M}$ should satisfy the following basic properties: (i) $\mathcal{M}$ should assume its maximum value one at $(x_0, y_0; t_0)$, (ii) $\mathcal{M}$ should assume high values in a small neighborhood of $(x_0, y_0; t_0)$, and (iii) $\mathcal{M}$ should decrease monotonically towards zero elsewhere. Additionally, $\mathcal{M}$ should not give preference to blobs of any particular size, position or amplitude, and should thus be invariant to scalings and translations in the image as well as local changes of the image contrast.

2.1   Scale-Space Representation

For any continuous signal $f : \mathbb{R}^D \mapsto \mathbb{R}$, the linear scale-space representation $L : \mathbb{R}^D \times \mathbb{R}_+ \mapsto \mathbb{R}$ is defined as the convolution of f with Gaussian kernels g

$$L(\cdot; t) = g(\cdot; t) * f(\cdot), \tag{1}$$

where $g(x; t) = \exp(-(x_1^2 + ... + x_D^2)/2t)/(2\pi t)^{D/2}$, and $x = (x_1, ..., x_D)^T$. One reason for considering such a representation is that the Gaussian derivatives

$$L_{x^m}(\cdot; t) = \partial_{x^m}(g * f) = (\partial_{x^m} g) * f = g * (\partial_{x^m} f) \tag{2}$$

(where m denotes the order of differentiation) constitute a canonical set of filter kernels given natural symmetry requirements on a visual front-end (Witkin 1983, Koenderink and van Doorn 1992, Lindeberg 1994, Florack 1997). Another reason is that the evolution over scales of a signal and its Gaussian derivatives provides important cues to local image structure. One such property, which we will make particular use of here, is based on the behavior over scales of γ-normalized Gaussian derivative operators (Lindeberg 1998)

$$L_{\xi^m, \gamma-norm}(\xi; t) = t^{m\gamma/2} L_{x^m}(x; t). \tag{3}$$

where $\xi = x/t^{\gamma/2}$ denotes γ-normalized coordinates. It can be shown both theoretically and experimentally that the scales at which such normalized differential entities assume local maxima over scales reflect characteristic scales of local image patterns and can thus be used for, for example, local size estimation.

2.2   Likelihood Map in the 1-D Case

When we construct the feature likelihood map, let us first consider the one-dimensional case and take a Gaussian function $f(x) = g(x; x_0, t_0)$ as a prototype for a blob of size t_0 centered at x_0 (see Figure 2(a)). Using the semi-group property of the Gaussian kernel, it follows that the scale-space representation of f is $L(x; t) = g(x; x_0, t + t_0)$, and its γ-normalized second-order derivative:

$$L_{\xi\xi}(\xi; t) = t^{\gamma_2} L_{xx}(x; t) = -\frac{t^{\gamma_2}(t + t_0 + (x - x_0)^2)}{\sqrt{2\pi(t + t_0)^5}} \, e^{-\frac{(x-x_0)^2}{2(t+t_0)}}. \tag{4}$$

If we choose $\gamma_2 = 3/4$, then it can be shown (Lindeberg 1998) that $L_{\xi\xi}$ assumes a local extremum over space and scale at the point (x_0, t_0) in scale-space that corresponds to the position x_0 and the size t_0 of the original blob f. Thus, $L_{\xi\xi}^2$ satisfies some of the required properties of the desired likelihood map $\mathcal{M}$, however, $L_{\xi\xi}^2$ is not invariant to the local amplitude of the signal (see Figure 2(b)).

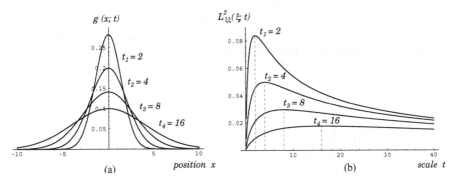

Fig. 2. (a): Gaussian kernels of various widths; (b): Evolution over scales of the second order normalized derivative operator $L_{\xi\xi}^2$ in the case when $\gamma_2 = 3/4$.

Quasi-quadrature. A standard approach for amplitude estimation in signal processing is in terms of quadrature filter pairs (h_+, h_-), from which the amplitude can be estimated as $\mathcal{Q} = (h_+ * f)^2 + (h_- * f)^2$. Strictly, a quadrature filter pair is defined from a Hilbert transform, in such a way that $\mathcal{Q}$ is phase-independent. Within the framework of scale-space derivatives, the quadrature entity $\mathcal{Q}$ for first- and second-order derivatives can be approximated by a pair of normalized first- and second-order Gaussian derivative operators (Lindeberg 1998):

$$\mathcal{Q}_1 L = A L_\xi^2 + L_{\xi\xi}^2 = A t^{\gamma_1} L_x^2 + t^{2\gamma_2} L_{xx}^2. \tag{5}$$

where A is a constant and $L_\xi = t^{\gamma_1/2} L_x(x; t)$ is the normalized first-order derivative operator, where we choose $\gamma_1 = 1/2$ to match $\gamma_2 = 3/4$. Moreover, the value of A can be chosen to $A \approx 4/e$, such that the response of the $\mathcal{Q}_1 L$ is approximately constant over space in the neighborhood of $(x_0; t_0)$ (Lindeberg 1998). This quadrature entity is, however, not phase-independent over scales.

Including Stability over Scales. To include the stability of image structures over scales (corresponding to low values of derivatives with respect to scale), and to also increase approximate phase invariance with respect to space and scale simultaneously, we propose to include the derivative of $L_{\xi\xi}$ with respect to effective scale $\tau = \log t$. Using $\partial_\tau = t\,\partial_t$ and the fact that all Gaussian derivatives satisfy the diffusion equation $\partial_t(L_{x^\alpha}) = 1/2\,\partial_{xx}(L_{x^\alpha})$, it follows that:

$$L_{\xi\xi\tau}(\xi;\,t) = t\,\partial_t L_{\xi\xi}(\xi;\,t) = \gamma_3 t^{\gamma_3}\,L_{xx} + t^{\gamma_3}\,L_{xxt} = \gamma_3 t^{\gamma_3}\,L_{xx} + \frac{t^{\gamma_3+1}}{2}\,L_{xxxx}. \quad (6)$$

By adding this expression to (5), we thus propose to extend $Q_1 L$ into

$$Q_2 L = A L_\xi^2 + B L_{\xi\xi\tau}^2 + L_{\xi\xi}^2. \quad (7)$$

Figures 3(a) and (b) illustrate the evolution of the components in this expression, i.e. L_ξ^2, $L_{\xi\xi\tau}^2$ and $L_{\xi\xi}^2$, over space and scale. As can be seen, the responses of L_ξ^2 and $L_{\xi\xi\tau}^2$ complement the response of $L_{\xi\xi}^2$ by assuming high values where $L_{\xi\xi}^2$ is low and vice versa. Thus, one can expect that by an appropriate choice of the weights A and B, $Q_2 L$ will approximately be constant in a neighborhood of (x_0, t_0). Such a behavior is illustrated in Figures 3(c) and (d).

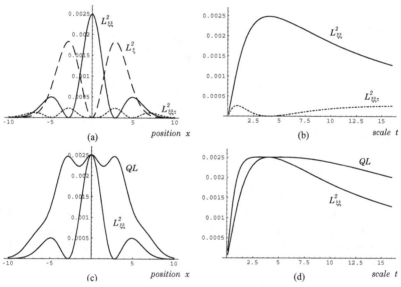

Fig. 3. (a)-(b): Evolution of $L_\xi^2, L_{\xi\xi}^2$ and $L_{\xi\xi\tau}^2$ over space and scale when applied to a Gaussian blob centered at $x_0 = 0$ and with variance $t_0 = 4$; (c)-(d): Evolution of $L_{\xi\xi}^2$ and $Q_2 L$ when using the parameter values $A = 1$ and $B = 2.8$. Note that $Q_2 L$ is approximately constant over space and scale in the neighborhood of (x_0, t_0).

Invariance Properties. If we consider the ratio $L_{\xi\xi}^2/Q_2 L$, it is apparent that the amplitude cancels between the numerator and the denominator. Thus, we achieve local contrast invariance. Moreover, since $Q_2 L \geq L_{\xi\xi}^2 \geq 0$, it follows that the ratio $L^2_{\xi\xi}/Q_2L$ will always be in the range $[0, 1]$. Scale invariance of Q_2 holds if we for $\gamma_2 = 3/4$ take $\gamma_1 = 1/2$. Moreover, it can be shown that for a Gaussian blob, the scale-space maximum of Q_2L is assumed at t_0 if and only if $\gamma_3 = 1$. The relative magnitudes of $L^2_{\xi\xi}$ and Q_2L are illustrated in Figures 3(c) and (d).

To conclude, the ratio $L^2_{\xi\xi}/Q_2L$ satisfies all the stated requirements on the feature likelihood map, and we define

$$\mathcal{M} = \frac{L^2_{\xi\xi}}{Q_2L} = \frac{L^2_{\xi\xi}}{AL^2_{\xi} + BL^2_{\xi\xi\tau} + L^2_{\xi\xi}}. \tag{8}$$

Determination of the Free Parameters A and B. Concerning the choice of A and B, it can be verified that $A \approx 1$ and $B \approx 3$ give an approximately constant behavior of the denominator of $\mathcal{M}$ around $(x_0; t_0)$. This was the original design criterion when the quasi quadrature entity (5) was proposed. Figure 4(a) shows the behavior of $\mathcal{M}$ in this case. Notably, the peak around $(x_0; t_0)$ is rather wide in the scale direction, and there are two quite strong side lobes in the spatial direction. For the purpose of dense scale selection with application to recognition, it is desirable to have a more narrow and localized response with respect to scale and space. For this reason, we increase the parameters to $A = 10$ and $B = 100$ and obtain a desired behavior of $\mathcal{M}$ as illustrated in Figure 4(b).

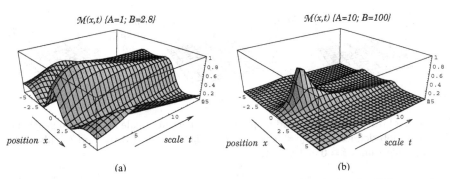

Fig. 4. Evolution of the likelihood map $\mathcal{M}$ over space and scale for the different values of parameters A and B when applied to a Gaussian blob ($x_0 = 0, t_0 = 4$).

2.3   Likelihood Map in the 2-D Case

The likelihood map defined in (8) can be easily extended to two dimensions. Consider again a Gaussian kernel $f = g(x, y; x_0, y_0, t_0)$ as a prototype image blob of size t_0 centered at (x_0, y_0). The scale-space representation of this signal is given by $L(x, y; t) = g(x, y; x_0, y_0, t + t_0)$ and the normalized Laplacian operator

$$\nabla^2_{norm}L = L_{\xi\xi} + L_{\eta\eta} = t^{\gamma_2}L_{xx}(x, y; t) + t^{\gamma_2}L_{yy}(x, y; t) \tag{9}$$

assumes a local extremum at (x_0, y_0, t_0) if $\gamma_2 = 1$. To construct a quadrature entity $\mathcal{Q}$, we consider the gradient magnitude (with $\gamma_1 = 1$)

$$|\nabla_{norm} L| = \sqrt{L_\xi^2 + L_\eta^2} = t^{\gamma_1/2}\sqrt{L_x^2 + L_y^2}, \qquad (10)$$

as the analogue to L_ξ in the one-dimensional case, and take

$$\partial_\tau(\nabla_{norm}^2 L) = L_{\xi\xi\tau} + L_{\eta\eta\tau} = \gamma_3 t^{\gamma_3}(L_{xx} + L_{yy}) + \frac{t^{\gamma_3+1}}{2}(L_{xxxx} + L_{yyyy} + 2L_{xxyy})$$

as the analogue to $L_{\xi\xi\tau}$. Then, we define the feature likelihood map as

$$\mathcal{M}_L = \frac{(L_{\xi\xi} + L_{\eta\eta})^2}{A(L_\xi^2 + L_\eta^2) + B(L_{\xi\xi\tau} + L_{\eta\eta\tau})^2 + (L_{\xi\xi} + L_{\eta\eta})^2}. \qquad (11)$$

Clearly, $\mathcal{M}_L$ is rotationally invariant, and invariant with respect to scale and local contrast; it assumes values in the range $[0, 1]$ and for a Gaussian blob the maximum value 1 is assumed at $(x_0, y_0; t_0)$. Hence, $\mathcal{M}_L$ has essentially similar properties as the likelihood map (8) in the one-dimensional case. Figures 5(a)-(c) illustrate how, with $A = 10$ and $B = 100$, $\mathcal{M}_L$ assumes a rather sharp maximum at (x_0, y_0, t_0) and rapidly decreases with deviations from this point.

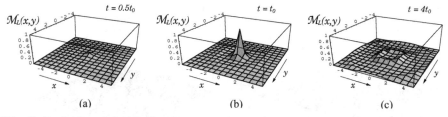

Fig. 5. Evolution of the likelihood map $\mathcal{M}_L$ over space and scale for a two-dimensional Gaussian blob defined by $(x_0 = 0, y_0 = 0, t_0 = 1)$. Plots in (a),(b) and (c) illustrate $\mathcal{M}_L$ for scale values $t = 0.5, 1$ and 4.

Suppression of Saddle Regions and Noise. Besides blobs and ridges, however, $\mathcal{M}_L$ will also respond to certain saddle points. This occurs when $\nabla_{norm} L = 0$ and $\partial_\tau(\nabla_{norm}^2 L) = 0$. To suppress such points, introduce a saddle suppression factor

$$\mu = \frac{\lambda_1^2 + \lambda_2^2 + 2\lambda_1\lambda_2}{\lambda_1^2 + \lambda_2^2 + 2|\lambda_1\lambda_2|} = \frac{L_{\xi\xi}^2 + L_{\eta\eta}^2 + 2L_{\xi\xi}L_{\eta\eta}}{L_{\xi\xi}^2 + L_{\eta\eta}^2 + 2L_{\xi\eta}^2 + 2|L_{\xi\xi}L_{\eta\eta} - L_{\xi\eta}^2|}, \qquad (12)$$

where λ_1 and λ_2 denote the eigenvalues of the Hessian matrix. Then, it can be seen that μ is equal to one when λ_1 and λ_2 have the same sign (i.e., for emphasized blob and ridge structures), while μ decreases towards zero if λ_1 and

λ_2 have equal magnitude and opposite sign. Moreover, to suppress the influence of spurious noise structures of amplitude lower than ε_N, we introduce a small normalising parameter ε_N in the denominator of the expression for the FLM. Thus, we define a saddle- and noise-suppressed feature likelihood map as

$$\tilde{\mathcal{M}}_L = \mu^k \mathcal{M}_L = \frac{\mu^k (L_{\xi\xi} + L_{\eta\eta})^2}{A(L_\xi^2 + L_\eta^2) + B(L_{\xi\xi\tau} + L_{\eta\eta\tau})^2 + (L_{\xi\xi} + L_{\eta\eta})^2 + \varepsilon_N^2} \quad (13)$$

Examples of other feature likelihood maps, with exclusive emphasis on specific types of image structures are presented in (Lindeberg 2001).

2.4   Experiments on Synthetic and Real Data

Figure 6 shows the result of computing this feature likelihood map for a synthetic image with three Gaussian blobs. As can be observed, the high values of $\mathcal{M}$ are well localized in space and scale, and the peaks over space and scale correspond to the positions and the sizes of the original blobs. Figure 6 shows the result of computing $\mathcal{M}$ for an image of a hand. Here, it can be seen that $\mathcal{M}$ responds not only to circular structures but also to elongated ridge-like structures, such as fingers. The reason for this is that the Laplacian operator, besides responding to circular blob-like structures, also gives a reasonably high response to elongated structures. From these results it can be clearly seen how $\mathcal{M}$ separates between small structures in the background, the fingers and the palm of a hand. Moreover, despite the varying contrast of the image structures, $\mathcal{M}$ gives equally high response to weak ridges in the background and to the fingers of higher contrast. In many cases, this is a desirable property of a recognition system aimed at classifying local image structures irrespective of illumination variations.

3   Hand Tracking and Recognition

To experimentally investigate the proposed direct approach for evaluation of feature hypotheses, we will in this section present an application of the feature likelihood map in combination with particle filtering for simultaneous tracking and recognition of hands in image sequences. By necessity the presentation is heavily condensed; more details can be found in (Laptev and Lindeberg 2001).

3.1   Hand Model

An image of a hand can be expected to give rise to blob and ridge features corresponding the fingers and the palm of a hand. These image structures together with information about their relative orientation, position and scale can be used for defining a simple but discriminative, view-based model of a hand. Thus, we represent a hand by a set of blob and ridge features as illustrated in Figure 7, and define different hand states, depending on the number of open fingers.

  To model translations, rotations and scalings of hands, we define a parameter vector $X = (x, y, s, \alpha, l)$ which describes the global position (x, y), the size s

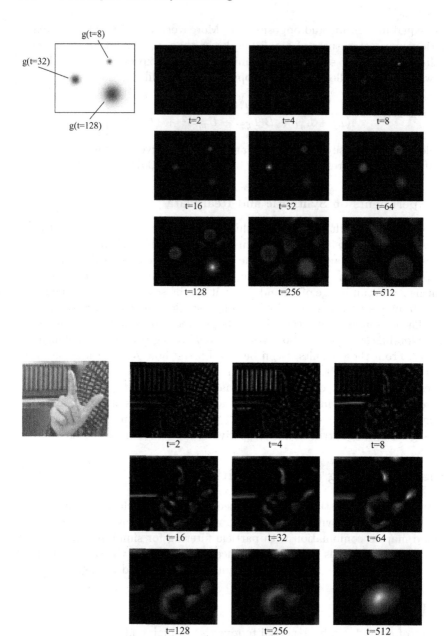

Fig. 6. The result of computing feature likelihood map on a synthetic image and a real image, where in the second case, the response of the FLM has been set to zero for points with $\nabla^2 L > 0$, in order to enhance the response to bright image structures. From the first image, it can be verified that the FLM gives a correct localization of blobs in space and scale. In the second image, it can be seen that the FLM clearly separates different image structures, such as the fingers and the palm of a hand, according to their size.

and the orientation α of a hand in the image, together with its discrete state $l = 1 \ldots 5$. The vector X uniquely identifies the hand configuration in the image and estimation of X from image sequences corresponds to simultaneous hand tracking and recognition.

Fig. 7. Feature-based hand models in different states. The circles and ellipses correspond to blob and ridge features. When aligning models to images, the features are translated, scaled and rotated according to the parameter vector X.

3.2 Model Evaluation

Given a feature-based object model, the feature likelihood map provides a *direct* way to evaluate the model on image data. To obtain the likelihood that a model configuration X gives rise to an image I, one can simply multiply the likelihood values for model features which are directly available from $\mathcal{M}_L$. Hence, we define the likelihood p for a model hypothesis X and an image I as

$$p(I|X) = (1 - \varepsilon)^{N-n} \prod_{i=1}^{n} \mathcal{M}_L(x_i, y_i, t_i), \tag{14}$$

where $\mathcal{M}_L$ is computed on the image I, x_i, y_i and t_i denote the position and the size of the ith feature in the model, while $\varepsilon \in (1, 0)$ accounts for a maximal admissible matching error and enables for comparison of models with the different number of features n ($N = \max_j (n_j)$). In addition, this likelihood is multiplied by a prior on skin colour computed from colour histograms of human hands.

Notably, the described evaluation does not involve any search and is simple and efficient to compute. Therefore it is highly useful for real-time applications.

3.3 Tracking and Recognition

To detect, recognize and track hands in image sequences, we search for a hand configuration defined by a parameter vector X_k that maximizes the posterior distribution $p(X_k|I_k)$ on a given image I_k at a time moment k. Using Bayes rule, the posterior can be estimated by

$$p(X_k|I_k) = h \, p(I_k|X_k) \, p(X_k|I_{k-1}) \tag{15}$$

where $p(I_k|X_k)$ is the likelihood of X_k given I_k, $p(X_k|I_{k-1})$ is the prior distribution of X_k derived from a previous time step and h is a normalization constant.

Since the likelihood distribution above has no closed-form expression, the desired posterior must be approximated. For this reason, we apply particle filtering to estimate and approximate the posterior by a set of N samples (here $N \approx 1000$) distributed in a parameter space (see (Isard and Blake 1996) for an introduction). Given the posterior $p(X_k|I_k)$, we compute its mean $X_{k,mean}$ and consider it as the estimate of a hand pose at time moment k.

Particle filters spend most of their time on evaluating the likelihood of model hypotheses (samples). As described in the previous section, the proposed feature likelihood map is highly efficient for this purpose and we use it for evaluating the likelihood of samples within the framework of particle filtering. The efficient evaluation enables recognition and tracking to be done in real-time (currently at the frame rate 5–10 Hz). Figure 8 illustrates the result of combined tracking and recognition using the described framework.

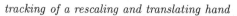

tracking of a rescaling and translating hand

simultaneous tracking and recognition of hand poses

Fig. 8. Results of combined hand tracking and pose recognition using particle filtering and evaluation of feature-based hand models on feature likelihood maps.

3.4   Implementation Details

In practice, the abovementioned scheme has been implemented in a pyramid framework using a fixed set of scale levels. The resolution at scale level t_i was obtained by sub-sampling the original image with a factor $\kappa_i = \sqrt{t_i/t_f}$, and the derivatives have been computed using filter kernels of fixed scale t_f. In the experiments, we found $t_f \approx 2.0$ to be sufficiently large for obtaining a satisfactory quality of $\mathcal{M}$ on one hand, while on the other hand being sufficiently small to enable fast computations. On a modest 550 MHz Pentium III processor our current implementation (without extensive optimization) requires about 0.1 s to compute the feature likelihood map on a 100×100 image and about 0.04 s to perform the particle filtering using 1000 hypotheses.

4   Related Work

The subject of this paper relates to multi-scale approaches for image representation, computation of differential invariants, detection of image features as well as tracking and recognition of view-based object models. Because of the scope of these areas, it is not possible to given an extensive review, and only a few closely related works will be mentioned. Crowley and Sanderson (1987) considered a graph-like image representation containing links between blobs at different scales. Pizer et al. (1994) proposed the use of multi-scale medial-axis representations computed directly from image patterns distributions. Multi-scale image differential invariants (Koenderink and van Doorn 1992, Lindeberg 1994, Florack 1997) have been computed by several authors, including Schmid and Mohr (1997) who apply such descriptors at interest points for image indexing and retrieval. Explicit scale selection for extraction of multi-scale image features has been investigated by Lindeberg (1998). A similar approach by Shokoufandeh et al. (1999) extracts extrema in a wavelet transform. Lindeberg (1998), Chomat et al. (2000) and Almansa and Lindeberg (2000) have computed dense descriptors for estimating the characteristic scale at any image point. With respect to object tracking, Isard and Blake (1996) developed a particle filtering approach for tracking contour-based models. Black and Jepson (1998) used eigenspace models of gray-value patterns for tracking deformable models. The approach by Bretzner and Lindeberg (1999) is closer to ours and applies a hierarchy of multi-scale features for representing and tracking hands.

5   Summary and Future Work

In this paper, we have presented a new approach for probabilistic and dense image representation by feature likelihood maps. Such maps are invariant to the amplitude of patterns and emphasize local structures in images by assuming high values at certain points in feature space. We derived the feature likelihood map for symmetric blob-like image structures and analyzed its behavior on synthetic and real images. Using the dense structure of the feature likelihood map, we have shown how it can be applied for direct and efficient evaluation of feature-based object hypotheses. Based on this evaluation procedure, we developed a particle filtering approach for recognizing and tracking hands in image sequences.

By analogy with the developed likelihood map for symmetric blob-like structures, similar maps can be constructed for other types of local image structures. For this purpose, the expression in (11) must be redefined by substituting the normalized Laplacian operator and its quadrature by other differential entities emphasizing the desired image properties. Examples of other feature likelihood maps constructed in this way are presented in (Laptev and Lindeberg 2001), as well as ways to incorporate colour information into this framework.

Another interesting direction of future research concerns the extension of feature likelihood maps to spatio-temporal domain. Here, the general ideas of this presentation could be combined with the concept of normalized derivatives in spatio-temporal scale-space. The resulting maps could then be used in order to analyze, capture and recognize temporal events in image sequences.

References

Almansa, A. and Lindeberg, T. (2000). Fingerprint enhancement by shape adaptation of scale-space operators with automatic scale-selection, *IEEE-IP*, **9**(12): 2027–2042.

Black, M. and Jepson, A. (1998). Eigen tracking: Robust matching and tracking of articulated objects using view-based representation, *IJCV* **26**(1): 63–84.

Bretzner, L. and Lindeberg, T. (1999). Qualitative multi-scale feature hierarchies for object tracking, *JVCIR* **11**: 115–129.

Chomat, O., de Verdiere, V., Hall, D. and Crowley, J. (2000). Local scale selection for gaussian based description techniques, *ECCV'00*, Dublin, Ireland, 117–133.

Crowley, J. and Sanderson, A. (1987). Multiple resolution representation and probabilistic matching of 2-D gray-scale shape, *IEEE-PAMI* **9**(1): 113–121.

Fleck, M., Forsyth, D. and Bregler, C. (1996). Finding naked people, *ECCV'96*, Cambridge, UK, II:593–602.

Florack, L. M. J. (1997). *Image Structure*, Kluwer.

Isard, M. and Blake, A. (1996). Contour tracking by stochastic propagation of conditional density, *ECCV'96*, Cambridge, UK, I:343–356.

Koenderink, J. J. and van Doorn, A. J. (1992). Generic neighborhood operators, *IEEE-PAMI*, **14**(6): 597–605.

Laptev, I and Lindeberg, T. (2001) "A multi-scale feature likelihood map for direct evaluation of object hypotheses", Technical report ISRN KTH/NA/P–01/03–SE. http://www.nada.kth.se/cvap/abstracts/cvap249.html

Lindeberg, T. (1994). *Scale-Space Theory in Computer Vision*, Kluwer.

Lindeberg, T. (1998). Feature detection with automatic scale selection, *IJCV*, **30**(2): 77–116.

Pizer, S. M., Burbeck, C. A., Coggins, J. M., Fritsch, D. S. and Morse, B. S. (1994). Object shape before boundary shape: Scale-space medial axis, *JMIV* **4**: 303–313.

Schmid, C. and Mohr, R. (1997). Local grayvalue invariants for image retrieval, *IEEE-PAMI* **19**(5): 530–535.

Shokoufandeh, A., Marsic, I. and Dickinson, S. (1999). View-based object recognition using saliency maps, *IVC* **17**(5/6): 445–460.

Witkin, A. P. (1983). Scale-space filtering, *Proc. IJCAI'83*, Karlsruhe, West Germany, 1019–1022.

Total Variation Based Oversampling of Noisy Images

François Malgouyres*

University of California Los Angeles, Dept. of Mathematics
Box 951555, Los Angeles, CA 90095-1555
http://www.math.ucla.edu/~malgouy/

Abstract. We propose a variational model which permits to simultaneously deblur and oversample an image. Indeed, after some recalls on an existing variational model for image oversampling, we show how to modify it in order to properly achieve our two goals. We discuss the modification both under a theoretical
point of view (the analysis of the preservation of some structural elements) and
the practical point of view of experimental results. We also describe the algorithm
used to compute a solution to this model.

1 Introduction

This paper deals with a variational methods whose aim is to both deblur and oversample
an image. More precisely, for $N \in \mathbb{N}$, noting $\mathbb{T}_N$ the torus of size N (the periodization
of $[0, N[^2)$, we expect to recover an image $v \in L^2(\mathbb{T}_N)$, from a data $u \in \mathbb{R}^{N^2}$, such
that

$$u_{m,n} = (s * v)(m, n) + b_{m,n}$$

where $s \in L^2(\mathbb{T}_N)$, $(m, n) \in \{0, ..., N - 1\}^2$ and $b \in \mathbb{R}^{N^2}$ is a Gaussian noise. Note
that here the convolution is made between two functions of $\mathbb{T}_N$. For commodity, in the
following, we will denote by $\mathbb{N}_N$ the periodization of $\{0, ..., N - 1\}$.

A very useful framework for this kind of problem is the Fourier domain. We define
the Fourier transform of a function $v \in L^2(\mathbb{T}_N)$ by

$$\hat{v}_{\frac{\xi}{N}, \frac{\eta}{N}} = \int_{\mathbb{T}_N} v(x, y) \, e^{-2i\pi \frac{(\xi x + \eta y)}{N}} \, dx dy \,,$$

for $(\xi, \eta) \in \mathbb{Z}^2$. The discrete Fourier transform of $u \in \mathbb{R}^{N^2}$ is defined by

$$\hat{u}_{\xi,\eta} = \sum_{m,n=0}^{N-1} u_{m,n} \, e^{-2i\pi \frac{\xi m + \eta n}{N}} \,,$$

for $(\xi, \eta) \in \{-\frac{N}{2} + 1, ..., \frac{N}{2}\}^2$.

---

* This work has been supported by ONR grant N00014-96-1-0277 and by NSF DMS-9973341.

M. Kerckhove (Ed.): Scale-Space 2001, LNCS 2106, pp. 111–122, 2001.
© Springer-Verlag and IEEE/CS 2001

Using the Poisson formula (see [10], pp 29), we can express the discrete Fourier transform of u in terms of the discrete Fourier transform of b and the Fourier transforms of s, v. This gives

$$\hat{u}_{\xi,\eta} = \sum_{k,l\in\mathbb{Z}} \hat{s}_{\frac{\xi}{N}+k,\frac{\eta}{N}+l}\hat{v}_{\frac{\xi}{N}+k,\frac{\eta}{N}+l} + \hat{b}_{\xi,\eta},$$

for any $(\xi,\eta) \in \{-\frac{N}{2}+1,...,\frac{N}{2}\}$. Therefore, we remark that if the function v satisfies, for any $(\xi,\eta) \in \{-\frac{N}{2}+1,...,\frac{N}{2}\}$, $v_{\frac{\xi}{N}+k,\frac{\eta}{N}+l} = 0$, for $k \neq 0$ or $l \neq 0$, this would be a deblurring problem. On the other hand, if we do not take into account the blurring and the noise but try to extrapolate the high frequencies, this is an interpolation problem. However, we do believe that these two issues cannot be separated and should be treated simultaneously. This is what we will propose in what follows.

There are only a few papers which deal with the possibility to simultaneously deblur and oversample an image. Although there is an extensive literature for both image deblurring and oversampling. Concerning image deblurring, the reader can refer to [3] for most of the linear methods, to [5, 12] for variational ones (respectively based on a regularization with the entropy and the total variation) and to [11, 8] for wavelet packet based methods. Concerning oversampling, most of the linear methods tend to compute or approximate the sinc-interpolation (see [14, 15]). Non-linear methods often try to adapt the filter to the particular behavior of the image (edge, smooth region,...) (see [2, 13]) or use a regularization approach [7, 8].

The paper is organized as follow , in Sect. 2, we make some recalls on a variational oversampling method introduced in [9]. Then, in Sect. 3, we show how to adapt this model in order to take into account the noise b. We also show that, with regard to the analysis of the preservation of a family of structural elements, this model has to be modified. We then explain the numerical scheme which is used to compute a solution of this model. Finally, in Sect. 4, we present some numerical experiments which confirm the importance of the modifications we have proposed in Sect. 3.

2   Variational Oversampling of Noise Free Images

All the results announced in this section are rigorously stated and proven in [9]. In this paper, we studied the possibility to oversample images by mean of a Maximum A Posteriori model. More precisely, we studied a variational oversampling method based on the minimization of the total variation. This method consists in finding an image $w \in L^2(\mathbb{T}_N)$ which

$$\text{minimizes} \int_{\mathbb{T}_N} |\nabla w|, \text{ among } w \in \mathcal{W}_{s,u}, \tag{1}$$

where, for any given data $u \in \mathbb{R}^{N^2}$ and any convolution kernel $s \in L^2(\mathbb{T}_N)$, we define

$$\mathcal{W}_{s,u} = \left\{ w \in L^2(\mathbb{T}_N), \forall(m,n) \in (\mathbb{N}_N)^2, s * w(m,n) = u_{m,n} \right\}.$$

Remark that, for simplicity, we note the total variation $\int_{\mathbf{T}_N} |\nabla w|$ instead of $|Dw|(\mathbf{T}_N)$.

We know that (1) has a solution as long as s is such that $\mathcal{W}_{s,u}$ is not empty and all the elements of $\mathcal{W}_{s,u}$ have the same mean. We cannot guaranty the uniqueness of this solution. However, we are sure that two different solutions have locally the same level lines at locations where these latter are properly defined and the solutions are C^1. We also know a discretization of (1) which permits to properly approximate one of its solutions. All these mathematical properties guaranty this problem to be well posed.

However, a drawback of this model is that if s is too much localized in space domain some points are not enough constrained by the data fidelity term. For instance if $s = \delta$ (the Dirac delta function), the points of $(\mathbb{N}_N)^2$ are the only one involved in the constraint in (1) and, since $(\mathbb{N}_N)^2$ is of measure zero in $\mathbf{T}_N$, the solutions of (1) are constant functions[1]. Therefore, arises the question of knowing whether s sufficiently spread the constraint over the whole domain or not.

We can give an answer to that question by investigating the preservation of structural elements that are the "cylindrical functions". These functions are basically 1D functions and was first introduced to model the ability of an oversampling methods to properly restore edges. They are rigorously defined by

Definition 1. *Let* $u \in \mathbb{R}^{N^2}$ *and* $(\alpha, \beta) \in \mathbb{Z}^2 \setminus \{(0,0)\}$. *$u$ is cylindrical along the direction* (α, β) *if and only if its Discrete Fourier Transform is supported by*

$$\left\{ (k, l) \in \{-\frac{N}{2} + 1, ..., \frac{N}{2}\}^2,\ \beta k - \alpha l = 0 \right\}.$$

Given this definition, we can state

Proposition 1. *Let* N *be an integer,* $(\alpha, \beta) \in \mathbb{R}^2 \setminus \{(0,0)\}$, $u \in \mathbb{R}^{N^2}$ *cylindrical along the direction* (α, β). *For any kernel* $s \in L^2(\mathbf{T}_N)$, *such that*

$$\hat{s}_{\frac{\xi}{N}, \frac{\eta}{N}} \begin{cases} \neq 0\,, \text{for } (\xi, \eta) \in \{-\frac{N}{2} + 1, ..., \frac{N}{2}\}^2 \\ = 0\,, \text{otherwise,} \end{cases}$$

(1) admits a solution cylindrical along the same direction (α, β).

Remark that this proposition can be extended to other kinds of convex regularity criterion such that the reformulation of (1) with this new regularity criterion has a solution. However, the advantage of the total variation is that it allows to reconstruct some high frequencies in a more complex manner than just filling them with 0. The strong and thin lines on Fig. 1 represent the spectrum of a variational oversampling (by (1)) of a cylindrical function. Once again, this has already been discussed in [9] where one can find lots of experiments on this property. Here, we interpret the possibility to preserve

---

[1] Note that here we cheat a little since when $s = \delta$ all the elements of $\mathcal{W}_{s,u}$ do not have the same mean and we are therefore not sure of the existence of a solution. Note also that this is coherent with the fact that constant functions (which are the "solutions" of (1) in this case) do, a priori, not belong to $\mathcal{W}_{s,u}$.

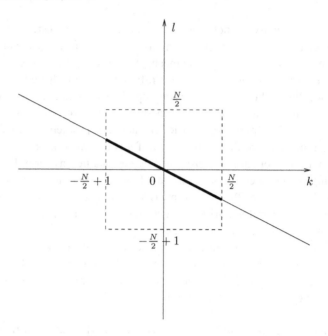

Fig. 1. The strong line represents the spectral support of a function cylindrical in the direction $(2, 1)$. The thin line represents the support of the spectrum of the oversampling of this image according to (1).

these 1D structure as a criterion to decide whether the constraint is sufficiently spread or not. Indeed, if it is not the case, we obtain artifacts such as the one presented on Fig. 3 and Fig. 4 where 1 structures are broken.

We are conscious of the fact that there could be more precise conditions on s in order to spread the constraint over $\mathbb{T}_N$ (indeed, we do not have any theoretical argument to assert that the condition given in Proposition 1 is necessary or optimal).

3   Variation Oversampling of Noisy Images

3.1   The Model

The model of the preceding section does not take into account the corruption of the image by noise. This leads us to introduce a model where the constraint is "weaker" than in (1). The following model is very close to the one of Rudin-Osher-Fatemi (see [12]) for the deblurring issue. However, this time, we do take into account the sampling and the aliasing as being part of the degradation process. This modification has already been evoked but not fully explored in [8].

More precisely an adaptation of Rudin-Osher-Fatemi method which would take into account the sampling process could be the minimization, among[2] $w \in BV(\mathbb{T}_N)$,

$$\int_{\mathbb{T}_N} |\nabla w| + \lambda \sum_{m,n=0}^{N-1} |s * w(m,n) - u_{m,n}|^2 , \qquad (2)$$

for a parameter $\lambda > 0$.

However, similarly to previously, a drawback of this model is that the data fidelity term may not be sufficiently spread over the whole torus (it may be concentrated in the vicinity of points with integer coordinates). We can, however, state a result similar to Proposition 1 for this model which suggests to modify (2) in such a way that we avoid this artifact.

Proposition 2. *Let N be an integer, $(\alpha, \beta) \in \mathbb{R}^2 \setminus \{(0,0)\}$, $u \in \mathbb{R}^{N^2}$ cylindrical along the direction (α, β). For any kernel $s \in L^2(\mathbb{T}_N)$, such that*

$$\hat{s}_{\frac{\xi}{N}, \frac{\eta}{N}} \begin{cases} \neq 0 \,, \text{for } (\xi, \eta) \in \{-\frac{N}{2} + 1, ..., \frac{N}{2}\}^2 \\ = 0 \,, \text{otherwise,} \end{cases}$$

the minimization of (2) admits a solution cylindrical along the same direction (α, β).

The proof of this proposition is very close to the one of Proposition 1 (see [8]).

Proposition 2 suggests to modify (2) and to minimize

$$\int_{\mathbb{T}_N} |\nabla w| + \lambda \sum_{m,n=0}^{N-1} |\tilde{s} * w(m,n) - u_{m,n}|^2 , \qquad (3)$$

where λ is a parameter and $\tilde{s}$ is defined by

$$\hat{\tilde{s}}_{\frac{\xi}{N}, \frac{\eta}{N}} = \begin{cases} \hat{s}_{\frac{\xi}{N}, \frac{\eta}{N}} \,, \text{if } (\xi, \eta) \in \{-\frac{N}{2} + 1, ..., \frac{N}{2}\}^2 \\ 0 \qquad , \text{otherwise.} \end{cases}$$

In order to understand the consequence of this modification, we express, using Poisson formula, the data fidelity term of (2) in frequency domain. We find that

$$\sum_{m,n=0}^{N-1} |s * w(m,n) - u_{m,n}|^2 = \sum_{\xi,\eta=0}^{N-1} \left| \sum_{k,l \in \mathbb{Z}} \hat{s}_{\frac{\xi}{N}+k, \frac{\eta}{N}+l} \hat{w}_{\frac{\xi}{N}+k, \frac{\eta}{N}+l} - \hat{u}_{\xi,\eta} \right|^2 . \quad (4)$$

Therefore, any change in the repartition of $\hat{u}_{\xi,\eta}$ over $(w_{\frac{\xi}{N}+k, \frac{\eta}{N}+l})_{k,l \in \mathbb{Z}}$, such that $\sum_{k,l \in \mathbb{Z}} \hat{s}_{\frac{\xi}{N}+k, \frac{\eta}{N}+l} \hat{w}_{\frac{\xi}{N}+k, \frac{\eta}{N}+l}$ remains unchanged, yields the same values for this data fidelity term. Therefore, the minimization of (2) may spread $\hat{u}_{\xi,\eta}$ over these co-efficient. This yields, in space domain, a result which looks like a sum of functions which are almost Dirac delta functions.

---

[2] One can refer to [6] for a definition of $BV(\mathbb{T}_N)$. It can heuristically be understood as the space of the functions $w \in L^2(\mathbb{T}_N)$, such that $\int_{\mathbb{T}_N} |\nabla w| < \infty$.

On the other hand, a formula similar to (4), for the model (3), shows that the data fidelity term deals only with low frequencies (the one in $\{-\frac{1}{2} + \frac{1}{N}, ..., \frac{1}{2}\}^2$). Therefore, we are sure to preserve the main structures of the image. The heuristic of this model is to consider the aliasing as a noise.

3.2   Numerical Implementation

In Sect. 4, we present some images which are solutions of (2) and (3). These solutions are computed using the same and more general algorithm: one which minimizes (2) for an arbitrary kernel s. Let us describe this algorithm.

The first issue in order to minimize (2) is to discretize it. Therefore, we have only considered oversampling of level $K \geq 2$. This means that in practice the result is simply an array of size $KN \times KN$. Moreover, we have discretize ∇w by a simple finite difference scheme and defined the partial derivatives

$$\Delta^x w_{m,n} = w_{m+1,n} - w_{m,n} \text{ and } \Delta^y w_{m,n} = w_{m,n+1} - w_{m,n}.$$

Moreover, in order to have a proper descent direction, we have replaced the total variation by

$$\sum_{i,j=0}^{KN-1} \sqrt{\beta^2 + (\Delta^x w_{m,n})^2 + (\Delta^y w_{m,n})^2},$$

for $\beta \in \mathbb{R}$. We call E_β the sum of this term and of the data fidelity term. Note that, in practice, we let β decrease to 0 during the iteration process. These ideas are now classical and are already discussed in [1, 4].

As we said previously, the main difference with the usual minimization of Rudin-Osher-Fatemi functional is that the data fidelity term now takes into account the sampling process. The computation of the data fidelity term and of its gradient are in this case simpler in Fourier domain. Therefore, we express it by an adaptation of (4).

More precisely, (4) becomes now

$$\sum_{m,n=0}^{N-1} |s * w(m,n) - u_{m,n}|^2 = \sum_{\xi,\eta=0}^{N-1} \left| \sum_{k,l=0}^{K-1} \hat{s}_{\xi+kN,\eta+lN} \hat{w}_{\xi+kN,\eta+lN} - \hat{u}_{\xi,\eta} \right|^2,$$

where the hats denote either the discrete Fourier transform of a signal of size $N \times N$ or $KN \times KN$.

Therefore, a simple computation permits to find that the Fourier transform of the gradient of this term is, at the frequency $(\xi + kN, \eta + lN)$, for $(\xi, \eta) \in \{0, ..., N - 1\}$ and $(k, l) \in \{0, ..., K - 1\}$,

$$2 \bar{\hat{s}}_{\xi+kN,\eta+lN} \left(\sum_{k',l'=0}^{K-1} \hat{s}_{\xi+k'N,\eta+l'N} \hat{w}_{\xi+k'N,\eta+l'N} - \hat{u}_{\xi,\eta} \right)$$

where the bar denotes the complex conjugate.

Finally, the discretization of the functional (2) is minimized with a gradient descent algorithm with an optimal step. More precisely, we start from the zero-padding (or sinc interpolation, see [15]) oversampling of the blurred image and call it u^0. To get u^{j+1} from u^j, for $j \in \mathbb{N}$, the gradient of the functional at u^j, $\nabla E_\beta(u^j)$, is calculated, as explained above, at each step of the algorithm. Then the optimal amplitude of the variation of the image in the direction $-\nabla E_\beta(u^j)$ is estimated by the resolution of

$$\min_{s>0} E_\beta(u^j - s \, \nabla E_\beta(u^j))$$

using a dichotomy method. Once the optimal amplitude s_0 is calculated, we let

$$u^{j+1} = u^j - s_0 \, \nabla E_\beta(u^j) \, .$$

We then iterate this process.

Note that in order to increase the speed of this algorithm, we can start from a de-blurred version of u^0, instead of u^0. Moreover, it is better to start with a large β and to let it decrease to 0.

4   Experiments

All the images presented here come from manipulations (degradations and reconstructions) of the image displayed on Fig. 2. Moreover, for simplicity of display, all the experiments deal with downsampling and oversampling of factor 2.

4.1   The Noise Free Case

We present in this section some experiments which show to evidence the relevance of our interpretation of Proposition 2 when there is no noise. Remark that in such a case, the choice of the parameter λ in (2) and (3) is arbitrary as long as λ is sufficiently large and the sampled image does not contain too much aliasing.

On Fig. 3, we display some extracted part of

- Up-Left: the reference image.
- Up-Right: the downsampled image (with $s = \delta$) of the reference image (without noise).
- Down-Left: an oversampling of the downsampled image by mean of (2), with $s = \delta$ and $\lambda = 10$. Since in (2) we took $s = \delta$, we clearly see on this image the points of the grid which are constrained. Note that this drawback is still present for all the values of λ we have tested.
- Down-Right: an oversampling of the downsampled image by mean of (3), with $\lambda = 10$. Note that the points which were visible on the previous image are no longer present on this image.

On Fig. 4, we display

Fig. 2. Reference Image. This is the image used in all the experiments of Section 4.

Fig. 3. Up-Left: The initial image. Up-Right: The downsampling of the initial image with $s = \delta$. Down-Left: Oversampling by minimizing (2). Down-Right: Oversampling by minimizing (3).

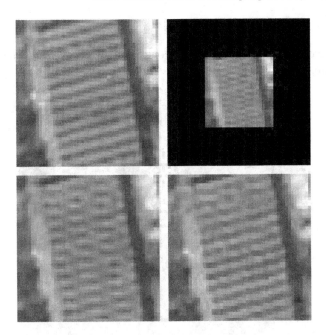

Fig. 4. Up-Left: The initial image. Up-Right: The downsampling of the initial image with $s = 1_{|[-\frac{1}{2},\frac{1}{2}]^2}$. Down-Left: Oversampling by minimizing (2). Down-Right: Oversampling by minimizing (3).

- Up-Left: the reference image.
- Up-Right: the downsampled image (with $s = 1_{|[-\frac{1}{2},\frac{1}{2}]^2}$) of the reference image (without noise).
- Down-Left: an oversampling of the downsampled image by mean of (2), with $s = 1_{|[-\frac{1}{2},\frac{1}{2}]^2}$ and $\lambda = 10$. The texture is distorted. Note that the only way to avoid this distortion is to remove the texture. We experimentally find that this occurs for $\lambda \leq 0.1$.
- Down-Right: an oversampling of the downsampled image by mean of (3), with $\lambda = 10$. This time the texture is preserved. This illustrates the interest of Proposition 2 and of the modification introduced in (3).

This latter experiment shows that even when the sequence $(s * w(m, n))_{(m,n) \in \mathbb{N}_N^2}$ depends on all the values[3] of $w(x, y)$, the modification suggested by Proposition 2 still permits to improve the method.

---

[3] More precisely, there does not exist any open set Ω such that, for any arbitrary modification of w on Ω, $(s * w(m, n))_{(m,n) \in \mathbb{N}_N^2}$ remains unchanged

4.2   The Noisy Case

Let us now investigate the possibility to remove a noise while oversampling and deblurring the image.

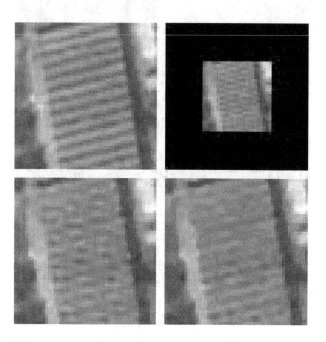

Fig. 5. Up-Left: The initial image. Up-Right: The downsampling of the initial image with $s = 1_{|[-\frac{1}{2},\frac{1}{2}]^2}$ plus a Gaussian noise of standard deviation 3. Down-Left: Oversampling by minimizing (2). Down-Right: Oversampling by minimizing (3).

In order to test our algorithm, we do the same experiment as for the creation of Fig. 4 (the one with $s = 1_{|[-\frac{1}{2},\frac{1}{2}]^2}$) except that we add a Gaussian noise of standard deviation 3. We display the results of this experiment on Fig. 5. For both reconstructed images the parameter λ is fixed in such a way that the amount of remaining noise is reasonable in an homogeneous region (see Fig. 6 where a larger part of the reconstruction by mean of (3) is displayed). We take $\lambda = 0.5$ for the oversampling by mean of (2) and $\lambda = 0.3$ for the one which uses (3). Note that the fact that for a comparable amount of noise we need a smaller λ with model (3) is not surprising, since the data fidelity term of (3) does more constrain the image than the one of (2). The main comment on these images is that, despite the noise, our interpretation of Proposition 2 still makes sense.

We also compare our results to the one obtained by a simple combination of linear algorithms. Once again, we compare them for the downsampling of the image displayed on Fig. 2 with $s = 1_{|[-\frac{1}{2},\frac{1}{2}]^2}$ and a Gaussian noise of standard deviation 3. Therefore, we display on Fig. 6, on left, an oversampling obtained by composing a wiener filter (see [3]) applied to the sampled image, to deblur and denoise it, and a sinc-interpolation

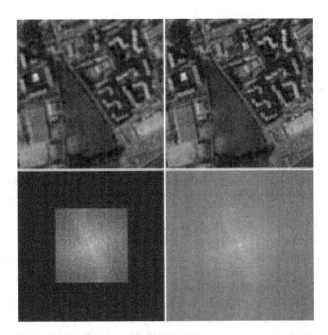

Fig. 6. Left: Oversampling with a linear filter (wiener filter + sinc-interpolation) (Up: The image, Down: Its spectrum). Right: Oversampling by mean of (3) (Up: The image, Down: Its spectrum).

(see [15]), in order to oversample it (Up: the result, Down: its spectrum). We tried to fix the parameter of the wiener filter (the assumed standard deviation of the noise) in order to have the same amount of noise on this image as on the oversampling by mean of (3). However, it is not possible to find such a value for the parameter without removing most of the informations contained in the image. Therefore, the left images displayed on Fig. 6 correspond to a value of $\sigma = 20$ and still contain a significant amount of noise.

The images on the right hand side of Fig. 6 correspond to the result and its spectrum when minimizing (3) for a parameter $\lambda = 0.3$. We clearly see here that (3) permits to obtain a result which contains less noise and is sharper than with the previous method. This is also visible on the spectrum of these images. In the first case, we just fill in the high frequencies with zero and with (3), we rebuild a realistic spectrum out of the initial spectral domain.

Acknowledgments

I would like to thank F. Guichard, J.M. Morel, B. Rougé and S. Durand for all the fruitful discussion we had on this subject.

References

[1] R. Acar and C. Vogel. Analysis of bounded variation methods for ill-posed problems. *Inverse Problems*, 10:1217–1229, 1994.

[2] J. Allebach and P. W. Wong. Edge-directed interpolation. In *Proceedings of the International Conference on Image Processing*, volume 3, pages 707–710, 1996.

[3] H.C. Andrews and B.R. Hunt. *Digital signal processing*. Technical Englewood Cliffs, NJ: Prentice-Hall, 1977.

[4] T. F. Chan and P. Mulet. On the convergence of the lagged diffusivity fixed method in total variation image restoration. *SIAM Journal of Numerical Analysis*, 36(2):354–367, 1999.

[5] G. Demoment. Image reconstruction and restoration: Overview of common estimation structures and problems. *IEEE Transactions on acoustics, speech and signal processing*, pages 2024–2036, 1989.

[6] L.C. Evans and R. F. Gariepy. *Measure Theory and Fine Properties of Functions*. Studies in Advanced Mathematics. CRC Press, Boca Raton, 1992.

[7] N. B. Karayiannis and A. N. Venetsnopoulos. Image interpolation based on variational principles. *Signal Processing*, 25(3):259–288, December 1991.

[8] F. Malgouyres. *Increase in the Resolution of Digital Images: Variational Theory and Applications*. PhD thesis, Ecole Normale Supérieure de Cachan, Cachan, France, 2000. available at http://www.math.ucla.edu/~malgouy.

[9] F. Malgouyres and F. Guichard. Edge direction preserving image zooming: a mathematical and numerical analysis. *SIAM, J. Num. Anal.*, 39(1):1–37, 2001. A preliminary version is available at: http://www.math.ucla.edu/~malgouy.

[10] S. Mallat. *A Wavelet Tour of Signal Processing*. Academic Press, Boston, 1998.

[11] B. Rougé. Fixed chosen noise restauration (fcnr). In *IEEE 95 Philadelphia*, 1995.

[12] L. Rudin, S. Osher, and E. Fatemi. Nonlinear total variation based noise removal algorithms. *Physica D*, 60:259–268, 1992.

[13] S. Thurnhofer and S. K. Mitra. Edge-enhanced image zooming. *Optical Engineering*, 35(7):1862–1870, July 1996.

[14] M. Unser, A. Aldroubi, and M. Eden. Enlargement or reduction of digital image with minimum loss of information. *IEEE Transactions on Image Processing*, 4(3):247–258, March 1995.

[15] L. Yaroslavsky. Efficient algorithm for discrete sinc interpolation. *Applied Optics*, 36(2):460–463, 1997.

Down-Scaling for Better Transform Compression

Alfred M. Bruckstein*, Michael Elad, and Ron Kimmel*

JiGami Research Division–Israel

Abstract. The most popular lossy image compression method used on the Internet is the JPEG standard. JPEG's good compression performance and low computational and memory complexity make it an attractive method for natural image compression. Nevertheless, as we go to low bit rates that imply lower quality, JPEG introduces disturbing artifacts. It appears that at low bit rates a down–scaled image when JPEG compressed visually beats the high resolution image compressed via JPEG to be represented with the same number of bits.

Motivated by this idea, we show how down–sampling an image to a low resolution, then using JPEG at the lower resolution, and subsequently interpolating the result to the original resolution can improve the overall PSNR performance of the compression process. We give an analytical model and a numerical analysis of the sub-sampling, compression and re-scaling process, that makes explicit the possible quality/compression trade-offs. We show that the image auto-correlation can provide good estimates for establishing the down-sampling factor that achieves optimal performance. Given a specific budget of bits, we determine the down sampling factor necessary to get the best possible recovered image in terms of PSNR.

1   Introduction

The most popular lossy image compression method used on the Internet is the JPEG standard. JPEG uses the Discrete Cosine Transform (DCT) on image blocks of size 8×8 pixels. The fact that the JPEG operates on small blocks is motivated by the non-stationarity of the image, and the need to approximate the Karhunen Loeve Transform (KLT) for 2D Markov processes. A quality measure determines the (uniform) quantization steps for each of the 64 DCT coefficients. The quantized coefficients of each block are then zigzag-scanned into one vector that goes through a run-length coding of the zero sequences, thereby clustering long insignificant low energy coefficients into short and compact descriptors. Finally, the run-length sequence is fed to an entropy coder, that can be a Huffman coding algorithm with either a known dictionary or a dictionary extracted from the specific statistics of the given image. A different alternative supported by the standard is arithmetic coding.

JPEG's good compression performance and low computational and memory complexity make it an attractive method for natural image compression. Nevertheless, as we go to low bit rates that imply lower quality, the JPEG compression algorithm introduces disturbing artifacts. It appears that at low bit rates a down–scaled image when

---

* Also affiliated with the Department of Computer Science, Technion–Israel Institute of Technology, Technion City, Haifa 32000, Israel.

M. Kerckhove (Ed.): Scale-Space 2001, LNCS 2106, pp. 123–136, 2001.

JPEG compressed and later interpolated, visually beats the high resolution image compressed directly via JPEG using the same number of bits. An experimental result displayed in Figure 1 shows that both visually and in terms of the Mean Square Error (or PSNR), one obtains better results using down-scaling compression and up-scaling after the decompression.

Fig. 1. Original image (on the left) JPEG compressed–decompressed image (middle), and down-scaled–JPEG compressed-decompressed and up scaled image (right). The down scaling factor - 0.5. In both cases, the compression ratio is 40. The MSE in the upper row is 219.5 (left) and 193.12 (right). Similarly, in the lower row: 256.04 (left) and 248.42 (right).

In this paper we propose an analytical explanation to the above phenomenon, along with a practical algorithm to automatically choose the optimal scaling factor for best PSNR. We derive an analytical model of the compression– decompression reconstruction error as a function of the memory (bits) budget, the (statistical) characteristics of the image, and the scale factor. We show that a simplistic second order statistical model provides a good estimate of the down-sampling factor that achieves optimal performance.

This report is organized as follows. Sections 2–3–4 present the analytic model, and explore its implications. Section 5 describes an experimental setup that validates the proposed model and its applicability for choosing best scaling factor for a given image with a given bits budget. Finally, Section 6 ends the paper with some concluding remarks.

2   Analysis of a Continuous "JPEG-Style" Image Representation Model

In this section we start building a theoretical model for analyzing the expected reconstruction error when doing compression–decompression as a function of the total bits budget, the characteristics of the image, and the scale factor. Our model considers the image over a continuous domain rather then a discrete one, in order to simplify the derivation. The steps we follow are:

- Derivation of the expected compression-decompression error for a general image representation process, based on slicing the image domain into M by N blocks.
- Derivation of an expression for the error by exploiting the fact that the coding is done in the transform domain using an orthonormal basis, and assuming that the error is due only to truncating the transform coefficients.
- Extension of the expression for the error to include quantization error of the non-truncated coefficients.
- Extension of the formal error to take into account the fact that the transform is the DCT, i.e. the orthonormal basis is cosine functions.
- Including in the expression for the error an approximation of the quantization errors due to various policies of allocation the total bits budget.

At the end of this process we obtain an expression for the error as a function of the bits budget, scale factor, and the image characteristics. This function eventually allows us to determine the optimal scale–down factor in JPEG-like image coding.

2.1   Compression-Decompression Expected Error

Assume we are given images on the unit square $[0, 1] \times [0, 1]$, $f_w(x, y) : [0, 1] \times [0, 1] \to \mathbf{R}$, realizations of a 2D random process $\{f_w(x, y)\}$, with second order statistics given by

$$E(f_w(x, y)) = 0, \qquad \mathcal{R}(x, y; x + \tau_x, y + \tau_y) = r_0^2 e^{-\alpha_x |\tau_x|} e^{-\alpha_y |\tau_y|}.$$

We assume that the image domain $[0, 1] \times [0, 1]$ is sliced into $M \cdot N$ regions of the form

$$\Delta_{ij} \equiv \left[\frac{i-1}{M}, \frac{i}{M} \right] \times \left[\frac{j-1}{N}, \frac{j}{N} \right] \quad \text{for} \quad i = 1, 2, .., M; j = 1, 2, .., N,$$

Assume that due to our coding of the original image $f_w(x, y)$ we obtain the compressed-decompressed result $\hat{f}_w(x, y)$, which is an approximation of the original image. We can measure the error in approximating $f_w(x, y)$ by $\hat{f}_w(x, y)$ as follows

$$\begin{aligned}
\mathcal{E}_w^2 &= \iint_{[0,1] \times [0,1]} (f_w(x, y) - \hat{f}_w(x, y))^2 dx dy \\
&= \sum_{i=1}^{M} \sum_{j=1}^{N} \iint_{\Delta_{ij}} (f_w(x, y) - \hat{f}_w(x, y))^2 dx dy
\end{aligned}$$

$$= \sum_{i=1}^{M}\sum_{j=1}^{N} \text{Area}(\Delta_{ij}) \frac{1}{\text{Area}(\Delta_{ij})} \iint_{\Delta_{ij}} (f_w(x,y) - \hat{f}_w(x,y))^2 dx dy$$

$$= \sum_{i=1}^{M}\sum_{j=1}^{N} \frac{1}{M \cdot N} \{MSE_{f_w}(\Delta_{ij})\},$$

where we define $MSE_{f_w}(\Delta_{ij}) \equiv \frac{1}{\text{Area}(\Delta_{ij})} \int_{\Delta_{ij}} (f_w(x,y) - \hat{f}_w(x,y))^2 dx dy$. We shall, of course, be interested in the expected mean square error of the digitization, i.e.,

$$E(\mathcal{E}_w^2) = \sum_{i=1}^{M}\sum_{j=1}^{N} \frac{1}{M \cdot N} E\left(\frac{1}{\text{Area}(\Delta_{ij})} \iint_{\Delta_{ij}} (f_w(x,y) - \hat{f}_w(x,y))^2 dx dy \right)$$

Note that the assumed wide–sense stationarity of the image process results in the fact that $E(MSE_f(\Delta_{ij}))$ is independent of (i,j), i.e., we have the *same* expected mean square error over each slice of the image. Thus we can write

$$E(\mathcal{E}_w^2) = M \cdot N \frac{1}{M \cdot N} E(MSE_{f_w}(\Delta_{11}))$$

$$= E\left(\frac{1}{\text{Area}(\Delta_{11})} \iint_{\Delta_{11}} (f_w(x,y) - \hat{f}_w(x,y))^2 dx dy \right).$$

Up to now we considered the quality measure to evaluate the approximation of $f_w(x,y)$ in the digitization process. We shall next consider the set of basis functions needed for representing $f_w(x,y)$ over each slice.

2.2 Bases for Representing $f_w(x,y)$ over Slices

In order to represent the image over each slice Δ_{ij}, we have to choose an orthonormal basis of functions. Denote this basis by $\{\Phi_{kl}(x,y)\}_{k,l=0,1,2,...}$. We must have

$$\iint_{\Delta_{ij}} \Phi_{kl} \Phi_{k'l'} dx dy = \delta_{kk'} \delta_{ll'} = \begin{cases} 1 \text{ if } (k,l) \equiv (k',l') \\ 0 \text{ otherwise.} \end{cases}$$

If $\{\Phi_{kl}\}$ is indeed a basis, then we can write $f_w(x,y) = \sum_{k=0}^{\infty}\sum_{l=0}^{\infty}\langle f_w(x,y), \Phi_{kl}(x,y)\rangle\Phi_{kl}(x,y)$, as a representation of $f_w(x,y)$ over Δ_{ij} in terms of an infinite set of coefficients

$$F_{kl} \equiv \langle f_w(x,y), \Phi_{kl}(x,y)\rangle = \iint_{\Delta_{ij}} f_w(x,y)\Phi_{kl}(x,y)dx dy.$$

Suppose now that we approximate $f_w(x,y)$ over Δ_{ij} by using only a finite set Ω of the orthonormal functions $\{\Phi_{kl}(x,y)\}$, i.e consider

$$\hat{f}_w(x,y) = \sum\sum_{(k,l)\in\Omega}\langle f_w(x,y), \Phi_{kl}(x,y)\rangle\Phi_{kl}(x,y),$$

(It is easy to see that the optimal coefficients in the approximation above turn out to be the corresponding F_{kl} 's from the infinite representation!). The mean square error of this approximation, over Δ_{11} say, will be

$$MSE_{f_w}(\Delta_{11}) = M \cdot N \left[\iint_{\Delta_{11}} f_w^2(x,y) dx dy \right.$$
$$\left. -2 \iint_{\Delta_{11}} f_w(x,y) \hat{f}_w(x,y) dx dy + \iint_{\Delta_{11}} \hat{f}_w^2(x,y) dx dy \right]$$

Hence,

$$MSE_{f_w}(\Delta_{11})$$
$$= M \cdot N \left[\iint_{\Delta_{11}} f_w^2(x,y) dx dy - \sum\sum_{(k,l) \in \Omega} \langle f_w(x,y), \phi_{kl}(x,y) \rangle^2 \right]$$

Now the expected $MSE_{f_w}(\Delta_{11})$ will be:

$$E(MSE_{f_w}(\Delta_{11}))$$
$$= M \cdot N \left[\iint_{\Delta_{11}} E f_w{}^2(x,y) dx dy - \sum\sum_{(k,l) \in \Omega} E\langle f_w(x,y), \phi_{k,l}(x,y) \rangle^2 \right]$$

Hence $E\mathcal{E}_w^2 = M \cdot N \cdot r_0^2 \cdot \frac{1}{M \cdot N} - M \cdot N \cdot \sum\sum_{(k,l) \in \Omega} E(F_{kl}^2) = r_0^2 - M \cdot N \cdot \sum\sum_{(k,l) \in \Omega} E[F_{k,l}^2]$.

2.3   The Effect of Quantization of the Expansion Coefficient F_{kl}

Suppose that in the approximation $\hat{f}_w(x,y) = \sum\sum_{(k,l) \in \Omega} F_{kl} \Phi_{k,l}(x,y)$ we can only use a finite number of bits in representing the coefficients $\{F_{kl}\}$ that take values in R. If F_{kl} is represented / encoded with b_{kl} -bits we shall be able to describe it via F_{kl}^Q that takes on $2^{b_{kl}}$ values only, i.e. $F_{kl}^Q = Q_{b_{kl}}(F_{kl}) : R \rightarrow$ set of $2^{b_{kl}}$ representation levels. The error in representing F_{kl} in this way is $\Gamma_{kl}^2 = (F_{kl} - F_{kl}^Q)^2$. Let us now see how the quantization errors affect the $MSE_{f_w}(\Delta_{11})$. We have

$$MSE_{f_w}^Q(\Delta_{11}) = \frac{1}{\frac{1}{M} \cdot \frac{1}{N}} \iint_{\Delta_{11}} \left(f_w(x,y) - \hat{f}_w^Q(x,y) \right)^2 dx dy$$

where $\hat{f}_{w(x,y)}^Q = \sum\sum_{k,l \in \Omega} F_{kl}^Q \phi_{kl}(x,y)$. Now

$$M \cdot N \iint_{\Delta_{11}} \left(f_w(x,y) - \hat{f}_w(x,y) + \hat{f}_w(x,y) - \hat{f}_w^Q(x,y) \right)^2 dx dy$$
$$= MSE_{f_w}(\Delta_{11}) + M \cdot N \cdot \sum\sum_{kl \in \Omega} \Gamma_{kl}^2 = MSE_{f_w}^Q(\Delta_{11}).$$

The expected $MSE_{f_w}^Q(\Delta_{11})$ is therefore given by:

$$E(MSE_{f_w}^Q)(\Delta_{11})$$

$$= r_0^2 - M \cdot N \cdot \sum\sum_{(k,l)\in\Omega} \cdot [F_{k,l}^2] + M \cdot N \sum\sum_{(k,l)\in\Omega} E[F_{kl} - F_{kl}^Q]^2$$

Hence, in order to evaluate $E[\mathcal{E}_w^Q]^2$ in a particular representation when the image is sliced into $M \cdot N$ pieces and over each piece we use a subset Ω of the possible basis functions (i.e. $\Omega \subset \{(k,l)|k,l = 0,1,2..\}$) and we quantize the coefficients with B_{kl}-bits we have to evaluate

$$r_0^2 - M \cdot N \cdot \sum\sum_{(k,l)\in\Omega} \{ \text{ variance of } F_{kl} \}$$
$$+ M \cdot N \cdot \sum\sum_{(k,l)\in\Omega} \{ \text{error in quantizing } F_{kl} \}$$

2.4   An Important Particular Case: Markov Process with Separable Cosine Bases

We have the statistics of $\{f_w(x,y)\}$ given by

$$E(f_w(x,y)) = 0, \quad E f_w(x,y) f_w(x+\tau_x, y+\tau_y) = r_0^2 e^{-\alpha_x |\tau_x|} e^{-\alpha_y |\tau_y|}$$

and we choose a separable cosine basis for the slices, i.e. over $[0, \frac{1}{M}] \times [0, \frac{1}{N}]$, $\Phi_{kl}(x,y) = \varphi_k(x)\varphi_l(y)$ where $\varphi_k(x) = \sqrt{M(2 - \delta_k)} \cos kM\pi x$, $k = 0,1,2,...$, and $\varphi_l(x) = \sqrt{N(2 - \delta_l)} \cos l N \pi x$, $l = 0,1,2,....$. To compute $E\mathcal{E}_w^2$ for this case we need to evaluate the variances of F_{kl} defined as $F_{kl} \equiv \int_{\Delta_{11}} f_w(x,y)\varphi_k(x)\varphi_l(y)dxdy$, we have

$$EF_{kl}^2 = E \iint_{\Delta_{11}} \iint_{\Delta_{11}} f_w(x,y) f_w(\xi,\eta)\varphi_k(x)\varphi_l(y)\varphi_k(\xi)\varphi_l(\eta)dxdyd\xi d\eta$$
$$= \iint_{\Delta_{11}} \iint_{\Delta_{11}} r_0^2 e^{-\alpha_x|x-\xi|} e^{-\alpha_y|y-\eta|} \cdot M(2 - \delta_k) \cos(k\pi Mx) \cos(k\pi M\xi)$$
$$\cdot N(2 - \delta_l) \cos(l\pi Ny) \cos(l\pi N\eta) dxdyd\xi d\eta.$$

Therefore, by separating the integrations we obtain

$$EF_{kl}^2 = r_0^2 (2 - \delta_k) \int_0^{\frac{1}{M}} \int_0^{\frac{1}{M}} e^{-\alpha_x|x-\xi|} \cos(k\pi Mx) \cos(k\pi M\xi) M dx d\xi$$
$$\cdot (2 - \delta_l) \int_0^{\frac{1}{N}} \int_0^{\frac{1}{N}} e^{-\alpha_y|y-\eta|} \cos(l\pi Ny) \cos(l\pi N\eta) N dy d\eta$$

Changing variables of integration to $\tilde{x} = Mx$ $\tilde{x} \in [0,1], \tilde{\xi} = M\xi$ $\tilde{\xi} \in [0,1], \tilde{y} = Ny$ $\tilde{y} \in [0,1]$, and $\tilde{\eta} = N\eta$ $\tilde{\eta} \in [0,1]$ yields

$$EF_{kl}^2 = r_0^2(2 - \delta_k)(2 - \delta_l) \cdot \frac{1}{M} \cdot \int_0^1 \int_0^1 e^{-\frac{\alpha_x}{M}|\tilde{x}-\tilde{\xi}|} \cos(k\pi\tilde{x}) \cos(k\pi\tilde{\xi}) d\tilde{x} d\tilde{\xi}$$
$$\cdot \frac{1}{N} \int_0^1 \int_0^1 e^{-\frac{\alpha_y}{N}|\tilde{y}-\tilde{\eta}|} \cos(l\pi\tilde{y}) \cos(l\pi\tilde{\eta}) d\tilde{y} d\tilde{\eta}$$

Let us define, for compactness, the following integral: $\int_0^1 \int_0^1 e^{-A|x-\xi|} \cos(k\pi x) \cos(l\pi \xi)dxd\xi \equiv \mathcal{M}(A; k, l)$ Then we see that

$$EF_{kl}^2 = r_0^2(2 - \delta_k^D) \cdot \frac{1}{M} \cdot \mathcal{M}(\frac{\alpha_x}{M}; k, k) \cdot (2 - \delta_l^D) \cdot \frac{1}{N} \cdot \mathcal{M}(\frac{\alpha_y}{N}; l, l)$$

We have that

$$\mathcal{M}(A; k, l) = (1 + \delta_k^D \text{ or } l)\delta_{|k-l|}^D \frac{A}{A^2 + k^2\pi^2}$$
$$- (1 + (-1)^{l+k}) \frac{A^2}{(A^2 + (l\pi)^2)(A^2 + (k\pi)^2)} \cdot \frac{(2 - e^{-A}[(-1)^k + (-1)^l])}{2}$$

Therefore some algebra yields

$$EF_{kl}^2 = \frac{4r_0^2}{M \cdot N} \left[\frac{(\frac{\alpha_x}{M})}{(\frac{\alpha_x}{M})^2 + k^2\pi^2} \right] \left(1 - (2 - \delta_k^D)(1 - (-1)^k e^{-(\frac{\alpha_x}{M})}) \frac{(\frac{\alpha_x}{M})}{(\frac{\alpha_x}{M})^2 + k^2\pi^2} \right) \cdot$$
$$\cdot \left[\frac{(\frac{\alpha_y}{N})}{(\frac{\alpha_y}{N})^2 + l^2\pi^2} \right] \left(1 - (2 - \delta_l^D)(1 - (-1)^l e^{-(\frac{\alpha_y}{N})}) \frac{(\frac{\alpha_y}{N})}{(\frac{\alpha_y}{N})^2 + l^2\pi^2} \right) \cdot$$

2.5   Incorporating the Effect of Coefficient Quantization

We have that $E[F_{kl} - F_{kl}^Q]^2 \sim \mathcal{K} \cdot \frac{\text{Var}\{F_{kl}\}}{2^{2b_{kl}}}$, where $\mathcal{K}$ is a constant in the range $[1, 3]$. According to rate-distortion theory (for uniform and Gaussian variables) the above formula for evaluating the error due to quantization describes well the behavior of the error as a function of the number of bits allocated for representing F_{kl}.

Putting the above results together, we get that the expected mean square error in representing images from the process $\{f_w(x, y)\}$ with Markov statistics, by slicing the image plane into $M \cdot N$ slices and using, over each slice, a cosine basis is given by:

$$E[\mathcal{E}_w^Q]^2$$
$$= r_0^2 \left\{ 1 - \sum\sum_{k,l \in \Omega} (2 - \delta_k^2)(2 - \delta_l^2) \, \mathcal{M}(\frac{\alpha_x}{M}; k, k)\mathcal{M}(\frac{\alpha_y}{N}; l, l) \, [1 - \frac{\mathcal{K}}{2^{2b_{kl}}}] \right\}$$

This expression gives $E[\mathcal{E}_w^Q]^2$ in terms of r_0, $\{\alpha_x, \alpha_y\}$ and $\{b_{kl}\}$ - the bits allocated to the coefficients F_{kl} where the subset of the coefficient is given via Ω.

3   The Slicing and Bit–Allocation Optimization Problems

Suppose we consider

$$E[\mathcal{E}_w^Q]^2$$
$$= r_0^2 \left\{ 1 - \sum\sum_{k,l \in \Omega} (2 - \delta_k^D) \, \mathcal{M}(\frac{\alpha_x}{M}; k, k)(2 - \delta_l^D)\mathcal{M}(\frac{\alpha_y}{N}; l, l) \, [1 - \frac{\mathcal{K}}{2^{2b_{kl}}}] \right\}$$

as a function of $M, N, \{b_{kl}\}$. We have that the total bit usage in representing the image is

$$B_{\text{TOT}} = \left(\sum\sum_{k,l \in \Omega} b_{kl} \right) \cdot M \cdot N$$

Now we can solve a variety of bit–allocation and slicing optimization problems.

3.1   Optimal Local Bit Allocation and Slicing Given Total Bit Usage

Given the constraint

$$\sum\sum_{(k,l)\in\Omega} b_{kl} = \frac{B_{\text{TOT}}}{M\cdot N},$$

find $\{b_{kl}^*\}$ that minimize the $E\mathcal{E}_w^2$. We need to minimize

$$\sum\sum_{k,l\in\Omega} \overbrace{(2-\delta_k^D)\mathcal{M}(\frac{\alpha_x}{M};k,k)(2-\delta_l^D)\mathcal{M}(\frac{\alpha_y}{N};l,l)}^{\tilde{\sigma}_{kl}^2}\mathcal{K}\,2^{-2b_{kl}}.$$

This is a classical bit allocation process and we have that the optimal bit allocation yields (theoretically) the same error for all terms in

$$\sum\sum_{k,l\in\Omega}\frac{\tilde{\sigma}_{kl}^2}{2^{2b_{kl}}} = \sum\sum_{k,l\in\Omega}\frac{\tilde{\sigma}_{kl}^2}{\Lambda_{kl}^2}$$

where we defined Λ_{kl} as the number of quantization levels, see [6]. Hence we need

$$\frac{\tilde{\sigma}_{kl}^2}{\Lambda_{kl}^2} = \text{Const} \Rightarrow \Lambda_{kl}^2 = \frac{\tilde{\sigma}_{kl}^2}{\text{Const}}$$

and we should have $2^{2\sum\sum b_{kl}} = \prod_{kl\in\Omega}\Lambda_{kl}^2 = 2^{2B_{TOT}/(MN)}$. The result is

$$b_{kl} = \frac{1}{2}\log_2\tilde{\sigma}_{kl}^2 + \frac{B_{\text{TOT}}}{M\cdot N}\cdot\frac{1}{|\Omega|} - \frac{1}{2}\log_2(\prod_{(kl)\in\Omega}\tilde{\sigma}_{kl}^2)^{\frac{1}{|\Omega|}}$$

With this optimal bit allocation the expression $\sum\sum_{(k,l)\in\Omega}\frac{\tilde{\sigma}_{kl}^2}{2^{2b_{kl}}}$ is minimized to

$$|\Omega|\cdot\text{Const} = |\Omega|\cdot 2^{\frac{-2B_{\text{TOT}}}{M\cdot N}}\left(\prod_{(kl)\in\Omega}\tilde{\sigma}_{kl}^2\right)^{\frac{1}{|\Omega|}}.$$

Hence,

$$E([\mathcal{E}_w^Q]^2)_{OPT} = r_0^2\left\{1 - \sum\sum_{k,l\in\Omega}(2-\delta_k^D)(2-\delta_l^D)\mathcal{M}(\frac{\alpha_x}{M};k,k)\mathcal{M}(\frac{\alpha_y}{N};l,l)\right.$$

$$\left. +|\Omega|2^{\frac{-2B_{\text{TOT}}}{M\cdot N}\cdot\frac{1}{|\Omega|}}\left(\prod_{(k,l)\in\Omega}\mathcal{K}\cdot(2-\delta_k^D)(2-\delta_l^D)\mathcal{M}(\frac{\alpha_x}{M};k,k)\mathcal{M}(\frac{\alpha_y}{N};l,l)\right)^{\frac{1}{|\Omega|}}\right\}$$

an error expression in terms of (B_{TOT}, M, N, Ω) and the second–order–statistics parameters r_0, α_x, α_y of the $\{f_w(x,y)\}$–process.

3.2   Effect of Slicing with Rigid Relative Bit Allocation

An alternative bit allocation strategy perhaps more in the spirit of the classical JPEG standard can also be thought of. Consider that Ω is chosen and the b_{kl}'s are also chosen a-priori for all $(k, l) \in \Omega$. Then we have

$$E[\mathcal{E}_w^Q]^2$$
$$= r_0^2 \left\{ 1 - \sum\sum_{k,l\in\Omega} (2 - \delta_k^D)(2 - \delta_l^D)\mathcal{M}(\frac{\alpha_x}{M}; k, k)\mathcal{M}(\frac{\alpha_y}{N}; l, l)[1 - \frac{\mathcal{K}}{2^{2b_{kl}}}] \right\}$$

as a function of M and N. This function clearly decreases with increasing M and N since more and more bits are allocated to the image, and here $B_{TOT} = M \cdot N \cdot \sum\sum_{k,l\in\Omega} b_{kl}$. Suppose now that for $M = N = 1$, we choose a certain bit allocation for a given Ω (say $\Omega = \{(k, l)|k + l \leq Limit, k, l = 0, 1, 2...\}$) i. e. we chose $\bar{b}_{kl}$ but now as we increase the number of slices (i.e. increase M and N) we shall modify the b_{kl}'s to keep B_{TOT} a constant by choosing $b_{kl}(M, N) = \bar{b}_{kl} \cdot \frac{1}{M \cdot N}$. Here B_{TOT} remains a constant and we can again analyze the behavior of $E[\mathcal{E}_w^Q]^2$ as M and N vary.

3.3   Soft Bit Allocation with Cost Functions for Error and Bit Usage

We could also consider cost functions of the form $C_{MSE}(E[\mathcal{E}_W^Q]^2) + C_B(M \cdot N \cdot$ Bits/slice) , where C_{MSE} and C_B are cost functions chosen according to the task in hand, and ask for the bit allocation that minimize the joint functionals, in the spirit of [5].

4   The Theoretical Predictions of the Model

In the previous sections we proposed a model for the compression error as a function of the image statistics $(r_0, \alpha_x, \alpha_y)$, the given total bits budget B_{TOT}, and the number of slicings M and N. Here, we fix these parameters according to the behaviour of natural images and typical compression setups and study the behaviour of the theoretical model.

Assume we have a gray scale image of size 512×512 with 8 bits/pixel, as our original image. JPEG considers 8×8 slices of this image and produces, by digitizing the DCT transform coefficients with a predetermined quantization table, approximate representation of these 8×8 slices. We would like to explain the observation that down-scaling the original image, prior to applying JPEG compression to a smaller image, produces with the same bit usage, a better representation of original image.

Suppose the original image is regarded as the 'continuous' image defined over the unit square $[0, 1] \times [0, 1]$, as we have done in the theoretical analysis. Then, the pixel width of a 512×512 image will be $1/512$. We shall assume that the original image is a realization of a zero mean 2D stationary random process with autocorrelation of the form

$$\mathcal{R}(|i - i'|, |j - j'|) = r_0^2 |\rho_1|^{|i-i'|}|\rho_2|^{|j-j'|},$$

with ρ_1, and ρ_2 in the range of $[0.8, 0.9]$, as is usually done (see [6]). From a single image, r_0^2 can be estimated via the expression

$$r_0^2 \approx \frac{1}{512 \times 512} \left(\sum_{i,j} (I(i,j) - \bar{I})^2 \right) = 2 \frac{1}{256} \left(\sum_0^{127} i^2 \right) = 32,385.00,$$

assuming an equalized histogram. If we consider that $\rho^{|i-i'|} \cong e^{-\alpha |\frac{i}{512} - \frac{i'}{512}|} = e^{-\frac{\alpha}{512}|i-i'|}$, we can obtain an estimate for α using $e^{-\frac{\alpha}{512}} = \rho \in [0.8, 0.9]$. This provides

$$-\frac{\alpha}{512} = \log_e \rho \longrightarrow \alpha = -512 \times \log_e \rho \in [50, 150].$$

The total number of bits for the image representation will range from 0.05bpp to about 2.0bpp, hence, B_{TOT} will be between $512 \times 512 \times 0.05 = 13,107$ to $512 \times 512 \times 2 = 524,288$ bits for 512×512 original images. Therefore, in the theoretical evaluations we shall take $\alpha_x, \alpha_y \in [50, 150]$, $r_o = 32500$ for 256 gray level images, with total bit usage between $10,000$ and $1,000,000$.

The symmetric x and y axis slicings considered will be $M, N = 1, 2, ...64$, and we shall evaluate

$$E[\mathcal{E}_w^Q]^2$$

$$\equiv r_0^2 \left\{ 1 - \sum \sum_{k,l \in \Omega} (2 - \delta_k^D)(2 - \delta_l^D) \mathcal{M}(\frac{\alpha}{M}, k, k) \mathcal{M}(\frac{\alpha}{N}, l, l)[1 - \frac{\mathcal{K}}{\Lambda_{kl}^2}] \right\}$$

with Λ_{kl}s provided by the optimal level allocation

$$\Lambda_{kl}^2$$
$$= (2 - \delta_k^D)(2 - \delta_l^D) \mathcal{M}(\frac{\alpha}{M}, k, k) \mathcal{M}(\frac{\alpha}{M}, l, l) \mathcal{K}(2^{2B_{TOT}/M^2})^{\frac{1}{|\Omega|}} \frac{1}{[\prod_{(k,l) \in \Omega} (\tilde{\sigma}_{kl}^2)]^{\frac{1}{|\Omega|}}}$$

Practically, the optimal level allocation Λ_{kl}^* should be given by $\Lambda_{kl}^* = \max(1, \lfloor \Lambda_{kl} \rfloor)$, a measure that automatically prevents the allocation of negative numbers of bits. Obviously this step must be followed by re-normalization of the bit allocation in order to comply with the bits budget constraint. $\mathcal{K}$ can be taken from 1 to 3, whereas Ω will be $\{(k,l) | k + l \leq 7, k, l = 0, 1, ..7\}$, simulating the standard JPEG approach which is coding of 8×8 transform coefficients, emphasizing the low frequency range via the precise encoding of only about $|\Omega| = 36$ coefficients.

Using the above described parameter ranges, we plot the predictions of the analytical model for the expected mean square error as a function of the slicings M with bit usage as a parameter. Figures 2 and 3 demonstrate the approximated error as a function of the number of slicings for various total number of bits. Figure 2 displays the predictions of the theoretical model in conjunction with optimal level allocation while Figure 3 uses the JPEG style rigid relative bit allocation. In both figures the left side shows the results of restricting the number of bits or quantization levels to integers, while the right side shows the results allowing fractional bit and level allocation.

These figures show that for every given total number of bits there is an optimal slicing parameter M indicating the optimal scaling factor. Note that the integer allocation cause in both cases non-smooth behaviour. Also, in Figure 2 it appears that the minimum points are local ones and the error tends to decrease as M increases. This phenomenon can be explained by the fact that we used an approximation of the quantization error which fails to predict the true error for a small number of bits at large scales.

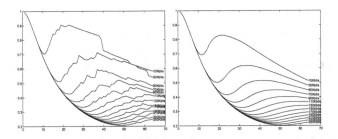

Fig. 2. Theoretical prediction based on optimal level allocation MSE versus number of slicings M with total bits usage as a parameter. Here, we used the typical values $\alpha = 150$, and $k = 3$.

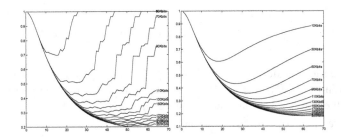

Fig. 3. Rigid relative bit allocation based prediction of MSE versus number of slicings M with total bits usage as a parameter. Here, we used the typical values $\alpha = 150$, and $k = 1$.

Figure 4 shows the theoretical prediction of PSNR versus bits per pixel curves for typical 512×512 images with different scales (different values of M, where scale= $8M/512$). One may observe that the curve intersections occur at similar locations as those of the experiments with real images shown in the next section.

5   Compression Results for Natural and Synthetic Images

In order to verify the validity of the analytic model and design a system for image transcoding we generate synthetic images for which the autocorrelation is similar to

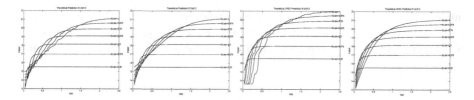

Fig. 4. Theoretical (two left frames) and rigid relative (two right frames) bit allocation based prediction of PSNR versus bits per pixel with image scaling as a parameter. Again, we used the typical values $\alpha = 150$, and $\kappa = 3$ for the theoretical prediction case, and $\kappa = 1$ for the JPEG-style case.

that of a given image. Next, we plot the PSNR/bpp JPEG graphs for all JPEG qualities, one graph for each given scaling ratio. The statistical model is considered valid if the behaviour is similar for the natural image and the synthesized one.

5.1 Image Synthesis

Assume that an image $g(m, n)$ autocorrelation function is that of a homogeneous random field of the form

$$R_{gg}(m, n) = \frac{1}{MN} \sum_{m'=0}^{M-1} \sum_{n'=0}^{N-1} g(m', n')g(m' + m, n' + n) = e^{-\alpha_x|m| - \alpha_y|n|}.$$

Define the Fourier transform $\hat{g}(k) = \mathcal{F}\{g(x)\}$. Then, the power spectrum of the real signal is given by $\mathcal{F}\{R_{gg}(x)\} = P_{gg}(k) = \langle \hat{g}(k)\hat{g}^*(k) \rangle$. Now, considering the $1D$ signal with the above given statistics, we have $\langle \hat{g}(k)\hat{g}^*(k) \rangle = \mathcal{F}\{e^{-\alpha|x|}\} = \frac{2\alpha}{\alpha^2 + k^2}$. Thus, we have that $\hat{g}(k) = \sqrt{2\alpha}\frac{\alpha - ik}{\alpha^2 + k^2}$, and

$$g(x) \equiv \mathcal{F}^{-1}\{\hat{g}(k)\} = \mathcal{F}^{-1}\left\{ \sqrt{\frac{\alpha}{2}}\frac{2\alpha}{\alpha^2 + k^2} \right\} + \mathcal{F}^{-1}\left\{ -\frac{1}{\sqrt{2\alpha}}ik\frac{2\alpha}{\alpha^2 + k^2} \right\}$$

$$= \sqrt{\frac{\alpha}{2}}e^{-\alpha|x|} - \frac{1}{\sqrt{2\alpha}}\frac{d}{dx}e^{-\alpha|x|} = \sqrt{\frac{\alpha}{2}}e^{-\alpha|x|}(1 + \text{sgn}(x))$$

$$= \begin{cases} \sqrt{2\alpha}e^{-\alpha|x|} & x > 0 \\ 0 & x \leq 0 \end{cases}$$

In order to generate synthetic images, we 'color' a uniform random (white) noise as follows. Let g_n be an $M \times N$ matrix in which each entry is a uniformly distributed random number. Next, let p and q be $M \times N$ matrices with elements

$$p(m, n) = \begin{cases} \sqrt{2\alpha_x}e^{-\alpha_x m} & n = \frac{N}{2}, m = 1, ..., M \\ 0 & \text{otherwise,} \end{cases},$$

$$q(m, n) = \begin{cases} \sqrt{2\alpha_y}e^{-\alpha_y n} & m = \frac{M}{2}, n = 1, ..., N \\ 0 & \text{otherwise.} \end{cases}$$

Our synthetic image is generated by the process $g(m,n) = \mathcal{F}_{2D}^{-1}\{\mathcal{F}_{2D}\{g_n\} \cdot \mathcal{F}_{2D}\{p\} \cdot \mathcal{F}_{2D}\{q\}\}$.

5.2   Estimating the Image Statistics α_x and α_y

In order to generate a synthetic image with the same statistics as that of the natural one, we have to first estimate the properties of the given image. Let us present a simple method for estimating the image statistics. We already used the relation $\mathcal{F}_{2D}\{R_{gg}(x,y)\} = P_{gg}(k,l) = \langle \hat{g}(k,l), \hat{g}^*(k,l)\rangle$. Explicitly, for our statistical image model we have that the power spectrum and the autocorrelation are given by

$$\frac{2\alpha_x}{\alpha_x^2 + k^2}\frac{2\alpha_y}{\alpha_y^2 + l^2} = \langle \hat{g}(k,l), \hat{g}^*(k,l)\rangle, \quad e^{-\alpha_x|x|-\alpha_y|y|} = \mathcal{F}_{2D}^{-1}\{\langle \hat{g}(k,l), \hat{g}^*(k,l)\rangle\}.$$

Thus, all we need to do is to estimate the slopes of the plane given by

$$\alpha_x|x| + \alpha_y|y| = -\ln(\mathcal{F}_{2D}^{-1}\{\langle \hat{g}(k,l), \hat{g}^*(k,l)\rangle\})$$
$$= -\ln(\mathcal{F}_{2D}^{-1}\{\langle \mathcal{F}_{2D}\{g(x,y)\}, (\mathcal{F}_{2D}\{g(x,y)\})^*\rangle\}).$$

This was the estimation implemented in our experiments.

5.3   Experimental Results

A JPEG compression performance comparison for a natural image and its random synthesized version is shown in Figure 5 for a 256×256 image (first row) and 512×512 image (second row). The figures show the compression results of synthetic versus natural images with similar statistics. Synthetic and original images and their corresponding autocorrelations are presented with their corresponding JPEG PSNR/bpp compression curves for 4 scales. The above experiments indicate that the crossing locations between scales in the synthetic images appear to be a good approximation of the crossings in the natural images. Thus, based on the second order statistics of the image we can predict the optimal scale factor. Moreover, the non-stationarity nature of images have a minor impact on the optimal scale factor. This is evident from the alignment of the results of the natural and the synthetic images. There appears to be a vertical gap (in PSNR) between the synthetic and the natural images. However, similar PSNR gaps appear also between different synthetic images.

6   Conclusions

We have presented an analytical model and a set of empirical results verifying our model and support the idea of scaling before transform coding for optimal compression. The numerical results prove the validity of the model, and the simple algorithms we introduced can be used in an on-line system, to (i) extract the image statistical coefficients (α_x and α_y). Next, (ii) use the image statistics, size, and bits budget to decide on the optimal scaling, e.g. for the JPEG compression in a transcoding system. In another report we will explore extensions and implementation issues, like extracting the image statistical characteristics from the JPEG DCT coefficients in an efficient way, obtaining second order statistics locally and using an hierarchical slicing of the image to various block sizes, and more.

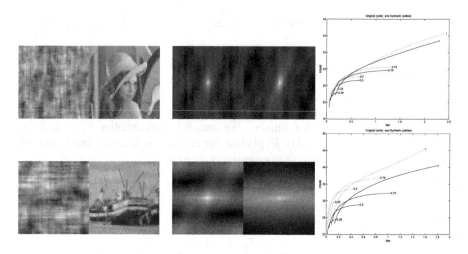

Fig. 5. Comparison between a natural and a synthesized image with similar autocorrelation.

References

1. W.B. Pennebaker and J.L. Mitchell. *JPEG Still Image Compression Standard.* Van Nostrand Reinhold, New York. 1992.
2. D. Taubman. High Performance Scalable Image Compression with EBCOT, *IEEE Trans. on Image Processing*, 9(7):1158–1170 2000.
3. A. Gersho and R.M. Gray. *Vector Quantization and Signal Compression,* Kluwer Academic,1992
4. A. Bruckstein. On Optimal Image Digitization *IEEE Trans. ASSP*, 35(4):553-555, 1987.
5. A. Bruckstein. On Soft Bit Allocation, *IEEE Trans. ASSP* 35(5):614-617, 1987.
6. A.K.Jain. *Fundamentals of Digit Image Processing,* Prentice Hall, 1989

Algebraic and PDE Approaches for Multiscale Image Operators with Global Constraints: Reference Semilattice Erosions and Levelings

Petros Maragos

National Technical University of Athens
Dept. of Electrical & Computer Engineering
Zografou, 15773 Athens, Greece
maragos@cs.ntua.gr

Abstract. This paper begins with analyzing the theoretical connections between levelings on lattices and scale-space erosions on reference semilattices. They both represent large classes of self-dual morphological operators that exhibit both local computation and global constraints. Such operators are useful in numerous image analysis and vision tasks ranging from simplification, to geometric feature detection, to segmentation. Previous definitions and constructions of levelings were either discrete or continuous using a PDE. We bridge this gap by introducing generalized levelings based on triphase operators that switch among three phases, one of which is a global constraint. The triphase operators include as special cases reference semilattice erosions. Algebraically, levelings are created as limits of iterated or multiscale triphase operators. The subclass of multiscale geodesic triphase operators obeys a semigroup, which we exploit to find a PDE that generates geodesic levelings. Further, we develop PDEs that can model and generate continuous-scale semilattice erosions, as a special case of the leveling PDE. We discuss theoretical aspects of these PDEs, propose discrete algorithms for their numerical solution which are proved to converge as iterations of triphase operators, and provide insights via image experiments.

1 Introduction

Nonlinear scale-space approaches that are based on morphological erosions and dilations are useful for edge-preserving multiscale smoothing, image enhancement and simplification, geometric feature detection, shape analysis, segmentation, motion analysis, and object recognition. Openings and closings are the basic morphological smoothing filters. The simplest openings/closings, which are compositions of Minkowski erosions and dilations, preserve well vertical image edges but may shift and blur horizontal edges/boundaries. A much more powerful class of filters are the *reconstruction* openings and closings which, starting from a *reference* signal consisting of several parts and a *marker* (initial seed) inside some of these parts, can reconstruct whole objects with exact preservation of their boundaries and edges [13,15]. In this reconstruction process they simplify

M. Kerckhove (Ed.): Scale-Space 2001, LNCS 2106, pp. 137–148, 2001.

the original image by completely eliminating smaller objects inside which the marker cannot fit. The reference signal plays the role of a *global constraint*. One disadvantage of both the simple as well as the reconstruction openings/closings is that they are not self-dual and hence they treat asymmetrically the image foreground and background. A recent solution to this asymmetry problem came from the development of a more general powerful class of morphological filters, the *levelings* introduced in [8] and further studied in [7,14], which include as special cases the reconstruction openings and closings. The levelings possess many useful algebraic and scale-space properties, as explored in [9], and can be generated by a nonlinear PDE introduced in [6].

A relatively new algebraic approach to self-dual morphology is based not on complete lattices but on inf-semillatices [5]. By using self-dual partial orderings the signal space becomes an inf-semilattice on which self-dual erosion operators can be defined [3,4] that have many interesting properties and applications.

In this paper we develop theoretical connections between levelings on lattices and erosions on semilattices, both from an algebraic and a PDE viewpoint. We begin in Section 2 with a brief background discussion on multiscale operators defined on complete lattices and inf-semilattices. In Section 3 we introduce and analyze algebraically multiscale *triphase* operators (which switch among 3 different states, one state being a global constraint) whose special cases are semilattice erosions and whose limits are levelings. The semigroup of *geodesic* triphase operators is discovered. Afterwards, in Section 4 we model both geodesic levelings and semilattice erosions using PDEs. The main ingredient here is the leveling PDE which we prove it can generate the multiscale geodesic operators and (as a special case) multiscale semilattice self-dual erosions. Section 5 extends the PDE ideas to 2D images signals. In both Sections 4,5 we also propose discrete numerical algorithms for solving the PDEs, prove their convergence using the semilattice operators of previous sections, and provide insights via experiments.

2   Signal Operators on Lattices and Inf-Semilattices

A poset is any set equipped with a partial ordering $\leq$. The supremum ($\bigvee$) and infimum ($\bigwedge$) of any subset of a poset is its lowest upper bound and greatest lower bound, respectively; both are unique if they exist. A poset is called a sup-(inf-) semilattice if the supremum (infimum) of any finite collection of its elements exists. A (sup-) inf-semilattice is called complete if the (supremum) infimum of arbitrary collections of its elements exist. A poset is called a (complete) lattice if it is simultaneously a (complete) sup- and an inf-semilattice. An operator ψ on a complete lattice is called: *increasing* if it preserves the partial ordering $[f \leq g \implies \psi(f) \leq \psi(g)]$; idempotent if $\psi^2 = \psi$; antiextensive (extensive) if $\psi(f) \leq f$ ($f \leq \psi(f)$). An operator ε (δ) on a complete inf- (sup-) semilattice is called an *erosion* (*dilation*) if it distributes over the infimum (supremum) of any collection of lattice elements. A *negation* ν is a bijective operator such that both ν and ν^{-1} are either decreasing or increasing and $\nu^2 = \mathsf{id}$, where id is the identity and $\nu \neq \mathsf{id}$. An operator ψ is called *self-dual* if it commutes with a negation ν.

In this paper, the signal space is the collection $\mathbb{V}^{\mathbb{E}}$ of all signals/images defined on $\mathbb{E}$ and assuming values in $\mathbb{V}$, where $\mathbb{E} = \mathbb{R}^d$ or $\mathbb{Z}^d$, $d = 1, 2, ...,$, and $\mathbb{V} \subseteq \overline{\mathbb{R}} = \mathbb{R} \cup \{-\infty, +\infty\}$. The value set $\mathbb{V}$ is equipped with some partial ordering that makes it a complete lattice or inf-semilattice. This lattice structure is inherited by the signal space by extending the partial order of $\mathbb{V}$ to signals pointwise. Classical lattice-based mathematical morphology [2] uses as signal space the *complete lattice* $\mathcal{L}(\mathbb{E}, \mathbb{V}) = (\mathbb{V}^{\mathbb{E}}, \vee, \wedge)$ of signals $f : \mathbb{E} \to \mathbb{V}$ with values in $\mathbb{V} = \overline{\mathbb{R}}$ or $\overline{\mathbb{Z}}$. In $\mathcal{L}$ the signal ordering is defined by $f \leq g \Leftrightarrow f(x) \leq g(x), \forall x$, and the signal infimum and supremum are defined by $(\bigwedge_i f_i)(x) = \sup_i f_i(x)$ and $\bigvee_i f_i)(x) = \inf_i f_i(x)$. Let B denote henceforth the d-dimensional *unit-radius ball* of $\mathbb{E}$, assuming the Euclidean metric, and let $tB = \{tb : b \in B\}$, $t \geq 0$, be its scaled version. The simplest multiscale dilation/erosion on $\mathcal{L}$ are the *Minkowski flat dilation/erosion* of a signal f by the sets tB:

$$\delta_B^t(f)(x) = (f \oplus tB)(x) = \bigvee_{a \in tB} f(x-a), \quad \varepsilon_B^t(f)(x) = (f \ominus tB)(x) = \bigwedge_{a \in tB} f(x+a) \tag{1}$$

We shall also need the *multiscale conditional dilation and erosion* of a *marker* ('seed') signal f within a *reference* ('mask') signal r:

$$\delta_{tB}(f|r) := (f \oplus tB) \wedge r, \quad \varepsilon_{tB}(f|r) := (f \ominus tB) \vee r \tag{2}$$

Iterating the conditional dilation (erosion) by a unit-scale B yields the *conditional reconstruction opening (closing)* of r from f.

Another important pair is the geodesic dilation and erosion. First we define them for sets $X \subseteq \mathbb{E}$ (binary images). Let $M \subseteq \mathbb{E}$ a *mask* set and consider its *geodesic metric* $d_M(x,y)$ equal to the length of the *geodesic path* connecting the points x, y inside M. If $B_M(x, t) = \{p \in M : d_M(x, p) \leq t\}$ is the geodesic closed ball with center x and radius $t \geq 0$, then the multiscale geodesic dilation and erosion of X within M are defined by $\delta^t(X|M) := \bigcup_{p \in X} B_M(p, t)$ and $\varepsilon^t(X|M) := [\delta^t(X^c|M^c)]^c$. By using threshold decomposition and synthesis of a signal f from its *threshold sets* $\Theta_h(f) := \{x \in \mathbb{E} : f(x) \geq h\}$ we can synthesize flat geodesic operators for signals by using as generators their set counterparts. The resulting *multiscale geodesic dilation and erosion* of f within a mask signal r are $\delta^t(f|r)(x) := \sup\{h \in \overline{\mathbb{R}} : x \in \delta^t(\Theta_h(f)|\Theta_h(r))\}$ and $\varepsilon^t(f|r)(x) := -\delta^t(-f|-r)$. An equivalent expression is

$$\delta^t(f|r)(x) = r(x) \wedge \bigvee_{d_{M_-}(x,p) \leq t} f(p), \quad \varepsilon^t(f|r)(x) = r(x) \vee \bigwedge_{d_{M_+}(x,p) \leq t} f(p) \tag{3}$$

where $M_- := \{x \in \mathbb{E} : f(x) \leq r(x)\}$ and $M_+ := \{x \in \mathbb{E} : f(x) \geq r(x)\}$. By letting $t \to \infty$ the geodesic dilation (erosion) yields the *geodesic reconstruction opening (closing)* of f within r:

$$\rho^-(f|r) := \bigvee_{t \geq 0} \delta^t(f|r), \quad \rho^+(f|r) := \bigwedge_{t \geq 0} \varepsilon^t(f|r) \tag{4}$$

In [5,3,4] a recent approach for a self-dual morphology was developed based on inf-semilattices. Now, the signal space is the collection of all signals $f : \mathbb{E} \to \mathbb{V}$, where $\mathbb{V} = \mathbb{R}$ or $\mathbb{Z}$. The value set $\mathbb{V}$ becomes a *complete inf-semilattice (cisl)* if equipped with the following partial ordering and infimum:

$$a \preceq_r b \Longleftrightarrow \begin{cases} r \wedge b \leq r \wedge a \\ r \vee b \geq r \vee a \end{cases}, \quad \overset{r}{\underset{i}{\curlywedge}}\, a_i = (r \wedge \bigvee_i a_i) \vee \bigwedge_i a_i$$

for some fixed $r \in \mathbb{V}$. The ordering $\preceq$ coincides with the *activity ordering* in Boolean lattices [10,2].

Given a reference signal $r(x)$, a valid signal cisl ordering is given by

$$f \preceq_r g \iff f(x) \preceq_{r(x)} g(x) \; \forall x \iff |f(x) - r(x) \leq |g(x) - r(x)| \; \forall x$$

and the corresponding signal cisl infimum becomes

$$\left(\overset{r}{\underset{i}{\curlywedge}}\, f_i \right)(x) = [r(x) \wedge \bigvee_i f_i(x)] \vee \bigwedge_i f_i(x) = [r(x) \vee \bigwedge_i f_i(x)] \wedge \bigvee_i f_i(x)$$

Under the above cisl infimum, the signal space becomes a cisl denoted henceforth by $\mathcal{F}_r(\mathbb{E}, \mathbb{V})$, or simply $\mathcal{F}_r$. Among all possible reference cisl's $\mathcal{F}_r$ that result from various choices of the reference signal $r(x)$, the cisl $\mathcal{F}_0$ with $r(x) = 0$ is of primary importance because it is isomorphic to any other $\mathcal{F}_r$. Specifically, the bijection $\xi : \mathcal{F}_0 \to \mathcal{F}_r$, given by $\xi(f) = f + r$, is a cisl isomorphism. Thus, if ψ_0 is an operator on $\mathcal{F}_0$, then its corresponding operator on $\mathcal{F}_r$ is given by

$$\psi_r(f) = \xi\psi_0\xi^{-1}(f) = r + \psi_0(f - r) \tag{5}$$

If ψ_0 is an erosion on $\mathcal{F}_0$ that is translation-invariant (TI) and self-dual, then ψ_r is also a self-dual TI erosion on $\mathcal{F}_r$. *Note:* the infimum, translation operator and negation operator on $\mathcal{F}_0$ are different from those on $\mathcal{F}_r$. For example, if $\nu_0(f) = -f$ is the negation on $\mathcal{F}_0$, then self-duality of ψ_0 means $\psi_0\nu_0 = \nu_0\psi_0$, whereas self-duality on $\mathcal{F}_r$ means $\psi_r\nu_r = \nu_r\psi_r$ where $\nu_r(f) = 2r - f$.

The simplest multiscale TI self-dual erosion on the cisl $\mathcal{F}_r$ is the operator

$$\psi_r^t(f)(x) = r(x) + \left([0 \wedge \bigvee_{a \in tB} (f(x - a) - r(x - a))] \vee \bigwedge_{a \in tB} (f(x - a) - r(x - a)) \right) \tag{6}$$

3   Lattice Levelings and Multiscale Semilattice Erosions

Defining levelings in $\mathcal{L}$ as in [8,7] requires a reference signal r, an input marker signal f, and a *parallel triphase* operator λ_p defined by:

(PT1) $\lambda_p(f, r, \alpha_p, \beta_p) := (r \wedge \beta_p(f)) \vee \alpha_p(f) = (r \vee \alpha_p(f)) \wedge \beta_p(f),$

(PT2) α_p, β_p are increasing and $\alpha_p(f) \leq f \leq \beta_p(f), \forall f$

where subscript 'p' denotes 'parallel'. In this paper we also define a more general triphase operator, the *serial triphase* operator λ_s, as follows:

(ST1) $\lambda_s(f|r, \alpha_s, \beta_s) := \alpha_s(f|\beta_s(f|r)),$

(ST2) α_s, β_s are increasing, $r \leq \alpha_s(f|r) \leq f \vee r$ and $r \geq \beta_s(f|r) \geq f \wedge r$

where the subscript 's' refers to 'serial' and the operators α_s and β_s have two arguments (f, r), written as $(f|r)$ to emphasize their different roles and provide a slightly different notation from the parallel case. *Any parallel triphase operator becomes a serial one by setting* $\alpha_s(f|r) = \alpha_p(f) \vee r$ *and* $\beta_s(f|r) = \beta_p(f) \wedge r.$ (However, the converse is not always true.) Thus, we henceforth drop the subscripts 's' and 'p' from α, β, λ (the difference will be clear from the context) and focus more on the serial case. The triphase operators depend on four parameters; if some of them are known and fixed, we shall omit them. Thus we may write $\lambda(f|r)$ or simply $\lambda(f)$. A signal f is a called a *parallel (serial) leveling* of r iff it is a fixed point of the parallel (serial) triphase operator, i.e. if $f = \lambda(f|r)$. The original definition in [8,7] corresponds to what we call here parallel leveling.

The definition of the serial triphase operator implies the following.

PROPOSITION 1 *For a serial triphase operator* $\lambda(f|r) = \alpha(f|\beta(f|r))$:
(a) $\alpha(r|r) = \beta(r|r) = r.$
(b) $\alpha(f|r) = \alpha(f \vee r|r)$ *and* $\beta(f|r) = \beta(f \wedge r|r).$
(c) At points where $f \geq r$, $f \geq \lambda(f|r) = \alpha(f|r) \geq r.$
(d) At points where $f \leq r$, $f \leq \lambda(f|r) = \beta(f|r) \leq r.$
(e) α *and* β *commute, i.e.* $\alpha(f|\beta(f|r)) = \beta(f|\alpha(f|r)).$
(f) $r \wedge \lambda = \beta(f|r)$ *and* $r \vee \lambda = \alpha(f|r).$

Thus, the operator α (β) affects only points where $f \geq r$ ($f \leq r$). Some general properties of triphase operators follow next.

PROPOSITION 2 *(a) Both parallel and serial triphase operators are antiextensive in the cisl* $\mathcal{F}_r$; *i.e.,* $\lambda(f|r) \preceq_r f.$
(b) Let (α_1, β_1) *and* (α_2, β_2) *create two (parallel or serial) triphase operators* λ_1 *and* λ_2, *respectively. If* $\alpha_1 \geq \alpha_2$ *and* $\beta_1 \leq \beta_2$, *then* $\lambda_2(f) \preceq_r \lambda_1(f), \forall f.$
(c) If α *and* β *are dual of each other, then* λ *is self-dual; i.e., if* $\alpha(-f|-r) = -\beta(f|r)$, *then* $\lambda(-f|-r) = -\lambda(f|r).$

Thus, a leveling of r from the marker f can be obtained by *iterating* any (parallel or serial) triphase operator λ to infinity, or equivalently by taking the cisl infimum $\bigwedge$ of all iterations of λ. Specifically, if $\psi^n(f) := \psi(\cdots \psi(f))$ denotes the n-fold composition of an operator ψ with itself, then

$$\Lambda(f|r) := \lambda^\infty(f|r) = \overset{r}{\underset{n \geq 1}{\bigwedge}} \; \lambda^n(f) \preceq_r \cdots \preceq_r \lambda^2(f) \preceq_r \lambda(f) \preceq_r f \qquad (7)$$

The map $r \mapsto \Lambda(\cdot|r)$ is called the *leveling operator* and is increasing and idempotent. The signal $g = \Lambda(f|r)$ is obviously a leveling of r from the marker f since $\lambda(g|r) = g.$

If we replace the operators α and β with the multiscale flat erosion and dilation by B of (1) we obtain a *multiscale conditional triphase* operator

$$\lambda_{tB}(f|r)(x) := [r(x) \wedge \delta_{tB}(f)(x)] \vee \varepsilon_{tB}(f)(x) = \overset{r}{\underset{a \in tB}{\lambda}} f(x-a) \qquad (8)$$

It is called 'conditional' because it can be written as a serial triphase operator, i.e., as a composition of conditional dilation and erosion:

$$\lambda_{tB}(f|r) = \varepsilon_{tB}(f|\delta_{tB}(f|r)) = \delta_{tB}(f|\varepsilon_{tB}(f|r)) \qquad (9)$$

Comparing (8) with (6) reveals that λ_{tB} becomes a multiscale TI semilattice erosion on $\mathcal{F}_r$ if r is constant. In particular, if $r = 0$, then λ_{tB} becomes a multiscale TI self-dual erosion on $\mathcal{F}_0$. For non-constant r, λ_{tB} is generally neither TI nor an erosion.

By replacing the conditional dilation and erosion in (9) with their geodesic counterparts from (3) we obtain a *multiscale serial geodesic triphase* operator

$$\lambda^t(f|r) = \varepsilon^t(f|\delta^t(f|r)) = \delta^t(f|\varepsilon^t(f|r)) \qquad (10)$$

This is the most important triphase operator because it obeys a semigroup. This will allow us later to find its PDE generator.

PROPOSITION 3 *(a) As $t \to \infty$, $\lambda^t(f|r)$ yields the geodesic leveling which is the composition of the geodesic reconstruction opening and closing:*

$$\Lambda(f|r) := \lambda^\infty(f|r) = \rho^-(f|\rho^+(f|r)) = \rho^+(f|\rho^-(f|r)) \qquad (11)$$

(b) The multiscale family $\{\lambda^t(\cdot|r) : t \geq 0\}$ forms an additive semigroup:

$$\lambda^t(\cdot|r)\lambda^s(\cdot|r) = \lambda^{t+s}(\cdot|r), \quad \forall t, s \geq 0. \qquad (12)$$

(c) For a zero reference ($r = 0$), the multiscale geodesic triphase operator becomes identical to its conditional counterpart and the multiscale semilattice erosion:

$$r = 0 \Longrightarrow \psi_0^t(f) = \lambda^t(f|0) = \lambda_{tB}(f|0) \qquad (13)$$

(d) For any r, the multiscale semilattice erosion $\psi_r^t = \xi\psi_0^t\xi^{-1}$ obeys a semigroup:

$$\psi_r^t\psi_r^s = \psi_r^{t+s} \quad \forall t, s \geq 0. \qquad (14)$$

The above result establishes that, for any positive integer n, the n-th iteration of the unit-scale geodesic triphase operator coincides with its multiscale version at scale $t = n$. The same is true for the multiscale semilattice erosions. It is not generally true, however, for the conditional triphase operator $\lambda_B(f|r)$, which does *not* obey a semigroup. Further, its iterations converge to the *conditional leveling* $\Lambda_B(f|r) = \lambda_B^\infty(f|r)$ which is smaller w.r.t. $\preceq_r$ than the geodesic leveling $\Lambda(f|r) = \lambda^\infty(f|r)$ of (11). Namely, $r \preceq_r \Lambda_B(f|r) \preceq_r \Lambda(f|r)$.

4   PDEs for 1D Levelings and Semilattice Erosions

Consider a 1D reference signal $r(x)$ and a marker signal $f(x)$, both real-valued and defined on $\mathbb{R}$. We start evolving the marker signal by producing the *multiscale geodesic triphase evolutions* $u(x,t) = \lambda^t(f|r)(x)$ of $f(x)$ at scales $t \geq 0$. The initial value is $u_0(x) = u(x,0) = f(x)$. In the limit we obtain the final result $u_\infty(x) = u(x,\infty)$ which will be the leveling $\Lambda(f|r)$. The mapping $u_0 \mapsto u_\infty$ is a *leveling filter*. In [6,9] it was explained that, if $f \leq r$ ($f \geq r$), the leveling $\Lambda(f|r)$ is a reconstruction opening (closing).

In an effort to find a generator PDE for the function u, we shall attempt to analyze the following evolution rule: $\partial u(x,t)/\partial t = \lim_{s \downarrow 0}[u(x,t+s) - u(x,t)]/s$. Since u satisfies the semigroup (12), the evolution rule becomes

$$\frac{\partial u}{\partial t}(x,t) = \lim_{s \downarrow 0} \frac{1}{s} \left[\bigwedge_{|a| \leq s}^{r} u(x-a,t) - u(x,t) \right] \tag{15}$$

We shall show later that, at points where the partial derivatives exist this rule becomes the following PDE: $u_t = -\text{sign}(u-r)|u_x|$. However, even if the initial signal f is differentiable, at finite scales $t > 0$, the above switched-erosion evolution may create shocks (i.e., discontinuities in the derivatives). One way to deal with shocks is to replace the standard derivatives with morphological sup/inf derivatives as in [1]. For example, let

$$\mathcal{M}^x u(x,t) := \lim_{s \downarrow 0} [\bigvee_{|a| \leq s} u(x+a,t) - u(x,t)]/s$$

be the sup-derivative of $u(x,t)$ along the x-direction, if the limit exists. If the right $u_x(x+,t)$ and left derivative $u_x(x-,t)$ of u along the x-direction exist, then its sup-derivative also exists and is equal to

$$\mathcal{M}^x u(x,t) = \max[0, u_x(x+,t), -u_x(x-,t)] \tag{16}$$

Obviously, if the left and right derivatives exist and are equal, then the sup-derivative becomes equal to the magnitude $|u_x(x,t)|$ of the standard derivative. The nonlinear derivative $\mathcal{M}$ leads next to a more general PDE that can handle discontinuities in $\partial u/\partial x$.

Theorem 1. [1] *Let $u(x,t) = \lambda^t(f|r)(x)$ be the scale-space function of multiscale geodesic triphase operations with initial condition $u(x,0) = f(x)$. Assume that f is continuous and possesses left and right derivatives at all x. (a) If the partial sup-derivative $\mathcal{M}^x u$ exists at some (x,t), then*

$$\frac{\partial u}{\partial t}(x,t) = \begin{cases} \mathcal{M}^x(u)(x,t), & \text{if } u(x,t) < r(x) \\ -\mathcal{M}^x(-u)(x,t), & \text{if } u(x,t) > r(x) \\ 0, & \text{if } u(x,t) = r(x) \end{cases} \tag{17}$$

---

[1] Due to space limitations, the proofs of all theorems and propositions will be given in a forthcoming longer paper.

(b) If the partial left and right derivatives $u_x(x\pm, t)$ exist at some (x, t), then

$$\frac{\partial u}{\partial t}(x, t) = \begin{cases} \max[0, u_x(x+, t), -u_x(x-, t)], & \text{if } u(x, t) < r(x) \\ \min[0, u_x(x+, t), -u_x(x-, t)], & \text{if } u(x, t) > r(x) \\ 0, & \text{if } u(x, t) = r(x) \end{cases} \tag{18}$$

(c) If the partial derivative $\partial u/\partial x$ exists at some (x, t), then u satisfies

$$\frac{\partial u}{\partial t}(x, t) = -\text{sign}[u(x, t) - r(x)] \left| \frac{\partial u}{\partial x}(x, t) \right| \tag{19}$$

Thus, assuming that $\partial u/\partial x$ exists and is continuous, the nonlinear PDE (19) can generate the multiscale evolution of the initial signal $u(x, 0) = f(x)$ under the action of the triphase operator. However, even if f is differentiable, as the scale t increases, this evolution can create shocks. In such cases, the more general PDE (18) that uses morphological derivatives still holds and can propagate the shocks provided the equation evolves in such a way as to give solutions that are piecewise differentiable with left and right limits at each point.

Consider now on the cisl $\mathcal{F}_0$ the *multiscale TI semilattice erosions* of a 1D signal $f(x)$ by 1D disks $tB = [-t, t]$:

$$v(x, t) = \psi_0^t(f)(x) = [0 \wedge \bigvee_{|a| \le t} f(x - a)] \vee \bigwedge_{|a| \le t} f(x - a) \tag{20}$$

This new scale-space function $v(x, t)$ becomes a special case of the corresponding function $u(x, t)$ for multiscale geodesic triphase operations when the reference r is zero. Thus, we can use the leveling PDE (19) with $r(x) = 0$ to generate the evolutions $v(x, t)$:

$$\begin{aligned} \partial v/\partial t &= -\text{sign}(v)|\partial v/\partial x| \\ v(x, 0) &= f(x) \end{aligned} \tag{21}$$

If $r(x)$ is not zero, then from the rule (5) that builds operators in $\mathcal{F}_r$ from operators in $\mathcal{F}_0$, we can generate multiscale TI semilattice erosions $\psi_r^t(f) = r + \psi_0^t(f - r)$ of f, defined explicitly in (6), by the following PDE system

$$\psi_r^t(f)(x) = r(x) + v(x, t), \quad \begin{aligned} \partial v/\partial t &= -\text{sign}(v)|v_x| \\ v(x, 0) &= f(x) - r(x) \end{aligned} \tag{22}$$

To find a *numerical algorithm* for solving the previous PDEs, let U_i^n be the approximation of $u(x, t)$ on a grid $(i\Delta x, n\Delta t)$. Similarly, define $R_i := r(i\Delta x)$ and $F_i := f(i\Delta x)$. Consider the forward and backward difference operators:

$$D^{+x}U_i^n := (U_{i+1}^n - U_i^n)/\Delta x, \quad D^{-x}U_i^n := (U_i^n - U_{i-1}^n)/\Delta x \tag{23}$$

To produce a shock-capturing and entropy-satisfying numerical method for solving the leveling PDE (19) we approximate the more general PDE (18) by replacing time derivatives with forward differences and left/right spatial derivatives with backward/forward differences. This yields the following algorithm:

$$\begin{aligned} U_i^{n+1} &= U_i^n - \Delta t[\ (P_i^n)^+ \max(0, D^{-x}U_i^n, -D^{+x}U_i^n) \\ &\quad + (P_i^n)^- \max(0, -D^{-x}U_i^n, D^{+x}U_i^n)] \\ \text{sign}(U_i^{n+1} - R_i) &= \text{sign}(F_i - R_i) \end{aligned} \tag{24}$$

where $P_i^n = \text{sign}(U_i^n - R_i)$, $q^+ = \max(0, q)$, and $q^- = \min(0, q)$. We iterate
the above scheme for $n = 1, 2, , \ldots$ starting from the initial data $U_i^0 = F_i$. For
stability, $(\Delta t / \Delta x) \leq 0.5$ is required. The above scheme can be expressed as
iteration of a conditional triphase operator Φ acting on the cisl $\mathcal{F}_R(\mathbb{Z}, \mathbb{R})$:

$$
\begin{aligned}
U_i^{n+1} &= \Phi(U_i^n), \quad \Phi(F_i) := [R_i \wedge \beta(F_i)] \vee \alpha(F_i), \\
\alpha(F_i) &= \min[F_i, \theta F_{i-1} + (1 - \theta)F_i, \theta F_{i+1} + (1 - \theta)F_i], \\
\beta(F_i) &= \max[F_i, \theta F_{i-1} + (1 - \theta)F_i, \theta F_{i+1} + (1 - \theta)F_i], \quad \theta = \Delta t / \Delta x.
\end{aligned}
\tag{25}
$$

By using ideas from methods of solving PDEs corresponding to hyperbolic conservation laws [12], we can easily show that this scheme is conservative and
monotone increasing (for $\Delta t / \Delta x < 1$), and hence satisfies the entropy condition.

There are also other possible approximation schemes such as the conservative
and monotone scheme proposed in [11] to solve the edge-sharpening PDE $u_t = -\text{sign}(u_{xx})|u_x|$. In order to solve the leveling PDE, we have modified this scheme
to enforce the sign consistency condition $\text{sign}(U_i^n - R_i) = \text{sign}(F_i - R_i)$. The
final algorithm can be expressed via the iteration of a discrete operator Φ as in
(25) but with different α and β:

$$
\begin{aligned}
\alpha(F_i) &= F_i - \theta\sqrt{[\max(F_i - F_{i-1}, 0)]^2 + [\min(F_{i+1} - F_i, 0)]^2}, \\
\beta(F_i) &= F_i + \theta\sqrt{[\min(F_i - F_{i-1}, 0)]^2 + [\max(F_{i+1} - F_i, 0)]^2}
\end{aligned}
\tag{26}
$$

This second approximation scheme is more diffusive and requires more computation per iteration than the first scheme (25). Thus, as the main numerical
algorithm to solve the leveling PDE, we henceforth adopt the first scheme (25),
which is based on discretizing the morphological derivatives. Examples of running this algorithm are shown in Fig. 1. An important question is whether the
two above algorithms converge. The answer is affirmative as proved next.

PROPOSITION 4 *If $\Phi(\cdot) = [R \wedge \beta(\cdot)] \vee \alpha(\cdot)$ and (α, β) are either as in (25) or
as in (26), the sequence $U^{n+1} = \Phi(U^n)$, $U^0 = F$, converges to a unique limit
$U^\infty = \Phi^\infty(F)$ which is a leveling of R from F.*

If $\Delta t = \Delta x$, then Φ of (25) becomes a discrete conditional triphase operator
with a unit-scale window $B = \{-1, 0, 1\}$, the PDE numerical algorithm coincides
with the iterative discrete algorithm of [8], and the limit of the algorithm is the
conditional leveling of R from F.

5   PDEs for 2D Levelings and Semilattice Erosions

A straightforward extension of the leveling PDE from 1D to 2D signals is to
replace the 1D dilation PDE with the PDE generating multiscale dilations by a
disk. Then the 2D leveling PDE becomes:

$$
\begin{aligned}
u_t(x, y, t) &= -\text{sign}[u(x, y, t) - r(x, y)]\|\nabla u(x, y, t)\| \\
u(x, y, 0) &= f(x, y)
\end{aligned}
\tag{27}
$$

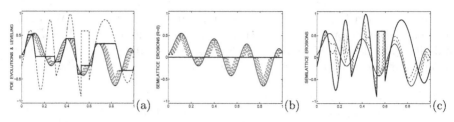

Fig. 1. (a) A reference signal r (dash line), a marker signal m (thin solid line) and its evolutions $u(x,t)$ (thin dash line) generated by the leveling PDE $u_t = -\text{sign}(u - r)|u_x|$, at $t = n25\Delta t$, $n = 1, 2, 3, 4$. (b) Multiscale semilattice erosions $v(x,t)$ of $m(x)$ w.r.t. zero reference, generated by the PDE $v_t = -\text{sign}(v)|v_x|$, $v(x,0) = m(x)$, at $t = n25\Delta t$, $n = 1, 2, 3, 4$. (c) Multiscale semilattice erosions $v(x,t) + r(x)$ of $m(x)$ w.r.t. reference $r(x)$, generated by the PDE $v_t = -\text{sign}(v)|v_x|$, $v(x,0) = m(x) - r(x)$, at $t = n25\Delta t$, $n = 1, 2$. ($\Delta x = 0.001$, $\Delta t = 0.0005$.)

Of course, we could select any other PDE modeling erosions by shapes other than the disk, but the disk has the advantage of creating an isotropic growth.

For discretization, let $U_{i,j}^n$ be the approximation of $u(x, y, t)$ on a computational grid $(i\Delta x, j\Delta y, n\Delta t)$ and set the initial condition $U_{ij}^0 = F_{ij} = f(i\Delta x, j\Delta y)$. Then, by replacing the magnitudes of standard derivatives with morphological derivatives and by expressing the latter with left and right derivatives which are approximated with backward and forward differences, we have developed the following entropy-satisfying scheme for solving the 2D leveling PDE (27):

$$U_{i,j}^{n+1} = \Phi(U_{i,j}^n), \quad \Phi(F_{ij}) := [R_{ij} \wedge \beta(F_{ij})] \vee \alpha(F_{ij}),$$
$$\alpha(F_{ij}) = F_{ij} - \Delta t \sqrt{\max^2[0, D^{-x}F_{ij}, -D^{+x}F_{ij}] + \max^2[0, D^{-y}F_{ij}, -D^{+y}F_{ij}]}$$
$$\beta(F_{ij}) = F_{ij} + \Delta t \sqrt{\max^2[0, -D^{-x}F_{ij}, D^{+x}F_{ij}] + \max^2[0, -D^{-y}F_{ij}, D^{+y}F_{ij}]}$$
$$(28)$$

For stability, $(\Delta t/\Delta x + \Delta t/\Delta y) \leq 0.5$ is required. This scheme is theoretically *guaranteed to converge to a leveling*. Examples of running the above 2D algorithm are shown in Fig. 2.

Why use PDEs for levelings and semilattice erosions? In addition to the well-known advantages of the PDE approach (such as more insightful mathematical modeling, more connections with physics, better approximation of Euclidean geometry, and subpixel accuracy), there are also some advantages over the discrete modeling that are specific for the operators examined in this paper. For levelings the desired result is mainly the final limit. The PDE numerical algorithms converge to a leveling Λ_{num}. The discrete (algebraic) algorithm of [8] converges to the conditional leveling Λ_{con}. If Λ is the sampled true (geodesic) leveling, then $r \preceq_r \Lambda_{con} \preceq_r \Lambda_{num} \preceq_r \Lambda$. Hence, the discrete algorithm result has a larger absolute deviation from the true solution than the PDE algorithm. Further, the discrete algorithm uses $\Delta t = \Delta x$ and hence it is unstable (amplifies small errors). In the 2D case we have an additional comparison issue: In

Reference   Marker $(t = 0)$

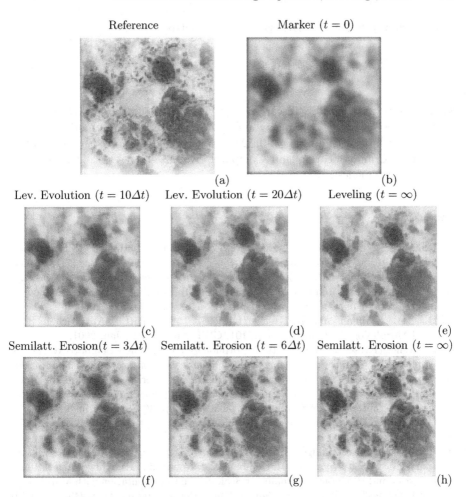

Lev. Evolution $(t = 10\Delta t)$ Lev. Evolution $(t = 20\Delta t)$ Leveling $(t = \infty)$

Semilatt. Erosion$(t = 3\Delta t)$ Semilatt. Erosion $(t = 6\Delta t)$ Semilatt. Erosion $(t = \infty)$

Fig. 2. Multiscale semilattice erosions and levelings of soilsection images generated by PDEs. (a) Reference image $r(x, y)$. (b) Marker image $m(x, y)$ obtained
from a 2D convolution of r with a 2D Gaussian of $\sigma = 4$. Images (c),(d),(e) show
evolutions $u(x, y, t)$ generated by the leveling PDE $u_t = -\text{sign}(u - r)||\nabla u||$.
Images (f),(g),(h) show multiscale semilattice erosions $v(x, y, t) + r(x, y)$ gen-
erated by the PDE $v_t = -\text{sign}(v)||\nabla v||$ with $v(x, y, 0) = m(x, y) - r(x, y)$.
$(\Delta x = \Delta y = 1, \Delta t = 0.25.)$

some applications we may need to stop the marker growth before convergence.
In such cases, the isotropy of the partially grown marker offered by the PDE is
an advantage.

For multiscale semilattice operators the final limit is not interesting since
it coincides with the reference; i.e., $\psi_r^\infty(f) = r, \forall f$. What is more interesting
in this case are the intermediate results. In this case producing 2D semilattice

erosions via the following PDE system yields isotropic results

$$\psi_r^t(f)(x,y) = r(x,y) + v(x,y,t), \quad \begin{array}{l} \partial v/\partial t = -\mathrm{sign}(v)\|\nabla v\| \\ v(x,y,0) = f(x,y) - r(x,y) \end{array} \quad (29)$$

Acknowledgments: This research work was supported by the Greek Secretariat for Research and Technology and by the European Union under the program $\Pi ENE\Delta$-99 with Grant # 99EΔ164. It was also supported by the NTUA Institute of Communication and Computer Systems under the basic research program 'Archimedes'.

References

1. R. Brockett and P. Maragos, "Evolution Equations for Continuous-Scale Morphological Filtering", *IEEE Trans. Signal Process.*, vol. 42, pp. 3377-3386, Dec. 1994.
2. H.J.A.M. Heijmans, *Morphological Image Operators*, Acad. Press, Boston, 1994.
3. H.J.A.M. Heijmans and R. Keshet, "First Steps Towards A Self-Dual Morphology", in *Proc. Int'l Conf. Image Processing*, Vancouver, Canada, Sep. 2000.
4. H.J.A.M. Heijmans and R. Keshet (Kresch), "Inf-Semilattice Approach to Self-Dual Morphology", Report PNA-R0101, CWI, Amsterdam, Jan. 2001.
5. R. Keshet (Kresch), "Mathematical Morphology On Complete Semilattices and Its Applications to Image Processing", *Fundamentae Informatica 41*, pp. 33-56, 2000.
6. P. Maragos and F. Meyer, "Nonlinear PDEs and Numerical Algorithms for Modeling Levelings and Reconstruction Filters", in *Scale-Space Theories in Computer Vision*, Lecture Notes in Computer Science 1682, pp. 363–374, Springer, 1999.
7. G. Matheron, "Les Nivellements", Technical Report, Centre de Morphologie Mathematique, 1997.
8. F. Meyer, "The Levelings", in *Mathematical Morphology and Its Applications to Image and Signal Processing*, H. Heijmans & J. Roerdink, Eds, Kluwer Acad., 1998.
9. F. Meyer and P. Maragos, "Nonlinear Scale-Space Representation with Morphological Levelings", *J. Visual Commun. & Image Representation*, 11, p.245-265, 2000.
10. F. Meyer and J. Serra, "Contrasts and Activity Lattice", *Signal Processing*, vol. 16, no. 4, pp. 303-317, Apr. 1989.
11. S. Osher and L.I. Rudin, "Feature-Oriented Image Enhancement Using Schock Filters", *SIAM J. Numer. Anal.*, vol. 27, no. 4, pp. 919–940, Aug. 1990.
12. S. Osher and J. Sethian, "Fronts Propagating with Curvature-Dependent Speed: Algorithms Based on Hamilton-Jacobi Formulations", *J. Comp.. Phys. 79*, 1988.
13. P. Salembier and J. Serra, "Flat Zones Filtering, Conected Operators, and Filters by Reconstruction", *IEEE Trans. Image Process.*, vol. 4, pp.1153-1160, Aug. 1995.
14. J. Serra, "Connections for Sets and Functions", *Fundamentae Informatica 41*, pp. 147-186, 2000.
15. L. Vincent, "Morphological grayscale reconstruction in image analysis: Applications and efficient algorithms", *IEEE Trans. Image Proces.*, 2(2), p.176-201, 1993.

Adjunctions in Pyramids and Curve Evolution

Renato Keshet (Kresch)[1] and Henk J.A.M. Heijmans[2]

[1] Hewlett-Packard Laboratories – Israel
Technion City, Haifa 32000, Israel
renato@hpli.hpl.hp.com

[2] Centre for Mathematics and Computer Science (CWI)
Kruislaan 413, 1098 SJ Amsterdam, The Netherlands
Henk.Heijmans@cwi.nl

Abstract. We have been witnessing lately a convergence among mathematical morphology and other nonlinear fields, such as curve evolution, PDE-based geometrical image processing, and scale-spaces. An obvious benefit of such a convergence is a cross-fertilization of concepts and techniques among these fields. The concept of adjunction however, so fundamental in mathematical morphology, is not yet shared by other disciplines. The aim of this paper is to show that other areas in image processing can possibly benefit from the use of adjunctions. In particular, it will be explained that adjunctions based on a curve evolution scheme can provide idempotent shape filters. This idea is illustrated in this paper by means of a simple affine-invariant polygonal flow.

1   Introduction

One of the most fundamental concepts in mathematical morphology is that of *adjunction*. An adjunction consists of an erosion/dilation pair, linked to each other in a unique way by a duality property. To define adjunctions, one merely needs to assume that the set of signals $\mathcal{S}$ (e.g., images, shapes, etc.) carries some partial ordering $\leq$.

Adjunctions have several simple but interesting algebraic properties. In particular, the concatenations of the dilation and erosion that form an adjunction give rise to idempotent operators known as opening and closing. As a result, adjunctions have become the most important theoretical concept in mathematical morphology, and despite (or perhaps, thanks to) their mathematical simplicity, their "adoption" has turned the research area of morphology into one with a strong mathematical foundation.

Despite their success in morphology, adjunctions have never been considered in the context of other image processing disciplines. Likely, this is due to the fact that adjunctions are often associated with dilations and erosions in their classical meaning. The work presented in [1] is a first attempt to alter this situation. In that paper, the first author suggested that an extended concept of adjunction can serve as a basis for signal processing in general, including the linear case! In fact, it is argued there that partially ordered sets and adjunctions can serve as

M. Kerckhove (Ed.): Scale-Space 2001, LNCS 2106, pp. 149–160, 2001.

a paradigm for signal processing tools in general. This paradigm consists of the following key ingredients:

- the information carried by various signals can be compared by using a properly chosen partial ordering;
- signal simplification and signal reconstruction, respectively, can be modeled by means of adjunctions;
- (idempotent) image filtering is achieved by an opening; the anti-extensivity of an opening guarantees that the filter reduces the information content.

The objective of this paper is to convey some of the ideas presented in [1], but focusing specifically on the area of scale-spaces in general, and pyramids and curve evolution in particular. Familiarity with [1] is not required for reading and understanding this paper.

After a brief review of the theoretical background, the first part of this paper shows the strong link between adjunctions and signal pyramids. The recent work in [3] is considered here as the basic framework for pyramids in general, and its axiomatic assumptions are proven to be closely related to those of an adjunction-based setting. Then, application of adjunctions in the context of curve evolution is considered. A simple case is studied, which illustrates the creation of an idempotent filter for shape denoising, derived from a curve flow.

2   Background on Adjunctions

The concept of adjunction was introduced by Heijmans and Ronse in [4] in the context of classical mathematical morphology. In that context, the set of signals is assumed to have a *complete lattice* structure (see [4,5] for definition of complete lattices and its rôle as a framework for classical mathematical morphology). However, the very same concept of adjunctions allows the extension of the theoretical morphology framework beyond complete lattices, first to complete *semilattices* [6], and then to generic partially ordered sets (posets) [1,2]. The latter framework is the one adopted here.

The above means that all that is required from a set of signals in order to enable the definition of adjunctions is a *partial ordering*.

Definition 1. (Partial Ordering) *A relation $\leq$ in a set S is a partial ordering if it is* reflexive *($s \leq s$), anti-symmetric (if $s \leq r$ and $r \leq s$, then $s = r$), and* transitive *(if $s \leq r$ and $r \leq q$, then $s \leq q$).*

A set ordered by a partial ordering is called a *partially ordered set* or *poset*. Adjunctions on posets are then defined as follows.

Definition 2. (Adjunctions) *Let $\leq_S$ and $\leq_R$ be two partial orderings defined on sets S and R respectively. Let $\varepsilon : S \mapsto R$ and $\delta : R \mapsto S$ be two operators. The pair (ε, δ) is called an* adjunction *between the posets $(S, \leq_S)$ and $(R, \leq_R)$ if $r \leq_R \varepsilon(s) \Leftrightarrow \delta(r) \leq_S s, \ \forall s \in S, r \in R$.*

In classical morphology, adjunctions are known to be related to the concepts of *erosion* and *dilation* [4]. Here we shall, for the sake of simplicity, actually *define* erosions and dilations in terms of adjunctions.

Definition 3. (Erosions and Dilations) *An operator $\varepsilon : \mathcal{S} \mapsto \mathcal{R}$ is called an erosion between $(\mathcal{S}, \leq_\mathcal{S})$ and $(\mathcal{R}, \leq_\mathcal{R})$ iff there exists an operator δ, such that (ε, δ) forms an adjunction between $(\mathcal{S}, \leq_\mathcal{S})$ and $(\mathcal{R}, \leq_\mathcal{R})$. Similarly, δ will be called a dilation iff there exists an operator ε, such that (ε, δ) is adjunction.*

Definition 4. (Morphological Opening and Closing) *Let (ε, δ) be an adjunction. The operator $\alpha = \delta\varepsilon$ is called the opening associated with the adjunction (ε, δ). Similarly, the operator $\beta = \varepsilon\delta$ is called the closing associated with the adjunction (ε, δ).*

We summarize some algebraic properties.

Proposition 1. (Uniqueness) *If (ε, δ_1) and (ε, δ_2) are adjunctions between $(\mathcal{S}, \leq_\mathcal{S})$ and $(\mathcal{R}, \leq_\mathcal{R})$, then $\delta_1 = \delta_2$. Similarly, if (ε_1, δ) and (ε_2, δ) are adjunctions, then $\varepsilon_1 = \varepsilon_2$.*

In other words, the dilation which forms an adjunction with a given erosion is unique, and we shall speak of the *adjoint dilation*. The *adjoint erosion* is defined in an analogous manner.

Proposition 2. *If (ε, δ) is an adjunction between $(\mathcal{S}, \leq_\mathcal{S})$ and $(\mathcal{R}, \leq_\mathcal{R})$, then*

1. *$\varepsilon\delta\varepsilon = \varepsilon$.*
2. *$\delta\varepsilon\delta = \delta$.*
3. *The erosion ε and the dilation δ are both increasing[1].*
4. *$\delta(r) = \inf\{s \in \mathcal{S} \mid r \leq_\mathcal{R} \varepsilon(s)\}, \forall r \in \mathcal{R}$.*
5. *$\varepsilon(s) = \sup\{r \in \mathcal{R} \mid \delta(r) \leq_\mathcal{S} s\}, \forall s \in \mathcal{S}$.*

The identity in 4 also involves the fact that the infimum (greatest lower bound) of $\{s \in \mathcal{S} \mid r \leq_\mathcal{R} \varepsilon(s)\}$ exists for all $r \in \mathcal{R}$. A similar remark applies to the identity in 5.

Proposition 3. *Let α and β be the morphological opening and closing, respectively, associated with an adjunction between $(\mathcal{S}, \leq_\mathcal{S})$ and $(\mathcal{R}, \leq_\mathcal{R})$. The following properties hold:*

1. *Both operators are idempotent (i.e., $\alpha\alpha = \alpha$ and $\beta\beta = \beta$).*
2. *Both operators are increasing.*
3. *Both operators are bounded by the input; $\alpha(s) \leq_\mathcal{S} s$ and $r \leq_\mathcal{R} \beta(r)$, for all $s \in \mathcal{S}$ and $r \in \mathcal{R}$. We say that α is anti-extensive and that β is extensive.*

---

[1] An operator $\psi : \mathcal{S} \to \mathcal{R}$ is called *increasing* if $s_1 \leq_\mathcal{S} s_2$ implies that $\psi(s_1) \leq_\mathcal{R} \psi(s_2)$.

3   Adjunctions and Pyramids

3.1   Background: Algebraic Axiomatics

In [3], a general framework for pyramidal signal decomposition is presented. It unifies linear and nonlinear multiresolution decompositions, by defining an axiomatic characterization of the analysis and synthesis operators that generate a pyramid. We briefly review this approach here.

A signal $s \in S_0$ is decomposed into a collection of coarse signals $s_j \in S_j$, $j = 1, 2, \ldots$, by means of a family of *analysis* operators $\psi_j^\uparrow : S_j \mapsto S_{j+1}$, such that $s_{j+1} = \psi_j^\uparrow(s_j)$. In linear pyramids, such as the Burt-Adelson pyramid, the analysis operator is usually a linear *decimation* process: Filtering (convolution) followed by downsampling.

Signal *synthesis*, or approximation, is obtained by a family of synthesis operators $\psi_j^\downarrow : S_{j+1} \mapsto S_j$, which generate an approximation signal $\hat{s}_j$ to the signal s_j, from the coarser one s_{j+1}, according to $\hat{s}_j = \psi_j^\downarrow(s_{j+1})$. In linear pyramids, the synthesis operator is usually a linear *interpolation* process: Upsampling followed by filtering.

In order to fulfill a series of intuitive conditions imposed on the analysis and synthesis operators, it was shown in [3] that a single axiomatic condition should hold for all j:

$$\psi_j^\uparrow \psi_j^\downarrow = \mathrm{id} \text{ on } S_{j+1}, \tag{1}$$

where id denotes the identity operator. Equation (1) is called the *pyramid condition*. This condition implies that

$$\psi_j^\uparrow \psi_j^\downarrow \psi_j^\uparrow = \psi_j^\uparrow \quad \text{and} \quad \psi_j^\downarrow \psi_j^\uparrow \psi_j^\downarrow = \psi_j^\downarrow \tag{2}$$

$$\psi_j^\uparrow \psi_j^\downarrow \text{ is idempotent.} \tag{3}$$

3.2   Relationship between the Pyramid Condition and Adjunctions

After a brief comparison, one may notice that pairs of analysis/synthesis operators and adjunctions have some common properties. For instance, compare (2) with items 1 and 2 in Proposition 2. Also, compare (3) with item 1 in Proposition 3. This lead us to wonder if there is a deeper relation between these structures.

In this section, we prove that any family of analysis and synthesis operators satisfying the pyramid condition forms a family of adjunctions between posets, with respect to an appropriate family of partial orderings. Even though it is not true that every adjunction satisfies the pyramid condition, the latter is satisfied if the erosion is surjective.

From Pyramids to Adjunctions.

Assume that the pyramid condition of Subsect. 3.1 holds. We shall next endow every space S_j with a partial ordering such that the analysis and synthesis operators become erosions and dilations, respectively. The operators $\psi_j^\uparrow$ and $\psi_j^\downarrow$ induce, on each set $\mathcal{S}_j$, the following partial ordering $\leq_j$:

$$\forall s', s \in \mathcal{S}_j, \; s' \leq_j s \Leftrightarrow \begin{cases} s' = s, \text{ or} \\ \exists J > j \mid s' = \hat{\psi}_{[j,J]}(s), \end{cases} \tag{4}$$

where $\hat{\psi}_{[j,J]} = \psi_{[j,J]}^\downarrow \psi_{[j,J]}^\uparrow$, with

$$\psi_{[j,J]}^\uparrow = \psi_{J-1}^\uparrow \cdots \psi_{j+1}^\uparrow \psi_j^\uparrow \quad \text{and} \quad \psi_{[j,J]}^\downarrow = \psi_j^\downarrow \psi_{j+1}^\downarrow \cdots \psi_{J-1}^\downarrow.$$

The above series of partial orderings are illustrated in Figure 1.

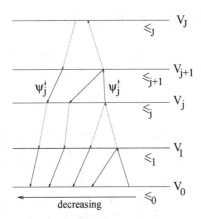

Fig. 1. Series of partial orderings generated by families of analysis/synthesis operators. Each partial ordering $\leq_j$ is depicted schematically on a horizontal line, which increases from left to right. For each $\leq_j$, a signal is smaller than another if it can be obtained from the latter by a same number of upstream and downstream analysis/synthesis operations.

Proposition 4. *For any j and any $J > j$, $(\psi_{[j,J]}^\uparrow, \psi_{[j,J]}^\downarrow)$ is an adjunction between $(\mathcal{S}_j, \leq_j)$ and $(\mathcal{S}_J, \leq_J)$.*

Proposition 5. *For any j and any $J > j$, $\hat{\psi}_{[j,J]}$ is the morphological opening associated with $(\psi_{[j,J]}^\uparrow, \psi_{[j,J]}^\downarrow)$.*

Corollary 1. *For any j, $(\psi_j^\uparrow, \psi_j^\downarrow)$ is an adjunction between $(\mathcal{S}_j, \leq_j)$ and $(\mathcal{S}_{j+1}, \leq_{j+1})$, and $\psi_j^\downarrow \psi_j^\uparrow$ is the associated morphological opening.*

We should note that the family of partial orderings defined in (4) is not necessarily the only one for which Propositions 4, 5, and Corollary 1, hold.

From Adjunctions to Pyramids.
Suppose that we are given a family of posets $(\mathcal{S}_j, \leq_j)$, and adjunctions $(\varepsilon_j, \delta_j)$ between $\mathcal{S}_j$ and $\mathcal{S}_{j+1}$. Suppose that ε_j is surjective, that is, any element s' in $\mathcal{S}_{j+1}$ is of the form $\varepsilon_j(s)$ for some $s \in \mathcal{S}_j$. We then get for all $s' \in \mathcal{S}_{j+1}$:

$$\varepsilon_j \delta_j(s') = \varepsilon_j \delta_j \varepsilon_j(s) = \varepsilon_j(s) = s'. \tag{5}$$

In other words:

$$\varepsilon_j \delta_j = \text{id on } \mathcal{S}_{j+1}, \tag{6}$$

which is the pyramid condition. Therefore, if ε_j is surjective, then the adjunction $(\varepsilon_j, \delta_j)$ consists of an analysis/synthesis pair.

4   Adjunctions for Curve Evolution

In this section, we consider the application of adjunctions and the pyramid condition in the area of curve evolution.

4.1   Motivation

The strength of curve evolution for shape filtering is well known and documented in the literature (see [8,9] for example). Important properties, like affine invariance, can be obtained by curve evolution methods, and they have been embedded and studied within a solid theoretical framework.

However, one disadvantage of classical curve evolution methods for denoising is the fact that the curve shrinks as time passes, and therefore the evolved curve gets farther and farther from the original one. For illustration, a discrete example can be seen in Fig. 2. There, a noisy C-shaped curve is submitted to several evolution iterations (a detailed description of this flow is given in the sequel), and the result is a nearly-elliptic, noiseless, shrinked version of the original curve. Although the noise is removed, the final shape does not resemble the original one; it is too distorted to consider this as a successful denoising operation.

In order to reduce this problem, one might (i) keep the number of iterations low, and (ii) rescale the final curve in order to have their contours match as much as possible, e.g., expand the final curve so it has the same area as the original one. Although this indeed yields an improvement, it does not solve the problem entirely: a small number of iterations may not remove enough noise energy, whereas rescaling keeps the final shape, possibly distorted.

An alternative approach to solve the problem is to apply the inverse flow to the outcome of the forward flow. This would bring the contour of the final curve somehow "close" to the original one. Others have disregarded this approach for two main reasons: First, in many important cases, the forward flow is mathematically invertible, which would make the forward/inverse composition equal to identity, and therefore useless. In practice though, and that is the second reason, the inverse flow is unstable, and the curve usually "explodes" after a few inverse iterations.

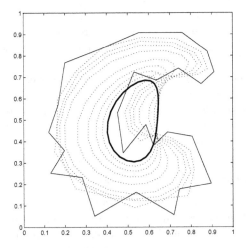

Fig. 2. Affine-invariant polygon evolution. The original curve is shown in thin, solid line, the curve after 30 iterations is shown bold-faced, and the dotted curves depict the evolution.

Some accepted ways to really avoid the above problem are (i) to use a switch to toggle between different flows [10], or (ii) to use a constrained optimization procedure [11]. The stable pseudo-inverse operators discussed in [13] for shape enhancement and exaggeration might also give fine results. Below we propose an alternative approach, using adjunction pyramids, which leads to an idempotent shape filter.

4.2   Proposed Approach – General Idea

The reason why the exact inverse flow is not achievable in finite-state machines is because the forward flow calculation is actually a composition of the filtering operation with *quantization*. This quantization is a result of arithmetic rounding in all steps of the computation, which slightly *distorts* the exact final results, but, more importantly, causes the whole operation to become non-invertible.

In order to obtain a stable inverse flow, our proposed approach is to design an adjunction pyramid $(\varepsilon_t, \delta_t)$, where the erosion ε_t describes the forward flow as well as the quantization from time t to $t + 1$, and the adjoint dilation δ_t is the (pseudo-) inverse flow step. Starting with a curve $\mathcal{C}_0$ at time 0 we obtain the curve $\mathcal{E}_t(\mathcal{C}_0) = \varepsilon_{t-1}\varepsilon_{t-2}\cdots\varepsilon_0(\mathcal{C}_0)$ at time t. From the theory on adjunctions we know that $\mathcal{E}_t$ is an erosion between $\mathcal{S}_0$ and $\mathcal{S}_t$ with adjoint dilation given by $\Delta_t = \delta_0\delta_1\cdots\delta_{t-1}$ mapping $\mathcal{S}_t$ into $\mathcal{S}_0$. Furthermore, we get that $(\mathcal{E}_t, \Delta_t)$ is an adjunction. Therefore, composition of the forward flow with the "inverse" flow, i.e., $\alpha_t = \Delta_t\mathcal{E}_t$, which is the associated morphological opening (of "size" t, in morphology jargon), will be stable, idempotent, and could be regarded as an ideal filter. Moreover, according to item 1 in Proposition 2, $\mathcal{E}_t\Delta_t\mathcal{E}_t$ is equal to $\mathcal{E}_t$, which means that the "inverse" flow Δ_t preserves the information retained by $\mathcal{E}_t$. Also, α_t is increasing and anti-extensive with respect to some partial ordering, and the latter *characterizes* the nature of the information removal performed by the forward flow $\mathcal{E}_t$.

The question is how to calculate the "inverse" flow step δ_t, given the forward one ε_t. In the next subsection we propose a guideline for adjunction design, using a given measure. A simple case where it is possible to calculate a closed-form solution is studied in Section 4.4. In general however this is not a straightforward task, and iterative solutions may be required.

4.3   Adjunction Design Using a Measure

Suppose there exists a *measure* (or *functional*) μ_t defined on $\mathcal{S}_t$, which characterizes in a satisfactory way the "simplicity" or "smoothness" of a shape or curve. For instance, μ_t could be the perimeter or the area of the shape. Define $\delta_t : \mathcal{S}_{t+1} \to \mathcal{S}_t$ by means of the minimization-problem formulation

$$\delta_t(s) = \arg\ \min\ \{\mu_t(r) \mid r \in \mathcal{S}_t \text{ and } \varepsilon_t(r) = s\}. \tag{7}$$

Note that this definition presupposes that the minimization problem has a unique solution for every $s \in \mathcal{S}_{t+1}$. In that case we have $\varepsilon_t \delta_t(s) = s$, hence $(\varepsilon_t, \delta_t)$ satisfies the pyramid condition, and is therefore an adjunction.

The proposed approach is therefore to use (7) to calculate the "inverse" flow, assuming that the required conditions of existence and uniqueness are satisfied. If these conditions are not satisfied, then other slightly different approaches could be considered, but these fall outside the scope of this paper.

The underlying partial ordering induced by the resulting adjunction is intimately related to the choice of measure μ_t. Specifically, let $(\varepsilon_t, \delta_t)$ be an adjunction obtained by means of (7), and associated to partial orderings $\leq_t$ in $\mathcal{S}_t$. Let $\leq$ be the usual ordering on the real numbers. Then, for all $s_1, s_2 \in \mathcal{S}_t$, the partial ordering $\leq_t$ satisfies:

$$s_1 \leq_t s_2 \Rightarrow \mu_t(s_1) \leq \mu_t(s_2). \tag{8}$$

In many cases, of which the example below is a particular example, the various steps ε_t whose composition yields the forward flow $\mathcal{E}_t$, are time-independent, i.e., $\varepsilon_t = \varepsilon$. In that case we have $\mathcal{E}_t = \varepsilon^t$, the t'th power of ε. If we choose the measures μ to be independent of t, we also get $\delta_t = \delta$, hence $\Delta_t = \delta^t$.

4.4   Case Study: Polygon Affine Evolution

In [7] Bruckstein, Sapiro, and Shaked presented a simple scheme for affine-invariant evolution of polygons. It can be regarded as a discrete, non-geometric version of affine evolution of continuous curves.

Given an N-vertex polygon $\mathcal{P}_0$ with vertex points $\boldsymbol{x}_0(i) \in \mathbb{R}^2$, $i = 0, \ldots, N-1$, perform an affine evolution using the rule:

$$\boldsymbol{x}_{t+1}(i) = \frac{1}{3}\left[\boldsymbol{x}_t(i-1) + \boldsymbol{x}_t(i) + \boldsymbol{x}_t(i+1)\right], \quad t = 0, 1, \ldots \tag{9}$$

where $x_t(i)$ are the vertices of the polygon after the t-th iteration and $i \pm 1$ are taken modulo N. It was shown in [7] that any polygon submitted to this flow converges to a vanishing polygonal ellipse. The discrete flow previously presented in Figure 2 is an example of polygon affine evolution. Equation (9) consists of a linear cyclic convolution of the polygon coordinates. If we write $x_t(i) = (x_t(i), y_t(i))$ for every i, then the evolution amounts to filtering the functions $x_t(i)$ and $y_t(i)$ separately by the filter $(\frac{1}{3}, \frac{1}{3}, \frac{1}{3})$. It can be shown that, if N is not a multiple of 3, then the above filtering operation is invertible. That means that, in principle, the polygon flow can be inverted. However, in practice, the inverse flow is unstable.

Because of the cyclic nature of the above convolution, this operation can be performed very easily in the Fourier domain. Henceforth we denote the vertex points of the N-vertex polygon $\mathcal{P}$ by $x_\mathcal{P}(i) = (x_\mathcal{P}(i), y_\mathcal{P}(i))$. Denote by $X_\mathcal{P}(k)$ the (coordinate-wise) Fourier transform of $x_\mathcal{P}(i)$. Th evolution process described by (9) can be reformulated by applying the Fourier transform at both sides. Then we arrive at:

$$X_{\mathcal{P}_{t+1}}(k) = F(k)X_{\mathcal{P}_t}(k), \tag{10}$$

where $F(k)$ is the frequency response of the filter $(\frac{1}{3}, \frac{1}{3}, \frac{1}{3})$, which is a real-valued function. Rather than using this cartesian representation, we will represent the Fourier transform of $\mathcal{P}$ by its polar form $[A_\mathcal{P}(k), \theta_\mathcal{P}(k)]$, where $A_\mathcal{P}$ is the amplitude and $\theta_\mathcal{P}$ the phase. When reformulated in terms of polar coordinates (10) looks as follows

$$A_{\mathcal{P}_{t+1}}(k) = |F(k)|A_{\mathcal{P}_t}(k) \tag{11}$$

$$\theta_{\mathcal{P}_{t+1}}(k) = \theta_{\mathcal{P}_t}(k) + \text{phase}(F(k)) \bmod 2\pi. \tag{12}$$

Since F is real-valued, its phase can only assume the values 0 and π. The expressions in (11)-(12) do not yet take quantization effects into account. Below we will give formal expressions for the erosion and dilation which constitute the pyramid associated with the affine evolution in (9) and which do also include quantization effects. Note however that, thanks to the fact that F is real-valued, we only need to deal with quantization of the amplitude term in (11). Note also that the spaces $\mathcal{S}_t$ which define the consecutive levels of the pyramid, do not depend on t, i.e., $\mathcal{S}_t = \mathcal{S}$ for all $t \geq 0$, and the same can be said for the erosions and dilations, i.e., $\varepsilon_t = \varepsilon$ and $\delta_t = \delta$. The latter means in particular that the evolution of a curve from time 0 to t is governed by ε^t, the t'th iterate of ε.

We define $q(k)$ to be the quantization step for the amplitude at frequency k. Let $\mathcal{S}$ be the set of N-vertex polygons $\mathcal{P}$ for which the amplitude function $A_\mathcal{P}(\cdot)$ is quantized, i.e., $A_\mathcal{P}(\cdot)/q(\cdot)$ is integer-valued. Define the erosion $\varepsilon : \mathcal{S} \to \mathcal{S}$ in terms of the polar representation $(A_\mathcal{P}, \theta_\mathcal{P})$ of the Fourier transform of $\mathcal{P}$:

$$A_{\varepsilon(\mathcal{P})}(k) = \left\lfloor \frac{|F(k)|A_\mathcal{P}(k)}{q(k)} \right\rfloor \cdot q(k) \tag{13}$$

$$\theta_{\varepsilon(\mathcal{P})}(k) = \theta_\mathcal{P}(k) + \text{phase}(F(k)) \bmod 2\pi, \tag{14}$$

where $\lfloor \cdot \rfloor$ denotes the floor function. Furthermore, we define the adjoint dilation δ using a minimization procedure like in (7) using for μ the energy

$$\mu(\mathcal{P}) = \left(\sum_{k=0}^{N-1} |A_{\mathcal{P}}(k)|^2 \right)^{\frac{1}{2}}. \tag{15}$$

This yields, in terms of $\boldsymbol{X}_{\mathcal{P}}$, the expression

$$\boldsymbol{X}_{\delta(\mathcal{P})}(k) = \tilde{F}^{-1}(k) \cdot \boldsymbol{X}_{\mathcal{P}}(k), \tag{16}$$

where $\tilde{F}^{-1}(k)$ is the pseudo-inverse of $F(k)$, i.e.,

$$\tilde{F}^{-1}(k) = \begin{cases} 1/F(k), & F(k) \neq 0, \\ 0, & F(k) = 0. \end{cases} \tag{17}$$

In Fig. 3, one can observe the result of applying the forward and inverse flows to "noisy" polygons (thin, solid line). The dotted curves are the result of 30 iterations of the forward affine flow. Our simulations were performed using Matlab with a uniform quantization step $q(k)$ equal to 10^{-10}. The bold-faced curves are the result of applying 30 iterations of the "inverse" flow on the dotted curves. In morphological terms, the bold-faced curves in Fig. 3 are the opening of the

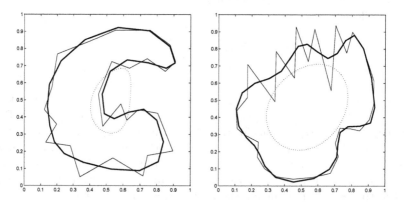

Fig. 3. Forward and inverse affine-invariant polygon flow. The original curves are presented in thin, solid lines. After 30 iterations of forward flow (erosion), the dotted curves are obtained. After further 30 iterations of inverse flow (adjoint dilation), one obtains the bold-face curves.

original curves with "size" 30. As stressed before, the opening can be regarded as an ideal filter; like any opening, it is idempotent, increasing and anti-extensive, where increasing and anti-extensive are with respect to the underlying partial ordering induced by $(\mathcal{E}_t, \Delta_t)$. In this case, anti-extensivity means producing a "smoother" curve, where the characteristics of this smoothing are dictated by the chosen energy measure minimization and the nature of the erosion operation (i.e., the affine flow). In the continuous case, the affine flow reduces the affine arc length of the curve; a similar quantity might be the reducing criterion for the polygon flow, but this is yet to be investigated.

Notice that, since $\mathcal{E}_t \Delta_t \mathcal{E}_t = \mathcal{E}_t$, the dotted curves are obtained again after further applying 30 iterations of the forward flow to the bold-faced curves.

The amount of smoothness produced by the opening operation is directly related to the "size" parameter, i.e., by the number of iterations of forward and inverse flows; see Fig. 4. For "size" 0, the opening is the identity operator. As "size" increases, the filtered curve becomes smoother, and later on (not shown) tends first to an ellipse, then to a circle, and, for an infinite "size", to a point.

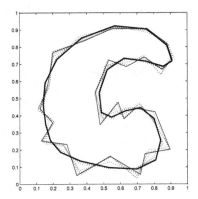

Fig. 4. Series of openings with increasing "size". The original curve is in thin, solid line, the bold-faced curve is the opening with parameter 30 (corresponding to 30 iterations of forward flow plus 30 iterations of inverse flow). The dotted curves show the result of openings with various "sizes".

Observe that in our approach one can distinguish two different scale-spaces. One is generated by the erosion (the forward flow), and evolves as the time parameter t increases; this is the scale-space illustrated in Fig. 2. The second scale-space is generated by the opening (the ideal filter), as its "size" parameter (which is identical to the time parameter t) increases. This scale-space is illustrated in Fig. 4. Notice that there exists a one-one correspondence between both scale-spaces: every level of the opening scale-space can be obtained from the corresponding one in the erosion scale-space by applying the "inverse" flow. Similarly, every level of the erosion scale-space can be obtained from the opening scale-space by using the forward flow again. This means that these two scale-spaces carry exactly the same information, differing only by their representations.

One of the main conclusions of this study is that, in many applications, such as denoising, one may be more interested in the opening scale-space, rather than the erosion one.

5   Conclusion

In this paper, we showed how the concept of adjunctions, so central in mathematical morphology, can be adopted by other disciplines as well. An intimate relationship between adjunctions and pyramids was proven, and the creation of idempotent shape filters based on curve evolution schemes was suggested and illustrated.

The close, intuitive relationship existing in general between pyramids and scale-spaces hints that adjunctions could also play a central rôle in scale-space theory in general. The study case described here also suggests such link, and the concepts of erosion scale-spaces vs. opening scale-spaces are devised. Hints regarding these entities can be also found in [12], where summation and supremal scale-spaces are defined and studied. Thus, an investigation of the relationship between adjunctions and scale-spaces is in order, and it is under way.

References

1. R. Keshet (Kresch), "A morphological view on traditional signal processing," *Mathematical Morphology and its Applications to Image and Signal Processing V (Proc. of ISMM'2000)*, Palo Alto, California, USA, June 2000.
2. H.J.A.M Heijmans and R. Keshet (Kresch), "Inf-semilattice Approach to Self-dual Morphology," *CWI Report PNA-R0101*, Amsterdam, January 2001.
3. J. Goutsias and H.J.A.M Heijmans, "Nonlinear multiresolution signal decomposition schemes: Part I: morphological pyramids," *IEEE Transactions on Image Processing*, Vol. 9, pp. 1862-1876, 2000.
4. H.J.A.M. Heijmans and C. Ronse, "The Algebraic Basis of Mathematical Morphology. I. Dilations and Erosions," *Comput. Vision Graphics Image Process.*, Vol. 50, pp. 245-295, 1990.
5. J. Serra, editor, *Image Analysis and Mathematical Morphology, Volume 2: Theoretical Advances.* New York: Academic Press, 1988.
6. R. Kresch, "Extension of Morphological Operations to Complete Semilattices and Its Applications to Image and Video Processing," *Mathematical Morphology and its Applications to Image and Signal Processing (Proc. of ISMM'98)*, H.J.A.M. Heijmans and J.B.T.M. Roerdink (eds.), pp. 35-42, June 1998.
7. A.M. Bruckstein, G. Sapiro, D. Shaked, "Evolutions of Planar Polygons", *Intern. J. of Pattern Recognition and Artificial Intelligence*, Vol. 9(6), pp. 991-1014, 1995.
8. G. Sapiro, "Geometric Partial Differential Equations in Image Analysis: Past, Present, and Future," *Proc. ICIP'95*, pp. 1-4, Vol. 3.
9. R. Kimmel, *Curve Evolution on Surfaces*, D.Sc. thesis, Technion–Israel Institute of Technology, June 1995.
10. Malladi, R. , and Sethian, J.A. , "Image Processing via Level Set Curvature Flow," *Proc. of the National Academy of Sciences*, Vol. 92(15), pp. 7046-7050, July 1995.
11. L. Rudin, S. Osher, and E. Fatemi, "Nonlinear Total Variation Based Noise Removal Algorithms," *Physica D*, 60:259-268, 1992.
12. H.J.A.M. Heijmans and R. van den Boomgaard, "Algebraic framework for linear and morphological scale-spaces," *CWI Report PNA-R0003*, Amsterdam, February 2000 (to appear in JVCIR).
13. A. Steiner, R. Kimmel, and A.M. Bruckstein,"Planar Shape Enhancement and Exaggeration," *Proc. ICPR 96'*, pp. 523-527, 1996.

Hierarchies of Partitions and Morphological Segmentation

Fernand Meyer

Centre de Morphologie Mathématique
Ecole des Mines de Paris, Fontainebleau, France

Abstract. Segmenting an image amounts to producing a partition, in which each tile represents an object of the image. Given an image, how to segment it into a predetermined number of regions ? How to select the objects to represent or discard when the number of regions varies ? Producing a series of nested partitions, or hierarchy is an answer to this question but is also central to practically all morphological segmentation approaches. In the present paper, we define, study, construct and show how to use for various segmention or filtering tasks such hierarchies.

1   Introduction

Segmenting an image amounts to producing a partition, in which each tile represents an object of the image. Segmentation is an extremely difficult task, as it requires some degree of semantic understanding of the images. The classical tool provided by mathematical morphology for segmenting images is the watershed, which sets the limits of the catchment basins of a topographic surface. The semantic analysis of the image is performed through the selection of a set of markers. By marker, we mean a binary set included in the object of interest ; it's exact location or shape has no importance. The strategies for finding markers are diverse and problem dependent ; many case studies are listed in [1] [2]. This classical segmentation process may be seen as a two stage process. In a first stage the watershed of the gradient image is constructed ; each frontier between two adjacent catchment basins is weighted by the altitude of its lowest pixel, which is a pass point between them. Suppressing all frontiers below some threshold λ produces a coarser partition. For increasing values of λ, one obtains a series of nested partitions, also called a hierarchy. The second stage of segmentation will then select the boundaries with the highest weight separating the markers. The quality of segmentation will depend upon the correct choice of markers and on the quality of the boundaries present in the hierarchy. Many efforts have focused on the selection of good markers and much less attention has been given to the construction of alternative hierarchies. It is the scope of the present paper to focus on the manifold of means to derive meaningful hierarchies from an image, in order to enrich the palette of available segmentation tools. We first define the hierarchies, study their algebraic structures and show how to construct new hierarchies by combination of preexisting ones. In a second section we show how the watershed line associated to increasing floodings of a topographic surface is able to construct hierarchies. We then present a series of particular modes of flooding and characterise the associated hierarchies. A third section shows new means

M. Kerckhove (Ed.): Scale-Space 2001, LNCS 2106, pp. 161–182, 2001.

to use hierarchies in segmentation. A last section considers another type of hierarchies associated to flooding, with the aim to simplify and filter images, without blurring or displacing contours.

2   The Lattice of Hierarchies

We are interested in segmenting images, that is functions of $\text{Fun}(E,\mathcal{T})$ where E represents the support of the images (a continuous domain or a discrete grid, in any number of dimensions) with value in $\mathcal{T}$ (in practice the set of reals or integers). The power set $\mathcal{P}(E)$ of E contains all subsets of E. The result of any segmentation of an image f of $\text{Fun}(E,\mathcal{T})$ will be a partition $\mathfrak{S}$ of E, that is a family (X_i) of elements of $\mathcal{P}(E)$ verifying: $X_i \wedge X_j = \infty$ for $i \neq j$ and $\bigcup X_j = E$. Often we are interested in representing an image not only as one partition but as a series of partitions with an increasing number of regions. Of particular interest is the case where these partitions are nested: every contour of a partition also belongs to all finer partitions. In such a case, coarser partitions are obtained by merging adjacent regions of finer partitions. Such nested partitions are called hierarchies. We now give an axiomatic definition of hierarchies [3] and study their properties.

2.1   Definition of a Hierarchy

2.1.1 Definition of a Tree and Its Elements. Let $\mathcal{A}$ be a subset of $\mathcal{P}(E)$, on which we consider the inclusion order relation. $\mathcal{A}$ is a dendrogram, if the following axiom is verified:

Axiom 1. *(Dendrogram Axiom)* $A, U, V \in \mathcal{A}$:
$A \subset U$ *and* $A \subset V \Rightarrow U \subset V$ *or* $V \subset U$

If $\mathcal{A}$ is a dendrogram, we may define:
- the summits: $\text{Sum}(\mathcal{A}) = \{A \in \mathcal{A} \mid \forall B \in \mathcal{A} : A \subset B \Rightarrow A = B\}$
- the leaves: $\text{Leav}(\mathcal{A}) = \{A \in \mathcal{A} \mid \forall B \in \mathcal{A} : B \subset A \Rightarrow A = B\}$
- the nodes: $\text{Nod}(\mathcal{A}) = \mathcal{A} - \text{Leav}(\mathcal{A})$
- the predecessors: $\text{Pred}(A) = \{B \in \mathcal{A} \mid B \subset A\}$
- the successors: $\text{Succ}(A) = \{B \in \mathcal{A} \mid A \subset B\}$

2.1.2 Definition of a Hierarchy. $\mathcal{A}$ is a hierarchy, if the two following axioms are verified:

Axiom 2. *(Intersection Axiom):* *two elements of $\mathcal{A}$ which are not comparable for the inclusion order have an empty intersection:* $A, B \in \mathcal{A}$: $A \cap B \in \{A, B, \emptyset\}$

Axiom 3. *(Union Axiom)* *Any element A of $\mathcal{A}$ is the union of all other elements of $\mathcal{A}$ contained in A:*
$\forall A \in \mathcal{A}: \bigcup \{B \in \mathcal{A} \mid B \subset A ; B \neq A\} = \{A, \emptyset\}$

Proposition 4. *The intersection axiom implies that A is a dendrogram for the inclusion order.*

Proof. If $A \subset U$ and $A \subset V$, then $U \cap V \neq \emptyset$, implying that $U \cap V = U$ or $U \cap V = V$, that is $V \subset U$ or $U \subset V$ showing that the dendrogram axiom is satisfied.

2.2   Stratified Hierarchies, Ultrametric Distances and Nested Partitions

$\mathcal{A}$ is a stratified hierarchy, if it is equipped with an index function st from $\mathcal{A}$ into $\mathcal{R}$ which is strictly increasing with the inclusion order: $\forall A, B \in \mathcal{A}$
$A \subset B$ and $B \neq A \Rightarrow \text{st}(a) < \text{st}(b)$

2.2.1 Ultrametric Distances on a Stratified Hierarchy.   Given a stratified hierarchy $\mathcal{A}$, for which the smallest stratification index st is equal to zero, a distance between the elements of $\mathcal{P}(E)$ is defined by $d(C, D)$, the index of the finest partition in which a tile contains both sets C and $D : \forall C, D \in \mathcal{P}(E)$
$d(C, D) = \inf \{\text{st}(A) \mid A \in \mathcal{A} : C \subset A \text{ and } D \subset A\}$
Properties : d is an ultrametric distance index:
$\forall A, B \in \mathcal{A} \quad d(A, B) = 0 \Rightarrow A = B$
$\forall C, D \in \mathcal{P}(E) \quad d(C, D) = d(D, C)$
$\forall B, C, D \in \mathcal{P}(E) \quad d(C, D) \leq \max \{d(C, B), d(B, D)\}$
    This last inequality is called ultrametric inequality, it is stronger than the triangular inequality. It expresses that the index of the smallest tile containing C and D is smaller or equal than the index or the smallest tile containing all three elements B, C and D.
    For $X \in \mathcal{P}(E)$ the closed ball of centre X and radius ρ is defined by $\text{Ball}(X, \rho) = \{D \in \mathcal{P}(E) \mid d(X, D) \leq \rho\}$. Each element of $\text{Ball}(X, \rho)$ is a centre of the ball. Furthermore the radius of a ball is equal to its diameter.
    Two closed balls $\text{Ball}(X, \rho)$ and $\text{Ball}(Y, \rho)$ with the same radius are either disjoint or identical: the balls of radius ρ form a partition. For increasing values of ρ we obtain nested partitions.

2.2.2 Stratification Associated to Nested Partitions.   Inversely the union of all tiles belonging to a series of nested partitions $(\mathfrak{S}_i)$ constitutes a hierarchy $\mathcal{A}$. Such a series of nested partitions $(\mathfrak{S}_i)$ may easily be generated from an initial fine partition $\mathfrak{S}_0 = \cup R_i$, $i = 1, \ldots, n$ on which a dissimilarity index δ is defined between neighboring tiles: if we merge all tiles of $\mathfrak{S}_0$ with a dissimilarity index below a given threshold λ, we obtain a coarser partition with a stratification index equal to λ. For increasing values of λ we obtain a series of nested partitions, forming a hierarchy $\mathcal{A}$. Of course, many different dissimilarity measures may be considered to weight the boundaries between adjacent tiles. If the tessellation is the result of the watershed construction on a gradient image, this dissimilarity measure can be defined as the lowest (or average) grey level value of the gradient image along the border separating the two regions. Other possible measures are color distances, various measures of local contrast, or even motion or texture dissimilarity.
    Such types of hierarchies can most economically be described as a weighted tree, defined as follows. The region adjacency graph (RAG) associated to $\mathfrak{S}_0$ is a non-directed graph $G = (X, U)$, where X is the set of nodes and U is the set of edges. Each element $x_i \in X$ represents a region $R_i \in \mathfrak{S}_0$. Two elements x_j and x_k are linked by an edge u_{jk} if and only if the corresponding regions R_j and R_k are neighbors ; the edge is assigned a weight $w_{jk} = \delta(x_i, x_j)$ measuring the dissimilarity between both regions. Let us suppose furthermore that all weights are different (this is not really a restriction, as in cases of equivalences it is always possible to introduce micro differences between

them.). A path on a graph is classically defined as a series of nodes $(x_1, x_2, ..., x_n)$ such that x_i and x_{i+1} are linked by an edge. We define the altitude of a path as the highest weight of the edges along this path ; this weight is called sup-section of the path. It is a well known result [4] that the union of all paths of smallest sup-section between two arbitrary nodes of the RAG is the minimum spanning tree (MST) T of the RAG:

* it spans the RAG: all nodes belong to it.

* it is a tree: it has no cycles. Between any two nodes there is a unique path on the tree.

* the total sum of weights of T is minimal among all possible spanning trees.

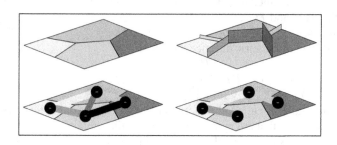

Fig. 1. 4 Equivalent Representations of Nested Partitions:
- as a fine partition with a dissimilarity index between neighboring regions
- as a topographic surface, where the height of the dam between regions represents their dissimilarity
- as a region adjacency graph
- as the minimum spanning tree of the RA.

There exists a unique path between the nodes x_i and x_j on the tree T. Let λ be the highest weight on this path. Merging all tiles of $\mathfrak{S}_0$ with a dissimilarity index below λ produces a coarser partition where x_i and x_j belong to different tiles ; merging also the tiles with dissimilarity equal to λ produces a still coarser partition for which now x, and x_j belong to the same tile. The smallest stratification index for which two regions R_i and R_j belong to a same tile of the hierarchy obviously constitutes an ultrametric distance between the corresponding nodes x_i and x_j. We call this ultrametric distance $\Theta(x_i, x_j) = \lambda$ or level distance between x_i and x_j, as it is the highest edge on the unique path of T between x_i and x_j. It is the greatest ultrametric distance which is below the dissimilarity δ and is called the subdominant ultrametric distance associated to δ.

Inversely, let us consider a spanning tree Θ. To any distribution of weights $W = (w_{jk})$ on the edges of Θ is associated an ultrametric distance $d_W(x_i, x_j)$, equal to the weight of the highest edge on the unique path between x_i and x_j. This property will be exploited intensively below in order to generate a manifold of useful hierarchies. In summary we have four equivalent representations for stratified hierarchies associated to a partition with a dissimilarity index (see fig.**??**). The first is the partition itself with the dissimilarity index δ between neighboring tiles. The second represents a topographic surface, in which a dam of 0 thickness separates adjacent tiles ; its height is equal to the distance δ between the tiles ; this representation will help unifying all morphological segmentation algorithms in terms of flooding. The third is the RAG and the last as the minimum spanning tree of the RAG.

2.3   The Lattice of Hierarchies

2.3.1 Supremum and Infimum of Two Hierarchies. Let $\mathcal{A}$ and $\mathcal{B}$ be two stratified hierarchies, with their associated distances: $d_{\mathcal{A}}$ and $d_{\mathcal{B}}$. The following relation defines an order relation between the hierarchies: $B < A \Leftrightarrow \forall C, D \in \mathcal{P}(E) \quad d_{\mathcal{A}}(C, D) \leq d_{\mathcal{B}}(C, D)$

With this order relation the stratified hierarchies of $\mathcal{P}(E)$ form a complete lattice. The maximal element is the hierarchy having E as only element and the smallest hierarchy contains all one pixel sets like $\{x\}$

The infimum of two hierarchies $\mathcal{A}$ and $\mathcal{B}$ is written $\mathcal{A} \wedge \mathcal{B}$ and is defined by its ultrametric distance $d_{\mathcal{A} \wedge \mathcal{B}} = d_{\mathcal{A}} \vee d_{\mathcal{B}}$. Its balls are defined by: $\text{Ball}_{\mathcal{A} \wedge \mathcal{B}}(X, \rho) = \text{Ball}_{\mathcal{A}}(X, \rho) \wedge \text{Ball}_{\mathcal{B}}(X, \rho)$

The supremum of two hierarchies $\mathcal{A}$ and $\mathcal{B}$ is written $\mathcal{A} \vee \mathcal{B}$ and is the smallest hierarchy larger than $\mathcal{A}$ and $\mathcal{B}$; as $d_{\mathcal{A}} \wedge d_{\mathcal{B}}$ is not an ultrametric distance, $d_{\mathcal{A} \vee \mathcal{B}}$ is the subdominant ultrametric distance associated to $d_{\mathcal{A}} \wedge d_{\mathcal{B}}$. If $\mathcal{A}_{\lambda}$, $\mathcal{B}_{\lambda}$ and $\mathcal{A}_{\lambda} \vee \mathcal{B}_{\lambda}$ are the partitions obtained by taking the balls of radius λ in each of the three hierarchies, then the boundaries of $\mathcal{A}_{\lambda} \vee \mathcal{B}_{\lambda}$ are all boundaries existing in both $\mathcal{A}_{\lambda}$ and $\mathcal{B}_{\lambda}$. The infimum and supremum of two hierarchies are illustrated in fig. 2

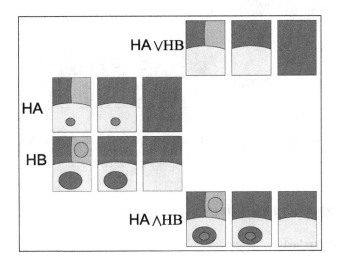

Fig. 2. Two Hierachies HA and HB and their Derived Supremumn and Infimum.

2.3.1 Lexicographic Fusion of Stratified Hierarchies. Let $\mathcal{A}$ and $\mathcal{B}$ be two stratified hierarchies, with their associated distances $d_{\mathcal{A}}$ and $d_{\mathcal{B}}$. In some cases, one of the hierarchies correctly represents the image to segment, but with a too small number of nested partitions. One desires to enrich the current ranking of regions as given by $\mathcal{A}$, by introducing some intermediate levels in the hierarchy. The solution is to combine the hierarchy $\mathcal{A}$ with another hierarchy $\mathcal{B}$ in a lexicographic order.

One produces the lexicographic hierarchy $\mathrm{Lex}(\mathcal{A}, \mathcal{B})$ by defining its ultrametric distance ; it is the largest ultrametric distance below the lexicographic distance $d_{\mathcal{A}, \mathcal{B}}$ classically defined by

$$d_{\mathcal{A}, \mathcal{B}}(C, D) > d_{\mathcal{A}, \mathcal{B}}(K, L) \Leftrightarrow$$
$$d_{\mathcal{A}}(C, D) > d_{\mathcal{A}}(K, L)$$
$$or$$
$$d_{\mathcal{A}}(C, D) = d_{\mathcal{A}}(K, L) \text{ and } d_{\mathcal{B}}(C, D) > d_{\mathcal{B}}(K, L)$$

Fig.3 present two hierarchies HA and HB and the derived lexicographic hierarchies $\mathrm{Lex}(\mathcal{A}, \mathcal{B})$ and $\mathrm{Lex}(\mathcal{B}, \mathcal{A})$.

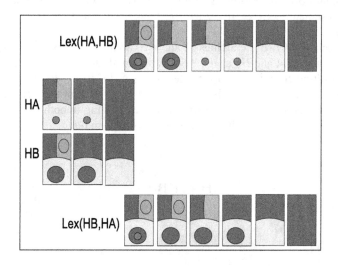

Fig. 3. Two Hierachies HA and HB and their Derived Lexigraphic Combinations.

3   Watershed and Floodings

3.1   The Watershed

We have now to describe how to derive hierarchies from images and how to use them for segmentation or filtering purposes. The answer will be flooding and watershed. The watershed line is a topographical entity ; a grey-tone image may indeed be considered as a topographical surface, where each pixel has an altitude proportional to its grey-tone. Let us now consider a drop of water falling on a topographic surface. If it falls outside a regional minimum, it will glide along a path of steepest descent until it reaches a minimum. The set of pixels drained by a given regional minimum forms the catchment basin of this minimum. The watershed line is the boundary between catchment basins. The trajectory of a drop of water falling on the surface is a geodesic line of a distance called topographic distance, defined in [5]. If two pixels p and q belong to such a geodesic line, the topographic distance between them is equal to the difference of altitudes between both pixels: $|f_p - f_q|$. Assigning to all regional minima the value 0 does not change the catchment basins, which may then be detected by a shortest distance algorithm: the catchment basin of a minimum is the set of pixels with a shorter topographic distance to this minimum than to any other minimum. In practice, a biased algorithm is used in order to create a partition: the pixels which are at an equal distance of two minima are assigned arbitrarily to one of the adjacent catchment basins. As a result of this choice, the union of the catchment basins forms a partition. This partition is the finest partition from which all other segmentations will be derived. In practice, an image is segmented by constructing the catchment basins of its gradient image, as illustrated in the following pictures.

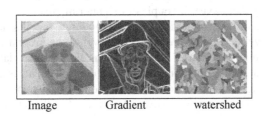

| Image | Gradient | watershed |

As each regional minimum generates a catchment basin, the obtained partition is often fragmented in a lot of tiny regions. We obtain a coarser partition if we reduce the number of minima. Flooding a topographic surface is an efficient way to reduce the number of its regional minima: after partial flooding, some catchment basins will be completely flooded and be absorbed by neighboring catchment basin. The next section defines and presents the properties of morphological flooding.

3.2   Definition of a Flooding

Notation: we write g_p for the value of the function g at pixel p. In what follows we consider that the domain E of the images is a discrete grid.

Definition 5. *A function g is a flooding of a function f if and only if $g \geq f$ and for any couple of neighboring pixels (p, q): $g_p > g_q \Rightarrow g_p = f_p$*

Definition 6. *Two pixels x, y belong to the same flat-zone of a function f if and only if there exists a n-tuple of pixels $(p_1, p_2, ..., p_n)$ such that $p_1 = x$ and $p_n = y$, and for all i, (p_i, p_{i+1}) are neighbours and verify $f_{p_i} = f_{p_i+1}$.*

"To belong to the same flat-zone" is an equivalence relation, whose equivalence classes are precisely the flat-zones.

Let g be a flooding of the function f. We call lake of g any flat-zone of g containing at least a pixel p for which $f_p > g_p$. Let L be such a lake. If all neighbors of L have a

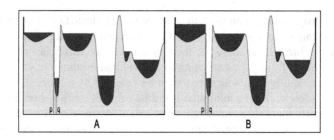

Fig. 4. A: A physically possible flooding; B: An impossible flooding, where a lake is limited by a wall of water at position p.

higher altitude, then L is a regional minimum. On the contrary, if L has a lower neighbor it is called full lake: there exists a couple of neighboring pixels (p, q), p belonging to L and $g_p > g_q$. According to the definition of floodings, this implies that $g_p = f_p$, meaning that the level of the flooding g and the level of the ground f are the same at pixel p ; hence the interpretation of the definition is simply that a lake cannot form a wall of water without solid ground in front to hold the water. This is clearly illustrated in fig.4, where the right figure cannot be a valid flooding, whereas the left figure is a valid one. The pixel p is then necessarily a pass point of g: the altitude of g decreases from p to the outside and the inside of the lake, and increases in both directions along the outside boundary of the lake (the altitude remains stable, if the lake has no higher neighbor).

By considering all neighbors of a central pixel, one easily derives the following criterion from the definition of a flooding.

Criterion *Flood*: A function g is a flooding of a function f if and only if $g = f \vee \varepsilon g$, where εg is the erosion of g with a structuring element equal to the central pixel and its first neighbors.

Remark: A flooding is a particular type of image filtering called leveling. There also exists a PDE implementation for constructing it.

3.3 Properties of Floodings

Creation of Lakes. Any flooding g of a function f creates a number of lakes on the topographic surface of f. All connected components where $g > f$ are flat, as shows the following property immediately derived from the definition:

for any couple of neighboring pixels (p, q): $\begin{vmatrix} g_q > f_q \\ g_p > f_p \end{vmatrix} \Rightarrow g_p = g_q$

Algebraic Properties. It is easy to check using their definition that:
* If g and h are two floodings of f, then $g \vee h$ and $g \wedge h$ also are floodings of f
* If g and h are floodings of f and $g \geq h$ then g is also a flooding of h. As a matter of fact, if h is a flooding of f then $h \geq f$. But $g \geq h$. Hence $g \geq h \geq f$.
On the other hand, g is a flooding of f, implying $\forall (p, q)$ neighbors: $g_p > g_q \quad\Rightarrow$ $f_p = g_p$ But since $g \geq h \geq f$, this implies $g_p = h_p$

* The relation $\{g$ is a flooding of $f\}$ is reflexive, antisymmetric and transitive: it is an order relation.

In particular, if f and h are two functions such that $f \leq h$, then the family of floodings (g^i) of f verifying $g^i \leq h$ form a complete lattice for this order relation. The smallest element is f itself. The largest is called flooding of f constrained by h (see fig. 5). It is obtained by repeating the geodesic erosion of h above f : $h^{(n+1)} = f \vee \varepsilon h^{(n)}$ until stability, that is until $h^{(n+1)} = h^{(n)}$. The criterion Flood given above shows that the result at convergence effectively is a flooding of f. Convergence may be obtained faster when using a recursive or a data driven implementation of the algorithm using hierarchical queues [6]. This operation also is known as reconstruction closing of f using h as marker.

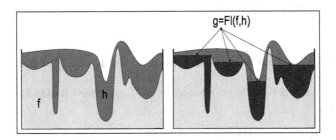

Fig. 5. $\text{Fl}(f, h)$ is the flooding of g (blue function) constrained by the function h (red function).

* These properties permit various constructions of increasing families of floodings (g^i): it is necessary and sufficient that g^j is a flooding .of g^{j-1}.

Construction of Floodings.

Uniform Flooding. A flooding of a function f is uniform if the level of all lakes is the same everywhere. A flooding f^λ at level λ is obtained simply by threshold:

$$f^\lambda = \begin{array}{l} f \text{ if } f > \lambda \\ \lambda \text{ if } f \leq \lambda \end{array}$$

Flooding with a Hierarchical Queue. A hierarchical queue is the ideal tool to implement floodings [6][5]. A hierarchical queue is a series of queues (working on a first in first out basis), each with a priority level ; lower altitudes meaning higher priority. A pixel entering the hierarchical queue is put in the queue with an altitude corresponding to its priority. Only one pixel is able to leave the queue at a time: it is the first pixel who entered the queue with highest priority. If we want to flood a surface f from a source X (a subset of E), we put all outside neighbors of X in the hierarchical queue. Each pixel leaving the queue is immediately flooded and all its unflooded neighbors are put into the queue. If the altitude of such a neighbor is below the current flooding level, the lake has attained the level of the smallest pass point on the boundary of the current catchment basin. If we stop after emptying the current queue, we will have produced a lake which is called full lake, as it is not a regional minimum anymore ; continuing the flooding will produce an overflood into the neighboring catchment basin.

Hierarchical queues naturally produce a flooding: lower pixels are flooded before higher pixels ; within a plateau, pixels are processed in the order of their distance to the lower border of the plateau. The same flooding mechanism is used for the construction of the watershed of a function f:

(a) Initialisation: give a label to each regional minimum put its inside boundary pixels in the hierarchical queue.

(b) If all queues are empty: END. Else, take a node j in the queue of lowest priority.

(c) For each unlabeled neighbouring node i of j do:

$\text{label}(i) = \text{label}(j)$;

put i in the queue with priority $p(i)$;

return to (b) ;

4   Hierarchy Associated to an Ordered Series of Floodings

4.1   Watershed and Floodings: Absorption of Catchment Basins During Flooding

If g is a flooding of f, how do the catchment basins of g relate to those of f ? We will call CB_f the catchment basins of f and CB_g those of g. Let m_i be a regional minimum of f and Y_i the associated CB_f. Two cases are possible. 1) m_i is not covered by a lake. m_i is then also a regional minimum of g and Y_i is included in a CB_g, which may have absorbed some full lakes of g 2) m_i is covered by a lake L. Then if L is a regional minimum of g, Y_i is included in the CB_g of L. On the contrary, if L is not a regional minimum of g, then L is a full lake and belongs to the same catchment basin as its lower neighbors. This analysis shows that in all cases each CB_f is included in a CB_g. Hence the partition of CB_f is finer than the partition of the CB_g.

4.2   Hierarchy of the Catchment Basins

Let us now consider a family of increasing floodings (g^i) of function f, verifying $g^i \leq g^j$ for $i < j$, and $g^0 = f$. As we have seen earlier, g^j is then a flooding of g^i for $i < j$. According to the previous section, the partition of CB_{g^i} is finer than the partition of the CB_{g^j} . The catchment basins of the family (g^i) are nested and form a hierarchy, for which we now characterise the associated ultrametric distance $d_{\mathcal{G}}$ and the minimum spanning tree $T_{\mathcal{G}}$. Consider two catchment basins of f, X_1 and X_2 associated to the minima m_1 and m_2. As we have seen in section 2.2.2, the ultrametric distance $d_{\mathcal{G}}(X_1, X_2)$ between them is the smallest index k such that X_1 and X_2 belong to the same catchment basin of g^k within the family (g^i) ; furthermore the hierarchy can be represented by a MST $T_{\mathcal{G}}$.

We will now state and establish an important property of all flooding hierarchies of a given function f.

Proposition: All minimum spanning trees representing a hierarchy associated to a series of increasing floodings of a given function f have the same nodes and edges ; they only differ by the distribution of weights.

In order to establish this result, we first characterize the minimum spanning tree T_f associated to the hierarchy produced by uniform flooding. We call T the unweighted tree having the same nodes and edges as T_f. We then come back to the general case of an arbitrary family of increasing floodings (g^i) and show how a new distribution of weights may be found on T in order to generate the hierarchy associated to (g^i).

4.2.1 Hierarchy Associated to Uniform Flooding.

Let G be the RAG of the topographic surface of f: its nodes are the CB_f, neighboring nodes are connected by an edge with a weight equal to the altitude of the smallest pass point between them. Between two minima m_1 and m_2 of the topographic surface f, there exist many paths ; among them there exists a path with lowest sup-section ; its highest point is a pass point p of f with altitude f_p. This path crosses a number of catchment basins of f, whose nodes also form a path of highest sup-section on the RAG G. Hence this path belongs to the minimum spanning tree T_f of G.

We now consider a uniform flooding of the function f, that is the family f^λ defined in section 3.3. The lowest level of flooding for which both minima m_1 and m_2 will be covered by a same lake and the associated catchment basins X_1 and X_2 be merged is then obviously equal to f_p, the highest altitude on the path with lowest sup-section between X_1 and X_2. This shows that the MST T_f effectively represents the hierarchy associated to uniform flooding.

4.2.2 Hierarchy Associated to Arbitrary Floodings.

Calling T the unweighted tree having the same nodes and edges as T_f, we now show that for an arbitrary series of increasing floodings (g^i) it is possible to find a distribution of weights on the edges of T, such that it represents the hierarchy associated to (g^i). This means that suppressing all edges of T with a weight superior to k produces a number of subtrees, representing each a catchment basin of g^k.

We first assign to all edges of T a weight equal to ∞. T is then able to represent the catchment basins of the zero flooding $g_0 = f$ suppressing all edges of the tree T with a positive weight creates isolated nodes, each of them representing a catchment basin of f. Let us now suppose that we have found a distribution of weights on T such that all hierarchies up to level i can be represented.

Let us show which weights have to be modified such that T also represents the catchment basins of g^{i+1}. Suppose that X and Y are catchment basins of g^i, which merge into a unique catchment basin Z of g^{i+1}. By hypothesis, X and Y can be correctly represented by the tree T. In order to show that it is also the case of Z, .we imagine a series of progressive floodings which transform g^i into g^{i+1} such that progressive fusions of catchment basins in this series of floodings can all be represented by edges of T:

1) Initialisation: $k = 0$; $h^k = g^i$;

2) chose a regional minimum W of h^k such that $h^k(W) < g^{i+1}(W)$.

* If such a minimum is found, flood the corresponding catchment basin until either (a) the level of $g^{i+1}(W)$ is reached or (b) until a full lake is created. As result we get a new flooding h^{k+1} of f. In case (a) h^k and h^{k+1} have the same catchment basins. In case (b) the full lake covering W has reached a pass point which corresponds to an

edge of T ; we assign to this edge a weight equal to $(i + 1)$ Like that the evolution of catchment basins between h^k and h^{k+1} can be expressed by the tree T.

* If there is none, this means that $h^k = g^{i+1}$ and we may exit, having produced a distribution of weights on T correctly representing g^{i+1}.

3) do $k = k + 1$ and go to (2).

The fact that a unique spanning tree is able to generate all hierarchies associated to increasing floodings is an important factor of speed and simplicity for morphological segmentation algorithms: it is sufficient to construct the tree T once and derive from it all morphological segmentation results, just by changing its weights. Furthermore, T represents a huge reduction in the amount of information to process: it is dimensionless whatever the number of dimensions of the domain E and each of its nodes represents a whole catchment basin of f. Being a tree, it has $N - 1$ edges for N nodes.

4.3   Useful Families of Floodings

We now have to indicate the principal and most useful families of floodings used in morphological and multiscale segmentations. As a matter of fact, the quality of segmentation will depend to a great extent on the family of floodings on which it is build. We already presented the uniform flooding, which is the simplest.

4.3.1 Size Oriented Flooding.   Size oriented flooding may be visualised as a process where sources are placed at each minimum of a topographic surface and pour water in such a way that all lakes share some common measure (height, volume or area of the surface). As the flooding proceeds, some lakes eventually become full lakes, as the level of the lowest pass point has been reached. Let L be such a full lake. The source of L stops pouring water and its lake is absorbed by a neighboring catchment basin X, where an active source is still present. Later the lake present in X will reach the same level as L, both lakes merge and continue growing together. Finally only one source remains active until the whole topographical surface is flooded. The series of floodings indexed by the measure of the lakes generates a size oriented hierarchy.

In fig.6, a flooding starts from all minima in such a way that all lakes always have uniform depth, as long as they are not full. The resulting hierarchy is called dynamics in case of depth driven flooding and has first been introduced by M.Grimaud[7]. Deep catchment basins represent objects which are contrasted ; such objects will take long before being absorbed by a neighboring catchment basin. The most contrasted one will absorb all others. This criterion obviously takes only the contrast of the objects into account and not their size. If we control the flooding by the area or the volume of the lakes, the size of the objects also is taken into consideration [8]; in multimedia applications, good results are often obtained by using as measure the volume of the lakes, as if each source would pour water with a constant flow This is illustrated by the following figures. The topographical surface to be flooded is a colour gradient of the initial image (maximum of the morphological gradients computed in each of the R, G and B colour channels). Synchronous volumic flooding has been used, and 3 levels of fusions have been represented, corresponding respectively to 15, 35 and 60 regions.

As a summary, the depth criterion ranks the region according to their contrast, the area according to their size and the volume offers a nice balance between size and contrast as illustrated in fig.7 where we have illustrated the differences between the criteria

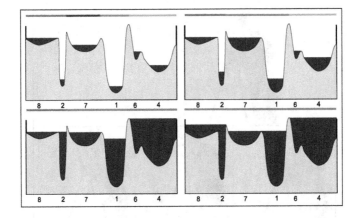

Fig. 6. Example of a height synchronous flooding. Four levels of flooding are illustrated; each of them is topped by a figuration of the corresponding catchment basins.

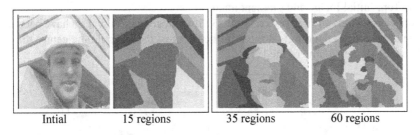

Intial   15 regions   35 regions   60 regions

used for controling the progression of the lakes. The initial image and its gradient are illustrated on the top row. Then 3 types of synchronous flooding are used. In the first (bottom left) the lakes grow with uniform depth, resulting in a pyramid where the most contrasted regions survive longest. In the second (bottom center) the area is used and the largest regions are favoured. In the last (bottom right) the volume of the lakes is used, offering a good balance between size and contrast of the regions. For each hierarchy the partition with 70 tiles is selected and each tile replaced by its mean grey tone, for the purpose of illustration.

4.3.2 Tailored Flooding for Favoring Some Types of Regions.

In some cases, while using one of the size criteria, it appears desirable to favor some regions. This happens if one knows beforehand that regions with some particular characteristics are important. As an example: in many cases, the topographic surface to be flooded is the gradient image ∂h of an image h. The catchment basins of ∂h correspond to flat zones in h, which may be regional minima, maxima or step zones. However minima and maxima of h are perceptually more important than transition flat zones. For this reason, it may be worthwhile to push minima and maxima of h higher in the hierarchy.

It is easy to obtain this result during synchronous flooding: by reducing the rate of flow in the corresponding minima. The more important a region is, the more the

Fig. 7. Top: Initial Image and gradient image
Bottom: 3 partitions with 70 regions each. 3 different geometric criteria have been used during synchronous flooding: on the left, the depth of the lakes, in the centre the area and on the left the volume of the lakes.

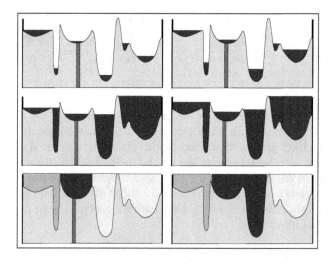

Fig. 8. 4 levels of tailored synchronous flooding, where the minimum marked red is slowed down by a factor 5. As a result we show the corresponding segmentation into 3 regions compared to the segmentation in 3 regions if no source is slowed down.

flow of its minima has to be reduced. In fig. 8 we have a case where depth synchronous flooding is performed. However the depth of the minimum marked by a black bar grows five times slower than the depth in the other catchment basins. For this reason, this particular minimum survives much longer any absorption. The interest of such markers is clearly illustrated in fig.9, where two segmentations without and with slowing down the flooding are compared. A fine partition is created first ; the color flat zones are detected and the largest of them serve as markers for flooding a colour gradient image (top right picture). Then a second gradient image is constructed on the boundaries of the fine partition and this new image is flooded according volumic criteria. The result is illustrated by the bottom pictures. On the left, the rate of flood is the same in all minima, on the right, regiona have been selected by hand in the faces of the angels, and their rate of flow reduced by a factor 50. Then 2 partitions have been selected in the hierarchy with the same number of regions showing that the faces of the angels merge with the background if their flooding is not slowed down.

4.3.3 Flooding in the Presence of Markers.

Markers are a limit case of the preceding situation. One wishes that the marked regions are present at the top of the hierarchy. This will be the case if the rate of flow in the marked minima is infinitely slowed down ; in other terms such minima have no source at all. Hence they stay minima for ever, and catch their neighboring basins as illustrated in fig. 10 If there are N minima, cutting the $N - 1$ highest edges of the MST yields a partition of N regions, containing a marker each. Cutting more than $N - 1$ edges shows how the regions are further subdivided in finer segmentations ; in this case, the criterion used for controling the flooding (depth, area or volume of the lakes) has an effect on the finer segmentations.

It is interesting to observe the resulting flooding at convergence: the only remaining minima are the marked minima, all others are full lakes. Let us consider two marked minima m_1 and m_2 for which the resulting catchment basins X_1 and X_2 are neighbors. The lowest pass point between X_1 and X_2 corresponds to an edge of the minimum spanning tree T_f of the RAG ; more precisely it is the edge with the highest valuation in the unique path joining m_1 and m_2 within T_f. From this we infer another method of segmenting with markers: cut the edge with the highest weight on the MST T_f between any couple of markers. Suppressing on each of these paths the edge with highest weight results produces a minimum spanning forest, where each tree is rooted in a marker. This method of segmentation with markers is extremely powerful as it only uses the minimum spanning tree. Of course, the minimum spanning tree representing the hierarchy of any series of increasing floodings can be used. Traditionaly morphological segmentation uses the hierarchy of uniform flooding ; however in some cases better results are obtained by using another hierarchy, for instance a size oriented hierarchy. This opens the way to a new segmentation mode with markers: in a first stage construct a hierarchy which is well adapted to the problem ; for instance use volumic size flooding, in order to obtain a hierarchy which better represents the relative importance of the different regions. And in a second stage, use the set of weights of this new hierarchy for segmenting with markers.

Finally, size oriented flooding, tailored flooding and flooding with markers may be regrouped: each minimum may be considered as a fuzzy marker, by assigning to it a fuzzy level: 1 means a hard marker, where no source is placed ; 0 means no marker at

Fig. 9. Top row: Initial image and fine segmentation
Bottom row: Segmentation without and with fuzzy markers placed in the faces of the angels.Both partitions have the same number of regions.

all, and the source is not slowed down ; λ means a fuzzy marker, and the corresponding source is slowed down by a factor λ. Fuzzy markers permit to establish a continuum between traditional multiscale segmentation and segmentation with markers.

4.3.4 Cataclysmic Floodings. A flooding g of a function f is cataclysmic if each catchment basin of f is occupied by a full lake. Some of these lakes are regional minima of g ; others are not. The catchment basins of g constitute the first level of the hierarchy (see fig.11). The resulting function g itself may then be submitted to a new cataclysmic flooding and again the number of catchment basins will be strongly reduced. Repeating this flooding in sequence a few times generally produces an image where only one region remains.

   A cataclysmic flooding of an image f is easy to produce through a constrained flooding. The constraining function is equal to f on the watershed line of f and equal

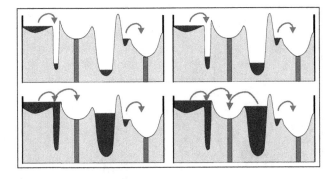

Fig. 10. Flooding in the presence of markers. The catchment basins with markers have no source at all. The arrows show in which order the catchment basins are absorbed one by another.

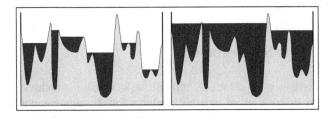

Fig. 11. Two levels of cataclysmic flooding of a topographic surface.

to ∞ everywhere else. The process is illustrated in 1 dimension in fig. 12 and also for a single basin in 2 dimensions in fig. 13.

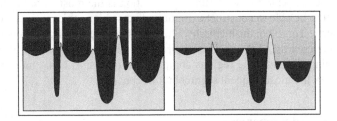

Fig. 12. Constrained flooding for producing a cataclysmic flooding.

Repeating the same extremal flooding on the result of the first extremal flooding again will drastically reduce the number of catchment basins. This process may then be repeated until a partition is created with only one catchment basin. Like that we obtain a series of nested partitions which decreases extremely rapidly.

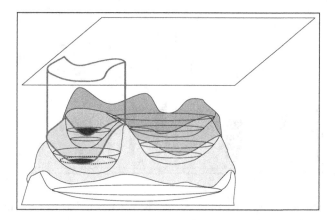

Fig. 13. Cataclysmic flooding: the constraining function is equal to 0 on the watershed line and to Ω everywhere else.

5   Application to Segmentation

Segmenting an image is an extremely difficult task. Using hierarchies offers a great help: a hierarchy offers a set of possible contours for the segmentation to construct. Instead of searching the contours blindly among all pixels of the image, segmenting through a hierarchy will select only contours present in one of the nested partition present in the hierarchy. Furthermore, each contour is weighted by the rank of the finest partition in which it does not exist anymore. For this reason, a number of segmentation tasks may be expressed as finding the strongest contours between a set of markers, or finding the best segmentation in a number of predefined regions. Hierarchical segmentation offers also new ways for interactive segmentation: For each part of the image, one is able to chose the scale for which the segmentation is the most easy. For this reason it is important to be able to construct extremely diverse hierarchies in order to offer for each segmentation problem the hierarchy which presents the best scale of contours : one may favour the contrast of the regions, their colour, their size. One may also, through tailored flooding, favour some regions compared to others, as being more important. We present now the most frequent segmentation scenarios.

5.1   Unsupervised Segmentation

The primary aim of a hierarchical approach is to be able to easily produce segmentations with an arbitrary number of regions. To the question "what is the best segmentation into n regions", the answer is easy. One produces through flooding the gradient of the image a hierarchy and choses the stratification index for which a partition with n tiles is produced. Such situations are met in object oriented coding applications: the image is encoded as a partition. To each degree of compression corresponds a partition with a given number of regions. Such an encoder must be able to segment an image in any number of regions.

5.2   Segmentation with Markers

Flooding with markers is the most used morphological segmentation method [1] [2], as it permits an easy and robust way to introduce semantics into the segmentation process: the objects to segment are first recognised and a marker is produced. It may be the segmentation produced in the preceding frame when one has to track an object in a sequence. It may also be some markers produced either by hand or automatically. Position and shape of the marker have no importance, yielding robustness. In a second phase the contours are found. We have seen earlier how to flood a topographic surface in presence of markers. The analysis of the result has shown that segmenting with markers amount to suppressing the highest edge on the unique path linking two markers within the MST T. Interactive situation may be implemented through markers: a first set of markers is defined by hand or automatically. The corresponding segmentation is constructed. Then the result is corrected by manually editing the set of markers. The update of the partition after each edition may be done without a new flooding.

As we have seen in section 4.3.3, segmenting with markers amouts to construct a minimum spanning forest, by cutting from T the edges with the highest weights between all couples of markers. An added marker m_i will belong to a tree of this forest, which is rooted in a marker m_k. Within this tree, there exists a unique path between m_k and m_i ; cutting the highest edge on this path yields the new segmentation. Alternatively, suppressing a marker m_k means assigning the corresponding tree to an adjacent tree, by adding to it the edge of T with lowest weight, leading to one of the neighboring trees.

5.3   Interactive Segmentation

Besides the traditional segmentation technique based on markers, new interactive segmentation techniques based on hierarchies are under development [9]. A hierarchy is constructed and explored with a pointing device such as a mouse. A mouse position is defined by its (x, y) coordinates in the image but also by its depth z in the segmentation tree. If the mouse is active, the whole tile containing the cursor is activated and added or suppressed from the segmentation mask. For the same (x, y) position, a mouse displacement towards lower levels of the hierarchy will result in a resegmentation of the region, whereas a displacement towards higher levels represents a fusion of adjacent regions. The desired segmentation is constructed as a painting process, in which the brush adapts its shape to the boundaries of the object: higher level of the hierarchy produce a larger brush, lower levels a smaller brush (see fig. 14)

6   Hierarchies and Filtering

Each morphological notion has a dual counterpart. Let us consider a grey tone image f. If we negate f, flood $-f$ and again negate the result, we will have suppressed some peaks of the topographic surface. This dual operation of flooding is called razing. To the constrained flooding presented earlier $\text{Fl}(f, h)$ corresponds a constrained razing $\text{Rz}(f, h)$. Similarly, if we construct the watershed line Wsh of the function $-f$ and negate the result, we obtain the thalweg line of f. As we have seen earlier, cataclysmic

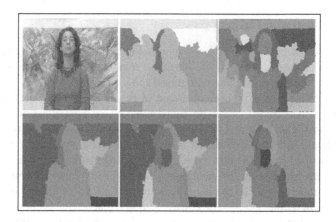

Fig. 14. Top row: a) initial image ; b) and c) two levels of the hierarchy associated to volumic flooding.
Bottom row: An initial partition of the hierarchy is selected. Some of its regions are split and others merged until the desired result is obtained.

flooding is the largest flooding of f below the constraining function equal to f on the watershed line of f and equal to the maximal value Ω everywhere else. After such a cataclysmic flooding, all CB contain a full lake. The dual operator would be cataclysmic razing.

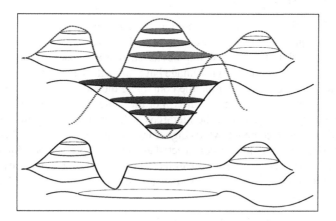

Fig. 15. Cataclysmic flooding and razing for filtering a topographic surface.

Fig.15 presents a CB in which a full lake has taken place. The boundary of this CB is a portion of the watershed line on which 3 regional maxima may be seen. These regional maxima are separated by portions of the thalweg line. As illustrated, the watershed line and the thalweg line intersect at the position of saddle points. The smallest saddle point on the boundary of a catchment basin becomes the level of the full lake whereas the highest saddle point on the piece of thalweg surrounding a regional maximum becomes the level of the full razing. So if a regional minimum and a regional maximum have a saddle point s in common then the full lake filling this regional minimum will be below or equal to f_s and the level of the full razing lowering the regional maximum will be higher than f_s. If a regional minimum and a regional maximum are neighbors but have no common saddle point, then the level of flooding in one and razing in the other are not coupled: it may then happen that the the altitude of a pixel should increase during cataclysmic flooding and at the same time decrease if a cataclysmic razing is done in parallel. For avoiding such situations we perform a cataclysmic flooding followed by a cataclysmic razing. Or alternatively a cataclysmic razing followed by a cataclysmic flooding. Both possibilities give the same result in all parts of the image were the watershed and thalweg lines cross. In fig. 16 we present 5 successice steps of simplification of the same image. In order to have a better control on the result, one may wish avoiding cataclysms: each step of cataclysmic razing fills a number of full lakes and suppresses a number of full blobs ; one may select a number of them for a reintroduction in the image. For instance, one may wish to keep the most contrasted ones and only suppress the smaller ones, corresponding to noise or less significant details. Other criteria, like area or volume of blobs and lakes also may be used.

7   Conclusion

Hierarchies of nested partitions offer a powerful representation of images as they convey all potential contours for a given segmentation task. We have established the link between floodings and hierarchies through the watershed transform. All traditional morphological segmentation methods may be expressed in this framework and new ones may be devised, as we have seen with interactive segmentation. As segmenting an image is extremely difficult, it is important to have a large toolbox of tools available. We do not pretend being able to segment every image. However we have large degrees of freedom in the choice of the right tools for a given task: choice of the best hierarchy, introduction of extraneous knowledge or semantics through fuzzy markers and possibility to implement a versatile mode of interaction.

References

1. S. Beucher. *Segmentation d'Images et Morphologie Mathématique*. PhD thesis, E.N.S. des Mines de Paris, 1990.
2. F. Meyer and S. Beucher. Morphological segmentation. 1(1):21–46, September 1990.
3. J. P. Benzécri. *L'analyse des données 1. La taxinomie*, chapter 3, pages 119–153. Dunod, 1973.
4. T.C. Hu. The maximum capacity route problem. *Operation research 9*, pages 898–900, 1961.
5. F. Meyer. Topographic distance and watershed lines. *Signal Processing*, pages 113–125, 1994.
6. F. Meyer. Algorithmes à base de files d'attente hiérarchique. Technical Report NT-46/90/MM, September 1990.

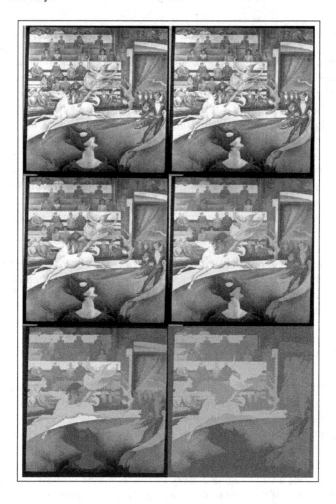

Fig. 16. 6 steps of cataclysmic filtering.

7. M. Grimaud. New measure of contrast : dynamics. *Image Algebra and Morphological Processing III, San Diego CA, Proc. SPIE*, 1992.
8. C. Vachier. *Extraction de Caractéristiques, Segmentation d'Image et Morphologie Mathématique*. PhD thesis, E.N.S. des Mines de Paris, 1995.
9. F. Meyer M. F. Zanoguera, B. Marcotegui. An interactive colour image segmentation system. In *Wiamis'99: Workshop on Image Analysis for Multimedia Interactive Services*, pages 137–141. Heinrich-Hertz Institut Berlin, 1999.

On the Behavior of Spatial Critical Points under Gaussian Blurring

A Folklore Theorem and Scale-Space Constraints

Marco Loog[1], Johannes Jisse Duistermaat[2], and Luc M.J. Florack[2]

[1] Image Sciences Institute, University Medical Center
Utrecht, The Netherlands
marco@isi.uu.nl
[2] Department of Mathematics, Utrecht University
Utrecht, The Netherlands

Abstract. The main theorem we present is a version of a "Folklore Theorem" from scale-space theory for nonnegative compactly supported functions from $\mathbb{R}^n$ to $\mathbb{R}$. The theorem states that, if we take the scale in scale-space sufficiently large, the Gaussian-blurred function has only one spatial critical extremum, a maximum, and no other critical points.

Two other interesting results concerning nonnegative compactly supported functions, we obtain are:

1. a sharp estimate, in terms of the radius of the support, of the scale after which the set of critical points consists of a single maximum;

2. all critical points reside in the convex closure of the support of the function.

These results show, for example, that all catastrophes take place within a certain compact domain determined by the support of the initial function and the estimate mentioned in 1.

To illustrate that the restriction of nonnegativity and compact support cannot be dropped, we give some examples of functions that fail to satisfy the theorem, when at least one assumption is dropped.

Keywords and Phrases. Large-scale behavior, loss of detail, nonnegative function, compact support, spatial critical point, deep structure.

1 Introduction

In this paper we discuss a "Folklore Theorem" from scale-space that could be roughly stated as follows: if a function $f : \mathbb{R}^n \to \mathbb{R}$ is blurred sufficiently, then the blurred function has a single critical point, which is an extremum. The intuitive idea behind this theorem is appealing: if scale is taken sufficiently large, every detail of the function will be lost (as scale increases "images become less articulated", one sees the "erosion of structure" as Koenderink calls it [7]), because they are too small with respect to the scale. All that is left is a blurred function virtually indistinguishable from a single Gaussian blob. This theorem, however, is false. *The principal aim of this article* is the formulation of certain

M. Kerckhove (Ed.): Scale-Space 2001, LNCS 2106, pp. 183–192, 2001.

restrictions on the functions considered, that leads to the Folklore Theorem to hold.

As we will see in Subsection 3.1, the falseness is already shown by a simple example like the nth order ($n > 0$) derivative of a one-dimensional Gaussian, or an arbitrary periodic function.

The theorem we present (Subsection 3.2) states that for nonnegative functions $f : \mathbb{R}^n \to \mathbb{R}_{\geq 0}$ (where $\mathbb{R}_{\geq 0}$ stands for the set of nonnegative real numbers) with compact support, it *does* hold that f_σ, which is f at scale σ, has only one critical point for all σ larger than a certain scale ς. To show that the restriction of nonnegativity or compact support cannot be dropped in general, we discuss in Subsection 3.3 some examples which illustrate this. Especially the example in which we retain the compact support, but drop the nonnegativity is counter-intuitive and an interesting observation.

A further result we present is a sharp estimate of the scale ς, in terms of the radius of the support, after which we certainly have a unique maximum. This, together with a result presented in Section 4, which states that all spatial critical points of a blurred function reside in the convex closure of the support of the initial function, gives us a certain bounded domain within scale-space to which attention can be restricted, when for example, tracking down catastrophes [1], finger-prints [9], or other potentially interesting features [3].

Most of the results are presented and proven in quite a formal way. However, the proofs of these results are postponed to Appendix A to keep the text more readable. The next section gives some definitions and notations, which are used in the remainder of the article. Section 5 provides the discussion and the conclusions.

2   Definitions and Notations

We start with the formal definitions of the support of a function, and the radius of the support.

Definition 1. *The support* supp(f) *of a function* $f : \mathbb{R}^n \to \mathbb{R}$ *is*

$$\operatorname{supp}(f) := \overline{\{x \in \mathbb{R}^n | f(x) \neq 0\}},$$

where the line indicates that the closure of the set is taken. The radius r(f) *of the support of the function* f, *is defined as the smallest radius of a ball containing* supp(f).

We also define Gaussian blurring of a function from which scale-space is generated.

Definition 2. *Let the Gaussian kernel* $g_\sigma : \mathbb{R}^n \to \mathbb{R}$, *for* $\sigma \in \mathbb{R}_{\geq 0}$, *be defined as:*

$$g_\sigma(x) := (2\pi\sigma^2)^{-\frac{n}{2}} e^{-\frac{\|x\|^2}{2\sigma^2}}.$$

Furthermore, given a function $f : \mathbb{R}^n \to \mathbb{R}$, *let the function* $f_\sigma : \mathbb{R}^n \to \mathbb{R}$ *be defined as:*

$$f_\sigma(x) := (f * g_\sigma)(x) = \int_{\mathbb{R}^n} f(y)\, g_\sigma(x - y)\, dy,$$

to which we refer as the blurred function f_σ at a fixed scale σ. Scale-space is defined as the complete family of functions f_σ, with $\sigma \in \mathbb{R}_{\geq 0}$.

3   Large-Scale Behavior of Critical Points

This section presents the theorem that states that for nonnegative functions f with compact support, it holds that f_σ has only one critical point for all σ larger than a certain scale ς. However, we first discuss shortly two simple examples, which show that the theorem cannot hold for general (integrable) functions.

3.1   Arbitrary Number of Critical Points

Example 1. Derivatives of the normalized Gaussian function define an autoconvolution algebra, i.e., if D_k denotes a partial derivative operator with multi-index order, $k = (k_1, \ldots, k_n)$, then $D_k g_\sigma * D_l g_\tau = D_{k+l} g_{\sqrt{\sigma^2 + \tau^2}}$. In particular this implies that derivatives of a normalized Gaussian are, topologically speaking, blur invariant, hence their critical points are preserved regardless of the amount of blurring.

Example 2. As a second example, note that $\sin(\langle \omega, x \rangle)$ and $\cos(\langle \omega, x \rangle)$, with $\omega, x \in \mathbb{R}^n$ are eigenfunctions under Gaussian blurring with eigenvalue $e^{-\frac{1}{2}\sigma^2 \|\omega\|^2}$. Thus the same conclusion can be drawn regarding their (infinite number of) critical points as in the previous example: the number of critical points remains equal for all scales and is infinite. Cf. [6], for an analysis of the behavior of the extrema at large scale, in which functions are considered that are periodic, band-limited, and one-dimensional.

Clearly, in general, the Folklore Theorem does not hold. Moreover, both examples in this section show that we can construct functions with an arbitrary number, ranging from one to infinite, of extrema at all scales. Hence, we look for restrictions on a function, that do lead to the behavior that only a single large-scale extremum exists beyond scale, say, ς. As Example 1 shows, requiring the function to satisfy: $\lim_{\|x\| \to \infty} f(x) = 0$ is not enough; it is still possible that an arbitrary number of critical points coexist to an arbitrarily large scale.

3.2   Nonnegative and Compactly Supported Functions

If we restrict the functions to compactly supported functions, it seems reasonable to expect the Folklore Theorem. Because the function is compactly supported, its support is bounded and has a maximal radius, say r, so, one expects that for scales that are large enough – proportional to r – there is not much more left of the blurred function then something similar to a Gaussian, in which one can no longer distinguish any kind of detail. However, as we will see in Subsection 3.3, this restriction is still too weak to make the theorem hold. We need an extra restriction, which is the requirement that the function is nonnegative.

Theorem 1. *Given a nonnegative function $f : \mathbb{R}^n \to \mathbb{R}$ with compact support. If $\mathrm{r}(f)$ equals r, then f_σ has exactly one critical point for every $\sigma > r$. This unique critical point is a maximum.*

Refer to Appendix A for the proof.

Remark 1. Without further proof, we mention that the foregoing estimate is sharp, in the sense that given a support with radius r, it is possible to construct a nonnegative, compactly supported function f such that f_σ has multiple extrema for all σ arbitrarily close to r. The idea is to construct a nonnegative function f that is compactly supported with $\mathrm{r}(f) = r$, and comes arbitrarily close to the sum of two Dirac functions on $\mathbb{R}^n$ separated by a distance equal to $2r$.

The result stated in Theorem 1, in combination with Remark 1, suggests that we should call 2σ, and not just σ, the scale of f_σ at which f is observed (cf. [4,7,8]).

Remark 2. Under much weaker assumptions, one has the following weaker result, which however still might be useful. The proof, of which we do not give the details here, starts with an estimate from below for the quantity $\int f(y) \, g_\sigma(x - y) \, dy$, which appears in the denominator of the mapping F in the proof of Theorem 1. In the estimate, we use the assumption that $x \in B_{\delta\sigma}$.

Theorem. *Assume that $\int_{\mathbb{R}^n} \|y\|^2 |f(y)| \, dy < \infty$ and $\int_{\mathbb{R}^n} f(y) \, dy > 0$ (the case that $\int_{\mathbb{R}^n} f(y) \, dy < 0$ can be treated analogously). Let B_r denote the ball with radius r and center at the origin. Then there exists a $\delta > 0$ and a $\sigma_0 > 0$ such that for every $\sigma > \sigma_0$ the restriction of f_σ to $B_{\delta\sigma}$ has precisely one critical point $\xi(\sigma)$, which is a maximum. Furthermore, if $\sigma \to \infty$, then $\xi(\sigma)$ converges to*

$$\frac{\int_{\mathbb{R}^n} y f(y) dy}{\int_{\mathbb{R}^n} f(y) dy}.$$

In the next subsection it is shown that the restrictions on the function cannot be dropped in general.

3.3   Nonnegative or Compactly Supported Functions

Dropping one of the requirements on the function in Theorem 1 can lead to examples of functions for which the theorem does not hold. We present three examples, which illustrate this. The first two are straightforward and are presented without rigorous proof. For the third one, it is demonstrated that the theorem does not hold.

Note that Examples 1 and 2 of Subsection 3.1 illustrate what can happen when both assumptions are dropped. The first and third example we present in this subsection do not require the initial function to be compactly supported. However, what we do require in the third example is that if $\|x\|$ goes to infinity that the value of the function goes to zero. In the second example we drop the nonnegativity assumption.

Example 3. As in Example 2, we consider periodic functions, however now we require the functions to be nonnegative. Hence, consider a bounded periodic function, and add a suitable constant so as to make it nonnegative. Note that a constant function is blur-invariant, and that its addition has no affect on critical points. Thus even positive functions may have multiple (in this case infinitely many) critical points that survive at all scales.

Example 4. In this example, we show that things can go wrong when dropping the nonnegativity assumption, but not the compactness requirement. We think that this result is quite counter-intuitive, because one would expect that if the support of the initial function is bounded, this restricts the size of the possible details that can be present in a function (e.g. an image) and so there should be a finite scale σ for which f_σ consists of one Gaussian-like blob. Hence f_σ should have a unique extremum.

However, it is quite easy to construct compactly supported functions that do not satisfy Theorem 1. To do so, let f be nonnegative, compactly supported, n-times differentiable, and one-dimensional. First, note that all derivatives of f are also compactly supported. Now, because f satisfies the assumptions of the theorem and hence has a single maximum for large scales, the nth-order derivatives still has, at least, $n + 1$ extrema for large scales.

Remark 3. Most images reflect a certain physical spatial and/or temporal measurements, and most of these measured physical quantities are nonnegative, because there is some clear absolute zero. So, there seems to be, at least in practice, hardly any loss of generality in restricting the class of admissible functions to nonnegative functions. However, quit often we do not study the function itself, but for example its first or second order derivative, or its Laplacian, and hence there are multiple critical points at large scales in general.

Example 5. A last example we give, is the function, $f := \sum_{k=0}^{\infty} 2^{-k\mu} \delta_{2^k} * g_s$ for some $s > 0$, here $\delta_{2^k} := \delta(\cdot - 2^k)$, which is the Dirac function situated in 2^k. Interesting about this function f is that its first mth-order moments, with $m < \mu$ are finite, i.e., $\int_{\mathbb{R}} x^m f(x)\, dx < \infty$ for all $m < \mu$, and f goes to zero when $|x|$ goes to infinity.

These two conditions do not hold for the function from Example 3, but do hold for the compactly supported functions in Theorem 1. One could think of these conditions as restrictions on the speed of growth of the function, and one might expect that these requirements are sufficient for the theorem to hold. In Appendix A, however, it is demonstrated that this nonnegative function has more than one extremum for large scales $\sigma \in \mathbb{R}_{\geq 0}$.

4 Spatial Constraints for Critical Points

In Section 3, we gave an explicit estimate of a scale ς beyond which there is only one spatial maximum for f_σ when $\sigma > \varsigma$. This gives a lower bound for the scale beyond which it might be needless to analyze the function f_σ any further, because further blurring does not bring further topological changes to the function as it remains a single blob upon succussive blurring.

In this section we present a result, Theorem 2, that also puts spatial constraints on the region of interest of scale-space. Again, it is required for the theorem to hold that the function is nonnegative. Moreover, the result becomes really useful, when the function is also compactly supported, which is exemplified by Corollary 1.

Theorem 2. *Let the function f be nonnegative, then every spatial critical point of f_σ is in the closure of the convex hull of* $\mathrm{supp}(f)$.

Refer to Appendix A for the proof.

As a direct consequence of Theorems 1 and 2, we can, for example, restrict the region in scale-space that would be of interest when we want to track down toppoints (i.e. scale-space catastrophes $(x, \sigma) \in \mathbb{R}^n \times \mathbb{R}_{\geq 0}$ for which

$$\mathrm{grad} f_\sigma(x) = 0 \wedge \det \left(\frac{\partial^2 f_\sigma}{\partial x_j x_k}(x) \right)_{jk} = 0,$$

see [1]) of compactly supported, nonnegative functions f.

Corollary 1. *For a nonnegative function f with compact support, all toppoints in scale-space are situated in $C \times [0, \mathrm{r}(f)] \subset \mathbb{R}^n \times \mathbb{R}_{\geq 0}$, where C is the convex closure of* $\mathrm{supp}(f)$.

5   Conclusions and Discussion

This article presented two theorems which, for example, enable us to restrict the interesting region in scale-space, with respect to toppoints.

The first, and main, theorem states that if a nonnegative function with compact support is blurred sufficiently, there is a scale for which any further blurring does not give rise to a topological change: the function is a single blob, and remains a single blob upon succussive blurring. This is a particular version of, what we called a "Folklore Theorem": if a function $f : \mathbb{R}^n \to \mathbb{R}$ is blurred sufficiently, then the blurred function has a single critical point, which is an extremum.

This result might be clear intuitively, because the function has only a bounded domain where one can distinguish details (or structure [7]), and so one expects that if scale is taken large enough every single detail is lost. However, based on the same reasoning, we could argue that the theorem is even true for not necessarily nonnegative functions; a conjecture that has to be rejected as Example 4 shows us. Hence the Folklore Theorem does not hold in all its generality. (Besides Example 4, we discussed some other examples, which show that the Folklore Theorem is not true in general.)

Furthermore, in the same theorem, we give a sharp estimate of the scale beyond which there are no more details distinguishable in the blurred function. This scale is equal to r, where r equals $\mathrm{r}(f)$, the radius of the support of the function nonnegative f. This, in combination with Remark 1, suggests that we should call 2σ the scale of f_σ at which a function f is observed.

The second theorem presented spatial constraints for the critical points. This result is complementary to Theorem 1, which can be interpreted as imposing scale constraints in scale-space (cf. Corollary 1), but now the constraints are in the spatial domain. Theorem 2 states that, for every nonnegative, compactly supported function f every spatial critical point of f_σ is in the closure of the convex hull of the support of the initial function f.

We conclude that the scale-space constraints we considered in this article are all based merely on the knowledge that the functions under consideration are nonnegative and compactly supported. Other function classes, for which comparable statements are possible, could be investigated. However, from the examples we give, it is clear that it can be hard to formulate such statements for different or broader classes of functions.

Another interesting direction for subsequent research is to generalize Theorem 1 and give explicit – and sharp – estimates of scales after which there are only 2 critical points, 3 critical points, etc. left, or to generalize Theorem 2 in such a way that one can restrict the "support of the spatial critical points for the function f_σ" to different domains than the convex closure of supp(f).

A   Proofs and Demonstrations

This appendix gives the proofs of both Theorems 1 and 2, as well as the proof of the statement in Example 5. We start with a definition of an inner product that is used in the proof of Theorem 1. Note that the domain of integration is omitted in the remainder of this appendix. One should read $\int_{\mathbb{R}^n}$ for $\int$.

Definition 3. *Given a nonnegative function f, a spatial coordinate x and a scale σ. Define the inner product $\langle \cdot, \cdot \rangle_x$ for two functions $a : \mathbb{R}^n \to \mathbb{R}$ and $b : \mathbb{R}^n \to \mathbb{R}$ as*

$$\langle a(y), b(y) \rangle_x := \frac{\int a(y)\, b(y)\, f(y)\, g_\sigma(x - y)\, dy}{\int f(y)\, g_\sigma(x - y)\, dy},$$

furthermore define $\overline{a(y)} := \langle a(y), 1 \rangle_x$.

Proof. (Theorem 1) To proof the theorem, we first derive a system of equations that is satisfied by a spatial critical point $\xi \in \mathbb{R}^n$ at a scale σ. Clearly, for ξ the following n equations hold:

$$\frac{\partial f_\sigma}{\partial x_j}(\xi) = \frac{1}{\sigma^2} \int (\xi_j - y_j)\, f(y)\, g_\sigma(\xi - y)\, dy = 0, \tag{1}$$

for all $j \in \{1, \ldots, n\}$. Hence, if ξ is a critical point:

$$\xi_j \int f(y)\, g_\sigma(\xi - y)\, dy = \int y_j f(y)\, g_\sigma(\xi - y)\, dy,$$

and we conclude that ξ satisfies $\xi = F(\xi; \sigma)$, where every $F_j : \mathbb{R}^n \times \mathbb{R}_{\geq 0} \to \mathbb{R}$ of F is defined as:

$$F_j(x; \sigma) := \frac{\int y_j f(y) g_\sigma(x - y)\, dy}{\int f(y) g_\sigma(x - y)\, dy} = \bar{y}_j.$$

Hence, ξ is a fixed point of $F(\cdot; \sigma)$.

$F(\cdot; \sigma)$ is a contraction if the operator norm of the matrix $\Phi(x) := (\frac{\partial F}{\partial x_k}(x; \sigma))_k$ is smaller than 1, i.e., $\|\Phi(x)\|$, for all $x \in \mathbb{R}^n$ [2]. Writing out the entries $\frac{\partial F_j}{\partial x_k}(x; \sigma)$ of $\Phi(x)$, we get:

$$
\begin{aligned}
\frac{\partial F_j}{\partial x_k}(x; \sigma) &= \frac{1}{\sigma^2}\left(\langle y_j, y_k\rangle_x - \langle y_j, 1\rangle_x \langle y_k, 1\rangle_x\right) \\
&= \frac{1}{\sigma^2}\langle y_j - \langle y_j, 1\rangle_x, y_k - \langle y_k, 1\rangle_x\rangle_x = \frac{1}{\sigma^2}\langle y_j - \bar{y}_j, y_k - \bar{y}_k\rangle_x.
\end{aligned}
\tag{2}
$$

From Equation (2), it follows that $\Phi(x)$ is a symmetric matrix and so its operator norm equals the maximum of the absolute values of the eigenvalues of $\Phi(x)$.

Rewrite $\Phi(x)$ as follows:

$$
\Phi(x) = \frac{1}{\sigma^2}\left(\langle y_j - \bar{y}_j, y_k - \bar{y}_k\rangle_x\right)_{jk} = \frac{\int (y - \bar{y})(y - \bar{y})^t f(y)\, g_\sigma(x - y)\, dy}{\sigma^2 \int f(y)\, g_\sigma(x - y)\, dy},
$$

and note that $\Phi(x)$ is positive semi-definite, because the matrix $(y - \bar{y})(y - \bar{y})^t$ is positive semi-definite and f is nonnegative. From this, it follows that the operator norm equals the maximum of the eigenvalues of $\Phi(x)$ [2]. Furthermore, it holds that the trace of the matrix $\Phi(x)$ is greater or equal to this maximum eigenvalue. Let λ be this eigenvalue, then the following holds:

$$
\begin{aligned}
\lambda \le \text{trace}(\Phi(x)) &= \sum_{j=1}^n \frac{1}{\sigma^2}\langle y_j - \bar{y}_j, y_j - \bar{y}_j\rangle_x \\
&= \frac{\sum_{j=1}^n \int (y_j - \bar{y}_j)^2 f(y)\, g_\sigma(x - y)\, dy}{\sigma^2 \int f(y)\, g_\sigma(x - y)\, dy}.
\end{aligned}
\tag{3}
$$

Furthermore, it is easy to verify that $\int \sum_j (y_j - \gamma_j)^2 f(y)\, g_\sigma(x - y)\, dy = \int \|y - \gamma\|^2 f(y)\, g_\sigma(x - y)\, dy$ attains its minimal value for $\gamma = \bar{y} \in \mathbb{R}^n$. Now, because the radius of the convex closure of $\text{supp}(f)$ equals r, there is an $m \in \mathbb{R}^n$ for which $\|y - m\| \le r$ for $y \in \text{supp}(y)$. And so from the last two statements, and Equation (3) we have:

$$
\begin{aligned}
\lambda \le \text{trace}(\Phi(x)) &= \frac{\sum_{j=1}^n \int (y_j - \bar{y}_j)^2 f(y)\, g_\sigma(x - y)\, dy}{\sigma^2 \int f(y)\, g_\sigma(x - y)\, dy} \\
&\le \frac{\int \sum_{j=1}^n (y_j - m_j)^2 f(y)\, g_\sigma(x - y)\, dy}{\sigma^2 \int f(y)\, g_\sigma(x - y)\, dy} \\
&\le \frac{\int r^2 f(y)\, g_\sigma(x - y)\, dy}{\sigma^2 \int f(y)\, g_\sigma(x - y)\, dy}
\end{aligned}
$$

As already stated, the function $F(\cdot; \sigma)$ is a contraction if $\lambda < 1$. The function $F(\cdot; \sigma)$ being a contraction directly implies that a spatial critical point ξ is unique. Hence f_σ has a unique spatial critical point if $\frac{r^2}{\sigma^2} < 1$. So for all $\sigma > r$, f_σ has a unique critical point, which is a maximum, because f_σ is nonnegative and $\lim_{\|x\| \to \infty} f_\sigma(x) = 0$. $\square$

Proof. (Theorem 2) Let $a \in \mathbb{R}^n$ and $c \in \mathbb{R}$, such that for every $y \in \text{supp}(f)$, we have: $\langle y, a \rangle \leq c$ (here $\langle \cdot, \cdot \rangle$ is the standard inner product between two vectors). Note that $\langle \cdot, a \rangle \leq c$ defines a half-space in $\mathbb{R}^n$, and so the foregoing states that $\text{supp}(f)$ is situated in this half-space.

Now assume ξ to be a critical point of f_ς (ς is fixed), then the n Equations (1), satisfied by a critical point, imply that

$$\langle \xi, a \rangle \int f(y) \, g_\varsigma(\xi - y) \, dy = \int \langle y, a \rangle f(y) \, g_\varsigma(\xi - y) \, dy$$
$$\leq c \int f(y) \, g_\varsigma(\xi - y) \, dy,$$

Here it is used that f is nonnegative to obtain the inequality. This inequality in turn implies that $\langle \xi, a \rangle \leq c$. Now, the intersection of all closed half-spaces determined by $\langle \cdot, a \rangle \leq c$ and containing $\text{supp}(f)$, equals the closure C of the convex hull of $\text{supp}(f)$ (see [5]). Furthermore, because for a critical point ξ we also have that $\langle \xi, a \rangle \leq c$ for all the former choices of $a \in \mathbb{R}^n$ and $c \in \mathbb{R}$, we conclude that all critical points reside within the same closure C. $\square$

Proof. (Example 5) Let $\phi := \sum_{k=0}^{\infty} 2^{-k\mu} \delta_{2^k}$. If this distribution has the property of having multiple extrema for all scales larger than a certain scale ς, then the function $f := \phi * g_s$ has the same property.

To show that ϕ possesses this property, we start by taking the derivative of ϕ_σ, which equals $\phi'_\sigma(x) = \frac{1}{\sigma^2} \sum_{k=0}^{\infty} 2^{-k\mu}(2^k - x) \, g_\sigma(x - 2^k)$, with $\sigma > 0$. Firstly, the function ϕ'_σ is positive for x smaller than 1. Secondly, for $\sigma > 0$, $\phi'_\sigma(2)$ is negative. To see this, note that for $x = 2$, the first summand equals $2^{-0\mu}(2^0 - x) \, g_\sigma(x - 2^0) = -g_\sigma(1)$, which is negative. Furthermore, for the other summand ($k \geq 1$), which are nonnegative, the following holds:

$$2^{-k\mu}(2^k - 2) \, g_\sigma(2 - 2^k) < 2^{-2k} 2^k g_\sigma(2^{k-1}) \leq 2^{-k} g_\sigma(1),$$

hence

$$\sum_{k=1}^{\infty} 2^{-k\mu}(2^k - x) \, g_\sigma(x - 2^k) < \sum_{k=1}^{\infty} 2^{-k} g_\sigma(1) = g_\sigma(1),$$

which shows that the latter statement holds.

Thirdly, for every σ there is an $x > 2$ for which $\phi'_\sigma(x)$ is positive. Proof: take $x = 2^p - \sigma$ ($p \in \mathbb{Z}_{>0}$), then the summand of ϕ'_σ, where $k = p$, equals $2^{-p\mu} \sigma e^{-\frac{1}{2}}$. Now, choose p such that $2^{p-2} > \sigma$ and such that $2^{\frac{p-3}{2}} > \sigma$ – implying that

$2\sigma^2 < 2^{p-2}$, then the following holds:

$$-\sum_{k=0}^{p-1} 2^{-k\mu}(2^k - 2^p + \sigma)\, g_\sigma(2^p - \sigma - 2^k) \leq$$

$$\sum_{k=0}^{p-1} 2^{-0\mu} 2^p g_\sigma(2^{p-1} + 2^{p-2} - 2^k) \leq$$

$$\sum_{k=0}^{p-1} 2^p g_\sigma(2^{p-2}) \leq$$

$$p\, 2^p\, e^{-\frac{(2^{p-2})^2}{2\sigma^2}} \leq p\, 2^p\, e^{-2^{p-2}}.$$

Because, $e^{-2^{p-2}}$ goes to 0 extremely rapidly when p goes to infinity, it follows that there is a $\rho \in \mathbb{Z}_{>0}$ for which

$$-\sum_{k=0}^{\rho-1} 2^{-k\mu}(2^k - 2^\rho + \sigma)\, g_\sigma(2^\rho - \sigma - 2^k) \leq \rho\, 2^\rho\, e^{-2^{\rho-2}} \leq 2^{-\rho\mu}\sigma e^{-\frac{1}{2}}.$$

Hence, taking $x = 2^\rho - \sigma$ gives $\phi'_\sigma(x) > 0$.

Now, from the three foregoing statements, we have that $\phi'_\sigma(0)$, $\phi'_\sigma(2)$, and $\phi'_\sigma(2^\rho - \sigma)$ are positive, negative, and positive, respectively. Finally, because $\lim_{x\to\infty} \phi'_\sigma(x)$ is negative, we conclude that for every scale $\sigma > 0$, ϕ_σ has at least three extrema.   □

References

1. J. Damon. Local morse theory for solutions to the heat equation and gaussian blurring. *Journal of Differential Equations*, 115(2):368–401, 1995.
2. J. A. Dieudonné. *Foundations of Modern Analysis*, volume 10 of *Pure and Applied Mathematics*. Academic Press, New York . London, 1960.
3. L. M. J. Florack. *Image Structure*, volume 10 of *Computational Imaging and Vision*. Kluwer Academic Publishers, Dordrecht . Boston . London, 1997.
4. L. M. J. Florack, B. M. Ter Haar Romeny, J. J. Koenderink, and M. A. Viergever. Linear scale-space. *Journal of Mathematical Imaging and Vision*, 4(4):325–351, 1994.
5. B. Grünbaum. *Convex Polytopes*, volume 16 of *Pure and Applied Mathematics*. Interscience Publishers, London, 1967.
6. P. Johansen, S. Skelboe, K. Grue, and J. Damgaard Andersen. Representing signals by their toppoints in scale-space. In *Proceedings of the 8th International Conference on Pattern Recognition*, pages 215–217, Paris, 1986.
7. J. J. Koenderink. The structure of images. *Biological Cybernetics*, 50:363–370, 1984.
8. T. Lindeberg and B. M. Ter Haar Romeny. *Linear Scale-Space I: Basic Theory*, volume 1 of *Computational Imaging and Vision*, chapter 1, pages 1–38. Kluwer Academic Publishers, Dordrecht . Boston . London, 1994.
9. A. L. Yuille and T. Poggio. Fingerprint theorems for zero-crossings. *Journal of the Optical Society of America. A, Optics and Image Science*, 2:683–692, 1985.

Scale-Space Theories for Scalar and Vector Images

Luc M.J. Florack

Utrecht University, PO Box 80010
NL-3584 CD Utrecht, The Netherlands
Luc.Florack@math.uu.nl
http://www.math.uu.nl/people/florack/index.html

Abstract. We define mutually consistent scale-space theories for scalar and vector images. Consistency pertains to the connection between the already established scalar theory and that for a suitably defined scalar field induced by the proposed vector scale-space. We show that one is compelled to reject the Gaussian scale-space paradigm in certain cases when scalar and vector fields are mutually dependent.

Subsequently we investigate the behaviour of critical points of a vector-valued scale-space image—*i.e.* points at which the vector field vanishes—as well as their singularities and unfoldings in linear scale-space.

1   Introduction

It has been argued by Koenderink [8] that a $C_1^2(\mathbb{R}^n \times \mathbb{R}^+)$ function[1] $u(\mathbf{x}; s)$—with scale parameter $s \in \mathbb{R}^+$—is a reasonable choice for a multiscale representation of a scalar image $f(\mathbf{x})$ if, at the location of spatial extrema,

$$u_s \Delta u > 0 \,.$$

Koenderink proposed to take the simplest instance of such a representation, which led him to consider the linear heat equation[2],

$$\begin{cases} \partial_s u &= \Delta u \,, \\ \lim_{s \to 0} u = f \,, \end{cases} \tag{1}$$

---

[1] A function $u : \mathbb{R}^n \times \mathbb{R}^+ \to \mathbb{R}$ is in $C_1^2(\mathbb{R}^n \times \mathbb{R}^+)$ if it is twice continuously differentiable with respect to $\mathbf{x} \in \mathbb{R}^n$ and once with respect to $s \in \mathbb{R}^+$. If $u \notin C_1^2(\mathbb{R}^n \times \mathbb{R}^+)$ then there are other possibilities, *cf.* Van den Boomgaard *et al.* [1, 2].

[2] Note that $\Delta u \neq 0$ at a spatial extremum.

M. Kerckhove (Ed.): Scale-Space 2001, LNCS 2106, pp. 193–204, 2001.

as the generating equation for a scale-space representation. Thus the argument pertains to the behaviour of extrema, and, in the case of the heat equation, basically boils down to the (strong) *maximum principle*[3] [4].

In this article we wish to generalise the scale-space paradigm to vector-valued images. A nontrivial demand to be reckoned with is *mutual consistency*: If the vector field implies the existence of a scalar field, as is for instance the case in a vector space endowed with a scalar product, then a multiscale representation of the latter must be consistent with the one induced by a multiscale representation of the former. We show that this implies that one is compelled to reject the Gaussian scale-space paradigm in certain cases.

Subsequently we concentrate on linear vector scale-space representations and investigate the behaviour of its critical points—*i.e.* points at which the vector field vanishes—as well as their singularities and unfoldings in scale-space.

2   Theory

2.1   Vector Scale-Space

Once one appreciates that the addition of first order terms on the right hand side of Eq. (1) does not violate Koenderink's causality principle, it becomes relatively straightforward to generalise the causality argument to vector images in such a way that consistency is manifest. That is to say, the scale-space of an arbitrary scalar field generated by the vector field (*e.g.* its magnitude) should be compatible with the already established theory for scalar images. In order to appreciate why first order terms are sometimes necessary, consider the following example.

Example 1. Suppose we would require the magnitude of a suitably defined multiscale vector-valued image to satisfy the linear Eq. (1), *i.e.* without a first order nonlinearity, then we are confronted with a dilemma: As the norm of the high-resolution vector image (at scale $s=0$, say) is a positive function[4] with isolated zeros only, its finite-scale representation must be everywhere *strictly positive* as a consequence of the maximum principle. Thus wherever defined, the scale-space representation of the vector field itself can have no critical points—spatial loci at which the vector field's components vanish for fixed scale $s>0$—not even at

---

[3] It should be stressed that this does *not* imply that extrema cannot be created as scale increases, as is sometimes claimed in the literature, *cf.* Simmons *et al.* [10]. Damon [3] has shown that such creations do in fact occur *generically*, although they are typically outnumbered by annihilations.

[4] A function f is called positive if $f(x)\geq 0$ for almost all $x\in\mathbb{R}^n$ and $\int f(x)\,dx\neq 0$.

"infinitesimal" scales. Elsewhere [6] it is explained that if the components v and w satisfy the following coupled system of p.d.e.'s

$$\begin{cases} \partial_s v = \Delta v - \dfrac{1}{v^2 + w^2}(w\nabla v - v\nabla w) \cdot \nabla w \\ \partial_s w = \Delta w - \dfrac{1}{v^2 + w^2}(v\nabla w - w\nabla v) \cdot \nabla v. \end{cases}$$

then $u = \sqrt{v^2 + w^2}$ indeed satisfies the linear Eq. (1). The problem alluded to above is reflected in the denominator occuring on the right hand sides. In fact, these equations *do not admit an initial condition with critical points*.

The scaling behaviour of the vector field's critical points outlined in the example is a highly undesirable situation, and so *we must reject Eq. (1) as a viable scale-space representation for the norm of a vector field* (or any other scalar induced by the vector field for that matter). Critical points of a vector field should be able to survive a range of physical scales. The Poincaré-Hopf theorem [11] bears witness to the fact that in spite of their zero measure they are *not* something "infinitesimal".

The way out of the dilemma is of course to relax the constraint on scalars induced by the vector field. None of these should be subjected to the linear heat equation for reasons amply discussed. Indeed, insisting on Koenderink's scale causality demand does not compel us to assume the existence of any scalar satisfying Eq. (1), notably linearity, as this is only a special case of a more general class. Only if the scalar image is not some quantity derived from another physical observable, *i.c.* a vector field, the simplifying assumption of linearity may be justified, as there is no additional consistency demand to be met in that case.

Vice versa, if we are given a scalar image and (thus) adopt Eq. (1) as our paradigm, the equations for the induced vector field $\mathbf{v} = \nabla u$ are obviously linear, too:

$$\begin{cases} \partial_s \mathbf{v} = \Delta \mathbf{v}, \\ \lim_{s \to 0} \mathbf{v} = \mathbf{v}_0, \end{cases} \tag{2}$$

in which $\mathbf{v}_0$ is the high resolution gradient image. We may subsequently adopt Eq. (2) as the paradigm for vector fields in general, *i.e.* beyond the class of gradient fields. Apart from being the most straightforward thing to do in the first place, it is easy to verify that this is indeed consistent with the scalar theory, provided we refrain from the linearity condition for vector-induced scalar fields. Indeed, any function of the magnitude $\rho = \sqrt{\mathbf{v} \cdot \mathbf{v}}$ satisfies an admissible semilinear diffusion equation. Let us consider some examples.

Example 2. In two dimensions we may introduce a complex scalar field, $u = v + iw \in \mathbb{C}$ (respectively $f = v_0 + iw_0$), where (v, w) are the Cartesian components of $\mathbf{v}$. The form of Eq. (2) then formally reduces to that Eq. (1). If we write $u = \varrho\, e^{i\phi}$ then we have

$$
\begin{cases}
\partial_s \varrho &= \Delta\varrho - \varrho \nabla\phi \cdot \nabla\phi, \\
\partial_s \phi &= \Delta\phi + \dfrac{2}{\varrho}\nabla\varrho \cdot \nabla\phi, \\
\lim_{s\to 0}(\varrho, \phi) &= (\varrho_0, \phi_0).
\end{cases}
$$

The first order terms in the equation for ϱ prevent the magnitude from becoming instantly everywhere positive, as opposed to the case in which they are absent. Thus critical points in the initial condition $(\varrho_0(\mathbf{x}_c) = 0)$ are able to survive a finite amount of blur, as it should. Note also that the weighted angle $\psi = \varrho\phi$ satisfies an equation of the same form as that of ϱ. Using this function instead of ϕ one may thus circumvent the singularity $\varrho = 0$ (implying ϕ is ill-defined but $\psi = 0$) on the right hand side.

We have seen that linear equations for the vector image imply nonlinear equations for induced scalar images. The example of a scalar image and its gradient illustrates the possibility of linearity in both domains. The next example, finally, shows that it may also be necessary to add nonlinear terms to the defining equations for a multiscale vector field derived from a linear scalar image.

Example 3. Elsewhere [7, 9] a theory has been proposed for multiscale motion extraction consistent with the scale-space paradigm for the underlying scalar image $u(\mathbf{x}; s)$. It has been noted that the operationally defined multiscale motion field $\mathbf{v}(\mathbf{x}; s)$ does *not* satisfy Eq. (2), but that the *flux field* $\mathbf{j}(\mathbf{x}; s) = u(\mathbf{x}; s)\mathbf{v}(\mathbf{x}; s)$ by construction does. From the fact that u and $\mathbf{j}$ satisfy the linear diffusion equation it follows that the motion field itself satisfies

$$
\begin{cases}
\partial_s \mathbf{v} &= \Delta\mathbf{v} + \dfrac{2}{u}\nabla u \cdot \nabla\mathbf{v}, \\
\lim_{s\to 0} \mathbf{v} &= \mathbf{v}_0.
\end{cases}
$$

Here the occurence of u in the denominator poses no problem since it is manifestly positive at scales $s > 0$, *cf.* Eq. (1).

All the examples given indicate that one must be cautious about *which* scalar or vector field one should subject to linear equations, Eq. (1) respectively Eq. (2), at least in cases where mutual dependencies exist (vector field *versus* magnitude field, scalar field *versus* motion field, *et cetera*). Otherwise a linear equation is the natural choice *a priori*.

2.2 Behaviour of Critical Points

Next we study the behaviour of critical points given Eq. (2). Recall that a critical point is defined as the spatial locus $\mathbf{x}_c$ at which $\mathbf{v}(\mathbf{x}_c; s) = \mathbf{0}$ for any fixed s.

In the generic case, assuming $\mathbf{v}(\mathbf{x}; s)$ is a Morse function for some given scale s, the critical points are all isolated. As scale increases each such point will move along a *critical path*. The situation is similar to that of critical points in a scalar image—in that context defined as spatial loci at which the image gradient vanishes—and can be analysed in a similar fashion [3, 5]. The situation for non-gradient fields is slightly more complicated, however.

Theorem 1. *Let $\mathbf{J}$ be the Jacobian matrix with components $v_i^{\mu} = \partial_i v^{\mu}$, with row and column indices $i, \mu = 1, \ldots, n$, respectively. Furthermore, let $\bar{\mathbf{J}}$ be its associated cofactor matrix, with components $\bar{v}_{\nu}^{j}$—in which upper indices are now row indices—and $\det \mathbf{J}$ the Jacobian determinant. A tangent to a parametrised critical path $\Gamma : \mathbb{R} \to \mathbb{R}^n \times \mathbb{R}^+ : \lambda \mapsto (\mathbf{x}(\lambda); s(\lambda))$ is then given by*

$$\begin{pmatrix} \dot{\mathbf{x}} \\ \dot{s} \end{pmatrix} = \begin{pmatrix} -\bar{\mathbf{J}}\,\Delta\mathbf{v} \\ \det \mathbf{J} \end{pmatrix}$$

in which a dot indicates differentiation with respect to λ. It is understood that the right hand side is evaluated at the location of the critical point.

Note that $\Delta\mathbf{v} = \partial_s \mathbf{v}$. The definition of the cofactor matrix is reviewed in Appendix A. The essential property is $\mathbf{J}\,\bar{\mathbf{J}} = \det \mathbf{J}\,\mathbf{I}$.

Proof. The derivation is essentially the same as presented elsewhere for critical paths in a scalar image [5]. The theorem is easily verified by noticing that the tangent must satisfy the n equations

$$\mathbf{J}\dot{\mathbf{x}} + \Delta\mathbf{v}\dot{s} = \mathbf{0}\,,$$

which follows by inspection of the first order Taylor terms of $\mathbf{v}$ at the location of a spatial critical point. Insertion of the right hand side in Theorem 1, using $\mathbf{J}\,\bar{\mathbf{J}} = \det \mathbf{J}\,\mathbf{I}$, readily shows that it indeed satisfies this constraint.

It follows from Theorem 1 that as long as the Jacobian does not degenerate the critical path intersects the planes of constant scale transversally. However, as soon as $\det \mathbf{J} = 0$, the critical path becomes horizontal, and the critical point changes its character as it "reverses in scale". This indicates either an annihilation or a creation—depending on the sign of curvature of the critical path at the singularity—of a pair of critical points with opposite Poincaré indices.

Theorem 1 applies to arbitrary dimensions. Let us scrutinise the 2-dimensional situation for simplicity. In that case the explicit form of the scale-space tangent to the critical path becomes

$$
\begin{pmatrix} \dot{x} \\ \dot{y} \\ \dot{s} \end{pmatrix} = \begin{pmatrix} \partial_y v \Delta w - \Delta v \partial_y w \\ \Delta v \partial_x w - \partial_x v \Delta w \\ \partial_x v \partial_y w - \partial_y v \partial_x w \end{pmatrix} .
$$

Note that the right hand side is just the outer product $\dot{\mathbf{x}} = \nabla v \times \nabla w$, in which ∇ is the scale-space gradient with components $(\partial_x, \partial_y, \partial_s)$, and in which v and w are the Cartesian components of the vector field.

Let us now consider the classification of possible critical points. The eigenvalue equation for $\mathbf{J}$ is

$$
\lambda^2 - \operatorname{tr} \mathbf{J} \, \lambda + \det \mathbf{J} = 0 ,
$$

with $\operatorname{tr} \mathbf{J} = \operatorname{div} \mathbf{v}$. Analysis then shows that we may distinguish the following cases (it is understood that $\mathbf{v} = \mathbf{0}$ in the points of interest):

1. If $\operatorname{tr}^2 \mathbf{J} < 4 \det \mathbf{J}$ then $\lambda_1, \lambda_2 \in \mathbb{C} \backslash \mathbb{R}$, $\lambda_1 = \lambda_2^*$, say $\lambda_{1,2} \equiv \lambda \pm i\mu$ with $\lambda, \mu \in \mathbb{R}$ and $\mu \neq 0$.
2. If $\operatorname{tr}^2 \mathbf{J} = 4 \det \mathbf{J}$ then $\lambda_1, \lambda_2 \in \mathbb{R}$, $\lambda_1 = \lambda_2 \equiv \lambda \neq 0$, so we have a *symmetric nodal point*:
   2a. If $\lambda < 0$ we have a *symmetric sink*.
   2b. If $\lambda > 0$ we have a *symmetric source*.
3. If $\operatorname{tr}^2 \mathbf{J} > 4 \det \mathbf{J}$ then $\lambda_1, \lambda_2 \in \mathbb{R}$, $\lambda_1 \neq \lambda_2$.

The first and last case can be further subdivided as follows.

1a. If $\lambda < 0$ we have a *spiral sink*.
1b. If $\lambda = 0$ we have a *central point*.
1c. If $\lambda > 0$ we have a *spiral source*.
3a. If $\det \mathbf{J} < 0$ then $\operatorname{sign} \lambda_1 = -\operatorname{sign} \lambda_2$, so that we have a *saddle point*.
3b. If $\det \mathbf{J} = 0$ then $\lambda_1 = 0$, $\lambda_2 = \operatorname{div} \mathbf{v}$ or *vice versa*, which corresponds to a *generic degeneracy*.
3c. If, finally, $\det \mathbf{J} > 0$ then $\operatorname{sign} \lambda_1 = \operatorname{sign} \lambda_2$, so that we have a *nodal point*. Still a further subdivision can be made (note that $\operatorname{sign} \lambda_{1,2} = \operatorname{sign} \operatorname{div} \mathbf{v}$):
   3c1. If $\lambda_1 < 0$ we have an *asymmetric sink*.
   3c2. If $\lambda_1 > 0$ we have an *asymmetric source*.

Figure 1 shows all types of nondegenerate critical points. (All figures may be arbitrarily rotated.)

The nature of the generic degeneracy (case **3b**) is particularly interesting, for it is precisely at such a point in scale-space that the vector field changes topologically. In two dimensions the vanishing of one eigenvalue of the Jacobian matrix along

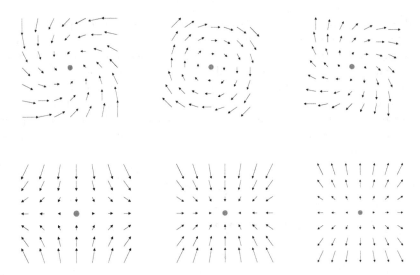

Fig. 1. Nondegenerate Critical Points. Upper row, from left to right: spiral sink, centre point, spiral source. Lower row: saddle, (asymmetric) sink, (asymmetric) source.

a critical path implies that the second eigenvalue must be real at the singularity, for if $\lambda_1 \in \mathbb{C} \backslash \mathbb{R}$ then $\lambda_2 = \lambda_1^*$. Moreover, in the generic case under consideration, λ_2 does not vanish at the same time as λ_1 does. This follows from the fact that if $\lambda_1 = 0$ then $\lambda_2 = \lambda_1 + \lambda_2 = \operatorname{tr} \mathbf{J} = \operatorname{div} \mathbf{v}$. In the generic case the common points of the scale-space surface $\det \mathbf{J} = 0$ and the curve $\mathbf{v} = \mathbf{0}$ are isolated. The probability that such a point lies within the surface $\operatorname{div} \mathbf{v} = 0$ is zero. This admits only one possible type of event, *viz.* a saddle point colliding with (*i.e.* annihilating with or emerging from) a nodal point, *i.e.* a sink or source node. Whether we have an annihilation or a creation depends on the (sign of the) curvature of the critical path at the singularity (*v.i.*). Figure 2 shows the vector field in the neighbourhood of a degenerate critical point.

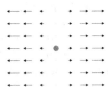

Fig. 2. Generic Degeneracy (Unperturbed).

The above analysis implies that a spiral node (case **1a** or **1c.**) is stable in the sense that it can only cease to exist by first transforming into a critical point of type **3c1**, respectively **3c2**, via a corresponding symmetric nodal point, *i.e.* case **2**, after which an annihilation with a saddle point may occur. This sequence of events corresponds to a pair of complex conjugate eigenvalues approaching the real axis and scattering off in horizontal direction after collision. As soon as one of the eigenvalues reaches 0 we get an event of type **3b**. *Vice versa*, spiral nodes cannot be created spontaneously; the abovesketched sequence must be traversed in opposite direction, starting out from a creation of a saddle and a nodal point, whereby the latter turns into a spiral node via an intermediate symmetric nodal point. See Figure 3.

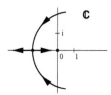

Fig. 3. Mutation diagram of (the eigenvalues associated with) a critical point in the $\mathbb{C}$-plane, showing a spiral node (nonreal complex conjugate points approaching the $\mathbb{R}$-axis) transforming into an asymmetric nodal point (pair of distinct real points moving along the $\mathbb{R}$-axis) via a symmetric nodal point (scatterpoint on the $\mathbb{R}$-axis). As soon as one of the scattered points reaches the origin we obtain a degeneracy. The velocities of corresponding points are mirror-symmetric relative to the real axis.

Theorem 1 implies that at the scale-space location of a catastrophe at which a saddle and a nodal point collide the tangent to the critical path is horizontal ($\dot{s}=0$). In order to distinguish between creation and annihilation events involving a saddle and a nodal point we need a higher order local analysis.

Example 4. Consider the vector field germs, together with their perturbations,

$$\mathbf{v}_a(x,y,s) = \begin{pmatrix} x^2 + 2s \\ 0 \end{pmatrix} + \begin{pmatrix} 0 \\ y \end{pmatrix} \quad \text{and} \quad \mathbf{v}_c(x,y,s) = \begin{pmatrix} x^2 - 2y^2 - 2s \\ -4xy \end{pmatrix} + \begin{pmatrix} 0 \\ y \end{pmatrix}.$$

The second term on each right hand side is the canonical form of a typical perturbation on a full scale-space neighbourhood of the fiducial origin, $(x,y,s) = (0,0,0)$. The field $\mathbf{v}_a(x,y,s)$ captures an annihilation, $\mathbf{v}_c(x,y,s)$ a creation event at the origin. The critical paths are given by $\Gamma_a : (x,y,s) = (\pm\sqrt{-2s},0,s)$, $s \le 0$, and $\Gamma_c : (x,y,s) = (\pm\sqrt{2s},0,s)$, $s \ge 0$, respectively. Figure 4 illustrates the behaviour of these fields near the origin.

These germs and their perturbations are analogous to those describing the unfoldings of corresponding annihilation and creation events in scalar images, *cf.* Damon [3].

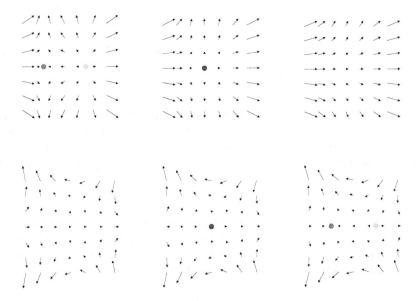

Fig. 4. Unfolding of Generic Singularities. Upper row: annihilation event. Lower row: creation event. Scale (resolution) increases (decreases) from left to right.

Critical points of a vector field all coincide with global minima of the vector field's magnitude, but the latter generally has additional critical points (maxima, saddles and local minima), *viz.* those points where $\mathbf{v} \cdot \nabla \mathbf{v} = 2\,\mathbf{J}^{\mathrm{T}}\,\mathbf{v} = 0$ and $\mathbf{v} \neq 0$, *i.e.* where the vector field itself happens to be nonvanishing and orthogonal to its gradient (note that this implies degeneracy of the Jacobian).

Inspection of the gradients and Hessian matrices of the scalar images $u_{\mathrm{a,c}}(x, y, s)$ $= \|\mathbf{v}_{\mathrm{a,c}}(x, y, s)\|^2$ as a function of scale reveals that at a singularity of the vector field there is an intersection of critical paths with the shape of a pitchfork pointing downward in the annihilation event and upward in the creation event. In the first case a saddle collides with two global minima (the critical points of $\mathbf{v}_{\mathrm{a}}$) at $(x, y, s) = (0, 0, 0)$, after which a single local minimum emerges. In the second case a local minimum spawns two global minima (the critical points of $\mathbf{v}_{\mathrm{c}}$) at $(x, y, s) = (0, 0, 0)$, together with a saddle. In both cases the Poincaré index of a spatial region containing (only) the critical points under consideration remains invariant, as it should: Figure 5. (In this argument "local minima" may be replaced by "local maxima" depending on the case of interest.)

The critical points of the vector field's magnitude that are not critical points of the vector field itself define critical paths in scale-space implicitly defined by

$$\mathbf{q}(\mathbf{x}; s) \stackrel{\mathrm{def}}{=} \mathbf{v}(\mathbf{x}; s) \cdot \nabla \mathbf{v}(\mathbf{x}; s) = 0 \,.$$

Fig. 5. Unfolding of the generic singularities of vector field's magnitude that correspond to those of the vector field itself. Left: annihilation event. Right: creation event. Scale (resolution) increases (decreases) upward. The singularity always involves two global minima as well as a saddle/local minimum/maximum pair.

In the two-dimensional case at hand we have two equations, one for each component of $\mathbf{v} = (v, w)$, and three unknowns, $(\mathbf{x}; s) = (x, y, s)$. Consequently we again expect to find critical paths in scale-space, which can be analysed as previously. If we expand the defining equation to second order we obtain

$$\mathbf{q}(\mathbf{x}; s) = \mathbf{q} + \nabla \mathbf{q} \cdot \mathbf{x} + \frac{1}{2} \mathbf{x}^{\mathrm{T}} \cdot \nabla \nabla^{\mathrm{T}} \mathbf{q} \cdot \mathbf{x} + \partial_s \mathbf{q}\, s + \text{h.o.t.}$$

in which the coefficients on the right hand side are partial derivatives evaluated at the origin. Setting the left hand side equal to zero, and defining the matrix

$$\mathbf{Q} \stackrel{\text{def}}{=} \nabla \mathbf{q}, \tag{3}$$

with components $q_{ij} = \partial_i\, (\mathbf{v} \cdot \partial_j \mathbf{v})$, it follows that a scale-space tangent to the critical path is given by the following theorem, the derivation of which is completely analogous to that of Theorem 1.

Theorem 2. *A tangent to a parametrised critical path* $\Gamma : \mathbb{R} \to \mathbb{R}^n \times \mathbb{R}^+ : \lambda \mapsto (\mathbf{x}(\lambda); s(\lambda))$ *through a local critical point of the magnitude field* $u(\mathbf{x}; s) = \|\mathbf{v}(\mathbf{x}; s)\|$ *is given by*

$$\begin{pmatrix} \dot{\mathbf{x}} \\ \dot{s} \end{pmatrix} = \begin{pmatrix} -\overline{\mathbf{Q}}\, \partial_s \mathbf{q} \\ \det \mathbf{Q} \end{pmatrix}$$

in which a dot indicates differentiation with respect to the curve parameter λ, *and in which* $\mathbf{Q}$ *is the matrix as defined in Eq. (3). It is understood that the right hand side is evaluated at the location of the critical point.*

Note that $\partial_s \mathbf{q} = \Delta \mathbf{v} \cdot \nabla \mathbf{v} + \mathbf{v} \cdot \nabla \Delta \mathbf{v}$.

The critical path is transversal to s-planes if and only if $\det \mathbf{Q} \neq 0$, in which case we may use $\lambda = s$ itself as a valid curve parameter. If $\det \mathbf{Q} = 0$ the curve becomes horizontal. Assuming that $\mathbf{v} \neq 0$ at that singularity (the other case has been discussed), we have either an annihilation or a creation of local critical points, one of which is a saddle, the other a maximum or local minimum. The criterion is again the sign of the critical path's curvature at the singularity. This case falls within the scope of Damon's analysis [3]. See Figure 6.

Fig. 6. Unfolding of the generic singularities of vector field's magnitude that do not involve critical points of the vector field itself. Left: annihilation event. Right: creation event. Scale (resolution) increases (decreases) upward. The singularity always involves a saddle/local minimum/maximum pair. The situation is similar to that encountered in scalar images.

A   Cofactor Matrix

Let $\mathbf{A}$ be a square $n \times n$ matrix with components $a_{\mu\nu}$. Then we define the transposed cofactor matrix $\overline{\mathbf{A}}$ as follows. In order to obtain the matrix entry $\overline{a}^{\mu\nu}$ skip the μ-th column and ν-th row of $\mathbf{A}$, evaluate the determinant of the resulting submatrix, and multiply by $(-1)^{\mu+\nu}$ ("checkerboard pattern"). Using tensor index notation,

$$\overline{\mathbf{A}}^{\mu\nu} \stackrel{\text{def}}{=} \frac{1}{(n-1)!} \, \varepsilon^{\mu\mu_1\cdots\mu_{n-1}} \, \varepsilon^{\nu\nu_1\cdots\nu_{n-1}} \, \mathbf{A}_{\mu_1\nu_1} \cdots \mathbf{A}_{\mu_{n-1}\nu_{n-1}} \, ,$$

in which $\varepsilon^{\mu_1\cdots\mu_n}$ is the spatial Lévi-Civita tensor, defined as the normalised, completely antisymmetric symbol with $\varepsilon^{1\cdots n} = 1$.

An important property of the cofactor matrix is

$$\overline{\mathbf{A}}\,\mathbf{A} = \mathbf{A}\,\overline{\mathbf{A}} = \det \mathbf{A}\,\mathbf{I} \, ,$$

in which $\mathbf{I}$ is the $n \times n$ identity matrix. Thus if a matrix is invertible, its cofactor matrix equals its inverse times its determinant. Unlike the inverse matrix, however, the cofactor matrix is always well-defined, because its coefficients are homogeneous polynomials of degree n–1 relative to the coefficients of the original matrix.

From the definition it follows that $\overline{\mathbf{I}} = \mathbf{I}$. Moreover, $\overline{r} = r$ for any number $r \in \mathbb{R}$, and if $\mathbf{B} = \overline{\mathbf{A}}$ then $\mathbf{A} = \overline{\mathbf{B}}$.

The following lemma has been used in the foregoing text.

Lemma 1. *For any matrix* $\mathbf{A}$ *we have*

$$\nabla \det \mathbf{A} = \operatorname{tr} \left(\overline{\mathbf{A}} \nabla \mathbf{A} \right) .$$

Proof. For invertible matrices the proof goes as follows. Write $\det \mathbf{A} = \exp \operatorname{tr} \ln \mathbf{A}$. Taking the gradient yields $\nabla \det \mathbf{A} = \nabla (\operatorname{tr} \ln \mathbf{A}) \exp(\operatorname{tr} \ln \mathbf{A}) = \operatorname{tr} (\nabla \ln \mathbf{A}) \det \mathbf{A}$ $= \operatorname{tr} (\mathbf{A}^{\mathrm{inv}} \nabla \mathbf{A}) \det \mathbf{A} = \operatorname{tr} (\overline{\mathbf{A}} \nabla \mathbf{A})$. If $\mathbf{A}$ is not invertible, consider the regularised, invertible matrix $\mathbf{A}_{\varepsilon} = \mathbf{A} + \varepsilon \mathbf{I}$ instead and apply the theorem. Left and right hand sides are polynomials in ε; taking the limit $\varepsilon \to 0$ establishes the result.

References

[1] R. van den Boomgaard. The morphological equivalent of the Gauss convolution. *Nieuw Archief voor Wiskunde*, 10(3):219–236, November 1992.

[2] R. van den Boomgaard and A. W. M. Smeulders. The morphological structure of images, the differential equations of morphological scale-space. *IEEE Transactions on Pattern Analysis and Machine Intelligence*, 16(11):1101–1113, November 1994.

[3] J. Damon. Local Morse theory for solutions to the heat equation and Gaussian blurring. *Journal of Differential Equations*, 115(2):368–401, January 1995.

[4] L. C. Evans. *Partial Differential Equations*, volume 19 of *Graduate Studies in Mathematics*. American Mathematical Society, Providence, Rhode Island, 1998.

[5] L. Florack and A. Kuijper. The topological structure of scale-space images. *Journal of Mathematical Imaging and Vision*, 12(1):65–79, February 2000.

[6] L. M. J. Florack. Non-linear scale-spaces isomorphic to the linear case. In B. K. Ersbøll and P. Johansen, editors, *Proceedings of the 11th Scandinavian Conference on Image Analysis (Kangerlussuaq, Greenland, June 7–11 1999)*, volume 1, pages 229–234, Lyngby, Denmark, 1999.

[7] L. M. J. Florack, W. J. Niessen, and M. Nielsen. The intrinsic structure of optic flow incorporating measurement duality. *International Journal of Computer Vision*, 27(3):263–286, May 1998.

[8] J. J. Koenderink. The structure of images. *Biological Cybernetics*, 50:363–370, 1984.

[9] M. Nielsen and O. F. Olsen. The structure of the optic flow field. In H. Burkhardt and B. Neumann, editors, *Proceedings of the Fifth European Conference on Computer Vision (Freiburg, Germany, June 1998)*, volume 1407 of *Lecture Notes in Computer Science*, pages 281–287. Springer-Verlag, Berlin, 1998.

[10] A. Simmons, S. R. Arridge, P. S. Tofts, and G. J. Barker. Application of the extremum stack to neurological MRI. *IEEE Transactions on Medical Imaging*, 17(3):371–382, June 1998.

[11] M. Spivak. *Differential Geometry*, volume 1. Publish or Perish, Berkeley, 1975.

Gaussian Convolutions
Numerical Approximations Based on Interpolation

Rein van den Boomgaard and Rik van der Weij

Intelligent Sensory Information Systems
University of Amsterdam, The Netherlands

Abstract. Gaussian convolutions are perhaps the most often used image operators in low-level computer vision tasks. Surprisingly though, there are precious few articles that describe efficient and accurate implementations of these operators.

In this paper we describe numerical approximations of Gaussian convolutions based on interpolation. We start with the continuous convolution integral and use an interpolation technique to approximate the continuous image f from its sampled version F.

Based on the interpolation a numerical approximation of the continuous convolution integral that can be calculated as a discrete convolution sum is obtained. The discrete convolution kernel is *not* equal to the sampled version of the continuous convolution kernel. Instead the convolution of the continuous kernel and the interpolation kernel has to be sampled to serve as the discrete convolution kernel .

Some preliminary experiments are shown based on zero order (nearest neighbor) interpolation, first order (linear) interpolation, third order (cubic) interpolations and sinc-interpolation. These experiments show that the proposed algorithm is more accurate for small scales, especially for Gaussian derivative convolutions when compared to the classical way of discretizing the Gaussian convolution.

1 Introduction

Gaussian convolutions are perhaps the most often used image operators in low-level computer vision tasks. Surprisingly though, there are precious few articles that describe efficient and accurate implementations of these operators.

Florack [2] recently published a paper comparing spatial sampling of the Gaussian convolution kernel with frequency sampling of the Gaussian convolution kernel. His findings are in accordance with the results of this paper. Florack heavily relied on the frequency domain analysis of the convolution operators, whereas in this paper the frequency domain analysis is not needed. Furthermore the analysis by Florack is restricted to the Gaussian convolution and does not include Gaussian derivative convolutions.

Efficient recursive approximation algorithms for Gaussian (derivative) convolutions are developed by Deriche [1] and Young and Van Vliet [7]. Although very fast they lack accuracy especially at small scales and for Gaussian derivatives.

M. Kerckhove (Ed.): Scale-Space 2001, LNCS 2106, pp. 205–214, 2001.

Another related approach is introduced by Lindeberg [4] who did not consider the task of discretizing the Gaussian convolution but instead opts for discretization of the diffusion equation. Again for large scales the Lindeberg approach is (almost) equal to the classical Gaussian convolution.

In this paper we describe numerical approximations of convolutions based on interpolation. We start with the continuous convolution integral and use an interpolation technique to approximate the continuous image f from its sampled version F. Based on the interpolation a numerical approximation of the continuous convolution integral is obtained that can be calculated as a discrete convolution sum. The discrete convolution kernel is in general *not* equal to the sampled version of the continuous convolution kernel. It proves to be the sampled version of the convolution of the continuous convolution kernel and the continuous interpolation kernel.

Some preliminary experiments are shown for Gaussian (derivative) convolutions based on several types of interpolation. The proposed algorithm is more accurate for small scales, especially for Gaussian derivative convolutions, compared to the classical approach of sampling the convolution kernel.

2   Sampling and Interpolation

An image f is a mapping from the continuous spatial domain $\mathbb{R}^d$ to the real numbers $\mathbb{R}$ (in this paper we only consider scalar images). The image f thus gives the value $f(\mathbf{x})$ for each location $\mathbf{x}$ as if we would have placed the observation probe at location $\mathbf{x}$.

In practice all that can be done is to sample the spatial domain in a finite number of locations. We assume the sampling grid is generated by the basis $B = (\mathbf{b}_1, \ldots, \mathbf{b}_d)$ leading to the observations $f(B\mathbf{k})$ for all integer multi-indices $\mathbf{k} \in \mathbb{Z}^d$.

Definition 1 (Sampling). *Let $f \in \mathrm{Fun}(\mathbb{R}^d, \mathbb{R})$ be an image and let B represent the sampling grid basis, then we define the sampling operator $\mathcal{S}_B : \mathrm{Fun}(\mathbb{R}^d, \mathbb{R}) \to \mathrm{Fun}(\mathbb{Z}^d, \mathbb{R})$ by:*

$$(\mathcal{S}_B f)(\mathbf{k}) = f(B\mathbf{k})$$

for all $\mathbf{k} \in \mathbb{Z}^d$.

In this report only the standard orthonormal sampling grid is considered, i.e. $B = I$, the identity matrix. Nevertheless we prefer to write $B\mathbf{k}$, to stress the fact that writing $B\mathbf{k}$ serves as a transition from $\mathbf{k} \in \mathbb{Z}^d$ (the discrete domain) to $B\mathbf{k} \in \mathbb{R}^d$ (the continuous domain).

The practical necessity to sample an image in only a small part of the entire space is not taken into account. Instead we consider infinite spatial domains; a simplification that does not greatly influence the results in this report.

Given a sampled version $F = \mathcal{S}_B f$ of an image f stored in computer memory, the goal is to process the image. In principle we are not interested in processing its representation F; we would like to process f and then sample the result again in order to store the result in computer memory as well. This approach thus concentrates on numerical approximations of the continuous operator instead of concentrating on sampling the images and applying a discrete operator. In section 3 we look at numerical approximations of continuous convolutions.

In order to numerically approximate the continuous convolution we need to be able to (approximately) reconstruct f given its sampled representation F. In this paper the restriction to linear and translation invariant interpolation schemes is made.

Definition 2 (Interpolation). *Let $F \in \mathrm{Fun}(\mathbb{Z}^d, \mathbb{R})$ be a sampled version $\mathcal{S}_B f$ of some continuous image $f \in \mathrm{Fun}(\mathbb{R}^d, \mathbb{R})$, then we define the interpolation $\mathcal{I}_{\phi,B} F$*

$$(\mathcal{I}_{\phi,B}F)(\mathbf{x}) = \sum_{\mathbf{k} \in \mathbb{Z}^d} \phi(\mathbf{x} - B\mathbf{k})F(\mathbf{k}) \tag{1}$$

where $\phi \in \mathrm{Fun}(\mathbb{R}^d, \mathbb{R})$ is called the interpolation kernel.

Note that $\mathcal{I}_{\phi,B}$ can only be truly called an interpolation in case $\mathcal{S}_B \mathcal{I}_{\phi,B} = \mathbf{id}$. This implies that for the interpolation kernel we have $\phi(B(\mathbf{k} - \mathbf{l})) = \delta_{\mathbf{k},\mathbf{l}}$ where $\delta_{\mathbf{k},\mathbf{l}} = 1$ iff $\mathbf{k} = \mathbf{l}$ and $\delta_{\mathbf{k},\mathbf{l}} = 0$ otherwise.

This requirement on interpolation means that interpolation followed by sampling should result in the original set of sample values (observe that in this case the identity operator $\mathbf{id}$ is in $\mathrm{Fun}(\mathbb{Z}^d, \mathbb{R})$). On the other hand, a sampling followed by an interpolation, i.e. $\mathcal{I}_{\phi,B}\mathcal{S}_B$ need not (and in general will not) result in the original function, i.e. $\mathcal{I}_{\phi,B}\mathcal{S}_B \neq \mathbf{id}$ (now the identity is in $\mathrm{Fun}(\mathbb{R}^d, \mathbb{R})$).

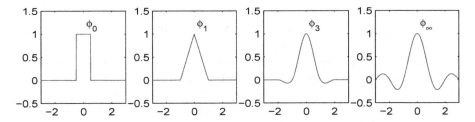

Fig. 1. Interpolation Kernels. Shown are 4 one-dimensional interpolation kernels for the unit sampling grid. The 0-order kernel ϕ_0 is 1 in the interval $[-0.5, 0.5]$ and 0 outside. The first order kernel ϕ_1 achieves a linear interpolation between the samples, the kernel ϕ_3 is a third order interpolating kernel and ϕ_∞ is the well-known sinc interpolation kernel $\phi_\infty(x) = \sin(\pi x)/(\pi x)$.

Well-known interpolation schemes like *nearest neighbor interpolation*, *bilinear interpolation*, *bicubic interpolation* and *sinc interpolation* all fit within this framework. These are all examples of polynomial interpolators (the subscript k in ϕ_k denotes the order of the interpolating polynomial).

The interpolation kernels depicted in Fig. 1 are defined as:

$$\phi_0(x) = \begin{cases} 1 : & |x| \leq \frac{1}{2} \\ 0 : & \text{elsewhere} \end{cases},$$

$$\phi_1(x) = \begin{cases} 1 - |x| : & |x| \le 1 \\ 0 & : \text{elsewhere} \end{cases},$$

$$\phi_3(x) = \begin{cases} 1 - \frac{5}{2}|x|^2 + \frac{3}{2}|x|^3 & : 0 \le |x| < 1 \\ 2 - 4|x| + \frac{5}{2}|x|^2 - \frac{1}{2}|x|^3 : & 1 \le |x| < 2 \\ 0 & : \text{ elsewhere} \end{cases}$$

and

$$\phi_\infty(x) = \frac{\sin \pi x}{\pi x}.$$

Note that ϕ_3 is only an example of a third order interpolation kernels.

The important property to note here is that all these interpolating schemes calculate the interpolated value as a linear combination of the sample values in the discrete representation of the image. For a comprehensive overview of linear interpolation techniques in (medical) image processing we refer to Meijering[5].

3   Discrete Approximations of Continuous Convolutions

In this paper we will make a explicit distinction between a continuous convolution integral and its discrete implementation. Therefore we give the formal definition of both the convolution integral and the discrete convolution sum.

Definition 3 (Continuous Convolution Integral). *The convolution of a continuous image $f \in \text{Fun}(\mathbb{R}^d, \mathbb{R})$ with a kernel $w \in \text{Fun}(\mathbb{R}^d, \mathbb{R})$ resulting in an image $f * w \in \text{Fun}(\mathbb{R}^d, \mathbb{R})$ is defined by:*

$$(f * w)(\mathbf{x}) = \int_{\mathbb{R}^d} f(\mathbf{x} - \mathbf{y}) w(\mathbf{y}) d\mathbf{y}. \tag{2}$$

In this definition (and throughout this paper) we assume that the functions involved in a convolution are defined in such a way that the convolution is well-defined.

Because only the discrete representation F of the image f is available we have to resort to an approximation of the convolution integral. The classical way to approximate the sampled version of $f * w$ in Eq. (2) is to sample both the image f (resulting in $F = \mathcal{S}_B f$) *and* the convolution kernel w (resulting in $W = \mathcal{S}_B w$) and then calculate a *discrete convolution sum*.

Definition 4 (Discrete Convolution Sum). *The convolution of a discrete image $F \in \text{Fun}(\mathbb{Z}^d, \mathbb{R})$ with a kernel $W \in \text{Fun}(\mathbb{Z}^d, \mathbb{R})$ resulting in an image $F \star W \in \text{Fun}(\mathbb{Z}^d, \mathbb{R})$ is defined by:*

$$(F \star W)(\mathbf{k}) = \sum_{\mathbf{l} \in \mathbb{Z}^d} F(\mathbf{k} - \mathbf{l}) W(\mathbf{l}). \tag{3}$$

The discrete image $F \star W$ is, in general, not the sampled version of the continuous convolution $f * w$, it is only a sampled approximation:

$$\mathcal{S}_B(f * w) \approx \mathcal{S}_B f \star \mathcal{S}_B w.$$

It is important to note that the above approximation for $\mathcal{S}_B(f * w)$ is just one of the possible approximations that will be presented in this paper. In the computer vision literature it is almost always the only approximation that is presented (and often without argumentation). In section 4 it will be argued that sampling both the image and the kernel is exact in case both the image f and the kernel w are band-limited. Sampling the kernel is most often not needed as it is known in analytical form (like the Gaussian kernel that we are interested in).

A second classical approach to approximate $\mathcal{S}_B(f * w)$ is to calculate the convolution integral in the—sampled—frequency domain (using a discrete Fourier transform). The main difference with the first approach is that sampling is not done in the spatial domain but in the frequency domain. For kernels that are poorly sampled in the spatial domain (because they are not band-limited) this may be advantageous (see Florack[2] and Oppenheimer et. al.[6]).

In this paper we propose not to sample the kernel w directly. Instead an interpolation is used to approximate the continuous image function f from its sampled representation F. The continuous convolution integral then becomes a sum of integrals. The integrals can be calculated analytically, whereas the sum turns out to be a discrete convolution.

Proposition 1 (From Continuous to Discrete Convolution). *The continuous convolution $f * w$ is approximated by the discrete convolution $F \star W_\phi$ where F is the sampling of f. The discrete kernel W_ϕ is the sampling of $w * \phi$, where ϕ is the interpolation kernel used to approximate f from its sampled representation F. I.e.*

$$\mathcal{S}_B(f * w) \approx \mathcal{S}_B f \star \mathcal{S}_B(w * \phi) = F \star W_\phi.$$

Proof. Because only the samples $F = \mathcal{S}f$ are known, we have to approximate f using an interpolation $\mathcal{I}_{\phi,B}F$ to obtain an approximation of the convolution integral:

$$f * w \approx \mathcal{I}_{\phi,B}F * w.$$

Let $\tau_\mathbf{y}$ be the translation operator over the vector $\mathbf{y}$ of an image in $\mathrm{Fun}(\mathbb{R}^d, \mathbb{R})$, then we can write:

$$\mathcal{I}_{\phi,B}F = \sum_{\mathbf{k} \in \mathbb{Z}^d} F(\mathbf{k})\tau_{B\mathbf{k}}\phi.$$

Substituting this into the above approximation of the convolution and using the fact that convolution is linear and translation invariant we get:

$$f * w \approx \left(\sum_{k \in \mathbb{Z}^d} F(k)\tau_{B\mathbf{k}}\phi \right) * w$$

$$= \sum_{\mathbf{k} \in \mathbb{Z}^d} F(\mathbf{k})\tau_{B\mathbf{k}}(w * \phi).$$

Sampling this function in $\mathrm{Fun}(\mathbb{R}^d, \mathbb{R})$ leads to

$$\mathcal{S}_B(f * w) \approx \sum_{\mathbf{k} \in \mathbb{Z}^d} F(\mathbf{k})\mathcal{S}_B\left(\tau_{B\mathbf{k}}(w * \phi)\right)$$

It can be easily shown that sampling commutes with translation (over a grid vector) such that $\mathcal{S}_B \tau_{B\mathbf{k}} = T_{\mathbf{k}} \mathcal{S}_B$, where $T_{\mathbf{k}}$ is the translation operator in discrete space. This leads to:

$$\mathcal{S}_B(f * w) \approx \sum_{\mathbf{k} \in \mathbb{Z}^d} F(\mathbf{k}) T_{\mathbf{k}} \mathcal{S}_B(w * \phi)$$

i.e. the discrete convolution of $F = \mathcal{S}_B f$ and $W_\phi = \mathcal{S}_B(w * \phi)$:

$$\mathcal{S}_B(f * w) \approx \mathcal{S}_B f \star \mathcal{S}_B(w * \phi) = F \star W_\phi.$$

QED.

The analysis in this section thus showed that

- A continuous convolution integral $f * w$ is approximated with a discrete convolution sum $F \star W_\phi$.
- The discrete kernel W_ϕ is, in general, not equal to the sampled version of the continuous kernel: it should be chosen to be the sampled version of the continuous kernel w convoluted with the interpolating kernel ϕ, i.e. $W_\phi = \mathcal{S}_B(w * \phi)$.
- The discrete approximation of a continuous convolution integral is tightly coupled with interpolation. The convolution integral can be approximated in any (subpixel) position $\mathbf{x} \in \mathbb{R}^d$.
- The analysis is not dependent on the choice of the kernel w (assuming the integral is well defined). Therefore the entire N-jet using Gaussian derivatives can be approximated at all scales at all (subpixel) positions.

4 Band-Limited Functions

The concept of band-limited functions rooted in the frequency domain analysis of signals and (linear) systems is so familiar to anyone working with sampled functions, that an analysis from this point of view on the convolution approximations discussed in the previous section is bound to be a fruitful exercise.

It has been shown in this paper that a discrete approximation of the convolution $f * w$ is obtained as a discrete convolution $F \star \mathcal{S}_B(w * \phi)$ where $F = \mathcal{S}_B f$ is the sampled version of f and $\mathcal{S}_B(w * \phi)$ is the sampled version of $w * \phi$.

In this section we assume that the sampling grid is generated by the standard orthonormal basis $B = I$, i.e. we sample f in the integer valued points:

$$F(\mathbf{k}) = f(B\mathbf{k}) = f(\mathbf{k}).$$

For a properly sampled band-limited function f the interpolation using the sinc function ϕ_∞ is exact and thus the convolution integral can be calculated and sampled without error.

Proposition 2 (Convolution of Band-Limited Function). *Let f be a band-limited function and let w be any kernel, then:*

$$\mathcal{S}_B(f * w) = \mathcal{S}_B f \star \mathcal{S}_B(w * \phi_\infty)$$

The proof of this proposition follows from the observation that in our approximation of the convolution integral in the previous section, the only approximation is of the function f itself (through the interpolation). For a properly sampled band-limited function, sinc-interpolation is exact and thus the convolution is exact.

The above proposition is true for any kernel w, *even for kernels w that are not band-limited.* In fact through the convolution $w * \phi_\infty$ we assure that the function to be sampled *is* band-limited.

Proposition 3 (Convolution of a Band-Limited Function with a Band-Limited Kernel). *Let f be a band-limited function and let w be a band-limited kernel, then:*

$$\mathcal{S}_B(f * w) = \mathcal{S}_B f \star \mathcal{S}_B w$$

Again the proof is trivial because for a band-limited function w we have that $w * \phi_\infty = w$. *In this case convolution and sampling commute* (be it that a continuous convolution is replaced by a discrete convolution).

In the practical use of scale-space techniques we often find that neither the image nor the convolution kernel (e.g. the Gaussian function at small scale) are band-limited. The results of the previous section then still provide a numerical sound way to approximate the convolution, even at small scales and in subpixel positions.

5   Separable Convolution Kernels

One of the practical advantages of using the Gaussian functions (and its derivatives) in computer vision is that the Gaussian function is separable. For a separable function $w \in \mathrm{Fun}(\mathbb{R}^d, \mathbb{R})$ we can find functions $w_i \in \mathrm{Fun}(\mathbb{R}, \mathbb{R})$ such that $w(\mathbf{x}) = w_1(x_1)w_2(x_2)\cdots w_d(x_d)$. The practical relevance is that the convolution of an image f with a separable kernel w is equivalent to the composition of d convolutions each using a 'one dimensional' convolution kernel.

Let w be a separable convolution kernel. The discrete convolution using kernel $\mathcal{S}_B(w * \phi)$ is separable as well in case the interpolation kernel ϕ is also separable.

In this paper the restriction to the discrete convolutions needed in Gaussian scale-space theory is made. All these convolutions using Gaussian kernels and derivatives of the Gaussian function are separable.

The interpolation methods that we will use are separable as well. Therefore in the remaining section of this paper we only look at one dimensional convolutions.

6   Gaussian Convolutions Based on Interpolation

No scale-space paper is complete without the definition of the Gaussian function. We only need the one dimensional Gaussian function:

$$g^s(x) = \frac{1}{s\sqrt{2\pi}} \exp\left(-\frac{x^2}{2s^2}\right).$$

In scale-space theory and practice, convolutions using Gaussian derivatives are just as important. The formalism developed in previous sections is valid for any kernel. Here we consider $\partial^n g^s$: the n-th order derivative of the one dimensional Gaussian function.

The interpolation schemes ϕ_0, ϕ_1, ϕ_3 and ϕ_∞ that are considered in this section are defined in section 2, see also Fig. 1.

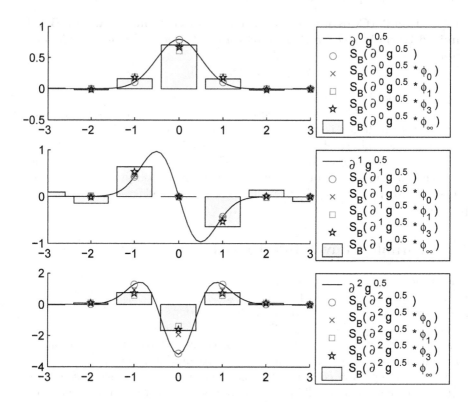

Fig. 2. Discrete Gaussian Convolution Kernels. Shown are the discrete kernels based on (normalized) sampling, zero order, first order interpolation, third order interpolation and sinc-interpolation. The scale of the Gaussian kernel is 0.5 (sampling grid distance).

The discrete kernels $\mathcal{S}_B(\partial^n g^s * \phi_k)$ for $n = 0, 1, 2$ and $k = 0, 1, 3, \infty$ at scale $s = 0.5$, are depicted in Fig. 2. The convolutions $\partial^n g^s * \phi_k$ are numerically approximated (with matlab).

For comparison we also give the sampled kernel $\bar{\mathcal{S}}(\partial^n g^s)$. We use the $\bar{\mathcal{S}}$ notation to indicate that the kernel is normalized (such that $\mathcal{S}_B(g^s)$ sums up to one).

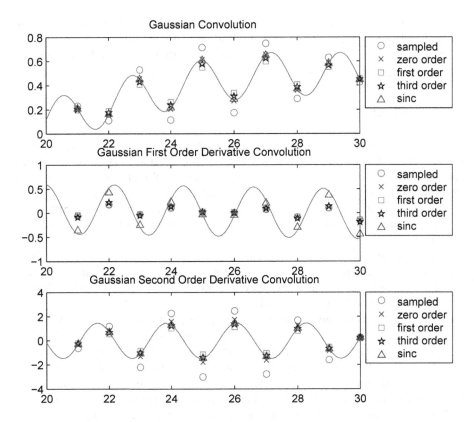

Fig. 3. Gaussian Convolution Approximation. Shown are the discrete convolutions approximating the Gaussian (derivative) convolution based on (normalized) sampling, zero order, first order interpolation, third order interpolation and sinc-interpolation. The scale of the Gaussian kernel is 0.5 (sampling grid distance).

As a test function we define:

$$f(x) = \sin(\frac{4x}{3}) \cos(\frac{3x}{2}).$$

For this function the convolutions $f * \partial^n g^s$ van be calculated analytically (using Mathematica). This allows us to compare the discrete convolution $\mathcal{S}_B f * \mathcal{S}_B(\partial^n g^s * \phi_k)$ with the true value $\mathcal{S}_B(f * \partial^n g^s)$. The discrete convolutions using a Gaussian kernel at scale $s = 0.5$ are depicted in Fig. 3.

For the function f the sinc interpolation based discrete convolution is most accurate (deviations from the true value are probably due to truncated support of the sinc kernel and due to the numerical approximations of the convolution integrals that are used.

From Fig. 3 it can also be concluded that for small scales, any interpolation is better then the classical sampling scheme. For larger scales this is not true anymore. Then $\partial^n g^s * \phi_i nfty \approx \partial^n g^s$ and thus sinc interpolation is equivalent with the classical sampling scheme. The other (simpler) interpolation schemes then introduce an unwanted smoothing effect (although the influence on the numerical approximations is negligible).

7   Conclusions

In this paper we presented a simple scheme for approximating Gaussian convolutions that outperforms the classical spatial convolutions (based on sampling the continuous convolution kernel). Especially at small scales and for Gaussian derivatives the performance (in terms of accuracy) is much better.

The presented formalism is tightly connected with interpolation. Sub-pixel accurate estimates of the Gaussian derivatives at small scales are therefore easily obtained.

The presented preliminary experiments are based on several types of (linear) interpolation. Future work will consider other more advanced interpolation methods as well. Furthermore we plan to compare our spatial sampling implementation with the frequency sampling method of Florack[2].

This paper presents accurate approximation algorithms for small scale Gaussian convolutions. To that end we presented a simple scheme that shows in what way any continuous convolution can be approximated with a discrete convolution. The importance of the sampling operator and the interpolation operator for discretizing continuous image processing operators seems to be new for linear operators (i.e. convolutions). In the morphological context it is not new (see Heijmans [3]), but in that context the operator that reconstructs a continuous image from its sampled representation is not called an interpolation.

References

1. Deriche, R., Using Canny's Criteria to Derive a Recursively Implemented Optimal Edge Detector, IJCV, Vol. 1, No. 2, May 1987, 167–187
2. Florack, L.,A Spatio-Frequency Trade-Off Scale for Scale-Space Filtering. IEEE-PAMI, Vol. 22, No. 9, September 2000, 1050–1055
3. Heijmans, H.J.A.M., Morphological Image Operators, Academic Press, 1994.
4. Lindeberg, T., Scale-Space Theory in Computer Vision, Kluwer Academic Publishers, The Netherlands, 1994.
5. Meijering, E.: Image Enhancement in Digital X-Ray Angiography, Ph.D. thesis, Utrecht University, 2000.
6. Oppenheim, A.V., Willsky, A.S., Young, I.T.: Systems and Signals. Vol. ISBN 0-13-809731-3. 1983, Englewood Cliffs, New Jersey: Prentice-Hall.
7. Young, I.I., van Vliet, L.J.: Recursive implementation of the Gaussian filter, Signal Processing, vol. 44, no. 2, 1995, 139–151.

Scale-Spaces, PDE's, and Scale-Invariance

Henk J.A.M. Heijmans

Centre for Mathematics and Computer Science (CWI)
Kruislaan 413, 1098 SJ Amsterdam, The Netherlands
Henk.Heijmans@cwi.nl

Abstract. In the literature an image scale-space is usually defined as the solution of an initial value problem described by a PDE, such as a linear or nonlinear diffusion equation. Alternatively, scale-spaces can be defined in an axiomatic way starting from a fixed-scale image operator (e.g. a linear convolution or a morphological erosion) and a group of scalings. The goal of this paper is to explain the relation between these two, seemingly very different, approaches.

1 Introduction

In two previous papers [9,24] we have presented an algebraic definition of scale-spaces. In our view a scale-space is the mathematical construct that describes the scale-dependent observation (probing) of images. We only look at the scale-space operators that are able of making observations at a finite scale *without* the necessity to make all observations at smaller scales as well.

Our construction technique for scale-space operators consists of three consecutive steps: (i) downscale the image by a factor $t > 0$ using a scaling operator $S(t)^{-1} = S(1/t)$, (ii) apply an image operator ψ at unit scale, and (iii) resize the image to its original scale using $S(t)$. Thus we arrive at

$$T(t) = S(t)\psi S(t)^{-1} \tag{1}$$

as the scale-space operator. The scaling operators $S(t)$ are assumed to form a group under composition. Refer to Section 3 for more details. In [9], where we have presented an exhaustive treatment of morphological scale-spaces of the form (1), we have made a distinction between between *additive scale-spaces* satisfying

$$T(t)T(s) = T(t+s)\,,\ t,s > 0\,,$$

and *supremal scale-spaces* satisfying

$$T(t)T(s) = T(t \vee s)\,,\ t,s > 0\,.$$

In this paper we will focus on additive scale-spaces since only these possibly allow a description by a PDE (partial differential equation).

At first sight, it appears that our approach is quite different from the PDE approach that has been advocated by various authors. In that approach one

M. Kerckhove (Ed.): Scale-Space 2001, LNCS 2106, pp. 215–226, 2001.

takes the evolution of the zero scale image modeled by a partial differential equation as the starting point. In this paper, we will demonstrate that the two approaches are not so different as it may seem at first sight. In fact, it is rather straightforward to formulate a condition on the differential operator governing the PDE (see (32) below) that guarantees that the corresponding solution family (often a C_0-semigroup) is of the form (1).

We conclude this section with an overview of this paper. In the next section we present a brief, and hence rather incomplete, discussion of some PDE's often encountered in the image processing and computer vision literature. In Section 3 we present our algebraic framework and apply it to two different linear scale-spaces. In Section 4 we consider the morphological scale-spaces governed by erosion and show that they can be associated with PDE's of Hamilton-Jacobi type. Section 5 is concerned with scale-invariance of PDE's. It is shown that the solution operator of a PDE which is invariant under scalings corresponds with a (additive) scale-space in the algebraic sense. Our treatment of scale-invariance in Section 5 is self-contained. Alternatively, one might also choose to use Lie groups [15] for the description of invariance under scalings and, possibly, other symmetries. We refer the reader to [14] for some work in this direction.

2   PDE's in Image Processing

In this section we list some of the PDE's that are often encountered in the image processing literature. We emphasise, however, that our list is far from exhaustive. A more comprehensive overview of various scale-spaces and the corresponding PDE's can be found in [22, 21, 27].

There can be no doubt that the PDE most often encountered in image processing is the *linear diffusion equation* or *heat equation*.

$$u_t = \Delta u \,. \tag{2}$$

Perona and Malik [18, 19] were the first to consider a nonlinear version of the form

$$u_t = \mathrm{div}\big(c(\|\nabla u\|)\nabla u\big)\,, \tag{3}$$

with the conductance function $c(\cdot)$ given by

$$c(s) = \exp(-s^2/k^2) \text{ or } c(s) = \big(1 + s^2/k^2\big)^{-1}\,. \tag{4}$$

The underlying idea is that by reducing the diffusivity in regions with high gradient, one could possibly avoid too strong blurring in such regions. Perona and Malik referred to equation (3) as the *anisotropic diffusion equation*. Unfortunately, (3) in combination with a choice for c such as in (4) is not well-posed as shown by Catté *et al.* [4]; see also Weickert [27].

Alvarez, Guichard, Lions and Morel [1,2] derived a family of nonlinear models of the form

$$u_t(t,x) = F(\nabla^2 u(t,x), \nabla u(t,x), u(t,x), x, t) \tag{5}$$

under the assumption that the multiscale analysis under consideration is causal and regular; refer to [1] for the precise meaning of the word 'causal'. Here F is a function mapping $M \times \mathbb{R}^2 \times \mathbb{R} \times \mathbb{R}^2 \times \mathbb{R}_+$ into $\mathbb{R}$, with M being the space of symmetric matrices, which is nondecreasing in its first argument with respect to the partial ordering of M. Alvarez *et al.* [1] showed that under the given assumptions, (5) allows a so-called *viscosity solution*. The linear diffusion equation (2) corresponds with the case where

$$F(w, v, u, x, t) = \text{trace}(w) \,.$$

If, in addition, the multiscale analysis is invariant under isometries (Euclidean invariance) and under changes of contrast, then (5) can be simplified to

$$u_t = \|\nabla u\| \, G\big(\text{div}(\nabla u/\|\nabla u\|), t\big) = \|\nabla u\| \, G\big(\text{curv}(u), t\big) \,. \tag{6}$$

Here $\text{curv}(u) = \text{div}(\nabla u/\|\nabla u\|)$ is the curvature of the level line of $u(t, x)$ passing through x. Furthermore, G is nondecreasing in its first argument. If G is identically -1, then we arrive at

$$u_t = -\|\nabla u\| \,, \tag{7}$$

which corresponds with the erosion with the Euclidean disk; see Example 4 in Section 4. This equation is a special case of the *Hamilton-Jacobi equation*

$$u_t = -H(\nabla u) \,, \tag{8}$$

where the Hamiltonian H is a convex function. In Section 4 we will explain that the solution of this equation can be obtained by means of a morphological grey-scale erosion.

Dually, putting $G \equiv +1$ in (6) yields

$$u_t = \|\nabla u\| \,, \tag{9}$$

which corresponds with a *dilation*. Equation (9) is also called *eikonal equation* [13]. Putting $G(s, t) = s$ in (6) we arrive at the so-called *mean curvature equation* [16]:

$$u_t = \|\nabla u\|\text{curv}(u) \,. \tag{10}$$

If the condition of Euclidean invariance is strengthened by assuming that the multiscale analysis is invariant under all affine transformations, then we arrive at the time-homogeneous equation

$$u_t = \nabla u \, \big(\text{curv}(u)\big)^{\frac{1}{3}} \,, \tag{11}$$

called the *affine morphological scale-space* (*AMSS*) model by Alvarez *et al.* [1]. Sapiro and Tannenbaum [20], who were following the curve evolution approach, arrived at the same equation independently.

We denote the solution operator of a PDE such as (5) by $U(t, s)$, where $t \geq s$. This means that the solution of the PDE endowed with initial condition $u(s, x) = f(x)$, is given by $u(t) = U(t, s)f$ for $t \geq s$. The family $U(t, s)$, which is sometimes called *multiscale analysis*, satisfies the evolution property $U(t, s)U(s, r) = U(t, r)$ for $r \leq s \leq t$. In this paper we shall be concerned exclusively with time-homogeneous PDE's. For the PDE in (5) this means that F does *not* depend on t, in which case it reduces to

$$u_t(t, x) = F(\nabla^2 u(t, x), \nabla u(t, x), u(t, x), x). \tag{12}$$

In this case the multiscale analysis $U(t, s)$ can be written as $T(t - s)$, where the family $T(t)$, $t \geq 0$, satisfies the semigroup property $T(t + s) = T(t)T(s)$. Below it will become clear that, under quite general assumptions, $T(t)$ defines a scale-space.

3   Algebraic Definition of Scale-Spaces

In [9, 24] we have proposed an algebraic definition of a scale-space. The ingredients of that definition are (i) a one-parameter family of scalings $S(t)$, and (ii) an image operator ψ which acts at images at a given unit scale.[1] With these ingredients we can define a family of operators which governs the action of ψ at various scales.

Let us describe this construction in more detail. Let $\mathcal{L}$ be the collection of images under consideration. For the time being, we take $\mathcal{L}$ to be the set of functions mapping $\mathbb{R}^2$ into $\overline{\mathbb{R}} = \mathbb{R} \cup \{-\infty, +\infty\}$. A one-parameter family $S = \{S(t) \mid t > 0\}$ of operators on $\mathcal{L}$ is called a *scaling* if

$$S(1) = \mathrm{id} \quad \text{and} \quad S(t)S(s) = S(ts), \quad s, t > 0.$$

Thus S is a commutative group with $S(t)^{-1} = S(1/t)$, $t > 0$. In [9] different methods for the construction of scalings have been discussed. In this paper, the family $S^{p,q}$ with $p, q \in \mathbb{R}$ given by

$$S^{p,q}(t)f = t^q f(\cdot/t^p), \quad t > 0 \tag{13}$$

plays an important role. Of particular interest are the following scalings:

- *spatial scaling*: $p = 1$, $q = 0$: a function f is scaled in the spatial domain but not in the grey-level domain.
- *quadratic scaling*: $p = 1/2$, $q = 0$.
- *umbral scaling*: $p = 1$, $q = 1$: the corresponding scaling $S^{1,1}$ scales the region in $\mathbb{R}^2 \times \overline{\mathbb{R}}$ beneath the graph of f (in the morphological literature, this region is called the *umbra* of f).

Furthermore, observe that the case $p = 0$ and $q = 1$ corresponds with a grey-level multiplication: $S^{0,1}(t)f = tf$.

Now suppose we are given a scaling S and an image operator ψ. Let $T_\psi(t)$ be the operator which governs the action of ψ at scale t; that is, to compute

---

[1] An inspiring discussion, from the physical viewpoint, about the role of scale in the description of the structure of images, can be found in the monograph of Florack [6].

$T_\psi(t)f$ for an input image f we first 'downscale' the image by the factor t to obtain $S(t)^{-1}f$, then we apply ψ, and finally we resize the image to its original scale by applying $S(t)$. Thus we get

$$T_\psi(t) = S(t)\psi S(t)^{-1}, \quad t > 0. \tag{14}$$

If the resulting family of operators $T_\psi(t)$ satisfies the additive semigroup property

$$T_\psi(t)T_\psi(s) = T_\psi(t+s), \quad s,t > 0, \tag{15}$$

then it is called a scale-space. Note that in [9] we have considered the more general case where the term at the right hand-side of (15) equals $T_\psi(t \dot{+} s)$, where $\dot{+}$ needs not be the addition on $(0,\infty)$ but may be some other semigroup operation such as the supremum. In this paper we will restrict ourselves to the additive case.

Substituting $t = 1$ in (14) and using that $S(1) = \mathrm{id}$, we get $T_\psi(1) = \psi$. Henceforth we omit the subscript ψ from $T_\psi(t)$ if no confusion is possible. We arrive at the following algebraic definition of a scale-space.

Definition 1. *Let S be a scaling on $\mathcal{L}$. The family $\{T(t)\}_{t>0}$ of operators on $\mathcal{L}$ is called an $(S,+)$-scale-space if*

$$T(t)T(s) = T(t+s), \ s,t > 0 \tag{16}$$
$$T(t)S(t) = S(t)T(1), \ t > 0. \tag{17}$$

If it is clear from the context which scaling is meant, then we shall call $\{T(t)\}_{t>0}$ a scale-space. If $\{T(t)\}_{t>0}$ is a scale-space and $T(1) = \psi$, then we call ψ the kernel operator *associated with $\{T(t)\}_{t>0}$.*

Assume that $\{T(t)\}_{t>0}$ is an $(S,+)$-scale-space, and let $s,t > 0$, then we get

$$T(t)S(s) = T(t)S(t)S(s/t) = S(t)T(1)S(s/t) = S(s)S(t/s)T(1)S(s/t)$$
$$= S(s)T(t/s)S(t/s)S(s/t) = S(s)T(t/s)$$

The following result, proved in [9], expresses that the definition of a scale-space is independent of the choice of the unit scale.

Proposition 1. *If ψ is the kernel of a scale-space, then the same holds for every operator $T_\psi(r)$, with $r > 0$.*

In fact, a straightforward computation shows that

$$S(t)T_\psi(r)S(t)^{-1} = T_\psi(rt),$$

hence that $T_\psi(r)$ is the kernel of the scale-space $\{T_\psi(rt)\}_{t>0}$.

In [9] we have explored linear as well as morphological scale-spaces. We conclude this section with a brief discussion of linear scale-spaces; see also [17]. In the next section we consider scale-spaces corresponding with morphological erosions.

Example 1. (Gaussian Scale-Space) The family $T(t)$ given by

$$(T(t)f)(x) = (2\pi t)^{-1} \int f(x-y) \exp(-\frac{\|y\|^2}{2t}) dy, \tag{18}$$

defines an $(S^{\frac{1}{2},0}, +)$-scale-space with kernel operator

$$\psi(f)(x) = (2\pi)^{-1} \int f(x-y) \exp(-\frac{\|y\|^2}{2}) dy.$$

The family $T(t)$ given by (18) is called a *Gaussian scale-space*. It is well-known that $u(t,x) = (T(t)f)(x)$ solves the linear diffusion equation in (2) with initial condition $u(0,x) = f(x)$.

Example 2. (Cauchy Scale-Space) The linear operator

$$(\psi(f)(x) = \pi^{-\frac{3}{2}} \Gamma(\frac{3}{2}) \int_{\mathbf{R}^2} \frac{f(x-y)}{[1+\|y\|^2]^{\frac{3}{2}}} dy.$$

is the kernel operator of the $(S^{1,0}, +)$-scale-space

$$(T_\psi(t)f)(x) = \pi^{-\frac{3}{2}} \Gamma(\frac{3}{2}) t \int_{\mathbf{R}^2} \frac{f(x-y)}{[t^2+\|y\|^2]^{\frac{3}{2}}} dy.$$

4   Erosion Scale-Spaces

In this section we discuss a particular family of scale-spaces, namely those governed by morphological erosions. Recall that an erosion is defined as an operator that distributes over arbitrary infima [7]. It is a well known fact (see e.g., [8]) that every translation invariant erosion ε in the set $\mathcal{L}$ of functions mapping $\mathbb{R}^2$ into $\overline{\mathbb{R}}$ is of the form

$$\varepsilon_b(f)(x) = \bigwedge_{h \in \mathbf{R}^2} [f(x-h) + b(h)]. \tag{19}$$

In this expression, the function b is called the *structuring function*. The expression for the erosion ε_b is a well-known operation in convex analysis, where it is called *infimal convolution* and denoted by $f \boxminus b$. Thus the erosion in (19) can be written as $\varepsilon_b(f) = f \boxminus b$. Often, we will omit the subscript b and write ε rather than ε_b. If b is the *indicator function* of a set $B \subseteq \mathbb{R}^2$, i.e., $b = I_B$ with $I_B(x) = 0$ if $x \in B$ and $+\infty$ if $x \notin B$, then

$$(f \boxminus b)(x) = \bigwedge_{h \in B} f(x-h),$$

which is also written as $f \ominus \check{B}$, where $\check{B} = -B$, the reflection of B. The erosion $\varepsilon(f) = f \ominus \check{B}$ is called a *flat erosion* [7].

Throughout the remainder of this section we assume that the function b is lower semi-continuous and convex, and satisfies $b(x) > -\infty$ for every $x \in \mathbb{R}^2$. A straightforward calculation shows that $T_\varepsilon(t)$ as defined by (14) equals

$$T_\varepsilon(t)f = f \boxminus S(t)b\,, \tag{20}$$

where $S = S^{p,q}$. In [9] we have analysed in great detail the exact conditions under which the erosion ε is the kernel of an $(S^{p,q}, +)$-scale-space. Before we state some of the major results obtained there, we give a definition. A convex function b is called *subpolynomial of degree k*, where $k \geq 1$, if

$$b(tx) = t^k b(x), \quad x \in \mathbb{R}^2, \ t > 0\,.$$

b is called subpolynomial of degree $+\infty$ if it is an indicator function.

Proposition 2. *The family $\{T_\varepsilon(t)\}_{t>0}$ given by (20) defines an $(S^{p,q}, +)$-scale-space in each of the following two cases:*

(a) $p = q = 1$;
(b) $q < p < 1$ or $1 < p < q$ and b is subpolynomial of degree k with $k = (1-q)/(1-p)$.

At first sight, this result might suggest that more than one scale-space can be associated with a structuring function b that is subpolynomial of degree k. For example, if $k = 2$ we can choose $p = \frac{1}{2}, q = 0$ or $p = \frac{3}{2}, q = 2$ (case (b)) and also $p = q = 1$ (case (a)). However, if b is subpolynomial of degree k and $k = (1-q)/(1-p)$, then

$$t^q b(x/t^p) = t^{q-k(p-1)} b(x/t) = tb(x/t)$$

which means that $S^{p,q}(t)b = S^{1,1}(t)b$. Therefore, in this case all scale-spaces given by Proposition 2 coincide. Putting

$$u(t, \cdot) = f \boxminus S(t)b\,, \tag{21}$$

where $S = S^{1,1}$, it is known [8] that u is a solution of the Hamilton-Jacobi equation (8), that is,

$$u_t = -H(\nabla u)\,, \tag{22}$$

where the Hamiltonian H is the *Young-Fenchel conjugate* (also called *Legendre transform*) of b:

$$H(x) = b^\star(x) = \bigvee_{y \in \mathbb{R}^2} [\langle x, y \rangle - b(y)]\,. \tag{23}$$

The structuring function b is called the *Lagrangian*. Since $(b^\star)^\star = b$, it follows that b can be recovered from H through $b = H^\star$. The solution formula in (21) is sometimes called the *Lax-Oleinik formula*.

If H is convex and *coercive*. i.e.,

$$\lim_{\|x\| \to +\infty} \frac{H(x)}{\|x\|} = +\infty\,,$$

then $u(t, \cdot)$ given by (21) is a so-called *viscosity solution* of (22); refer to [5] for more details. We consider two examples in more detail.

Example 3. Quadratic Structuring Functions
Consider the quadratic scaling S corresponding with $p = 1/2$ and $q = 0$. Proposition 2 tells us that $\varepsilon(f) = f \boxminus b$ is the kernel of an $(S, +)$-scale-space $T_\varepsilon(t)$ if b is subpolynomial of degree 2. It is given by

$$(T_\varepsilon(t)f)(x) = \bigwedge_{y \in \mathbf{R}^2} [f(x - y) + b(y/\sqrt{t})] .$$

Note that in this expression, $b(y/\sqrt{t})$ may be replaced by $t^{-1} b(y)$ or $tb(y/t)$. A typical example of a convex function which is subpolynomial of degree 2 is

$$b_Q(x) = \frac{1}{2} \langle Qx, x \rangle ,$$

where Q is a symmetric positive semi-definite matrix. It is known that

$$b_Q \boxminus b_R = b_{Q \times R} ,$$

where $Q \times R = (Q^{-1} + R^{-1})^{-1}$. The erosion $T_\varepsilon(t)$ is given by $T_\varepsilon(t)f = f \boxminus b_{t^{-1}Q}$ and the semigroup property $T_\varepsilon(t)T_\varepsilon(s) = T_\varepsilon(t + s)$ can also be derived from the fact that

$$b_{t^{-1}Q} \boxminus b_{s^{-1}Q} = b_{t^{-1}Q \times s^{-1}Q} = b_{(t+s)^{-1}Q} .$$

This scale-space has been called the *parabolic morphological scale-space*; see [25, 26] as well as [11, 12]. The function u given by

$$u(t, x) = (f \boxminus b_{t^{-1}Q})(x)$$

is a solution of the Hamilton-Jacobi equation (22) with $H(x) = b_Q^\star(x) = \frac{1}{2} \langle Q^{-1}x, x \rangle$; see [10, Part II, Sect.X.1]. If we choose $Q = I$, (22) reduces to

$$u_t = -\frac{1}{2} \|\nabla u\|^2 . \tag{24}$$

Example 4. Flat Structuring Functions
Consider the spatial scaling given by $p = 1$ and $q = 0$. From Proposition 2 we derive that b has to be a subpolynomial of degree $+\infty$, that is $b = I_B$, where B is a closed convex set. The scale-space induced by $\varepsilon(f) = f \boxminus b$ is given by

$$(f)(x) = \bigwedge_{y \in tB} f(x - y) .$$

In other words, $T_\varepsilon(t)$ is a flat erosion with structuring element tB. The function $u(t, \cdot) = T_\varepsilon(t)f$ satisfies the PDE

$$u_t = -H_B(\nabla u) ,$$

where $H_B(x) = I_B^\star(x) = \bigvee_{y \in B} \langle x, y \rangle$ is the *support function* of the convex set B; see e.g. [10]. If B is symmetric (i.e. $B = \check{B}$) and contains the origin in its interior, then H_B is the norm associated with the unit ball $B°$, the *polar set* of B, defined by

$$B° = \{x \in \mathbb{R}^2 \mid \langle y, x \rangle \le 1 \text{ for all } y \in B\}.$$

For example, if B is the Euclidean unit disk in $\mathbb{R}^2$, then $B° = B$ and $H_B(x) = \|x\|$, the Euclidean norm. The resulting PDE for u is

$$u_t = -\|\nabla u\|, \tag{25}$$

which we have already encountered in (7). If B is the square $\|x\|_\infty \le 1$, where $\|x\|_\infty = \max(|x_1|, |x_2|)$, then $B°$ is the diamond shape $\|x\|_1 \le 1$ where $\|x\|_1 = |x_1| + |x_2|$, and in this case the resulting PDE is

$$u_t = -\|\nabla u\|_1 = -(|\frac{\partial u}{\partial x_1}| + |\frac{\partial u}{\partial x_2}|).$$

PDE's of this type were first considered by Brockett and Maragos [3].

Equations (24) and (25) correspond with the cases $m = 2$ and $m = 1$ in the one-parameter family of PDE's

$$u_t = -\frac{1}{m}\|\nabla u\|^m, \quad m \ge 1. \tag{26}$$

If $m > 1$, then the Hamiltonian $H_m(x) = \frac{1}{m}\|x\|^m$ has a conjugate $b_m = H_m^*$ given by

$$b_m(x) = \frac{m-1}{m}\|x\|^{\frac{m}{m-1}}.$$

Furthermore, b_1 is the indicator function of the Euclidean unit disk. Therefore, the solution of (26) at time instant t is obtained through the erosion of the input function f with structuring function $S^{1,1}(t)b_m$. It is easy to verify that the erosion with structuring function b_m is also the kernel of an $(S^{\frac{1}{m},0}, +)$-scale-space if $m > 1$.

5   Scale-Invariance of PDE's

In Section 2 we have expressed our interest in initial value problems of the form

$$\begin{cases} u_t = A(u) \\ u(0, x) = f(x), \end{cases} \tag{27}$$

where the initial condition f corresponds with the input image. Here A is the differential operator

$$A(u)(x) = F(\nabla^2 u(x), \nabla u(x), u(x), x), \tag{28}$$

where F has the properties listed in Section 2.

An important problem, and often very difficult, concerns the existence and uniqueness of solutions of the initial value problem (27). The difficulty of such problems depends not only on the specific PDE involved but also on the properties of the underlying function space. In this paper we will not deal with the existence and uniqueness problem, but assume that there is a space $\mathcal{L}$ such that for every input image $f \in \mathcal{L}$ the initial value problem (27) has a solution $u(t) = T(t)f$ in $\mathcal{L}$. Note that the exact meaning of the concept "solution" needs to be specified. In particular, if A is the infinitesimal generator of a C_0-semigroup $T(t)$ on a Banach space $\mathcal{L}$, then the solution concept has a specific meaning for initial conditions $f \in D(A)$, the domain of A, which is known to lie dense in the underlying space $\mathcal{L}$ [28].

Throughout the remainder of this section we assume that we can associate a solution $u(t) = T(t)f$ with the initial value problem (27). Since the underlying PDE is autonomous, the one-parameter family $\{T(t) \mid t > 0\}$ of operators on $\mathcal{L}$ forms a semigroup, i.e., $T(t+s) = T(t)T(s)$, for $t, s > 0$. Recalling our definition of a scale-space from Definition 1 we see that $T(t)$ defines an $(S, +)$-scale-space if (17) holds, or equivalently, if

$$T(t)S(s) = S(s)T(t/s), \quad t, s > 0. \tag{29}$$

Here $S(\cdot)$ is a scaling and, as before, we shall restrict ourselves to scalings $S^{p,q}$. Relation (29) can be formulated in terms of the initial value problem (27). Assume that $u(t, x)$ is a solution of (27), fix $s > 0$, and define

$$\tilde{u}(t, x) = s^q u(t/s, x/s^p). \tag{30}$$

In order for (29) to hold, it is necessary and sufficient that $\tilde{u}$ is a solution of the initial value problem (27) with initial function f replaced by $S(s)f$. Note indeed that

$$\tilde{u}(0, x) = s^q u(0, x/s^p) = s^q f(x/s^p).$$

Thus it remains to be verified that $\tilde{u}$ satisfies $\tilde{u}_t = A(\tilde{u})$. This yields the following relation for A:

$$S(s)AS(s)^{-1} = sA, \quad \text{for } s > 0. \tag{31}$$

Note that this equation can also be obtained by differentiating (29) with respect to t and substituting $t = 0$.

If we assume in addition that A is of the form (28), then we arrive at the equation

$$s^{q-1}F(w, v, u, x) = F(s^{q-2p}w, s^{q-p}v, s^q u, s^p x). \tag{32}$$

We consider some examples.

Example 5. (*a*) For the linear diffusion equation we have $F(w, v, u, x) = \text{trace}(w)$, and (32) yields $q - 1 = q - 2p$, that is $p = \frac{1}{2}$. Notice that in this case, like in all linear cases, the value of q is irrelevant.
(*b*) The Hamilton-Jacobi equation (8) corresponds with $F(w, v, u, x) = -H(v)$ and (32) yields

$$s^{q-1}H(v) = H(s^{q-p}v).$$

If H is subpolynomial of degree ℓ, then the right hand-side equals $s^{\ell(q-p)}H(v)$ and we find

$$q - 1 = \ell(q - p) \,.$$

These values of p, q, ℓ correspond with those that follow from Proposition 2 with $b = H^*$. Note that H is subpolynomial of degree ℓ if and only if $b = H^*$ is subpolynomial of degree k where $1/\ell + 1/k = 1$.

(c) The anisotropic diffusion equation (3) gives rise to a scale-space if c is of the form

$$c(v) = \|v\|^{-m} \,,$$

for some $m \geq 0$. In that case (32) gives rise to the relation

$$2p + m(q - p) = 1 \,.$$

PDE's of this type have been investigated by Tsurkov [23] for the one-dimensional case.

References

1. L. Alvarez, F. Guichard, P. L. Lions, and J. M. Morel. Axioms and fundamental equations of image processing. *Archive for Rational Mechanics and Analysis.*, 16(9):200–257, 1993.
2. L. Alvarez and J.M. Morel. Formalization and computational aspects of image analysis. *Acta Numerica*, pages 1–59, 1994.
3. R.W. Brockett and P. Maragos. Evolution equations for continuous-scale morphological filtering. *IEEE Transactions on Signal Processing*, 42(12):3377–3386, 1994.
4. F. Catté, P.-L. Lions, J.-M. Morel, and T. Coll. Image selective smoothing and edge detection by nonlinear diffusion. *SIAM J. numerical analysis*, 29(1):182–193, 1992.
5. M. Crandall, H. Ishii, and P. Lions. User's guide to viscosity solutions of second order partial differential equations. *Bull. Amer. Math. Soc.*, 27:1–67, 1992.
6. L. M. J. Florack. *Image Structure*, volume 10 of *Computational Imaging and Vision Series*. Kluwer Academic Publishers, Dordrecht, 1997.
7. H. J. A. M. Heijmans. *Morphological Image Operators*. Academic Press, Boston, 1994.
8. H. J. A. M. Heijmans and P. Maragos. Lattice calculus of the morphological slope transform. *Signal Processing*, 59(1):17–42, 1997.
9. H. J. A. M. Heijmans and R. van den Boomgaard. Algebraic framework for linear and morphological scale-spaces. Research Report PNA-R0003, CWI, 2000 (to appear in JVCIR).
10. J.-B. Hiriart-Urruty and C. Lemaréchal. *Convex Analysis and Minimization Algorithms*. Parts I and II. Springer, Berlin, 1993.
11. P. T. Jackway. Properties of multiscale morphological smoothing by poweroids. *Pattern Recognition Letters*, 15:135–140, 1994.
12. P. T. Jackway. Gradient watersheds in morphological scale-space. *IEEE Transactions on Image Processing*, 5(6):913–921, 1996.

13. P. Maragos and M.A. Butt. Curve evolution, differential morphology, and distance transforms applied to multiscale and eikonal problems. *Fundamenta Informaticae*, 41(1-2):91–129, 2000.

14. P. Olver, G. Sapiro, and A. Tannenbaum. Differential invariant signatures and flows in computer vision: A symmetry group approach. In B. M. ter Haar Romeny, editor, *Geometry Driven Diffusion in Computer Vision*, pages 255–306. Kluwer Academic Publishers, Dordrecht, 1994.

15. P. J. Olver. *Applications of Lie Groups to Differential Equations*. Springer Verlag, New York, 1986.

16. S. Osher and J. A. Sethian. Fronts propagating with curvature-dependent speed: Algorithms based on Hamilton-Jacobi formulations. *J. Comput. Phys.*, 79(1):12–49, 1988.

17. E. J. Pauwels, L. J. Van Gool, P. Fiddelaers, and T. Moons. An extended class of scale-invariant and recursive scale space filters. *IEEE Trans. Pattern Analysis and Machine Intelligence*, 17(7):691–701, 1995.

18. P. Perona and J. Malik. Scale space and edge detection using anisotropic diffusion. In *Workshop on Computer Vision, (Miami Beach, FL, November 30 – December 2, 1987)*, pages 16–22, Washington, DC., 1987. IEEE Computer Society Press.

19. P. Perona and J. Malik. Scale-space and edge detection using anisotropic diffusion. *IEEE Transactions on Pattern Analysis and Machine Intelligence*, 12(7):629–639, July 1990.

20. G. Sapiro and A. Tannenbaum. On affine plane curve evolution. *Journal of Functional Analysis*, 119:79–120, 1994.

21. J. A. Sethian. *Level Set Methods: Evolving Interfaces in Geometry, Fluid Mechanics, Computer Vision and Materials Science*. Cambridge University Press, Cambridge, 1996.

22. B. M. ter Haar Romeny, editor. *Geometry-Driven Diffusion in Computer Vision*. Kluwer Academic Publishers, Dordrecht, 1994.

23. V. I. Tsurkov. An analytical model of edge protection under noise suppression by anisotropic diffusion. *J. Computer and Systems Sciences International*, 39(3):437–440, 2000.

24. R. van den Boomgaard and H. J. A. M. Heijmans. Morphological scale-space operators: an algebraic approach. In J. Goutsias, L. Vincent, and D. S. Bloomberg, editors, *Mathematical Morphology and its Applications to Image and Signal Processing*, ISMM 2000, pages 283–290, Boston, 2000. Kluwer Academic Publishers.

25. R. van den Boomgaard and A. Smeulders. The morphological structure of images: the differential equations of morphological scale space. *IEEE Transactions on Pattern Analysis and Machine Intelligence*, 16:1101–1113, 1994.

26. R. van den Boomgaard and A. W. M. Smeulders. Towards a morphological scale-space theory. In Y-L. O, A. Toet, D. Foster, H. J. A. M. Heijmans, and P. Meer, editors, *Proceedings of the Workshop "Shape in Picture", 7–11 September 1992, Driebergen, The Netherlands*, pages 631–640, Berlin, 1994. Springer.

27. J. Weickert. *Anisotropic Diffusion in Image Processing*. Teubner-Verlag, Stuttgart, 1998.

28. K. Yosida. *Functional Analysis*. Springer, Berlin, 1980.

Generic Multi-scale Segmentation and Curve Approximation Method

Marielle Mokhtari and Robert Bergevin

Computer Vision and Systems Laboratory
Department of Electrical and Computer Engineering
Laval University, Ste-Foy, Qc, Canada, G1K 7P4
marielle.c.mokhtari@ca.abb.com, bergevin@gel.ulaval.ca

Abstract. We propose a new complete method to extract significant description(s) of planar curves according to constant curvature segments. This method is based *(i)* on a multi-scale segmentation and curve approximation algorithm, defined by two grouping processes (polygonal and constant curvature approximations), leading to a multi-scale covering of the curve, and *(ii)* on an intra- and inter-scale classification of this multi-scale covering guided by heuristically-defined qualitative labels leading to pairs (scale, list of constant curvature segments) that best describe the shape of the curve. Experiments show that the proposed method is able to provide salient segmentation and approximation results which respect shape description and recognition criteria.

1 Introduction

In order to easily manipulate a planar curve or databases composed of planar curves, it would be interesting to represent data according to primitives which describe them in a way that respects their actual shape for recognition and compression purposes. In this paper, we present an improved version of the multi-scale segmentation and curve approximation method introduced in [1][6]. It is related to the category of the methods favoring shape *recovery* [2][3][8]. However, this new method tries to go behind limitations generated by the other methods by identifying in a formal way the requirements related to the problem of segmentation and approximation of a planar curve [1][7]. The associated algorithm represents a generalization of the paradigm *recover-and-select* established by Leonardis and Bajcsy [4].

The original method that we propose in order to extract significant description(s) of planar curves into lists of constant curvature segments (such as straight line segments and/or circular arcs) is based on MuscaGrip (which stands for *MUlti-scale Segmentation and Curve Approximation based on the Geometry of Regular Inscribed Polygons*), a multi-scale segmentation and curve approximation algorithm, leading to a multi-scale covering of the curve. The MuscaGrip algorithm is defined by two grouping processes: *(i)* a polygonal approximation (from points to straight line segments), and *(ii)* a constant curvature approximation (from straight line segments to straight line segments and/or circular arcs).

M. Kerckhove (Ed.): Scale-Space 2001, LNCS 2106, pp. 227–235, 2001.

MuscaGrip repeats the first grouping process using each point on the curve as its starting point and the second grouping process using each straight line segment provided by the first process as its starting segment. These repetitions lead to a complete description of the curve composed of lists of constant curvature segments at different scales. Although they increase the computational load of the algorithm, these repetitions are necessary in order to respect invariance criteria. In order to find a set of pairs composed of one scale and one list of constant curvature segments that best describe the shape of the curve, a global combinatorial method of the multi-scale covering is introduced, guided by heuristically-defined qualitative labels leading to a single non-redundant subset.

In the following, the description of the complete method is presented. The MuscaGrip grouping processes are first described. The method to extract the minimal set of adequate pairs (scale, list of constant curvature segments) is then introduced in details with its inter- and intra-scale classification steps. Finally, experimental results are presented for open and closed planar curves.

2   MuscaGrip: Point Grouping Process

The generic process first splits a planar curve into several sub-curves, each of which is approximated by a straight line segment. The associated point grouping criterion is equivalent to a *co-circularity* criterion among the connected points of the sub-curve. A *scale parameter*, acting as a maximum deviation criterion, is associated with a scale measure.

It is assumed that a point chain of two points forms an uniform sub-curve. A chain of three or more points forms an uniform sub-curve if and only if the perpendicular distance of each point of the chain relative to the straight line joining the two endpoints of the chain is less than or equal to the scale parameter. The computation of this step is repeated at a number of scales to provide a multi-scale set of polygonal approximations, and using all points on the curve as a starting point.

More formally, let $\mathcal{C}$ be an open or closed planar curve, an ordered list of n points $p_i(x_i, y_i)$, for $i \in [1, n]$, where p_i, p_{i+1} are consecutive points along sampled curve, then $\mathcal{C} = \{ p_i(x_i, y_i) \,|\, i \in [1, n] \wedge x_i \in \mathcal{R} \wedge y_i \in \mathcal{R} \}$. When $\mathcal{C}$ is open, p_1 is obtained from the first point of the curve and p_n from the last point. Otherwise, p_1 (consequently p_n) is obtained from an arbitrarily selected point of $\mathcal{C}$. Let $\mathcal{S}$ be an ordered list of m scales s_j, for $j \in [1, m]$, where s_j, s_{j+1} are consecutive scales, then $\mathcal{S} = \{ s_j \,|\, j \in [1, m] \wedge s_j \in \mathcal{R} \}$ with s_1 the finest scale, and s_m the coarsest scale.

At a given scale $s_j \in \mathcal{S}$, $PA_{\mathcal{C}}(s_j, p_i)$, a polygonal approximation associated to a planar curve $\mathcal{C}$ and generated from point $p_i \in \mathcal{C}$ is defined by an ordered list of p straight line segments $sls_k(p_q, p_r)$, for $k \in [1, p]$, whose p_q and p_r are the first and last points of an uniform sub-curve of $\mathcal{C}$. We thus have:

$$PA_{\mathcal{C}}(s_j, p_i) = \{ sls_k(p_q, p_r) \,|\, k \in [1, p] \wedge p_q, p_r \in \mathcal{C} \}. \tag{1}$$

For a closed planar curve, $PA_{\mathcal{C}}(s_j, p_i)$ is defined by $PA_{\mathcal{C}}^{clkw}(s_j, p_i)$ in the clockwise direction and $PA_{\mathcal{C}}^{cclkw}(s_j, p_i)$ in the counter-clockwise direction (overshoot can occur).

3   MuscaGrip: Straight Line Segment Grouping Process

For a polygonal approximation, the constant curvature approximation process aims at grouping $n \geq 2$ adjacent straight line segments into circular arcs whenever feasible. The associated uniformity criterion is based on the model of a *regular polygon*, formed of $n \geq 2$ segments, approximating the circular arc (noted *ca* in most figures) into which it is *inscribed*. Let a be the radius of the inscribed circular arc, and let R be the radius of the circumscribed circular arc, the difference between R and a is related to s_j, the scale parameter. The constant curvature approximation is then obtained using a merging process of consecutive straight line segments of the polygonal approximation.

Given a polygonal approximation and a regular polygon whose features are induced by a sublist of this polygonal approximation, is it possible that, by adding to this sublist a straight line segment being adjacent to it, the new sublist still be at the basis of a regular polygon whose features are similar to those of the old instance? If such is the case after consideration of a set of uniformity criteria, a new straight line segment adjacent to the sublist is targeted whenever possible.

More formally, let $\mathcal{P}'$ be a sublist of a polygonal approximation composed of p straight line segments. $\mathcal{P}'$ is defined by an ordered list of $\wp'$ segments, with $\wp' \leq p$. If $\wp'$ is equal to 1, $\mathcal{P}'$ is only composed of one straight line segment, then $\mathcal{P}'$ is uniform. Before continuing, let us note that a regular polygon $\mathcal{RP}'$ originating from an uniform sublist $\mathcal{P}'$ is entirely described by *(i)* the angle θ' between two consecutive sides, *(ii)* the length l' of each side and *(iii)* n', its number of sides. Derived features are deduced, *(i)* R', the value of the radius of the circumscribed circular arc, and *(ii)* a', the value of the radius of the inscribed circular arc, commonly called apothem. If $\wp'$ is equal to 2, $\mathcal{P}'$ composed by two straight line segments, sls_1 and sls_2, will be considered uniform if and only if the regular polygon $\mathcal{RP}'$ originating from this one is validated by the following uniformity criteria:

1● $s_j - \delta s \leq R' - a'$ and $R' - a' \leq s_j + \delta s$. δs corresponds to the step between two consecutive scales of $\mathcal{S}$,

2● the features (l_{sls_1} and l_{sls_2}, the lengths of the segments, and $\theta_{(sls_1, sls_2)}$, the angle between the two segments) describing $\mathcal{P}'$ must be validated by the features describing two regular control polygons, $\mathcal{RP}'_{s_j - \delta s}$ and $\mathcal{RP}'_{s_j + \delta s}$. These latter are induced by R' and the scales $s_j - \delta s$ and $s_j + \delta s$.

When $\mathcal{P}'$ is uniform, a first instance of a regular polygon $\mathcal{RP}'$ inscribed into the approximating circular arc is created.

If $\mathcal{P}'$ is uniform then the sublist $\mathcal{P}$ composed of $\wp$ ($\wp = \wp' + 1$) straight line segments, and defined by $\mathcal{P} = \{\mathcal{P}' \cup \{sls\} \,|\, sls \in PA\}$ is also uniform if and only if a regular polygon $\mathcal{RP}$, defined by θ, l and n, can be deduced from $\mathcal{P}$ and $\mathcal{RP}'$ according to various uniformity criteria:

1• $\wp$ is equal to or higher than 2,

2• $\wp$ is lower than or equal to n', the number of sides of $\mathcal{RP}'$, the regular polygon induced by $\mathcal{P}'$,

3• $s_j - \delta s \leq R - a$ and $R - a \leq s_j + \delta s$,

4• the features (length of the segments, angle between two consecutive segments) describing $\mathcal{P}$ must be validated by the features describing two regular control polygons, $\mathcal{RP}_{s_j - \delta s}$ and $\mathcal{RP}_{s_j + \delta s}$. These latter are induced by R and the scales $s_j - \delta s$ and $s_j + \delta s$.

At a given scale $s_j \in \mathcal{S}$, $CCA_{\mathcal{C}}(s_j, p_i, sls_k)$, a constant curvature approximation related to a polygonal approximation $PA_{\mathcal{C}}(s_j, p_i)$ and initiated by the straight line segment sls_k is defined by an ordered list of $q+r$ constant curvature segments ccs_s for $s \in [1, q+r]$: q straight line segments sls_u for $u \in [1, q]$ and r circular arcs ca_v for $v \in [1, r]$. ca_v is provided by the grouping of an ordered list of straight line segments according to the uniformity criteria listed above. We thus have:

$$CCA_{\mathcal{C}}(s_j, p_i, sls_k) = \{ ccs_s \mid s \in [1, q+r] \land (ccs_s \in PA_{\mathcal{C}}(s_j, p_i) \lor ccs_s = \cup sls) \}. \quad (2)$$

Overlap can occur inside $CCA_{\mathcal{C}}(s_j, p_i, sls_k)$. Once again, this step is repeated using all straight line segments provided by the polygonal approximation as a starting segment.

4 Extraction of the Best Descriptions

A significant computational load results from the proposed multi-scale segmentation and approximation of a planar curve $\mathcal{C}$. This multi-scale method leads to many representations. Among them, only the more salient ones should be considered. For that purpose, we define an intra- and inter-scales classification of this multi-scale description, guided by heuristically-defined qualitative labels leading to a set of representation(s) which respect shape description and recognition criteria.

4.1 Labeling of Polygonal Approximations

A classification of the results obtained from the first grouping process is a good starting point for extracting salient approximations. We associate a *qualitative label* to each polygonal approximation associated with both open and closed curves. Three labels are defined, label VG_{PA} for *Very Good Polygonal Approximation*, label G_{PA} for *Good Polygonal Approximation*, and label A_{PA} for *Acceptable Polygonal Approximation*.

In the case of an open curve $\mathcal{C}$, at scale s_j, (i) label VG_{PA} means that endpoints of $\mathcal{C}$, p_1 and p_n, are *real* endpoints of $PA_{\mathcal{C}}(s_j, p_i)$, (ii) label G_{PA} means that p_1 or p_n is a *virtual* endpoint of $PA_{\mathcal{C}}(s_j, p_i)$, the other being real, and (iii) label A_{PA} means that p_1 and p_n are both virtual endpoints of $PA_{\mathcal{C}}(s_j, p_i)$. In the same way, for a closed curve $\mathcal{C}$, at scale s_j, (i) label VG_{PA} means that p_i is the starting and ending point of $PA_{\mathcal{C}}^{clkw}(s_j, p_i)$ and $PA_{\mathcal{C}}^{cclkw}(s_j, p_i)$, (ii) label G_{PA} means that p_i is the starting and ending point of $PA_{\mathcal{C}}^{clkw}(s_j, p_i)$ or

$PA_{\mathcal{C}}^{cclkw}(s_j, p_i)$, and *(iii)* label A_{PA} means that p_i is the starting and ending point of neither $PA_{\mathcal{C}}^{clkw}(s_j, p_i)$ and $PA_{\mathcal{C}}^{cclkw}(s_j, p_i)$. In the latter two cases, overshoot occurs. If

$$\begin{aligned}
\mathcal{S}(VG_{PA_{\mathcal{C}}}) &= \{PA_{\mathcal{C}}(s_j, p_i) \mid label = VG_{PA}\}, \\
\mathcal{S}(G_{PA_{\mathcal{C}}}) &= \{PA_{\mathcal{C}}(s_j, p_i) \mid label = G_{PA}\}, \\
\mathcal{S}(A_{PA_{\mathcal{C}}}) &= \{PA_{\mathcal{C}}(s_j, p_i) \mid label = A_{PA}\},
\end{aligned} \tag{3}$$

where $\mathcal{S}(X_{PA_{\mathcal{C}}})$ is a set composed of polygonal approximations of $\mathcal{C}$ labeled X, then,

$$\begin{aligned}
\mathcal{S}(VG_{PA_{\mathcal{C}}}) \cap \mathcal{S}(G_{PA_{\mathcal{C}}}) &= \emptyset \\
\mathcal{S}(G_{PA_{\mathcal{C}}}) \cap \mathcal{S}(A_{PA_{\mathcal{C}}}) &= \emptyset \\
\mathcal{S}(VG_{PA_{\mathcal{C}}}) \cap \mathcal{S}(A_{PA_{\mathcal{C}}}) &= \emptyset.
\end{aligned} \tag{4}$$

Therefore,

$$\mathcal{S}(VG_{PA_{\mathcal{C}}}) \cup \mathcal{S}(G_{PA_{\mathcal{C}}}) \cup \mathcal{S}(A_{PA_{\mathcal{C}}}) = PA_{\mathcal{C}}(s_j). \tag{5}$$

4.2 Labeling of Constant Curvature Approximations

Following the first grouping process, a labeled polygonal approximation $PA_{\mathcal{C}}(s_j, p_i)$ leads to $CCA_{\mathcal{C}}(s_j, p_i)$ composed of p $CCA_{\mathcal{C}}(s_j, p_i, sls_k)$. Each one can in turn be qualitatively labeled: label VG_{CCA} for *Very Good Constant Curvature Approximation*, label G_{CCA} for *Good Constant Curvature Approximation*, and label A_{CCA} for *Acceptable Constant Curvature Approximation*.

For both open and closed curves, *(i)* label A_{CCA} means that overlap (and overshoot if $\mathcal{C}$ is closed) occurs into $CCA_{\mathcal{C}}$ (s_j, p_i, sls_k), *(ii)* label G_{CCA} means that no overlap (and no overshoot if $\mathcal{C}$ is closed) occurs into $CCA_{\mathcal{C}}(s_j, p_i, sls_k)$ but the ratio between the number of constant curvature segments and the number of straight line segments from $PA_{\mathcal{C}}$ (s_j, p_i) is close to 1.0, consequently $CCA_{\mathcal{C}}(s_j, p_i, sls_k)$ is composed principally of straight line segments and then

$$CCA_{\mathcal{C}}(s_j, p_i, sls_k) \cong PA_{\mathcal{C}}(s_j, p_i), \tag{6}$$

and *(iii)* label VG_{CCA} means that no overlap (and no overshoot if $\mathcal{C}$ is closed) occurs into $CCA_{\mathcal{C}}(s_j, p_i, sls_k)$ and the ratio (also called *compression rate*) between the number of circular arcs and the number of constant curvature segments is high. When s_j is coarse, G_{CCA} is used more often than VG_{CCA} because searching to group adjacent straight line segments into circular arcs is less feasible, the number of straight line segments into $PA_{\mathcal{C}}(s_j, p_i)$ decreasing with increasing scale s_j. If

$$\begin{aligned}
\mathcal{S}(VG_{CCA_{\mathcal{C}}}) &= \{CCA_{\mathcal{C}}(s_j, p_i, sls_k) \mid label = VG_{CCA}\}, \\
\mathcal{S}(G_{CCA_{\mathcal{C}}}) &= \{CCA_{\mathcal{C}}(s_j, p_i, sls_k) \mid label = G_{CCA}\}, \\
\mathcal{S}(A_{CCA_{\mathcal{C}}}) &= \{CCA_{\mathcal{C}}(s_j, p_i, sls_k) \mid label = A_{CCA}\},
\end{aligned} \tag{7}$$

where $\mathcal{S}(X_{CCA_{\mathcal{C}}})$ is a set composed of constant curvature approximations of $\mathcal{C}$ labeled X, then

$$\begin{aligned}
\mathcal{S}(VG_{CCA_{\mathcal{C}}}) \cap \mathcal{S}(G_{CCA_{\mathcal{C}}}) &= \emptyset \\
\mathcal{S}(G_{CCA_{\mathcal{C}}}) \cap \mathcal{S}(A_{CCA_{\mathcal{C}}}) &= \emptyset \\
\mathcal{S}(VG_{CCA_{\mathcal{C}}}) \cap \mathcal{S}(A_{CCA_{\mathcal{C}}}) &= \emptyset.
\end{aligned} \tag{8}$$

Therefore,

$$\mathcal{S}(VG_{CCA_C}) \cup \mathcal{S}(G_{CCA_C}) \cup \mathcal{S}(A_{CCA_C}) = CCA_C(s_j, p_i). \qquad (9)$$

The most interesting description for a curve is a set of one or several VG_{CCA} provided by a VG_{PA}. If no VG_{PA} exists, then the most interesting description for a curve is a set of one or several VG_{CCA} provided by a G_{PA}. The compression rate allows to partition $\mathcal{S}(CCA_C)$. If several $CCA_C(s_j, p_i, sls_k)$ have the same compression rate then they form a partition of $\mathcal{S}(CCA_C)$, and they can in turn be classified according to the accumulation of the errors (also called *error rate*) generated between each pair of adjacent constant curvature segments. A good compression rate and a weak error rate are thus significant factors.

5   Results

This section presents results for various open and closed curves. To generate results, the algorithm proceeds as follows: for each curve $\mathcal{C}$, at each scale $s_j \in \mathcal{S}$, search for $PA_C(s_j, p_i)$ labeled VG_{PA}, then search by intra-and inter-scales classification for the most significant $CCA_C(s_j, p_i, sls_k)$ labeled VG_{CCA}.

Fig.1(a) provides for a spiral of Archimede-shaped open curve $\mathcal{C}$ the best constant curvature approximation hypothesis for one scale. In order to highlight the span of the circular arcs, grey lines are drawn. Best description hypothesis for a semi-limacon of Pascal-shaped open curve is shown in Fig.1(b) for working scales $s_j \in [1.0, 3.0]$ with $\delta s = 1.0$. For these two results, we can appreciate the excellent compression rate of data.

Invariance to similarity transformations such as translation, rotation and scaling is an important criterion to which a good algorithm of segmentation and approximation of planar curves must conform to in order to provide similar descriptions under various conditions. In order to show invariance, four different orientations are used on an ellipse-shaped closed curve and results are shown on Fig.2. For this curve and under any condition, each obtained description, formed by four circular arcs, is representative of the geometrical shape. Let us note that the origin of each circular arc is located on the axes of symmetry of the curves. In order to visualize the behavior of the algorithm more adequately in the presence of the same curve at several scales, we chose to show results on one set made up of astroids. Whatever the scale to which the curve appears, its general description must remain the same. The results shown on Fig.3(a) illustrate the very good behavior of the algorithm relative to scaling.

An interesting aspect of the MuscaGrip algorithm is the conservation of existing symmetries. Fig.3(b) illustrates this fact by experimenting on a rose-shaped closed curve whose complexity is high. The rose is formed by ten petals and the constant curvature approximation hypothesis is particularly convincing. Each petal is described in the same way. Only circular arcs are included in the description. The conservation of symmetries is also visible on Fig.2 and Fig.3(a). A polygonal approximation of recursive subdivision type, [5], can reduce the overall process only when a planar curve is composed of symmetries. On the other hand, in the case of an unspecified curve, a polygonal approximation as recommended in MuscaGrip is necessary and impossible to circumvent.

When noise is added along the curve, the method has to find a final description including the same number of primitives and the same type of primitives as description that one would have obtained without noise. In the presence of noise, it is obvious that a multi-scale method is more suitable and more robust because no matter what occurs, there always exists one scale likely to attenuate it. Results shown on Fig.4 for an ellipse-shaped closed curve are very satisfactory because, in spite of the more or less significant irregularity in the signal, the algorithm is able to provide an acceptable description.

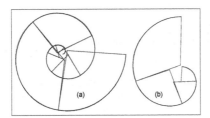

Fig. 1. Best constant curvature approximation hypothesis. (a) For a spiral of Archimede-shaped open curve $\mathcal{C}$ composed of 1440 points, at scale $s_j = 1.0$ with $\delta s = 0.15$, for $PA_\mathcal{C}(s_j, p_i)$ $(= 45sls)$ labeled VG_{PA}, $CCA_\mathcal{C}(s_j, p_i, sls_k) = (3sls, 8ca)$. (b) For a semi-limacon of Pascal-shaped open curve $\mathcal{C}$ composed of 360 points, at scales $s_j \in [1.0, 3.0]$ with $\delta s = 1.0$, for $PA_\mathcal{C}(s_j, p_i)$ labeled VG_{PA}, $CCA_\mathcal{C}(s_j, p_i, sls_k) = (0sls, 4ca))$.

6   Conclusion

A complete method to extract significant descriptions of planar curves as ordered lists of constant curvature segments was presented. This method is based *(i)* on MuscaGrip, a multi-scale segmentation and curve approximation algorithm, defined by two grouping processes leading to a multi-scale covering of the curve, and *(ii)* on an intra- and inter-scale classification of this multi-scale covering, guided by qualitative labels, leading to a single non-redundant subset. The goal is to find a minimal set of pairs composed of *(scale, ordered list of constant curvature segments)* to best describe the shape of the curve. Experiments on synthetic curves have shown that the proposed method is able to provide salient segmentation and approximation results which respect shape description and recognition criteria, and which have a good data compression rate. A more exhaustive experimental evaluation of algorithms on curves of various types, ideal and noisy, and contours from real $2D$ illuminance images is presented in [7] and confirm the good behavior of the method. Furthermore, this research work is part of a more generic project for detecting and describing 3D objects in a

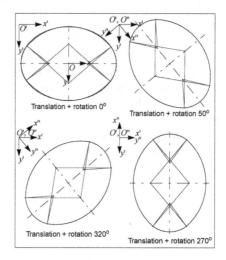

Fig. 2. Invariance to translation and rotation for an ellipse-shaped closed curve, composed of 720 points, at scale $s_j = 3.0$.

single 2D image based on high-level structures obtained by perceptual grouping of constant curvature segments [7].

References

1. Bergevin, R. and Mokhtari, M., "Multiscale Contour Segmentation and Approximation: An Algorithm Based on the Geometry of Regular Inscribed Polygons", in *Computer Vision and Image Understanding*, 71(1):55-73, July 1998.
2. Etemadi, A. "Robust Segmentation of Edge Data", in *Fourth IEE International Conference on Image Processing and Its Applications*, April 7-9, Maastricht, The Netherlands, 1992.
3. Jacot-Descombes, A. and Pun, T., "Asynchronous Perceptual Grouping: From Contours to Relevant 2D Structures", in *Computer Vision and Image Understanding*, 66(1):1-24, April 1997.
4. Leonardis, A. and Bajcsy, R., "Finding Parametric Curves in an Image", in *Second European Conference on Computer Vision*, May 19-22, Santa Margherita Ligure, Italy, 1992.
5. Lowe, D.G., "Three-Dimensional Object Recognition from Single Two-Dimensional Images", in *Artificial Intelligence*, 31(3):355-395, March 1987.
6. Mokhtari, M. and Bergevin, R., "Multi-scale Compression of Planar Curves using Constant Curvature Segments", in *Proc. of the 14th International Conference on Pattern Recognition*, Vol. 1, August 16-20, Brisbane, Australia, pp. 744-746, 1998.
7. Mokhtari, M., "Segmentation multi-échelles et approximation de courbes planes: application à la localisation de structures 3D génériques," *Ph.D Thesis*, Dept. of Electrical and Computer Eng., Laval University, Qc, Canada, Dec. 2000.
8. Rosin, P. and West, G.A.W., "Non-parametric Segmentation of Curves into Various Representations", in *Trans. on Pattern Analysis and Machine Intelligence*, 17(12):1140-1153, December 1995.

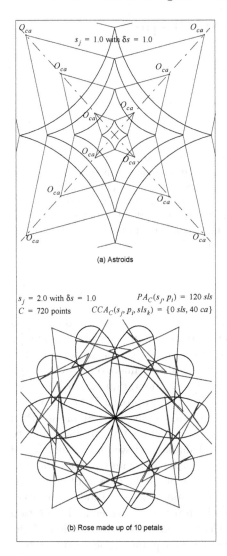

(a) Astroids

$s_j = 2.0$ with $\delta s = 1.0$ $PA_C(s_j, p_i) = 120\ sls$
$C = 720$ points $CCA_C(s_j, p_i, sls_k) = \{0\ sls, 40\ ca\}$

(b) Rose made up of 10 petals

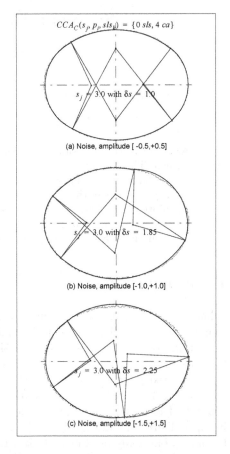

$CCA_C(s_j, p_i, sls_k) = \{0\ sls, 4\ ca\}$

$s_j = 3.0$ with $\delta s = 1.0$

(a) Noise, amplitude [-0.5,+0.5]

$s_j = 3.0$ with $\delta s = 1.85$

(b) Noise, amplitude [-1.0,+1.0]

$s_j = 3.0$ with $\delta s = 2.25$

(c) Noise, amplitude [-1.5,+1.5]

Fig. 4.   Behavior face to adding noise along the curve.

Fig. 3.   (a) Invariance to scaling for a set of closed curves: astroids. (b) Conservation of existing symmetries on a closed curve: a rose made up of ten petals.

Segmentation of Shapes*

Jayant Shah

Mathematics Department, Northeastern University, Boston, MA

Abstract. An algorithm for segmenting 2D shapes into parts is described. The segmentation is constructed from the local symmetry axes of the shape. The local symmetry axes are determined by analyzing the local symmetries of the level curves of a function which is the solution of an elliptic PDE. The segmentation has the structure of a directed graph. The shapes need not be presmoothed and the algorithm may be applied to a complex scene consisting of many objects.

1 Introduction

What is meant by shape segmentation in this paper is decomposition of a 2D shape into ribbons. The basic idea is to delineate the main body of the shape by segmenting out protrusions. The inclusion relations among protrusions induce the structure of a directed graph on the segmentation, analogous to the graph structure associated with shape skeletons. A finer segmentation may be obtained by segmenting the shape across narrow necks. The approach is based on the concept of local symmetry axes which was developed by Tari, Shah and Pien in [3] and further developed in [4]. Axes of local symmetry are analogous to the more commonly used medial axes. If a 2D shape is viewed as a collection of ribbons glued together, then the medial axis of each ribbon may be thought of as a local symmetry axis. In contrast to the usual use of medial axes to obtain shape skeletons, here they are used to segment the shape. The set of local symmetry axes is found by analyzing the level curves of a function, v, which is the solution of an elliptic PDE. The function v smooths the characteristic function of the shape boundary. A point on a level curve of v is a point of local symmetry if the level curve is locally symmetric about the gradient vector of v at that point upto second order. The local symmetry axes may also be described as the ridges and the valleys of the graph of v. The rationale underlying this approach is that if a shape has certain symmetries, then the solution of the PDE ought to reflect these symmetries.

One of the motivations behind this approach was to carry out noise suppression and extraction of shape properties simultaneously. In this spirit, the level curves of v may be thought of as successive smoothings of the shape boundary and thus the approach described above has close similarities with that based on curve evolution. However, the advantage here is that the necessary properties of the level curves are calculated from the differential properties of the function v

---

* This work was supported by NIH Grant I-R01-NS34189-04.

itself, without having to locate the level curves of v. This is not true in the case of curve evolution because the time of arrival of the evolving curve at various points in the domain almost never defines a function over the domain. (The evolving curve may cross a given point several times.) Moreover, differential derivatives needed in the case of curve evolution are one order higher than in the approach proposed here, making the numerical calculations more sensitive to noise. Like curve evolution, there is a smoothing parameter in the elliptic PDE and as it tends to zero, function v tends to the (rescaled) distance function. Of course, shape analysis based on distance function has a long history. (For some recent developments, see the [2].) Local symmetry axes may be used to extract shape skeletons, but as in the case of curve evolution, smoothing built into the process disconnects the skeleton. It is more useful to employ local symmetry axes to segment the shape instead.

The work described here is also related to that of Zhu [5] who has formulated a segmentation functional to draw optimal chords. The optimal chords determine ribbon like portions of the shape whose medial axes determine a partial shape skeleton. The shape skeleton is completed by joining the medial axes in an optimal way. The advantage of this approach is that the segmentation functional provides a goodness criterion for evaluating optimality of shape skeletons and also permits a statistical framework. However, the technique requires calculation of the shape normals and thus shape has to be presmoothed.

The version of the algorithm described here extracts the longest possible ribbon from the shape by segmenting out protrusions. There are several obvious refinements that can be made. It might be necessary to further segment the ribbon segments found by the algorithm. The algorithm does provide the option of further segmenting each of the ribbon segments by creating cuts originating at the saddlepoints of v. However, this may or may not be desirable depending on the application. For example, in shapes with a long neck, a saddlepoint will be formed at its narrowest point and the neck will be segmented there. However, it might be preferrable to isolate the whole neck as one object. The algorithm is not sensitive to special symmetries such as those exhibited by a square or a rectangle. It has to be modified if these special coincidences have to be taken into account. For instance, depending on the numerical choices made, it will segment out two of the corners of a rectangle as protrusions, identifying the rest as the longest ribbon that can be extracted. Such a segmentation would appear reasonable in the case of a parallelogram in which case the two obtuse angles will be segmented out as protrusions and a long ribbon around the long diagonal will be extracted. Since the algorithm does not recognize special cases, it treats the rectangle as a generic parallelogram. Another example where the algorithm does not recognize symmetry is provided by the star-shape shown in Fig. 1. Instead of treating all the arms on the same footing, the algorithm picks out two of them to make up the longest possible ribbon and segments out the others.

2   Smoothing of the Shape Boundary

A shape is described by specifying its boundary in the form of a collection of curves, Γ, inside a bounded domain D of the plane. All that is necessary is that Γ be sufficiently regular for the solution of the differential equation given below to exist. We consider the usual L^2 functional for smoothing the characteristic function of Γ :

$$E_\rho(v) = \int_D \left[\rho \|\nabla v\|^2 + \frac{(v - \chi_\Gamma)^2}{\rho} \right] \tag{1}$$

$$= \int_D \left[\rho \|\nabla v\|^2 + \frac{v^2}{\rho} \right] \tag{2}$$

with the boundary condition $v = 1$ along Γ where

$$\text{the characteristic function } \chi_\Gamma = \begin{cases} 1 \text{ along } \Gamma \\ 0 \text{ elsewhere} \end{cases} \tag{3}$$

Alternative smoothing strategies are possible. The advantage of this particular functional is that it behaves correctly in the limit as $\rho \to 0$:

$$\lim_{\rho \to 0} \inf E_\rho(v) = length(\Gamma) \tag{4}$$

The minimizer of E_ρ satisfies the elliptic differential equation

$$\nabla^2 v = \frac{v}{\rho^2} \tag{5}$$

with boundary conditions $v = 1$ along Γ and $\frac{\partial v}{\partial n} = 0$ along the boundary of D. The parameter ρ plays the role of the smoothing radius.

Although what is relevant here is the global behavior of v which determines the axes of local symmetries, it is interesting to note that when ρ is small compared to the local width of the shape and the local radius of curvature of Γ, the level curves of v locally capture the smoothing of Γ by curve evolution. As shown in Appendix (3) of [1], when ρ is small,

$$v(x,y) = -\rho \left(1 + \frac{\rho \kappa(x,y)}{2} \right) \frac{\partial v}{\partial n}(x,y) + O(\rho^3) \tag{6}$$

where $\kappa(x, y)$ is the curvature of the level curve passing through the point (x, y) and n is the direction of the gradient. If we imagine moving from a level curve to a level curve along the normals, then a small change of δv in the level requires movement

$$\delta r \approx -\frac{\rho}{v}(1 + \frac{\rho \kappa}{2})\delta v \tag{7}$$

where r denotes the arc length along the gradient lines of v. Define time t such that $\frac{dt}{\rho^2} = \frac{dv}{2v}$. Then

$$\frac{dr}{dt} \approx \frac{2}{\rho} + \kappa \tag{8}$$

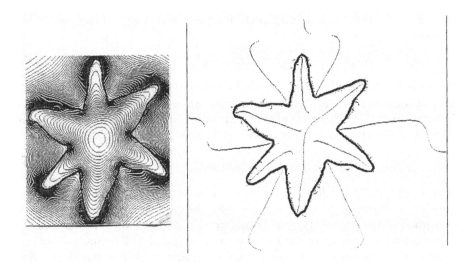

Fig. 1. Left: Level Curves of v.   Right: S_1^+.

As pointed out above, the global behavior of the level curves is radically different from that of curve evolution since the value of v at a point cannot be determined by its values in a local neighborhood. For example, consider a closed level curve with large width and small curvature everywhere so that its evolution mimics the curve evolution. As the level curve shrinks and narrows, interaction between its opposite sides becomes significant and the gradient of v will be less than what it would be without the interaction. For instance, the level curve speeds up as it nears a saddlepoint.

3   Local Symmetries, Medial Axes, and Skeletons

Loci of local symmetries are now defined by analyzing the local symmetries of the level curves of v. These loci consist of one-dimensional branches and their terminal points. The level curves of v inside a starlike shape are shown on the left in Fig. 1. (In all the figures, most of the region in the frame D outside the shape is not shown.) Notice that along the apparent medial axes of protrusions, the level curves are further separated than they are in the neighborhood of indentations. The tips of protrusions are in some sense furthest away from the apparent center of the shape. Now the distance between two adjacent level curves is given by $\frac{dv}{\|\nabla v\|}$. If we define the semimetric

$$\frac{dv/dl}{\|\nabla v\|} dl \qquad (9)$$

where dl is the infinitesimal Euclidean distance, then the geodesics satisfy the equation

$$\frac{d\,\|\nabla v\|}{ds} = 0 \qquad (10)$$

where s is the arc-length along the level curves of v. The symmetry of the level curve at a point P where $\frac{d\|\nabla v\|}{ds} = 0$ is revealed by the missing $\eta\xi$-term in the Taylor expansion of v in terms of the local coordinates η and ξ where η is in the direction of ∇v and ξ is tangent to the level curve:

$$v = a_{00} + a_{10}\eta + a_{01}\xi + a_{20}\eta^2 + a_{02}\xi^2 + \cdots \qquad (11)$$

Thus locally at P, the level curve $v = a_{00}$ is approximately a conic section whose one of the principal axes coincides with the gradient vector. An equivalent description of the symmetry at P is that the Hessian of v at P is diagonalized when expressed in terms of the local coordinates η and ξ. This means that the gradient vector ∇v is an eigenvector of the Hessian at P. The last description may be generalized to define partial symmetries of shapes in dimensions > 2 [4].

As explained above, along the middle of protrusions, the distance between adjacent level curves is the greatest, that is, $\|\nabla v\|$ is minimum along the level curve. So let S_1^+ denote the closure of the set of zero-crossings of $\frac{d\|\nabla v\|}{ds}$ where $\frac{d^2\|\nabla v\|}{ds^2}$ is positive and let S_1^- denote the closure of the set of zero-crossings of $\frac{d\|\nabla v\|}{ds}$ where $\frac{d^2\|\nabla v\|}{ds^2}$ is negative. The connected components of $S_1 \backslash (S_1^+ \cap S_1^-)$ are called the branches of S_1. The direction of each branch is in the direction of increasing v. The locus S_1^+ in the case of the star-like shape is shown on the right in Fig. 1. (Note the characteristic behavior as a branch of S_1^+ approaches the boundary of D.)

The set $S_1^+ \cap S_1^-$ consists of the terminal points of the branches of S_1 and it is the union of two sets, S_0 and J. The set S_0 is defined by the equation $\|\nabla v\| = 0$ and the set J is defined by the equations $\frac{d\|\nabla v\|}{ds} = \frac{d^2\|\nabla v\|}{ds^2} = 0$. The set S_0 may be further subdivided into the set S_0^+ of elliptic points where the determinant of the Hessian of v is positive, the set S_0^- of hyperbolic points where it is negative and the set S_0^0 of parabolic points where it is zero. At an elliptic point, v has a local minimum and has the Taylor expansion of the form $a_{00} + a_{20}x^2 + a_{02}y^2 +$ *higher order terms*. By applying the definition of S_1^+ and S_1^- to this local expression, it is easy to see that at an elliptic point, there are two branches of S_1^+ directed away from the point in the direction of the maximum second derivative and two branches of S_1^- directed away in the direction of the minimum second derivative. At a hyperbolic point, v has the Taylor expansion of the form $a_{00} + a_{11}xy +$ *higher order terms* and calculations show that at a hyperbolic point, there are four branches of S_1 all of which belong to S_1^+. Hyperbolic points are of course saddlepoints in that two of these branches are directed away from the saddlepoint and two are directed towards it. In theory, the set S_0^0 of parabolic points may be one-dimensional, but numerically it is impossible to identify such points without setting some kind of a numerical threshold. What we find is that a parabolic line is seen numerically as a series of elliptic and hyperbolic points, making analysis

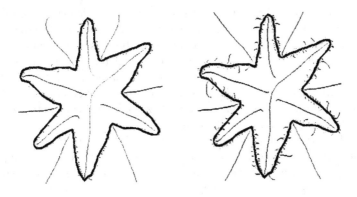

Fig. 2. Left: S_1^+ with $\rho = 128$.   Right: S_1^+ with $\rho = 8$.

of parabolic points difficult. However, from the point of view of segmentation, all that is needed is determination of the kind of branches of S_1 that are present in a tubular neighborhood.

Generically, a point in J is a junction of a branch from S_1^+ and a branch from S_1^-. As in the case of parabolic lines, in the absence of a numerical threshold, all points in J are numerically regarded as belonging to this category. A point in J belongs to the subset J^+ if the two branches of S_1 are directed away from it and it belongs to the subset J^- if they are directed towards it. At points of J, v has a local maximum or a local minimum when restricted to S_1. It is minimum if the point belongs to J^+ and maximum if it belongs to J^-. Junctions of type J^- arise when a parabolic line breaks up into a series of elliptic and hyperbolic points or when there is protrusion present near a neck. The latter case can be seen in Fig. 1. Shape protrusions narrow the space between the shape and boundary of D, creating saddlepoints along the boundary of D. A branch of S_1^+ from such a saddlepoint is linked to a branch of S_1^+ emanating from a nearby shape indentation by a segment of S_1^-. (Note that an indentation in the shape behaves like a protrusion when seen from outside the shape.) In principle, there should be exactly one point of J^+ and one point of J^- in this linkage. However, there is numerical degeneracy due to the fact that the level curves $\frac{d\|\nabla v\|}{ds} = 0$ and $\frac{d^2\|\nabla v\|}{ds^2} = 0$ are nearly coincident over some distance creating a series of points numerically identified as points of J, (see the saddlepoint on the right).

Since there are only four branches at an elliptic point, most branches of S_1 end up at points in J. The smaller the protrusion, the shorter the branch. Notice the extremely short branches near the shape boundary, created by the noise in the boundary. The two branches of S_1^+ meeting at the elliptic point inside the star define the medial axis of the longest ribbon that can be extracted from the shape.

The construction described above depends on the choice of the smoothing parameter ρ. The locus S_1^+ shown in Fig. 1 was obtained with $\rho = 32$ pixels.

(The size of the frame D is 400×400 pixels.) Figure 2 depicts the same locus determined using $\rho = 8$ and $\rho = 128$. The features that are sensitive to the choice of ρ are the location of the points in J and the number of saddlepoints. The larger the value of ρ, the shorter the protrusion axes. What recedes are the portions of these axes projecting outside the protrusions, and the points in J move closer to the corresponding shape projections. Since the function v emulates the distance function more and more closely as ρ tends to zero, it begins to detect even very wide necks by creating more saddlepoints.

We conclude this section with the definition of the shape skeleton:

Definitions: A *medial axis* is a branch of S_1^+ which starts at an elliptic point or at a point in J^+ and ends either at the shape boundary or at a saddlepoint. A medial axis starting at an elliptic point is called a *main axis* while a medial axis starting at a point in J^+ is called a *protrusion axis*. The *skeleton* of the shape is the union of its medial axes.

As noted before, a shape skeleton need not be connected.

4   Segmentation

The medial axes detect the "corners" of the shape. The saliency or the extent of each corner may be guaged by the length of the associated medial axis. However, the main objective of this paper is to segment protrusions and indentations by means of their medial axes. The basic idea is to find the two nearest points on the shape boundary from the terminal point of the protrusion axis, one on each side of the axis and connect these two points to segment the protrusion. The important point is to restrict the search to a suitable neighborhood of the protrusion axis. To solve this problem, we use the fact that S_1 segments the frame D and inside each connected component of $D \backslash S_1$, $\frac{d\|\nabla v\|}{ds}$ is either positive or negative. Segmentation of D by the zero-crossings of $\frac{d\|\nabla v\|}{ds}$ in the case of the star-figure is shown on the left in Fig. 3. Each protrusion axis neighbors exactly two of these components. Therefore the search for the nearest boundary points is restricted to the interior of these two components adjoining the axis. Admittedly, the boundary points found in this way depend on where the terminal point of the protrusion axis is which in turn depends on the choice of ρ. However, if the ends of protrusion are marked by a sharp change in the local width of the shape, the boundary points are insensitive to ρ. In the special cases when this is not true as in the case of a parallelogram, the larger the value of ρ, the further away the boundary points from the obtuse corners which are interpreted as protrusions.

It is possible to segment shapes across necks by means of the associated saddlepoints. This is a more delicate construction. Here the problem is to avoid spurious saddlepoints arising from the numerical break-up of parabolic lines. The difficulty is that there may be irrelevant small segments of $D \backslash S_1$ adjoining the saddlepoint. Therefore, a hyperbolic point is called a *true saddlepoint* if it adjoins at least three segments of $D \backslash S_1$ which touch the shape boundary and if the saddlepoint is not a point on the boundary of D. (The last condition avoids saddlepoints artificially introduced by the frame D.) Going through each

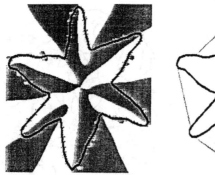

Fig. 3. Left: $\frac{d\|\nabla v\|}{ds} > 0$ dark, < 0 light.   Right: Segmentation.

saddlepoint is a medial axis, directed away from it, and the problem is to find the two nearest boundary points, one each side of the medial axis. Restrict the search for the nearest boundary points to only these adjoining segments of $D \backslash S_1$. Once the two boundary points are found, one on each side of the medial axis, connect the saddlepoint to each of them. This construction may still produce double segmentation lines. This happens if there are two branches of S_1 leaving the theoretical parabolic line from two different points to meet the shape boundary or another true saddlepoint. The solution in this case is to search in an appropriately chosen tubular neighhood of the medial axis through the saddlepoint and treat the two terminal points on the parabolic line as a single unit.

Figure 3 on the right shows the segmentation of the star figure. The shape is segmented from inside as well as from outside. As noted before, in its attempt to extract the longest possible ribbon, the algorithm disregards the approximate symmetry of the star and includes in the main ribbon two of what would normally be perceived as protrusions.

The segmentation has the structure of a directed graph. Its set of vertices consists of the true saddlepoints and one vertex for each of the shape segments. If a segment X is a protrusion with a medial axis originating at a point in J^+ which is contained in another segment Y, then YX is an edge in the graph. (The direction of an edge is always in the direction of increasing v.) Each segmentation line through a saddlepoint is the common boundary between two shape segments. The vertices correponding to these two segments are connected to the vertex corresponding to the saddlepoint by edges directed towards the saddlepoint.

Additional examples of shape segmentation are shown in Fig. 4. All the quantities needed in the algorithm were computed using 3×3 neighborhoods except the sign of $d^2 \|\nabla v\| / ds^2$ which required 4×3 neighborhooods. (Each shape was scaled to make sure that it was nowhere less than 4 pixels wide.) In Fig. 4, the top row on the left shows the S_1^+ loci while the bottom row shows the corresponding segmented shapes. The example of the brain segmentation shown on

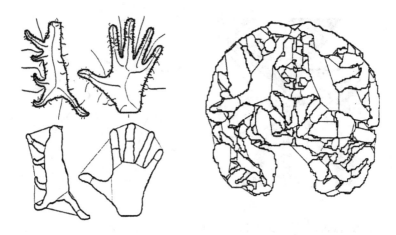

Fig. 4. Left: top row: S_1^+, bottom row: Segmentation. Right: Complex Shape.

the right illustrates the case of a complex of shapes involving non-simply connected shapes and triple junctions. Note that the shape boundary is outlined by thick jagged lines while the segmentation lines are straight and thinner.

References

1. D. Mumford and J. Shah, Optimal approximations by piecewise smooth functions and associated variational problems, *Comm. Pure Appl. Math,* **XLII**, 1989, 577-684.
2. K. Siddiqi, A. Shokoufandeh, S. Dickinson and S. Zucker, Shock graphs and shape matching, *Intl. J. Computer Vision,* **35 (1)**, 1999, 13-32.
3. S. Tari, J. Shah and H. Pien, Extraction of shape skeletons from grayscale images, *Computer Vision and Image Understanding,* **66**, 1997, 133-146.
4. S. Tari and J. Shah, Local symmetries of shapes in arbitrary dimension, *Sixth Intl. Conf. Computer Vision,* 1998.
5. S.C. Zhu, Stochastic jump-diffusion process for computing medial axes in markov random fields, *IEEE Trans. Pattern Analysis and Machine Intelligence,* **21 (11)**, 1999.

The Influence of the γ-Parameter on Feature Detection with Automatic Scale Selection

Peter Majer

Institute for Statistics and Econometrics, University of Göttingen
correspondence: Bitplane AG, Badenerstr. 682, 8048 Zürich, Switzerland
majer@bitplane.com

Abstract. A method to automatically select locally appropriate scales for feature detection, proposed by Lindeberg [8], [9], involves choosing a so-called γ-parameter. The implications of the choice of γ-parameter are studied and it is demonstrated that different values of γ can lead to qualitatively different features being detected. As an example the range of γ-values is determined such that a second derivative of Gaussian filter kernel detects ridges but not edges. Some results of this relatively simple ridge detector are shown for two-dimensional images.
Keywords: Scale selection, ridge detection.

1 Introduction

The response of a local operator to an image depends on just how local the operator is. Figure (1) demonstrates this scale-dependence for an operator that computes the principal curvature of the image intensity. At small scales the edges of the diamonds produce a strong response, at larger scales the long axis of each diamond is particularly pronounced, and at still larger scales the rows of diamonds stand out.

Scale-dependence has received much attention during the last two decades. On one hand it creates the problem of having to deal with all scales whenever there is no prior information available about the scales that occur in an image. On the other hand it creates the possibility to automatically determine the scales of structures in an image.

In medical image processing, for example, several studies have demonstrated the possibility to determine both the position and the width (scale) of linelike structures such as blood vessels [5], [6], [10], [12]. The selection of locally appropriate scales along such structures not only yields local estimates of the width but it also allows to track structures whose width varies considerably.

The method for automatic scale-selection employed in these studies was proposed by Lindeberg [8], [9]. It requires choosing one parameter, called the γ-parameter. In [5], [6], [9], [10] the parameter was chosen in such a way that for some model structure the automatically selected scale exactly reproduced the known scale of the model. All these studies also report that "the most serious problem in the application of these [linear, second derivative of Gaussian] filters is their response to other features, such as edges or 'sheets' in 3D." [5, page 40].

M. Kerckhove (Ed.): Scale-Space 2001, LNCS 2106, pp. 245–254, 2001.

The aim of this article is to demonstrate that the choice of γ determines not only quantitatively the scales of detected features but also qualitatively the type of features that are detected. In the case of linelike structures feature detection with automatic scale selection can be accomplished with a simple second derivative of Gaussian filter kernel. While at fixed scales this detector suffers from the abovementioned problem of also detecting edges, the appropriate choice of γ allows to avoid edge detection in the variable scale setting.

The article is organized as follows. First the method for automatic scale-selection by Lindeberg [8] is briefly reviewed. Then the influence of the γ-parameter on feature detection is studied in general. Next a short catalog of critical γ-values for several one-dimensional model structures is created. This catalog suggests a range of γ-values at which a second derivative of Gaussian operator detects ridges but not edges. This possibility is studied in detail in one dimension. Finally the problem of detecting linelike structures in two-dimensional images is studied and examples are given.

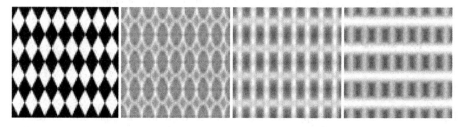

Fig. 1. Original image (left) and principal curvature computed at three different scales. The image has 512 by 512 pixels and the scales are $\sqrt{t} = 8$, $\sqrt{t} = 16$, $\sqrt{t} = 24$ pixels.

2   Scale-Selection Using γ-Normalized Derivatives

A method for automatic scale-selection that deals with positions and scales simultaneously was proposed by Lindeberg in 1993 [8]. It is a generalization of the idea to normalize the response of edge-detectors described earlier by Korn [7].

The method deals with derivative of Gaussian operators

$$G^{\mathbf{n}}(\mathbf{x}; t) = \partial_1^{n_1} ... \partial_N^{n_N} \frac{e^{-\frac{\mathbf{x}^T \mathbf{x}}{2t}}}{(2\pi t)^{N/2}}$$

where $\partial_i^{n_i}$ denotes the n_i-th order derivative along the i-th Cartesian coordinate, N is the dimension of the image, usually 2 or 3, and t is the scale-parameter. The response of these operators to an image f is computed by convolution and will be denoted as

$$L_{\mathbf{n}}(\mathbf{x}; t) = (G^{\mathbf{n}}(\circ; t) * f)(\mathbf{x}) \quad .$$

It should be noted that the response of a derivative of Gaussian operator computed in Cartesian coordinates does not itself capture useful structural information about an image because the Cartesian coordinates are generally not related to image structures. Useful structural operators can be constructed from combinations of the response of several derivative of Gaussian operators as described in [2].

In analogy to feature detection where local extrema of the operator response are computed with respect to space, one might wish to select scales in terms of local extrema of the operator response with respect to scale. Unfortunately, for derivative of Gaussian operators this makes little sense because the amplitude of a derivative tends to decrease with increasing scale as a simple consequence of the fact that with increasing scale the response is increasingly smoothed.

This prompted Lindeberg to consider γ-*normalized derivatives*

$$t^{\gamma n/2} L_{\mathbf{n}}(\mathbf{x}; t) = t^{\gamma n/2}(G^{\mathbf{n}}(\circ; t) * f)(\mathbf{x}) \tag{1}$$

where $n = n_1 + ... + n_N$. The amplitude of γ-*normalized derivatives* is obviously greater than that of regular derivatives when $t > 1$ and $\gamma > 0$. Lindeberg proposed the following heuristic principle [8]:

> In the absence of other evidence, a scale level at which some (possibly non-linear) combination of normalized derivatives assumes a local maximum can be treated as reflecting the characteristic length of a corresponding structure in the data.

In combination with feature detection this method of scale selection amounts to finding those (position,scale)-pairs $(\mathbf{x}, t)$ where the γ-normalized operator response has an extremum with respect to position and scale.

The idea proved to be very useful and it has since been applied to detect blood vessels [5], [6], [10], and other structures whose size is of interest [9], [12], [13], [3].

3   Implications of Different γ

To analyze the influence of γ on scale selection consider the necessary conditions for $t^{\gamma n/2} L_{\mathbf{n}}(\mathbf{x}; t)$ to have a local extremum with respect to position and scale:

$$\begin{aligned}
0 &= \partial_i L_{\mathbf{n}}(\mathbf{x}; t) \qquad i = 1, ..., N \\
0 &= \frac{\gamma n}{2} t^{-1} L_{\mathbf{n}}(\mathbf{x}; t) + \partial_t L_{\mathbf{n}}(\mathbf{x}; t)
\end{aligned} \tag{2}$$

Figure (2) shows solutions to these equations for a second derivative of Gaussian operator applied to a one-dimensional image. The zero-crossings of the derivative with respect space are independent of γ. The zero-crossings of the derivative with respect to scale show a tendency to move to larger scales with increasing γ. The negative-most pit at $x \approx 40$ for example is assigned the three different scales $\sqrt{t} = 5$, $\sqrt{t} = 10$, $\sqrt{t} = 21$ at the γ-values $\gamma = .5$, $\gamma = 1.5$, $\gamma = 2.5$ respectively.

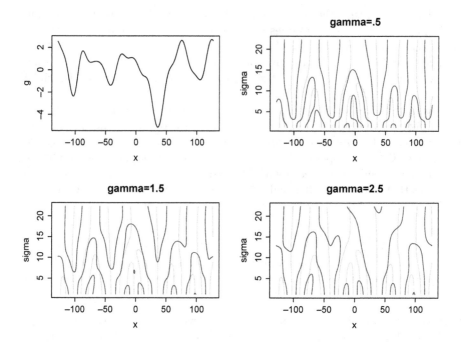

Fig. 2. Original one-dimensional image and zero-crossings of the response of the second derivative of Gaussian as functions of $\mathbf{x}$ and sigma= $\sqrt{t}$ for three different values of γ. The solutions of $0 = \partial_i L_\mathbf{n}(\mathbf{x}; t)$ are shown in light gray, those of $0 = \frac{\gamma n}{2} t^{-1} L_\mathbf{n}(\mathbf{x}; t) + \partial_t L_\mathbf{n}(\mathbf{x}; t)$ in dark gray.

This influence of γ on the selected scales suggests that the value of γ may be adjusted such that some "correct" scale is selected for a model feature whose scale is known or defined a priori. Most previous work on scale-selection motivates the choice of γ in this way. To give an example consider the one-dimensional model $e^{-\frac{x^2}{2w}} / \sqrt{2\pi w} = G(x; w)$ of width w. Suppose one attempts to detect such structures in one dimensional images and one chooses to do so with a second derivative of Gaussian operator. The response of the γ-normalized second derivative of Gaussian to this model is $t^\gamma G^2(\mathbf{x}; t + w) = t^\gamma(\frac{x^2}{(t+w)^2} - \frac{1}{t+w})G(\mathbf{x}; t + w)$. The maximum over scales at the center $x = 0$, which is the position of interest, occurs at $t = \frac{\gamma}{3/2-\gamma} w$. To achieve a one to one correspondence between the selected scale and the width of the model γ must be set to $\gamma = 3/4$.

A more far reaching consequence of the choice of γ-value is the following. For any specific image structure there is a certain range of γ-values within which the structure is assigned a finite scale by the γ-normalized operator used for detection. For values of γ greater than some *critical* γ the extrema with respect to scale are pushed to infinity so that above this critical γ the structure cannot be detected. In other words, *the choice of γ determines which structures can be detected and which not.*

The implications are equally evident and surprising: A feature detection operator applied at some fixed scale generally responds to a number of different structures, e.g. edges and ridges. At variable scales the γ-normalized operator responds only to a subset of the structures detected at fixed scales. The γ-parameter can be used to adjust this subset. For example, in the application considered in section 5 where ridges are of interest and edges not, γ can be adjusted such that only ridges but not edges are detected.

4   A Short Catalog of Critical γ-Values

In order to apply scale-selection to "turn off" specific features that are not of interest we briefly report the critical γ-values for a few one-dimensional model structures and derivative of Gaussian operators. A more detailed treatment might be given elsewhere.

Step Edge. For all derivative of Gaussian operators $\gamma = 1$ is the critical γ-value of a step edge θ, where $\theta(x) = 1$ for $x < 0$ and $\theta(x) = 0$ for $x \geq 0$.

Gaussian Edge. For all derivative of Gaussian operators $\gamma = 1$ is the critical γ-value of a Gaussian edge $g(x; w) = \int_x^\infty dx\ G^0(x; w^2)$ of width w, which is simply a step edge smoothed with a Gaussian filter kernel.

Lindeberg [9] determined this critical γ-value in the context of edge detection and suggested to use $\gamma = 1/2$ in order to detect the edge at its "correct" scale $t = w$. Here we wish to emphasize the use of values $\gamma < 1$ to enable detection of edges and values $\gamma > 1$ to avoid detection of edges.

Step Ridge. The response of a derivative of Gaussian operator G^n to a step ridge $r(x; w)$ of width w, defined by $r(x; w) = 1$ for $-w < x < w$, $r(x; w) = 0$ otherwise, is the difference of two step edge responses.

For a second derivative of Gaussian operator G^2 the critical γ-value is $\gamma = 3/2$. For $n = 4$ the critical γ-value is $\gamma = 5/4$. One may conjecture that the critical γ-values of derivative of Gaussian operators applied to the step ridge are $\gamma = \frac{n+1}{n}$.

Gaussian Ridge. The response of a derivative of Gaussian operator G^n to a Gaussian ridge $G^0(x; w^2)$ of width w is simply $G^n(x; t + w^2)$. The critical γ-value of a derivative of Gaussian operator G^n applied to a Gaussian ridge is $\gamma = \frac{n+1}{n}$.

5   Ridges versus Edges

The critical γ-values shall now be applied to demonstrate how a second derivative of Gaussian operator can be used to detect ridges but not edges. This allows to avoid detecting the edges that naturally occur on both sides of a ridge.

For a second derivative of Gaussian operator G^2 the critical γ-value of an edge is $\gamma = 1$ and the critical γ-value of a ridge is $\gamma = 1.5$. Consequently within the range $1 < \gamma < 1.5$ this operator detects only ridges and not edges. In other words, the operator responds to a ridge with only a single extremum over position and scale (x, t) and this extremum occurs at the center of the ridge.

Figure (3) displays the response of a second derivative of Gaussian operator to a step ridge for different values of γ. The response $t^\gamma L_{xx}$ is drawn as a surface. Below the surface zero-crossings of the first derivatives along space and scale are shown in order to aid the visual inspection of local extrema.

It can be seen clearly that the maximum response corresponding to the center of the ridge is "pushed" towards larger scales with increasing γ, until at $\gamma = 1.5$ it disappears. Moreover, as expected, the maxima corresponding to the edges occur at small scales ($t = 0$) as long as $\gamma < 1$ and disappear when $\gamma >= 1$. Hence of the displayed γ-values the only value at which the ridge is detected and the edges are not is $\gamma = 1.25$.

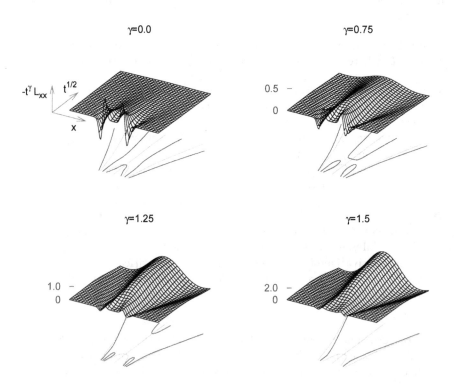

Fig. 3. Response of second derivative ridge detector $-t^\gamma L_{xx}$ to a step ridge model. Zero-crossings of the first derivative along space and scale are shown below each surface. With increasing γ the central maximum is "pushed" to larger scales.

6   Linelike Structures in Two Dimensions

Several methods for the detection of linelike structures in two or three dimensional images have been proposed in the context of fixed scales (see e.g.[1], [4], and [13]) and still more differences exist when scales are to be selected automatically [5], [6], [10], [9], [12]. In the following a brief description is given of a local approach that uses a second derivative of Gaussian operator and profits from the critical γ-values for edges and ridges described above.

The detection of ridges in two-dimensional images proceeds in two steps. First at each point a set of orthogonal directions is chosen, one pointing along the hypothetical ridge and the other perpendicular to the ridge. Then, at each point, the image intensity is analyzed in the direction across the hypothetical ridge to see if the point is on a ridge or not.

The direction along which a ridge extends is defined as the direction of maximum second derivative and is denoted as $\mathbf{q}$. The orthogonal axis of minimum second derivative traverses the ridge and is denoted by $\mathbf{p}$. Within these local coordinates a ridge at fixed scales is defined as the set of points where L_{pp} is a local minimum along $\mathbf{p}$ and additionally the conditions $L_{pp} < 0$ as well as $|L_{pp}| \geq |L_{qq}|$ are satisfied. In terms of zero-crossings the defining equations are:

$$L_{ppp} = 0 \quad , \quad L_{pppp} > 0 \quad , \quad L_{pp} < 0 \quad , \quad |L_{pp}| \geq |L_{qq}| \tag{3}$$

Figure (4) shows the ridges of the diamond image computed from definition (3) at three different scales. (For computational details refer to [11] or [1].)

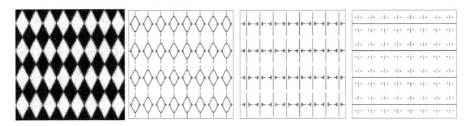

Fig. 4. Original image (left) and ridges computed at three different scales. The image has 512 by 512 pixels and the chosen scale levels are $\sqrt{t} = 8$, $\sqrt{t} = 16$, $\sqrt{t} = 24$.

From figure (4) it is clear that the results of fixed scale ridge computations can significantly depend on the choice of scale. Worse still, at scales that are relatively small compared to the size of the image structures the method detects edges instead of ridges.

Previous studies of line detection with automatic scale selection have reported that edges also pose a problem in the variable scale context [5], [10]. A number of approaches have been proposed to avoid these "false" responses. Koller [5] suggests a nonlinear operator that combines the response of two edge-detectors on both sides of a ridge. Lorenz et al. [10] use an edge-indicator to suppress the response to edges. Lindeberg [9] proposes to compute positions of ridges in terms of extrema of one operator and scales in terms of extrema of another operator.

The considerations of the previous sections suggest that a "correct" choice of γ-parameter allows to use a simple second derivative of Gaussian operator in order to detect ridges without running into the problem of also detecting edges. In particular, if one defines a *second derivative scale-space ridge* to be the set of points where $t^\gamma L_{pp}$ has a local minimum along $\mathbf{p}$ as well as along the scale-dimension t and additionally the conditions $L_{pp} < 0$ as well as $|L_{pp}| \geq |L_{qq}|$ are satisfied, then the results of section 5 can be applied directly. In other words a γ-value of $\gamma = 1.25$ allows to detect ridges and "escape" edges.

Figures (5) and (6) display the second derivative scale-space ridges computed from the diamond image for $\gamma = 1.25$. Figure (5) shows a projection of the results onto the image plain. Figure (6) displays the ridges from two points of view that also show the scale axis. Evidently, edges are not detected even though the range of scales covers the value $\sqrt{t} = 8$ at which edges pose a problem in the fixed scale setting of figure (4).

Concerning ridges the variable scale approach finds both the ridges corresponding to the long axes of each diamond and the ridges corresponding to the rows of diamonds. Notably, although these ridges cross each other in the projection of figure (5), they occur at separate scales as can be seen in figure (6). These merits of the variable scale approach are well known [14] and not at the focus of attention here. In the present context figures (5) and (6) should only serve to illustrate that in the variable scale setting the response to edges of a second derivative of Gaussian operator can be "turned off" simply by a suitable choice of γ-parameter.

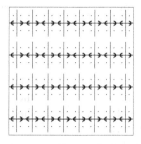

Fig. 5. Second derivative scale-space ridges projected onto the image plain. The original image has 256 by 256 pixels. Ridges were computed for $\gamma = 1.25$ and scales in the range 1 to 28 in steps of 1.0 (unit length=1 pixel width/height).

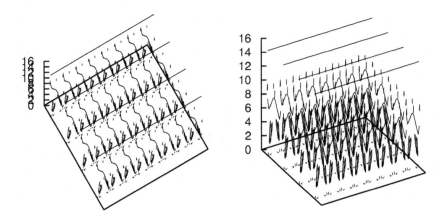

Fig. 6. Second derivative scale-space ridges projected along different directions. The scale-axis is the one with tics and numerical values.

7   Summary

Given some γ-normalized operator to be used for detection there is for any specific image structure a certain range of γ-values within which the structure is assigned a finite scale. For values of γ greater than some *critical* γ the extrema of the operator response with respect to scale disappear so that above this critical γ the structure cannot be detected. In other words, the choice of γ determines which structures can be detected and which not.

References

1. D. Eberly. *Ridges in Image and Data Analysis*. Computational Imaging and Vision. Kluwer Academic Publishers, 1996.
2. W. T. Freeman and E. H. Adelson. The design and use of steerable filters. *IEEE PAMI*, 13(9):891–906, 1991.
3. D. Fritsch, S. Pizer, B. Morse, D. Eberly, and A. Liu. The multiscale medial axis and its applications in image regestration. *Pattern Recognition Letters*, 15:445–452, 1994.
4. J.J. Koenderink and A. van Doorn. Two-plus-one-dimensional differential geometry. *Pattern Recognition Letters*, 15(5):439–444, 1994.
5. T. M. Koller. *From Data to Information: Segmentation, Description and Analysis of the Cerebral Vascularity*. PhD thesis, Swiss Federal Institute of Technology, Zürich, 1995.
6. T. M. Koller, G. Gerig, G. Szekely, and D. Dettwiler. Multiscale detection of curvilinear structures in 2d and 3d medical images. In *Fifth International Conference on Computer Vision ICCV 95*, pages 864–869, Cambridge, MA, USA, 1995.
7. Axel F. Korn. Toward a symbolic representation of intensity changes in images. *IEEE PAMI*, 10(5):610–625, 1988.
8. T. Lindeberg. On scale selection for differential operators. In K. Heia, A. Hœgdra, and B. Braathen, editors, *8th Scandinavian Conference on Image Analysis*, pages 857–866, Tromsœ, Norway, 1993.

9. T. Lindeberg. Edge detection and ridge detection with automatic scale selection. *International Journal of Computer Vision*, 30(2):117–156, 1998.

10. C. Lorenz, I.-C. Carlsen, T.M. Buzug, C. Fassnacht, and J. Weese. A multi-scale line filter with automatic scale selection based on the hessian matrix for medical image segmentation. In B. ter Haar Romeny, L. Florack, J. Koenderink, and M. Viergever, editors, *Scale-space theory in Computer Vision, ScaleSpace '97*, volume 1252 of *Lecture Notes in Computer Science*. Springer, 1997.

11. P. Majer. *A Statistical Approach to Feature Detection and Scale Selection in Images*. PhD thesis, University of Göttingen, 2000.

12. S. Pizer, D. Eberly, B. Morse, and D. Fritsch. Zoom-invariant figural shape: the mathematics of cores. *Computer Vision and Image Understanding*, 69:55–71, 1998.

13. S.M. Pizer, C.A. Burbeck, J.M. Coggins, D. Fritsch, and B. Morse. Object shape before boundary shape: Scale-space medial axis. *J. Math. Im. Vis.*, 4:303–313, 1994.

14. J. Staal, S. Kalitzin, B. ter Haar Romeny, and M. Viergewer. Detection of critical structures in scale space. In M. Nielsen, P. Johansen, O. Olsen, and J. Weickert, editors, *Scale-Space Theories in Computer Vision*, 1999.

Scale-Time Kernels and Models

Bart M. ter Haar Romeny[1], Luc M.J. Florack[2], and Mads Nielsen[3]

[1] Image Sciences Institute, Utrecht University, Utrecht, The Netherlands
B.terHaarRomeny@isi.uu.nl, http://www.isi.uu.nl
[2] Utrecht University, Mathematics Dept, Utrecht, The Netherlands
L.Florack@math.uu.nl
[3] IT-University, University of Copenhagen, Denmark
malte@it-c.dk

Abstract. Receptive field sensitivity profiles of visual front-end cells in the LGN and V1 area in intact animals can be measured with increasing accuracy, both in the spatial and temporal domain. This urges the need for mathematical models. Scale-space theory, as a theory of (multiscale) apertures as operators on observed data, is concerned with the mathematical modeling of front-end visual system behaviour. This paper compares recent measurements on the spatio-temporal respons of LGN cell and V1 simple cell receptive fields [1] with Koenderink's results from axiomatic reasoning for a real-time measuring spatio-temporal differential operator [2]. In this model time must be logarithmically remapped to make the operation causal in the temporal domain.

1 Scale-Space Kernel Derivation from Entropy Maximization

The Gaussian kernel as the fundamental linear scale-space kernel for an uncommitted observation is now well established. Many fundamental derivations have been proposed (see for an extensive and complete overview Weickert [3]). In this paper we present an alternative way to derive the Gaussian kernel as the scale-space kernel of an uncommitted observation. It is based on the notion that the 'uncommittedness' is expressed in a statistical way using the entropy of the observed signal. The reasoning is due to Mads Nielsen, IT-University Copenhagen [4]:

First of all, we want to do a measurement, i.e. we have a device which has some integration area with a finite width by necessity. The measurement should be done at all locations in the same way, i.e. with either a series of identical detectors, or the same detector measuring at all places: the measurement should be invariant for translation. We want the measurement to be linear in the signal to be measured (e.g. the intensity): invariance for translation along the intensity axis. These requirements lead automatically to the formulation that the observation must be a convolution: $h(x) = \int_{-\infty}^{\infty} L(\alpha)g(x - \alpha)d\alpha$. $L(x)$ is the observed variable, e.g. the luminance, $g(x)$ is the aperture function, $h(x)$ the result of the measurement.

M. Kerckhove (Ed.): Scale-Space 2001, LNCS 2106, pp. 255–263, 2001.

The aperture function $g(x)$ should be a unity filter, i.e. normalized, which means that the integral over its weighting profile should be unity: $\int_{-\infty}^{\infty} g(x)dx = 1$. The mean of the filter $g(x)$ should be at the location where we measure, e.g. at x_0, so the expected value (or first moment) should be x_0 : $\int_{-\infty}^{\infty} xg(x)dx = x_0$. Because we may take any point for x_0, we may take for our further calculations as well the point $x_0 = 0$.

The size of the aperture is an essential element. We want to be free in choice of this size, so at least we want to find a family of filters where this size is a free parameter. We can then monitor the world at all these sizes by 'looking through' the complete set of kernels simultaneously. We call this 'size' σ. It has the dimension of length, and is the yardstick of our measurement. We call it the inner scale. Every physical measurement has an inner scale. It can be μm or lightyears, we need for every dimension a yardstick: σ. If we weight distances $r(x)$ with our kernel, so we get $\int_{-\infty}^{\infty} r(x)g(x)dx$, we will use $r(x) = x^2$ since with this choice we separate the dimensions: two orthogonal vectors fullfill $r(a + b) = r(a) + r(b)$. We call the weighted metric σ^2: $\int_{-\infty}^{\infty} x^2 g(x)dx = \sigma^2$.

Finally we incorporate the request to be as uncommitted as possible. We want no filter with some preference at this first stage of the observation. We want, in statistical terms, the 'orderlessness' or disorder of the measurement as large as possible. There should be no ordering, ranking, structuring or whatsoever. Physically the measure for disorder is expressed through the entropy $H = \int_{-\infty}^{\infty} g(x) \ln g(x)dx$ where $\ln x$ is the natural logarithm. We look for the $g(x)$ for which the entropy is maximal, given the constraints derived before:

$$\int_{-\infty}^{\infty} g(x)dx = 0, \quad \int_{-\infty}^{\infty} x\, g(x)dx = 0, \quad \int_{-\infty}^{\infty} x^2 g(x)dx = \sigma^2$$

To find a maximum under a set of given constraints, we apply the method of Euler-Lagrange equations. The Lagrangian e becomes:

The condition to be minimal for a certain $g(x)$ is given by the vanishing of the first variation (corresponding to the first derivative, but in this case with respect to a function) to $g(x)$: $\frac{\partial e}{\partial g} = 0$. This gives us: $-1 + \lambda_1 + x\lambda_2 + x^2\lambda_3 - \ln g(x) = 0$ from which we can easily solve $g(x)$:

```
g[x_]= y . Solve[Log[y]==-1+λ₁+x λ₂+x²λ₃,y]  // First
```

$$e^{-1+\lambda_1+x\lambda_2+x^2\lambda_3}$$

So, $g(x)$ is an exponential function with constant, linear and quadratic terms of x in the exponent. At least λ_3 must be negative, otherwise the function explodes, which is physically unrealistic. We need the explicit expressions for our constraints, so we make the following set of constraint equations, simplified with the condition of $\lambda_3 < 0$:

```
{eqn1 = Simplify[ ∫∞₋∞ g[x] dx ==1, λ₃ < 0],
 eqn2 = Simplify[ ∫∞₋∞ x g[x] dx ==0, λ₃ < 0],
 eqn3 = Simplify[ ∫∞₋∞ x² g[x] dx == σ², λ₃ < 0 }
```

$$\left\{ \frac{e^{-1+\lambda_1-\frac{\lambda_2^2}{4\lambda_3}}\sqrt{\pi}}{\sqrt{-\lambda_3}} == 1, \quad \frac{e^{-1+\lambda_1-\frac{\lambda_2^2}{4\lambda_3}}\sqrt{\pi}\lambda_2}{2(-\lambda_3)^{3/2}} == 0, \quad \frac{e^{-1+\lambda_1-\frac{\lambda_2^2}{4\lambda_3}}\sqrt{\pi}(\lambda_2^2-2\lambda_3)}{4(-\lambda_3)^{5/2}} == \sigma^2 \right\}$$

Now we can solve for all three λ's:

```
Off[Solve::ifun]; solution = Solve[{eqn1,eqn2,eqn3},{λ₁,λ₂,λ₃}]
```

$$\left\{\left\{\lambda_1 \rightarrow \tfrac{1}{4}\,\mathrm{Log}[\tfrac{e^4}{4\pi^2\sigma^4}], \quad \lambda_2 \rightarrow 0, \quad \lambda_3 \rightarrow -\tfrac{1}{2\sigma^2}\right\}\right\}$$

```
g[x_] = Simplify[E^{-1+λ₁+xλ₂+x²λ₃} /. Flatten[solution], σ > 0]
```

$$\frac{e^{-\frac{x^2}{2\sigma^2}}}{\sqrt{2\pi}\sigma}$$

which is the Gaussian function as the unique solution to the set of constraints, which in principle are a formal statement of the uncommitment of the observation.

2 Scale-Time

In the time domain we encounter sampled data just as in the spatial domain. E.g. a movie is a series of frames, samples taken at regular intervals. In the spatial domain we need an integration over a spatial area, in the temporal domain we need to have an aperture in time integrating for some time to perform the measurement. This is the integration time. Systems with a short resp. long integration time are said to have a fast resp. slow respons. The integration time by necessity needs to have a finite duration (temporal width) in time, a scale-space construct is a phyical necessity again. Furthermore, time and space are incommensurable dimensions, so we need a scale-space for space and a scale-space for time.

Time measurements can essentially be processed in two ways: as pre-recorded frames or instances, or realtime. Temporal measurements stored for later replay or analysis, on whatever medium, fall in the first catagory. Humans perform continuously a temporal analysis with their senses, they measure real-time and are part of the second category. The scale-space treatment of these two categories will turn out to be essentially different.

Prerecorded sequences can be analyzed in a manner completely analogous with the spatial treatment of scaled operators, we just interchange space with time. The notion of temporal scale σ_τ then naturally emerges, which is the temporal resolution, a device property when we look at the recorded data (it is the inner scale of the data), and a free parameter in the multiscale analysis.

In the real-time measurement and analysis of temporal data we have a serious problem: the time axis is only a half axis: the past. There is a sharp and unavoidable boundary on the time axis: the present moment. This means that we can no longer apply our standard Gaussian kernels, because they have an (in theory) infinite extent in both directions. There is no way to include the future in our kernel, it would be a strong violation of causality. But there may be a way

out when we derive from first principles a new kernel that fulfils the constraint
of causality: a kernel defined on a logarithmically remapped time axis. From
this new causal kernel we might again derive the temporal and spatio-temporal
family of scaled derivative operators. Koenderink [2] has presented the reasoning
to derive the theory, and we will discuss it in detail below.

There have appeared some other fine papers discussing the real-time causal
scale-space in detail by Florack [5] and Lindeberg, Fagerstrom and Bretzner
[6,7,8,9]. Lindeberg also discusses the automatic selection of temporal scale [10].

3   Causal Time-Scale Is Logarithmic

For realtime systems the situation is completely different. We noted in the previous section that we can only deal with the past, i.e. we only have the half
time-axis. This is incompatible with the infinite extent of the Gaussian kernel
to both sides. With Koenderink's words: "Because the diffusion spreads influ-
ences with infinite speed any blurring will immediately spread into the remote
future thereby violating the principle of temporal causality. It is clear that the
scale-space method can only lead to acceptable results over the complete axis,
but never over a mere semi-axis. On the other hand the diffusion equation is the
unique solution that respects causality in the resolution domain. Thus there can
be no hope of finding an alternative. The dilemma is complete" [2].

The solution, proposed by Koenderink, is to *remap* (reparametrize) the half
t-axis into a full axis. The question is then how this should be done. We follow
here Koenderink's original reasoning to come to the mapping function, and to
derive the Gaussian derivative kernels on the new time axis.

We call the remapping $s(t)$. We define t_0 the present moment, which can
never be reached, for as soon as we try to measure it, it is already later. It
is our absolutely defined referencepoint, our fiducial moment. Every realtime
measurement is relative to this point in time. Then s should be a function of
$\mu = t_0 - t$, so $s(\mu) = s(t_0 - t)$. We choose the parameter μ to be dimensionless,
and $\mu = 0$ for the present moment and $\mu = -\infty$ for the infinite past. So we
get $s(\mu) = s(\frac{t_0-t}{\tau})$. The parameter τ is some time constant and is essentially
arbitrary. It is the scale of our measurement, and we should be able to give it
any value, so we want the diffusion to be scale-invariant on the μ-domain.

We want shift invariance on this time axis and the application of different
clocks, so we require that a transformation $t' = at + b$ leaves $s(t)$ invariant. μ is
invariant if we change clocks.

On our new time-axis $s(t)$ the diffusion should be a normal causal diffusion.
On every point of the s-axis we have the same amount of diffusion, i.e. the
diffusion is homogeneous on the s-domain. The 'inner scale' or resolution of our
measurement has to become smaller and smaller when we want to approach
the present moment. But even if we use femtosecond measuring devices, we will
never catch the present moment. On the other side of the s-axis, a long time
ago, we don't want that high resolution. An event some centuries ago is placed
with a resolution of say a year, and the moment that the dinasaurs disappeared
from earth, say some 65 million years ago, is referred to with an accuracy of a
million years or so.

This intuitive reasoning is an expression of the requirement that we want our time-resolution τ on the s-axis to be proportional to μ, i.e. $\tau \simeq \mu$ or $\frac{\tau}{\mu} =$ constant. So for small μ we have a small resolution, for large μ a large one.

Normal causal diffusion on the s-axis means that the 'magnification' $\|\frac{ds}{d\mu}\|$ should be proportional to $\frac{\tau}{\mu}$. Then the s-axis is 'stretched' for every μ in such a way that the scale (or 'diffusion length' as Koenderink calls it) in the s-domain is a constant relative diffusion length in the μ-domain. Uniform sampling in the s-domain gives a graded resolution history in the t- or μ-domain. In formula : $\|\frac{ds}{d\mu}\| \simeq \frac{\tau}{\mu}$ or $\|\frac{ds}{d\mu}\| = \frac{\alpha}{\mu}$. From this partial differential equation we derive that the mapping $s(\mu)$ must be logarithmic: $s(\mu) = \alpha \ln \mu + c_1$.

So our mapping for s is now: $s = \alpha \ln(\frac{t_0-t}{\tau})+$ constant. The constant is an arbitrary translation, for which we defined t_0 to be invariant, so we choose this constant to be zero. We choose the arbitrary scaling parameter α to be unity, so we get: $s = \ln(\frac{t_0-t}{\tau})$.

This is a fundamental result. For a causal interpretation of the time axis we need to sample time in a logarithmic fashion. It means that the present moment is mapped to infinity, which conforms to our notion that we can never reach it. We can now freely diffuse on the s-axis, as we have a well defined scale at all moments on our transformed time axis. See figure 1.

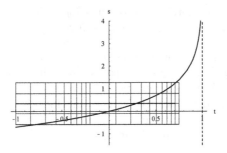

Fig. 1. The logarithmic mapping of the horizontal t-time half-axis onto the vertical s-time full axis. The present moment t_0, at $t = 1$ in this example (indicated by the vertical dashed line) can never be reached. The s-axis is now a full axis, and fully available for diffusion. The inset shows a typical working area for a realtime system. The response time delimits the area at the right, the lifetime at the left. Figure adapted from [5].

In the s-domain we can now run the diffusion equation without violation of temporal causality.

4 A Causal Semi-axis Is Logarithmic

Florack [5] came to the same result from a different perspective, from abstract mathematics. He used a method from group theory. A group is formally defined as a set of similar transformations, with a member that does the unity operation (projects on itself, i.e. does nothing, e.g. rotation over zero degrees, an enlargement of 1, a translation of zero etc.), it must have an inverse (e.g. rotation clockwise, but also anti-clockwise) and one must be able to concatenate its members (e.g. a total rotation which consists of two separate rotations after each other).

Florack studied the group properties of whole and half axes of real numbers. The group of summations is a group on the whole axis, which includes the positive and the negative numbers. This group however is *not* a group on the half axis. For we might be able to do a summation which has a result outside the allowed domain. The group of multiplications however is a group on the positive half axis. Two numbers multiplied from the half axis give a result on the same half axis. If we could make all multiplications into sums, we would have an operation that makes it a group again. The formal transformation from multiplications into sums is the logarithmic function: $\ln(a*b) = \ln(a) + \ln(b)$ and its inverse: $e^{a+b} = e^a * e^b$. The zero element is addition of zero, or multiplication with one. So the result is the same logarithmic function as the function of choice for the causal parametrization of the half axis.

Lindeberg and Fagerstrom [6] derived the causal temporal differential operator from the non-creation of local extrema (zero-crossings) with increasing scale.

Interestingly, we encounter more often a logarithmic parametrization of a half axis when the physics of observations is involved:

- Light intensities are only defined for positive values, and form a half axis. It is well known e.g that the eye performs a logarithmic transformation on the intensity measured by its receptors on the retina.
- Scale is only defined for positive values, and form a half axis (scale-space). The natural scalestep τ on the scale-axis in scale-space is the logarithm of the diffusion scale σ: $\tau = \ln(\sigma) - \ln(\sigma_0)$.

5   Real-Time Receptive Fields

We have now all information to study the shape of the causal temporal derivative operators. The kernel in the transformed s-domain was given above. The kernel in the original temporal domain t becomes

$$K(t, t_0; \tau) = \frac{1}{\sqrt{2\pi\tau}} e^{-\frac{1}{2\tau^2} \ln(\frac{t_0-t}{\tau})^2}$$

In figure 2 we see that the Gaussian kernel and its temporal derivatives are skewed, due to the logarithmic time axis remapping. It is clear that the present moment t_0 can never be reached. The zerocrossing of the first order derivative (and thus the peak of the zeroth order kernel) is just at $t = -\tau$.

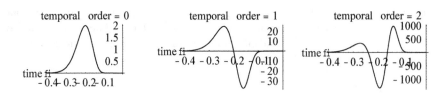

Fig. 2. Left, middle right: the zeroth, first and second Gaussian temporal derivative operator in causal time. The timescale in each plot runs from the past, to the right. The temporal scale $\tau = 200$ ms, the right boundary is the present, $t_0 = 0$. Note the pronounced skewness of the kernels.

6   A Scale-Space Model for Time-Causal Spatio-Temporal Cortical Receptive Fields

Precise measurements of the spatio-temporal properties of macaque monkey and cat LGN and cortical receptive fields are possible [11,12] [1]. They give support for the scale-time theory for causal time sampling. De Valois, Cottaris, Mahon, Elfar and Wilson [1] applied the method of reverse correlation and multiple receptive field mapping stimuli (m-sequence, maximum length white noise stimuli) to map numerous receptive fields with high spatial and temporal resolution. Some of the resulting receptive fields maps are shown in figure 3.

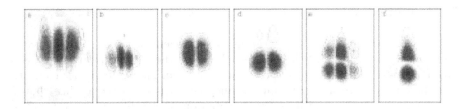

Fig. 3. Examples of spatio-temporal receptive field maps of a sample of V1 simple cells of macaque monkey. Vertical axis in each plot: time axis from 0 ms (bottom) to 200 ms (top). Horizontal axis per plot: space (in degrees), a: 0-0.9, b: 0-1.2, c,d: 0-0.6, e: 0,1.9, f: 0-1.6 degrees. Note the skewed sensitivity profiles in the time direction, especially in subfigures e and f. Every 'island' has opposite polarity to its neighboring 'island' in each plot. Due to black and white reproduction the sign of the response could not be reproduced. The scale-space models for the plots are respectively: a: $\frac{\partial^2 L}{\partial x^2}$, b: $\frac{\partial^3 L}{\partial x^3}$, c: $\frac{\partial L}{\partial x}$, d: $\frac{\partial L}{\partial x}$, e: $\frac{\partial^3 L}{\partial x^2 \partial t}$, f: $\frac{\partial^2 L}{\partial x \partial t}$. Adapted from [1].

---

[1] See also totoro.berkeley.edu/Demonstrations/VSOC/teaching/RF/LGN.html

If we plot the predicted sensitivity profiles according to Gaussian scale-space theory we get remarkably similar results. In figure 4 the space-time plots are shown for zeroth to second spatial and temporal differential order. Note the skewness in the temporal direction.

```
Clear[gt,gs,n]; t=0.3; σ = 2;
gt[n_] = D[1/√(2π τ²) Exp[-1/(2t²) Log[-(t₀-t)/τ]²], {t,n}],
gs[n_] = D[1/√(2π τ²) Exp[-1/(2t²) x²], {t,n}];
Block[{$DisplayFunction=Identity},
p=Table[ContourPlot[Evaluate[gt[i] gs[j]],{x,-15,15},{t,.01,.8},
PlotPoints->30],{i,0,1},{j,0,2}]; Show[GraphicsArray[Flatten[p]];
```

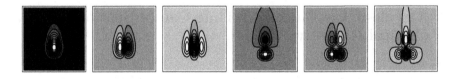

Fig. 4. Model for time-causal spatio-temporal receptive field sensitivity profiles from Gaussian scale-space theory. From left to right: a: L, b: $\frac{\partial L}{\partial x}$, c: $\frac{\partial^2 L}{\partial x^2}$, d: $\frac{\partial L}{\partial t}$, e: $\frac{\partial^2 L}{\partial x \partial t}$, f: $\frac{\partial^3 L}{\partial x^2 \partial t}$. Vertical axis: time. Horizontal axis: space.

7   Conclusion

The causal-time multiscale temporal differential operator model from Gaussian scale-space theory has not yet been tested against the wealth of currently available receptive field measurement data. It may be an interesting experiment, to test the quantitative similarity, and to find the statistics of the applied spatial and temporal scales, as well as the distribution of the differential order. The Gaussian scale-space model is especially attractive because of its robust physical underpinning by the principal of temporal causality, leading to the natural notion of the logarithmic mapping of the time axis in a realtime measurement (see also [13]).

The distributions of the locations of the different scales and the differential order has not been mapped yet on the detailed cortical orientation column with the pinwheel structure. Orientation has been clearly charted due to spectacular developments in optical dye high resolution recording techniques in awake animals. Is the scale of the operator mapped along the spokes of the pinwheel? Is the central singularity in the repetitive pinwheel structure the largest scale? Is differential order coded in depth in the column?

These are all new questions arising from a new model. The answer to these questions can be expected within a reasonable time, given the fast developments, both in high resolution recording techniques, and the increase in resolution of non-invasive mapping techniques as high-field functional magnetic resonance imaging (fMRI) [14].

In summary: When a time sequence of data is available in stored form, we can apply the regular symmetric Gaussian derivative kernels as causal multiscale differential operators for temporal analysis, in complete analogy with the spatial case. When the measurement and analysis is realtime, we need a reparametrization of the time axis in a logarithmic fashion. The resulting kernels are skewed towards the past. The present can be never reached, the new logarithmic axis guarantees full causality. The derivation is performed by the first principle of a scale of observation on the new time axis which is proportional to the time the event happened. This seems to fit well in the intuitive perception of time by humans.

Recent physiological measurements of LGN cell receptive fields and cortical V1 simple cell receptive fields suggest that the biological system may employ the temporal and spatiotemporal differential operators. Especially striking is the observed skewness in the temporal domain, giving support for the working of the biological cells as time-causal temporal differential operators.

References

1. R. L. De Valois, N. P. Cottaris, L. E. Mahon, S. D. Elfar, and J. A. Wilson, "Spatial and temporal receptive fields of geniculate and cortical cells and directional selectivity," *Vision Research*, vol. 40, pp. 3685–3702, 2000.
2. J. J. Koenderink, "Time-scale," *Biological Cybernetics*, vol. 58, pp. 159–162, 1988.
3. J. Weickert, S. Ishikawa, and A. Imiya, "Linear scale-space has first been proposed in japan," *J. Math Imaging and Vision*, vol. 10, pp. 237–252, 1999.
4. M. Nielsen, *From paradigm to algorithms in computer vision*. PhD thesis, DIKU Copenhagen University, Denmark, 1995.
5. L. M. J. Florack, *Image Structure*. Computational Imaging and Vision Series, Dordrecht: Kluwer Academic Publishers, 1997.
6. L. Lindeberg and D. Fagerstrom, "Scale-space with causal time direction," in *Lecture Notes in Computer Science*, vol. 1064, pp. 229–240, 1996.
7. L. Lindeberg, "Linear spatio-temporal scale-space," in *Lecture Notes in Computer Science*, vol. 1252, 1997.
8. L. Bretzner and L. Lindeberg, "On the handling of spatial and temporal scales in feature tracking," in *Lecture Notes in Computer Science*, vol. 1252, July 2-4 1997.
9. L. Bretzner and L. Lindeberg, "Feature tracking with automatic selection of spatial scales," *Comp. Vision and Image Understanding*, vol. 71, pp. 385–392, 1998.
10. L. Lindeberg, "On automatic selection of temporal scales in time-causal scale-space," in *Lecture Notes in Computer Science*, vol. 1315, pp. 94–113, 1997.
11. G. C. DeAngelis, I. Ohzawa, and R. D. Freeman, "Receptive field dynamics in the central visual pathways," *Trends Neurosci.*, vol. 18, pp. 451–458, 1995.
12. D. L. Ringach, G. Sapiro, and R. Shapley, "A subspace reverse correlation technique for the study of visual neurons," *Vision Research*, vol. 37, no. 17, pp. 2455–2464, 1997.
13. E. Poppel, *Handbook of Sensory Physiology*, ch. Time perception, pp. 713–729. Berlin: Springer, 1978.
14. N. K. Logothetis, H. Guggenberger, S. Peled, and J. Pauls, "Functional imaging of the monkey brain," *Nature Neuroscience*, vol. 2, no. 6, pp. 555–562, 1999.

Exploring Non-linear Diffusion: The Diffusion Echo

Erik Dam and Mads Nielsen

The IT University, Glentevej 67
DK – 2400 Copenhagen NV, Denmark
{erikdam,malte}@it-c.dk
http://www.it-c.dk

Abstract. The Gaussian serves as Green's function for the linear diffusion equation and as a source for intuitive understanding of the linear diffusion process. In general, non-linear diffusion equations have no known closed form solutions and thereby no equally simple description. This article introduces a simple, intuitive description of these processes in terms of the *Diffusion Echo*. The Diffusion Echo offers intuitive visualisations for non-linear diffusion processes.

In addition, the Diffusion Echo has potential for offering simple formulations for grouping problems. Furthermore, the Diffusion Echo can be considered a deep structure summary and thereby offers an alternative to multi-scale linking and flooding techniques.

1 Introduction

Linear scale-space [5,10,6] is the canonical un-committed scale-space with appealing theoretical properties. Among these are the existence of a Green's function for the PDE (partial differential equation) in terms of the Gaussian. Besides providing a closed form solution to the PDE, the Gaussian yields a clear, intuitive understanding of the local filtering process.

Non-linear scale-spaces are appropriate for enhancement of desired features and for extraction of certain deep structure features (in for instance edge detection [7] and segmentation). These diffusion schemes can typically be formulated as PDE's where a diffusion tensor determines the non-linear nature [9]. In general, these PDE's have no known closed form solutions. This necessitates iterative numerical approximation schemes which offer less intuition.

Section 2 contains a presentation of the diffusion schemes used in the article. The Diffusion Echo is introduced in section 3 with examples of how the Diffusion Echo can be used for visualisation of the diffusion schemes. Finally, potential applications of the Diffusion Echo are presented:

- Grouping of features, for instance used for segmentation (section 4).
- As a deep structure summary that can serve as an alternative to multi-scale linking or flooding techniques (section 5).

M. Kerckhove (Ed.): Scale-Space 2001, LNCS 2106, pp. 264–272, 2001.

2   Diffusion Schemes

A number of diffusion schemes are explored. All schemes use a PDE to define a scale-space $L(\boldsymbol{x}; t)$, where $\boldsymbol{x}$ are spatial coordinates and t the scale parameter. The PDE's have an image I as initial condition: $L(\boldsymbol{x}; 0) = I(\boldsymbol{x})$.

Linear diffusion [5,10] can be defined by: $L_t(\boldsymbol{x}; t) = \Delta L(\boldsymbol{x}; t)$, the heat diffusion equation. The Gaussian with standard deviation $\sigma = \sqrt{2t}$ is Green's function for the PDE.

The isotropic non-linear Perona-Malik scheme preserves edges during the diffusion [7]: $L_t(\boldsymbol{x}; t) = div(\ p(|\nabla L_\sigma|^2)\ \nabla L\ )$ where $p(|\nabla L_\sigma|^2) = 1/(1 + \frac{|\nabla L_\sigma|^2}{\lambda^2})$. The regularisation parameter σ is due to [2]. The notation ∇L_σ means the gradient evaluated at scale σ. The parameter λ is a soft threshold for the gradient magnitude required to locally slow the diffusion and preserve an edge. Following the terminology of Weickert [9], the scheme is termed "isotropic" since the diffusivity function p is scalar-valued.

2.1   Generalised Anisotropic Diffusion

Weickert [9] defines the *anisotropic non-linear diffusion equation*:

$$L_t(\boldsymbol{x}; t) = div(\ D(J_\rho(\nabla L_\sigma))\ \nabla L\ )$$

The diffusion tensor $D \in C^\infty(R^{2\times 2}, R^{2\times 2})$ is assumed to be symmetric and uniform positive definite. The *structure tensor* J_ρ is evaluated at *integration scale* ρ (set to zero in the following), and the gradient ∇L_σ at *sampling scale* σ.

Diffusion schemes can be defined in terms of the eigenvalues λ_1 and λ_2 for the corresponding eigenvectors $\bar{v}_1 \parallel \nabla L_\sigma$, $\bar{v}_2 \perp \nabla L_\sigma$ for the diffusion tensor D. A large number of diffusion schemes (including the previous) are generalized by the *Generalized Anisotropic Non-linear* scheme (GAN) [3,4], where the diffusion tensor eigenvalues are defined:

$$w(m, \lambda, s) = \begin{cases} 1 & |\nabla L_\sigma| = 0 \\ 1 - exp\left(\frac{-C_m}{\left(\frac{s^2}{\lambda}\right)^m}\right) & |\nabla L_\sigma| > 0 \end{cases} \tag{1}$$

$$\lambda_1 = w(m, \lambda, |\nabla L_\sigma|)$$
$$\lambda_2 = \theta + (1 - \theta)\ \lambda_1 \tag{2}$$

The scheme is "anisotropic" when the eigenvalues are not equal (then D can not simply be replaced by a scalar-valued function). The global parameter θ determines the degree of anisotropy (0 is isotropic diffusion and 1 is full anisotropic), λ is the soft edge threshold, and m is the "aggressiveness" that the edges are preserved with.

The GAN scheme has the following schemes as special cases:

- Linear Gaussian diffusion is defined by $\lambda \to \infty$.
- The regularised Perona-Malik scheme is approximated by $\theta = 0$ and $m = 0.75$ (which implies $C_m = 3.31488$ [3]).
- Weickert's *Edge Enhancing diffusion* (EED) is defined by $\theta = 1$ and $m = 4$ (which implies $C_m = 3.31488$ [9]).

2.2   Corner Enhancing Diffusion

Near "edges" the Perona-Malik scheme slows diffusion in all directions. For image enhancement, EED is appropriate since diffusion is full along edges.

However, the EED scheme tend to round corners due to the full diffusion along the edge. Therefore, while full anisotropic diffusion is desirable at edge-like structures, a diffusion scheme with a milder degree of anisotropy is desired at corners. A local steering of the degree of anisotropy therefore seems sensible.

The following *Corner Enhancing Diffusion* scheme (CED) is similar to GAN but steers the anisotropy locally using a corner measure: the isophote curvature κ times the gradient to a power k.

$$\lambda_1 = w(m_g, \lambda_g, |\nabla L_\sigma|)$$
$$\theta = w(m_i, \lambda_i, |\kappa_\sigma| \, |\nabla L_\sigma|^k)$$
$$\lambda_2 = \theta + (1 - \theta) \, \lambda_1 \tag{3}$$

The Corner Enhancing scheme is similar to the CID scheme from [3].

3   Visualisations

It takes a strong mathematician to get intuition about the differences between the diffusion schemes above. A standard way of illustrating the schemes is to visualise the local diffusion at key points in an image like in the following.

The non-linear diffusion processes are implemented using iterative numerical approximation schemes. For each iteration a diffusion tensor is determined for each point in the scale-space image. This diffusion tensor can be visualized by an ellipse where the orientation and the size are determined by the eigenvectors and corresponding eigenvalues.

In figure 1 EED is illustated like this. Isolated, the third image seems to offer an understanding of the intensions of the diffusion scheme. However, the illustrated diffusion tensors are deceiving since they evolve during the diffusion. Furthermore, they fail to capture the interaction with the surrounding area.

Fig. 1. Visualisations of diffusion tensors for EED scheme. Left: test image (64x64 pixels, intensities 0-255, SN ratio 2.5). Right three images: the local diffusion tensors illustrated as ellipses at five points for three different iterations ($t = 0.4, 20, 100$). An explicit approximation scheme with a nonnegativity discretisation was used [9].

3.1   The Diffusion Echo

The Diffusion Echo is inspired by the Gaussian that defines the local filtering in linear diffusion. The equivalent is obtained for non-linear schemes in two steps:

Diffusion Echo: Source
  For a fiducial point p construct an auxiliary image with the value 1 at the point p and zero otherwise: the discrete impulse function.
  For each iteration in a diffusion process for an image I, the values are computed by assigning each pixel a weighted average of a neighbourhood of pixels.
  The auxiliary image is treated with the same weighting as the image I. The result is a distribution that has recorded the flux that propagates from the source pixel p. This is the *Diffusion Echo source distribution* and is denoted $S_p(\cdot)$.

Diffusion Echo: Drain
  The *Diffusion Echo drain distribution* is the opposite of the source. For a point q, the value for the drain distribution at a given point p is defined in terms of the source at p. Specifically, the drain distribution $D_q(\cdot)$ is $D_q(p) \equiv S_p(q)$.
  Note that the drain for a point requires the sources for the entire image.
  The Diffusion Echo drain distribution is the local filter for the diffusion process equivalent to the Gaussian filter for the linear diffusion process.

Diffusion Echo Properties
  For linear diffusion both the source and the drain distributions are Gaussian distributions. However, in general the distributions are not equal.
  The Diffusion Echo drain distribution is the local convolution filter for the diffusion process: $L(\boldsymbol{x};t) = \int L(q;0) \, D_{\boldsymbol{x}}(q) \, dq = \int I(q) \, D_{\boldsymbol{x}}(q) \, dq$
  The distributions can be interpreted as affinity measures. However, note that in general both $S_p(q) \neq S_q(p)$ and $D_q(p) \neq D_p(q)$.
  Since both source and drain are unity distributions they can also be interpreted as probabilistic distributions. The source distribution $S_p(q)$ (or the drain distribution $D_q(p)$) states the probability for an "atom" originating at point p to end at point q as a result of the diffusion.
  The maximum for both source and drain distributions remain at the origin for the distribution. Mean and higher order moments are in general not located at the origin and can be used to characterise the distributions.
  The definitions are applicable for images of arbitrary dimensions.

3.2   Diffusion Echo Visualisations

The Diffusion Echo is a summary of the diffusion process up to a certain time/scale. In the following we show that illustrations using this principle offer significantly more information than the illustrations in the previous section.

Basic Comparison. In figure 2 we illustrate this for the four diffusion schemes presented in section 2. The figure displays the Diffusion Echo drain distributions for the five selected points in the test image from figure 1. These are equivalent to the local convolution filters that would yield the diffusion directly.
  The ellipses in figure 2 highlight the properties of the diffusion schemes. Linear diffusion uses the same diffusion tensor at all points. The isotropic non-linear

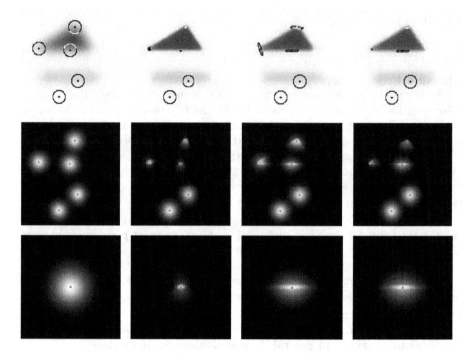

Fig. 2. Diffusion Echo drain distributions. The top row shows ellipse-illustrations for the four diffusion schemes (linear, Perona-Malik, EED, and CED). The center row shows the corresponding drain distributions. Note that the distribution is computed separately at each point — the illustrations are mosaics of these separate illustrations. By definition, each distribution has the same total energy (they are unity filters), but they are scaled individually for better visual appearance. The bottom row shows close-ups of the distributions for the point right below the center of the triangle.

An explicit approximation scheme with a nonnegativity discretisation was used with $t = 20$ [9]. The edge threshold parameter is set to 220 for all schemes. This corresponds to characterising the contour around the triangle as edge and the contour around the rectangle as non-edge. The regularisation scale is 1.2.

Perona-Malik reduces the diffusion gradually determined by the gradient magnitude compared to a soft threshold value. The anisotropic EED scheme reduces diffusion across edges quite agressively but maintains full diffusion along the edges. Finally, the CED scheme reduces diffusion perpendicular to the gradient as well at corner-like structures. However, the Diffusion Echo distributions reveal that differences between the schemes are not quite as characteristic. Apparently, there is more like a smooth transitition between the schemes — like the existence of the GAN scheme implies. Even though the Perona-Malik scheme is isotropic it has a preferred diffusion direction along the edge. This is much more pronounced for the anisotropic EED scheme but not qualitatively different.

Effects of Discretisation Scheme. Apart from the relative differences between the schemes, it appears that the Edge Enhancing scheme is not quite able to enhance the straight edges as well as in previous publications [9]. This is simply because of the numerical approximation scheme. For the previous illustrations we used the implementation that ensures non-negative weights in the local diffusion stencil ([9] page 95). This restricts the spectral condition number of the diffusion tensor to be below 5.8284 — meaning that the local degree of anisotropy is limited. The eigenvectors are correspondingly limited such that $\lambda_1 < 5.8284\,\lambda_2$. For the Edge Enhancing scheme where $\lambda_1 \equiv 1$ this sets a lower limit on λ_2 and thereby some diffusion across the edges is allowed.

In figure 3 the same diffusion processes have been repeated using the non-restricted, standard approximation scheme [9,8]. It is apparent that a more effective preservation of the edges is possible. The shapes of the distributions are especially interesting at the corners. The different abilities of the schemes with respect to supporting diffusion along the edge through the corner is evident.

The illustration clearly reveals that the change of discretisation scheme has a major effect on the diffusion for some of the schemes.

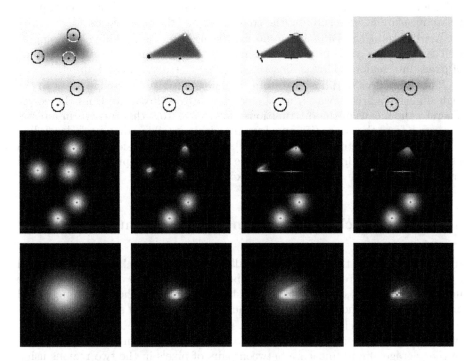

Fig. 3. Diffusion Echo drain distributions for the four diffusion schemes (linear, Perona-Malik, Edge Enhancing, and Corner Enhancing) where the nonnegativity approximation scheme used in figure 2 is replaced with the simpler standard approximation scheme. The standard scheme allows more pronounced anisotropy. The bottom row is here close-ups for the point inside the left corner of the triangle.

The Visualisation Ability. The previous illustrations show that the Diffusion Echo is able to visualize properties of the diffusion schemes that are not otherwise apparent. Extended experiments with the diffusion schemes allows similar intuition but the Diffusion Echo illustrations offer this understanding directly.

In the following sections we offer a few appetisers indicating that the Diffusion Echo can be used for more than just illustrations.

4   Diffusion Echo Application: Grouping

The Diffusion Echo expresses affinity between points in an image. This affinity measure can be used for grouping of pixels into regions or grouping of feature points in general.

Since the affinity measure is defined in terms of the underlying diffusion, the diffusion scheme needs to be appropriate for the specific grouping task.

Edge detectors often produce edge pieces with small gaps in-between. The Diffusion Echo for the Edge Enhancing diffusion scheme would be a very appropriate measure for determining the connectivity of the edge pieces.

Attributes of the Diffusion Echo can be used for determining grouping as well. An example could be using the shape of the distribution to guide grouping of pixels into regions. This is illustrated by the distributions in figure 4.

The differences in diffusivity from the low diffusivity near-edge areas to the high diffusivity areas away from the edges causes a flux away from the edges. Thereby the means of the distributions move away from their origins in a direction away from the edges (if any edges are within "striking distance" depending on diffusion parameters, especially regularisation and diffusion time). This can be used to create a drift field that can be used to group the pixels. The field will create a *sink* in each region that the pixels drift towards.

5   Diffusion Echo Application: Deep Structure Summary

Instead of grouping the pixels individually, the Diffusion Echo can also be used for grouping image regions. This could be an alternative to existing multi-scale linking schemes. An example of this is shown in figure 5 where grouping based on the Diffusion Echo is compared to multi-scale watershed segmentation.

The Diffusion Echo grouping uses a simple threshold to determine whether two neighbouring regions are merged into one region. This threshold is compared to the average affinity measure between pairs of pixels in the two regions using the affinity measure directly from the Diffusion Echo source distribution. The result is a simple flooding-like algorithm.

Even though both examples are quite simple, they illustrate that the Diffusion Echo distributions capture what can be considered a deep structure summary to such an extent that even simple attributes offer powerful grouping abilities.

 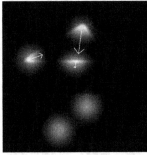

Fig. 4. Diffusion Echo grouping drift fields. For the five points a vector from the point to the mean for the drain distribution gives a drift field that can be used for grouping. For visualisation purposes, the vectors have been scaled to 10 times their actual lengths. The vectors from the points just inside the corners aim towards the center of the triangle. The vector for the point just below the triangle (it is a single pixel outside) aims away from the triangle. The remaining vectors are practically zero-vectors since the parameters for the Edge Enhancing scheme dictate that there are no edges near them — their distributions are approximately Gaussian with means at their origins.

6   Conclusion

We introduce the Diffusion Echo: the distributions that equip non-linear diffusion schemes with what corresponds to the Gaussian for linear diffusion.

The Diffusion Echo offers illustrations of non-linear diffusion schemes that reveal the true local diffusion in an intuitive manner.

Furthermore, we argue that the affinity nature of the distributions can be used effectly for grouping. This is demonstrated through two examples. First, the Diffusion Echo distributions are used to generate a drift field, where each pixel is equipped with a vector stating the preferred direction of grouping. Secondly, we group regions by the average affinity between pixels in the regions. This proves to be a simple but effective region grouping scheme.

Computation time and memory requirement for the computation of the Diffusion Echoes are quadratic in the number of image pixels — this obviously is problematic for larger images. However, this article is only an introduction of the principles. Future applications will not use the basic definition directly. Where linear attributes of the Diffusion Echo distributions are needed, these can be computed directly during the diffusion iterations (in linear time and memory).

Diffusion Echo based methods imply a shift from the diffusion scheme being an underlying information-simplifying step to being the central information-collecting process. The basic principle behind Diffusion Echo based methods is *the diffusion knows*. Future work will reveal the application tasks where the proper non-linear diffusion scheme really is omnipotent.

Acknowledgements: Part of the implementations used for this article are based on code originally developed by Joachim Weickert, University of Mannheim, and Ole Fogh Olsen, The IT University of Copenhagen.

Fig. 5. Segmentation by grouping of watershed regions using the Diffusion Echo. Top row shows a simple example where the segmentation task is to capture the rectangle. First the test image followed by a watershed segmentation at low scale. Third image shows the multi-scale linking of the regions where the underlying diffusion is 30 levels of the edge enhancing scheme from $t = 1$ to $t = 600$ [3]. The rightmost image is the result of flooding with the threshold 0.0025 using the average Diffusion Echo source affinity between neighbouring regions.

Bottom row is equivalent where the segmentation task is to capture the ventricles from a data set from the Internet Brain Segmentation Repository [1]. Here, the linking uses 10 levels from $t = 0.6$ to $t = 80$ in 10 levels. The flooding threshold is 0.0059.

The Diffusion Echo flooding method groups the desired regions for both images.

References

1. The internet brain segmentation repository, 1999. MR brain data set 788_6_m and its manual segmentation was provided by the Center for Morphometric Analysis at MGH, http://neuro-www.mgh.harvard.edu/cma/ibsr.
2. F. Catté, P.-L. Lions, J.-M. Morel, and T. Coll. Image selective smoothing and edge detection by nonlinear diffusion. *SIAM J. of Num. An.*, 29:182–193, 1992.
3. Erik Dam. Evaluation of diffusion schemes for watershed segmentation. Master's thesis, University of Copenhagen, 2000. Technical report 2000/1 on http://www.diku.dk/research/techreports/2000.htm.
4. Erik Dam and Mads Nielsen. Non-linear diffusion for interactive multi-scale watershed segmentation. *MICCAI 2000*, vol 1935 of *LNCS*, 216–225. Springer, 2000.
5. Jan J. Koenderink. The structure of images. *Biol. Cybern.*, 50:363–370, 1984.
6. Tony Lindeberg. *Scale-Space Theory in Computer Vision*. Kluwer, 1994.
7. Pietro Perona and Jitendra Malik. Scale-space and edge detection using anisotropic diffusion. *IEEE PAMI*, 12(7):629 – 639, July 1990.
8. H. Scharr and J. Weickert. An anisotropic diffusion algorithm with optimized rotation invariance. *Mustererkennung 2000, DAGM*, pp 460–467. Springer, 2000.
9. Joachim Weickert. *Anisotropic Diffusion in Image Processing*. Teubner, 1998.
10. Andrew P. Witkin. Scale-space filtering. In *Proceedings of International Joint Conference on Artificial Intelligence*, pages 1019–1022, Karlsruhe, Germany, 1983.

Bilateral Filtering and Anisotropic Diffusion: Towards a Unified Viewpoint

Danny Barash

Hewlett-Packard Laboratories Israel, Technion City
Haifa 32000, Israel

Abstract. Bilateral filtering has recently been proposed as a noniterative alternative to anisotropic diffusion. In both these approaches, images are smoothed while edges are preserved. Unlike anisotropic diffusion, bilateral filtering does not involve the solution of partial differential equations and can be implemented in a single iteration. Despite the difference in implementation, both methods are designed to prevent averaging across edges while smoothing an image. Their similarity suggests they can somehow be linked. Using a generalized representation for the intensity, we show that both can be related to adaptive smoothing. As a consequence, bilateral filtering can be applied to denoise and coherence-enhance degraded images with approaches similar to anisotropic diffusion.

1 Introduction

In a wide variety of applications, it is necessary to smooth an image while preserving its edges. Simple smoothing operations such as low-pass filtering, which does not take into account intensity variations within an image, tend to blur edges. Anisotropic diffusion [4] was proposed as a general approach to accomplish edge-preserving smoothing. This approach has grown to become a well-established tool in early vision.

This paper examines the relation between bilateral filtering, a recent approach proposed in [7], and anisotropic diffusion. The paper is divided as follows. Section II presents the connection between anisotropic diffusion and adaptive smoothing. The goal is to suggest a viewpoint in which adaptive smoothing serves as the link between bilateral filtering and anisotropic diffusion. In Section III, adaptive smoothing is extended, which results in bilateral filtering. The possible unification of bilateral filtering and anisotropic diffusion is then discussed. Sections IV and V take advantage of the resultant link, borrowing the use of the geometric interpretation to anisotropic diffusion and applying it in bilateral filtering. Section IV examines the convolution kernel of a bilateral filter, from the standpoint that color images are 2D surfaces embedded in 5D (x,y,R,G,B) space. In Section V, conclusions are drawn and suggestions are given for future examination of the proposed unified viewpoint.

M. Kerckhove (Ed.): Scale-Space 2001, LNCS 2106, pp. 273–280, 2001.

2   Anisotropic Diffusion and Adaptive Smoothing

We first examine the connection between anisotropic diffusion and adaptive smoothing, which was outlined in [5]. Given an image $I^{(t)}(\boldsymbol{x})$, where $\boldsymbol{x} = (x_1, x_2)$ denotes space coordinates, an iteration of adaptive smoothing yields:

$$I^{(t+1)}(\boldsymbol{x}) = \frac{\sum_{i=-1}^{+1} \sum_{j=-1}^{+1} I^{(t)}(x_1 + i, x_2 + j) w^{(t)}}{\sum_{i=-1}^{+1} \sum_{j=-1}^{+1} w^{(t)}} \tag{1}$$

where the convolution mask $w^{(t)}$ is defined as:

$$w^{(t)}(x_1, x_2) = \exp\left(-\frac{\left|d^{(t)}(x_1, x_2)\right|^2}{2k^2}\right) \tag{2}$$

where k is the variance of the Gaussian mask. In [5], $d^{(t)}(x_1, x_2)$ is chosen to depend on the magnitude of the gradient computed in a 3×3 window:

$$d^{(t)}(x_1, x_2) = \sqrt{G_{x_1}^2 + G_{x_2}^2} \tag{3}$$

where,

$$(G_{x_1}, G_{x_2}) = \left(\frac{\partial I^{(t)}(x_1, x_2)}{\partial x_1}, \frac{\partial I^{(t)}(x_1, x_2)}{\partial x_2}\right) \tag{4}$$

noting the similarity of the convolution mask with the diffusion coefficient in anisotropic diffusion [4], [8].

It was shown [5] that equation (1) is an implementation of anisotropic diffusion. Briefly sketched, lets consider the case of a one-dimensional signal $I^t(x)$ and reformulate the averaging process as follows:

$$I^{t+1}(x) = c_1 I^t(x - 1) + c_2 I^t(x) + c_3 I^t(x + 1) \tag{5}$$

with

$$c_1 + c_2 + c_3 = 1 \tag{6}$$

Therefore, it is possible to write the above iteration scheme as follows:

$$I^{t+1}(x) - I^t(x) = c_1(I^t(x - 1) - I^t(x)) + c_3(I^t(x + 1) - I^t(x)) \tag{7}$$

Taking $c_1 = c_3$, this reduces to:

$$I^{t+1}(x) - I^t(x) = c_1(I^t(x - 1) - 2I^t(x) + I^t(x + 1)) \tag{8}$$

which is a discrete approximation of the linear diffusion equation:

$$\frac{\partial I}{\partial t} = c\nabla^2 I \tag{9}$$

However, when the weights are space-dependent, one should write the weighted averaging scheme as follows:

$$I^{t+1}(x) = c^t(x - 1)I^t(x - 1) + c^t(x)I^t(x) + c^t(x + 1)I^t(x + 1) \tag{10}$$

with

$$c^t(x-1) + c^t(x) + c^t(x+1) = 1 \tag{11}$$

This can be rearranged as:

$$
\begin{aligned}
I^{t+1}(x) - I^t(x) &= c^t(x-1)(I^t(x-1) \\
&\quad - I^t(x)) + c^t(x+1)(I^t(x+1) - I^t(x))
\end{aligned} \tag{12}
$$

or

$$
\begin{aligned}
I^{t+1}(x) - I^t(x) &= c^t(x+1)(I^t(x+1) \\
&\quad - I^t(x)) - c^t(x-1)(I^t(x) - I^t(x-1))
\end{aligned} \tag{13}
$$

which is an implementation of anisotropic diffusion, proposed by Perona and Malik [4]:

$$\frac{\partial I}{\partial t} = \nabla(c(x_1, x_2)\nabla I) \tag{14}$$

where $c(x_1, x_2)$ is the nonlinear diffusion coefficient, typically taken as:

$$c(x_1, x_2) = g(\|\nabla I(x_1, x_2)\|) \tag{15}$$

where $\|\nabla I\|$ is the gradient magnitude, and $g(\|\nabla I\|)$ is an "edge-stopping" function. This function is chosen to satisfy $g(x) \to 0$ when $x \to \infty$ so that the diffusion is stopped across edges.

Thus, a link between anisotropic diffusion (14) and adaptive smoothing (1) is established. In the next section, we show the link between adaptive smoothing and bilateral filtering.

3   Bilateral Filtering and Adaptive Smoothing

Bilateral filtering was introduced [7] as a nonlinear filter which combines domain and range filtering. Given an input image $f(x)$, using a continuous representation notation as in [7], the output image $h(x)$ is obtained by:

$$h(x) = \frac{\int_{-\infty}^{\infty} \int_{-\infty}^{\infty} f(\xi)c(\xi, x)s(f(\xi), f(x))d\xi}{\int_{-\infty}^{\infty} \int_{-\infty}^{\infty} c(\xi, x)s(f(\xi), f(x))d\xi} \tag{16}$$

where $x = (x_1, x_2), \xi = (\xi_1, \xi_2)$ are space variables and $f = (f_R, f_G, f_B)$ is the intensity. The full vector notation is used in order to avoid confusion in what follows. The convolution mask is the product of the functions c and s, which represent 'closeness' (in the domain) and 'similarity' (in the range), respectively.

Effectively, we claim that a discrete version of bilateral filtering can be written as follows (using the same notation as in the previous section, only I is now a 3-element vector which describes color images):

$$I^{(t+1)}(x) = \frac{\sum_{i=-S}^{+S} \sum_{j=-S}^{+S} I^{(t)}(x_1 + i, x_2 + j)w^{(t)}}{\sum_{i=-S}^{+S} \sum_{j=-S}^{+S} w^{(t)}} \tag{17}$$

with the weights given by:

$$w^{(t)}(\boldsymbol{x}, \boldsymbol{\xi}) = \exp(\frac{-(\boldsymbol{\xi} - \boldsymbol{x})^2}{2\sigma_D^2}) \exp(\frac{-(I(\boldsymbol{\xi}) - I(\boldsymbol{x}))^2}{2\sigma_R^2}) \tag{18}$$

where S is the window size of the filter, which is a generalization of (1). In order to prove our claim and demonstrate the relation to (1), we use a generalized representation for the intensity $\boldsymbol{I}$. In principle, the first element corresponds to the range and the second element corresponds to the domain of the bilateral filter. Defining the generalized intensity as:

$$\widehat{\boldsymbol{I}} \equiv \left\{ \frac{\boldsymbol{I}(\boldsymbol{x})}{\sigma_R}, \frac{\boldsymbol{x}}{\sigma_D} \right\} \tag{19}$$

we now take $d^{(t)}(\boldsymbol{x})$ to be the difference between generalized intensities at two points in a given $S \times S$ window, $\left| \widehat{\boldsymbol{I}}(\boldsymbol{\xi}) - \widehat{\boldsymbol{I}}(\boldsymbol{x}) \right|$, the latter being a global extension to (3). In (3), the gradient, being the local difference between two neighboring points in a 3×3 window, was taken as a distance measure. Starting from (2), and setting $k = 1$ since the variances σ_D and σ_R are already included in the generalized intensity, we obtain:

$$w^{(t)}(\boldsymbol{x}) = \exp(-\frac{1}{2} \left| \widehat{\boldsymbol{I}}(\boldsymbol{\xi}) - \widehat{\boldsymbol{I}}(\boldsymbol{x}) \right|^2) =$$

$$= \exp(-\frac{1}{2} \left| \left\{ \frac{\boldsymbol{I}(\boldsymbol{\xi})}{\sigma_R}, \frac{\boldsymbol{\xi}}{\sigma_D} \right\} - \left\{ \frac{\boldsymbol{I}(\boldsymbol{x})}{\sigma_R}, \frac{\boldsymbol{x}}{\sigma_D} \right\} \right|^2)$$

$$= \exp(-\frac{1}{2} \left| \left\{ \frac{\boldsymbol{I}(\boldsymbol{\xi}) - \boldsymbol{I}(\boldsymbol{x})}{\sigma_R}, \frac{\boldsymbol{\xi} - \boldsymbol{x}}{\sigma_D} \right\} \right|^2)$$

$$= \exp(-\frac{1}{2} \left(\frac{(\boldsymbol{I}(\boldsymbol{\xi}) - \boldsymbol{I}(\boldsymbol{x}))^2}{\sigma_R^2} + \frac{(\boldsymbol{\xi} - \boldsymbol{x})^2}{\sigma_D^2} \right))$$

$$= \exp(\frac{-(\boldsymbol{\xi} - \boldsymbol{x})^2}{2\sigma_D^2}) \exp(\frac{-(I(\boldsymbol{\xi}) - I(\boldsymbol{x}))^2}{2\sigma_R^2}) \tag{20}$$

Because these are the weights used in the bilateral filter, as can be verified in (18), equation (20) provides a direct link between adaptive smoothing and bilateral filtering. In a general framework of adaptive smoothing, one can take spatial and spectral distance measures along with increasing the window size, abandoning the need to perform several iterations. Taken as such, we get the bilateral filtering implementation of [7] which can be viewed as a generalization of adaptive smoothing.

4   Geometric Interpretation

In the previous two sections, it was shown that anisotropic diffusion and bilateral filtering can be linked through adaptive smoothing. Specifically, the diffusion coefficient in (14) relates to the convolution mask and in particular to the distance measure which is used in the bilateral filter. Similarly, the relation between anisotropic diffusion and robust statistics was described in [1].

For illustration, Figure 2 demonstrates two different ways of performing edge-preserving smoothing on the original image in Figure 1. The result of using nonlinear diffusion filtering and the result of bilateral filtering is similar but not identical, since the parameters are different and it was intentionally chosen to use a large window size with the bilateral filter and several iterations with anisotropic diffusion. That is the most natural setup for the two to be used.

Fig. 1. Original Image: Laplace.

In color images, it was demonstrated in [6] that the image can be represented as 2D surface embedded in the 5D spatial-color space and denoising can be achieved by using the Beltrami flow. Related ideas can be found in [10], [3]. It is possible to borrow this notion outlined in [6] and choose the following spectral distance measure for the bilateral filter:

$$|I(\boldsymbol{x}) - I(\boldsymbol{\xi})| = \sqrt{(\Delta R)^2 + (\Delta G)^2 + (\Delta B)^2} \qquad (21)$$

Note that only the spectral distance measure of the range part is given in (21) and can directly be installed in the similarity function s of the bilateral filter as implemented in [7]. The spatial distance measure of the domain part remains the same as with grey-level images. Written that way, one can distinguish between closeness in the domain and similarity in the range, with the advantage of treating the two separately. However, it is also possible to write (21) equivalently by combining the spatial and spectral distance terms. Using the generalized inten-

Fig. 2. Edge-preserving smoothing: Anisotropic diffusion with 20 time-steps of $\tau = 1.0$ (left) and Gaussian bilateral filtering with a 30×30 window size, $\sigma_D = 5.0$ and $\sigma_R = 30.0$ (right). σ_D and σ_R are bilateral filtering parameters, see [6] for details.

sity defined in (19), the full distance measure can be written as:

$$\left| d^{(t)}(x_1, x_2) \right|^2 = \left| \sigma_D(\widehat{I(\boldsymbol{x})} - \widehat{I(\boldsymbol{\xi})}) \right|^2 = \tag{22}$$
$$(\varDelta x_1)^2 + (\varDelta x_2)^2 + \beta^2((\varDelta R)^2 + (\varDelta G)^2 + (\varDelta B)^2)$$

where $\beta = \sigma_D/\sigma_R$. Note that this distance measure can be plugged into the convolution mask of adaptive smoothing (2) as one term with $k = \sigma_D$. It is now possible to take advantage of a geometric interpretation in which color images are $2D$ surfaces embedded in the $5D$ (x, y, R, G, B) space. Equation (22) is then analogous to the local measure:

$$ds^2 = dx^2 + dy^2 + \beta^2(dR^2 + dG^2 + dB^2) \tag{23}$$

which is the geometric arclength in the hybrid spatial-color space discussed in [2], [6].

5 Conclusions

The nature of bilateral filtering resembles that of anisotropic diffusion. It is therefore suggested the two are related and a unified viewpoint can reveal the similarities and differences between the two approaches. Once such an understanding is reached, it is possible to choose the desired ingredients which are common to the two frameworks along with the implementation method. The method can be either applying a nonlinear filter or solving a partial-differential equation.

Adaptive smoothing serves as a link between the two approaches, each of which can be viewed as a generalization of the former. In anisotropic diffusion, the diffusion coefficient can be generalized to become a 'structure tensor' [8] which then leads to phenomena such as edge-enhancing and coherence-enhancing diffusions. In bilateral filtering, the kernel (which plays the same role as the diffusion coefficient) is extended to become globally dependent on intensity, whereas a gradient can only yield local dependency among neighboring pixels. Thus, the window of the filter becomes much bigger in size than the one used in adaptive smoothing and there is no need to perform several iterations. We note that this extension is general on its own right, meaning that a variety of yet unexplored possibilities exist for constructing a kernel with an optimal window size, as well as designing the best closeness and similarity functions for a given application.

The general hybrid spatial-color formulation [2], [6] provide a geometric interpretation with which the bilateral convolution kernel can be viewed as an approximation to the geometric arclength in the 5D hybrid spatial-color space. Ideas that are based on the geometric interpretation, such as coherence-enhancement, can be borrowed from anisotropic diffusion and applied to some degree of approximation in bilateral filtering.

Two practical goals seem to come up from comparing between anisotropic diffusion and bilateral filtering. The first is a further trial to reduce the number of iterations needed in anisotropic diffusion (which can be achieved by efficient numerical schemes such as [9], less proned to stability problems) while retaining the same accuracy as in bilateral filtering. The second is to reduce the window size and investigate other means which aim at minimizing computations associated with bilateral filtering. Both approaches are related to each other, and an exchange of new ideas between one another can be rewarding.

Acknowledgments

The author would like to thank Ron Kimmel, from the computer science department at the Technion - Israel Institute of Technology, for his assistance in all aspects of this work.

References

1. Black M.J., Sapiro G., Marimont D., Heeger D., "Robust Anisotropic Diffusion," *IEEE Transactions on Image Processing*, Vol. 7, No. 3, p.421, 1998.
2. R. Kimmel, R. Malladi, N. Sochen, "Images as Embedded Maps and Minimal Surfaces: Movies, Color, Texture, and Volumetric Medical Images," *International Journal of Computer Vision*, 39(2), p.111, 2000.
3. J.J. Koenderink, A.J. Van Doorn, "The Structure of Locally Orderless Images," *International Journal of Computer Vision*, 21(2/3), p.159, 1999.

4. P. Perona and J. Malik, "Scale-Space and Edge Detection Using Anisotropic Diffusion," *IEEE Transactions on Pattern Analysis and Machine Intelligence*, Vol. 12, No. 7, p.629, 1990.

5. P. Saint-Marc, J.S. Chen, G. Medioni, "Adaptive Smoothing: A General Tool for Early Vision," *IEEE Transactions on Pattern Analysis and Machine Intelligence*, Vol. 13, No. 6, p.514, 1991.

6. N. Sochen, R. Kimmel, R. Malladi, "A Geometrical Framework for Low Level Vision," *IEEE Transactions on Image Processing*, Vol. 7, No. 3, p.310, 1998.

7. C. Tomasi and R. Manduchi, "Bilateral Filtering for Gray and Color Images," *Proceedings of the 1998 IEEE International Conference on Computer Vision*, Bombay, India, 1998.

8. J. Weickert, *Anisotropic Diffusion in Image Processing,* Tuebner Stuttgart, 1998. ISBN 3-519-02606-6.

9. J. Weickert, B.M. ter Haar Romeny, M. Viergever, "Efficient and Reliable Schemes for Nonlinear Diffusion Filtering," *IEEE Transactions on Image Processing*, Vol. 7, No. 3, p.398, 1998.

10. A. Yezzi, "Modified Curvature Motion for Image Smoothing and Enhancement," *IEEE Transactions on Image Processing*, Vol. 7, No. 3, p.345, 1998.

An Accurate Operator Splitting Scheme for Nonlinear Diffusion Filtering

Danny Barash[1], Moshe Israeli[2], and Ron Kimmel[2]

[1] Hewlett-Packard Laboratories Israel
Technion City, Haifa 32000, Israel
[2] Computer Science Department, Technion-Israel Institute of Technology
Haifa 32000, Israel

Abstract. Efficient numerical schemes for nonlinear diffusion filtering based on additive operator splitting (AOS) were introduced in [10]. AOS schemes are efficient and unconditionally stable, yet their accuracy is low. Future applications of nonlinear diffusion filtering may require additional accuracy at the expense of a relatively modest cost in computations and complexity.

To investigate the effect of higher accuracy schemes, we first examine the Crank-Nicolson and DuFort-Frankel second-order schemes in one dimension. We then extend the AOS schemes to take advantage of the higher accuracy that is achieved in one dimension, by using symmetric multiplicative splittings. Quantitative comparisons are performed for small and large time steps, as well as visual examination of images to find out whether the improvement in accuracy is noticeable.

1 Introduction

There are various applications of nonlinear diffusion filtering [6,9] in image processing. Such 'filters' can be used for denoising, gap completion and computer aided quality control among many other tasks. These kind of applications demand high processing capabilities. The balance between high accuracy and computational efficiency is therefore an important issue in the design of such filters, that is expected to play an increasing role in future applications.

In this paper, an accurate numerical scheme is proposed which is an extension to Weickert-Romeny-Viergever's additive operator splitting (AOS) schemes [10]. These schemes are efficient and reliable, in the sense that they permit the use of larger time steps, whereas the straight-forward explicit schemes, that were proposed originally in Perona and Malik's classical paper [6], are restricted to small time steps in order to ensure stability. However, the AOS schemes are limited in their accuracy to first order in time even for the linear case. We therefore examine the possibility of increasing the accuracy in one- dimension, along with preserving this increase in accuracy by a suitable split-operator scheme. Our approach closely resembles the use of alternating direction implicit (ADI) type schemes [5], which are second order in time for the linear case. We show that for large time steps the gain in accuracy can be visualized. These ADI-like

M. Kerckhove (Ed.): Scale-Space 2001, LNCS 2106, pp. 281–289, 2001.

schemes can be applied in certain cases with a single iteration, effectively a large time-step, or very few number of iterations in order to better approximate many iterations with smaller time-steps.

2   Nonlinear Diffusion Filtering

Let us first provide a model for nonlinear diffusion in image filtering. We briefly describe the filter proposed by Catté, Lions, Morel and Coll [1]. The CLMC filter is a version of the Perona and Malik model [6] for image selective smoothing that was used in [10] as a benchmark for studying various numerical schemes. The basic equation which governs nonlinear diffusion filtering is

$$\frac{\partial u}{\partial t} = \nabla \cdot (g(|\nabla u_\sigma|^2)\nabla u), \tag{1}$$

where $u(x, t)$ is a filtered version of the original image. The original image $f(x)$ is given as the initial condition

$$u(x, 0) = f(x), \tag{2}$$

and reflecting boundary conditions are used

$$\frac{\partial u}{\partial n} = 0 \ \text{ on } \ \partial \Omega, \tag{3}$$

where n is the normal to the image boundary $\partial\Omega$.

The goal of selective smoothing in edge-preserving applications is to reduce smoothing across edges. In order to achieve this goal, the diffusivity g is chosen as a rapidly decreasing function of the gradient magnitude (edge indicator). Specifically, the following form for the diffusivity is suggested in the CLMC filter

$$g(s) = \begin{cases} 1 & (s \leq 0) \\ 1 - \exp\left(\frac{-3.315}{(s/\lambda)^4}\right) & (s > 0), \end{cases} \tag{4}$$

where $\lambda = 10.0$ throughout this paper. In addition, CLMC suggest at each time step a presmoothing mechanism, in which the image u is convolved with a Gaussian of standard deviation σ to obtain u_σ. This can be achieved by solving the linear diffusion filtering ($g \equiv 1$)

$$\frac{\partial u_\sigma}{\partial t} = \nabla \cdot (\nabla u_\sigma), \tag{5}$$

for a very small time step of size $T = \sigma^2/2$. This step is called regularization, or presmoothing, and can be approximated by any of the splitting schemes that will be mentioned in the paper. For example, a simple locally one-dimensional (LOD) scheme is a convenient choice. In the remaining of this paper, $\sigma = 0.25$ is chosen for the presmoothing, except when quantitative comparisons are performed and presmoothing is excluded.

3   One-Dimensional Schemes

This section relies on [10], where the one-dimensional explicit and semi-implicit schemes were described. Here we add the Crank-Nicolson and the DuFort-Frankel, as possible schemes to perform nonlinear diffusion in one-dimension. For more details and theoretical considerations regarding the framework for discrete nonlinear diffusion scale-spaces, the reader is referred to [9,10].

Both the explicit scheme and the semi-implicit scheme are first order in time. A scheme which is a combination of the two and is second order in time for the linear case is the Crank-Nicolson scheme

$$(I - \frac{\tau}{2}A(u^k))u^{k+1} = (I + \frac{\tau}{2}A(u^k))u^k. \tag{6}$$

Another candidate scheme to try and achieve higher accuracy is the DuFort-Frankel method [2]. However, its inconsistency results (see Figure 2) in a scheme that is not reliable from a certain time step onwards. Nevertheless, an extended DuFort-Frankel in higher dimensions that averages the fluctuations at higher time steps might perform well in the anisotropic cases like the Beltrami framework [7], or coherence enhancement [9]. Experimental results with all schemes are shown in Figures 1,2,3,4, in which a 1D cross-section of a natural image was taken (Figure 1) and edge-preserving smoothing was applied using small and large time steps. It is seen in Figure 1 (right) that the Forward-Euler scheme becomes unstable for larger time steps. Reducing the time-step by two orders of magnitude can recover an edge-preserved smoothed signal (Figure 1 middle), but this is inefficient. We are left with Backward-Euler and Crank-Nicolson for obtaining a robust nonlinear diffused signal at large time steps. An l_2 norm error comparison between the different output signals (see Section 4 on how this is calculated for images) reveals that in the nonlinear case, the 1D Crank-Nicolson scheme as is remains first-order accurate in time. This is because the nonlinear diffusivity term, calculated at a specific time step, interferes with achieving higher order accuracy in time. In order to retain second-order accuracy, extrapolation is needed such that the diffusivity is calculated according to two levels of time step. Table 1 indicates that a simple extrapolation along with the Crank-Nicolson, in the form of $g_i^{new} = 2 \cdot g_i^{new} - g_i^{old}$ for each time step, can boost the accuracy. We will refer to some more involved extrapolation procedures, such as the Douglas Jones predictor-corrector method proposed in [9], in Section 4.

4   Accurate Operator Splitting Schemes

Motivated by ADI [5] which is known as a favorable splitting scheme for the linear diffusion equation, we wish to combine the merits of the AOS scheme as a symmetric scheme, together with the family of multiplicative operator splittings. Multiplicative operator splittings are known in general to be more accurate than the AOS schemes. We therefore propose a symmetric scheme, mentioned by Strang in [8], which is both additive and multiplicative operator splitting

Table 1. l_2 Norm Error Estimation.

τ	Linear CN	Nonlin CN	Extrapolation
0.4	0.0079	0.052	0.0262
0.2	0.002	0.024	0.0068
0.1	$4.94 \cdot 10^{-4}$	0.0113	0.0024
0.05	$1.22 \cdot 10^{-4}$	0.0052	$5.6 \cdot 10^{-4}$
0.025	$2.9 \cdot 10^{-5}$	0.0022	$1.18 \cdot 10^{-4}$
0.0125	$5.81 \cdot 10^{-6}$	$7.34 \cdot 10^{-4}$	$2.37 \cdot 10^{-5}$
0.00625	0	0	0

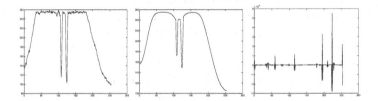

Fig. 1. Explicit Scheme (Forward-Euler). Left: Original Noisy Signal. Middle: 100 Time Steps of $\tau = 0.5$. Right: 5 Time Steps of $\tau = 10.0$.

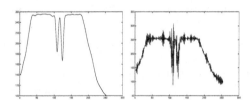

Fig. 2. DuFort-Frankel. Left: 8 Time Steps of $\tau = 0.4$. Right: 4 Time Steps of $\tau = 0.8$.

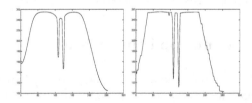

Fig. 3. Semi-implicit Scheme (Backward Euler). Left: 5 Time Steps of $\tau = 10.0$. Right: Same as Left, Except the Diffusivity $g(s) = (1 + 3s^8)^{-1}(s > 0)$ Was Used.

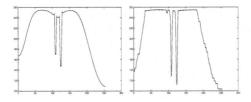

Fig. 4. Crank-Nicolson. Left: 5 Time Steps of $\tau = 10.0$. Right: Same as Left, Except the Diffusivity $g(s) = (1 + 3s^8)^{-1}(s > 0)$ Was Used.

(AMOS)

$$u^{k+1} = \frac{1}{2}[(I - \tau A_1(u^k))^{-1}(I - \tau A_2(u^k))^{-1}$$
$$+ (I - \tau A_2(u^k))^{-1}(I - \tau A_1(u^k))^{-1}]u^k \qquad (7)$$

Equation (7) applies the AMOS scheme to the semi-implicit scheme. Such a combination is known in the literature [2] as the approximate factorization implicit (AFI) scheme, which is first order accurate in time. However, even in the case where it is built upon the semi-implicit scheme, the AMOS scheme is expected to be more accurate than the AOS scheme while preserving symmetry. Furthermore, it is possible to try to achieve better accuracy by applying the AMOS scheme on the Crank-Nicolson scheme. At each time step, two calculations are performed

$$\left(I - \frac{\tau}{2}A_1(u^k)\right)u^{k*} = \left(I + \frac{\tau}{2}A_1(u^k)\right)u^k$$
$$\left(I - \frac{\tau}{2}A_2(u^k)\right)u^{k+1} = \left(I + \frac{\tau}{2}A_2(u^k)\right)u^{k*}, \qquad (8)$$

and

$$\left(I - \frac{\tau}{2}A_2(u^k)\right)u^{k*} = \left(I + \frac{\tau}{2}A_2(u^k)\right)u^k$$
$$\left(I - \frac{\tau}{2}A_1(u^k)\right)u^{k+1} = \left(I + \frac{\tau}{2}A_1(u^k)\right)u^{k*}. \qquad (9)$$

After the time step is completed, the two results are averaged together which ensures a symmetric splitting. Although the directions are not alternating in each of the two calculations, i.e. the forward and backward Euler are performed on the same direction, in effect this scheme belongs to the family of alternating direction implicit (ADI) type methods. In our experiments, alternating the directions as in the classical ADI, produced no better results when applied to nonlinear diffusion filtering. Therefore, we refer to (8),(9) as ADI, whereas (7) is AFI. We also note that adding the extrapolation suggested in the one-dimensional case, as in Table 1, did not increase the order of accuracy to exactly second when performing quantitative calculations with very small time steps in two dimensions. At the expense of more computations, one can try to improve the extrapolation procedure by using the Wynn extrapolation or predictor-corrector methods, such as Adams Bashforth [2] or Douglas Jones [9], in which the Crank-Nicolson is the corrector. While these more complicated procedures are costly, it is not obvious how much accuracy will be gained as a consequence for larger time steps and whether this will be justifiable. However, practical use in applications requires mostly large time steps to do the filterting, and it turns out the ADI scheme in (8),(9) leads to visually better results for such time steps as can be seen in Figures 5,6. We take 2000 time steps of 0.1 as a reference, then decrease the number of iterations to check the deviation from the reference. As we decrease the number of iterations, we observe that the deviation from the converged result is smaller with the ADI scheme than with the AOS scheme. Filtering effect becomes stronger in the ADI scheme, while preserving fine details, which is an indication that the ADI scheme is visually more accurate than the AOS scheme. Quantitative examination of the deviations from the reference is calculated as follows. We start from the original image in Figure 5 (left), which is a texture image taken from a neutron diffraction experiment. Figures 5,6 show the comparison in terms of accuracy between the AOS, AFI and ADI schemes, which are discussed next. In terms of speed, the AOS and AFI schemes in actual simulations indicate that the AFI scheme takes roughly 1.5 the time it takes the AOS scheme to perform the filtering. The ADI scheme is roughly a factor of 2 to 3 longer in processing some test images relative to the AOS scheme. We note that simply decreasing the time step with the AOS scheme by this ratio does not produce the fine filtering that is achieved with the ADI scheme. This fact can be visually observed in practice and will not be reflected in the results of Table 2, as will be explained in the next paragraph.

Fig. 5. Left: Original Texture Image. Middle and Right: Reference for ADI and AOS/AFI, respectively. In all, nonlinear diffusion filtering was performed with 2000 time steps of $\tau = 0.1$.

In Table 2, the relative l_2 norm errors are calculated for the example in Figures 5,6 as follows. Let v denote the reference solution: AOS, $\tau = 0.1$, in the case of the AOS and AFI schemes, and ADI, $\tau = 0.1$, in the case of the ADI scheme. Let u denote the approximate solution in each of the schemes. The

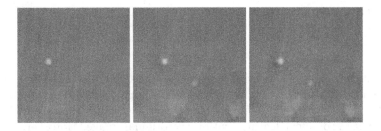

Fig. 6. Left:ADI. Middle: AFI. Right: AOS. In all, nonlinear diffusion filtering was performed with four time step of $\tau = 50.0$.

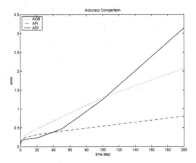

Fig. 7. Comparison of error estimation for different time steps based on Table 2: AOS, AFI, ADI. However, note that for the ADI, a different reference image was used.

Table 2. l_2 Norm Error Estimation.

τ	AOS	AFI	ADI
0.25	0.09 %	0.06 %	0.08 %
0.5	0.13 %	0.1 %	0.11 %
1.0	0.17 %	0.14 %	0.13 %
2.0	0.22 %	0.17 %	0.17 %
5.0	0.29 %	0.24 %	0.19 %
10	0.36 %	0.27 %	0.21 %
20	0.47 %	0.32 %	0.23 %
50	0.79 %	0.41 %	0.47 %
100	1.3 %	0.54 %	1.25 %
200	2.07 %	0.81 %	3.14 %

relative error percentages are calculated by

$$\frac{\|u - v\|_2}{\|v\|_2}. \tag{10}$$

Note that the small relative error percentage values do not completely reflect the strength of the deviations and accuracies, since large propagation times produce smooth images, where the differences between the schemes appear only in small regions near prominent features within the original image. Moreover, the comparison with the ADI scheme is done for a separate reference frame, since even with a small time step the ADI scheme acts as a better filter, as can be seen in several test images, and hence its reference to measure deviations should be different. Therefore, Table 2 and the plot in Figure 7 should be analyzed with caution, especially with respect to the comparison between the ADI and the AOS/AFI. From Table 2 and Figure 7 it can be observed that up to a time step of $\tau = 50.0$, the ADI scheme is the most accurate, which is expected because the Crank-Nicolson is used as its building block. With very large time steps of more than $\tau = 50.0$, the AFI scheme is the most balanced scheme in deviations from the corresponding references, probably because the higher order error terms affect the closeness of the ADI scheme to its reference in Figure 5. Among the schemes which are based on the semi-implicit scheme as their building block, the AFI scheme will produce more accurate results than the AOS scheme since the AMOS scheme is a more accurate splitting scheme than the AOS scheme at the expense of some increase in computations. Finally, we tried to obtain better accuracy out of the results in Figure 6 by using Richardson's extrapolation [2] for our case

$$R_I(\tau/2) = \frac{4R(\tau/2) - R(\tau)}{3}, \tag{11}$$

where $R_I(\tau/2)$ denotes an improved result, using a time grid with a spacing of $\tau/2$ or coarser. $R(\tau/2)$ and $R(\tau)$ are the results of applying nonlinear diffusion filtering for time steps $\tau/2$ and τ, respectively. Our trials failed to show an improvement of $R_I(\tau/2)$ relative to $R(\tau/2)$. An improvement is not guaranteed to begin with, since our equation is nonlinear and the solution is non-smooth.

5   Conclusions

In this paper, accurate splitting operator schemes were proposed for performing nonlinear diffusion filtering. They are gradually constructed by reviewing schemes which are relevant and have been suggested in this context to other applications. Comparing two splitting schemes, it is found that higher order of accuracy can be visually inspected and might become a desirable feature in some future applications.

The two splitting methods which unconditionally satisfy all discrete scale-space criteria are Weickert et al's [10] AOS scheme and our proposed scheme, the AMOS scheme. The AOS scheme is more efficient than the AMOS scheme in its first-order form, the AFI scheme, by approximately a factor of 1.5, and the AMOS scheme in its second-order form, the ADI scheme, by a factor of 2 to 3, depending on the efficiency of the implementation. Although the AOS remains the simplest and most efficient choice for implementation, in the arsenal of numerical schemes for performing nonlinear diffusion filtering the AMOS scheme can be considered as an extension for applications that require high accuracy. Multiplicative operator schemes are in general more accurate than their additive counterparts, and the combination of the two in the AMOS schemes ensures both symmetry and better accuracy at the expense of an increase in execution time.

Acknowledgments

We thank Joachim Weickert from the department of mathematics and computer science at the University of Mannheim, Germany, for providing us the original image of the veneer used in an extended version of this paper.

References

1. F. Catté, P.L. Lions, J.M. Morel, T. Coll, "Image Selective Smoothing and Edge Detection by Nonlinear Diffusion," *SIAM J. Numer. Anal.*, Vol. 29, No. 1, p.182, 1992.
2. J.D. Hoffman, *Numerical Methods for Engineers and Scientists,* McGraw-Hill, Inc., 1992.
3. R. LeVeque, *Numerical Methods for Conservation Laws,* Birkhuser Verlag, Basel, 1990.
4. G.I. Marchuk, "Splitting and Alternating Direction Methods," *Handbook of Numerical Analysis, P.G. Ciarlet, J.L. Lions (Eds.),* Vol. 1, p.197, 1990.
5. D.W. Peaceman and H.H. Rachford, "The Numerical Solution of Parabolic and Elliptic Differential Equations," *Journal Soc. Ind. Appl. Math,* Vol. 3, p.28, 1955.
6. P. Perona and J. Malik, "Scale-Space and Edge Detection Using Anisotropic Diffusion," *IEEE Transactions on Pattern Analysis and Machine Intelligence,* Vol. 12, No. 7, p.629, 1990.
7. N. Sochen, R. Kimmel, R. Malladi, "A Geometrical Framework for Low Level Vision," *IEEE Transactions on Image Processing,* Vol. 7, No. 3, p.310, 1998.
8. G. Strang, "On the Construction and Comparison of Difference Schemes," *SIAM J. Numer. Anal.,* Vol. 5, No. 3, p.506, 1968.
9. J. Weickert, *Anisotropic Diffusion in Image Processing,* Tuebner, Stuttgart, 1998.
10. J. Weickert, B.M. ter Haar Romeny, M. Viergever, "Efficient and Reliable Schemes for Nonlinear Diffusion Filtering," *IEEE Transactions on Image Processing,* Vol. 7, No. 3, p.398, 1998.
11. N.N. Yanenko, *The Method of Fractional Steps: the solution of problems of mathematical physics in several variables,* Springer, New York, 1971.

Selection of Optimal Stopping Time
for Nonlinear Diffusion Filtering

Pavel Mrázek*

Center for Machine Perception
Faculty of Electrical Engineering, Czech Technical University
Technická 2, 166 27 Praha 6, Czech Republic
http://cmp.felk.cvut.cz
mrazekp@cmp.felk.cvut.cz

Abstract. We develop a novel time-selection strategy for iterative image restoration techniques: the stopping time is chosen so that the correlation of signal and noise in the filtered image is minimised. The new method is applicable to any images where the noise to be removed is uncorrelated with the signal; no other knowledge (e.g. the noise variance, training data etc.) is needed. We test the performance of our time estimation procedure experimentally, and demonstrate that it yields near-optimal results for a wide range of noise levels and for various filtering methods.

1   Introduction

If we want to restore noisy images using some method which starts from the input data and creates a set of possible filtered solutions by gradually removing noise and details from the data, the crucial question is when to stop the filtering in order to obtain the optimal restoration result. The restoration procedures needing such a decision include the linear scale space [3], the nonlinear diffusion filtering [6,1], and many others. We employ a modified version of the Weickert's edge-enhancing anisotropic diffusion [9] for most experiments in this paper.

The stopping time T has a strong effect on the diffusion result. Its choice has to balance two contradictory motivations: small T gives more trust to the input data (and leaves more details and noise in the data unfiltered), while large T means that the result becomes dominated by the (piecewise) constant model which is inherent in the diffusion equations. The scale-space people often set T to a large value (ideally infinity) and observe how the diffused function evolves with time (and converges to a constant value). As we are more concerned with image restoration and we want to obtain nontrivial results from the diffusion filter, we will have to pick a single (finite) time instant T and stop the diffusion evolution there.

We work with the following model (see Fig. 1): let $\tilde{\mathbf{f}}$ be an ideal, noise-free (discrete) image; this image is observed by some imprecise measurement device

---

* This research was supported by the Czech Ministry of Education under project LN00B096.

M. Kerckhove (Ed.): Scale-Space 2001, LNCS 2106, pp. 290–298, 2001.

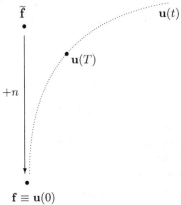

Fig. 1. Model of the time-selection problem for the diffusion filtering. We want to select the filtered image $\mathbf{u}(T)$ which is as close as possible to the ideal signal $\widetilde{\mathbf{f}}$.

to obtain an image $\mathbf{f}$. We assume that some noise n is added to the signal during the observation so that

$$\mathbf{f} = \widetilde{\mathbf{f}} + n. \tag{1}$$

Furthermore, we assume that the noise n is uncorrelated with the signal $\widetilde{\mathbf{f}}$, and that the noise has zero mean value, $E(n) = 0$.[1]

The diffusion filtering starts with the noisy image as its initial condition, $\mathbf{u}(0) = \mathbf{f}$, and the diffusion evolves along some trajectory $\mathbf{u}(t)$. This trajectory depends on the diffusion parameters and on the input image; the optimistic assumption is that the noise will be removed from the data before any important features of the signal commence to deteriorate significantly, so that the diffusion leads us somewhere 'close' to the ideal data. This should be the case if the signal adheres to the piecewise constant model inherent in the diffusion equation.

The task of the stopping time selection can be formulated as follows: select that point $\mathbf{u}(T)$ of the diffusion evolution which is nearest to the ideal signal $\widetilde{\mathbf{f}}$. Obviously, the ideal signal is normally not available; the optimal stopping time T can only be estimated by some criteria, and the distance[2] between the ideal and the filtered data serves only in the experiments to evaluate the performance of the estimation procedure.

---

[1] Let us review the statistical definitions used in the paper (see e.g. Papoulis [5]). For the statistical computations on images, we treat the pixels of an image as independent observations of a random variable.

The *mean* or *expectation* of a vector x is $\overline{x} = E(x) = \frac{1}{N} \sum_{i=1}^{N} x_i$.

We define the *variance* of a signal x as $\mathrm{var}(x) = E\left[(x - \overline{x})^2\right]$.

The *covariance* of two vectors x, y is given by $\mathrm{cov}(x, y) = E\left[(x - \overline{x}) \cdot (y - \overline{y})\right]$.

The normalized form of the covariance is called the *correlation coefficient*, $\mathrm{corr}(x, y) = \frac{\mathrm{cov}(x,y)}{\sqrt{\mathrm{var}(x) \cdot \mathrm{var}(y)}}$.

[2] In the experiments below, we measure the distance of two images by the *mean absolute deviation*, $\mathrm{MAD}(x - y) = E(|x - y|)$.

In the following paragraphs we first cite the approaches to stopping time selection which have appeared in the literature, and comment on them. Then we develop a novel and reliable time-selection strategy based on signal–noise decorrelation.

2   Previous Work

In the diffusion model of Catté *et al.* [1], the image gradient for the diffusivity computation is regularized by convolution with a Gaussian smoothing kernel G_σ. The authors argue that this regularization introduces a sort of time: the result of convolution is the same as the solution to the linear heat equation at time $t = \frac{\sigma^2}{2}$, so it is coherent to correlate the stopping time T and the 'time' of the linear diffusion. However, the equality $t = \frac{\sigma^2}{2}$ is rather a lower estimate of the stopping time: because of the diffusion process inhibited near edges, the nonlinear diffusion is always slower than the linear one, and needs a longer time to reach the desired results.

Dolcetta and Ferretti [2] recently formulated the time selection problem as a minimization of the functional

$$E(T) = \int_0^T E_c + E_s \tag{2}$$

where E_c is the computing cost and E_s the stopping cost, the latter encouraging filtering for small T. The authors provide a basic example $E_c = c$, $E_s = -\left(\int_\Omega |\mathbf{u}(x,T) - \mathbf{u}(x,0)|^2 dx\right)^2$ where the constant c balancing the influence of the two types of costs has to be computed from a typical image to be filtered.

Sporring and Weickert in [7] study the behaviour of generalized entropies, and suggest that the intervals of minimal entropy change indicate especially stable scales with respect to evolution time. They estimate that such scales could be good candidates for stopping times in nonlinear diffusion scale spaces. However, as the entropy can be stable on whole *intervals*, it may be difficult to decide on a single stopping instant from that interval; we are unaware of their idea being brought to practice in the field of image restoration.

Weickert mentioned more ideas on the stopping time selection, more closely linked to the noise-filtering problem, in [10]. They are based on the notion of relative variance.

The variance $\mathrm{var}(\mathbf{u}(t))$ of an image $\mathbf{u}(t)$ is monotonically decreasing with t and converges to zero as $t \to \infty$. The *relative variance*

$$r(\mathbf{u}(t)) = \frac{\mathrm{var}(\mathbf{u}(t))}{\mathrm{var}(\mathbf{u}(0))} \tag{3}$$

decreases monotonically from 1 to 0 and can be used to measure the distance of $\mathbf{u}(t)$ from the initial state $\mathbf{u}(0)$ and the final state $\mathbf{u}(\infty)$. Prescribing a certain value for $r(\mathbf{u}(T))$ can therefore serve as a criterion for selection of the stopping time T.

Let again $\widetilde{\mathbf{f}}$ be the ideal data, the measured noisy image $\mathbf{f} = \widetilde{\mathbf{f}} + n$, and let the noise n be of zero mean and uncorrelated with $\widetilde{\mathbf{f}}$. Now assume that we know the variance of the noise, or (equivalently, on the condition that the noise and the signal are uncorrelated) the *signal-to-noise ratio*, defined as the ratio between the original image variance and the noise variance,

$$\mathrm{SNR} \equiv \frac{\mathrm{var}\big(\widetilde{\mathbf{f}}\big)}{\mathrm{var}(n)}. \tag{4}$$

As the signal $\widetilde{\mathbf{f}}$ and the noise n are uncorrelated, we have

$$\mathrm{var}(\mathbf{f}) = \mathrm{var}\big(\widetilde{\mathbf{f}}\big) + \mathrm{var}(n). \tag{5}$$

Substituting from this equality for $\mathrm{var}(n)$ into (4), we obtain by simple rearrangement that

$$\frac{\mathrm{var}\big(\widetilde{\mathbf{f}}\big)}{\mathrm{var}(\mathbf{f})} = \frac{1}{1 + \frac{1}{\mathrm{SNR}}}. \tag{6}$$

We take the noisy image for the initial condition of our diffusion filter, $\mathbf{u}(0) = \mathbf{f}$. An ideal diffusion filter would first eliminate the noise before significantly affecting the signal; if we stop at the right moment, we might substitute the filtered data $\mathbf{u}(T)$ for the ideal signal $\widetilde{\mathbf{f}}$ in (6). Relying on this analogy, we can choose the stopping time T such that the relative variance satisfies

$$r(\mathbf{u}(T)) = \frac{\mathrm{var}(\mathbf{u}(T))}{\mathrm{var}(\mathbf{u}(0))} = \frac{1}{1 + \frac{1}{\mathrm{SNR}}}. \tag{7}$$

Weickert remarks that the criterion (7) tends to underestimate the optimal stopping time, as even a well-tuned filter cannot avoid influencing the signal before eliminating the noise.

So far the Weickert's suggestions from [10]: knowing the SNR, we decide to filter the image until some distance from the noisy data is reached, and the formula (7) tells us when to stop the diffusion. This idea seems natural and resembles also that used in the total variation minimizing methods (see overview in [9, pp. 50-52]). However, our experiments indicate that this approach does not usually yield the optimal stopping time. Let us study in more detail why the problems occur.

3   Decorrelation Criterion

The equality (5) and hence the equation (6) are valid only if the signal and the noise are uncorrelated. This assumption holds for $\widetilde{\mathbf{f}}$ and n, but not necessarily for the filtered signal $\mathbf{u}(T)$ and the difference $\mathbf{u}(0) - \mathbf{u}(T)$; the latter is needed for the equation (7) to be justified. In other words (if we substitute mentally the filtered function $\mathbf{u}(T)$ for $\widetilde{\mathbf{f}}$, the difference $n_u \equiv \mathbf{u}(0) - \mathbf{u}(T)$ for the noise n, and $\mathbf{u}(0)$ for $\mathbf{f}$ in (5) and (6)), the formula (7) is useful only if the random variables $\mathbf{u}(T)$ and $(\mathbf{u}(0) - \mathbf{u}(T))$ are uncorrelated.

Fig. 2. Experimental Data. Left: Cymbidium image (courtesy Michal Haindl). Right: Noisy input image ($[0, 127]^2 \rightarrow [0, 255]$) for the 'Triangle and rectangle' experiment. Noise with uniform distribution in the range $[-255, 255]$ was added to two-valued synthetic data.

Inspired by these observations, we arrive to the following idea: if the unknown noise n is uncorrelated with the unknown signal $\widetilde{\mathbf{f}}$, wouldn't it be reasonable to minimize the covariance of the 'noise' $(\mathbf{u}(0) - \mathbf{u}(t))$ with the 'signal' $\mathbf{u}(t)$, or – better – employ its normalized form, the correlation coefficient

$$\mathrm{corr}\big(\mathbf{u}(0) - \mathbf{u}(t), \mathbf{u}(t)\big) = \frac{\mathrm{cov}\big(\mathbf{u}(0) - \mathbf{u}(t), \mathbf{u}(t)\big)}{\sqrt{\mathrm{var}\big(\mathbf{u}(0) - \mathbf{u}(t)\big) \cdot \mathrm{var}\big(\mathbf{u}(t)\big)}} \tag{8}$$

and choose the stopping time T so that the expression (8) is as small as possible? This way, instead of determining the stopping time so that $(\mathbf{u}(0) - \mathbf{u}(T))$ satisfies a quantitative property and its variance is equal to the known variance of the noise n, we try to enforce a qualitative feature: if the ideal $\widetilde{\mathbf{f}}$ and n were uncorrelated, we require that their artificial substitutes $\mathbf{u}(T)$ and $(\mathbf{u}(0) - \mathbf{u}(T))$ reveal the same property, to the extent possible, and select

$$T = \arg\min_t \mathrm{corr}\big(\mathbf{u}(0) - \mathbf{u}(t), \mathbf{u}(t)\big). \tag{9}$$

Let us test and validate this new stopping time criterion experimentally.

4   Experiments

We added various levels of Gaussian noise to the cymbidium image shown in Fig. 2 left, filtered by nonlinear diffusion (more precisely a modified version of the Weickert's edge-enhancing anisotropic diffusion [9], numerically implemented

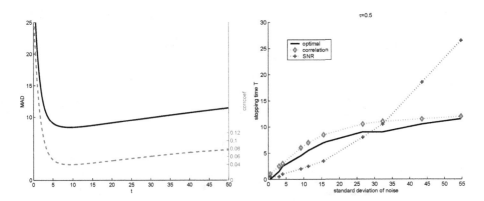

Fig. 3. Left: The distance $\mathrm{MAD}(\mathbf{u}(t) - \widetilde{\mathbf{f}})$ (solid line) and the correlation coefficient $\mathrm{corr}(\mathbf{u}(0) - \mathbf{u}(t), \mathbf{u}(t))$ (dashed line) developing with the diffusion time. Right: The stopping time T_{SNR} determined by the SNR method (dotted with crosses), and T_{corr} obtained through the covariance minimization (dotted with diamonds) compared to the optimal stopping time T_{opt} (solid line). The graphs are plotted against the standard deviation of noise in the input image.

using the AOS scheme [8]), and observed how the signal–noise correlation measured by equation (8) develops with the diffusion time. A typical example is drawn in Fig. 3 left: you can observe that the plot of the MAD criterion of the filtering quality coincides very well with the graph of the correlation coefficient $\mathrm{corr}(\mathbf{u}(0) - \mathbf{u}(t), \mathbf{u}(t))$.

A more thorough study of the performance of the stopping time selection criteria (measured again on the cymbidium data) is seen in figures 3 right and 4. The former compares three stopping times: the optimal T_{opt} is the time instant for which the filtered image $\mathbf{u}(t)$ is closest to the noise-free $\widetilde{\mathbf{f}}$ in the MAD distance; obviously, T_{opt} can be found only in the artificial experimental setting, the noise-free $\widetilde{\mathbf{f}}$ is normally not available. The second stopping time T_{SNR} is determined using the criterion (7) (which requires the knowledge of the noise variance or SNR). The stopping time T_{corr} minimizes the correlation coefficient of equation (8). All alternative stopping times are computed for a series of input images with varied amount of noise present. While the SNR method easily underestimates or overestimates the optimal stopping time (depending on the amount of noise in the input data), the correlation minimization leads to near-optimal results for all noise levels. The graph is plotted for iteration time step $\tau = 0.5$, other choices $\tau \in \{0.1, 1\}$ gave similar results.

The actually obtained quality measure $\mathrm{MAD}(\mathbf{u}(T) - \widetilde{\mathbf{f}})$ is shown in Fig. 4, again with $\tau = 0.5$. You can see that for all noise levels the correlation-estimated time leads to filtering results very close to the optimal values obtainable by the nonlinear diffusion.

Let us return for a moment to Fig. 3 left. At the beginning of the diffusion filtering, the correlation coefficient declines fast until it reaches its minimum.

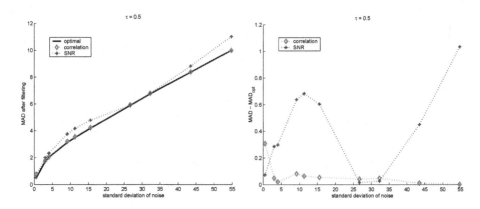

Fig. 4. Left: The MAD distance of the filtered data from the ideal noise-free image, $\mathrm{MAD}(\mathbf{u}(T) - \widetilde{\mathbf{f}})$, using the SNR and the correlation-minimization time selection strategies. Right: the difference between the estimated result and the optimal one, $\mathrm{MAD}(\mathbf{u}(T) - \mathbf{u}(T_{\mathrm{opt}}))$.

If for some data the graph behaves differently, it may serve as a hint on some problems. As an example, we observed that if there is only a small amount of noise in the input image, the correlation $\mathrm{corr}\big(\mathbf{u}(0) - \mathbf{u}(t), \mathbf{u}(t)\big)$ might grow from the first iterations. In such a case, the iteration time step τ has to be decreased adaptively and the diffusion restarted from time $t = 0$ until the correlation plot exhibits a clear minimum.

Another experiment compares the results of different diffusion algorithms filtering an originally black and white image with non-Gaussian additive noise. The input data are shown in Fig. 2 right: the noisy image was obtained by adding noise of uniform distribution in the range $[-255, 255]$ to the ideal input, and by restricting the noisy values into the interval $[0, 255]$.

In Fig. 5, the noise is smoothed by linear diffusion, isotropic nonlinear diffusion, and two anisotropic diffusion filters; the grey-values are stretched to the whole interval $[0, 255]$ so that a higher contrast between the dark and bright regions corresponds to a better noise-filtering performance. In all cases, the stopping time was determined autonomously by the signal–noise decorrelation criterion (9). You can see that in all cases, although quite different filtering algorithms were employed, the stopping criterion leads to results where most of the noise is removed and the ideal signal becomes apparent or suitable for further processing; we support this statement by showing the thresholded content of the filtered images in Fig. 6.

The stopping criterion was designed to minimize the MAD distance from the ideal function. If visual quality was the goal to be achieved, we would probably stop the diffusion later, especially as linear diffusion (Fig. 5a) and the Weickert's edge-enhancing anisotropic diffusion [9] with maximum amount of diffusion in the coherence direction ($\varphi_2 = 1$, Fig. 5c) are concerned. We find however that the MAD distance and the visual quality are in a good agreement in Fig. 5d which

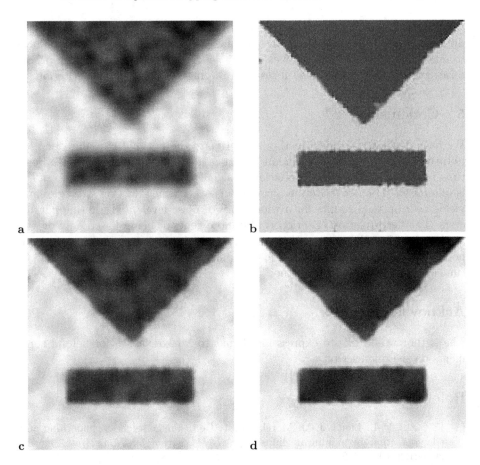

Fig. 5. Comparing the different diffusion algorithms on the noisy data of Fig. 2 right, all with the stopping time selected autonomously by minimizing the criterion (8): (a) linear diffusion, $T = 3.8$; (b) isotropic nonlinear diffusion, $T = 125$; (c) anisotropic NL diffusion, $\varphi_2 = 1$, $T = 15$; (d) anisotropic NL diffusion, $\varphi_2 = 0.2$, $T = 32$.

In (b)–(d), the parameters $\sigma = 1$, $\tau = 1$ were employed, and the parameter λ was estimated using the Perona-Malik procedure from percentile $p = 0.9$ in each step.

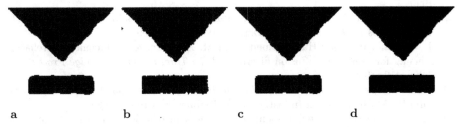

Fig. 6. Thresholded versions of the images in Fig. 5.

represents the result of the edge-enhancing diffusion with a smaller amount of diffusion in the coherence direction, $\varphi_2 = 0.2$. Because of limited space, we have to refer the reader to Pavel Mrázek's thesis [4] for details on the filtering procedures and for more experimental results verifying the decorrelation criterion.

5   Conclusion

We have developed a novel method to estimate the optimal stopping time for iterative image restoration techniques such as nonlinear diffusion. The stopping time is chosen so that the correlation of signal $\mathbf{u}(T)$ and 'noise' $(\mathbf{u}(0) - \mathbf{u}(T))$ is minimised. The new criterion outperforms other time selection strategies and yields near-optimal results for a wide range of noise levels and filtering parameters. The decorrelation criterion is also more general, being based only on the assumption that the noise and the signal in the input image are uncorrelated; no knowledge on the variance of the noise, and no training images are needed to tune any parameters of the method.

Acknowledgements

The author would like to express his thanks to Mirko Navara for helpful comments on the manuscript.

References

1. F. Catté, P.-L. Lions, J.-M. Morel, and T. Coll. Image selective smoothing and edge-detection by nonlinear diffusion. *SIAM Journal on Numerical Analysis*, 29(1):182–193, 1992.
2. I. Capuzzo Dolcetta and R. Ferretti. Optimal stopping time formulation of adaptive image filtering. *Applied Mathematics and Optimization*, 2000. To appear.
3. Tony Lindeberg. *Scale-Space Theory in Computer Vision*. Kluwer Academic Publishers, 1994.
4. Pavel Mrázek. *Nonlinear Diffusion for Image Filtering and Monotonicity Enhancement*. PhD thesis, Czech Technical University, 2001. To appear.
5. Athanasios Papoulis. *Probability and Statistics*. Prentice-Hall, 1990.
6. P. Perona and J. Malik. Scale-space and edge-detection using anisotropic diffusion. *IEEE Transactions on Pattern Analysis and Machine Intelligence*, 12(7):629–639, 1990.
7. Jon Sporring and Joachim Weickert. Information measures in scale-spaces. *IEEE Transactions on Information Theory*, 45:1051–1058, 1999.
8. J. Weickert, B.M. ter Haar Romeny, and M. A. Viergever. Efficient and reliable schemes for nonlinear diffusion filtering. *IEEE Transactions on Image Processing*, 7:398–410, 1998.
9. Joachim Weickert. *Anisotropic Diffusion in Image Processing*. European Consortium for Mathematics in Industry. B. G. Teubner, Stuttgart, 1998.
10. Joachim Weickert. Coherence-enhancing diffusion of colour images. *Image and Vision Computing*, 17:201–212, 1999.

Complex Diffusion Processes for Image Filtering

Guy Gilboa[1], Yehoshua Y. Zeevi[1], and Nir A. Sochen[2]

[1] Department of Electrical Engineering, Technion - Israel Institute of Technology
Technion City, Haifa 32000, Israel
gilboa@tx.technion.ac.il, zeevi@ee.technion.ac.il
[2] Department of Applied Mathematics, University of Tel-Aviv
Ramat-Aviv, Tel-Aviv 69978, Israel
sochen@math.tau.ac.il

Abstract. A framework that naturally unifies smoothing and enhancement processes is presented. We generalize the linear and nonlinear scale spaces in the complex domain, by combining the diffusion equation with the simplified Schrödinger equation. A fundamental solution for the linear case is developed. Preliminary analysis of the complex diffusion shows that the generalized diffusion has properties of both forward and inverse diffusion. An important observation, supported theoretically and numerically, is that the imaginary part can be regarded as an edge detector (smoothed second derivative), after rescaling by time, when the complex diffusion coefficient approaches the real axis. Based on this observation, a nonlinear complex process for ramp preserving denoising is developed.
Keywords: Scale-space, image filtering, image denoising, image enhancement, nonlinear diffusion, complex diffusion.

1 Introduction

The scale-space approach is by now a well established multi-resolution technique for image structure analysis (see [6],[2],[5]). Originally, the Gaussian representation introduced a scale dimension by convolving the original image with a Gaussian of a standard deviation $\sigma = \sqrt{2t}$. This is analogous to solving the linear diffusion equation

$$I_t = c\nabla^2 I, \quad I|_{t=0} = I_0, \quad 0 < c \in \mathbb{R}, \tag{1}$$

with a constant diffusion coefficient $c = 1$.

Perona and Malik (P-M) [4] proposed a nonlinear adaptive diffusion process, where diffusion takes place with a variable diffusion coefficient in order to reduce the smoothing effect near edges. The P-M nonlinear diffusion equation is of the form: $I_t = \nabla \cdot (c(|\nabla I|)\nabla I), \quad c(\cdot) > 0$, where c is a decreasing function of the gradient. Our aim is to see if the linear and nonlinear scale-spaces can be viewed as special cases of a more general theory of complex diffusion-type processes.

Complex diffusion-type processes are encountered i.e. in quantum physics and in electro-optics. The time dependent *Schrödinger equation* is the fundamental

M. Kerckhove (Ed.): Scale-Space 2001, LNCS 2106, pp. 299–307, 2001.

equation of quantum mechanics. In the simplest case for a particle without spin
in an external field it has the form

$$i\hbar\frac{\partial\psi}{\partial t} = -\frac{\hbar^2}{2m}\Delta\psi + V(x)\psi \quad , \tag{2}$$

where $\psi = \psi(t, x)$ is the wave function of a quantum particle, m is the mass
of the particle, $\hbar$ is Planck's constant, $V(x)$ is the external field potential, Δ is
the Laplacian and $i \doteq \sqrt{-1}$. With an initial condition $\psi|_{t=0} = \psi_0(x)$, requiring
that $\psi(t, \cdot) \in L_2$ for each fixed t, the solution is $\psi(t, \cdot) = e^{-\frac{i}{\hbar}tH}\psi_0$, where the
exponent is a shorthand for the corresponding power series, and the higher order
terms are defined recursively by $H^n\Psi = H(H^{n-1}\Psi)$. The operator

$$H = -\frac{\hbar^2}{2m}\Delta + V(x), \tag{3}$$

called the *Schrödinger operator*, is interpreted as the energy operator of the particle under consideration. The first term is the kinetic energy and the second is
the potential energy. The duality relations that exist between the Schrödinger
equation and diffusion theory have been studied in [3]. Another important complex PDE in the field of phase transitions of traveling wave systems is the *complex
Ginzburg-Landau equation* (CGL): $u_t = (1 + i\nu)u_{xx} + Ru - (1 + i\mu)|u|^2u$. Note
that although these flows have a diffusion structure, because of the complex
coefficient, they retain wave propagation properties.

In both cases a non-linearity is introduced by adding a potential term while
the kinetic energy stays linear. In this study we employ the equation with zero
potential (no external field) but with non-linear "kinetic energy". To better understand the complex flow, we study in Section 2 the linear case and derive the
fundamental solution. We show that for small imaginary part the flow is approximately a linear real diffusion for the real part while the imaginary part behaves
like a second derivative of the real part. Indeed as expected, the imaginary part
is directly related to the localized phase and zero crossings of the image, and
this is one of the important properties obtained by generalizing the diffusion
approach to the complex case. The non-linear case is studied in Section 3 and
the intuition gained from the linear case is used in order to construct a special
non-linear complex diffusion scheme which preserves ramps. The advantage over
higher order PDE's and over the P-M algorithm is demonstrated in one- and
two-dimensional examples.

2   Linear Complex Diffusion

2.1   Problem Definition

We consider the following initial value problem:

$$I_t = cI_{xx}, \qquad t > 0, \qquad x \in \mathbb{R} \tag{4}$$
$$I(x; 0) = I_0 \in \mathbb{R}, \quad c, I \in \mathbb{C}.$$

This equation is a generalization of two equations: the linear *diffusion* equation (1) for $c \in \mathbb{R}$ and the simplified *Schrödinger* equation, i.e. $c \in \mathbb{I}$ and $V(x) \equiv 0$. When $c \in \mathbb{R}$ there are two cases: for $c > 0$ the process is a well posed forward diffusion, whereas for $c < 0$ an ill posed inverse diffusion process is obtained.

2.2   Fundamental Solution

We seek the complex fundamental solution $h(x;t)$ that satisfies the relation:

$$I(x;t) = I_0 * h(x;t) \tag{5}$$

where $*$ denotes convolution. We rewrite the complex diffusion coefficient as $c \doteq re^{i\theta}$, and, since there does not exist a stable fundamental solution of the inverse diffusion process, restrict ourselves to a positive real value of c, that is $\theta \in (-\frac{\pi}{2}, \frac{\pi}{2})$. Replacing the real time variable t by a complex time $\tau = ct$, we get $I_\tau = I_{xx}$, $I(x;0) = I_0$. This is the linear diffusion equation with the Gaussian function being its fundamental solution. Reverting back to t, we get:

$$h(x;t) = \frac{K}{2\sqrt{\pi tc}} e^{-x^2/(4tc)}, \tag{6}$$

where $K \in \mathbb{C}$ is a constant calculated according to the initial conditions. For $c \in \mathbb{R}$ we have $K = 1$. Separating the real and imaginary exponents we get:

$$h(x;t) = \frac{Ke^{-i\theta/2}}{2\sqrt{\pi tr}} e^{-x^2 \cos\theta/(4tr)} e^{ix^2 \sin\theta/(4tr)}$$
$$= KAg_\sigma(x;t)e^{i\alpha(x;t)},$$
$$\text{where } A = \frac{e^{-i\theta/2}}{\sqrt{\cos\theta}}, \quad g_\sigma(x;t) = \frac{1}{\sqrt{2\pi}\sigma(t)} e^{-x^2/2\sigma^2(t)},$$

and

$$\alpha(x;t) = \frac{x^2 \sin\theta}{4tr}, \quad \sigma(t) = \sqrt{\frac{2tr}{\cos\theta}}. \tag{7}$$

Satisfying the initial condition $I(x;0) = I_0$ requires $h(x;t \to 0) = \delta(x)$. Since $\lim_{t \to 0} g_\sigma(x;t)e^{i\alpha(x;t)} = \delta(x)$, we should require $K = 1/A$ (indeed $K = 1$ for the case of positive real c $(\theta = 0)$). The fundamental solution is therefore:

$$h(x;t) = g_\sigma(x;t)e^{i\alpha(x;t)}, \tag{8}$$

with the Gaussian's standard deviation σ and exponent function α as in (7).

2.3   Approximate Solution for Small Theta

We will now show that as $\theta \to 0$ the imaginary part can be regarded as a smoothed second derivative of the initial signal, factored by θ and the time t. Generalizing the solution to any dimension with Cartesian coordinates $\mathbf{x} \doteq (x_1, x_2, ..x_N) \in \mathbb{R}^N$, $I(\mathbf{x};t) \in \mathbb{C}^N$ and denoting that in this coordinate system $\mathbf{g}_\sigma(\mathbf{x};t) \doteq \prod_i^N g_\sigma(x_i;t)$, we show that:

$$\lim_{\theta \to 0} \frac{Im(I)}{\theta} = t\Delta \mathbf{g}_{\tilde{\sigma}} * I_0, \tag{9}$$

where $Im(\cdot)$ denotes the imaginary value and $\tilde{\sigma} = lim_{\theta \to 0}\sigma = \sqrt{2t}$. For convenience we use here a unit complex diffusion coefficient $c = e^{i\theta}$. We use the following approximations for small θ: $cos\theta = 1 + O(\theta^2)$ and $sin\theta = \theta + O(\theta^3)$. Introducing an operator $\tilde{H}$, which is similar to the *Schrödinger operator*, we can write equation (4) (in any dimension) as: $I_t = \tilde{H}I$; $I|_{t=0} = I_0$, where $\tilde{H} = c\Delta$. The solution is $I = e^{t\tilde{H}}I_0$, and is the equivalent of (5), (8). Using the above approximations we get:

$$I(\mathbf{x}, t) = e^{ct\Delta}I_0 = e^{e^{i\theta}t\Delta}I_0$$
$$\approx e^{(1+i\theta)t\Delta}I_0 = e^{t\Delta}e^{i\theta t\Delta}I_0$$
$$\approx e^{t\Delta}(1 + i\theta t\Delta)I_0 = (1 + i\theta t\Delta)\mathbf{g}_{\tilde{\sigma}} * I_0.$$

A thorough analysis of the approximation error with respect to time and θ will be presented elsewhere. We should comment that part of the error depends on the higher order derivatives (4th and higher) of the signal, but, as these derivatives are decaying exponentially by the Gaussian convolution, this error diminishes quickly with time. Numerical experiments show that for $\theta = \pi/30$ the peak error is $\sim 0.1\%$ for the real part and $3 - 5\%$ for the imaginary part (depending on the signal). Though the peak value error of the imaginary part seems large, the zero crossing location remains essentially accurate.

Some further insight into the behavior of the small theta approximation can be gained by separating real and imaginary parts of the signal and diffusion coefficient in to a set of two equations. Assigning $I = I_R + iI_I$, $c = c_R + ic_I$, we get

$$\begin{cases} I_{Rt} = c_R I_{Rxx} - c_I I_{Ixx} & , I_R|_{t=0} = I_0 \\ I_{It} = c_I I_{Rxx} + c_R I_{Ixx} & , I_I|_{t=0} = 0, \end{cases} \tag{10}$$

where $c_R = \cos\theta$, $c_I = \sin\theta$. The relation $I_{Rxx} \gg \theta I_{Ixx}$ holds for small enough θ, which allows us to omit the right term of the first equation to get the small theta approximation:

$$I_{Rt} \approx I_{Rxx} \quad ; \quad I_{It} \approx I_{Ixx} + \theta I_{Rxx}. \tag{11}$$

In (11) I_R is controlled by a linear forward diffusion equation, whereas I_I is affected by both the real and imaginary equations. We can regard the imaginary part as $I_{It} \approx \theta I_{Rxx} + ("$a smoothing process$")$.

2.4   Examples

We present examples of 1D and 2D signal processing with complex diffusion processes characterized by small and large values of θ. In Fig. (1) a unit step is processed with small and large θ ($\frac{\pi}{30}, \frac{14\pi}{30}$ respectively). In Figs. (2) and (3) the cameraman image is processed with same θ values. The edge detection (smoothed second derivative) qualitative properties are clearly apparent in the imaginary part for the small θ value, whereas the real value depicts the properties of ordinary Gaussian scale-space. For large θ however, the imaginary part feeds back into the real part significantly, creating wave-like structures. In addition, the signal exceeds the original maximum and minimum values, violating the "Maximum-minimum" principle - a property suitable for sharpening purposes.

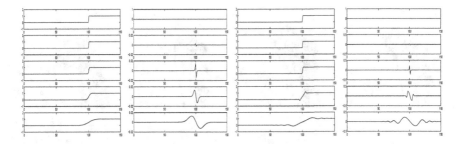

Fig. 1. Complex diffusion applied to a step signal. From left to right: small θ ($\theta = \pi/30$) real and imaginary values, large θ ($\theta = 14\pi/30$) real and imaginary values. Each frame depicts from top to bottom: original step, diffused signal after times: 0.025, 0.25, 2.5, 25.

3   Nonlinear Complex Diffusion

Nonlinear complex processes can be derived from the above mentioned properties of the linear complex diffusion for purposes of signal and image denoising or enhancement. We suggest an example of a nonlinear process for ramp edges denoising purposes (different from the widely used step edges denoising methods).

We are looking for a general nonlinear diffusion equation

$$I_t = \frac{\partial}{\partial x}\left(c(\cdot)I_x\right) \tag{12}$$

that preserves smoothed ramps. Following the same logic that utilized a gradient measure in order to slow the diffusion near step edges, we search for a suitable differential operator $\mathcal{D}$ for ramp edges. Eq. (12) with a diffusion coefficient $c(|\mathcal{D}I|)$ which is a decreasing function of $|\mathcal{D}I|$ can be regarded as a ramp preserving process. We begin by examining the gradient, as a possible candidate, concluding that it is not a suitable measure for two reasons: The gradient does not detect the ramp main features - namely its endpoints; Moreover, it has a nearly uniform value across the whole smoothed ramp, causing a nonlinear gradient-dependent diffusion to slow the diffusion process in that region, thus not being able to properly reduce noise within a ramp (creating staircasing effects). The second derivative (Laplacian in multiple dimensions) is a suitable choice: It has a high magnitude near the endpoints and low magnitude everywhere else - and thus enables the nonlinear diffusion process to reduce noise within a ramp.

We formulate $c(s)$ as a decreasing function of s:

$$c(s) = \frac{1}{1 + s^2}, \text{ where } c(s) = c(|I_{xx}|). \tag{13}$$

Using the c of (13) in (12) we get:

$$I_t = \frac{\partial}{\partial x}\left(\frac{I_x}{1 + I_{xx}^2}\right) = \frac{1 + I_{xx}^2 - 2I_x I_{xxx}}{(1 + I_{xx}^2)^2}I_{xx}. \tag{14}$$

Fig. 2. Complex diffusion of the cameraman image for small theta ($\theta = \pi/30$). Top - real values, bottom - imaginary values (factored by 20). Each frame (from left to right): original, image after times: 0.25, 2.5, 25.

Fig. 3. Complex diffusion of the cameraman image for large theta ($\theta = 14\pi/30$). Top - real values, bottom - imaginary values (factored by 20). Each frame (from left to right): original, image after times: 0.25, 2.5, 25.

There are two main problems in this scheme. The first and more important one is the fact that noise has very large (theoretically unbounded) second derivatives. Secondly, a numerical problem arises as third derivatives should be computed, with large numerical support and noisier derivative estimations. These two problems are solved by using the nonlinear complex diffusion.

Following the results of the linear complex diffusion (Eq. 9) we estimate by the imaginary value of the signal divided by θ, the smoothed second derivative multiplied by the time t.

Whereas for small t this terms vanish, allowing stronger diffusion to reduce the noise, with time its influence increases preserving the ramp features of the signal. We should comment that these second derivative estimations are more biased than in the linear case, as we have a nonlinear process.

The equation for the multidimensional process is

$$I_t = \nabla \cdot (c(Im(I))\nabla I),$$
$$c(Im(I)) = \frac{e^{i\theta}}{1 + \left(\frac{Im(I)}{k\theta}\right)^2}, \tag{15}$$

where k is a threshold parameter. The phase angle θ should be small ($\theta << 1$). Since the imaginary part is normalized by θ, the process is not affected much by changing the value of θ as long as it stays small.

We implement this flow with forward Euler scheme with central difference approximation for the spatial derivatives and backward time derivative. Care should be exercised when choosing the time step. The fundamental solution includes a Gaussian with variance $\sigma^2 = \frac{2tr}{\cos\theta}$. Implementing Gaussian convolution of time τ by incremental time steps where $\sigma^2 = 2\tau$ requires the time step bound to be: $\Delta\tau \leq 0.25h^2$ (in 2 dimensions, where h is the spatial step). Here we have $\tau = \frac{tr}{\cos\theta}$ and hence in the general case we require: $\Delta t \leq 0.25h^2\frac{\cos\theta}{r}$, and for our case where $r = 1$, $h = 1$: $\Delta t \leq 0.25\cos\theta$.

This means that when θ approaches $\pi/2$ it is very inefficient to implement complex diffusion with incremental time-steps. For small θ there is essentially no difference than real diffusion (works also in the nonlinear case).

In Figs. 4 and 5 we show an example of a noisy ramp denoised by a P-M process in comparison to the above process (with $\theta = \frac{\pi}{30}$). One can notice that the known P-M's staircasing effect does not happen in our nonlinear complex scheme. In Fig. 6 the process is applied to an apple image that contains both sharp (step) and gradual (ramp) edges. Note that using the regularized P-M version of Catte et al. [1] produces staircasing results similar to the original P-M process.

4   Conclusion

The fundamental solution for the linear complex diffusion indicates that there exists a stable process for $\theta \in (-\frac{\pi}{2}, \frac{\pi}{2})$. In the case of small θ two observations are relevant to the application of the complex diffusion process in image processing:

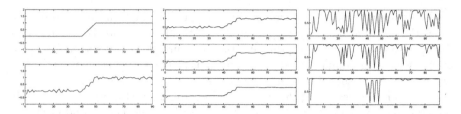

Fig. 4. Perona-Malik nonlinear diffusion of a ramp edge ($k = 0.1$). Left - original (top) and noisy ramp signal (white Gaussian, SNR=15dB) . Middle - denoised signal at times $0.25, 1, 2.5$, from top to bottom, respectively. Right - respective values of c coefficient.

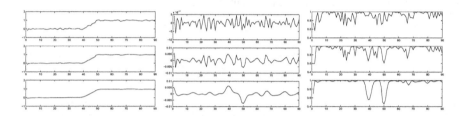

Fig. 5. Nonlinear complex diffusion of a ramp edge ($\theta = \pi/30$, $k = 0.07$). Left - real values of denoised signal at times $0.25, 1, 2.5$, from top to bottom, respectively. Middle - respective imaginary values, right - respective real values of c.

The real function equation is effectively decoupled from the imaginary one, and behaves like a real linear diffusion process; The imaginary part is approximately a smoothed second derivative of the real part. Therefore, we can regard the Gaussian and Laplacian "pyramids" (scale-spaces) as results of a single complex diffusion equation.

Although the nonlinear scheme remains to be better analyzed and understood, a ramp preserving denoising process was demonstrated as an example of possible applications of complex diffusion schemes.

Acknowledgments: This research has been supported in part by the Ollendorf Minerva Center, by the Fund for the Promotion of Research at the Technion and by the Israeli Ministry science.

References

1. F. Catte, P. L. Lions, J. M. Morel and T. Coll, "Image selective smoothing and edge detection by nonlinear diffusion", SIAM J. Num. Anal., vol. 29, no. 1, pp. 182-193, 1992.

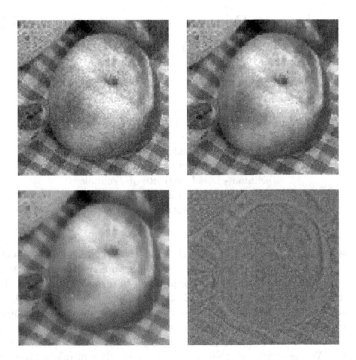

Fig. 6. Nonlinear diffusion of an apple image: Top: left - image corrupted by white Gaussian noise (SNR=13dB), right - image denoised by Perona-Malik process ($k = 3$, $time = 2.5$). Bottom: image denoised by complex nonlinear scheme ($\theta = \pi/30$, $k = 2$, $time = 2.5$), left - real part, right - imaginary part. One can see that the apple is better denoised in the complex scheme, where staircasing effects appear in the P-M process. Trying to increase the P-M threshold in order to avoid staircasing causes the whole apple to get diffused with the background. Another observation is that the complex scheme denoises faster (due to its implicit time dependency).

2. J.J. Koenderink, "The structure of images", *Biol. Cybern.*, 50: 363-370, 1984.
3. M. Nagasawa, *S*chrödinger equations and diffusion theory, Monographs in mathematics, vol. 86, Birkhäuser Verlag, Basel, Switzerland 1993.
4. P. Perona and J. Malik, "Scale-space and edge detection using anisotropic diffusion", IEEE Trans. Pat. Anal. Machine Intel., vol. PAMI-12,no. 7, pp. 629-639, 1990.
5. B M ter Haar Romeny Ed., *G*eometry Driven Diffusion in Computer Vision, Kluwer Academic Publishers, 1994.
6. A. P. Witkin, "Scale space filtering", Proc. Int. Joint Conf. On Artificial Intelligence, pp. 1019-1023, 1983.

Combing a Porcupine via Stereographic Direction Diffusion

Nir A. Sochen[1] and Ron Kimmel[2]

[1] Department of Applied Mathematics, University of Tel Aviv
Ramat-Aviv, Tel-Aviv 69978, Israel
sochen@math.tau.ac.il
[2] Department of Computer Science
Technion - Israel Institute of Technology
Technion City, Haifa 32000, Israel
ron@cs.technion.ac.il

Abstract. This paper addresses the problem of feature enhancement in noisy images when the feature is known to be constrained to a manifold. As an example, we study the problem of direction denoising. This problem was treated recently and several solutions were proposed. The various solutions share the same structure. They are composed of two terms: A diffusion term and a projection term. Analytically, the solutions differ in the diffusion part. The projection part is equivalent in all works. Yet, as it is often the case, the analytically equivalent projection terms differ from a numerical viewpoint. We present in this work a new parameterization of the problem that enables us to work always in a numerically stable way.

1 Introduction

Many objects of low-level vision are scalar and vector fields of various types. This is the case for gray-value images, color images, movies, 3D volumetric images and disparity in stereo vision to name just a few examples. These vector fields are considered traditionally as taking value in $\mathbb{R}^n$. Several types of vector fields, though, are constrained in a non-trivial way. When the constraint can be expressed via the vanishing of a smooth function, i.e. a polynomial, the vector fields take their values in a non-Euclidean manifold. One notable example is the direction vector field that assigns to each pixel in the image a local direction. These directions are unit length vectors that span the unit n-dimensional sphere $\mathbb{S}^n$. Other classes of non-Euclidean vector fields are perceptually treated color images [13], and gradients [8]. The relation to non-linear filters, and short-time kernels is studied in [9,12]. Here we study the n-dimensional direction vector fields and spherically constrained color models via the Beltrami framework [11,4].

Almost all works that try to minimize a functional with respect to a constrained quantity embed the constrained feature in a higher dimensional Euclidean space and perform the minimization for the coordinates of this unconstrained space. The common approach is to alternate minimization of an unconstrained function and a projection on the constraint manifold. The treatment

M. Kerckhove (Ed.): Scale-Space 2001, LNCS 2106, pp. 308–316, 2001.

of direction diffusion was recently addressed, along these lines, in the low-level vision community [7,1,14,15]. The projection in these works was incorporated in the PDE directly but the dynamical coordinates are the unconstrained ones and we are still facing the problem of projection due to *numerical* errors.

We proposed recently [3] to work directly on the constraint's manifold. Once a local coordinate system is chosen for the embedding space and the optimization is done directly in these coordinates we can never leave the feature manifold and avoid the problem of projection. The difficulty represented in the problem of projection is transformed to the problem of the choice of local coordinate system, and the appearance of parametric singularities. Since a compact manifold demands at least two charts to cover it, we face the problems of choosing the charts and deciding locally on which of the charts to work. In our previous publication we treated the $\mathbb{S}^1$ problem. We generalize, in this paper, the analysis to $\mathbb{S}^n$ and describe two different possible choices for the charts. We describe the hemispheric and the stereographic coordinate systems and show the *numerical* advantage of the later. Our solution produces an adaptive smoothing process, which preserves orientation discontinuities by the projection of the mean curvature flow in the non-Euclidean space to the feature coordinates. The proposed solution works for all dimensions and codimensions, and overcomes possible parameterization singularities by introducing several internal coordinates on different charts.

2   The Beltrami Framework

Let us briefly review the Beltrami geometric framework for non-linear diffusion in image processing and analysis [11].

Representation and Riemannian Structure: We represent an image and other local features as an embedding map of a Riemannian manifold in a higher dimensional space (see [2] for the earliest time this idea was put forward for color images). In general a n-dimensional (Riemannian) manifold is defined by a collection of maps from charts of the manifold to $\mathbb{R}^n$. Each chart covers part of the manifold. Their union covers the whole manifold and the transformation of the coordinates on the intersection between any two charts is smooth. The Riemannian structure transforms in a proper way under any change of the coordinate system. We denote the coordinates on the two-dimensional surface by (x^1, x^2), the coordinates on a chart of the embedding space by $(Y^1, \ldots, Y^n)$. The embedding space is a hybrid spatial-feature space. The first two coordinates (Y^1, Y^2) are the spatial coordinates and the rest $(Y^3, \ldots, Y^n)$ are the feature coordinates. The simplest example is the image itself which is represented as a 2D surface embedded in $\mathbb{R}^3$. We denote the map by $Y : \Sigma \to \mathbb{R}^3$. Where Σ is a two-dimensional surface. The map Y is given in this example by $(Y^1 = x^1, Y^2 = x^2, Y^3 = I(x^1, x^2))$. We choose on this surface a Riemannian structure, namely, a metric. The metric is a positive definite and a symmetric 2-tensor that may be defined through the local distance measurements

$$ds^2 = g_{11}(dx^1)^2 + 2g_{12}dx^1dx^2 + g_{22}(dx^2)^2. \tag{1}$$

We use below the Einstein summation convention in which the above equation reads $ds^2 = g_{\mu\nu}dx^\mu dx^\nu$ where repeated indices are summed over. We denote the inverse of the metric by $g^{\mu\nu}$.

Selecting the Induced Metric as the Image Metric: A reasonable assumption is that distances we measure in the embedding spatial-feature space, such as distance between pixels and difference between gray-levels, correspond directly to the distance measured on the image manifold. This is the assumption of isometric embedding under which we can calculate the image metric in terms of the embedding maps Y^i and the embedding space metric h_{ij}. This follows directly from the fact that the length of infinitesimal distances on the manifold can be calculated in the manifold and in the embedding space with the same result. Formally, $ds^2 = g_{\mu\nu}dx^\mu dx^\nu = h_{ij}dY^i dY^j$. By the chain rule, $dY^i = \partial_\mu Y^i dx^\mu$, we get $ds^2 = g_{\mu\nu}dx^\mu dx^\nu = h_{ij}\partial_\mu Y^i \partial_\nu Y^i dx^\mu dx^\nu$. From which we have

$$g_{\mu\nu} = h_{ij}\partial_\mu Y^i \partial_\nu Y^j. \tag{2}$$

Polyakov Action, a Measure on the Space of Embedding Maps: Denote by (Σ, g) the image manifold and its metric, and by (M, h) the space-feature manifold and its metric. Then the functional $S[\cdot, \cdot, \cdot]$ attaches a real number to a map $Y : \Sigma \to M$

$$S[Y^i, g_{\mu\nu}, h_{ij}] = \int dV \langle \nabla Y^i, \nabla Y^j \rangle_g h_{ij}, \tag{3}$$

where $dV = dx^1 dx^2 \cdots dx^m \sqrt{g}$ is a volume element, and the scalar product $\langle, \rangle_g$ is defined with respect to the image metric, i.e. $\langle \nabla Y^1, \nabla Y^2 \rangle_g = g^{\mu\nu}\partial_\mu Y^1 \partial_\nu Y^2$. This functional, for $m = 2$ (two-dimensional image manifold) and $h_{ij} = \delta_{ij}$, was first proposed by Polyakov [6] in the context of *string theory* in high energy physics. Note that the image metric and the feature coordinates, i.e., intensity, color, orientation etc. are independent variables. The minimization of the functional with respect to the image metric can be solved analytically in the two-dimensional case (see for example [10]). The minimizer is the induced metric. If we choose, a-priory, the image metric induced from the metric of the embedding spatial-feature space M, then the Polyakov action is reduced to an area (volume) of the image manifold.

Using standard methods in the calculus of variations (see [10]), the Euler-Lagrange equations with respect to the embedding are

$$-\frac{1}{2\sqrt{g}}h^{il}\frac{\delta S}{\delta Y^l} = \frac{1}{\sqrt{g}}\partial_\mu(\sqrt{g}g^{\mu\nu}\partial_\nu Y^i) + \Gamma^i_{jk}\langle \nabla Y^j, \nabla Y^k \rangle_g. \tag{4}$$

Since $(g_{\mu\nu})$ is positive definite, $g \equiv \det(g_{\mu\nu}) > 0$ for all x^μ. The $1/\sqrt{g}$ factor is the simplest one that does not change the minimization solution while giving a reparameterization invariant expression. The operator that is acting on Y^i in the first term is the natural generalization of the Laplacian from flat spaces to manifolds and is called the *Laplace-Beltrami operator*, and is denoted by Δ_g. The second term involves the Levi-Civita connection whose coefficients are given in terms of the metric of the embedding space

$$\Gamma_{jk}^i = \frac{1}{2} h^{il} \left(\partial_j h_{lk} + \partial_k h_{jl} - \partial_l h_{jk} \right). \tag{5}$$

This is the term that takes into account the fact that the image surface flows in a non-Euclidean manifold and not in $\mathbb{R}^n$.

A map that satisfies the Euler-Lagrange equations $-\frac{1}{2\sqrt{g}} h^{il} \frac{\delta S}{\delta Y^l} = 0$ is a **harmonic map**. The one- and two-dimensional examples are a geodesic curve on a manifold and a minimal surface.

The non-linear diffusion or "scale-space" equation emerges as the gradient descent minimization flow

$$Y_t^i = \frac{\partial}{\partial t} Y^i = -\frac{1}{2\sqrt{g}} h^{il} \frac{\delta S}{\delta Y^l} = \Delta_g Y^i + \Gamma_{jk}^i \langle \nabla Y^j, \nabla Y^k \rangle_g. \tag{6}$$

This flow evolves a given surface towards a minimal surface, and in general, it changes continuously a map towards a harmonic map.

3   Hemispheric Parameterization

Fiber Geometry: We are interested in the case where the fiber feature space is the hypersurface $\mathbb{S}^n$. We choose to represent the hyper-sphere $\mathbb{S}^n$ as a n-dimensional manifold embedded in $\mathbb{R}^{n+1}$, with Cartesian coordinate system $\{U^i\}_{i=3}^{n+3}$, as the constrained hyper-surface

$$\sum_{i=3}^{n+3} (U^i)^2 = 1. \tag{7}$$

We work in $n + 1$ charts (with $2(n + 1)$ arcwise connected parts), where $\{Y^i\}_{\substack{i=3 \\ i \neq j}}^{n+3}$ are local coordinates. On this chart $U^i = Y^i$, $i = 3, \ldots, n+3$, $i \neq j$ and $U^j = \pm\sqrt{1 - \sum_{\substack{i=3 \\ i \neq j}}^{n+3}(Y^i)^2}$. The points $U^j = 0$ do not belong to this chart and it has two unconnected components, the positive and negative values of U^j. We compute below the flow for the chart $j = n + 3$. Other charts are computed similarly.

Denote the metric elements, for the feature space only, by $\tilde{h}_{ij}$. The metric elements, and the inverse metric elements, are given by

$$\tilde{h}_{ij} = \sum_{k=3}^{n+3} \frac{\partial U^k \partial U^k}{\partial Y^i \partial Y^j} = \delta^{ij} + \frac{Y^i Y^j}{1 - \sum_{k=3}^{n+2}(Y^k)^2}$$
$$\tilde{h}_{ij}^{-1} = \delta^{ij} - Y^i Y^j. \tag{8}$$

The Induced Metric: Now we are in a position to compute the induced metric on the image surface. The embedding map is $(Y^1 = x^1, Y^2 = x^2, Y^3(x^1, x^2), \ldots,$

$Y^{n+2}(x^1, x^2)$). The induced metric is given by

$$g_{\mu\nu} = \delta_{\mu\nu} + \sum_{i,j=3}^{n+2} \tilde{h}_{ij} \partial_\mu Y^i \partial_\nu Y^j \tag{9}$$

where $\partial_\mu Y^i = \partial Y^i / \partial x^\mu$.

The Flow Equations: The non-zero Levi-Civita coefficients for this parameterization derived directly from substitution of Eq. (8) in Eq. (5). The simple result is

$$\Gamma^i_{jk} = Y^i \tilde{h}_{jk}(Y^3, \ldots, Y^{n+2}), \quad i, j, k = 3, \ldots, n+2. \tag{10}$$

The minimization of the Polyakov action leads to the following evolution equations

$$Y^i_t = \Delta_g Y^i + 2Y^i - Y^i \mathrm{Tr}(g^{\mu\nu}) \qquad i = 1, \ldots, n. \tag{11}$$

where $\mathrm{Tr} X$ is the trace of the matrix X.

One- and Two-Dimensional Directions: Two charts are needed to cover $\mathbb{S}^1$. The charts are $\{(Y^3, Y^4) | (Y^3)^2 + (Y^4)^2 = 1, Y^3 \neq 0\}$ and $\{(Y^3, Y^4) | (Y^3)^2 + (Y^4)^2 = 1, Y^4 \neq 0\}$. In each chart we have one coordinate (Y^3 and Y^4 respectively) that parameterize that chart. The flows in the charts are

$$Y^3_t = \Delta_g Y^3 + Y^3 \frac{g-1}{g} \tag{12}$$

and

$$Y^4_t = \Delta_g Y^4 + Y^4 \frac{g-1}{g}. \tag{13}$$

The metric in the two charts is identical in its form and depends on the corresponding coordinate that parameterize each chart. In the implementation we compute the diffusion for Y^3 and Y^4 simultaneously and determine the updated values as follows: We take the values $(Y^3, \mathrm{sign}(Y^4)\sqrt{1 - (Y^3)^2})$ for the range $(Y^3)^2 \leq (Y^4)^2$, and the values $(\mathrm{sign}(Y^3)\sqrt{1 - (Y^4)^2}, Y^4)$ for the range $(Y^4)^2 \leq (Y^3)^2$. The switching point is $Y^i = 1/\sqrt{2}$.

Similarly for the two-dimensional sphere $\mathbb{S}^2$ we have three charts. The charts are North-South, East-West, and front-rear hemispheres. The corresponding flows for the three charts are

$$(Y^i)_t = \Delta_g Y^i + 2Y^i - Y^i(g^{11} + g^{22}) \qquad i = 1, 2, 3. \tag{14}$$

At each point we find the largest component and compute the update of the value in the patch that is locally parameterized by the other two components. This way we always perform the computation as far as possible from the singularities. The largest component serves as its own sign holder. The switching point is $Y^i = 1/\sqrt{3}$.

In general we need more and more charts as n increases. Note that the singular point in the chart j is $Y^j = 0$. The switching point is therefor $1/\sqrt{n}$ and we are forced to work closer and closer to the singularity as n increases. In the following section we present different parameterization in which we work always in the furthest point from the singularity.

4   Stereographic Parameterization

Fiber Geometry: The hypersphere $\mathbb{S}^n$ is realized as the place of all the points in $\mathbb{R}^{n+1}$ that satisfy the constraint $\sum_{i=3}^{n+3} U^i U^i = 1$. We denote by Y^i for $i = 3, \ldots, n+2$ the Cartesian coordinate system on the unit disk $D^n = \{ U \in \mathbb{R}^{n+1} | \sum_{i=3}^{n+2} U^i U^i \leq 1, U^{n+1} = 0 \}$. The intersection of the line between the north pole and a point on the south hemisphere, and the the the D^n disk serves as a parameterization of the south hemisphere. Similarly, for the north hemisphere and the south pole (see Fig.(1) for the one- and two-dimensional coordinate systems).

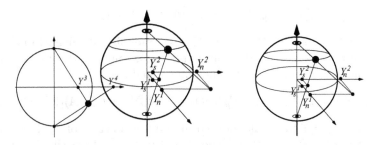

Fig. 1. The one-dimensional (left) and two-dimensional (right) stereographic coordinate systems.

Explicitly, these transformations are given by

$$Y^i = \frac{U^i}{1 \mp U^{n+3}} \quad i = 3, \ldots, n+2.$$

Inverting these relations we find

$$U^i = \frac{2Y^i}{A+1} \quad i = 3, \ldots, n+2 \quad \text{and} \quad U^{n+3} = \pm \frac{A-1}{A+1} \tag{15}$$

where $A = \sum_{k=3}^{n+2} (Y^k)^2$, and the upper (lower) sign is for the south (north) hemispheres.

The Induced Metric and Flow Equations: Now we are ready to compute the induced metric of our feature space,

$$\tilde{h}_{ij} = \sum_{k=3}^{n+3} \frac{\partial U^k \partial U^k}{\partial Y^i \partial Y^j} = \frac{4}{(1+A)^2} \delta_{ij} \quad i, j = 3, \ldots, n+2. \tag{16}$$

The image surface metric is the induced one

$$g_{\mu\nu} = \sum_{i=1}^{n+2} h_{ij} \frac{\partial Y^i \partial Y^j}{\partial x^\mu \partial x^\nu} = \delta_{\mu\nu} + \frac{4}{(1+A)^2} \sum_{i=3}^{n+2} \frac{\partial Y^i \partial Y^i}{\partial x^\mu \partial x^\nu} \quad \mu, \nu = 1, 2.$$

The Levi-Civita connection is obtained by Eq. (16) and Eq. (5) to be

$$\Gamma^i_{jk} = \frac{4}{1+A} \left(Y^i \delta_{jk} - Y^k \delta_{ij} - Y^j \delta_{ki} \right) \quad i,j,k = 3,\ldots,n+2.$$

The resulting diffusion equations are

$$Y^i_t = \Delta_g Y^i + \sum_{j,k=3}^{n+3} \frac{4}{1+A} \left(Y^i \delta_{jk} - Y^k \delta_{ij} - Y^j \delta_{ki} \right) \partial_\mu Y^j \partial_\nu Y^k g^{\mu\nu} \qquad (17)$$

($i = 3,\ldots,n+2$). This can be rearranged to

$$Y^i_t = \Delta_g Y^i - 4g^{\mu\nu}(\partial_\mu \log(1+A))(\partial_\nu Y^i) + (1+A)(2 - g^{11} - g^{22})Y^i \qquad (18)$$

($i = 3,\ldots,n+2$). **One- and Two-Dimensional Directions:** We denote our coordinate system by the subscripts s (for south) and n (for north). The equations are, therefor, for the one-dimensional case

$$(Y_s)_t = \Delta_g Y_s - 4g^{\mu\nu}(\partial_\mu \log(1+A))(\partial_\nu Y_s) + (1+A)(2 - g^{11} - g^{22})Y_s, \qquad (19)$$

where $A = Y_s^2$ and the induced metric is a function of Y_s. Identical equation is written for Y_n. We solve the north and south equations simultaneously for values *smaller* than 1. Each iteration we update the values which are greater than 1 by the simple relation $Y_s = 1/Y_n$. Note that the problematic zone(s), i.e. ± 1, are as far as possible from the singularities, i.e. the poles.

The two-dimensional case is managed similarly via

$$(Y_s^1)_t = \Delta_g Y_s^1 - 4g^{\mu\nu}(\partial_\mu \log(1+A_s))(\partial_\nu Y_s^1) + (1+A_s)(2 - g^{11} - g^{22})Y_s^1$$
$$(Y_s^2)_t = \Delta_g Y_s^1 - 4g^{\mu\nu}(\partial_\mu \log(1+A_s))(\partial_\nu Y_s^2) + (1+A_s)(2 - g^{11} - g^{22})Y_s^2 \quad (20)$$

where $A_s = (Y_s^1)^2 + (Y_s^2)^2$ and the induced metric is a function of Y_s^i. As in the one-dimensional case we solve simultaneously for the south and north patches and work with Y^is which are smaller than 1. The update for values who are greater than 1 after the diffusion (in each iteration) is done by $Y_s^i = A_s Y_n^i$. The decision zone along the equator, is the most numerically stable region since it is the furthest from the poles where singularities may appear.

5   Color Diffusion and Experimental Results

First, we use machine color space as our spectral model, where we first restrict the colors to a unit sphere in the RGB space. The sphere is centered at the RBG box as shown in Figure 2. The filter in this case is based on a flow on the $\mathbb{S}^2$ sphere, while the magnitude is kept fix. A coupled magnitude-chroma process as discussed in [3] may be envisaged as well.

In all these examples the noise was introduced in the chromatic channels only. Note that although the chromatic channels carry a small fraction of the energy of the signal it has very pronounced perceptual effect. Popular denoising techniques which are luminosity based are doomed to fail in this situation.

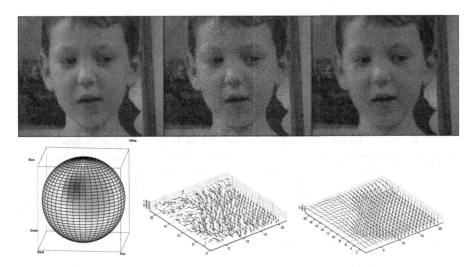

Fig. 2. Colors are restricted to a unit sphere, $\mathbb{S}^2$, in the RGB unit box, while the magnitude is treated separately. The original image (left), the noisy image (middle), and the filtered image (right). The vector fields of part of the images, before (left) and after (right) the flow.

6   Concluding Remarks

There are three important issues in the process of denoising a constrained feature field. The first is to make the process compatible with the constraint in such a way that the latter is never violated along the flow. The second is the type of regularization which is applied in order to preserve significant discontinuities of the feature field while removing noise. The third is numerical accuracy and stability.

We studied, in this paper, the direction diffusion flow where the feature manifold is the hypersphere $\mathbb{S}^n$. We proposed to use *intrinsic* coordinates of the constraint's manifold in order to be compatible with the constraint along the flow. We used the Beltrami flow that projects the mean curvature on the feature space coordinates. This operation preserves edges while removing the noise. Finally we analyzed the hemispheric and stereographic parameterizations for the hypersphere geometry. We showed that the stereographic parameterization is numerically superior since the decision between the two charts (North and South hemispheres) is done along the equator, far away from the singularities which are located in the North and South poles.

The result of this algorithm is an adaptive smoothing process for a constrained feature space in every dimension and codimension. Application to a model of color space was used to demonstrate the flows and their edge preserving properties.

References

1. T. Chan and J. Shen, "Variational restoration of non-flat image features: Models and algorithms", SIAM J. Appl. Math., to appear.
2. A. Cumani, "Edge detection in multi-spectral images", CVGIP: Graphical Models and Image Processing 53 (1991) no.1 40-51.
3. R. Kimmel and N. Sochen, "Orientation Diffusion or How to Comb a Porcupine?", special issue on PDEs in Image Processing, Computer Vision and Computer Graphics, Journal of Visual Communication and Image Representation, to appear.
4. R. Kimmel and R. Malladi and N. Sochen, "Images as Embedding Maps and Minimal Surfaces: Movies, Color, Texture, and Volumetric Medical Images", International Journal of Computer Vision 39(2) (2000) 111-129.
5. E. Kreyszig, "Differential Geometry", Dover Publications, Inc., New York, 1991.
6. A. M. Polyakov, "Quantum geometry of bosonic strings", *Physics Letters*, **103B** (1981) 207-210.
7. P. Perona, "Orientation Diffusion" *IEEE Trans. on Image Processing*, 7 (1998) 457-467.
8. N. Sochen and R. M. Haralick and Y. Y. Zeevi, "A Geometric functional for Derivatives Approximation" EE-Technion Report, April 1999.
9. N. Sochen and R. Kimmel and A. M. Bruckstein, "Diffusions and confusions in signal and image processing", accepted to *Journal of Mathematical Imaging and Vision*.
10. N. Sochen and R. Kimmel and R. Malladi, "From high energy physics to low level vision", Report, LBNL, UC Berkeley, LBNL 39243, August, Presented in ONR workshop, UCLA, Sept. 5 1996.
11. N. Sochen and R. Kimmel and R. Malladi, "A general framework for low level vision", *IEEE Trans. on Image Processing*, 7 (1998) 310-318.
12. N. Sochen, "Stochastic processes in vision I: From Langevin to Beltrami", CCIT Technion technical report No. 245
13. N. Sochen and Y. Y. Zeevi, "Representation of colored images by manifolds embedded in higher dimensional non-Euclidean space", Proc. IEEE ICIP'98, Chicago, 1998.
14. B. Tang and G. Sapiro and V. Caselles, "Direction diffusion", International Conference on Computer Vision, 1999.
15. B. Tang and G. Sapiro and V. Caselles, "Color image enhancement via chromaticity diffusion" Technical report, ECE-University of Minnesota, 1999.

Inverse Scale Space Theory for Inverse Problems

Otmar Scherzer and Chuck Groetsch

[1] Angewandte Mathematik,Universität Bayreuth
D-95440 Bayreuth, Germany
otmar.scherzer@uni-bayreuth.de
[2] Department of Mathematics, University of Cincinnati
Cincinnati, Ohio 45221-0025, USA
groetsch@uc.edu

Abstract. In this paper we derive scale space methods for inverse problems which satisfy the fundamental axioms of fidelity and causality and we provide numerical illustrations of the use of such methods in deblurring. These scale space methods are asymptotic formulations of the Tikhonov-Morozov regularization method. The analysis and illustrations relate diffusion filtering methods in image processing to Tikhonov regularization methods in inverse theory.

1 Introduction

scale space methods in *signal* and *image processing* and *regularization methods* for the solution of *inverse problems* have developed rather independently. In fact, there are major philosophical differences between the image processing and regularization communities as to what constitutes adequate numerical methods for solving problems in the respective fields. This is quite surprising since there are many problems which are relevant both in image processing and inverse problems.

In order to discuss different approaches to numerical methods in the two areas we relate two paradigms:

- *diffusion filtering* methods in image processing and
- *Tikhonov-type regularization* methods in inverse problems.

Moreover, we show that there are adequate modifications of both methods which allow their application in the other area. In particular, we derive scale space methods for inverse problems.

One of the most important scale space methods in image processing and *computer vision* is diffusion filtering (see e.g. [16]). Let $\Omega = [0,1]^2$. To analyze an image u^δ defined on Ω the diffusion process

$$\frac{\partial u}{\partial t} = \nabla \cdot (g(|\nabla u|^2)\nabla u) \text{ on } \Omega\,, \quad \frac{\partial u}{\partial n} = 0 \text{ on } \partial\Omega\,, \quad u(0) = u^\delta \text{ on } \Omega \quad (1)$$

is solved. The sequence of *filtered* or *diffused* images $\mathcal{D} := \{u(\cdot,t) : t \geq 0\}$ is used to analyze u^δ. When it is helpful to specify the dependence of u on the initial data u^δ, we write $u_{u^\delta}(\cdot,t)$.

M. Kerckhove (Ed.): Scale-Space 2001, LNCS 2106, pp. 317–325, 2001.

The sequence of images $\mathcal{D}$ defined by the diffusion process has the following properties:

Fidelity: $u(\cdot, t) \to u^\delta$ as $t \to 0$.
Causality: Given $0 < t_0 < T$, $u(\cdot, T)$ is completely determined by $u(\cdot, t_0)$.
Euclidean Invariance: If A is an isometry, then $u_{u^\delta \circ A}(\cdot, t) = u_{u^\delta}(\cdot, t) \circ A$.

Diffusion filtering methods are closely related to (iterative) Tikhonov-type regularization methods. The *implicit* Euler method for the solution of (1) is

$$\frac{\hat{u}(t_n) - \hat{u}(t_{n-1})}{t_n - t_{n-1}} = \nabla \cdot (g(|\nabla \hat{u}|^2) \nabla \hat{u})(t_n) . \tag{2}$$

If there exists a convex function h satisfying $h' = g$, then the minimizer $\hat{u}$ of

$$\|\hat{u} - \hat{u}(t_{n-1})\|_{L^2(\Omega)}^2 + (t_n - t_{n-1}) \int_\Omega h(|\nabla \hat{u}|^2) \tag{3}$$

provides an approximation of $u(t_n)$. Using just *one* implicit time step α is known as the method of Tikhonov regularization. This method consists in minimizing the functional

$$f_{\text{Tik}}(\hat{u}) := \|\hat{u} - u^\delta\|_{L^2(\Omega)}^2 + \alpha \int_\Omega h(|\nabla \hat{u}|^2) . \tag{4}$$

Tikhonov regularization violates the causality principle: let $\mathcal{R} := \{\hat{u}(\cdot, \alpha) : \alpha \geq 0\}$ be the set of *regularized* images then it is *not* possible to calculate $\hat{u}(\cdot, \alpha)$ from the knowledge of $\hat{u}(\cdot, \alpha_1)$ for $0 < \alpha_1 < \alpha$. Tikhonov regularization is a widely used method for solving *ill–posed* operator equations

$$F(\hat{u}) = y^0 . \tag{5}$$

where F is an operator which lacks a continuous inverse. The generalization of (4) for solving (5) is to minimize the functional

$$f_F(\hat{u}) := \|F(\hat{u}) - y^\delta\|_{L^2(\Omega)}^2 + \alpha \int_\Omega h(|\nabla \hat{u}|^2) . \tag{6}$$

For some survey references concerned with Tikhonov regularization for the solution of linear ill–posed problems we refer to [13,6,2,10,9,11]; for the solution of nonlinear ill–posed problems see [15,12,1,3].

The concept of diffusion filtering *cannot* be used for the solution of ill–posed operator equations. Arguing as before, the optimality criterion for the minimizer of (6) is $F'(\hat{u})^{*2}(F(\hat{u}) - y^\delta) = \alpha \nabla \cdot (h'(|\nabla \hat{u}|^2) \nabla \hat{u})$, where $F'(\hat{u})^{*2}$ denotes the L^2-adjoint of $F'(\hat{u})$, i.e., $\int_\Omega F'(\hat{u})^{*2}(v) w = \int_\Omega v F'(\hat{u})(w)$ for all $v \in L^2(\Omega), w \in H^1(\Omega)$ In the case of noise–free attainable data, i.e., for $y^\delta = y^0 = F(\hat{u}^\dagger)$, we have

$$F'(\hat{u})^{*2}(F(\hat{u}) - F(\hat{u}^\dagger)) = \alpha \nabla \cdot (h'(|\nabla \hat{u}|^2) \nabla \hat{u})$$

and there exists an associated diffusion-type methodology

$$F'(u)^{*2} F'(u) \frac{\partial u}{\partial t} = \nabla \cdot (h'(|\nabla u|^2) \nabla u), \quad u(0) = \hat{u}^\dagger . \tag{7}$$

Due to the ill–posedness of the operator equation (5) there will generally not exist a solution of (5) when y^0 is replaced by $y^\delta \neq y^0$. The ill-posedness thus prohibits an a-priori estimation of an approximation of $\hat{u}^\dagger$. Thus method (7) is inappropriate for calculating a scale space of an inverse problem.

We find it convenient to use the abstract formulation of Tikhonov regularization (6). Let $F : X \to Y$ be an operator between two Hilbert spaces X and Y. Then the abstract setting of Tikhonov regularization requires minimization of the functional $f(\hat{u}) := \|F(\hat{u}) - y^\delta\|_Y^2 + \alpha\|\hat{u}\|_X^2$, where $\|\cdot\|_X$ and $\|\cdot\|_Y$ denote the associated norms on X, Y, respectively. The optimality condition for a minimum of this functional is $F'(\hat{u})^{*XY}(F(\hat{u}) - y^\delta) + \alpha\hat{u} = 0$, where $F'(\hat{u})^{*XY}$ denotes the adjoint of $F'(\hat{u})$ with respect to the spaces X and Y, i.e., $\langle F'(\hat{u})^{*XY} v, w\rangle_X = \langle v, F'(\hat{u})w\rangle_Y$ for all $v \in Y$ and $w \in X$. The relation to diffusion filtering becomes apparent if we use $F = I$, $Y = L^2(\Omega)$ and let X be the Sobolev space $H^1(\Omega)$ of one time differentiable functions on Ω, and use the $H^1(\Omega)$-seminorm on X: $\|\cdot\|_X^2 = \|\cdot\|_{H_s^1}^2 := \int_\Omega |\nabla \cdot|^2$. In this setting the minimizer $\hat{u}$ of the Tikhonov functional satisfies

$$\hat{u} - u^\delta - \alpha\Delta\hat{u} = 0 \text{ on } \Omega, \quad \frac{\partial\hat{u}}{\partial n} = 0 \text{ on } \partial\Omega.$$

This implies that in a formal sense $F'(x)^{*XY} = -\Delta^{-1}F'(x)^{*2}$.

The *iterative Tikhonov-Morozov method* is a variant of Tikhonov regularization for solving inverse problems. This method consists of iteratively minimizing the sequence of functionals

$$f_n(\hat{u}) := \|F(\hat{u}) - y^\delta\|^2 + \alpha_n\|\hat{u} - \hat{u}_{n-1}\|^2 \quad n = 1, 2, \cdots \tag{8}$$

If the functionals are convex, then the minimizers $\hat{u}_n$ are characterized as the solutions of

$$F'(\hat{u}_n)^{*XY}(F(\hat{u}_n) - y^\delta) + \alpha_n(\hat{u}_n - \hat{u}_{n-1}) = 0, \quad n = 1, 2, \cdots \tag{9}$$

Typically in the Tikhonov-Morozov method one sets $\hat{u}_0 = 0$. But any other choice is suitable as well. For example, a–priori information on the solution may be incorporated in the initial approximation $\hat{u}_0$.

Taking $\alpha_n = 1/(t_n - t_{n-1})$ shows that $\hat{u}_n$ and $\hat{u}_{n-1}$ can be considered as approximations of the solution u of the *asymptotic Tikhonov–Morozov* filtering technique

$$F'(u)^{*XY}(F(u) - y^\delta) + \frac{\partial u}{\partial t} = 0, \text{ with } u(0) = 0. \tag{10}$$

For $F = I$ the identity mapping from $H^1(\Omega)$ into the $L^2(\Omega)$ the iterative Tikhonov-Morozov method generates minimizers $\hat{u}_n$ of the functionals

$$f_n(\hat{u}) := \|\hat{u} - u^\delta\|_{L^2(\Omega)}^2 + \alpha_n\|\hat{u} - \hat{u}_{n-1}\|_{H_s^1(\Omega)}^2 \quad n = 1, 2, \cdots. \tag{11}$$

Accordingly, the asymptotic Tikhonov-Morozov method consists in solving the differential equation of third order $u - u^\delta = \Delta\frac{\partial u}{\partial t}$ with $u(0) = 0$. In [5] we established the following properties of via semi-group theory **causality, Euclidean invariance** and

inverse fidelity: $u(\cdot, t) \to u^\delta$ as $t \to \infty$.

These three properties justify the name *inverse scale space* method for (10).

In Section 2 we discuss the asymptotic Tikhonov-Morozov method for *deblurring* images. In this case F is a linear integral operator. For this particular model problem we can motivate preferences of different numerical methods in inverse problems and image processing.

2   Deblurring with a Scale Space Method

In this section we consider a problem of *deblurring* data. We aim to recover a function $\hat{u}^\dagger$ on $\Omega = [0,1]^2$ given (blurred) data

$$y^\delta = K\hat{u}^\dagger + \text{noise} := \int_\Omega k(\|x - y\|)\hat{u}^\dagger(y)\, dy + \text{noise}$$

on Ω. To formulate the Tikhonov-Morozov method we have to specify a *similarity measure* for the data and an appropriate function space containing $\hat{u}^\dagger$.

In this section we restrict our attention to those $\hat{u}^\dagger$ in one of the following two spaces:

1. the Banach space $W^{1,p}(\Omega)$, with $p > 1$, of functions u satisfying

$$\|u\|_{W^{1,p}} := \left(\int_\Omega |\nabla u|^p + \omega |u|^p \right)^{1/p} < \infty,$$

with an appropriate positive weighting parameter $\omega > 0$.
2. the space $BV(\Omega)$ of functions of bounded variation. That is, the class of functions u satisfying

$$\|u\|_{BV(\Omega)} := \int_\Omega (|\nabla u| + \omega |u|) < \infty .$$

For a function $u \in BV(\Omega)$ the term $\int_\Omega |\nabla u|$ has to be understood as a measure (see [4]).

An appropriate choice for the similarity measure is the $L^2(\Omega)$-norm. Depending on a–priori information on $\hat{u}^\dagger$ it is instructive to study the Tikhonov-Morozov method in a variety of settings.

- For $\hat{u}^\dagger \in W^{1,p}(\Omega)$, $p > 1$, the corresponding Tikhonov-Morozov method consists in minimizing the functional

$$f_{W^{1,p}}(\hat{u}) := \|K\hat{u} - y^\delta\|_{L^2(\Omega)}^2 + \alpha_n \|\hat{u} - \hat{u}_{n-1}\|_{W^{1,p}(\Omega)}^p . \qquad (12)$$

- For $\hat{u}^\dagger \in BV(\Omega)$ the Tikhonov-Morozov method consists in minimizing

$$f_{BV}(\hat{u}) := \|K\hat{u} - y^\delta\|_{L^2(\Omega)}^2 + \alpha_n \|\hat{u} - \hat{u}_{n-1}\|_{BV(\Omega)} , \qquad (13)$$

Since the operator K is self-adjoint on $L^2(\Omega)$, the asymptotic Tikhonov-Morozov method in the $H^1 = W^{1,2}$-setting reads as follows

$$K(Ku(x,t) - y^\delta(x)) = (\Delta - \omega I)\frac{\partial u}{\partial t}(x,t) \text{ for } (x,t) \in \Omega \times (0,\infty)$$

$$\frac{\partial u}{\partial n}(x,t) = 0 \text{ for } (x,t) \in \partial\Omega \times (0,\infty), \qquad u(0) = 0 \text{ for } x \in \Omega. \tag{14}$$

The minimizer $\hat{u}$ of $f_{W^{1,p}}$ has to satisfy

$$K(K\hat{u}_n - y^\delta) = \alpha_n \frac{p}{2}\nabla \cdot \left(\|\nabla(\hat{u} - \hat{u}_{n-1})\|^{p-2}\nabla(\hat{u} - \hat{u}_{n-1})\right) - $$
$$\alpha_n \frac{p}{2}\omega\|\hat{u} - \hat{u}_{n-1}\|^{p-2}(\hat{u} - \hat{u}_{n-1}). \tag{15}$$

Introducing the relation

$$\alpha_n = \frac{2}{p}\frac{1}{(t_n - t_{n-1})^{p-1}} \tag{16}$$

between the regularization parameters and the time discretization we derive the asymptotic Tikhonov-Morozov method on $W^{1,p}(\Omega)$:

$$K(Ku - y^\delta) = \nabla \cdot \left(\left\|\nabla\left(\frac{\partial u}{\partial t}\right)\right\|^{p-2}\nabla\left(\frac{\partial u}{\partial t}\right)\right) - \omega\left\|\frac{\partial u}{\partial t}\right\|^{p-2}\frac{\partial u}{\partial t}. \tag{17}$$

For $p = 1$ the relation (16) degenerates, indicating that there is *no* asymptotic integro-differential equation for the Tikhonov-Morozov method on $BV(\Omega)$.

One of the most significant differences between diffusion filtering and iterative Tikhonov-Morozov regularization is that a small time step-size in the diffusion filtering method results in very *large* regularization parameters. This is not inconsistent with standard regularization theory since we consider an iterative regularization technique which uses the information of the previous iteration cycle. In our numerical simulations an exponentially decreasing sequence α_n leads to more visually attractive image sequences. This in turn implies that the time steps t_n of the diffusion filtering method are exponentially increasing. This compensates for the fact that in the beginning the diffusion process is rather strong and a small step size is required. As the diffusion progresses the image starts stagnating and a large time step size becomes appropriate.

Typically in inverse problems the main objective of regularization techniques is to obtain a reasonable reconstruction which are resistant to noise. Moreover, especially for nonlinear ill–posed problems, the calculation of a scale can be significantly more expensive than just calculating one regularized solution.

2.1 Numerical Simulations

In this subsection we discuss the numerical implementation of the Tikhonov-Morozov method and present some numerical simulations for deblurring images. In the numerical simulations presented below we have used the kernel function

$$k(t) = \frac{(t^2 - \varepsilon^2)^4}{\varepsilon^8} \text{ for } t \in [-\varepsilon, \varepsilon] \text{ and } k(t) = 0 \text{ otherwise}.$$

For the numerical solution of the *integro-differential* equation (14) we discretize in time and use a finite element ansatz of products of linear splines on Ω. Let $v(\cdot, t_n) = \sum_{i,j=0}^{N} c_{ij}(t_n) v_{ij}$ be the approximation of the solution of (14) where $v_{ij}(x, y) = v_i(x) v_j(y)$ and v_i is a spline of order 1, i.e., $v_i(j/n) = \delta_{ij}$ for $i = 0, \cdots, N$ and v_i is piecewise linear on $[0, 1]$. For the approximation of the time derivative of v we use a *backward difference* operator, i.e., $\frac{v(x, t_n) - v(x, t_{n-1})}{t_n - t_{n-1}} \approx \frac{\partial v}{\partial t}(x, t_n)$. Using $\alpha_n = 1/(t_n - t_{n-1})$ the discretized system for an approximation of (14) at time t_n requires solving the following linear equation for the coefficients $c_{ij}(t_{n+1})$ from given coefficients $c_{ij}(t_n)$

$$\sum_{ij} c_{ij}(t_{n+1})(\mathcal{K} + \alpha_n \mathcal{I}_\omega) = \int_\Omega y^\delta K(v_k v_l) + \alpha_n \sum_{ij} c_{ij}(t_n) \mathcal{I}_\omega \qquad (18)$$

for all $l, k \in \{0, \cdots, N\}$. Here $\mathcal{I}_\omega = \int_\Omega [(v_i)_x (v_k)_x (v_j)_y (v_l)_y + \omega v_i v_k v_j v_l]$ and $\mathcal{K} = \left[\int_\Omega K(v_i v_j) K(v_k v_l) \right]_{ij,kl}$. In general the matrix $\mathcal{K}$ is not sparse - it is only sparse if the essential support of the kernel function k is small. Thus in general the setup of $\mathcal{K}$ is computationally expensive. For example, if k has infinite essential support, then the setup of the matrix for an image of size $n \times n$ requires $O(n^6)$ operations. The solution of the unregularized equation (18) (i.e., with $\alpha_n = 0$) is ill-conditioned. This becomes clear when the singular values of the matrix $\mathcal{K}$ are calculated; most of the singular values are comparatively small. Errors in components of the data corresponding to singular functions with singular value near zero are then exceedingly amplified. Thus it is prohibitive to calculate the solution of the unregularized equation.

Example 1. In the first example we aimed to reconstruct the pattern (left images in Figure 1) from the blurred and additionally noisy data (cf. Figure 1). Figures 2, 3 show the inverse scale space method for reconstructing the pattern from blurred data (cf. Figure 2). When the blurred data is additionally distorted with Gaussian noise the ill-posedness of the problems becomes apparent. Only for a relatively short time period is the reconstruction visually attractive. For $t \to \infty$ the reconstruction becomes useless. One of the major concerns in regularization theory is the estimation of appropriate regularization parameters needed to stop the iteration process before the image becomes hopelessly distorted by noise. For some references on appropriate stopping rules for the Tikhonov-Morozov method we refer to [7,14,8,5].

Example 2. Here we aim to compare the Tikhonov-Morozov method on $H^1(\Omega)$ and $BV(\Omega)$. We have chosen a piecewise constant function on a rectangle as a paradigm of a function that is in $BV(\Omega)$ but not in $H^1(\Omega)$. This has the effect that the reconstruction with the (asymptotic) Tikhonov-Morozov on $H^1(\Omega)$ always has a blurry character (cf. Fig. 5). Figure 6 shows the reconstruction with the Tikhonov-Morozov method on $BV(\Omega)$.

Conclusions

In this paper the iterative nonstationary Tikhonov-Morozov method and its asymptotic formulations for the solution of inverse problems were studied and diffusion filtering and regularization have been related. Different formulations of the Tikhonov-Morozov method have been numerically compared and several arguments explaining why scale space methods have so far not been used in general inverse problem theory have been presented.

References

1. A.B. Bakushinskii and A.V. Goncharskii. *Ill–Posed Problems: Theory and Applications*. Kluwer Academic Publishers, Dordrecht, Boston, London, 1994.
2. M. Bertero and P. Boccacci. *Introduction to Inverse Problems in Imaging*. IOP Publishing, London, 1998.
3. H.W. Engl, M. Hanke, and A. Neubauer. *Regularization of Inverse Problems*. Kluwer Academic Publishers, Dordrecht, 1996.
4. L.C. Evans and R.F. Gariepy. *Measure Theory and Fine Properties of Functions*. CRC–Press, Boca Raton, 1992.
5. C. W. Groetsch and O. Scherzer. Nonstationary iterated tikhonov-morozov method and third order differential equations for the evaluation of unbounded operators. *Math. Meth. Appl. Sci.*, 23:1287–1300, 2000.
6. C.W. Groetsch. *The Theory of Tikhonov Regularization for Fredholm Equations of the First Kind*. Pitman, Boston, 1984.
7. C.W. Groetsch and O. Scherzer. Optimal order of convergence for stable evaluation of differential operators. *Electronic Journal of Differential Equations*, 4:1–10, 1993. http://ejde.math.unt.edu.
8. M. Hanke and C.W. Groetsch. Nonstationary iterated Tikhonov regularization. *J. Optim. Theory and Applications*, 98:37–53, 1998.
9. B. Hofmann. *Mathematik inverser Probleme. (Mathematics of inverse problems)*. Teubner, Stuttgart, 1999.
10. A. Kirsch. *An Introduction to the Mathematical Theory of Inverse Problems*. Springer–Verlag, New York, 1996.
11. A.K. Louis. *Inverse und Schlecht Gestellte Probleme*. Teubner, Stuttgart, 1989.
12. V.A. Morozov. *Methods for Solving Incorrectly Posed Problems*. Springer Verlag, New York, Berlin, Heidelberg, 1984.
13. M. Z. Nashed, editor. *Generalized Inverses and Applications*. Academic Press, New York, 1976.
14. O. Scherzer. Stable evaluation of differential operators and linear and nonlinear milti-scale filtering. *Electronic Journal of Differential Equations*, 15:1–12, 1997. http://ejde.math.unt.edu.
15. A. N. Tikhonov and V. Y. Arsenin. *Solutions of Ill-Posed Problems*. John Wiley & Sons, Washington, D.C., 1977. Translation editor: Fritz John.
16. J. Weickert. *Anisotropic Diffusion in Image Processing*. Teubner, Stuttgart, 1998.

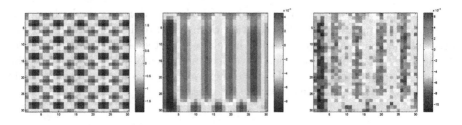

Fig. 1. The test pattern, the blurred data with and without noise. From the blurred data we intend to recover the test patter.

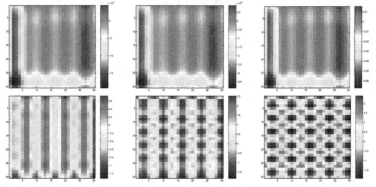

Fig. 2. Reconstruction from blurred data without noise by the inverse scale space method (14)

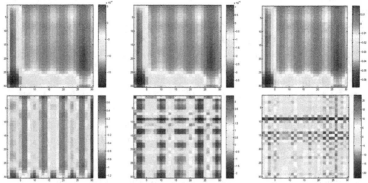

Fig. 3. Reconstruction from blurred data with high noise using the inverse scale space method (14)

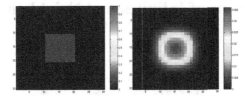

Fig. 4. Test-data for comparing the Tikhonov-Morozov method on $H^1(\Omega)$ and $BV(\Omega)$. The left image shows the data to be reconstructed; the right data shows the available blurred data.

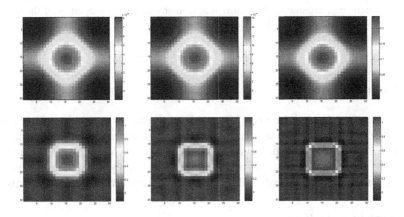

Fig. 5. Reconstruction with the Tikhonov-Morozov method on $H^1(\Omega)$.

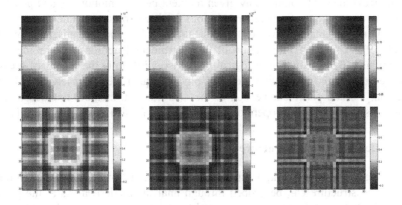

Fig. 6. Reconstruction with the Tikhonov-Morozov method on $BV(\Omega)$

Histograms of Infinitesimal Neighbourhoods

Lewis D. Griffin

King's College, London
Lewis.Griffin@kcl.ac.uk

Abstract. Image analysis methods that use histograms defined over non-zero-sized local neighbourhoods have been proposed [1-4]. To better understand such methods, one can study the histograms of infinitesimal neighbourhoods. In this paper we show how the properties of such histograms can be derived through limit arguments. We show that in many cases the properties of these histograms are given by simple expressions in terms of spatial derivatives at the point   analyzed.

1   Introduction

Assorted results, that build on previous work on the use of local histogram methods for image processing [2-5], are reported. The introduction reviews relevant background material and establishes some formalism. The body of the paper contains new results on: averages and moments of local histograms, analytic solutions of the mode filtering equation, and information theoretic measures applied to local histograms

1.1   Structure at a Point

The observation that 'structure at a point' is seemingly essential for Physics and yet apparently incoherent can be traced back to Zeno's discussion [6] of the paradox of how an arrow in flight could at any given moment be both motionless and possessing of a particular velocity. Proposed resolutions of this paradox include the method of limits [7], instrumental approaches to physical theory [8], and formalisations of infinitesimals [9]. A modern formulation of the instrumental approach is the method of distributions [10] in which, in a logical positivist spirit, only the results of measurement are dealt with, rather than idealised physical quantities themselves [11]. Scale space analysis is a particular version of the distributional method, founded upon the use of Gaussian apertures as operators for measuring physical scalar functions [12].

1.2   Differential Point Structure

In the scale space framework, as in the standard calculus of infinitesimal neighbourhoods, local structure can be probed through analysis of derivatives at the point of interest [13-19]. In the scale space approach these values are obtained by application of derivatives of the aperture function. Raw derivatives are poor descriptors of image structure as they vary with the coordinate system. Instead, satisfactory descriptors can

M. Kerckhove (Ed.) : Scale-Space 2001, LNCS 2106, pp. 326-334, 2001.

be obtained through combination of derivative values into coordinate system independent quantities such as the gradient magnitude $\left(L_x^2 + L_y^2\right)^{\frac{1}{2}}$.

When the emphasis is on invariant quantities, it is convenient to employ gauge coordinates. In particular, in w,v-gauge coordinates where the w-direction is uphill along the gradient and the v-direction is tangent to the isophote, the expression for the gradient magnitude simplifies to L_w. The w,v-system will be used in what follows.

1.3   Statistical Point Structure

An alternative way to probe local structure is consider the histogram of values visible within an aperture [2-4] (see figure 1). For a Gaussian aperture $\left(G_s\left(\vec{r}\right) = \left(4\pi s\right)^{-1} e^{\frac{\vec{r}\cdot\vec{r}}{4s}}\right)$ of scale s centred on the origin, the histogram is given by $H_s\left[L\right](p) := \int_{\mathbb{R}^2} G_s\left(\vec{r}\right).\delta\left(L\left(\vec{r}\right) - p\right) d\vec{r}$. In so far as this histogram depends upon the underlying image, it is dependent upon the image derivatives at the origin, but in a complex manner. The relationship does, however, simplify in the limit as the aperture size goes to zero [5].

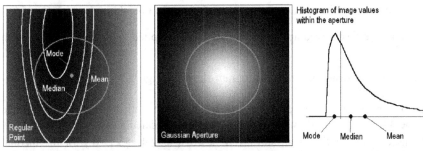

Fig. 1. The left panel shows an example image region centred on a regular point. The central panel shows a gaussian aperture. The right panel shows the histogram of the image at left within the aperture shown in the centre. The mean, median and mode of the histogram are marked, as are the corresponding isophotes in the underlying image on the left. The median isophote divides the image into two regions with equal integral of the aperture weighting.

As scale tends to zero, the histogram tends to a delta function (i.e. $\lim_{s\downarrow 0} H_s\left[L\right](p) = \delta\left(p - L\left(\vec{0}\right)\right)$), which obscures analysis of its limiting form. To better study the limit, we can use the trick of fixing the aperture scale and resizing the image in the spatial and intensive dimensions. Following this procedure one discovers that in the zero scale limit, the local histogram is Gaussian in form with a width related to the gradient (i.e. the coordinate-invariant part of the 1st order differential structure):

$$\lim_{s\to 0} \ H_1\left[s^{-\frac{1}{2}}L\left(s^{\frac{1}{2}}.\_\right)\right](p) = G_{L_w^2}\left(p - L\left(\vec{0}\right)\right)$$

The first-order manner in which this histogram evolves as the scale is increased from 0 is captured by an expression that depends upon the second order structure:

$$\left\{ s^{\frac{1}{2}} \frac{\partial}{\partial s} H_1 \left[s^{-\frac{1}{2}} L \left(s^{\frac{1}{2}}.\_ \right) \right] (p) \right\}_{s=0} = \frac{-1}{4L_w^2} \left(2L_w^2 \left(L_{vv} - 2L_{ww} \right) + p^2.L_{ww} \right).G'_{L_w^2} \left(p - L(\vec{0}) \right)$$

2   Averages and Moments of Local Histograms

As has been presented elsewhere [5], from the equations in section 1.4 one can compute the mean $(\mu_2 [H_s [L]] = L(\vec{0}) + (L_{vv} + L_{ww})s + o(s^2))$, median $(\mu_1 [H_s [L]] = L(\vec{0}) + (L_{vv})s + o(s^2))$ and mode $(\mu_0 [H_s [L]] = L(\vec{0}) + (L_{vv} - 2L_{ww})s + o(s^2))$ of local histograms for small s. It is also possible to calculate moment-based measures of local histograms for small s. For example, the variance (second moment) depends on the local gradient $v(s) = 2L_w^2 s + o(s^3)$, while the skewness (third moment normalized by the second) depends on the second derivative in the gradient direction $k(s) = 6L_{ww}s + o(s^2)$.

These results can be used for the troublesome task of estimating the median and the mode of sparse image histograms (such as result from 3×3 neighbourhoods). Consider, for example, the discretized aperture $\frac{1}{36}\begin{pmatrix} 1 & 4 & 1 \\ 4 & 16 & 4 \\ 1 & 4 & 1 \end{pmatrix}$ [20], applied to a patch of image with values $\begin{pmatrix} 100 & 40 & 25 \\ 79 & 44 & 13 \\ 59 & 28 & 0 \end{pmatrix}$, resulting in the histogram shown in figure 2. Using a standard approach, the mean would be calculated to be 42.4, but both the median and mode would be 44. Instead the skew of the histogram can be calculated to be 12.6 and this can be used to adjust the mean and arrive at $40.3 (= 42.4 - \frac{1}{6} \times 12.6)$ for the median and $36.1 (= 42.4 - \frac{1}{2} \times 12.6)$ for the mode.

Alternatively, the skewness and the mean can be used to estimate L_{ww} and L_{vv}. To do this, the scale of the aperture must be known, but this can be readily calculated using the expression $s = \frac{1}{4} \int_{-\infty}^{\infty} \int_{-\infty}^{\infty} (x^2 + y^2) G_s (x, y) \, dx \, dy$) which, applied to the mask above, gives an equivalent scale of $s_D = \frac{1}{6}$. Thus $L_{ww} = \frac{12.6}{6 s_D} = 12.6$ and $L_{vv} = \frac{1}{s_d} (42.4 - 44 - \frac{1}{6} 12.6) = -22.2$

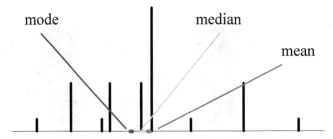

Fig. 2. The sparse histogram corresponding to a 3×3 aperture applied to a typical image region (see text above). The mean has been calculated in the normal manner. Under a literal interpretation of the histogram, the median and mode would both be located at the main spike; however, the skew-based method described in the text places them at the marked locations.

3   Image Simplification

The concept of progressively simplifying an image is well established [21]. The obvious technique is iteratively to replace simultaneously the value at each point of the image by the average of the values within an aperture around the point. The effect of such filtering will depend upon the size and shape of the aperture. To remove this dependency one can to consider the limiting process as smaller apertures are used and the number of iterations is increased. In the limit, the apertures become infinitesimal and the iteration number is replaced by a continuous time parameter. At the limit, the effect of filtering can only be dependent on differential measures of the image and so infinitesimal filtering is always describable by a partial differential equation.

3.1   Mean, Median, and Mode Filtering

Different definitions of average, result in different filtering schemes [22-24]. Using the mean as the averaging operator results in a scheme equivalent to linear diffusion [12], described by $L_{t_2} = L_{vv} + L_{ww}$ – where t_2 is the time parameter. Using the median causes the image to evolve (at regular points) according to $L_{t_1} = L_{vv}$, also know as mean curvature flow [25]. Using the mode results in the image evolving according to $L_{t_0} = L_{vv} - 2L_{ww}$ at regular points, and $L_{t_0} = 0$ at critical points [5].

   Mode filtering is distinctly different in effect from mean or median. As mode filtering progresses, the $-2L_{ww}$ term has the effect of de-blurring and so enhancing edges, while the $+L_{vv}$ term stabilizes this process and prevents the developing loci of discontinuity from becoming too ragged. Away from developing edges, the image changes in value towards nearby critical points. The final result seems to be a mosaic of plateaus separated by discontinuities, though this has not been proved. At this point, the image is unaffected by further applications of the mode filtering procedure.

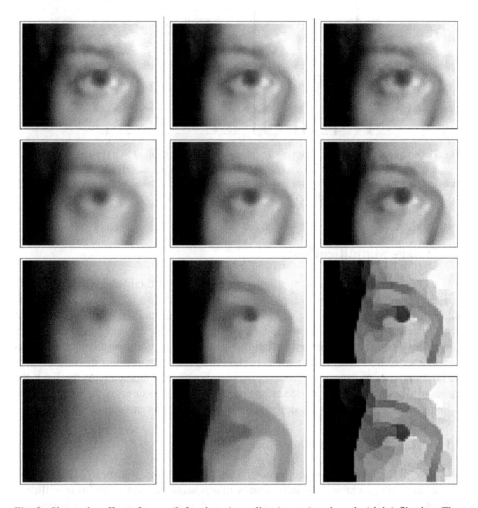

Fig. 3. Shows the effect of mean (left column), median (centre) and mode (right) filtering. The first row shows the original image; the other rows reading downwards show the progressive effect of repeated filtering after 4, 16 and 64 iterations. The mode-filtered image at bottom right is the final state for this image; further mode filtering has no effect.

Mean-filtering, being linear, is straightforward to implement; median- and mode-filtering, being non-linear, are not. Results from attempted numerical implementations of these filtering schemes are shown in figure 3. The qualitative effect of median filtering is similar to results presented by other authors under the guises of mean curvature flow [26] as well as median filtering [25]. For mode filtering, although the results are in rough qualitative agreement with expectation, the algorithm can only truly be assessed by comparison to explicit solutions of the evolution equations. In the next section we report progress on identifying such explicit solutions.

3.2   Analytic Solutions to the Mode Filtering Equations

An exact solution to the mode filtering equation is provided by a family of erf functions $E(x;t_0 < c) = \mathrm{erf}\left(x(8(c-t_0))^{-\frac{1}{2}}\right)$. Since these functions are 1D, the mode filtering equation reduces to $E_{t_0} = -2E_{xx}$, the truth of which is easily established. As this family evolves, a blurred step edge becomes increasingly sharp until at $t_0 = c$ it becomes a sharp step edge ($E(x;t_0 \geq c) = \mathrm{sgn}(x)$), after which point there is no further change.

The above solution is of some use in evaluating our numerical implementation, but it does not feature any extrema. A 1D solution that does includes extrema, but is however only approximate, is $S(x;t_0 \leq 0) = \sum_{i=0}^{\infty} \frac{1}{2i+1} e^{2(2i+1)^2 t_0} \cos\left((2i+1)x\right)$. As figure 4 shows, this describes the formation of a square wave (at $t_0 = 0$) from a blurred square wave (at $t_0 < 0$). At regular points ($x \neq n\pi$) the family of functions satisfy the evolution equation $S_{t_0} = -2S_{xx}$ exactly as required. Unfortunately, the extremum change value slightly with t_0, which should not occur with proper mode filtering. The movement is small though (less than 0.1% for $t_0 \in [-0.05, 0]$).

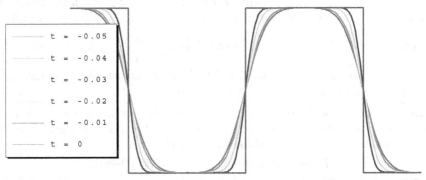

t = -0.05	
t = -0.04	
t = -0.03	
t = -0.02	
t = -0.01	
t = 0	

Fig. 4. Shows a blurred square wave evolving into a sharp square wave. The evolution satisfies the mode filtering equations except at the extrema, which change value slightly.

4   Information Theoretic Measures

Image registration methods based upon information theoretic measures are becoming common [27, 28]. In this context, information measures are used to quantify the degree to which two images are in correct registration. Optimisation routines are then used to explore an appropriate space of transformations to discover the best possible registration according to the measure.

At the heart of any information theoretic approach is Shannon's measure (H) of the entropy of a distribution D, defined as $H[D] = -\int D(\vec{p}) \ln\left(D(\vec{p})\right) d\vec{p}$ [29]. Entropy measures something similar to variance, especially for unimodal distributions. For example, the entropy of a Gaussian distribution is $H[G_s(\_)] = \frac{1}{2}(1 + \ln(4\pi s))$.

For image registration purposes, a measure 'mutual information', that is defined in terms of entropy but that applies to joint distributions, is used. The joint distribution (J) of a pair $(U,V:\mathbb{R}^2 \to \mathbb{R})$ of registered images is defined as $J(u,v) = |\Omega|^{-1} \int_{\Omega} \delta(U(\vec{r})-u)\delta(V(\vec{r})-v) d\vec{r}$; where Ω is the region of overlap. The mutual information (M) of J measures the degree to which a value of one variable (e.g. u) of the joint histogram is predictable from the value of the other variable (v). Good registration corresponds to high mutual information i.e. the values of one image can be well predicted from the values of the other. The formula for mutual information is:

$$M[J] = H[J(\_,\_)] - \left(H\left[\int J(u,\_) du \right] + H\left[\int J(\_,v) dv \right] \right)$$

While mutual information gives good registration results most of the time, it has been observed that it can result in obvious mis-registration even with images not specially constructed to fool the algorithm [30]. It has been suggested that this can be prevented by using a global mutual information measure combined by multiplication with a local measure integrated across the image domain [31]. We describe below how such local measures can be understood within an information theoretic framework.

4.1   Mutual Information Defined for an Infinitesimal Aperture

As a preliminary result, we first build on the equations given above for (i) the entropy of a Gaussian distribution, and (ii) mutual information of a 2D distribution. These equations allow one to calculate the mutual information of a 2D gaussian distribution

$$E(u,v) = \frac{1}{\pi}\sqrt{AC - B^2}\, e^{-(Au^2 + 2Buv + Cv^2)} \quad \text{to be} \quad M[E] = \frac{1}{2}\ln\left(\frac{AC}{AC - B^2} \right). \text{ Our next step is}$$

to consider two registered images (U and V), both regular and (for convenience) zero-valued at the origin i.e. $U(x,y) = ax + by + ...$ and $V(x,y) = \alpha x + \beta y + ...$. Just as we can define the histogram of a single image within an aperture, so we can define the joint histogram within an aperture of a pair of images. For a Gaussian aperture of scale s centred at the origin, the joint histogram of U and V is:

$$H_s(u,v) = \int G_s(\vec{r})\delta(U(\vec{r})-u)\delta(V(\vec{r})-v) d\vec{r}$$

In the limit, as we reduce the scale of the aperture down to zero, the joint histogram becomes dependent upon only the first order structure of the two images and the joint histogram tends to the form of a two-dimensional gaussian:

$$\lim_{s\downarrow 0} H_s(u,v) = \lim_{s\downarrow 0} \left(4\pi s|a\beta - \alpha b|\right)^{-1} e^{-\frac{(u\ v)\begin{pmatrix} \alpha^2+\beta^2 & -(a\alpha+b\beta) \\ -(a\alpha+b\beta) & a^2+b^2 \end{pmatrix}\begin{pmatrix} u \\ v \end{pmatrix}}{4s(a\beta-\alpha b)^2}}$$

So, using the already stated expression for the mutual information of a two-dimensional Gaussian one arrives at:

$$\lim_{s\downarrow 0} M[H_s(u,v)] = -\frac{1}{2}\ln\left(\frac{(a^2+b^2)(\alpha^2+\beta^2)}{(a\beta - b\alpha)^2} \right)$$

Finally, if the angle between the two gradient vectors $\begin{pmatrix} a \\ b \end{pmatrix}$ and $\begin{pmatrix} \alpha \\ \beta \end{pmatrix}$ is denoted θ, then the expression for mutual information simplifies to:

$$\lim_{s \downarrow 0} M\left[H_s\left(u, v\right)\right] = -\ln\left(\left|\sin\theta\right|\right).$$

This expression reminds us of the expression $\frac{1}{2}(1 + \cos(2\theta))$ used as a measure of local registration quality in a recently proposed [31] improvement to standard global mutual information measures. The two measures are compared in figure 5.

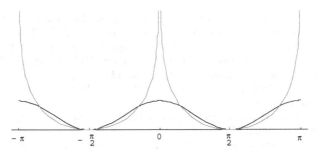

Fig. 5. Compares two measures of local registration. The sinusoidal dark curve is $\frac{1}{2}(1 + \cos(2\theta))$, the paler curves are our alternative $-\ln\left(\left|\sin\theta\right|\right)$.

5   Concluding Remarks

In this paper, we have defined *local histograms* as the limit of histograms defined for gaussian apertures as the scale of the aperture tends to zero. We have shown how properties of these local histograms are, in many cases, given by simple expressions in terms of spatial derivatives of the image at the aperture centre.

We have given examples of the use of local histogram operations in three areas: image measurement, image filtering and image registration. In all three cases, the details of the actual implementation of these methods on a discrete grid of pixels is *ad hoc*.

Several questions are raised by this approach. Consider, for example, the following. The equation that was presented for the first order deviation of the local histogram from gaussian form depended upon L_w, L_{ww} and L_{vv} but not L_{wv}. Which other derivatives is the form of the local histogram unaffected by? Or to turn the question around, what characterizes the portion of the differential structure at a point that is discoverable from examination of the local histogram at the point?

References

[1] Noest, A.J., Koenderink, J.J.: Visual coherence despite visual transparency or partial occlusion. Perception 19 (1990) 384
[2] Griffin, L.D.: Scale-imprecision space. Image Vis. Comput. 15(5) (1997) 369-398
[3] Koenderink, J.J., Van Doorn, A.J.: The structure of locally orderless images. Int. J. Comput. Vis. 31(2-3) (1999) 159-168

[4] van Ginneken, B., ter Haar Romeny, B.M.: Applications of locally orderless images. J. Vis. Comm. Imag. Rep. 11(2) (2000) 196-208

[5] Griffin, L.D.: Mean, Median and Mode Filtering of Images. Proc. Roy. Soc. A 456(2004) (2000) 2995-3004

[6] Russell, B.: The Principles of Mathematics. Routledge, London (1903)

[7] Newton, I.: Principia. (1687)

[8] Leibniz, G.W.: Mathematical Works. Open Court, London (1920)

[9] Diener, F., Diener, M., ed.: Nonstandard Analysis in Practice. Springer-Verlag, Berlin (1995)

[10] Richards, J.I., Youn, H.K.: Theory of Distributions. Cambridge University Press, Cambridge (1990)

[11] Florack, L.M.J., ter Haar Romeny, B.M., Koenderink, J.J., Viergever, M.A.: Images: Regular Tempered Distributions, In: Shape in Picture. vol. 126 (O, Y.-L., Toet, A., Foster, D., Heijmans, H.J.A.M., Meer, P., eds.), Springer-Verlag, Berlin, pp. 651-660.

[12] Koenderink, J.J.: The Structure of Images. Biol. Cybern. 50(5) (1984) 363-370

[13] Koenderink, J.J.: What is a feature? J. Intell. Syst. 3(1) (1993) 49-82

[14] Koenderink, J.J.: Operational Significance of Receptive-Field Assemblies. Biol. Cybern. 58(3) (1988) 163-171

[15] Koenderink, J.J., van Doorn, A.J.: Receptive Field Assembly Specificity. J. Vis. Comm. Imag. Rep. 3(1) (1992) 1-12

[16] Koenderink, J.J., van Doorn, A.J.: Generic Neighborhood Operators. IEEE Trans. Patt. Anal. Mach. Intell. 14(6) (1992) 597-605

[17] Koenderink, J.J., van Doorn, A.J.: Receptive-Field Families. Biol. Cybern. 63(4) (1990) 291-297

[18] Koenderink, J.J., van Doorn, A.J.: Representation of Local Geometry in the Visual-System. Biol. Cybern. 55(6) (1987) 367-375

[19] Romeny, B.M.T., Florack, L.M.J., Salden, A.H., Viergever, M.A.: Higher-Order Differential Structure of Images. Image Vis. Comput. 12(6) (1994) 317-325

[20] Lindeberg, T.: Scale-Space for Discrete Signals. IEEE Trans. Patt. Anal. Mach. Intell. 12(3) (1990) 234-254

[21] Marr, D.: Vision. W H Freeman & co, New York (1982)

[22] Davies, E.R.: On the noise suppression and image enhancement characteristics of the median, truncated median and mode filters. Patt. Recog. Lett. 7(2) (1988) 87-97

[23] Evans, A.N., Nixon, M.S.: Mode filtering to reduce ultrasound speckle for feature extraction. IEE Proc. Visual. Image & Sig. Process. 142(2) (1995) 87-94

[24] Torroba, P.L., Cap, N.L., Rabal, H.J., Furlan, W.D.: Fractional order mean in image processing. Opt. Eng. 33(2) (1994) 528-533

[25] Guichard, F., Morel, J.-M.: Partial differential equations and image iterative filtering, CEREMADE, Université Paris IX, Paris.

[26] Weickert, J.: Anisotropic Diffusion in Image Processing. Teubner, Stuttgart (1998)

[27] Viola, P.A.: Alignment by Maxsimization of Mutual Information, In: Artificial Intelligence Laboratory, Massachusetts Institute of Technology, pp. 156.

[28] Maintz, J.B.A., Viergever, M.A.: A survey of medical image registration. Med. Image Anal. 2(1) (1998) 1-36

[29] Cover, T.M., Thomas, J.A.: Elements of Information Theory. John Wiley & Sons (1991)

[30] Studholme, C., Hill, D.L.G., Hawkes, D.J.: An overlap invariant entropy measure of 3D medical image alignment. Pattern Recognit. 32(1) (1999) 71-86

[31] Pluim, J.P.W., Maintz, J.B.A., Viergever, M.A.: Image registration by maximization of combined mutual information and gradient information. IEEE Trans. Med. Imaging 19(8) (2000) 809-814

Indentation and Protrusion Detection
and Its Applications

Tim K. Lee[1,2], M. Stella Atkins[2], Ze-Nian Li[2]

[1] BC Cancer Agency, Cancer Control Research Program, Vancouver, BC, Canada, V5Z 4E6
tlee@bccancer.bc.ca
[2] Simon Fraser University, School of Computing Science, Burnaby, BC, Canada, V5A 1S6
{tklee,stella,li}@cs.sfu.ca

Abstract. In this paper, we investigated the mechanism of dividing a 2D-object border into a set of local and global indentation and protrusion segments by extending the classic curvature scale-space filtering method. The resultant segments, arranged in hierarchical structures, can represent the object shape. Applying this technique, we derived a border irregularity measure for pigmented skin lesions. The measure correlated well with experienced dermatologists' evaluations and may be useful for measuring the malignancy of the lesion. Furthermore, we can use the method to discover all the bays in an aerial map.

1 Introduction

Shape decomposition is an important technique for computer vision or image understanding systems. Dividing an object into parts forms a logical hierarchical structure of the part shapes, which can help us understand the object.

There are many approaches to partition an object. Generalized-cylinders [1] and superquadrics [2, 3] methods model shape parts by predefined geometric primitives. Blum and Nagal [4] proposed to divide an object according to its symmetric axes. The high curvature points of an object border, which are considered to possess *high information content* [5], have also been used for shape decomposition. Hoffman and Richards [6, 7] partitioned an object border at the concave tips. Siddiqi and Kimia's [8] neck-based and limb-based approach to object decomposition also put the terminals of part-lines at the concave tips. However, the above methods cannot produce a full set of indentation and protrusion segments.

In this paper, we present an algorithm, which is an extension of the classic curvature scale-space filtering technique, to partition a 2D planar curve into two sets of local and global indentation and protrusion segments. Then we discuss two applications for such a boundary decomposition technique. The first application is to measure the border irregularity of a pigment skin lesion, which may indicate the malignancy of the lesion. Another application is to detect a set of bays, arranged in a hierarchical structure, from aerial maps.

The paper is organized as follows: Sect. 2 briefly describes the classic curvature scale-space filtering technique. Sect. 3 defines indentation and protrusion segments.

M. Kerckhove (Ed.) : Scale-Space 2001, LNCS 2106, pp. 335-343, 2001.

Sect. 4 presents the algorithm of detecting all indentation and protrusion segments. Sect. 5 shows the duality between the classic and the extended curvature scale-space images. Sect. 6 discusses the two applications and Sect. 7 concludes the discussion.

2 Classic Curvature Scale-Space

The classic curvature scale-space filtering technique extracts curvature zero-crossing points from a 2D-object border in a multi-scale environment [9, 10]. The idea begins with a smoothing process of the object border $L(t)$, which is parameterized by the path length variable t and is in C^2. The smoothing process is achieved by a series of Gaussian convolutions with a family of kernels $g(t, \sigma)$ of increasing σ. The curvature function $K(t, \sigma)$ of the smoothed border $L(t, \sigma)$ is defined as:[1]

$$K(t,\sigma) = \frac{\dfrac{\partial X}{\partial t}\dfrac{\partial^2 Y}{\partial t^2} - \dfrac{\partial^2 X}{\partial t^2}\dfrac{\partial Y}{\partial t}}{\{(\dfrac{\partial X}{\partial t})^2 + (\dfrac{\partial Y}{\partial t})^2\}^{3/2}}. \tag{1}$$

During the smoothing process, σ controls the amount of smoothing. At some large σ, all concavities on the border are removed and the process is terminated. Fig. 1 demonstrates the smoothing process of a planar closed curve.

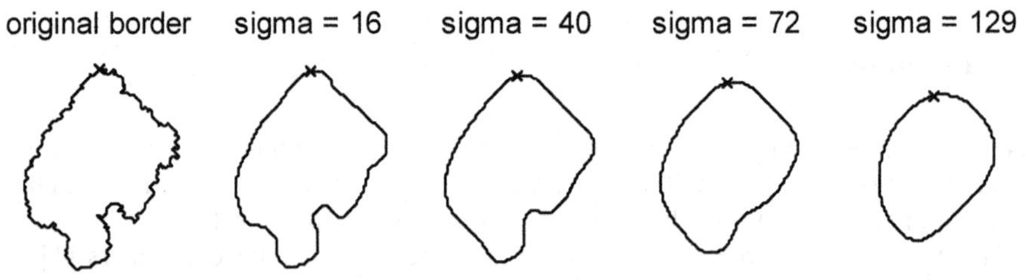

original border   sigma = 16   sigma = 40   sigma = 72   sigma = 129

Fig. 1. Gaussian smoothing process for a planar closed curve. The initial parameterization point is marked as 'x' in each subfigure. The smoothing σ level is specified at the top of the subfigure. The σ_{term}, the σ level when all concavities are removed, for this example is 129.

For a smoothed border, the curvature zero-crossings are the points that satisfy the following conditions:

$$K(t,\sigma) = 0, \qquad \frac{\partial K(t,\sigma)}{\partial t} \neq 0. \tag{2}$$

Zero-crossings of all smoothed borders are computed and a 2D scale-space image is employed to record the captured feature points. Fig. 2a shows the classic curvature scale-space image for Fig. 1.

---

[1] With our convention, using counterclockwise tracing along the border and image coordinate system (i.e. the origin is in the top-left corner), positive curvature values imply concavity, while negative curvature values imply convexity.

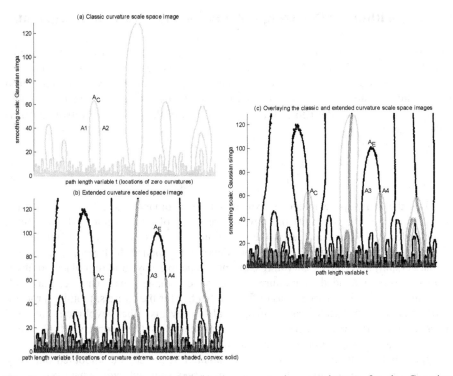

Fig. 2. The classic (a) and extended (b) curvature scale-space images for the Gaussian smoothing process shown in Fig. 1. (c) The overlay of (a) and (b).

The classic curvature scale-space image has been used to match 2D objects from a database [9, 10] and to detect corners from an image [11]. However, these systems are not designed to analyse indentation and protrusion curve segments.

3   Definition of Indentation and Protrusion Segments

To define indentation and protrusion curve segments, we exploit the characteristics of the curvature function $K(t)$ of a curve function $L(t)$. The curvature function portrays the curve in two ways. The sign of $K(t)$ indicates the type of bending (concavity or convexity) at the point t and the magnitude denotes the amount of bending. Local curvature extrema, located by the zero-crossings of the first derivative of $K(t)$ with respect to t ($K'(t)=0$, $K''(t) \neq 0$), mark the tip points of the curve segment, whose type is determined by the corresponding sign of $K(t)$. Therefore, we define an indentation/protrusion segment as a curve segment composed of three consecutive local curvature extrema $[t_1, t_2, t_3]$. The middle curvature extremum t_2 determines the segment tip point and the segment type. For example, when t_2 is a concave curvature extremum, $K(t_2) > 0$, the corresponding segment is an indentation segment. The local curvature extrema t_1 and t_3 delimit the extent of the segment. $K(t_1)$ and $K(t_3)$ have the same sign, which are different from $K(t_2)$.

4   Algorithm for Detecting Indentation and Protrusion Segments

The details of the algorithm for detecting all indentation and protrusion segments have been published elsewhere [12]; therefore, only an overview is presented here.

To analyse indentation/protrusion segments, local curvature *extrema* are chosen to be the investigated feature of our extended curvature scale-space image. These curvature extrema are defined as the zero-crossings of the partial derivative of $K(t,\sigma)$ with respect to t, i.e.

$$\frac{\partial K(t,\sigma)}{\partial t} = 0, \qquad \frac{\partial^2 K(t,\sigma)}{\partial t^2} \neq 0. \tag{3}$$

Also, the scale-space image is extended from a binary image to a three-valued image to encode the concavity or convexity property of the curvature extrema. Such an extended scale-space image for the smoothing process of Fig. 1 is depicted in Fig. 2b, where concave curvature extrema are denoted by shaded thick points (red in the online version) and convex curvature extrema are denoted by solid thin black points.

From our extended curvature scale-space image, we can capture all indentation/protrusion segments as defined in Sect. 3 for the entire smoothing process. Furthermore, our scale-space image also reveals the evolution of the indentation/protrusion segments. Because of the causality property of Gaussian smoothing [13, 14], segments are smoothed out in a 'proper' order: small ones disappear before larger ones. When some smaller segments are smoothed out, they may merge into some larger segments. The larger segments are considered as the *global* segments to the smaller *local* ones. Hence, indentation/protrusion segments can be grouped into hierarchical structures. In addition, the *true* location of an indentation/protrusion segment can be pinpointed by coarse-to-fine tracking of the segment to the zeroth-scale, the original non-smoothed curve.

5   Classic and Extended Curvature Scale-Space Images

The classic and the extended curvature scale-space images form a dual space because these two images are constructed by different feature points of the smoothed borders. Fig. 2c depicts the overlay of Fig. 2a and 2b. In this section, we present the parallel properties and the differences for these two images.

Property 1a: *In classic curvature scale-space images, the apex of a contour arc is the point (τ,ξ) such that $K(\tau,\xi)=0$ and $\partial K(\tau,\xi)/\partial t=0$.*[2]

For any σ in the internal of $[0, \xi)$ in the classic curvature scale-space image, let the points t_1 and t_2 be the curvature zero-crossings at the two sides of the contour arc. Since $K(t_1, \sigma) = K(t_2, \sigma) = 0$ and K is a continuous function, according to Rolle's Theorem, there exists a point t_3 such that $t_1 < t_3 < t_2$ and $\partial K(t_3, \sigma)/\partial t = 0$ in K-t space.

---

[2] Note that the apex point (τ,ξ) of a contour arc is not selected in the classic curvature scale-space process due to the definition of the process as expressed in Eqn 2. However, the property of the point can be derived.

At the smoothing level ξ, the points t_1, t_2 and t_3 merge together to the point τ. Because K is continuous, $K(\tau,\xi)=0$ and $\partial K(\tau,\xi)/\partial t=0$.

Property 1b: *In extended curvature scale-space images, the apex of a contour arc is the point* (τ, ζ) *such that* $\partial K(\tau,\xi)/\partial t=0$ *and* $\partial^2 K(\tau,\xi)/\partial t^2=0$.[3]

For any σ in the internal of $[0, \xi)$ in the extended curvature scale-space image, let the points t_1 and t_2 be the curvature extrema at the two sides of the contour arc. Since $\partial K(t_1, \sigma)/\partial t = \partial K(t_2, \sigma)/\partial t = 0$ and $\partial K/\partial t$ is a continuous function, according to Rolle's Theorem, there exists a point t_3 such that $t_1 < t_3 < t_2$ and $\partial^2 K(t_3, \sigma)/\partial t^2 = 0$ in $\partial K/\partial t$-t space. At the smoothing level ξ, the points t_1, t_2 and t_3 merge together to the point τ. Because $\partial K/\partial t$ is continuous, $\partial K(\tau,\xi)/\partial t=0$ and $\partial^2 K(\tau,\xi)/\partial t^2=0$.

Property 2a: *In classic curvature scale-space images, excluding the apex point, one side of a contour arc has the property* $\partial K/\partial t > 0$ *and the other side of the contour arc has the property* $\partial K/\partial t < 0$.

Assume the contour apex is the point (τ,ξ) in the classic curvature scale-space image. For any σ in the internal of $[0, \xi)$ of the smoothing axis, let the points t_1 and t_2 be the curvature zero-crossings at the two sides of the contour arc. By definition, $K(t_1, \sigma) = 0$ and $\partial K(t_1, \sigma)/\partial t \neq 0$. Without loss of generality, we assume $\partial K(t_1, \sigma)/\partial t > 0$. In other words, K crosses the zero from below at t_1 in the K-t space. Because K is continuous, for K to cross the next zero at t_2, K must crosses the zero from above, $\partial K(t_2, \sigma)/\partial t < 0$. Otherwise, there exists a curvature zero-crossing in between t_1 and t_2, which contradicts the classic curvature scale-space process. Therefore, the partial derivatives of $\partial K(t_1, \sigma)/\partial t$ and $\partial K(t_2, \sigma)/\partial t$ must have different sign.

To complete our argument for the property, we have to show that if $\partial K(t_1, \sigma)/\partial t > 0$, all curvature zero-crossings in the same side of the contour arc must have the property $\partial K/\partial t > 0$. Since $\partial K(t_1, \sigma)/\partial t > 0$ and $\partial K/\partial t = 0$ only at the contour apex (τ,ξ), moving along the contour arc from (t_1, σ) to (τ,ξ) in the $\partial K/\partial t$ surface cannot go to negative because $\partial K/\partial t$ is continuous. Therefore, the curvature zero-crossings along the same side as t_1 have the property $\partial K/\partial t > 0$.

Property 2b: *In extended curvature scale-space images, excluding the apex point, one side of a contour arc has the property* $\partial^2 K/\partial t^2 > 0$ *and the other side of the contour arc has the property* $\partial^2 K/\partial t^2 < 0$.

The argument is parallel to property 2a if we can show $\partial^2 K/\partial t^2$ is a continuous function. Since the border L_0 is C^2, the smoothed border $L(t, \sigma)$ and curvature K are C^3 and $\partial^2 K/\partial t^2$ is C^1. Therefore, $\partial^2 K/\partial t^2$ is a continuous function.

Assume the contour apex is the point (τ,ζ) in the extended curvature scale-space image. For any σ in the internal of $[0, \zeta)$ of the smoothing axis, let the points t_1 and t_2 be the curvature extrema at the two sides of the contour arc. By definition, $\partial K(t_1, \sigma)/\partial t = 0$, $\partial^2 K(t_1, \sigma)/\partial t^2 \neq 0$. Without loss of generality, we assume $\partial^2 K(t_1, \sigma)/\partial t^2 > 0$. In other words, ∂K crosses the zero from below at t_1 in the $\partial K/\partial t$-t space. Because $\partial K/\partial t$ is continuous, for $\partial K/\partial t$ to cross the next zero at t_2, $\partial K/\partial t$ must cross the zero from above, i.e., $\partial^2 K(t_2, \sigma)/\partial t^2 < 0$. Otherwise, there exists a curvature extrema in

---

[3] Note that the apex point (τ,ξ) of a contour arc is not selected in the extended curvature scale-space process due to the definition of the process as expressed in Eqn 3. However, the property of the point can be derived.

between t_1 and t_2, which contradicts the extended curvature scale-space process. Therefore, $\partial^2 K(t_1, \sigma)/\partial t^2$ and $\partial^2 K(t_2, \sigma)/\partial t^2$ must have different sign.

To complete our argument for the property, we have to show that if $\partial^2 K(t_1, \sigma)/c t^2 > 0$, all curvature extrema in the same side of the contour arc must have the property $\partial^2 K/\partial t^2 > 0$. Since $\partial^2 K(t_1, \sigma)/\partial t^2 > 0$ and $\partial^2 K/\partial t^2 = 0$ only at the contour apex (τ, ζ), moving along the contour arc from (t_1, σ) to (τ, ξ) in the $\partial^2 K/\partial t^2$ surface cannot go to negative because $\partial^2 K/\partial t^2$ is continuous. Therefore, the curvature extrema along the same side as t_1 have the property $\partial^2 K/\partial t^2 > 0$.

Property 3: *In the contours of an extended curvature scale-space image, the points where the concave extrema and convex extrema meet are the zero curvature points.*

The curvature of a convex curvature extremum is less than 0 and the curvature of a concave curvature extremum is greater than 0; hence, the meeting point has the property of zero curvature. The Points A_C and A4 in Fig. 2b are the examples of such points.

Even though the extended curvature scale-space process computes the locations of curvature extrema, some curvature zero-crossings can be easily identified using the three-valued scale-space image. However, there is no corresponding property for the classic curvature scale-space image.

Property 4a: *In classic curvature scale-space images, all curvature zero-crossings disappear at σ_{term}.*

When a Gaussian smoothing process terminates at σ_{term}, the object border is transformed into an oval shape with convex curvature for the entire border (i.e. $K(t, \sigma_{term}) < 0$ for all t); therefore, all curvature zero-crossings disappear.

Property 4b: *In extended curvature scale-space images, all curvature extrema may disappear (a special case of a circle) or at least 4 curvature extrema remain at σ_{term}.*

When a Gaussian smoothing process terminates at σ_{term}, the object border is transformed into an oval shape with convex curvature for the entire border (i.e. $K(t, \sigma_{term}) < 0$ for all t). In a special case, $K(t, \sigma_{term})$ is a negative constant (i.e. a circle) and there will be no curvature extremum. Otherwise, curvature extrema must exist. Since an ellipse has 4 curvature extrema, there must be at least 4 curvature remains at σ_{term} for the oval shaped border.

6   Applications

6.1   Differentiating Malignant Melanomas from Benign Nevi

The indentation and protrusion segments obtained from an object border can be used to describe the object shape. One of the applications for the technique is to analyse the border irregularity of the 2D projection of an object. In particular, this technique has been used to measure the border irregularity of skin pigmented lesions, commonly known as moles, which may indicate the malignancy of the lesion [12, 15, 16].

Moles are mostly benign; however, some of them are malignant melanomas, the most fatal form of skin cancer. Benign moles usually have a round or oval shape with regular contour and uniform colour. Fig. 3a shows a typical benign nevus. On the other hand, malignant melanomas are usually described as enlarged lesions with multiple shades of colours. Furthermore, their borders tend to be irregular and asymmetric with protrusions and indentations [17, 18]. Fig. 3b shows a malignant melanoma.

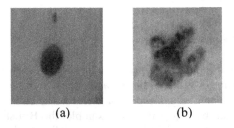

(a)   (b)

Fig. 3. Pigmented skin lesion (a) Benign nevus (b) Malignant melanoma.

Among the clinical characteristics (size, colour and irregular border shape) of skin pigmented lesions, border irregularity is one of the important clinical features differentiating benign nevi from malignant melanomas. There are two types of border irregularity: texture and structure irregularities. Texture irregularities are the small variations along the border, while structure irregularities are the global indentations and protrusions that may suggest either the unstable growth in a lesion or regression of a melanoma. An accurate measurement of structure irregularities is essential to detect the malignancy of melanoma [19].

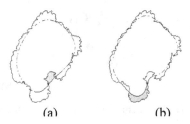

(a)   (b)

Fig. 4. The largest indentation (a) and protrusion (b) for a lesion border.

Our extended curvature scale-space filtering technique can be used to measure the structure border irregularity of a pigmented skin lesion by locating a set of global indentation/protrusion segments along the border. An area-based index, called irregularity index, is generated to measure the severity of irregularity for each segment. We compare the area difference between the smoothed segment at the smooth-out sigma level and the original non-smoothed segment. The ratio of the affected area difference over the area of the smoothed object is used to define the irregularity index of a segment [12]. For example, Fig. 4 shows the affected area difference (shaded) of a segment in the smoothing process, between the lesion border (shown by the solid line) and a smoothed border (shown by the dashed line) at the smooth-out level for the largest indentation (a) or protrusion (b). The overall irregularity index is computed by summing all individual irregularity indices. Because all global irregular segments are analysed, the measure is sensitive to structure irregularities. A user study showed that the overall irregularity index correlated well with experienced dermatologists' evaluations of the malignancy of a lesion. The preliminary results of the user study have been reported in [16].

6.2 Detecting Bays from Aerial Maps

To analyse aerial maps, one may represent a bay of the landmass by an indentation segment of the coastline. When all local and global indentation segments of the coastline are computed and organized in a hierarchical structure, the hierarchical structure of the bays can be detected.[4] For example, the British coastline, shown in Fig. 5a, can be divided into 7 global bay areas, according to the algorithm discussed in Sect. 4. As we move down the hierarchical structure of one of the global bays in the west side of the British coastline as shown in Fig. 5b, smaller bays are discovered.

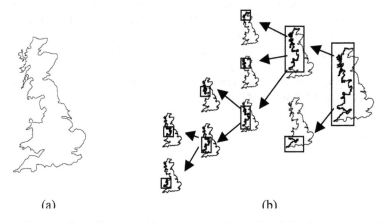

(a)   (b)

Fig. 5. (a) British coastline. (b) Hierarchical structure of bays (highlighted) at the west side of the British coastline.

7   Conclusions

We presented an extended curvature scale-space filtering technique to partition a 2D planar-closed curve into a set of indentation and protrusion segments, which can be used to describe the shape of the object. The extended and classic techniques form a dual space and their similarities and differences have been compared. Two applications for the extended technique have been discussed. A stable border irregularity index for skin pigmented lesion can be derived. Preliminary results showed that the index correlated well with experienced dermatologists' evaluations of

---

[4] A set of peninsulas can also be detected if the protrusion segments are analysed.

the malignancy of a lesion.   Also, we can discover the bays of a coastline by computing all indentation segments and organized them into a hierarchical structure.

References

1. Nevaita, R., Binford, T.O.: Description and recognition of curved objects. Artificial Intelligence 8 (1977) 77-98.
2. Pentland, A.P.: Recognition by parts. In: IEEE International Conference on Computer Vision (1987) 612-620.
3. Lou, S.L., Chang, C.L., Lin, K.P., Chen, T.S.: Object-based deformation technique for 3D CT lung nodule detection. In: SPIE Medical Imaging, San Diego (1999) 1544-1552.
4. Blum, H., Nagel, R.N.: Shape description using weighted symmetric axis features. Pattern Recognition 10 (1978) 167-180.
5. Attneave, F.: Some informational aspects of visual perception. Psychol. Rev. 61 (1954) 183-193.
6. Hoffman, D.D., Richards, W.A.: Parts of recognition. Cognition 18 (1985) 65-96.
7. Richards, W., Hoffman, D.D.: Condon Constraints on Closed 2D Shapes. Computer Vision, Graphics, and Image Processing 31 (1985) 265-281.
8. Siddiqi, K., Kimia, B.B.: Parts of visual form: computational aspects. IEEE Transactions on Pattern Analysis and Machine Intelligence 17 (1995) 239-251.
9. Mokhtarian, F., Mackworth, A.: Scale-based description and recognition of planar curves and two-dimensional shapes. IEEE Transactions on Pattern Analysis and Machine Intelligence 8 (1986) 34-43.
10. Mokhtarian, F.: Silhouette-based object recognition through curvature scale space. IEEE Transactions on Pattern Analysis and Machine Intelligence 17 (1995) 539-544.
11. Mokhtarian, F., Suomela, R.: Robust image corner detection through curvature scale space. IEEE Transactions Pattern Analysis and Machine Intelligence 20 (1998) 1376-1381.
12. Lee, T.K., Atkins, M.S.: A new approach to measure border irregularity for melanocytic lesions. In: SPIE Medical Imaging 2000, San Diego (2000) 668-675.
13. Mokhtarian, F., Mackworth, A.K.: A theory of multiscale, curvature-based shape representation for planar curves. IEEE Transactions on Pattern Analysis and Machine Intelligence 14 (1992) 789-805.
14. Lindeberg, T.: Scale-space Theory in Computer Vision Kluwer Academic Publishers, Boston (1994).
15. Lee, T., Atkins, S., Gallagher, R., MacAulay, C., Coldman, A., McLean, D.: Describing the structural shape of melanocytic lesions. In: SPIE Medical Imaging 1999, San Diego (1999) 1170-1179.
16. Lee, T.K., Atkins, M.S.: A new shape measure for melanocytic lesions. In: Medical Image Understanding and Analysis 2000, London, England (2000) 25-28.
17. Maize, J.C., Ackerman, A.B.: Pigmented Lesions of the Skin Lea & Febiger, Philadelphia (1987).
18. Rivers, J.K.: Melanoma. Lancet 347 (1996) 803-807.
19. Claridge, E., Hall, P.N., Keefe, M., Allen, J.P.: Shape analysis for classification of malignant melanoma. Journal Biomed. Eng. 14 (1992) 229-234.

Geodesic Active Contours Applied to Texture Feature Space

Chen Sagiv[1], Nir A. Sochen[1], and Yehoshua Y. Zeevi[2]

[1] Department of Applied Mathematics
University of Tel Aviv
Ramat-Aviv, Tel-Aviv 69978, Israel
chensagi@post.tau.ac.il, sochen@math.tau.ac.il
[2] Department of Electrical engineering
Technion - Israel Institute of Technology
Technion City, Haifa 32000, Israel
zeevi@ee.technion.ac.il

Abstract. Gabor Analysis is frequently used for texture analysis and segmentation. Once the Gaborian feature space is generated it may be interpreted in various ways for image analysis and segmentation. Image segmentation can also be obtained via the application of "snakes" or active contour mechanism, which is usually used for gray-level images. In this study we apply the active contour method to the Gaborian feature space of images and obtain a method for texture segmentation. We calculate six localized features based on the Gabor transform of the image. These are the mean and variance of the localized frequency,orientation and intensity. This feature space is presented, via the Beltrami framework, as a Riemannian manifold. The stopping term, in the geodesic snakes mechanism, is derived from the metric of the features manifold. Experimental results obtained by application of the scheme to test images are presented.

1 Introduction

Gaborian approach to image processing and analysis has been motivated by biological principles of image representation at the level of the primary visual cortex. The Gabor framework has been extensively used over the last fifteen years for texture analysis and segmentation [15,11,1].

The motivation for using Gabor filters in texture analysis is double fold. First, it appears as though simple cells in the visual cortex can be well modeled by Gabor functions [12,4], and that the Gabor scheme provides a suitable representation for visual information in the combined frequency-position space [14]. Second, the Gabor representation is optimal in the sense of minimizing the joint two-dimensional uncertainty in the combined spatial-frequency space [5].

Once the Gabor feature space of an image is generated, it may be used for texture segmentation. The fundamental question is how to extract the features which enable us to discriminate between textures. Porat and Zeevi have proposed [15] to extract six localized features that can describe textures: the first

M. Kerckhove (Ed.): Scale-Space 2001, LNCS 2106, pp. 344–352, 2001.
© Springer-Verlag and IEEE/CS 2001

two moments of the spatial frequency, orientation of the spatial frequency and intensity information. The six resulting features were used for texture analysis and synthesis.

Segmentation is another important task in image processing. Since the introduction of "snakes" or active contours [6], this method has been extensively used for boundary detection in gray-level images. In this framework an initial contour is deformed towards the boundary of an object to be detected. The evolution equation is derived from minimization of an energy functional, which obtains a minimum for a curve located at the boundary of the object.

The geodesic or geometric active contours model [3,7] offers a different perspective for solving the boundary detection problem; It is based on the observation that the energy minimization problem is equivalent to finding a geodesic curve in a Riemannian space whose metric is derived from the image contents. The geodesic curve can be found via a geometric flow. Utilization of the Osher and Sethian level set numerical algorithm [16] allows automatic handling of changes of topology.

This snakes' model was extended to the vector valued active contours to handle more complex scenery such as color images [17] and multi-texture images. Some recent related work includes the one of Paragios and Deriche [13] who generate the image texture feature space by filtering the image using Gabor filters. Texture information is then expressed using statistical measurements, and segmentation is achieved by application of geodesic snakes to the statistical feature space. Shah [18] developed and applied curve evolution and segmentation algorithms where anisotropic metrics were considered. Lorigo et al [10] used both image intensity and its variance for MRI image segmentation.

It was shown recently that the Gaborian spatial-feature space can be described, via the Beltrami framework, as a 4D Riemannian manifold embedded in R^6 [8]. Based on this approach we aim to generalize the intensity based geodesic active contours method to the Gabor-feature space of images. The stopping term, in the geodesic snakes mechanism, is generalized and derived from the metric of the Gabor spatial-feature manifold. We treat the localized texture features suggested in [15] as a multi-valued image and apply the geodesic snakes mechanism to it.

2   Geodesic Active Contours

In this section we review the geodesic and geometric active contours method in the context of gray-level images [3,7].

Let $\mathbf{C}(\mathbf{q}) : [0, 1] \to R^2$ be a parametrized curve, and let $I : [0, a] \times [0, b] \to R^+$ be the given image. Let $E(r) : [0, \infty[\to R^+$ be an inverse edge detector, so that E approaches zero when r approaches infinity. Minimizing the energy functional proposed in the classical snakes is generalized to finding a geodesic curve in a Riemannian space by minimizing:

$$L_R = \int E(|\nabla I(\mathbf{C}(q))|) \, |\mathbf{C}'(q)| dq. \tag{1}$$

The resultant evolution equation is the gradient descent flow:

$$\frac{\partial \mathbf{C}(t)}{\partial t} = E(|\nabla I|)k\mathbf{N} - (\nabla E \cdot \mathbf{N})\,\mathbf{N}, \tag{2}$$

where k denotes curvature.

Defining a function U, such that $\mathbf{C} = ((x, y)|U(x, y) = 0)$, we may use the Osher-Sethian Level-Sets approach [16] and obtain an evolution equation for the embedding function U:

$$\frac{\partial U(t)}{\partial t} = |\nabla U|\mathrm{Div}\left(E(|\nabla I|)\frac{\nabla U}{|\nabla U|}\right). \tag{3}$$

A popular choice for the stopping function $E(|\nabla I|)$ is given by:

$$E(I) = \frac{1}{1 + |\nabla I|^2}, $$

but other functions have been considered as well.

3   Feature Space and Gabor Transform

The Gabor scheme and Gabor filters have been studied by numerous researchers in the context of image representation, texture segmentation and image retrieval. A Gabor filter centered at the 2D frequency coordinates (U, V) has the general form of:

$$h(x, y) = g(x', y')\exp(2\pi i(Ux + Vy)) \tag{4}$$

where

$$(x', y') = (x\cos(\phi) + y\sin(\phi), -x\sin(\phi) + y\cos(\phi)), \tag{5}$$

the $2D$ Gaussian window is

$$g(x, y) = \frac{1}{2\pi\sigma^2}\exp\left(-\frac{x^2}{2\lambda^2\sigma^2} - \frac{y^2}{2\sigma^2}\right), \tag{6}$$

λ is the aspect ratio between x and y scales, σ is the scale parameter, and the major axis of the Gaussian is oriented at angle ϕ relative to the x-axis and to the modulating sinewave gratings.

The Fourier transform of the Gabor function is, accordingly :

$$H(u, v) = \exp\left(-2\pi^2\sigma^2((u' - U')^2\lambda^2 + (v' - V')^2)\right), \tag{7}$$

where, (u', v') are rotated frequency axes and (U', V') are the rotated coordinates of the central frequency. Thus, $H(u, v)$ is a bandpass Gaussian with minor axis oriented at angle ϕ from the u-axis, and the radial center frequency F is defined by : $F = \sqrt{(U^2 + V^2)}$, with orientation $\theta = \arctan(V/U)$. Since maximal resolution in orientation is desirable, the filters whose sine gratings are cooriented with the major axis of the modulating Gaussian are usually considered ($\phi = \theta$ and $\lambda > 1$), and the Gabor filter is reduced to: $h(x, y) = g(x, y) \exp(2\pi i F x)$.

It is possible to generate Gabor-Morlet wavelets from a single mother-Gabor-wavelet by transformations such as: translations, rotations and dilations. We can generate, in this way, a set of filters for a known number of scales, S, and orientations K. We obtain the following filters for a discrete subset of transformations:

$$h_{mn}(x, y) = a^{-m} h(\frac{x'}{a^m}, \frac{y'}{a^m}), \tag{8}$$

where (x', y') are the spatial coordinates rotated by $\frac{\pi n}{K}$ and $m = 0...S - 1$. Alternatively, one can obtain Gabor wavelets by logarithmically distorting the frequency axis [14] or by incorporating multiwindows [20]. In the latter case one obtains a more general scheme wherein subsets of the functions constitute either wavelet sets or Gaborian sets.

The feature space of an image is obtained by the inner product of this set of Gabor filters with the image:

$$W_{mn}(x, y) = R_{mn}(x, y) + i J_{mn}(x, y) = I(x, y) * h_{mn}(x, y). \tag{9}$$

Next, we follow Porat and Zeevi [15] and extract six localized texture features from the Gabor feature space: dominant localized frequency (denoted MF), variance of the dominant localized frequency (VF), dominant orientation (MT), variance of the dominant orientation (VT), mean of the local intensity (MI) and variance of the localized intensity level (VI). This selection is based on the assumption that the primitives of natural textures are localized frequency components in the form of Gabor elementary functions. Therefore, texture analysis takes the form of inner product or correlation of such primitives with textured images.

The spatial frequencies are determined by the scale parameter a and a base frequency F_0 as: $F_m = F_0 * a^m$, where m is an integer. The dominant localized frequency is given by:

$$MF(x, y) = \frac{\sum_{i=1}^{m} \sum_{i=1}^{n} W_{mn}(x, y) F_m(x, y)}{\sum_{i=1}^{m} \sum_{i=1}^{n} W_{mn}(x, y)} \tag{10}$$

The variance of the localized frequency VF is

$$VF(x, y) = \frac{\sum_{i=1}^{m} |F_m(x, y) - MF(x, y)|}{m} \tag{11}$$

This feature represents the bandwidth of the localized spatial frequency. If it is normalized by the mean localized frequency we obtain a scale invariant feature.

$$VF_{normalized}(x, y) = \frac{VF(x, y)}{MF(x, y)} \tag{12}$$

The mean and variance of the orientation are defined by

$$MT(x, y) = \frac{\sum_{i=1}^{m} \sum_{i=1}^{n} W_{mn}(x, y) T_n(x, y)}{\sum_{i=1}^{m} \sum_{i=1}^{n} W_{mn}(x, y)} \tag{13}$$

$$VT(x,y) = \frac{\sum_{i=1}^{n} |T_n(x,y) - MT(x,y)|}{n} \tag{14}$$

where $T_n = \frac{\pi n}{K}$.

The local mean intensity and its variance are extracted to complete the set of features. If the image contains smooth segments then the gray level information is the only way to separate these regions. The locality of these features is accomplished by averaging the intensity level using a filter equal in size to the Gabor filter used to generate the Gabor-feature-space:

$$MI(x,y) = \frac{\sum_{x,y \in A} I(x,y)}{N}, \tag{15}$$

where A is the set of N pixels belonging to the area defined by the averaging filter window centered at (x,y) and $I(x,y)$ is the intensity image. The variance of the intensity level is given by

$$VI(x,y) = \frac{\sum_{x,y \in A} |I(x,y) - MI(x,y)|}{N} \tag{16}$$

4   Application of Geodesic Snakes to the Localized-Texture-Features-Space

Application of the geodesic snakes mechanism to the localized texture feature space, derived from the Gabor space of images, is achieved by generalizing the inverse edge indicator function E, which attracts in turn the evolving curve towards the boundary in the classical and geodesic snakes schemes. A special feature of our approach is the metric introduced in the localized texture feature space, and used as the building block for the stopping function E in the geodesic active contours scheme.

Sochen et al [19] proposed to view images and image feature space as Riemannian manifolds embedded in a higher dimensional space. For example, a gray scale image is a 2-dimensional Riemannian surface (manifold), with (x,y) as local coordinates, embedded in R^3 with (X,Y,Z) as local coordinates. The embedding map is $(X = x, Y = y, Z = I(x,y))$, and we write it, by abuse of notations, as (x,y,I). When we consider feature spaces of images, e.g. color space, statistical moments space, and the Gaborian space, we may view the image-feature information as a N-dimensional manifold embedded in a $N + M$ dimensional space, where N stands for the number of local parameters needed to index the space of interest and M is the number of feature coordinates. In our case, we may view the localized features image as a 2D manifold with local coordinates (x,y) embedded in a 8D feature space. The embedding map is (x,y,MF,VF,MT,VT,MI,VI).

MF,VF,MT,VT,MI,VI are functions of the local coordinates (x,y) and are the localized texture features, as described in the previous section.

A basic concept in the context of Riemannian manifolds is distance. For example, we take a two-dimensional manifold Σ with local coordinates (σ_1, σ_2).

Since the local coordinates are curvilinear, the distance is calculated using a positive definite symmetric bilinear form called the metric whose components are denoted by $g_{\mu\nu}(\sigma_1, \sigma_2)$: $ds^2 = g_{\mu\nu}d\sigma^\mu d\sigma^\nu$, where we used the Einstein summation convention : elements with identical superscripts and subscripts are summed over. The metric on the image manifold is derived using a procedure known as pullback [19]. The manifold's metric is then used for various geometrical flows. We shortly review the pullback mechanism [19].

Let $X : \Sigma \to M$ be an embedding of Σ in M, where M is a Riemannian manifold with a metric h_{ij} and Σ is another Riemannian manifold. We can use the knowledge of the metric on M and the map X to construct the metric on Σ. This pullback procedure is as follows:

$$(g_{\mu\nu})_\Sigma(\sigma^1, \sigma^2) = h_{ij}(X(\sigma^1, \sigma^2))\frac{\partial X^i}{\partial \sigma^\mu}\frac{\partial X^j}{\partial \sigma^\nu}, \qquad (17)$$

where we used the Einstein summation convention, $i, j = 1, \ldots, dim(M)$, and σ^1, σ^2 are the local coordinates on the manifold Σ.

If we pull back the metric of a $2D$ image manifold from the Euclidean embedding space (x,y,I) we get:

$$(g_{\mu\nu}(x, y)) = \begin{pmatrix} 1 + I_x^2 & I_x I_y \\ I_x I_y & 1 + I_y^2 \end{pmatrix}. \qquad (18)$$

The determinant of $g_{\mu\nu}$ yields the expression : $1 + I_x{}^2 + I_y{}^2$. Thus, we can rewrite the expression for the stopping term E in the geodesic snakes mechanism as follows:

$$E(|\nabla I|) = \frac{1}{1 + |\nabla I|^2} = \frac{1}{\det(g_{\mu\nu})}. \qquad (19)$$

The exact geometry of texture feature space is not known. Therefore, for simplicity, we assume it is Euclidean. Moreover, since we have no previous knowledge on the $2D$ feature-manifold metric, we assume that the distances measured on the $2D$ manifold are the same as those measured in the $8D$ embedding space. Thus, we may use the pullback mechanism to obtain the following metric:

$$(g_{\mu\nu}) = \begin{pmatrix} 1 + \sum_i(C_i A_x^i)^2 & \sum_i C_i C_i A_x^i A_y^i \\ \sum_i C_i C_i A_x^i A_y^i & 1 + \sum_i(C_i A_y^i)^2 \end{pmatrix} \qquad (20)$$

where $\mathbf{A} = (\mathbf{MF}, \mathbf{VF}, \mathbf{MT}, \mathbf{VT}, \mathbf{MI}, \mathbf{VI})$, C_i are regularization factors which account for the different physical dimensions for each parameter, and i goes over all members of this set.

The metric g derived in this section is strictly used for the purpose of calculating an edge detector. It is used to measure distances on manifolds and its components indicate the rate of change of the manifold given a certain direction. Therefore, the determinant of the metric is used as a positive definite edge indicator: A large value indicates a strong gradient, while a small value indicates where the manifold is almost flat. Thus, it is reasonable to set E to be the inverse of the determinant of $g_{\mu\nu}$.

5   Results and Discussion

In our application of geodesic snakes to textural images, we have used the
mechanism offered by Lee [9] to generate the Gabor wavelets for five scales
and eight orientations. In the geodesic snakes mechanism U was initiated to
be a signed distance function [3]. For simplicity, we have set the values of C_i
discussed in section 4 to be 1. Following are the results for a few test im-

Fig. 1. a. A synthetic image made up of 2D sinewave gratings containing background and object of different orientations (left). b. The stopping function E
(middle). c. The resultant boundary(right).

ages. For the complete set of full size images and a demo see the web-page:
`http://www-visl.technion.ac.il/scalespace01`.

In the first example (Fig. 1) the test image is a synthesized texture composed
of vertical and horizontal lines. Application of the geodesic snakes algorithm results in an accurate boundary. In the second example the test image is composed
of two textures which differ in their scale (Fig. 2). The resultant boundary is
located at the interior of the circles rather than on their exact boundary. The
reason for that might be that since the two textures are quite similar, the change
of scale is noted by the Gabor filters only when they are properly located within
the internal texture.

Our next example is composed of two different textures taken from the Brodatz album (Fig. 3). Since these textures are characterized by small variations
in their dominant scale and orientation the six localized features are submitted
to non linear smoothing prior to the generation of the stopping term E which
is also in turn smoothed by the same process. The non linear smoothing procedure used is the Beltrami flow as described in [19]. The degree of smoothing was
empirically determined to obtain satisfactory results.

We have shown that it is useful to extend the definition of the stopping term
E used in the geodesic snakes scheme to features other than intensity gradients.
In the original work the six localized features are used as vector components to
determine distance between textures [15]. This allows for determining the mean
value of these features for each texture. In the proposed segmentation process
the localized features are calculated for each pixel and therefore hold a large

Fig. 2. a. A synthetic image made up of 2D sinewave gratings containing background and object of different scales (left). b. The stopping function E (middle). c. The resultant boundary(right).

degree of intra-variation. Thus, if the texture is not homogeneous we may need higher statistical moments such as kurtosis of the localized texture features. Yet, we have shown that this algorithm can be successfully applied to textures that are characterized by a small degree of intra-variation.

Fig. 3. a. An image comprised of two textures taken from Brodatz album of textures [2] (left). b. The stopping function E (middle). c. The resultant boundary(right).

Acknowledgments: This research has been supported in part by the Israeli Ministry of Science, by the Ollendorff Minerva Center of the Technion, and by the Fund for Promotion of Research at the Technion.

References

1. A.C. Bovik and M. Clark and W.S. Geisler "Multichannel Texture Analysis Using Localized Spatial Filters", *IEEE Transactions on PAMI*, 12(1), 1990, 55-73.
2. P. Brodatz, Textures: A photographic album for Artists and Designers, New York, NY, Dover, 1996.

3. V. Caselles and R. Kimmel and G. Sapiro, "Geodesic Active Contours", *International Journal of Conputer Vision*, 22(1), 1997, 61-97.

4. J.G. Daugman, "Uncertainty relation for resolution in space, spatial frequency, and orientation optimized by two-dimensinal visual cortical filters", *J. Opt. Soc. Amer.* 2(7), 1985, 1160-1169.

5. D. Gabor "Theory of communication"*J. IEEE* , 93, 1946, 429-459.

6. M. Kaas, A. Witkin and D. Terzopoulos, "Snakes : Active Contour Models", *International Journal of Computer Vision*, 1, 1988, 321-331.

7. S. Kichenassamy, A. Kumar, P. Olver, A. Tannenbaum and A. Yezzi, "Gradient Flows and Geometric Active Contour Models",*Proceedings ICCV'95*, Boston, Massachusetts, 1995, 810-815.

8. R. Kimmel, R. Malladi and N. Sochen, "Images as Embedded Maps and Minimal Surfaces: Movies, Color, Texture, and Volumetric Medical Images",*International Journal of Computer Vision*, 39(2), 2000, 111-129.

9. T.S. Lee, "Image Representation using 2D Gabor-Wavelets", *IEEE Transactions on PAMI*, 18(10), 1996, 959-971.

10. L.M. Lorigo, O. Faugeras, W.E.L. Grimson, R. Keriven, R. Kikinis, "Segmentation of Bone in Clinical Knee MRI Using Texture-Based Geodesic Active Contours", *Medical Image Computing and Computer-Assisted Intervention*, 1998, Cambridge, MA, USA.

11. B.S. Manjunath and W.Y. Ma, "Texture features browsing and retrieval of image data", *IEEE Transactions on PAMI*, 18(8), 1996, 837-842.

12. S. Marcelja, "Mathematical description of the response of simple cortical cells", *J. Opt. Soc. Amer.*, 70, 1980, 1297-1300.

13. N. Paragios and R. Deriche, "Geodesic Active Regions for Supervised Texture Segmentation", *Proceedings of International Conference on Computer Vision*, 1999, 22-25.

14. M. Porat and Y.Y. Zeevi, "The generalized Gabor scheme of image representation in biological and machine vision", *IEEE Transactions on PAMI*, 10(4), 1988, 452-468.

15. M. Porat and Y.Y. Zeevi, "Localized texture processing in vision: Analysis and synthesis in the gaborian space", *IEEE Transactions on Biomedical Engineering*, 36(1), 1989, 115-129.

16. S.J. Osher and J.A. Sethian, "Fronts propagating with curvature dependent speed: Algorithms based on Hamilton-Jacobi formulations", *J of Computational Physics*, 79, 1988, 12-49.

17. G. Sapiro, "Vector Valued Active Contours", *Proc. IEEE Conference on Computer Vision and Pattern Recognition*, 680-685, 1996.

18. Jayant Shah, "Riemannian Drums, Anisotropic Curve Evolution and Segmentation",*Proceedings of Scale-Space 1999.*, Eds. Nielsen, P. Johansen, O.F. Olsen, J. Weickert, Springer, 129-140.

19. N. Sochen, R. Kimmel and R. Malladi , "A general framework for low level vision", *IEEE Trans. on Image Processing*, 7, (1998) 310-318.

20. M. Zibulski and Y.Y. Zeevi, "Analysis of multiwindow Gabor-type schemes by frame methods", *Applied and Computational Harmonic Analysis*, 4, 1997, 188-221.

Color Differential Structure

Bart M. ter Haar Romeny[1], Jan-Mark Geusebroek[2], Peter Van Osta[3],
Rein van den Boomgaard[2], and Jan J. Koenderink[4]

[1] Image Sciences Institute, Utrecht University, The Netherlands
[2] Intelligent Sensory Information Systems
University of Amsterdam, The Netherlands
[3] Biological Imaging Laboratory, Janssen Research Foundation, Beerse, Belgium
[4] Dept. Physics of Man, Utrecht University, The Netherlands

Abstract. The scale-space approach to the differential structure of color images was recently introduced by Geusebroek et al. [1,2], based on the pioneering work of Koenderink's Gaussian derivative color model [5]. To master this theory faster, we present the theory as a practical implementation in the computer algebra package Mathematica for the extraction of color differential structure. Many examples are given, the practical code examples enable easy extensive experimentation. High level programming is now fast: all examples run with 5-15 seconds on typical images on a typical modern PC.

1 Color Image Formation and Color Invariants

Color is an important extra dimension. Information extracted from color is useful for almost any computer vision task, like segmentation, surface characterization, etc. The field of color science is huge [6], and many theories exist. It is far beyond the scope of this paper to cover even a fraction of the many different approaches. We will focus on a single recent theory, based on scale-space models for the color sensitive receptive fields in the front-end visual system. We are especially interested in the extraction of multi-scale differential structure (derivatives) in the spatial and the wavelength domain of color images. What is color invariant structure? To understand that notion, we first have to study the process of color image formation.

The light spectrum falling onto the eye results from interaction between a light source, the object, and the observer. Color may be regarded as the measurement of spectral energy, and will be handled in the next section. Here, we only consider the interaction between light source and material. Before we see an object as having a particular color, the object needs to be illuminated. After all, in darkness objects are simply black. The emission spectra $l(\lambda)$ of common light sources are close to Planck's formula [6] (NB: λ in nm):

$$\mathrm{h} = 6.626176\ 10^{-34}; \mathrm{c} = 2.99792458\ 10^{8}; \mathrm{k} = 2.9979245810^{8};$$
$$\mathrm{l}[\lambda_-, \mathrm{T}_-] = 8\pi\mathrm{hc}(10^{-9}\lambda)^{-5}$$

where h is Planck's constant, k Boltzmann's constant, and c the velocity of light in vacuum. The *color temperature* of the emitted light is given by T, and typically

M. Kerckhove (Ed.): Scale-Space 2001, LNCS 2106, pp. 353–361, 2001.

ranges from $2500K$ (warm red light) to $10,000K$ (cold blue light). Note that the terms "warm" and "cold" are given by artists, and refer to the sensation caused by the light. Representative white light is, by convention, chosen to be at a temperature of $6500K$. However, in practice, all light sources between $10,000K$ and $2500K$ can be found. Planck's equation is adequate for incandescent light and halogen. The spectrum of daylight is slightly different, and is represented by a *correlated color temperature*. Daylight is close enough to the Planckian spectrum to be characterized by a equivalent parameter.

The part of the spectrum reflected by a surface depends on the surface *spectral reflection function*. The spectral reflectance is a material property, characterized by a function $c(\lambda)$. For planar, matte surfaces, the spectrum reflected by the material $e(\lambda)$ is simplified as the multiplication between the spectrum falling onto the surface $l(\lambda)$ and the surface spectral reflectance function $c(\lambda)$: $e(\lambda) = c(\lambda)l(\lambda)$.

At this point it is meaningful to introduce spatial extent, hence to describe the spatio-spectral energy distribution $e(x, y, \lambda)$ that falls onto the retina. Further, for three-dimensional objects the amount of light falling onto the object's surface depends on the energy flux, thus on the local geometry. Hence *shading* (and shadow) may be introduced as being a wavelength independent multiplication factor $m(x, y)$ in the range $[0, 1]$: $e(x, y, \lambda) = c(x, y, \lambda)l(\lambda)m(x, y)$. Note that the illumination $l(\lambda)$ is independent of position. Hence the equation describes spectral image formation of matte objects, illuminated by a single light source. For shiny surfaces the image formation equation has to be extended with an additive term describing the Fresnel reflected light, see [3] for more details.

The *structure* of the spatio-spectral energy distribution is due to the three functions c, l, and m. By making some general assumptions, these quantities may be derived from the measured image. Estimation of the object reflectance function c boils down to deriving material properties, the "true" color invariant which does not depend on illumination conditions. Estimation of the light source l is well known as the color constancy problem. Determining m is in fact estimating the shadows and shading in the image, and is closely related to the shape-from-shading problem.

For the extraction of color invariant properties from the spatio-spectral energy distribution we search for algebraic or differential expressions of e, which are independent of l and m. Hence the goal is to solve for differential expressions of e which results in a function of c only.

To proceed, note that the geometrical term m is only a function of spatial position. Differentiation with respect to λ, and normalization reduces the problem to only two functions: $e(\mathbf{x}, \lambda) = c(\mathbf{x}, \lambda)l(\lambda)m(\mathbf{x}) \Rightarrow \frac{1}{e(\mathbf{x},\lambda)}\frac{\partial e(\mathbf{x},\lambda)}{\partial \lambda} = \frac{l_\lambda}{l} + \frac{c_\lambda}{c}$ (indices indicate differentiation). After additional differentiation to the spatial variable x or y, the first term vanishes, since l only depends on λ

$$e[x_-,\lambda_-] = c[x, \lambda] \; l[\lambda] \; m[x];$$

$$\partial_x \left(\frac{\partial_\lambda e[x,\lambda]}{e[x,\lambda]} \right) //\text{shortnotation}$$

$$\frac{c c_{xy} - c_x c_y}{c^2}$$

The spatial derivative of the normalized wavelength derivative, after applying the chain rule,

$$D\left[\frac{D[e[x,y,\lambda],\ \lambda]}{e[x,y,\lambda]},x\right]\ //\texttt{shortnotation}$$

$$\frac{e\,e_{x\lambda}-e_x\,e_\lambda}{e^2}$$

is completely expressed in spatial and spectral derivatives of the observable spatio-spectral energy distribution.

We develop the differential properties of the invariant color-edge detector $\mathcal{E}=\frac{1}{e}\frac{\partial e}{\partial\lambda}$, where the measured spectral intensity $e=e(x,y,\lambda)$. Spatial derivatives of $\mathcal{E}$, like $\frac{\partial\mathcal{E}}{\partial c}$, contain derivatives to the spatial as well as to the wavelength dimension due to the chain rule. In the next section we will see that the zero-th, first and second order derivative-to-λ kernels are acquired from the transformed RGB space of the image directly. The derivatives to the spatial coordinates are acquired in the conventional way, i.e. convolution by a spatial Gaussian kernel.

2   Koenderink's Gaussian Derivative Color Observation Model

Spatial structure can be extracted from the data in the environment by measuring the N-jet of (scaled) derivatives to some order. For the spatial domain this has led to the family of Gaussian derivative kernels, sampling the spatial intensity distribution. These derivatives naturally occur in a local Taylor expansion of the signal.

Koenderink [5] proposed to take a similar approach to the sampling of the color dimension, i.e. the spectral information contained in the color. If we construct the Taylor expansion of the spatio-spectral energy distribution $e(x,y,\lambda)$ of the measured light to wavelength, in the fixed spatial point (x_0,y_0), and around a central wavelength λ_0 we get (to second order):

$$\texttt{Series[e[x0, y0, }\lambda\texttt{], \{}\lambda\texttt{, }\lambda\texttt{0, 2\}]}$$

$$\texttt{e[x0, y0, }\lambda\texttt{0]}+\texttt{e}^{(0,0,1)}\texttt{[x0, y0,}\lambda\texttt{0]}(\lambda-\lambda0)+$$

$$\frac{1}{2}\texttt{e}^{(0,0,2)}\texttt{[x0, y0, }\lambda\texttt{0]}(\lambda-\lambda0)^2+O[\lambda-\lambda0]^3$$

A physical measurement with an aperture is mathematically described with a convolution. So for a measurement of the luminance a with aperture function $G(x,\sigma)$ in the (here in the example 1D) spatial domain we get: $L(x;\sigma)=\int_{-\infty}^{\infty}L(x-y)G(y;\sigma)dy$ where y is the dummy spatial shift parameter running over all possible values. For the temporal domain we get $L(t;\sigma)=\int_{-\infty}^{\infty}L(t-s)G(s;\sigma)ds$ where s is the dummy temporal shift parameter running over all possible values in time. Based on this analogy, we might expect a measurement along the color dimension to look like: $L(\lambda;\sigma)=\int_{-\infty}^{\infty}L(\lambda-\mu)G(\mu;\sigma)d\mu$ where λ is the wavelength and μ is the dummy wavelength shift parameter.

In the scale-space model for vision the front-end visual system has implemented the shifted spatial kernels with a grid on the retina with receptive fields, so the shifting is implemented by the simultaneous measurement of all the neighboring receptive fields. The temporal kernels are implemented as time-varying lateral geniculate nucleus (LGN) and cortical receptive fields. However, in order to have a wide range of receptive fields which shift over the wavelength axis in sensitivity, would require a lot of different photo-sensitive dyes (rhodopsines) in the receptors with these different—shifted—color sensitivities. The visual system has opted for a cheaper solution: The convolution is calculated at just a single position on the wavelength axis, at around $\lambda_0 = 520$nm, with a standard deviation of the Gaussian kernel of about $\sigma_\lambda = 55$ nm. The integration is done over the range of wavelengths that is covered by the rhodopsines, i.e. from about 350 nm (blue) to 700 nm (red). The values for λ_0 and σ_0 are determined from the best fit of a Gaussian to the spectral sensitivity as measured psychophysically in humans, i.e. the Heering model.

So we get for the spectral intensity

$$e(\mathbf{x}, \lambda_0; \sigma_0) = \int_{\lambda_{\min}}^{\lambda_{\max}} e(\mathbf{x}, \lambda) G(\lambda, \lambda_0; \sigma_\lambda) d\lambda.$$

This is a 'static' convolution operation (i.e. inner product in function space). It is not a convolution in the familiar sense, because we don't shift over the whole wavelength axis. We just do a single measurement with a Gaussian aperture over the wavelength axis at the position a. Similarly, the derivatives to λ:

$$\frac{\partial e(\mathbf{x}, \lambda_0)}{\partial \lambda} = \sigma_\lambda \int_{\lambda_{\min}}^{\lambda_{\max}} e(\mathbf{x}, \lambda) \frac{\partial^2 G(\lambda, \lambda_0, \sigma_\lambda)}{\partial \lambda^2} d\lambda$$

and

$$\frac{\partial^2 e(\mathbf{x}, \lambda_0)}{\partial \lambda^2} = \sigma_\lambda^2 \int_{\lambda_{\min}}^{\lambda_{\max}} e(\mathbf{x}, \lambda) \frac{\partial^2 G(\lambda, \lambda_0, \sigma_\lambda)}{\partial \lambda^2} d\lambda$$

describe the first and second order spectral derivative respectively. The factors σ_λ and σ_λ^2 are included for the normalization, i.e. to make the Gaussian spectral kernels dimensionless.

In Fig. 1 the graphs of the 'static' normalized Gaussian spectral kernels to second order as a function of wavelength are given.

Color sensitive receptive fields come in the combinations red-green and yellow-blue center-surround receptive fields. The subtraction of yellow and blue in these receptive fields is well modeled by the first order derivative to λ, the subtraction of red and green minus the blue is well modeled by the second order derivative to λ. Alternatively, one can say that the zero-th order receptive field measures the luminance, the first order the 'blue-yellowness', and the second order the 'red-greenness'.

Note: the wavelength axis is a half axis. It is known that for a *half axis* (such as with positive-only values) a logarithmic parameterization is the natural way to 'step along' the axis. E.g. the scale axis is logarithmically sampled in scale-space (remember the 'orders of magnitudes'), the intensity is logarithmically

```
gaussλ[λ_,σ_] = D[gauss[λ,σ],λ];
gaussλλ[λ_,σ_] = D[gauss[λ,σ],{λ,2}];
λ0 = 520; σ0 = 55;
```

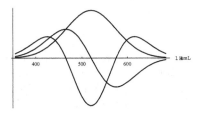

Fig. 1. The zero-th, first and second derivative of the Gaussian function with respect to wavelength as models for the color receptive field's wavelengths sensitivity in human color vision. After [Koenderink 1998a]. The central wavelength is 520 nm, the standard deviation 55 nm.

transformed in the photoreceptors, and the time axis can only be measured causally when we sample it logarithmically. We might conjecture here a better fit to the Heering model with a logarithmic wavelength axis.

The Gaussian color model needs the first three components of the Taylor expansion of the Gaussian weighted spectral energy distribution at λ_0 and scale σ_0. An RGB camera measures the red, green and blue component of the incoming light, but this is not what we need for the Gaussian color model. We need a method to extract the Taylor expansion terms from the RGB values.

An RGB camera approximates the CIE 1964 XYZ basis for colorimetry by the linear transformation matrix `rgb2xyz`, while Geusebroek et al. [2] give the best linear transform from the XYZ values to the Gaussian color model, i.e. matrix `xyz2e`:

$$
\mathbf{rgb2xyz} = \begin{pmatrix} 0.621 & 0.113 & 0.194 \\ 0.297 & 0.563 & 0.049 \\ -0.009 & 0.027 & 1.105 \end{pmatrix} \qquad \mathbf{xyz2e} = \begin{pmatrix} -0.019 & 0.048 & 0.011 \\ 0.019 & 0.000 & -0.016 \\ 0.047 & -0.052 & 0.000 \end{pmatrix}
$$

The resulting transform from the measured RGB input image to the sampling ' la human vision' is the product of the above matrices: `colorRF=xyz2e . rgb2xyz`.

The Gaussian color model is an approximation, but has the attractive property of fitting very well into Gaussian scale-space theory. The notion of image structure is extended to the wavelength domain in a very natural and coherent way. The similarity with human differential-color receptive fields is more than a coincidence.

Now we have all the tools to come to an actual implementation. The RGB values of the input image are transformed into Gaussian color model space, and plugged into the spatio-spectral formula for the color invariant feature. Next to the derivatives to wavelength we need spatial derivatives, which are computed in the regular way with spatial Gaussian derivative operators. The full machinery of e.g. gauge coordinates and invariance under specific groups of transformations is also applicable here. The next section details the implementation.

3   Implementation

In *Mathematica* a color image is represented as a two dimensional array of color triplets. The RGB triples are converted into measurements through the color receptive fields in the retina with the transformation matrix `colorRF` defined in the previous section. To transform every RGB triple we map the transformation to our input image as a pure function at the second list level:
`observedimage = Map[Dot[colorRF,#]&, im, 2];`.

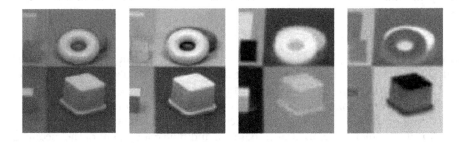

Fig. 2. The input image (left) and the observed images e, e_λ and $e_{\lambda\lambda}$ with the color differential receptive fields. Image resolution 228x179 pixels.

The color image data set can be smartly resliced by a reordering `Transpose`:

$$\texttt{obs = Transpose[observedimage, 2,3,1];}.$$

The resulting data set is a list of three scalar images, allowing us to access the measurements e, e_λ and $e_{\lambda\lambda}$ individually as scalar images (see Fig. 2).

We now develop the differential properties of our invariant color-edge detector $\mathcal{E} = \frac{1}{e}\frac{\partial e}{\partial \lambda}$, where the spectral intensity $e = e(x, y, \lambda)$. The derivatives to the spatial and spectral coordinates are easily found with the chainrule. Here are the explicit forms:

$$\mathcal{E} := \frac{\texttt{D[e[x,y,\lambda], \lambda]}}{\texttt{e[x,y,\lambda]}};$$
$$\texttt{shortnotation[}\quad \partial_x\mathcal{E}, \ \partial_y\mathcal{E}, \ \partial_\lambda\mathcal{E} \quad \texttt{]}$$
$$\left\{ \frac{ee_{x\lambda} - e_x e_\lambda}{e^2}, \frac{ee_{y\lambda} - e_y e_\lambda}{e^2}, \frac{-e_\lambda^2 + ee_{\lambda\lambda}}{e^2} \right\}$$

The gradient magnitude (detecting yellow-blue transitions) becomes:

$$\mathcal{G} = \texttt{Simplify[}\ \sqrt{(\partial_x \mathcal{E})^2 + (\partial_y \mathcal{E})^2}\ \texttt{]}$$

$$\mathcal{G}\ \texttt{// shortnotation}$$

$$\sqrt{\frac{(e\,e_{x\lambda} - e_x\,e_\lambda)^2 + (e\,e_{y\lambda} - e_y\,e_\lambda)^2}{e^4}}$$

The second spectral order gradient (detecting purple-green transitions) becomes:

$$\mathcal{W} = \texttt{Simplify[}\ \sqrt{(\partial_{x,\lambda}\mathcal{E})^2 + (\partial_{y,\lambda}\mathcal{E})^2}\ \texttt{]}$$

Finally, the total edge strength $\mathcal{N}$ (for all color edges) in the spatio-spectral domain becomes:

$$\mathcal{N} = \texttt{Simplify[}\ \sqrt{(\partial_x \mathcal{E})^2 + (\partial_y \mathcal{E})^2 + (\partial_{x,\lambda}\mathcal{E})^2 + (\partial_{y,\lambda}\mathcal{E})^2}\ \texttt{]};$$

As an example, we implement this last expression for discrete images. First we replace each occurrence of a derivative to λ with the respective plane in the observed image $\texttt{rf}$ (by the color receptive fields). Note that we use $\texttt{rf[[n}\lambda\texttt{+1]]}$ because the zero-th list element is the $\texttt{Head}$ of the list.

We will look for derivative patterns in the *Mathematica* expression for $\mathcal{N}$ and replace them with another pattern. We do this pattern matching with the command $\texttt{/.}$ ($\texttt{ReplaceAll}$). We call the observed image at this stage $\texttt{rf}$, without any assignment to data, so we can do all calculations symbolically first:

```
Clear[rf0, rf1, rf2, σ]; rf = {rf0, rf1, rf2};
𝒩 = 𝒩 /. { Derivative[nx_, ny_, nλ_][e][x, y, λ]
     :→ Derivative[nx, ny][rf[[nλ+1]]][x,y], e[x,y,λ]]
        :→ rf[[1]] } // Simplify;
```

Note that we do a delayed rule assignment here ($:\to$ instead of $\to$) because we

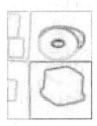

Fig. 3. The color-invariant $\mathcal{N}$ calculated for our input image at spatial scale $\sigma = 1$ pixel. Primarily the red-green color edges are found, as expected, with little edge detection at intensity edges. Image resolution 228x179 pixels.

want to evaluate the right hand side only after the rule is applied. We finally replace the spatial derivatives with the spatial Gaussian derivative convolution gD at scale σ:

$$\mathcal{N} = \mathcal{N} \ /. \ \{ \ \mathtt{Derivative[nx\_,ny\_][rf\_][x, \ y]}$$
$$\mathtt{:\rightarrow gD[rf,nx,ny,\sigma], \ rf1[x, \ y] :\rightarrow rf1,rf2[x, \ y] :\rightarrow rf2}\}$$

The resulting expression for the total edge strength can now safely be calculated on the discrete data (see Fig. 3). Equivalent expressions can be formulated for the yellow-blue edges $\mathcal{G}$ and the red-green edges $\mathcal{W}$, the results of these detectors are given in Fig. 4.

Fig. 4. Left: original color image. Middle: The yellow-blue edge detector $\mathcal{E}$ calculated at a spatial scale $\sigma = 1$ pixel. Note that there is hardly any red-green edge detection. Right: output of the red-green edge detector $\mathcal{W}$. Image resolution 249x269.

4   Combination with Spatial Constraints

Interesting combinations can be made when we combine the color differential operators with the spatial differential operators. E.g. when we want to detect specific blobs with a specific size and color, we can apply feature detectors that are best matching the shape to be found. We end the paper with one examples: locating PAS stained material in a histological preparation. This examples illustrates the possible use of color differential operators and spatial differential operators in microscopy.

Blobs are detected by calculating those locations (pixels) where the Gaussian curvature $\mathtt{lgc} = L_{xx}L_{yy} - L_{xy}^2$ on the black-and-white version ($\mathtt{imbw}$) of the image is greater then zero. This indicates a convex 'hilltop'. Pixels on the boundaries of the 'hilltop' are detected by requiring the second order directional derivative in the direction of the gradient $(L_x^2 L_{xx} + 2L_x L_{xy} + L_y^2 L_{yy})/(L_x^2 + L_y^2)$ to be positive. Interestingly, by using these invariant shape detectors we are largely independent of image intensity. For the color scheme we rely on $\mathcal{E}$ and its first and second order derivative to λ.

In Fig. 5 we detect stained carbohydrate deposits in a histological application using this combined color and spatial structure detection mechanism.

The Mathematica functions not described in the text and the images are available from the first author.

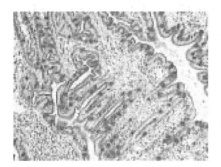 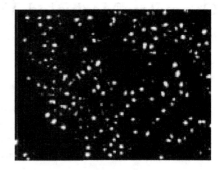

Fig. 5. Detection of carbohydrate stacking in the mucus in intestinal cells, that are specifically stained for carbohydrates with periodic acid Schiff (P.A.S.). The carbohydrate deposits are in magenta, cell nuclei in blue. The blob-like areas are detected with positive Gaussian curvature and positive second order directional derivative in the gradient direction of the image intensity, the magenta with a boolean combination of the color invariant $\mathcal{E}$ and its derivatives to λ. Scale = 4 pixels. Example due to P. Van Osta. Image taken from http://www.bris.ac.uk/Depts/PathAndMicro/CPL/pas.html.

References

1. Geusebroek, J.M., Dev, A., van den Boomgaard, R., Smeulders A.W.M., Cornelissen, F., and Geerts H., Color Invariant edge detection. In: Scale-Space theories in Computer Vision, Lecture Notes in Computer Science, vol. 1252, pp. 459—464, Springer-Verlag, 1999.
2. Geusebroek, J.M., van den Boomgaard, R., Smeulders A.W.M., and Dev, A., Color and scale: the spatial structure of color images. In: Eur. Conf. on Computer Vision 2000, Lecture Notes in Computer Science, Vol. 1842, Springer, pp. 331—341, June 26 - July 1, 2000.
3. Geusebroek, J.M., Smeulders A.W.M., and van den Boomgaard, R., Measurement of Color Invariants. Proc. CVPR, vol. 1, pp. 50—57, June 13-15, 2000.
4. Hering, E., Outlines of a theory of the light sense, Harvard University Press, Cambridge, 1964.
5. Koenderink, J.J., Color Space. Utrecht University, the Netherlands, 1998.
6. Wyszecki, G., and Stiles, W.S., Color science: concepts and methods, quantitative data and formulae, Wiley, New York, NY, 2nd edition, 2000.

Geometry Motivated Variational Segmentation for Color Images

Alexander Brook[1], Ron Kimmel[2], and Nir A. Sochen[3]

[1] Dept. of Mathematics, Technion, Israel
sova@math.technion.ac.il
[2] Dept. of Computer Science, Technion, Israel
[3] Dept. of Applied Mathematics, Tel-Aviv University, Israel

Abstract. We propose image enhancement, edge detection, and segmentation models for the multi-channel case, motivated by the philosophy of processing images as surfaces, and generalizing the Mumford-Shah functional. Refer to http://www.cs.technion.ac.il/~sova/canada01/ for color figures.

1 Introduction

We provide a general variational framework for color images, generalizing the Mumford-Shah functional. Our goal is to provide a theoretical background for the model proposed and implemented in [25].

In Section 2 we give a review of variational segmentation and color edge detection. Section 3 offers a summary of the theory of the Mumford-Shah functional and of numerical minimization methods devised for this functional. We propose two generalizations of the Mumford-Shah functional in Section 4 and show some numerical results.

A few words on the notation. The norm $|\cdot|$ is the usual Euclidean norm of *any* object: a number, a vector, or a matrix. In particular, for a function $u : \mathbb{R}^n \to \mathbb{R}^m$ we put $|\nabla u| = \left(\sum \left(\frac{\partial u^i}{\partial x_j}\right)^2\right)^{1/2}$. $\mathcal{L}^n$ is the Lebesgue measure on $\mathbb{R}^n$. $\mathcal{H}^{n-1}$ is the $(n-1)$-dimensional *Hausdorff measure*, which is a generalization of the area of a submanifold.

2 Image Segmentation

We consider images as functions from a domain in $\mathbb{R}^2$ into some set, that will be called the *feature space*. When needed, we suppose that the domain is $[0,1]^2$. Some examples of feature spaces are $[0, 255]$ or $[0, \infty)$, for gray-level images, or $[0,1]^3$ for color images in RGB.

In [28] Mumford and Shah suggested segmenting an image by minimizing a functional of the form $\int_{\Omega \setminus K} (\|\nabla u\|^2 + \alpha \|u - w\|^2) + \beta \operatorname{length}(K)$, where K is the union of edges in the image. Thay conjectured that there are minimizers over

M. Kerckhove (Ed.): Scale-Space 2001, LNCS 2106, pp. 362–370, 2001.

$u \in C^1(\Omega \setminus K)$ and K being finite union of smooth arcs, and decribed possible conjectured configurations for endpoints and crossings in K.

The minimization of the Mumford-Shah functional poses a difficult problem, both theoretical and numerical, because it contains both area and length terms and is minimized with respect to two variables: a function $f : \Omega \to \mathbb{R}$ and a set $K \subset \Omega$. This kind of functionals was introduced in [18].

The usual mean of providing coupling between the color channels is by defining a suitable *edge indicator function* e, that is supposed to be small in the smooth parts of the image and large in the vicinity of an edge. A typical example is $e(x) = |\nabla f(x)|^2$, and the integral $\int e$ usually constitutes the smoothing term.

One of the promising frameworks to derive and justify edge indicators is to consider images as embedded manifolds and to look at the induced metric for qualitative measurements of image smoothness. This idea first appeared in [21], and was extended in [16].

This interpretation was formulated in the most general way and implemented in [31]. The n-dimensional m-valued image is considered as an n-dimensional manifold in $(\mathbb{R}^{n+m}, h)$ given by $(x_1, \ldots, x_n, f_1(x_1, \ldots, x_n), \ldots, f_m(x_1, \ldots, x_n))$, and $\sqrt{\det g}$, where g is the metric on the manifold induced by the metric h from $\mathbb{R}^{n+m}$, is taken to be the edge indicator function. The integral $\int \sqrt{\det g}$ gives the n-dimensional volume of the manifold, and its minimization brings on a kind of non-isotropic diffusion, which the authors called the Beltrami flow.

As pointed out in [31], when implementing such a diffusion, one must decide what is the relationship between unit lengths along the x_i axes and along the f_j axes. The significance of the ratio of the scales is discussed in detail in [31]. We will denote this coefficient by γ.

In the case of gray-level images this framework was first introduced in [22]. Here the image is a surface in $\mathbb{R}^3$, the edge indicator is the area element $(1 + f_x^2 + f_y^2)^{1/2}$, and the flow is closely related to the mean curvature flow.

In a number of works (e.g. [11, 32]) another problem is considered, leading to very similar equations. It is the problem of smoothing, scaling and segmenting an image in a "non-flat" feature space, like a circle, a sphere or a projective line.

Other related formulations and models for color images were proposed in [26, 5, 30, 16, 12, 7, 8]

3   Mumford-Shah Functional

The core difficulty in proving this conjecture is that the functional is a sum of an area and a curvilinear integrals, and the curve of integration is one of the variables.

There is yet another problem, namely that the proposed domain of u and K is too restrictive and lacks some convenient properties (compactness, lower semicontinuity of the functionals in question). This one, however, is ordinary; instead of imposing that K is a finite union of smooth arcs, we should drop this requirement, and prove later that a minimizing K must be smooth. This also necessitates replacing length(K) with something defined on non-smooth sets; the most natural replacement is $\mathcal{H}^1(K)$, the one-dimensional Hausdorff measure of K.

The crucial idea in overcoming the difficulties of interaction between the area and the length terms is to use a weak formulation of the problem. First, we let K be the set of jump points of u: $K = S_u$. The functional thus depends on u only. Second, we relax the functional in L^2, that is, we consider

$$\bar{E}(u) = \inf\{\liminf_{k\to\infty} E(u_k, S_{u_k}) : u_k \xrightarrow{L^2} u, u_k \in C^1(\Omega \setminus \overline{S_{u_k}}), \mathcal{H}^1(\overline{S_{u_k}} \setminus S_{u_k}) = 0\}.$$

It turns out (see [4]) that this functional has an integral representation

$$\bar{E}(u) = \int_\Omega (|\nabla u|^2 + \alpha|u - w|^2) + \beta \mathcal{H}^1(S_u)$$

and if $\bar{E}(u)$ is finite then $u \in$ SBV, the space of special functions of bounded variation. For the definition of SBV, and also of BV, GBV, and GSBV spaces we refer the reader to the book [2]

In this weak setting it was shown in [19] that there are indeed minimizers of $\bar{E}$ and that at least some of them are regular enough (with K closed and $u \in C^1(\Omega \setminus K)$). Actually, it was proven for the more general case of $\Omega \subset \mathbb{R}^n$, $n \geq 2$, and $F(u) = \int_\Omega (|\nabla u|^2 + \alpha|u - w|^2) + \beta \mathcal{H}^{n-1}(S_u)$.

An interesting and important limiting case of the Mumford-Shah functional is the problem

$$\bar{F} = \int_\Omega \alpha|u - w|^2 + \beta \mathcal{H}^{n-1}(S_u), \quad \nabla u = 0 \text{ on } \Omega \setminus S_u$$

of approximating g by a piecewise-constant function. For this functional, the Mumford-Shah conjecture was proved already in the original paper [28]; an elementary constructive proof can be found in [27]. Existence of minimizers for any $n \geq 2$ was shown in [15].

The main difficulty that hampers attempts to minimize the Mumford-Shah functional $E(u, K)$ numerically is the necessity to somehow store the set K, keep track of possible changes of its topology, and calculate it's length. Also, the number of possible discontinuity sets is enormous even on a small grid.

We can, however, try to find another functional approximating the Mumford-Shah functional that will also be more amenable to numerical minimization. The framework for this kind of approximation is Γ-convergence, introduced in [20] (also see the book [17]).

Consider a metric space (X, d). A sequence of functionals $F_i : X \to \mathbb{R}_+$ is said to Γ-converge to $F : X \to \mathbb{R}_+$ (Γ-lim $F_i = F$) if for any $f \in X$

$$\forall f_i \to f : \liminf F_i(f_i) \geq F(f) \quad \text{and} \quad \exists f_i \to f : \limsup F_i(f_i) \leq F(f).$$

We can extend this definition to families of functionals depending on a continuous parameter $\varepsilon \downarrow 0$, requiring convergence of F_{ε_i} to $F(x)$ on every sequence $\varepsilon_i \downarrow 0$.

It is important to notice that Γ-limit depends on what kind of convergence we have on X. Sometimes, to avoid ambiguities, it is designated as $\Gamma(X)$- or $\Gamma(d)$-limit. For us, the most important property of Γ-convergence is that if $\Gamma\text{-lim } F_i = F$, f_i minimizes F_i and $f_i \rightarrow f$, f minimizes F.

We come back to the task of approximating the Mumford-Shah functional by a nicer functional. However, we can not approximate $F(u)$ with functionals of the usual local integral form $F_\varepsilon(u) = \int_\Omega f_\varepsilon(\nabla u, u)$ for $u \in W^{1,1}$ (see [10, p. 56]). One of the possibilities to overcome this is to introduce a second auxiliary variable, which was done in [3, 4].

The approximation proposed in [4] is

$$F_\varepsilon(u, v) = \int_\Omega \left[v^2 |\nabla u|^2 + \beta \left(\frac{(v-1)^2}{4\varepsilon} + \varepsilon |\nabla v|^2 \right) + \alpha |u - w|^2 \right] dx. \quad (1)$$

The meaning of v in this functional is clear—it approximates $1 - \chi_{S_u}$, being close to 0 when $|\nabla u|$ is large and 1 otherwise. This functional is elliptic and is relatively easy to minimize numerically. A finite-element discretization was proposed in [6], with a proof that the discretized functionals also Γ-converge to $F(u)$ if the mesh-size is $o(\varepsilon)$.

Other works, suggesting approximations and numerical methods for the Mumford-Shah functional are [10, 29, 9, 33, 27, 13, 14].

4   Generalizing Mumford-Shah Functional to Color

The most obvious way to generalize the Mumford-Shah functional to color images $u : \Omega \rightarrow \mathbb{R}^3$ is to use

$$F(u) = \int_\Omega (|\nabla u|^2 + \alpha |u - w|^2) + \beta \mathcal{H}^{n-1}(S_u). \quad (2)$$

In this case the only coupling between the channels is through the common jump set S_u. The approximation results from Section 3 translate to this case without change (as noted in [4]) and we can use the elliptic approximation

$$F_\varepsilon(u, v) = \int_\Omega \left[v^2 |\nabla u|^2 + \beta \left(\frac{(v-1)^2}{4\varepsilon} + \varepsilon |\nabla v|^2 \right) + \alpha |u - w|^2 \right] dx, \quad (3)$$

to find minimizers of $F(u)$. We minimize F_ε by steepest descent. A result of numerical minimization is shown in Figure 1. The original image was a noisy color image also shown in Figure 1.

We want to generalize the Mumford-Shah functional

$$\int_\Omega (|\nabla u|^2 + \alpha |u - w|^2) + \beta \mathcal{H}^{n-1}(S_u)$$

to color images, using the "image as a manifold" interpretation, while the length term $\mathcal{H}^{n-1}(S_u)$ remains the same.

Fig. 1. Results with $\varepsilon = 0.05$, $\alpha = 0.7$, $\beta = 0.022$, $t = 20$ and the original image.

The fidelity term that is most consistent with the geometric approach would be the Hausdorff distance between the two surfaces, or at least $\int_\Omega d(u(x), w(x))$, where $d(\cdot, \cdot)$ is the geodesic distance in the feature space, as in [8]. Yet, both these approaches seem computationally intractable. The suggestion of $\int_\Omega \|u - w\|_h^2$, made in [25], (here h_{ij} is the metric on the feature space, and $\|\cdot\|_h$ is the corresponding norm on the tangent space) is easy to implement, but lacks mathematical validity: $u - w$ is not in the tangent space. We will use the simplest reasonable alternative, $\int_\Omega |u - w|^2$.

The smoothing term is the area $\int_\Omega \sqrt{\det g}$ or the energy $\int_\Omega \det g$, where g is the metric induced on the manifold by h—the metric on the feature space. In the case where h is a Euclidean metric on $\Omega \times [0, 1]^3$ and

$$U(x, y) = (x, y, R, G, B) = (x, y, u^1(x, y), u^2(x, y), u^3(x, y))$$

is the embedding, we get

$$\det g = \det(dU^* \circ h \circ dU) = \gamma^2 + \gamma \sum_i |\nabla u^i|^2 + \sum_{i,j} |\nabla u^i \times \nabla u^j|^2$$

$$= \gamma^2 + \gamma(|u_x|^2 + |u_y|^2) + |u_x \times u_y|^2 = \gamma^2 + \gamma|\nabla u|^2 + |u_x \times u_y|^2.$$

Thus, we have two models:

$$F^1(u) = \int_\Omega \sqrt{\gamma^2 + \gamma|\nabla u|^2 + |u_x \times u_y|^2} + \alpha \int_\Omega |u - w|^2 + \beta \mathcal{H}^{n-1}(S_u),$$

$$F^2(u) = \int_\Omega (\gamma|\nabla u|^2 + |u_x \times u_y|^2) + \alpha \int_\Omega |u - w|^2 + \beta \mathcal{H}^{n-1}(S_u).$$

Note that γ^2 was dropped in the second functional, since in this case it merely adds a constant to the functional.

However, the theory of functionals on SBV or GSBV seems to be unable to deal with these models at the moment. It is necessary to establish lower semicontinuity of the functionals, both to ensure existence of minimizers, and as an important component in the Γ-convergence proofs. Though, theorems on lower semicontinuity of functionals on SBV exist only for isotropic functionals (depending only on $|\nabla u|$ and not on ∇u itself), or at least functionals with constant rate of growth, i.e. $c|\nabla u|^r \leqslant f(\nabla u) \leqslant C(1 + |\nabla u|)^r$ for some $C > c > 0$ and $r > 1$. The term $|u_x \times u_y|^2$ is of order $|\nabla u|^4$, yet we can not bound it from below by $c|\nabla u|^4$ for some $c > 0$, therefore we can not use these theorems.

The role of the term $|u_x \times u_y|^2$ is explored in [24]. If we assume the Lambertian light reflection model, then $u(x, y) = (n(x, y) \cdot l)\rho(x, y)$, where $n(x, y)$ is the unit normal to the surface, l is the source direction, and $\rho(x, y)$ captures the characteristics of the material. Assuming that for any given object $\rho(x, y) = \rho =$ const we have $u(x, y) = (n(x, y) \cdot l)\rho$, hence $\mathrm{Im}\, u \subset \mathrm{span}\{\rho\}$ and $\mathrm{rank}\, du \leqslant 1$. This is equivalent to $u_x \times u_y = 0$.

Thus, the term $|u_x \times u_y|^2$ in the edge indicator enforces the Lambertian model on every smooth surface patch. It also means that taking rather small γ makes sense, since we expect $|u_x \times u_y|^2$ to be (almost) 0, and $|\nabla u|^2$ to be just small.

A generalization of the Mumford-Shah functional proposed here is an attempt to combine the nice smoothing-segmenting features of the geometric model with the existing Γ-convergence results for the elliptic approximation of the original Mumford-Shah functional. We pay for that by the loss of some of the geometric intuition behind the manifold interpretation. The proposed models are just F^1 and F^2 with $|u_x \times u_y|^2$ replaced by $|u_x \times u_y|$, that is

$$G^1(u) = \int_\Omega (\gamma |\nabla u|^2 + |u_x \times u_y|) + \alpha \int_\Omega |u - w|^2 + \beta \mathcal{H}^{n-1}(S_u),$$

$$G^2(u) = \int_\Omega \sqrt{\gamma^2 + \gamma |\nabla u|^2 + |u_x \times u_y|} + \alpha \int_\Omega |u - w|^2 + \beta \mathcal{H}^{n-1}(S_u).$$

Note that $|u_x \times u_y|$ enforces the Lambertian model, just as $|u_x \times u_y|^2$.

The new functional G^2 seems to violate another important requirement, necessary for lower semicontinuity with respect to L^1 convergence: being quasiconvex. Besides, since the smoothing term is of linear growth, approximation similar to those in Section 3 will converge to a functional with more interaction between the area and the length terms, and depending on the Cantor part of Du. We thus propose the functional

$$G^3(u) = \int_\Omega \sqrt{\gamma + |\nabla u|^2} + \alpha \int_\Omega |u - w|^2 + \beta \int_{S_u} \frac{|u^+ - u^-|}{1 + |u^+ - u^-|} d\mathcal{H}^{n-1} + |D^c u|(\Omega).$$

The elliptic approximation for G^1 is provided in [23]:

$$G^1_\varepsilon(u, v) = \int_\Omega v^2(\gamma |\nabla u|^2 + |u_x \times u_y|) + \beta \left(\varepsilon |\nabla v|^2 + \frac{(v - 1)^2}{4\varepsilon} \right) + \alpha |u - w|^2.$$

Results of numerical minimization by steepest descent are shown in Figure 2.

A functional similar to the Mumford-Shah functional, but with linear growth in the gradient is examined in [1], and it is proved in particular that $\Gamma\text{-}\lim G_\varepsilon = G$

Fig. 2. Results for G^1 with $\varepsilon = 0.25$, $\alpha = 0.05$, $\beta = 0.002$, $\gamma = 0.01$, $t = 20$.

(with respect to L^1 convergence), where

$$G_\varepsilon(u, v) = \int_\Omega \left[v^2 f(|\nabla u|) + \beta \left(\varepsilon |\nabla v|^2 + \frac{(1-v)^2}{4\varepsilon} \right) \right]$$

if $u, v \in H^1(\Omega)$ and $0 \leqslant v \leqslant 1$ a.e., and $+\infty$ otherwise,

$$G(u, v) = \int_\Omega f(|\nabla u|) + \beta \int_{S_u} \frac{|u^+ - u^-|}{1 + |u^+ - u^-|} \, d\mathcal{H}^1 + |D^c u|(\Omega)$$

if $u \in \mathrm{GBV}(\Omega)$ and $v = 1$ a.e., and $+\infty$ otherwise,

and $f : [0, +\infty) \to [0, +\infty)$ is convex, increasing, and $\lim_{z \to \infty} f(z)/z = 1$. With the aim of generalizing this result to color images we define $f(z) = \sqrt{\gamma + z^2}$,

$$G^3(u) = \int_\Omega \sqrt{\gamma + |\nabla u|^2} + \alpha \int_\Omega |u - w|^2 + \beta \int_{S_u} \frac{|u^+ - u^-|}{1 + |u^+ - u^-|} \, d\mathcal{H}^{n-1} + |D^c u|(\Omega),$$

$$G_\varepsilon^3(u, v) = \int_\Omega \left[v^2 \sqrt{\gamma + |\nabla u|^2} + \alpha |u - w|^2 + \beta \left(\varepsilon |\nabla v|^2 + \frac{(1-v)^2}{4\varepsilon} \right) \right],$$

with domains as above.

Upon inspection of the proofs in [1], it seems that everything remains valid for the vectorial case, except one part, that establishes the lower inequality for the one-dimensional case ($n = 1$) in a small neighborhood of a jump point. We can, however, provide a "replacement" for this part (the second part of Proposition 4.3 in [1], beginning with (4.4)).

A result of numerical minimization of G_ε^3 is shown in Figure 3.

References

[1] R. Alicandro, A. Braides, and J. Shah. Free-discontinuity problems via functionals involving the L^1-norm of the gradient and their approximation. *Interfaces and Free Boundaries*, 1(1):17–37, 1999.

[2] L. Ambrosio, N. Fusco, and D. Pallara. *Functions of Bounded Variation and Free Discontinuity Problems*. Oxford Mathematical Monographs. Oxford University Press, 2000.

Fig. 3. Results for G^3 with $\varepsilon = 0.01$, $\alpha = 3$, $\beta = 0.02$, $\gamma = 0.001$, $t = 4$.

[3] L. Ambrosio and V. M. Tortorelli. Approximation of functionals depending on jumps by elliptic functionals via Γ-convergence. *Comm. Pure Appl. Math.*, 43(8):999–1036, 1990.

[4] L. Ambrosio and V. M. Tortorelli. On the approximation of free discontinuity problems. *Boll. Un. Mat. Ital. B (7)*, 6(1):105–123, 1992.

[5] C. Ballester and M. González. Texture segmentation by variational methods. In *ICAOS '96. 12th International Conference on Analysis and Optimization of Systems. Images, Wavelets and PDEs*, pages 187–193. Springer Verlag, 1996.

[6] G. Bellettini and A. Coscia. Discrete approximation of a free discontinuity problem. *Numer. Funct. Anal. Optim.*, 15(3-4):201–224, 1994.

[7] P. Blomgren and T. F. Chan. Color TV: total variation methods for restoration of vector-valued images. *IEEE Trans. Image Processing*, 7(3):304–309, 1998.

[8] A. Bonnet. On the regularity of edges in image segmentation. *Ann. Inst. H. Poincaré Anal. Non Linéaire*, 13(4):485–528, 1996.

[9] B. Bourdin and A. Chambolle. Implementation of an adaptive finite-element approximation of the Mumford-Shah functional. *Numer. Math.*, 85(4):609–646, 2000.

[10] A. Braides. *Approximation of free-discontinuity problems.* Lecture Notes in Math., 1694. Springer-Verlag, Berlin, 1998.

[11] T. Chan and J. Shen. Variational restoration of non-flat image features: models and algorithms. Technical Report 99-20, UCLA CAM, 1999.

[12] T. F. Chan, B. Y. Sandberg, and L. A. Vese. Active contours without edges for vector-valued images. *J. Visual Communication Image Representation*, 11(2):130–141, 2000.

[13] T. F. Chan and L. A. Vese. An active contour model without edges. In M. Nielsen, P. Johansen, O. F. Olsen, and J. Weickert, editors, *Scale-Space Theories in Computer Vision, Second International Conference, Scale-Space'99*, volume 1682 of *Lecture Notes in Comp. Sci.*, pages 141–151. Springer, 1999.

[14] T. F. Chan and L. A. Vese. Image segmentation using level sets and the piecewise-constant Mumford-Ssah model. Technical Report 00-14, UCLA CAM, 2000.

[15] G. Congedo and I. Tamanini. On the existence of solution to a problem in multidimensional segmentation. *Ann. Inst. Henri Poincaré Anal. Non Linéaire*, 8(2):175–195, 1991.

[16] A. Cumani. Edge detection in multispectral images. *CVGIP: Graphical Models and Image Processing*, 53(1):40–51, 1991.

[17] G. Dal Maso. *An introduction to Γ-convergence.* Birkhäuser Boston Inc., Boston, MA, 1993.

[18] E. De Giorgi and L. Ambrosio. New functionals in the calculus of variations. *Atti Accad. Naz. Lincei Rend. Cl. Sci. Fis. Mat. Natur. (8)*, 82(2):199–210 (1989), 1988.

[19] E. De Giorgi, M. Carriero, and A. Leaci. Existence theorem for a minimum problem with free discontinuity set. *Arch. Rational Mech. Anal.*, 108(3):195–218, 1989.

[20] E. De Giorgi and T. Franzoni. Su un tipo di convergenza variazionale. *Atti Accad. Naz. Lincei Rend. Cl. Sci. Fis. Mat. Natur. (8)*, 58(6):842–850, 1975.

[21] S. Di Zenzo. A note on the gradient of a multi-image. *Computer Vision, Graphics, and Image Processing*, 33(1):116–125, 1986.

[22] A. I. El-Fallah and G. E. Ford. The evolution of mean curvature in image filtering. In *Proceedings of IEEE International Conference on Image Processing*, volume 1, pages 298–302, 1994.

[23] M. Focardi. On the variational approximation of free-discontinuity problems in the vectorial case. Technical report, SNS, Pisa, 1999.

[24] R. Kimmel, R. Malladi, and N. Sochen. Images as embedded maps and minimal surfaces: Movies, color, texture, and volumetric medical images. *Int. J. Computer Vision*, 39(2):111–129, 2000.

[25] R. Kimmel and N. Sochen. Geometric-variational approach for color image enhancement and segmentation. In M. Nielsen, P. Johansen, O. F. Olsen, and J. Weickert, editors, *Scale-space theories in computer vision*, volume 1682 of *Lecture Notes in Comp. Sci.*, pages 294–305. Springer, 1999.

[26] T. S. Lee, D. Mumford, and A. Yuille. Texture segmentation by minimizing vector-valued energy functionals: the coupled-membrane model. In G. Sandini, editor, *Computer vision – ECCV '92*, volume 558 of *LNCS*, pages 165–173. Springer Verlag, 1992.

[27] J.-M. Morel and S. Solimini. *Variational methods in image segmentation*. Birkhäuser Boston Inc., Boston, MA, 1995. With seven image processing experiments.

[28] D. Mumford and J. Shah. Optimal approximations by piecewise smooth functions and associated variational problems. *Comm. Pure Appl. Math.*, 42(5):577–685, 1989.

[29] M. Negri. The anisotropy introduced by the mesh in the finite element approximation of the Mumford-Shah functional. *Numer. Funct. Anal. Optim.*, 20(9-10):957–982, 1999.

[30] G. Sapiro and D. L. Ringach. Anisotropic diffusion of multivalued images with application to color filtering. *IEEE Trans. Image Processing*, 5(11):1582–1586, Oct. 1996.

[31] N. Sochen, R. Kimmel, and R. Malladi. A general framework for low level vision. *IEEE Trans. Image Processing*, 7(3):310–318, 1998.

[32] B. Tang, G. Sapiro, and V. Caselles. Diffusion of general data on non-flat manifolds via harmonic maps theory: The direction diffusion case. *Int. J. Computer Vision*, 36(2):149–161, 2000.

[33] A. Tsai, A. Yezzi, and A. S. Willsky. Curve evolution, boundary value stochastic processes, the Mumford-Shah problem, and missing data applications. In *IEEE International Conference on Image Processing*, volume 3, pages 588–591. IEEE, 2000.

Hierarchical Segmentation Using Dynamics of Multiscale Color Gradient Watersheds

Iris Vanhamel, Ioannis Pratikakis, and Hichem Sahli

Vrije Universiteit Brussel - ETR0 - IRIS
Pleinlaan 2, 1050 Brussels, Belgium
{iuvanham,hsahli}@etro.vub.ac.be
http://www.etro.vub.ac.be/Research/IRIS/iris.htm

Abstract. In this paper, we describe and compare two multiscale color segmentation schemes based on the *Gaussian* multiscale and the *Perona and Malik* anisotropic diffusion. The proposed segmentation schemes consist of an extension to color images of an earlier multiscale hierarchical watershed segmentation for scalar images. Our segmentation scheme constructs a hierarchy among the watershed regions using the principle of dynamics of contours in scale-space. Each contour is valuated by combining the *dynamics of contours* over the successive scales. We conduct experiments on the scale-space stacks created by the *Gaussian* scale-space and the *Perona and Malik* anisotropic diffusion scheme. Our experimental results consist of the comparison of both schemes with respect to the following aspects: size and information reduction between successive levels of the hierarchical stack, dynamics of contours in scale space and computation time.

1   Introduction

Color image segmentation refers to the partitioning of a multi-valued image into meaningful objects. The additional information, which is provided by color along with the continuously increasing number of applications that deal with analysis tasks of color images, advocate its prominent position among the interests of the image processing community. Recent segmentation methods tend to take the multiscale nature of images into account, which allows the integration of both the superficial and the deep image structure. The majority of the existing multiscale schemes employ a *Gaussian* scale-space and subsequently suffer from its inherent drawbacks such as the *correspondence problem*: Edges at coarser scales are displaced, which results in the need to trace them to the original image in order to find their exact location. For this reason, non-linear scale-space were investigated. Currently, the use of anisotropic scale-space methods, which do not suffer or suffer less from the *correspondence problem* and thus allow the immediate localization of the edges, is increasing. Its numerical restrictions to preserve stability and its architectural properties often led to unacceptable computation times in the past. This problem has been resolved by better numerical methods [14]. Most of the existing segmentation schemes employ the anisotropic diffusion

M. Kerckhove (Ed.): Scale-Space 2001, LNCS 2106, pp. 371–379, 2001.

as an enhancement step. In [12] an image enhancement based on the anisotropic diffusion is used before applying a hierarchical watershed segmentation. A similar approach is given in [6] for color images. In [2] a watershed-pyramid, which is based on a morphological scale-space, is used to automatically segment multivalued images. In this technique, the watershed is applied to a coarse level where after the edges are propagated down to the finer layers of the pyramid.

In this paper, we extend, to color images an earlier multi-resolution scheme [10] which is based upon principles of the watershed analysis and the *Gaussian* scale-space. The main motivation was the duality of the catchment basins in the gradient magnitude image along with the simplification processes which occurs during the creation of scale-space. In our approach we examine the multiscale behavior of the catchment basins and the gradient watersheds. The *dynamics of contours* [1] is used for the valuation, over the successive scales, of the watershed lines. An extension for color images of the *Perona and Malik* anisotropic diffusion [9] is proposed. Furthermore, the numerical scheme given by *Perona and Malik* in [9] is replaced by the Additive Operator Splitting (AOS) scheme [14]. The linear and non-linear multi-resolution schemes are compared on the following aspects: (i) the size and the information reduction between successive levels of the hierarchical stack, (ii) dynamics of contours in scale space (iii) the computation time.

The paper is organized as follows: In section 2 we present an overview of the hierarchical multi-resolution segmentation scheme and explain the both scale-space generators and their implementation for color, the dynamics of contours in scale-space and the hierarchical scheme. The comparative study of the *Gaussian* - with the *Perona and Malik* based multiscale segmentation is explained and illustrated with experimental results in section 3. And finally, some conclusions are made in section 4 concerning the performance of both methods and the continuation of the research.

2   Multiscale Watershed Segmentation Scheme

2.1   Introduction

Similar to the grey level case, the segmentation of color images using the watershed transformation can be translated as elimination of its main drawback, namely over-segmentation. Without being an exception to the rule of the grey level case, the oversegmentation problem in color images has been treated by following for main approaches: *markers* [7], *flat zones*[4] and *waterfall* [5], and *dynamics of contours* [8].

In this paper we present a hierarchical segmentation scheme using dynamics of multiscale color gradient watersheds [10]. A hierarchical segmentation of an image is a tree structure by inclusion of connected regions. In our approach the tree structure construction follows a model which consists of two modules (see Figure 1): the *salient measure* module and *stopping criterion* module. The first module is dedicated to valuate each contour arc with a *salient measure* while the second identifies the different hierarchical levels by using a hypothesis testing.

Utilizing this algorithm enables us to construct a hierarchy among the regions which are produced by the gradient watersheds, integrating three types of information into a single algorithm, namely homogeneity, contrast and scale. It has a superior behavior compared to hierarchies constructed by considering either the superficial or the deep image structure alone.

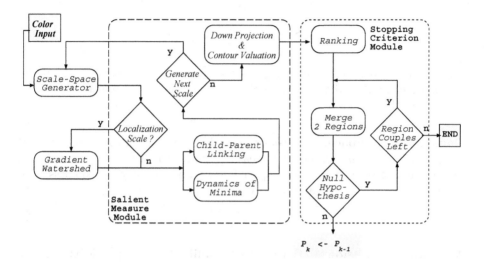

Fig. 1. Flowchart of the *constrained dynamics of contours in scale space* for color images.

2.2   The Salient Measure Module

The cooperation of watershed analysis and scale-space' main motivation is the duality of the catchment basins of the watershed with their respective minima in the gradient image and the simplification process which occurs during the creation of a scale-space. The used scheme relies on the concept of the dynamics of contours in scale-space, which incorporates a segment linking that has been advocated by a study of the topological changes of the critical point configuration [10]. The entire process to retrieve a salient measure for the gradient watershed requires three steps: (i) scale generation, (ii) linking, and (iii) contour valuation by downward projection.

On the localization scale S_o, which in our case is the original image, a gradient watershed is performed. This produces the minima that are used for the linking scheme. In our approach the linking entities are regions and not pixels.

Dynamics of Contours in Scale Space. The linking process (parent-child relationship) for successive levels is applied using the *proximity* criterion [10].

Once the parent-child relations are made, a linking list $L(p, q)$ for each region couple (p, q) at the localization scale is created, the next step is to valuate the gradient watersheds at the localization scale S_o using the notion of *dynamics of contours in scale-space* ($DCSS$). The $DCSS$ for an adjacent region couple (p, q) is defined as the integration of all the valuations of the dynamics of contours ($DC_i^{L(p,q)}$) during the evolution in scale-space. Formally:

$$DCSS(p, q) = \sum_{i=S_o}^{S_a-1} DC_i^{L(p,q)} \tag{1}$$

where p and q denote adjacent regions at the localization scale S_o, S_a is the annihilation scale; the difference $S_a - S_o$ is the scale space life time of the contour, and $L(p, q)$ the linking list.

Gaussian Scale-Space. The *Gaussian* scale generator convolves the original image with *Gaussian* kernels of increasing width. To ensure scale invariance, the sampling of the generate scale-space follows a linear and dimensionless scale parameter $\delta\tau$, which is related to σ by:

$$\sigma_N = e^{\tau_o + N\delta\tau} \tag{2}$$

Anisotropic Diffusion of Perona and Malik. Inherent problems of linear scale-space methods led to the investigation of their non-linear counterparts. The idea was to deal with problems such as the dislocation of edges, the similar treatment of information and noise, etc. In non-linear methods, extra information is added to guide the diffusion process. In [9], Perona and Malik propose an anisotropic diffusion filtering for scalar images that avoids blurring and localization problems of the linear diffusion filtering. They apply an inhomogenous process that reduces the amount of diffusion at those locations, which have a larger likelihood to be edges. This likelihood is measured by a decreasing function of the squared gradient and is denoted the *diffusivity* or *diffusion tensor*. In this paper we adopted for a function that favors wide regions over smaller ones:

$$g(|\nabla(u)|^2) = \frac{1}{1 + \frac{|\nabla(u)|^2}{K^2}} \tag{3}$$

where the constant K$>$ 0 is a contrast parameter that separates forward (low contrast) from backward (high contrast) diffusion. The value of K is problem dependent and needs to be determined experimentally. The diffusion scheme proposed in [9] is ill-posed and subsequently we estimated the *diffusion tensor* on the gradient of a Gaussian smoothed image as was proposed by Catte et al. in [3]. In our experiments this regularization technique was applied using a Gaussian kernel of 0.5. In the following sections the non-linear scheme is referred to as the *Perona-Malik-Catte* scheme (PMC).

The numerical scheme, given in [9], is replaced with the AOS scheme [14] to increase the computational performance. However, even tough this removes the stability restriction on the time step, one now ought to restricted the time step to avoid visible errors in approximation of the diffused image. During our experiments the time step never exceeds 10.

For a better comparative analysis, only those scales that are equivalent to the ones produced in the *Gaussian* scale space (Eq. 2) are considered. Using the relationship between the size of the *Gaussian* kernel and the scale-parameter t of the diffusion equation [13], we construct a selection scheme to determine the scales in which the dynamics of contours should be estimated. The time step λ is adapted at each scale N as follows:

$$\lambda = t_{N+1} - t_N = \frac{e^{2(\tau_o + N\delta\tau)}}{2} \cdot (e^{2\delta\tau} - 1) \tag{4}$$

The extension of the scheme for color images is obtained by diffusing each color channel separately using a common diffusion tensor, which is estimated using the Euclidean distance between the color vectors of neighboring pixels.

2.3 The Stopping Criterion Module

This module identifies the hierarchical levels. When the contour valuation of adjacent region couples has terminated, a ranking of the values providing the priority of merging is applied. The hierarchical segmentation algorithm will be completed after the application of the merging stopping criterion phase which retrieves the different hierarchical levels HL_k. For this purpose, a statistical decision is employed through a *hypothesis test*, leading to the creation of a new hierarchical level in the case that the homogeneity constraint imposed in the regions is violated during the region merging process [11].

3 Comparative Study

The proposed segmentation schemes are compared on the following aspects: (i) Evolution of the dynamics of contours in scale-space, (ii) size and information reduction between successive levels of the hierarchical stack and (iii) computation time. Both schemes use the same discretization of scale-space stack (2, 4). This way we ensure that the comparison is performed on equivalent scales, however this also implies that we do not use an optimal discretization of the *PMC* based scale-space stack. Similar remarks can be issued concerning the localization scale, for which in case of the *PMC* a much coarser scale can be chosen. Figures 2 and 3 give an inside to the scale generator and the scheme used to link the local minima over the scales. In figure 2 we see an cross-section of the scale-space stack, which is - as expected - decaying faster for the linear scale generator. Figure 3 shows some mosaic images, which can be obtained after the linking of the local minima. One notices that the segmentation quality of the mosaic images for the non-linear scale generator is relatively high. The linear scale generator, on the other hand, rapidly loses several important details.

The dynamics of contours in scale-space combine scale and contrast measure. The scale-space lifetime of all significant details is longer for the *PMC* scheme

Fig. 2. Scale-space stack in RGB color-space. Top: *Gaussian* scale generator, from left to right: $N = 0,4,7,10$. Bottom: *PMC* diffusion with k = 4.5. $N = 0,4,7,10$.

than for the *Gaussian* scheme. This is demonstrated in Figure 4, which shows the number of regions retained at each scale. The reduction of information is significantly slower at the finer scales for the *PMC* scheme, subsequently the majority of regions have a larger scale-space lifetime. Figure 5 displays the evolution of the dynamic for two contours in scale. The first contour is the fairly weak contour separating two green regions, which are located is the grass in front of the house (Figure 6). The second is a very salient one, which separates the house and the sky (Figure 6). For the *Gaussian* scheme both contours have a fast exponential decrease. In the *PMC* scheme the dynamic of salient contour is more or less constant with an enhancement at coarser scales. For the weak contour the dynamic decreases stepwise with an increasing step until it disappears. Hence, the dynamics of contours in scale-space for the *PMC* scheme can be discriminated better, which results in a more robust hierarchy among the regions.

The homogeneity test, which does not employ the scale-space stack, uses the uniformity information retrieved from the localization scale only. It aims to extract the hierarchical levels, which contain regions of similar saliency. The hierarchical stack and the information reduction between the successive hierarchical levels (number of regions) are demonstrated in Figure 4 and Figure 6, where a selection of hierarchical levels is shown. On first sight the results of both schemes seem very similar. Both schemes result in a hierarchical stack that has to many oversegmented levels and does not really contain an optimal level. However, the hierarchical stack of the *PMC* scheme is qualitatively better since it has a better treatment of almost similar regions and small but salient details. Some examples can be found in Figure 6 at $P_k = 10$ and $P_k = 12$.

Fig. 3. Mosaic images obtained after linking. Top: *Gaussian* scale generator, from left to right: N = 2, 5, 10, 13 with 1988, 232, 25 and 12 regions. Bottom: *PMC* diffusion with k = 4.5. N = 4, 8, 12, 16 with 2887, 1196, 609 and 273 regions.

The computation time of the *PMC* scheme would be significantly longer than the *Gaussian* scheme if one where to use the explicit numerical scheme. However, the usage of the *AOS* numerical scheme decreases the computation time significantly. The non-linear scheme is still slower due to diffusion-quality restriction on the time step and due to a higher amount of regions at the finer scales. The latter increases the computation time for the linking of the local minima and calculation of the dynamics of contours in scale-space but can be resolved by selecting an appropriate localization scale [1]

4   Conclusions

The hierarchical stack of both schemes is more or less similar: The higher hierarchical levels for the *PMC* scheme are slightly better and the lower hierarchical levels are in both schemes severely oversegmented. At turning point between over- and undersegmented in the hierarchical stack, the *PMC* results in a better hierarchical retrieval. The dynamics of contours retrieved using the *PMC* scheme show a quantitative superiority, which leads us to believe that the used homogeneity test causes the similarity of the hierarchical stacks. This is a reasonable assumption since the used homogeneity test only conveys the uniformity information of the regions at the localization scale. Therefore, we suggest that in our future work we attempt to include uniformity information from the whole scale-space stack. Furthermore, an analytical investigation of the color gradient

---

[1] Color versions of Figures 2, 3 and 6 are available at
http://www.etro.vub.ac.be/~iuvanham/pubs/ScaleSpace01.html.

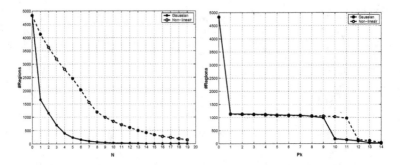

Fig. 4. Left: Number of regions retained at each scale. Right: Number of regions at each hierarchical level.

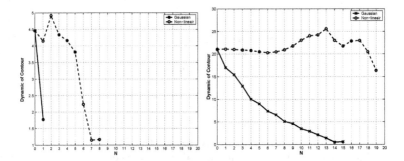

Fig. 5. Evolution of the dynamic of contour in scale-space. Left: weak contour. Right: very salient contour.

Fig. 6. Hierarchical Levels in RGB color-space. Top: *Gaussian* scale generator, from top to bottom: $P_k = 0,10,11,12$. Bottom: *PMC* diffusion with k = 4.5. $P_k = 0,10,11,12$.

watersheds retrieved in the *PMC* scale-space is needed to optimize the parent-child linking and the manner in which the dynamics of contours over the scales are combined. The selection of the localization scale and the measurement scales in non-linear scale-space also requires further study.

References

1. S. Beucher. *Watershed, hierarchical segmentation and waterfall algorithm.* In J. Serra and P. Soille, editors, *Mathematical Morphology and its applications on Image and Signal processing (ISMM'94)*, pages 69–76. Kluwer Academic Press, 1994.
2. J. Bosworth, T. Koshimizu and S.T. Acton. *Automated Segmentationof Surface Soil Moisture From Landsat TM Data*, In *Proc. of the IEEE Southwest Symposium on Image Analysis and Interpretation*, Tucson, April 6-7, 1998.
3. F. Catte, P.-L. Lions, J.-M. Morel, and T. Coll. *Image Selective Smoothing and Edge Detection by Nonlinear Diffusion. SIAM J. Numer. Anal.*, vol. 29(1):182–193, 1992.
4. J. Crespo and R. Schafer. *The flat zone approach and color images.* In J. Serra and P. Soille, editors, *Mathematical Morphology and its applications on Image and Signal processing (ISMM'94)*, pages 85–92. Kluwer Academic Press, 1994.
5. C.H. Demarty and S. Beucher. *Color segmentation algorithm using an HLS transformation.* In H. Heijmans and J. Roerdink, editors, *Mathematical Morphology and its applications on Image and Signal processing (ISMM'98)*, pages 231–238. Kluwer Academic Press, 1998.
6. P. De Smet, R. Pires, D. De Vleeschauwer, I. Bruyland. *Activity driven non-linear diffusion for color image watershed segmentation. Journal of Electronic Imaging (SPIE)*, Volume 08(03), 1999.
7. F. Meyer. *Color image segmentation.* In *4th IEEE Conference on Image Processing and applications*, volume 354:53
8. L. Najman and M. Schmitt. *Geodesic Saliency of Watershed Contours and Hierarchical Segmentation. IEEE Transactions on Pattern Analysis and Machine Intelligence*, vol. 18(12):1163-1173, 1996.
9. P. Perona and J. Malik. *Scale-space and edge detection using anisotropic diffusion. IEEE Transactions on Pattern Analysis and Machine Intelligence*, volume 12(7):629-639, 1990.
10. I. Pratikakis, H. Sahli, and J. Cornelis. *Hierarchical segmentation using dynamics of multiscale gradient watershed. 11th Scandinavian Conference on Image Analysis 99*, pp. 577–584, 1999.
11. I. Vanhamel, I. Pratikakis, H. Sahli. *Automatic Watershed segmentation of color images.* In J. Goutsia, L. Vincent and Dan S. Bloomberg, editors, *Mathematical Morphology and its applications on Image and Signal processing (ISMM'00)*, pp. 207-214. Kluwer Academic Press, 2000.
12. J. Weickert. *Fast segmentation methods based on partial differential equations and the watershed transformation.* In. P. Levi, R-J. Ahlers, F. May, M. Shanz, editors. *Mustererkennung 1998*, Springer, Berlin, pp. 93-100, 1998.
13. J. Weickert. *Anisotropic Diffusion in Image Processing* ECMI Series, Teubner, Stuttgart, 1998.
14. J. Weickert, B.M. ter Haar Romeny, M.A. Viergever. *Efficient and Reliable Schemes for Nonlinear Diffusion Filtering. IEEE transactions on image processing*, volume 7(3):398-410, 1998

Fast Statistical Level Sets Image Segmentation for Biomedical Applications

Sophie Schüpp, Abderrahim Elmoataz,
Mohamed-Jalal Fadili, and Daniel Bloyet

Groupe de Recherche en Informatique, Image et Instrumentation de Caen UMR 6072
GREYC-ISMRA 6, Bd Maréchal Juin, F-14050 Caen, France
sophie.schupp@greyc.ismra.fr

Abstract. In medical microscopy, image analysis offers to pathologist a modern tool, which can be applied to several problems in cancerology: quantification of DNA content, quantification of immunostaining, nuclear mitosis counting, characterization of tumor tissue architecture. However, these problems need an accurate and automatic segmentation. In most cases, the segmentation is concerned with the extraction of cell nuclei or cell clusters. In this paper, we address the problem of the fully automatic segmentation of grey level intensity or color images from medical microscopy. An automatic segmentation method combining fuzzy clustering and multiple active contour models is presented. Automatic and fast initialization algorithm based on fuzzy clustering and morphological tools are used to robustly identify and classify all possible seed regions in the color image. These seeds are propagated outward simultaneously to refine contours of all objects. A fast level set formulation is used to model the multiple contour evolution. Our method is illustrated through two representative problems in cytology and histology.

Keywords: Segmentation, active contour models, level set method, fuzzy clustering, medical microscopy.

1 Introduction

Image analysis offers a modern tool to pathologist, which can be applied to several problems in cancerology : quantification of DNA content, quantification of immunostaining, nuclear mitosis counting, characterization of tumor tissue architecture, etc... However, its introduction in clinical daily practice implies complete automation and standardization of procedures, together with the evaluation of the clinical interest of measured parameters. One of the bringing out steps is the segmentation process, which has to provide the interesting objects to be measured.

Segmenting medical images of soft tissues to form regions related to meaningful biological structures (such as cells, nuclei or organs) is a difficult problem, due to the wide variaty of structures characteristics. Many strategies can be used; their performances depend largely on images to be processed and on a priori knowledges relative to the object features. Efforts have been made towards the unification of the contour and region based approaches, and level

M. Kerckhove (Ed.): Scale-Space 2001, LNCS 2106, pp. 380–388, 2001.

set theories have been used in the formulation of the unification of these approaches [6][5][4][7]. To the best of our knowledge, the only work applying level set approach to medical microscopy images is reported by Sarti in [8]. In this work a partial differential equation based analysis is used as a methodology for computer-aided cytology. All the approaches using the level set approach for active contours can deal with gradient or regions information and can handle topological changes automatically. However, when an automatic segmentation or a quantitative segmentation such as studies in medical microscopy [9] is needed, robust and automatic specification of initial curves is required.

In this paper, we present a method for automatic segmentation of biomedical microscopic sections as a combination of fast level set approach and fuzzy clustering based on global color information. An initial automatic detection algorithm based on fuzzy clustering is used to robustly identify and classify all possible seed regions in the image. These seeds are propagated outward simultaneously to localize the final contours of all objects in the image.

The originality of the method is to classify markers obtained by morphological operators. The technique is fast, because the markers represent only 1 to 5% of the total number of pixels in the image. These markers resulting from this classification, are distributed symmetrically inside the objects of interest. They provide a good automatic initialization of the contours which allows to active contours and level set methods to operate in good conditions.

This paper is organized as follows. In section 2, the level set algorithm is reviewed. Section 3 presents a fast level set algorithm called the Group Marching Algorithm [10]; it describes how we extend the later to deal with multiple active contour evolution. In section 4, we consider the problem of automatic initialization of level set, and propose automatic fuzzy clustering combined with local morphology tools as an automatic initialization algorithm. As a conclusion, section 5 illustrates the robustness of the proposed method with two representative problems of color quantitative segmentation in medical image microscopy.

2   The Original Level Set Approach

Since its introduction, the level set approach has been successfully applied to a wide collection of problems that arise in computer vision and image processing. Let us describe the original level set idea of Osher and Sethian [11] for tracking the evolution of an initial front Γ_0 as it propagates in a direction normal to itself with a speed function F. The main idea is to match the one-parameter family of fronts $\{\Gamma_t\}_{t>=0}$, where Γ_t is the position of the front at time t, with a one-parameter family of moving surfaces in such a way that the zero level set of the surface always yields the moving front. To determine the front propagation, it is necessary to solve a partial differential equation for the motion of the evolving surface. Assume that the so-called *level set function* $u : \mathbb{R}^n \times \mathbb{R}^+ \to \mathbb{R}$ is such that at time $t \geq 0$ the zero level set $u(x,t)$ is the front Γ_t. The derivations described in [12] yield the time-dependant level set equation:

$$\frac{\partial u}{\partial t} = F \left| \nabla u \right|$$
$$u\left(x, t = 0 \right) = \pm d \left(x, \Gamma_0 \right) \tag{1}$$

where $d\left(x, \Gamma_0\right)$ is the distance from x to the curve Γ_0. The distance is positive if x is inside Γ_0 and negative if x is outside. If the non-regularized model given by equation (1) is considered, this leads to an interesting and fast model being able to take into account the simultaneous evolution of several contours. In this model, the speed function F is either always positive or always negative. We can introduce a new variable (the arrival time function) $T(x)$ defined by $u\left(x, T\left(x\right)\right) = 0$. In other words, $T\left(x\right)$ is the time when $u\left(x, t\right) = 0$. If $\frac{dx}{dt} \neq 0$, T satisfy the stationary eikonal equation

$$\left| \nabla T \right| . F = 1$$
$$T_{d(x)=0} = 0 \tag{2}$$

This equation states that the gradient of the arrival time function is inversely proportional to the velocity of the contour at any given point. The advantage of this formulation is that it can be numerically solved by fast techniques. Sethian [12] combined heap sort algorithm with variant of Dijkstra algorithm to solve equation (2), this method is known as the fast marching method (*FMM*). The heap sort algorithm is used to update T at any specified pixel in an increasing order. If N is the number of image pixels, the complexity goes as $O(N\log(N))$. Lately, an alternative sweeping strategy was suggested and used by Kim [10] to derive fast algorithm known as Group Marching Methods (*GMM*); its cost is $O(N)$. The latter is used in this paper.

3   The Group Marching Algorithm

Now let us derive a discrete version of the Eikonal equation (2). The easiest way to obtain such discretization is to replace the gradient by the first-order approximation [12] :

$$\sqrt{\left(max\left(D_{ij}^{-x}T, -D_{ij}^{+x}T, 0\right)\right)^2 + \left(max\left(D_{ij}^{-y}T, -D_{ij}^{+y}T, 0\right)\right)^2} = \frac{1}{F_{ij}} \tag{3}$$

where the standard finite differences are given by: $D_{ij}^{-x} = T_{ij} - T_{i-1j}$ and $D_{ij}^{+x} = T_{i+1j} - T_{ij}$, where T_{ij} is the value of T for each pixel (i, j). Expressions of D_{ij}^{-y} and D_{ij}^{-y} in the other direction are similar.

Consider a neighborhood Γ of the front Γ_t, in the current stage of *GMM*, a group of points G is selected from Γ. Some pixels of Γ are included in G and are already labeled "completed". For the other pixels of Γ the equation (3) is solved.

The evolution of the set of active pixels is done by choosing, at the initial time, a subset G of Γ which corresponds to all the points that have to be processed. The formal definition of this principle is given by:

$$F_{\Gamma,min} = min \left\{ \frac{1}{F_{i,j}} : (i,j) \in \Gamma \right\} \tag{4}$$

$\delta\tau = \frac{1}{\sqrt{2}} F_{\Gamma,min}$, $\tau_{\Gamma,min} = min\left\{\tau_{ij} : (i,j) \in \Gamma\right\}$ and select G as follows:
$G = \{p = (i,j) \in \Gamma, \tau_p < \tau_{\Gamma,min} + \delta\tau\}$. Proceeding as in [10], the Group Marching Method goes as follows:

- **Initialization**
  - **Processed pixels**: *All pixels under markers; assign a distance transform value of zero to them $T(i,j)=0$ and label them $idT(i,j)=2$*
  - **Active pixels**: *Pixels at the outside boundary of the markers; their distance transform is known $T(i,j)=1/F(i,j)$*
    - *label them as $idT(i,j)=1$*
    - *save those point indices to the interface indicator array $\Gamma(i,j)$ set TM to be the minimum of T on those points*
  - **Unprocessed pixels**: *Pixels away from the markers $T(i,j) = \infty$; label them as $idT(i,j) = 0$,*
  - *Set $\delta\tau = \frac{1}{\sqrt{2}} \cdot \underset{i,j}{min} \left(\frac{1}{F_{i,j}} \right)$*
- **Marching Forward:**
  (M1) *Set $TM = TM + \delta\tau$*
  (M2) *For each (i,j) in $\Gamma(i,j)$, in the reverse order, if $T(i,j) \leq TM$, update the solution at neighboring points (l,m) where $idT(l,m) \leq 1$;*
  (M3) *For each (i,j) in Γ, in the forward order, if $T(i,j) \leq TM$,*
     (a) *update the solution at neighboring points (l,m) where $idT(l,m) \leq 1$;*
     (b) *if $idT(l,m) = 0$ at a neighboring point (l,m), set $idT(i,j) = 1$ and save (l,m) into Γ;*
     (c) *remove the index (i,j)) from Γ; set $idT(i,j) = 0$;*
  (M4) *if $\Gamma \neq \emptyset$, go to (M1);*

The *GMM* is in fact an iterative update procedure, converging in two iterations. Rouy and Tourin [13] have chosen all the grid points as one group and carried out iterations up to convergence. *GMM* can be viewed as an intermediate algorithm between *FMM* ($\delta\tau \to 0$) and the purely iterative algorithm of Rouy and Tourin ($\delta\tau \to \infty$).

This algorithm can be easily extended to deal with evolution and labeling of multiple curves. Let us assume we have C seed regions G_i, to deal with the evolution. Any of the independent contours possibly propagates with different speeds, we label all seeds with C labels according to the results of fuzzy classification, and then we propagate these labels while computing G_i, by solving the equation:

$$\begin{aligned} |\nabla T| &= \frac{1}{F(I)} \\ T_{/G_i} &= 0 \end{aligned} \tag{5}$$

For each pixel, two properties are calculated: the arrival time and the region label that reached that pixel first. All curves are thus allowed to evolve simultaneously and no limiting evolution time is necessary.

The implementation of this algorithm is at the root of a wide range of image processing applications to do various image analysis tasks that one typically encounters in the study of medical microscopic images.

4   Automatic Initialization

An essential step of the whole framework consists in estimating features associated with different labels and in determining the initial seed regions.

Our method consists of two steps:

1) A detection of a set of germs, located in a symmetrical way inside all the interesting objects in the image. Mathematical morphology operators are mainly used to extract these germs.

2) All or a part of these germs is gathered in classes of germs according to their color, by using a fuzzy classification. These seeds are classified according to their color and characterized by region information : the mean and variance of each class i. The latter can be supervised or unsupervised using the available a priori information on the images considered.

4.1   Feature Extraction

A 2D color image I is a function where each pixel (x_1, x_2), by three grey level values in the RGB color space. The gradient amplitude is obtained by the contour information I defined by : $|\nabla I| = \sqrt{\lambda_+ + \lambda_-}$. λ_+, λ_- are the largest, (resp. smallest) eigenvalues of the quadratic form associated to f. The local minima or the h-minima of this contrast image give a set of seed regions placed nearly symmetrically with respect to the object boundaries. The h-minima of the image can be formulated by :

$$h_{min}(U_0) = \left\{ P \; / \; \left(U_0(P) - \gamma^{(rec)}(U_0, U_0 + h)(P) \right) < 0 \right\}$$

where $\gamma^{(rec)}(U_0, U_0 + h)$ denotes the morphological reconstruction by erosion of the $U_0 + h$ image with U_0.

4.2   Fuzzy Classification of Seed Regions

For classification, a modified fuzzy c-mean algorithm [14] is applied to classify all seed pixels in a given image into C classes by minimizing the following objective function :

$$J = \sum_{i=1}^{C} \sum_{j=1}^{N} (u_{ij})^m \, d^2(x_j, c_i) - \alpha \sum_{i=1}^{C} p_i \log(p_i)$$

where u_{ij} is the membership value at pixel j in the class i such that $\sum_{i=1}^{C} u_{ij} = 1$

$\forall \, j \in [0, N]$. $p_i = \frac{1}{N} \sum_{j=1}^{N} u_{ij}$ is interpreted as "the probability" of all the pixels

j to belong to the class i. c_i is the centroid of class i, N is the total number of pixels in image, $d^2(x_j, c_i)$ is the standard Euclidian distance and the fuzziness index m is a weighting coefficient on each fuzzy membership, $m=2$ is an usual value.

In the algorithm, the number of classes C can be known or automatically determined by choosing initially a high value of C and eliminating the class i with the smallest probability p_i.

5   Localization

In order to take into account the information about regions and contours obtained in the classification step , we consider an adaptive speed function F. This function is defined in each point by the following equation:

$$F^i(I)(x,y) = 1 - e^{\frac{1}{2}\left(\sum_{k=1}^{3} |I_k(x,y)-\mu_i^k|^2 + |\nabla_C I(x,y)|^2\right)} \tag{6}$$

where I_k is the kth channel of color image μ_i^k is the mean of classes i on channel k and ∇I_C is the color gradient amplitude.

6   Biomedical Applications

6.1   Color Cytology

For this first biomedical application, images from serous cytology are considered. The images are from a database of digitized cells images, collected from pleural and peritoneal effusions with different pathologies. In this class of images, both cytoplasm and nuclei have to be segmented. Once segmented, the cells can be classified among cellular types (ranging from normal to abnormal). Figure 1(b) gives the set of minima extracted from the amplitude of the gradient. From these ones, markers are obtained for each class : nuclei, cytoplasm and background (figure 1 (c), (d), (e), respectively). Figure 1(f) presents the final result.

6.2   Color Histology

In the second example, acquisitions were performed on sections of immunohisto-chemically stained tissues (figure 2 (a)). The markers involve a brown coloration for positive nuclear locations and a blue coloration for unmarked nuclei (negative locations). Images of this class are more complex than in the previous case. One could be interested by many categories of objects : the clusters of tumoral cells (called lobules in carcinoma),the marked and unmarked tumor nuclei presenting specific characteristics inside the clusters. The goal of this analysis is to evaluate the immunostaining ratio defined as the positive nuclear area to the whole nuclear area within the the lobules limits.

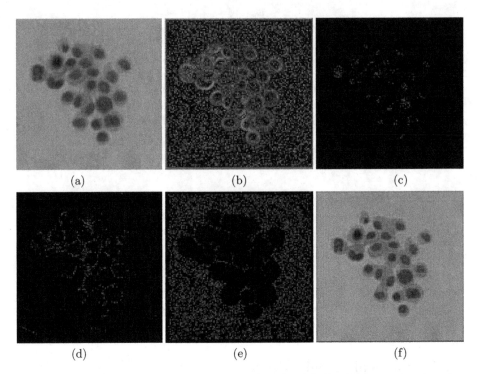

Fig. 1. (a) A serous cytology color image ($\times 20$) . (b) Gradient amplitude minima. (c) Nuclei markers. (d) Cytoplasm markers. (e) Background markers. (f) Final segmentation.

Segmentation of Lobules. The tumoral lobules are made of clusters which can be characterized by a small inter-cellular distance and whose nuclei have a greater size than the other cell categories (lymphocytes or stroma cells for example). The processing goes according to the the following: a)Image simplification is used to remove lymphocytes and to make the clustering of other cells easier. This step uses morphological closing performed on each color plane (i ranging from 1 to 3): $\gamma_B(I_i) = \varepsilon_B \circ \delta_B(I_i)$, where δ_B and ε_B are the dilation and erosion of the ith plane of the color image I by a flat structuring element B.

b)The fuzzy clustering algorithm provides reliable markers for the two different classes of pixels to be used in the localization. The result is a binary mask I_b displaying the lobules (figure 2 (b)).

Detection of the Nuclei Inside the Lobules. This process is twofold:

a) Extraction of the nuclei by residual analysis on the luminance component (I_L) provides a monochromatic image I_R whose positive and negative values form a binary image of nuclei I_a.
b) An inverted image of distance I_d is computed from I_a and the watershed transformation is applied to split nuclei initially merged. The distance and

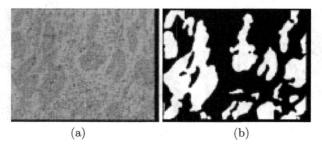

(a)   (b)

Fig. 2. (a) Original histological breast cancer image ($\times 33$). (b) Segmentation result : binary mask of lobules.

the watershed transformations are computed by setting $F=1$ and $F = |\nabla I_d|$ respectively, in equation (5).

The process is limited to the lobule area, by the means of a logical intersection between the image of lobules and that of all nuclei (figure 3 b).

Immunostaining Characterization. A simple binary thresholding, which represents the degre of membership to the class of marked nuclei, allows to detect the positive pixels (brown pixels). To extract the marked nuclei, the segmented objects are reconstructed from the positive pixels in order to assess the total area of positive profiles.

7   Conclusion

A fast statistical level set method for color image segmentation was presented. This method is based on the integration of two attractive techniques : the fuzzy clustering and the level set active contours. They can both take into account local information, such as the gradient modulus, and statistical information, such as the mean color levels in an object. According to their properties, the initialization and localization can be easily extended from 2D images to 3D images, provided by a confocal microscope.

Acknowledgments

Mrs. Herlin from Baclesse Center (Caen) and Mr Helie (Hospital of Cherbourg) have kindly provide applications and images.

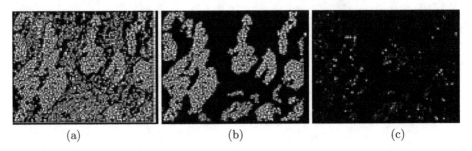

| (a) | (b) | (c) |

Fig. 3. Segmentation of nuclei inside the lobules. (a) Residual analysis of the luminance. (b) Intersection image. (c) Marked nuclei inside the lobules.

References

1. J. Morel, S. Soleimini, *Variational. Methods in Image Segmentation.* Progress in Nonlinear Differential Equations Equations and their application, Birkhaüser 1995.
2. V. Caselles, F. Catte, T. Coll , F. Dibos, A geometric model of active contours", Numerische Mathematick, 66·(1993) 1-3.
3. S. Kichenassamy, A. Kumar, P.J. Olver, A. Tannenbaum, A. Yezzi, Gradient flows and geometric active contours, *Proceeding of Fifth International Conference on Computer Vision, Cambridge,* (1995) 810-815.
4. C. Samson, L. Blanc-Feraud, G. Aubert, J. Zerubia, A level set model for image classification", *rapport de recherche, INRIA,* France, RR-3662 (1999).
5. T. Chan, B. Y. Sandberg, L. Vese, Active Contours without Edges for Vector-Valued Images, *J. of Visual Communication and Image Representation,* 11 (2000) 130-141.
6. T. Chan, B. L. Vese, Active Contours and Segmentations Models Using Geometric PDE's for Medical Imaging, *UCLA CAM Report* (2000).
7. R. Malladi, B. J.A Sethian, , A Real-time Algorithm for Meduical Shape Recovery, *Proceeding of International Conference on Computer Vision,Mubai, India* (1998) 304-310.
8. A. Sarti, C. Ortiz, S. Lockett, R. Malladi, A Geometric Model for 3D Confocal Microscope Image Analysis , *Preprint, Lurence Berkeley National Laboratory, LBLNL-41740,* 1999.
9. A. Elmoataz, S. Schüpp, R. Clouard, P. Herlin, D. Bloyet, Using active contours and mathematical morphology tools for quantification of immunohistochemical images, *Signal Processing,* 71 (1998) 215-226.
10. S. Kim, O(N) Level set , *Math-Report, University of Kentuckey,* (2000).
11. S. Osher, J.A. Sethian, Fronts propagating with curvature-dependent speed: algorithms based on Hamilton-Jacobi formulations, *Journal of computational physics,* 79 (1988) 12-49,.
12. J. Sethian, *Level Set Methods: Evolving interfaces in geometry, fluid mechanics, computer vision, and material science.* Cambridge University Press, (1996).
13. E. Rouy, A. Tourin, " A viscosity solutions approach to shape-from-shading, SIAM J. Numer. Anal., (1992) 29 867-884.
14. A. Lorette, X. Descombes, J. Zerubia, Urban areas extraction based on texture analysis through a markovian modelling, *International Journal of Computer Vision* 36 (2000) 219-234.

Robust Multi-scale Non-rigid Registration of 3D Ultrasound Images

Ioannis Pratikakis, Christian Barillot, and Pierre Hellier

IRISA, INRIA-CNRS, ViSTA Project
Campus universitaire de Beaulieu, 35042 Rennes Cedex, France
i.pratikakis@ieee.org, cbarillo@irisa.fr, phellier@irisa.fr

Abstract. In this paper, we embed the minimization scheme of an automatic 3D non-rigid registration method in a multi-scale framework. The initial model formulation was expressed as a robust multiresolution and multigrid minimization scheme. At the finest level of the multiresolution pyramid, we introduce a focusing strategy from coarse-to-fine scales which leads to an improvement of the accuracy in the registration process. A focusing strategy has been tested for a linear and a non-linear scale-space. Results on 3D Ultrasound images are discussed.

1 Introduction

Non-rigid registration can be considered as a motion estimation problem which can be solved by minimizing an objective function. This function is the energy which usually consists of two terms. The first term represents the interaction between the unknown variables and the data while the second one explores some kind of prior information. In the context of dense motion field estimation, Mémin and Pérez [8] proposed a motion estimator which makes use of the optical flow constraint along with an associated smoothness regularizing prior. Both terms have been constructed with an outlier rejection mechanism, originated from robust statistics. For the minimization of their functional they use a multiresolution and multigrid scheme. The multiresolution part is dedicated to grasp large displacements while the multigrid approach is invoked for accelerating the estimation. Extension of this work to treat 3D data has been done by Hellier et al [5].

In this paper, we embed the above mentioned minimization scheme in a multi-scale framework aiming to improve the estimates by making them less sensitive to noise of acquisition. In the same spirit, Weber and Malik [7] propose a model for multi-scale motion estimation. They convolve an image sequence with a set of linear, separable spatiotemporal filter kernels and apply a robust version of the total least squares on the filtered responses in a two step method. Niessen et al. [11] report a reconciliation of optical flow and scale-space theory. They compute both zeroth and first order optic flow at multiple spatial and temporal scales and they apply a scale selection criterion which attributes in each pixel the optic flow at the chosen scale. Alvarez et al. [1] present an interpretation of a classic optical flow method by Nagel and Enkelmann [10] as a tensor-driven

M. Kerckhove (Ed.): Scale-Space 2001, LNCS 2106, pp. 389–397, 2001.

anisotropic diffusion approach. They avoid convergence to irrelevant local minima by embedding their method in a linear scale-space framework.

Our work was motivated by the application of tissue deformation tracking during surgery using 3D ultrasound. The problem of registration (motion estimation) in ultrasound images has been treated by different researchers. Morcy and Von Ramm [9] investigate the implementation of a correlation search scheme to estimate the 3D motion vectors and demonstrate the advantages over 2D correlation search using the Sum Absolute Difference (SAD) as a similarity measure. Strintzis and Kokkinidis [14] introduce a maximum likelihood block matching technique which corresponds to an accurate statistical description of ultrasound images. In [16] an adaptive mesh has been proposed for non-rigid tissue motion estimation from ultrasound image sequences. A deformable blocking matching algorithm has been developed which takes into consideration both similarity measures and strain energy caused by mesh deformation. In [12], Pennec et al. disseminate results regarding 3D Ultrasound registration using the demon's algorithm and a straightforward minimization of the sum of square of intensity differences criterion.

Non-rigid registration of 3D Ultrasound images poses a significant challenge due to the following shortcomings: (i) Low SNR of ultrasound images which are characterized by Rayleigh-governed speckle noise and corrupted by Gaussian-distributed electronic noise; (ii) motion ambiguities which arise when there is insufficient representation of spatial information. This holds in regions of image saturation or specular reflection and in homogeneous regions of weak acoustic scatterers; (iii) Speckle decorrelation. Since speckle patterns result from the constructive and destructive interference of ultrasonic echoes from numerous subresolvable elements, nonuniform movement of these scatterers in the tissue volume can cause temporal decorrelation of the speckle patterns.

The algorithm which is presented in this paper is designed to overcome the above shortcomings and lead to an accurate registration.

The paper is organized as follows. In Section 2 we present in detail the multiresolution and multigrid optimization scheme. Section 3 describes the multiscale framework that the optimization scheme is embedded. Section 4 is dedicated to experimental results and conclusions are drawn in Section 5.

2   Primary Registration Model

2.1   Formulation of the Registration Problem

In this work, the registration problem is considered as a motion estimation problem. The optical flow hypothesis, introduced by Horn et Schunck [6], leads then to the minimization of the following cost function:

$$U(\boldsymbol{w}; f) = \sum_{s \in S} [\boldsymbol{\nabla} f(s, t) \cdot \boldsymbol{w}_s + f_t(s, t)]^2 + \alpha \sum_{<s,r> \in \mathcal{C}} ||\boldsymbol{w}_s - \boldsymbol{w}_r||^2, \qquad (1)$$

where s is a voxel of the volume, t is the temporal index of the volumes, f is the luminance function, $\boldsymbol{w}$ is the expected $3D$ displacement field, S is the voxel lattice, $\mathcal{C}$ is the set of neighboring pairs and α controls the balance between the two energy terms. The first term is the first order Taylor-expansion of the luminance conservation equation and represents the interaction between the field and the data, whereas the second term expresses the smoothness constraint.

Shortcomings of this formulation are well-known:

(a) The optical flow constraint (OFC) is not valid in case of large displacements because of the linearization.
(b) The OFC might not be valid everywhere, because of the noise, the intensity non-uniformity, and occlusions.
(c) The "real" field probably contains discontinuities that might not be pre-served.

To cope with (b) and (c) limitations, the quadratic cost has been replaced by robust functions. To face problem (a), a multiresolution and multigrid strategy has been designed.

2.2   Robust Estimators

Cost function (1) does not make any difference between relevant data and in-consistent data, and it is sensitive to noise. Therefore, robust M-estimators have been introduced in the formulation [2]. An M-estimator is a function ρ that is increasing on $\mathbb{R}^+$, such that (i) $\phi(u) \triangleq \rho(\sqrt{u})$ is strictly concave on $\mathbb{R}^+$ and (ii) $\lim_{x \to \infty} \rho'(x) < \infty$. The main benefit of robust M-estimators is the semi-quadratic formulation that can be deduced from (i):

$$\exists \psi \in C^1([0, M], \mathbb{R}) : \forall u, \rho(u) = \min_{z \in [0, M]} \left(zu^2 + \psi(z) \right) \qquad (2)$$

Two robust estimators have therefore been introduced: the first one on the data term (ρ_1) and the second one on the regularization term (ρ_2). According to (2), the minimization of the cost function (1) is equivalent to the minimization of the augmented function, noted $\overset{*}{U}$:

$$\overset{*}{U}(\boldsymbol{w}; f) = \sum_{s \in S} \delta_s \left(\boldsymbol{\nabla} f(s, t) \cdot \boldsymbol{w}_s + f_t(s, t) \right)^2 + \psi_1(\delta_s)$$

$$+ \alpha \sum_{<s, r> \in \mathcal{C}} \beta_{sr} \left(||\boldsymbol{w}_s - \boldsymbol{w}_r|| \right)^2 + \psi_2(\beta_{sr}), \qquad (3)$$

where δ_s and β_{sr} are auxiliary variables acting as "weights". This cost function has the advantage to be quadratic with respect to $\boldsymbol{w}$. Furthermore, when the adequation of a data with the model is not correct, its contribution gets lower as the associated weight δ_s decreases ($\delta_s = \phi_1'([\boldsymbol{\nabla} f(s, t) \cdot \boldsymbol{w}_s + f_t]^2)$, and function ϕ' decreases), making this formulation more robust.

2.3   Multiresolution and Multigrid Minimization

In order to cope with large displacements, a classical incremental multiresolution procedure has been developed. A pyramid of volumes $\{f^k\}$ is constructed by successive Gaussian smoothing and subsampling. At the coarsest level, the linearization of the conservation equation can be hopefully used. For the next resolution levels, only an increment $\mathbf{dw}^k$ is estimated to refine estimate $\hat{\mathbf{w}}^k$, obtained from the previous level (Equation 4).

$$
\overset{*}{U}^k(\mathbf{dw}^k; f^k, \hat{\mathbf{w}}^k) = \sum_{s \in S^k} \delta_s^k \left(\boldsymbol{\nabla} f^k(s + \hat{\mathbf{w}}_s^k, t_2)\mathbf{dw}_s^k + f^k(s + \hat{\mathbf{w}}_s^k, t_2) - f^k(s, t_1) \right)^2
$$

$$
+\psi_1(\delta_s^k) + \alpha \sum_{<s,r> \in \mathcal{C}^k} \beta_{sr}^k \left(||(\hat{\mathbf{w}}_s^k + \mathbf{dw}_s^k) - (\hat{\mathbf{w}}_r^k + \mathbf{dw}_r^k)|| \right)^2 + \psi_2(\beta_{sr}^k), \qquad (4)
$$

Furthermore, at each level of resolution, a multigrid minimization based on successive partitions of the initial volume is achieved (see Fig. 1). For each cube of a given grid level ℓ (partition of cubes), a 12-parametric increment field is estimated. The result over the grid level is a rough estimate of the desired solution, and it is used to initialize the next grid level. This hierarchical minimization strategy improves the quality and the convergence rate.

The partition at the coarsest grid level is initialized with a binary segmentation mask of the structure of interest (template). The octree partition which is thus defined is anatomically relevant. When we change grid level, each cube is adaptively divided. The criterion of subdivision may be either the measure of the way that model fits the data, or a prior knowledge such as the presence of an important anatomical structure where estimation must be accurate. Consequently, we can distinguish between the regions of interest where the estimation must be precise and the other regions where computation efforts are useless.

3   Embedded Multi-scale Framework

The multigrid scheme which has already been described is bound to a good initialization of the flow. To improve the quality of the initial estimates we propose to incorporate the scale of image measurements by exploring the scale-space of the data-derived information. Specifically, since we deal with the optical flow constraint we experiment with two scale-spaces which are characterized by the luminance conserving principle. These are the linear scale-space [15] and the one which is constructed by the regularized version [4] of Perona-Malik (P&M) algorithm [13]. Let f_τ^0 be the luminance of a voxel at the finest spatial resolution which has been diffused at the scale quantization level τ. Then, a linear scale-space is denoted as:

$$
f_\tau = f_o * G_\sigma \qquad (5)
$$

where $*$ denotes convolution, f_o is the original image and G_σ is the Gaussian kernel for standard deviation σ.

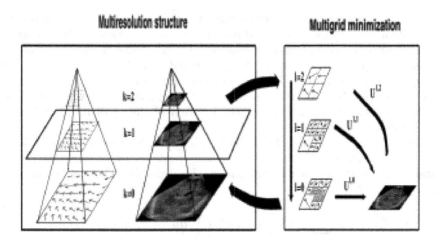

Fig. 1. Example of multiresolution/multigrid minimization. For each resolution level (on the left), a multigrid strategy (on the right) is performed. For clarity reasons, this is a 2D illustration of our 3D algorithm.

If no scale is preferred, the natural way to travel through a linear multi-scale can be realized via a sampling which should follow a linear and dimensionless scale parameter $\delta\lambda$ which is related to σ by :

$$\sigma_\tau = e^{\lambda_0 + \tau\delta\lambda} \tag{6}$$

where τ denotes the scale quantization levels.

The regularized P&M scale-space in its discretized form is denoted as:

$$f_\tau = f_{\tau-1} + \lambda \sum c_i (G_\sigma * \Delta_i f) \tag{7}$$

where $i \in \{N, S, E, W, F, B\}$ and N,S,E,W,F,B denote Northern, Southern, Eastern, Western, Forward and Backward neighbor respectively.

$$c_i = g \parallel G_\sigma * \Delta_i f \parallel \tag{8}$$

c_i is a decreasing function of the image gradient that has been determined at a scale σ to compensate for noise and to assure well-posedness of the diffusion equation. $\Delta_i f = f_i - f_\star$ where $f_\star$ denotes the central pixel in a 3-dimensional mask with 6-neighbor connectivity.

$$g \parallel \Delta_i f \parallel = e^{-\left(\frac{\Delta_i f^2}{k}\right)} \tag{9}$$

$$g \parallel \Delta_i f \parallel = \frac{1}{\left(1 + \frac{\Delta_i f^2}{k}\right)} \tag{10}$$

where k is a contrast parameter and can be interpreted as a threshold, which determines whether a gradient is significant or not.

For non-linear diffusion schemes there is no global scale parameter because they adapt the diffusion locally. However, we may synchronize their scale parameter with the one of linear diffusion. This holds due to the fact that the scalar diffusivity c_i in Equation 8 is constructed such that $\| c \| \leq 1$. Therefore, an upper bound is derived for the nonlinear schemes which permits us to recall the relation between the evolution parameter and the standard deviation of the Gaussian $\tau_n = (1/2)\sigma_n^2$ for the creation of the regularized P&M scale quantization space.

The construction of any of the above scale-spaces leads to a stack of volumes $\{f_\tau^0\}$ which is the source of the data measurements for every successive quantization scale during a coarse-to-fine parameter estimation. This can be explained by Equation 11.

$$\overset{\star}{U}_\tau^0(d\boldsymbol{w}^0; f_\tau^0, \hat{\boldsymbol{w}}^0) = \sum_{s \in S^0} \delta_s^0 \left(\boldsymbol{\nabla} f_\tau^0(s + \hat{\boldsymbol{w}}_s^0, t_2) \cdot d\boldsymbol{w}_s^0 + f_\tau^0(s + \hat{\boldsymbol{w}}_s^0, t_2) - f_\tau^0(s, t_1) \right)^2$$

$$+ \psi_1(\delta_s^0) + \alpha \sum_{<s,r> \in \mathcal{C}^0} \beta_{sr}^0 \left(\|(\hat{\boldsymbol{w}}_s^0 + d\boldsymbol{w}_s^0) - (\hat{\boldsymbol{w}}_r^0 + d\boldsymbol{w}_r^0)\| \right)^2 + \psi_2(\beta_{sr}^0), \tag{11}$$

f_τ^0 denotes the data measurement at the finest pyramid resolution and the τ scale quantization level.

Our goal is the estimation of parameter $\hat{\boldsymbol{w}}^0$ which is refined at each quantization scale by only an increment $d\boldsymbol{w}_s^0$. Minimization remains in the same multigrid fashion.

4   Experimental Results

We have already mentioned in Section 1 that our efforts were motivated by the application of tissue deformation tracking which can result in brain shift correction. In view of this, we have conducted a number of experiments using an original 3D Ultrasound image (256x256x128) of the brain of an 8 months old baby and its deformed counterpart. The acquired original volume is the result of an examination through the fontanella. In the ideal case, the accuracy of our algorithm in registering volumes should be tested in a situation that the actual motion should be known. Due to the difficulty to produce known non-rigid motion fields in biological tissues we have chosen to simulate this phenomenon. We have created an artificially deformed volume by using a Thin Plate Spine deformation [3]. Although this approach produces a global smooth deformation, we were very careful in the distribution of the point landmarks over the whole volume to cope with local deformations. The produced deformed volume and velocity field can be seen in Figure 2(b) and Figure 2(c), respectively.

In our experimental work we strived towards an overall comparison between the primary non-rigid registration model of Section 2 and the model with an embedded scale-space framework of Section 3. Our evaluation is both qualitative and quantitative. As a qualitative measure we have chosen to use the difference image between the original volume and the reconstructed one. All of the registration models produced difference images without significant differences, implying a visually correct registration (Figure 3(b)). For the sake of comparison we provide you the difference image between the original volume and the deformed one in Figure 3(a). The difference image in Figure 3(b) has come out after the application of the algorithm which uses the embedded regularized P&M scale-space.

For a quantitative evaluation we have considered the following measures : (i)Mean square error (MSE); (ii) the average angular error between correct $\overrightarrow{v_c}$ and estimated $\overrightarrow{v_e}$ velocity : $\psi = \arccos(\overrightarrow{v_c} \cdot \overrightarrow{v_e})$ along with (iii) its standard deviation. Table 1 demonstrates the improvement in velocity estimation which

Table 1. Quantitative Comparison Measures.

	MSE	Mean angular error	Std deviation
Without multi-scale framework	10.2772	14.112656^{o}	24.254787^{o}
Embedded Linear scale-space	9.73472	13.878700^{o}	23.987515^{o}
Embedded Regularized P&M scale-space	9.6945	13.791579^{o}	23.959972^{o}

has been achieved for all three above measures in the case of the embedded scale-space framework for both the linear and the regularized P&M case. The latter one has a slightly better behavior than the linear one.

Our basic argumentation for the advantageous use of a multi-scale framework was that it can lead to improvement in quality of the initial estimates at the multigrid optimization scheme which subsequently will improve the quality of the final estimates. A verification of this is presented in Figure 3(c) which shows in terms of MSE the improvement that occurs during successive multigrid levels at the finest spatial resolution for all the three examined cases. We may observe that in the case of the absence of a multi-scale framework we get an initial estimate with an MSE equals to 15.1756 while in the case of linear scale-space we get an initial estimate with an MSE equals to 11.9146 and in the case of regularized P&M scale-space we get an initial estimate with an MSE equals to 12.1082. The higher quality of the initial estimates was preserved till the final stage at the multigrid optimization scheme.

5   Conclusions

In this paper, we propose a methodology which embeds a multi-scale framework in a multiresolution and multigrid optimization scheme that can lead to a successful non-rigid registration of 3D Ultrasound images. It grasps its power from three fundamental features which operate as the remedy in the basic shortcomings of ultrasound images. Its multigrid nature responds to motion ambiguities in the case of insufficient representation of spatial information, its estimate smoothness functional term can fight the speckle decorrelation which characterizes ultrasound while low SNR can be less disastrous for the estimates in the case of embedding a multi-scale framework.

In our last word will keep on defending the use of a multi-scale framework but it will not provide any definite clue about the superiority of either the linear or a non-linear scale-space. We opt on experimenting with more non-linear scale-spaces in order to reach a definite and generalized conclusion.

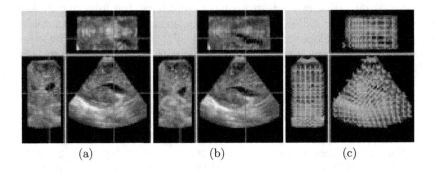

(a)   (b)   (c)

Fig. 2. (a) Preoperative 3D Ultrasound; (b) Simulated intraoperative (Deformed) 3D Ultrasound; (c) The artificial deformation field.

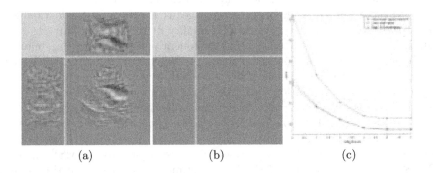

(a)   (b)   (c)

Fig. 3. (a) Difference between the original and the deformed volume; (b) Difference between the original and the reconstructed volume; (c) MSE improvement wrt to multigrid levels at the finest spatial resolution.

Acknowledgments. The 3D US image of the baby was provided by Prof. Auer and his colleagues at ISM (Austria) in the framework of the EC-funded ROBO-SCOPE project (HC 4018), a collaboration between the Fraunhofer Institute (Germany), Fokker Control System (Netherlands), Imperial College (UK), IN-RIA (France), ISM-Salzburg and Kretz Technik (Austria). This work has been granted by INRIA within the Cooperative Action Framework which involved the Epidaure and ISA projects of INRIA. Finally, we are grateful to Xavier Pennec and Nicholas Ayache for their support in this work.

References

1. L. Alvarez, J. Weickert, and J. Sanchez. A scale-space approach to nonlocal optical flow calculations. In *Scale-Space '99*, pages 235–246, 1999.
2. M. Black and A. Rangarajan. On the unification of line processes, outlier rejection and robust statistics with applications in early vision. *International Journal of Computer Vision*, 19(1):57–91, 1996.
3. F.L. Bookstein. Principal warps: Thin-plate slines and the decomposition of defomations. *IEEE Transactions on Pattern Analysis and Machine Intelligence*, 11(6):567–585, 1989.
4. F. Catté, P.L. Lions, J.M. Morel, and T. Coll. Image selective smoothing and edge detection by nonlinear diffusion. *SIAM Journal on Numerical analysis*, 29:182–193, 1992.
5. P. Hellier, C. Barillot, E. Mémin, and P. Pérez. An energy-based framework for dense 3D registration of volumetric brain images. In *IEEE Conf. on Computer Vision and Pattern Recognition (CVPR)*, volume II, pages 270–275, Hilton Head Island, South Carolina, USA, June 2000.
6. B. Horn and B. Schunck. Determining optical flow. *Artificial Intelligence*, 17:185–203, August 1981.
7. J.Weber and J. Malik. Robust computation of optical flow in a multi-scale differential framework. *International Journal of Computer Vision*, 14:67–81, 1995.
8. E. Mémin and P. Pérez. Dense estimation and object-based segmentation of the optical flow with robust techniques. *IEEE Transactions on Image Processing*, 7(5):703–719, 1998.
9. A. Morsy and O. VonRamm. 3D ultrasound tissue motion tracking using correlation search. *Ultrasonic Imaging*, 20:151–159, 1998.
10. H.H. Nagel and W. Enkelmann. An investigation of smoothness constraints for the estimation of displacement vector fields from image sequences. *IEEE Transactions on Pattern Analysis and Machine Intelligence*, 8:565–593, 1986.
11. W.J. Niessen, J.S. Duncan, M. Nielsen, L.M.J. Florack, ter Haar Romeny B.M, and M.A. Viergever. A multiscale approach to image sequence analysis. *Computer Vision and Image Understanding*, 65(2):259–268, 1997.
12. X. Pennec, P. Cachier, and N. Ayache. Understanding the "demon's algorithm": 3D non-rigid registration by gradient descent. In *MICCAI*, pages 597–605, September 1999.
13. P. Perona and J. Malik. Scale-space and edge detection using anisotropic diffusion. *IEEE Transactions on Pattern Analysis and Machine Intelligence*, 12(7):629–639, 1990.
14. M. Strintzis and I. Kokkinidis. Maximum likelihood motion estimation in ultrasound image sequences. *IEEE Signal Processing Letters*, 4(6):156–157, 1997.
15. A.P. Witkin. Scale-space filtering. In *International Joint Conference on Artificial intelligence*, pages 1019–1023, Karlsruhe, W. Germany, 1983.
16. F. Yeung, S. Levinson, D. Fu, and K. Parker. Feature-adaptive motion tracking of ultrasound image sequences using a deformable mesh. *IEEE Transactions on Medical Imaging*, 17(6):945–956, 1998.

Segmentation-Free Estimation of Length Distributions Using Sieves and RIA Morphology

Cris L. Luengo Hendriks and Lucas J. van Vliet

Pattern Recognition Group, Delft University of Technology
Lorentzweg 1, 2628 CJ Delft, The Netherlands
cris@ph.tn.tudelft.nl

Abstract. Length distributions can be estimated using a class of morphological sieves constructed with a so-called Rotation-Invariant, Anisotropic (RIA) morphology. The RIA morphology can only be computed from an (intermediate) morphological orientation space, which is produced by a morphological operation with rotated versions of an anisotropic structuring element. This structuring element is defined as an isotropic region in a subspace of the image space (i.e. it has fewer dimensions than the image). A closing or opening in this framework discriminates on various object lengths, such as the longest or shortest internal diameter. Applied in a sieve, they produce a length distribution. This distribution is obtained from grey-value images, avoiding the need for segmentation. We apply it to images of rice kernels. The distributions thus obtained are compared with measurements on binarized objects in the same images.

1   Introduction

The fraction of broken rice kernels in a batch is used to determine its quality. The milling process used to extract the kernels from their husk breaks a certain amount of them. Broken rice causes the consumer's perception of quality to decrease, and so does the price. This makes it economically important to determine the fraction of broken kernels.

Because manual counting is both expensive and subjective (different people apparently produce different results!), an automated system is required. A flatbed scanner is an ideal instrument to image rice, but it takes a lot of time to distribute the rice kernels on it in such a way that segmentation is possible. Therefore, we have applied a segmentation-free measurement technique to estimate the length distribution of kernels in an image, which can be used to derive the fraction of broken ones. It involves morphological filtering (RIA morphology) at different scales, from which a particle length distribution is obtained. The length of a kernel can be used to determine if it is broken or not. This multi-scale morphological filtering is called sieving.

A sieve is a technique that builds a scale-space using a single morphological operation with a scale parameter. This operation has to be chosen carefully. The morphological operations that are allowed to be used in a sieve must satisfy three properties: increasingness, extensivity and absorption [1]. In this scale-space, image features

M. Kerckhove (Ed.) : Scale-Space 2001, LNCS 2106, pp. 398-406, 2001.

are separated into different levels according to some size measure. The chosen morphological operation determines to what level each feature is assigned.

Since our application requires the measurement of object length, we need a morphological operation that discriminates features based on their length. To this end, we have developed a morphological framework based on a structuring element that is isotropic in a subspace of the image, and thus anisotropic in the image space itself. Since the structuring element has full rotational freedom, this framework is rotation-invariant. It also possesses most of the properties of regular morphology. We name it Rotation-Invariant Anisotropic (RIA) morphology. An RIA opening removes an object in the image if it cannot encompass the structuring element under any orientation. This allows the RIA opening to discriminate objects on their characteristic lengths (supposing convex objects). In the case of an ellipsoid, these would be the principal axes. On an N-dimensional (hyper-)ellipsoid, a 1-dimensional structuring element finds the longest axis, a 2-dimensional one the second longest, etc. An N-dimensional structuring element is isotropic in the image space, and therefore has no rotational freedom; its usage reverts to regular isotropic morphology.

2   The Sieve

Morphological sieves were first proposed by Matheron [1]. They have been extensively used with both binary and grey-value morphology to measure particle-size distributions. Since a sieve has an increasing scale parameter, it results in a scale-space. Many theoretical studies have been made, linking it with linear scale-space theory and other non-linear scale-spaces (see for example Alvarez and Morel [2], or Park and Lee [3]). A sieve can be built with any closing or opening operation Ψ that satisfies these three axioms [1]:

- Extensivity ($\Psi(f) \geq f$) or anti-extensivity ($\Psi(f) \leq f$),

- Increasingness (if $f \leq g$, then $\Psi(f) \leq \Psi(g)$), and

- Absorption (if $\lambda > v$ then $\Psi_\lambda(\Psi_v(f)) = \Psi_v(\Psi_\lambda(f)) = \Psi_\lambda(f)$).

By definition, all openings and closings satisfy the first two axioms, but many do not satisfy the third one [1]. In the next section we will introduce a closing that we use in the application in Sect. 4, and which does satisfy all three axioms. In this section we illustrate the notion of sieving with a generic isotropic closing.

2.1   The Closing Scale-Space

We construct a (continuous) scale-space by closing (ϕ) the image at all scales $r \in (0, \infty)$,

$$F(x,r) = \phi_{D(r)} f(x) \quad .$$

(1)

Each image $F(x,r_0)$ contains only dark features larger than r_0. This is the closing scale-space. We define $F(x,0) = f(x)$. Sampling at discrete scales $r = s[i]$ denoted by $i \in \mathbb{N}$ produces a sampled scale-space,

$$F[x,i] = \phi_{D(s[i])} f(x) \quad .$$

(2)

For uniform scale sampling, $s[i] = i + 1$. However, if the relative error should be kept constant, logarithmic sampling suffices. In this case, $s[i] = b^i$ with $b = 2^{1/n}$, in which n denotes the number of samples per octave.

Some structures contain different scales. Think about a telephone cable, composed of many bundles, each of which is made out of hundreds of thin wires. The wires are part of two structures at different scales. The morphological scale-space as described in this section is capable of finding both scales.

2.2   Size Distributions

The grey-value sum of each of the images in the closing scale-space generates a cumulative size distribution, which is rotation and translation invariant, since the closing is too [4]. By normalization, the cumulative distribution is made independent from the image size, contrast, and the fraction of objects. It is thus defined as

$$H[i] = \frac{\sum_x F[x,i] - \sum_x F[x,0]}{\sum_x F[x,\infty] - \sum_x F[x,0]} \quad ,$$

(3)

where $F[x,\infty]$ is the original image closed with an infinitely large structuring element, and is thus equal to an image filled with its maximum grey-value.

2.3   Implementation Aspects

When looking at the description of a sieve, it is obvious that image features composed of grey-value ramps will be separated into many scales. This can be dealt with by an appropriate pre-processing step (e.g. high pass-filtering, line or edge detection).

Another important question is how to sample the scale-space. There is relatively little literature on this topic, and in most articles, one-pixel increments are used as a default solution. However, we believe it makes sense to use logarithmic sampling, since we might want to distinguish between 3-pixel features and 4-pixel ones, but not between 100-pixel features and 101-pixels ones. This causes the relative error to remain constant across the scales. We will be using four samples per octave for the current application, which means that $s[i] = 2^{i/4}$.

3   RIA Morphology

As stated in the introduction, this morphological framework is based on structuring elements that are isotropic in a subspace of the image, and thus anisotropic in the image space itself. By allowing these structuring elements to rotate, we can create rotation-invariant operators. The operators in this framework that are comparable to the dilation and erosion are actually not a dilation and erosion in the strict morphological sense, since they don't distribute with the intersection and union, respectively. Therefore we will name them *sedimentation* and *wear*, two words with a similar meaning, but without the morphological connotations. The other two operations defined in this framework are the closing and the opening.

In this section, we use δ as the symbol for dilation, ε for erosion, and, as in the previous section, ϕ for closing. As subscripts to these, we provide its structuring element. Translation is also denoted with a subscript: $f_x(t) = f(t-x)$.

3.1   Sedimentation and Wear

By decomposing the dilation with an isotropic structuring element D with radius r into a union of dilations with rotated one-dimensional isotropic elements L_φ with radius r and orientation φ, we get

$$\delta_D f = f \oplus D = f \oplus \bigcup_\varphi L_\varphi = \bigvee_\varphi \delta_{L_\varphi} f \quad . \tag{4}$$

Note that here φ is taken as a multi-dimensional orientation, or *orientation vector*. If, instead of taking the maximum over the dilations, we take the minimum, we get a new operator, which we will call RIA sedimentation,

$$\delta_L^{\prec} = \bigwedge_\varphi \delta_{L_\varphi} f \quad . \tag{5}$$

Here L can be any isotropic support with less dimensions than the image itself, and thus does not need to be a line. This operator takes the maximum of the image over the structuring element, rotated in such a way as to minimize this maximum. Fig. 1 gives an example of the effect that this operator has on an object boundary. Note that a convex object boundary is not changed, but a concave one is.

In the 2D case, in which L is a line, we can compare this sedimentation operator with a train running along a track. The train wagons (which are joined at both ends to the track) require some extra space at the inside of the curves. This sedimentation, applied to a train track, and using a structuring element with the length of the wagons, reproduces the area required by them. Note that this analogy is only true if the length of the structuring element is small compared to the curvature of the boundary. This is always true for a train track, but not necessarily so for a grey-value image.

By duality, one can define the RIA wear as the maximum of a set of erosions with rotated line segments.

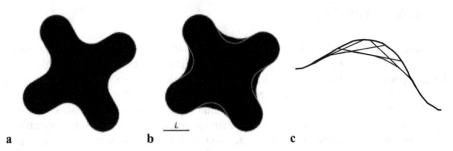

a   b   c

Fig. 1. Effect of the RIA dilation on an object boundary. The white line in *b* represents the original object boundary. In *c*, its construction

3.2   Opening and Closing

The closing is usually defined as a dilation followed by an erosion. However, it is easier to understand (and modify) if we see it as the maximum of the image over the support of the structuring element D, after shifting it in such a way that it minimizes this maximum, but still hits the point t at which the operation is being evaluated. Or, in other words, the 'lowest' position we can give D by shifting it over the 'landscape' defined by the function f,

$$\phi_D f = \bigwedge_{x \in D} \bigvee_{y \in D_x} f_y \quad \left[= \bigwedge_{x \in D} \left(\bigvee_{y \in D} f_y \right)_x = \varepsilon_D \delta_D f \right] \quad . \tag{6}$$

In accordance to this, we define a new morphological operation, RIA closing, as the 'lowest' position we can give the subspace structuring element L, by shifting and rotating it over the 'landscape' f, such that it still hits the point x being evaluated. It is defined by

$$\phi_L^\alpha f = \bigwedge_\varphi \bigwedge_{x \in L_\varphi} \bigvee_{y \in L_{\varphi,x}} f_y \quad . \tag{7}$$

This turns out to be the same as the minimum of the closings, at all orientations, with the structuring element L (but not equal to an RIA sedimentation followed by an RIA wear),

$$\phi_L^\alpha f = \bigwedge_\varphi \bigwedge_{x \in L_\varphi} \left(\bigvee_{y \in L_\varphi} f_y \right)_x = \bigwedge_\varphi \varepsilon_{L_\varphi} \delta_{L_\varphi} f = \bigwedge_\varphi \phi_{L_\varphi} f \quad . \tag{8}$$

According to Matheron, this operation is an algebraic closing since it is an intersection of morphological closings [1]. This implies that extensivity, increasingness and absorption are satisfied, and they can be used in a sieve. The two-dimensional case is an intersection of closings with rotated lines, which have been used before (see for example Soille [4]), and we will use in the next section.

By duality, one can define the RIA opening as the maximum of openings with rotated line segments.

3.3 Morphological Orientation Space and RIA Morphology

The morphological operation ψ by rotated versions of an anisotropic structuring element L can be used to construct a morphological orientation space

$$f_{\Psi,L}(x,y,\varphi) = \Psi_{L_\varphi} f(x,y) \quad . \tag{9}$$

The RIA sedimentation and closing now result from a maximum projection along the orientation axes,

$$\Psi_L^\triangleleft f(x,y) = \bigwedge_\varphi f_{\Psi,L}(x,y,\varphi) \quad . \tag{10}$$

The RIA wear and opening result from a minimum projection. In a sieve, this orientation space would be extended with a scale dimension.

4 Length Measurement of the Rice Kernels

Fig. 2 shows two images of rice kernels obtained by placing the rice on a flatbed scanner. The image on the left has all kernels manually separated before acquisition, which takes about 15 minutes. The one on the right contains the same kernels randomly scattered on the scanning surface. As stated before, it is not trivial to correctly segment such an image. Thus, the classical measuring paradigm (threshold, label, measure the segmented objects) is not easily applied.

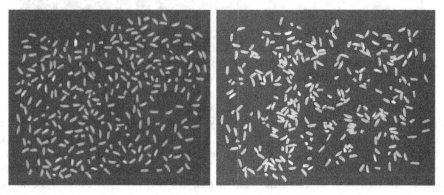

Fig. 2. Two images of rice kernels. The image on the left has been made after carefully separating all kernels to make segmentation easy

In total we have 10 images of the same sample, 20% of which consists of broken kernels:

- two images with only the broken kernels (one touching, one separated),
- two images with only the intact kernels (again, one touching, one separated), and
- six images with all kernels (two touching, four separated).

Accurate and reliable measurements can be obtained by applying the sieve with an RIA opening to an image with all kernels separated (as the image on the left of Fig. 2). However, that is the easy problem. An image with touching kernels will produce an over-estimation of the particle sizes, since groups of rice kernels can accommodate larger line segments than single rice kernels. The solution would be to use 'thick lines' (ellipses). If these are thick enough not to fit through the union point between touching rice kernels (which is usually thinner than the kernels themselves), the measurements produce the same results as on the first image.

4.1   Preprocessing

To increase the accuracy of the measurements we do some preprocessing on the images (see Fig. 3 for the results of these steps). The goals are twofold:

1. remove imaging artifacts, and
2. remove kernels that are thinner than the structuring element to avoid an underestimation of the lengths.

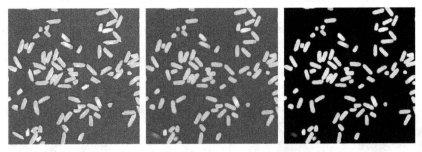

Fig. 3. Preprocessing of the images: first, an opening removes thin elements, which are not counted in de length distributions (*middle*). Then, an error-function clip is applied (*right*)

Because we use thick line segments as structuring elements, all kernels and portions of kernels that are thinner than these will be put into the smallest scale of the granulometry. To overcome this we remove these features by an opening with a disk of diameter equal to the width of the line segments. Since very few rice kernels are too thin, removing them introduces only a very small imprecision in the measurements. The thinner portions of the kernels that are also removed cause these to be somewhat shorter. This yields a systematic error, an average underestimation of the lengths of four pixels (result obtained experimentally). This causes a shift to the left of the cumulative length distribution. This error would, however, also be produced by the introduction of thick line segments (in addition to an overestimation of the smallest scale).

The second operation that is applied to the images is an error-function clip. This is a clipping that introduces less aliasing than hard clipping [5]. Its need is two-fold: removing noise in the background, and equalizing the grey-value over the rice kernels. Some of these contain a chalky portion, caused by an unbalanced growing process. This chalky portion is imaged whiter than the rest of the kernel, and would influence the length distribution by adding weight to the smaller scales.

4.2   The Classical Measuring Paradigm

To compare our results with those obtained with an existing algorithm, we measured the length distribution using the Feret length measure [6] on the thresholded and segmented image. This works well on the images where the kernels have been manually separated before acquisition, but produces poor results on the images with touching kernels. The algorithm we used to determine the Feret length uses a chain-code representation of the object boundary, which can be easily rotated. The longest projection of the boundary is used as the object length.

4.3   Results

The length distributions of the two images in Fig. 2, obtained by the proposed sieve as well as the Feret length, are plotted in Fig. 4. The results for both images using the sieve are almost identical and only slightly different from the measurement obtained using the classical method applied to the image with separated kernels. However, the classical method applied to the image with touching kernels produces a very large over-estimation of the sizes. Fig. 5 shows the results obtained by the sieve on the ten images. In all cases, the sieve applied to the images with touching kernels produces only a minimal overestimation of the kernel length.

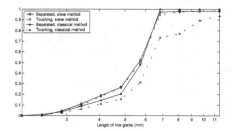

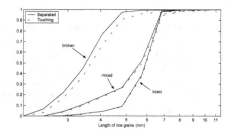

Fig. 4. Comparison of the classical segment and measure method, and the sieve with the RIA opening. For the latter, touching rice kernels do not influence the measurement very much. Note the logarithmic scaling of the horizontal axis

Fig. 5. Cumulative distribution measured for the images. This figure shows that it is easy to measure the fraction of broken kernels in this way. The difference induced by the contact between rice kernels is very small

5 Conclusion

For the application discussed in this article, as well as many other applications, segmentation is very difficult or not possible at all. Segmentation-free measurement techniques are therefore desirable. Sieves, a form of multi-scale morphological filtering, are very useful in this context. Sieves produce size distributions from grey-value images, and the measure for the size of the image features is determined by the chosen morphological operation. Since this application requires length measurement, RIA openings have been used in a sieve to obtain length distributions.

RIA (Rotation-Invariant Anisotropic) openings are the openings in a new morphological framework that results from decomposing an isotropic structuring element into rotated lower-dimensional isotropic structuring elements. An RIA opening only removes an image feature if the chosen structuring element does not fit under any orientation.

The proposed sieve is applied to measure the length distribution of rice kernels acquired with a flatbed scanner. These were scattered quickly onto the scanning surface, so that many are touching. To minimize the influence of the touching kernels, we have modified the RIA openings slightly, using line segments of certain width, instead of using one-pixel thin line segments. With this modification, the obtained distributions are almost identical for the images with separated and touching kernels. In contrast, the classical measuring paradigm (which uses a threshold, segmentation of the objects, and measuring the length based on these binarized shapes) produces incorrect results for the image with the touching kernels.

References

1.   G. Matheron, Random Sets and Integral Geometry. New York: Wiley, 1975.
2.   L. Alvarez and J.-M. Morel, Morphological Approach to Multiscale Analysis: From Principles to Equations, in Geometry-Driven Diffusion in computer Vision, M. A. Viergever (ed). Dordrecht: Kluwer Academic Publishers, 1994.
3.   K.-R. Park and C.-N. Lee, Scale-Space Using Mathematical Morphology, IEEE Transactions on Pattern Analysis and Machine Intelligence, vol. 18, pp. 1121-1126, 1996.
4.   P. Soille, Morphological Image Analysis. Berlin: Springer-Verlag, 1999.
5.   L. J. van Vliet, Grey-Scale Measurements in Multi-Dimensional Digitized Images. Ph.D. Thesis, Delft University of Technology, Delft, 1993.
6.   L. R. Feret, La grosseur des grains, Assoc. Intern. Essais Math. 2D, Zurich, 1931.

Morphological Tools for Robust Key-Region Extraction and Video Shot Modeling*

Javier Ruiz Hidalgo and Philippe Salembier

Technical University of Catalonia, Barcelona, Spain
{jrh,philippe}@gps.tsc.upc.es

Abstract. In recent years, the use of multimedia content has experienced an exponential growth. In this context, the need of new image/video sequence representation is becoming a necessity for many applications. This paper deals with the structuring of video shots in terms of various foreground key-regions and a background mosaic. Each key-region represents different foreground objects that appear through the entire sequence in a similar manner the mosaic image represents the background information of the complete sequence. We focus on the interest of morphological tools such as connected operators or watersheds to perform the shot analysis and the computation of the key-regions and the mosaic. It will be shown that morphological tools are particularly attractive to improve the robustness of the various steps of the algorithm.

1 Introduction

Images and video sequences modeling is experiencing important developments. Part of this evolution is due to the need to support a large number of new multimedia services. Traditionally, digital images were represented as rectangular arrays of pixels and digital video was seen as a flow of frames. New multimedia applications can rely on indexing or content-based coding that allow a representation that is more structured and hopefully closer to the real word.

The most straightforward way of representing video shots is to consider them as a set of contiguous frames. An alternative approach is to represent them by a subset of representative frames called key-frames. A more sophisticated approach for shot representation involves the analysis of the spatio-temporal content of the video shot. In [5] and [7], for instance, the representation of a video shot is composed of a set of layers representing the background information and various foreground layers. An attractive background representation relies on mosaic images [5,1]. Mosaics are panoramic views of the background components that are visible during the shot [5,7]. Mobile foreground objects can then be superimposed to the mosaic representation. In the sequel, these foreground objects will be represented by *key-regions*. A typical example of shot representation based on background mosaic and key-regions is shown in Fig. 1. The background mosaic

---

* The authors would like to thank the support of the European Commission and in particular, the ACTS DICEMAN Project.

M. Kerckhove (Ed.): Scale-Space 2001, LNCS 2106, pp. 407–416, 2001.

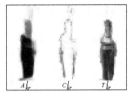

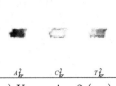

a) Background Mosaic   b) Key-region 1 (girl)   c) Key-region 2 (car)

Fig. 1. Video shot representation with a background mosaic a) and two key-regions b) and c). Key-regions are represented from left to right by an appearance image A_{kr}, a contour image C_{kr} and a texture image T_{kr}.

is presented in Fig. 1.a and two key-regions are shown in Fig. 1.b and 1.c. Each key-region is represented here by an appearance image A_{kr}^k, a contour image C_{kr}^k and a texture image T_{kr}^k, where kr stands for key-region and k the key-region number. The meaning and computation of these images will be presented in this paper. Note that the motion trajectories of the key-regions are also drawn (as white lines) on the background mosaic.

The extraction of foreground regions in video sequences is an active research topic. Classical approaches [5,7] mainly rely on motion information. However, pure motion-based algorithms fail when shots present rapidly changing backgrounds, when foreground objects present little motion with respect to the camera or when foreground objects have a low contrast with respect to the background. The shot representation technique proposed in this paper builds, in a first step, a background mosaic and then uses this mosaic to extract key-regions. Beside the explanation of the complete algorithm, the main focus of this paper is to highlight the use of morphological tools such as connected operators [4] and watersheds to improve the robustness of the algorithm [2,6].

This paper is organized as follows. Section 2 gives an overview of the proposed algorithm. Section 3 presents the use of motion-oriented connected operators for outliers detection in the mosaic creation algorithm. Section 4 explains the foreground segmentation algorithm and section 5 the creation of key-regions. The representation and modeling of key-regions are discussed in section 6. Finally, conclusions are drawn on section 7.

2   Overview of the Algorithm

The algorithm is highlighted in Fig. 2 and involves three steps. The first one is the background mosaic computation (top blocks of Fig. 2). The second step extracts the shape of each key-region at each time instant (middle blocks) and the last step combines the information obtained at each time instant and builds the key-region models (bottom blocks). Next sections will describe each step.

The background mosaic computation follows a classical approach [1]. The first step is to compute the dominant motion between successive input images, $I(t)$ and $I(t-1)$. The dominant motion, $m(t)$, is assumed to represent the camera

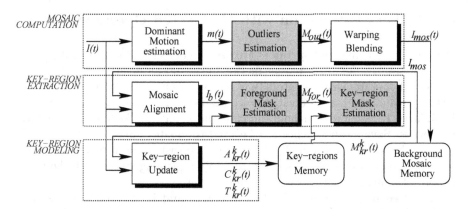

Fig. 2. Overview of the algorithm. Blocks in gray represent steps where morphological tools are used (only the major input and output signals are represented).

motion and is used to warp the original frames in the same coordinate system. The warped images are blended to produce the mosaic image, I_{mos}. In order to be robust, the blending should only take into account pixels belonging to the background. As a result, before the warping and blending step, outliers that do not follow the dominant motion are identified. They are represented by an outliers mask $M_{out}(t)$. In section 3, we will show how morphological connected operators efficiently allow the identification of outliers.

The second step extracts, for each key-region k at time t, a key-region mask $M_{kr}^k(t)$. This extraction starts by the mosaic alignment. Its goal is to produce an estimation of the background information, $I_b(t)$, at time t. Taking into account the dominant motion, the relevant part of the mosaic is un-warped to be compared to the current image $I(t)$. A foreground mask, $M_{for}(t)$, is computed by comparing the original image $I(t)$ with the background estimation $I_b(t)$. A watershed algorithm (section 4) is used for this step. The foreground mask $M_{for}(t)$ is an estimation of the key-regions at time t. However, this estimation is not very reliable because it is obtained on the basis of the observation of a single time instant. To improve the robustness of the analysis, the last step combines the contour information of the foreground masks extracted at each past time instant and selects the most reliable sections that have been observed to create the mask of the key-region, $M_{kr}^k(t)$. A watershed algorithm can be also used to combine a set of contours taking into account their reliability (section 5).

Finally, the last step of the algorithm takes into account the key-region masks, $M_{kr}^k(t)$, as well as the original image, $I(t)$, to update the key-region models (see section 6 for more details). In the following sections, we explain the use of morphological tools for the outliers estimation (section 3), the foreground mask estimation (section 4) and the key-region mask estimation (section 5).

3   Outliers Estimation with Connected Operators

Morphological connected operators are used to detect and remove outliers that do not follow the dominant mosaic motion in the mosaic creation step. Gray level connected operators are operators that act by merging elementary regions called *flat zones* [4]. They cannot create new contours or modify the position of existing boundaries between regions and, therefore, have very good contour preservation properties. Several approaches can be used to create connected operators. We will use the one discussed in [3]. The strategy consists in creating a region-based tree representation of the image and to apply a pruning strategy on the tree to simplify the image (in this case, without the outliers).

The tree representation is called Max-tree and is oriented towards signal maxima. Each node $\mathcal{N}_i$ in the tree represents a connected component of the space that is extracted by the following thresholding process: for a given threshold value T, consider the set of pixels X that have a gray level value larger than T and the set of pixels Y that have a gray level value equal to T:

$$X = \{x, \text{ such that } f(x) \geq T\} \text{ and } Y = \{x, \text{ such that } f(x) = T\} \tag{1}$$

The nodes $\mathcal{N}_i$ represent the connected components of X such that $X \bigcap Y \neq \emptyset$.

The filtering strategy consists in pruning the tree and in reconstructing the image from the resulting pruned tree. The simplification is governed by a criterion which may involve simple notions such as size, contrast or more complex ones such as texture, motion or even semantic criteria. Here, the detection of outliers is based on a motion criterion. For all input frames, the corresponding max-tree is created. A recursive version of the mean displaced frame difference is computed for all nodes of the trees using the dominant mosaic motion $m(t)$ [3]. Nodes of the tree that do not follow the given motion produce a high displaced difference and should be removed. The criterion is not increasing: there is no constraint stating that if a node has to be removed, its children have also to be removed. Therefore, a dynamic programming strategy based on the Viterbi algorithm is used. We refer the reader to [3] for a complete description of the max-tree creation and the morphological filtering involved.

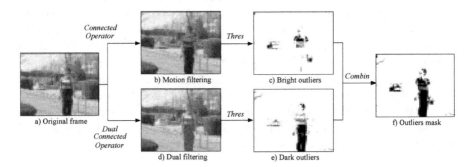

Fig. 3. Estimation of outliers with connected operators

Fig. 3 shows an example of outliers estimation. Connected operators remove maxima of the image that do not follow the dominant mosaic motion. Fig. 3.b and 3.c show an original frame and the output of the connected filter. The filter has removed the bright components of the outliers (the girl and the car) and has preserved the background information. Comparison between the original and filtered frames gives the mask corresponding to bright outliers. The estimation of dark outliers can be done using the dual connected operator. The dual operator ψ^* is defined by: $\psi^*(f) = -\psi(-f)$ and has the same effects as ψ but on minima. Fig. 3.e and 3.f show the filtered output and the mask corresponding to dark outliers. The final outliers mask is shown in Fig. 3.g.

On the other hand, classical mosaic creation algorithms try to remove outliers by defining a map assigning to each pixel a value representing whether it belongs to the foreground or to the background. The classical value assigned to each pixel of the weight map image is:

$$w(t)[x] = \frac{c}{c + |I(t)[x] - I(t-1)[x - m(t)[x]]|^2} \tag{2}$$

Fig. 4. Comparison of mosaic creation without a) and with b) connected operators.

Fig. 4 compares the classical solution with the one proposed using connected operators. The classical approach does not allow the elimination of outliers that occupy a significant portion of the image (as the girl). A dark shadow is clearly visible in the lower right part of the mosaic of Fig. 4. Moreover, the partial elimination of outliers has a strong effect on the successive warping and blending steps: strong geometrical deformations appear on the lower right part of Fig. 4.a.

4   Foreground Mask Estimation with Watershed

The foreground mask extraction process is outlined in Fig. 5. Using the dominant motion, the relevant part of the mosaic is un-warped to produce an estimation of the background $I_b(t)$ at time t, that can be compared to the current image $I(t)$. All the relevant information is concentrated in the image: $I(t) - I_b(t)$. The foreground mask, $M_{for}(t)$, is computed by using a watershed algorithm [6]. The watershed algorithm is applied on a gradient image and uses markers to initiate the propagation process.

The gradient image should indicate the contours of the foreground mask. It is mainly computed from the image gradient of $I(t) - I_b(t)$. However, this gradient

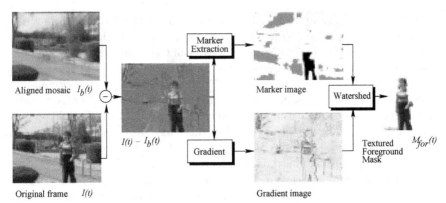

Fig. 5. Estimation of the foreground mask

highlights contours but also textured areas. To solve this drawback, the gradient is weighted (pixel by pixel) by a temporal gradient: $\mathcal{G}\{I(t) - I(t-1)\}$, where $\mathcal{G}$ denotes the gradient operator:

$$G(t) = \mathcal{G}\{I(t) - I_b(t)\} \cdot (\mathcal{G}\{I(t) - I(t-1)\} \vee \mathcal{G}_0) \qquad (3)$$

where $\vee$ denotes the maximum and $\mathcal{G}_0$ is used as lower-bound of the weighting gradient so that the weight is not too low on static areas.

Markers are obtained by thresholding $|I(t) - I_b(t)|$ and by erosion of the resulting masks. Two different thresholds, t_{for} and t_{back}, are used to extract foreground and background makers. Assume that $\epsilon_s\{\cdot\}$ denotes a binary erosion with a structuring element, s. The foreground and background markers are defined by $M_{for}(t) = \epsilon_s\{|I(t) - I_b(t)| > t_{for}\}$ and $M_{back}(t) = \epsilon_s\{|I(t) - I_b(t)| < t_{back}\}$ respectively. The threshold values were empirically chosen to be $t_{for} = 35$, $t_{back} = 10$ and s an square structuring element whose length is 2 per cent of the original image size. Results have shown these values to be very robust even across different type of sequences. Foreground and background markers are combined in a single image called *Marker image* in Fig. 5. In this image, the dark (grey) areas correspond to foreground (background) markers.

Finally, the watershed is applied to the gradient image $G(t)$ using the markers, $M_{for}(t)$ and $M_{back}(t)$. A final step groups all connected regions into the same connected masks and considers non-connected regions as different foreground regions. The segmentation can be seen on the right side of Fig. 5 where the girl has been successfully segmented from the background.

5   Key-Region Mask Definition with Watershed

The foreground mask $M_{for}(t)$ is an estimation of the key-regions at time t. However, this estimation is not very reliable because it is obtained on the basis of the observation of a single time instant. To improve the robustness of the analysis, the key-region mask estimation step combines the contour information of the foreground masks extracted at past time instants and selects the most reliable sections to create the mask of the key-region k, $M_{kr}^k(t)$.

The first step of the algorithm is to associate connected components of the background mask $M_{for}(t)$ to key-regions that are already stored in the key-region memory. A connected component of the foreground mask is assigned to an existing key-region if it sufficiently overlaps with the last assigned foreground mask of the corresponding key-region. This approach works well on common scenes where changes between frames (at 25 or 30 fps) are usually small. If the current foreground mask does not correspond to any known key-region, a new key-region is created.

Once a connected component of the foreground mask is assigned to an existing key-region, it should be aligned to the same coordinate system. This alignment is performed by estimating the motion between the foreground mask and the stored key-region. After alignment, let us denote by $\hat{M}_{for}(t)$ and $\hat{I}(t)$ the motion compensated version of the foreground mask and the motion compensated input image. These images can be seen on the left side of Fig. 6. Note that, in this example, the contour of the foreground mask is not always reliable. Our goal is to combine this contour information with the contour information of the same key-region extracted at previous time instants taking into account the reliability of contours in time. The update of the foreground shape starts from the compensated foreground mask $\hat{M}_{for}(t)$ and is performed as follows. Assume that I is an image and M a mask, $\mathcal{C}\{I, M\}$ denotes an image equal to zero except on the contours of M where it takes the values of I. The contour reliability of the foreground mask $\hat{M}_{for}(t)$ is obtained by:

$$\hat{C}_{for}(t) = \mathcal{C}\left\{\mathcal{G}\{\hat{I}(t)\}, \hat{M}_{for}(t)\right\} \tag{4}$$

The pixels value of this contour image is a confidence measure of the contours of the current foreground mask $\hat{M}_{for}(t)$. Low values imply that the corresponding contour does not correspond to contrasted edges. This can occur, for instance, when the foreground occludes a background region of the same color. High values on the contour measure correspond to strong edges on the original image and therefore to reliable contours. Fig. 6 illustrates the use of the contour image to correct possible segmentation errors in the foreground mask extraction algorithm. In this example, the foreground mask extracted at frame 2039 of the *nhkvideo7* sequence of the *MPEG-7* database is of poor quality due to a low contrast between the girl and the background in that specific time instant.

The two images on the left side of Fig. 6 show the extracted foreground mask $\hat{M}_{for}(t)$ and the measure of contours reliability $\hat{C}_{for}(t)$ (as in Equ. (4)). This measure of the contour confidence on the current foreground mask is compared with the same accumulated measures from the previous foreground masks assigned to the same key-region, $C_{kr}^k(t-1)$. This accumulated contour image is part of the key-region model (see section 6). The corresponding accumulated contours measure of the key-region is shown on the bottom image of Fig. 6. The combination of the current contour $\hat{C}_{for}(t)$ and the accumulated contours $C_{kr}^k(t-1)$ is done by a maximum operation:

$$\hat{C}_u(t) = a\hat{C}_{for}(t) \vee (1-a)C_{kr}^k(t-1) \tag{5}$$

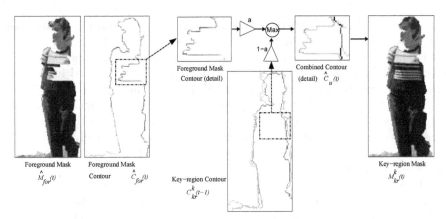

Fig. 6. Creation of the key-region mask $M_{kr}^k(t)$ taking into account the reliability of the current foreground mask $\hat{M}_{for}(t)$ and of past contour information $C_{kr}^k(t-1)$.

The parameter $a \in [0, 1]$ controls the memory of the allowed modifications to the shape of extracted foreground masks. If $a \simeq 0$, previously segmented key-region contours are trusted more than the current contours from the foreground mask. In this case, errors in the foreground mask are easier to fix but tracking non-rigid foreground regions becomes more difficult. On the other hand, if $a \simeq 1$, non-rigid regions are easier to track but segmenting errors are also more difficult to correct. In our case, a value of $a = 0.5$ has been used for all examples. Note that resulting contour values of $\hat{C}_u(t)$ are only used locally as the gradient image for the watershed of the key-region mask definition (see Figure 6) so the implied lowered of the gradient when using $a < 1$ is not propagated on following frames.

The estimation of the final mask of the foreground region: $M_{kr}^k(t)$ is done with a watershed algorithm. The markers for this watershed consist of two points, one inside the foreground mask and one outside (in the background). The output of the watershed algorithm is the new foreground mask $M_{kr}^k(t)$ where the most reliable contour parts from the foreground mask and from the assigned key-region have been used. The resulting mask is shown on the right side of Fig. 6. The initial error in the foreground mask shape has been eliminated and replaced by the most reliable contour observed in the past. In general, this procedure allows the progressive improvement of the key-region contours on a frame by frame basis taking into account the reliability of past extracted key-region contours.

6   Key-Region Modeling

The final step of the algorithm creates and updates a model for each key-region observed in the scene (Key-region update block of Fig. 2). The key-region model consists of a template of three images. An appearance image, a contours image and a texture image. The appearance image $A_{kr}^k(t)$ shows the frequency with

Fig. 7. Modeling of key-region k with, from left to right, an appearance image $A_{kr}^k(t)$, a contour image $C_{kr}^k(t)$ and a texture image $T_{kr}^k(t)$.

which a pixel has been estimated as belonging to key-region k. The contour image $C_{kr}^k(t)$ stores the confidence of the key-region contours and is used to modify the input foreground masks in a frame basis as seen in the previous section. Finally, the texture image $T_{kr}^k(t)$ represents the overall texture of the key-region.

If the key-region mask $M_{kr}^k(t) = 1$ denotes pixels that have been extracted and assigned to key-region k at time t and, $\hat{C}_{for}(t)$ is the contour confidence of the extracted foreground mask (as in Equ. (4)). The equations that update each template image are (pointwise operations are implied):

$$T_{kr}^k(t) = \frac{A_{kr}^k(t-1)T_{kr}^k(t-1) + M_{kr}^k(t)\hat{I}(t)}{A_{kr}^k(t)} \qquad C_{kr}^k(t) = \frac{A_{kr}^k(t-1)C_{kr}^k(t-1) + \hat{C}_{for}(t)}{A_{kr}^k(t)}$$

$$A_{kr}^k(t) = A_{kr}^k(t-1) + M_{kr}^k(t) \tag{6}$$

Fig. 7 shows the key-region template images from a scene where a person walks in front of the camera. The appearance, contour and texture template images contain information of the activity followed by the key-region. In this case, higher body parts (body, chest) show no relative movement while lower parts (legs) show a considerable amount of relative motion. This representation is particularly attractive to analyze the activity of non-rigid regions.

Fig. 1 shows a complete shot representation of the *nhkvideo7* sequence. The background information is separated from the key-regions of the scene. In the original sequence, the camera follows the walking girl while a car crosses the road in the background. Two key-regions have been extracted corresponding to the girl and the car. Fig. 1.b and 1.c show the corresponding template images of the two key-regions. Superimposed to the final mosaic image, the relative motion respect to the camera is drawn.

7   Conclusion

A method for representing and structuring video shots has been presented. A robust outliers detection algorithm based on connected operators is used to estimate and create a mosaic image of the background information of the scene. This background information can then be used to extract representative foreground key-regions that appear in the shot. The proposed approach uses a watershed algorithm to extract the foreground mask on a frame by frame basis. These foreground regions are refined using the reliability of previous extracted contours and are progressively combined into key-region templates. At this step, the watershed algorithm turned out to be again an attractive solution. Both key-regions templates and mosaic image create a compact and useful representation of the content and of the activity of the scene allowing the possibility of further representation, indexing and analysis of the shot.

References

1. J. Davis. Mosaics of scenes with moving objects. In *Proceedings of Computer Vision and Pattern Recognition*, pages 354–360, Santa Barbara, USA, June 1998.
2. F. Meyer and S. Beucher. Morphological segmentation. *Journal of Visual Computing and Image Representation*, 1(1):21–45, 1990.
3. P. Salembier, A. Oliveras, and L. Garrido. Antiextensive connected operators for image and sequence processing. *IEEE Trans. on IP*, 7(4):555–570, April 1998.
4. P. Salembier and J. Serra. Flat zones filtering, connected operators and filters by reconstruction. *IEEE Trans. on IP*, 3(8):1153–1160, August 1995.
5. H.S. Sawhney and S. Ayer. Compact representation of videos through dominant multiple motion estimation. *IEEE Trans. on PAMI*, 18(8):814–830, 1996.
6. L. Vincent and P. Soille. Watersheds in digital spaces: an efficient algorithm based on immersion simulations. *IEEE Trans. on PAMI*, 13:583–598, 1991.
7. J. Wang and E. Adelson. Representing moving images with layers. *IEEE Trans. on IP*, 3(5):625–638, September 1994.

Polyhedral Set Operations for 3D Discrete Object Deformation

Yukiko Kenmochi[1]* and Atsushi Imiya[2]

[1] School of Information Science, JAIST, Japan
[2] Department of Information and Image Sciences, Chiba University, Japan
kenmochi@jaist.ac.jp,imiya@ics.tj.chiba-u.ac.jp

Abstract. In 3D and 4D digital image analysis, deformable objects are considered for object recognition and shape analysis. In this paper, we study for an algebraic framework for 3-dimensional object deformation in a discrete space by defining polyhedral sets and their set operations.

1 Introduction

In digital image analysis, not only still objects but moving/deforming objects are currently considered for object recognition and shape analysis. For instance, we use deformable object models for object segmentation from digital images such as active contours [1], object deformation description of a sequence of digital images [2], and thinning and skeletonization for topological-based object analysis [3].

In this paper, given a sequence of 3-dimensional(3D) digital images, we consider to obtain a sequence of the shape features via a sequence of polyhedral representation of a deformable object. We use polyhedral object representation because we consider geometric and topological shape analysis for the final outputs. In this paper, we focus on the first stage in which we obtain a sequence of deformable polyhedra from a sequence of 3D digital images. We make an algebraic framework for 3-dimensional object deformation in a discrete space by defining polyhedral sets and their set operations in a 3-dimensional discrete space. The efficient extraction algorithms for topological features from a sequence of deformable polyhedra are presented in [4].

There are two different representations for polyhedral sets: a set of all points in a polyhedral region in the 3-dimensional Euclidean space and another is a set of polygons which are the boundary of a polyhedral region. We choose the boundary representation to obtain the advantage of data compression. Algebraic consideration on polyhedral set operations with such boundary representation are studied in the fields such as computer-aided design [5] and mathematical morphology [6,7] to obtain the guarantee of correct results by operations; if polyhedral sets are algebraically closed, we can obtain such guarantee. In this paper, we have a similar algebraic consideration on our polyhedral sets and set operations for 3D and 4D digital image analysis.

---

* The current address of the first author is Laboratoire A2SI, ESIEE, Cité Descartes, B.P. 99, 93162 Noise-Le-Grand Cedex, France thanks to JSPS Postdoctoral Fellowships for Research Abroad from 2000.

M. Kerckhove (Ed.): Scale-Space 2001, LNCS 2106, pp. 417–425, 2001.

2   Primitives of Discrete Polyhedra

Let $\mathbf{Z}$ be a set of the integers. Then, $\mathbf{Z}^3$ is a set of points whose coordinates are all integers in the three-dimensional Euclidean space $\mathbf{R}^3$. Those points are called lattice points and $\mathbf{Z}^3$ a lattice space hereafter. In this paper, we define the set of all polyhedra in $\mathbf{Z}^3$ which we call discrete polyhedra such that their vertices are all lattice points and neighboring to each other in the sense of classical neighborhood systems such as 6-, 18- and 26-neighborhood in $\mathbf{Z}^3$ [3]. For any point $\boldsymbol{x} \in \mathbf{Z}^3$, they are defined such as

$$\mathbf{N}_m(\boldsymbol{x}) = \{\boldsymbol{y} \in \mathbf{Z}^3 \; : \; \|\boldsymbol{x} - \boldsymbol{y}\| \leq \sqrt{t}\}$$

where $t = 1, 2, 3$ for $m = 6, 18, 26$, respectively. This section is devoted to define the set of primitives of discrete polyhedra. We show that the finite number of primitives are obtained due to the above constraints of discrete polyhedra.

2.1   Construction for Primitives of Discrete Polyhedra

Let us consider a unit cubic region which contains eight lattice points including $\boldsymbol{x} = (i, j, k)$ such that

$$\mathbf{D}(\boldsymbol{x}) = \{(i + \epsilon_1, j + \epsilon_2, k + \epsilon_3) \in \mathbf{Z}^3 \; : \; \epsilon_l = 0 \text{ or } 1, \; l = 1, 2, 3\}.$$

First, let us consider that each point in $\mathbf{D}(\cdot)$ has either one or zero of its value and the point is called a 1- or 0-point, respectively. The number of possible arrangements of 1- and 0-points in $\mathbf{D}(\cdot)$ will be 23 as shown in Table 1 of the 26-neighborhood, if we omit the arrangements which differ from those by rotations for counting. For each of the 23 arrangements, a convex hull of all 1-points $\boldsymbol{x}_1$, $\boldsymbol{x}_2$, ..., and $\boldsymbol{x}_p$ is constructed in $\mathbf{D}(\cdot)$ such that

$$\mathbf{CH}(\{\boldsymbol{x}_1, \boldsymbol{x}_2, \dots, \boldsymbol{x}_p\}) = \{\boldsymbol{x} \in \mathbf{R}^3 \; : \; \boldsymbol{x} = \sum_{i=1}^{p} \lambda_i \boldsymbol{x}_i, \; \sum_{i=1}^{p} \lambda_i = 1, \; \lambda_i \geq 0\}.$$

The dimension of $\mathbf{CH}(\{\boldsymbol{x}_1, \boldsymbol{x}_2, \dots, \boldsymbol{x}_p\})$ depends on the number and arrangement of 1-points in $\mathbf{D}(\cdot)$. For instance, $\mathbf{CH}(\{\boldsymbol{x}_1, \boldsymbol{x}_2, \dots, \boldsymbol{x}_p\})$ becomes an 0-dimensional isolated points when $p = 1$, a 1-dimensional line segment when $p = 2$, and a 2-dimensional triangle when $p = 3$. When $p = 4$, $\mathbf{CH}(\{\boldsymbol{x}_1, \boldsymbol{x}_2, \dots, \boldsymbol{x}_4\})$ becomes a 2-dimensional rectangle if $\boldsymbol{x}_1$, $\boldsymbol{x}_2$, ..., $\boldsymbol{x}_4$ lie on a plane, and otherwise a 3-dimensional tetrahedron. When $p \geq 5$, $\mathbf{CH}(\{\boldsymbol{x}_1, \boldsymbol{x}_2, \dots, \boldsymbol{x}_p\})$ becomes a 3-dimensional polyhedron with p vertices. Note that any 1-point $\boldsymbol{x}_i$ for $i = 1, 2, \dots, p$ becomes the vertex of $\mathbf{CH}(\{\boldsymbol{x}_1, \boldsymbol{x}_2, \dots, \boldsymbol{x}_p\})$. We then classify every $\mathbf{CH}(\{\boldsymbol{x}_1, \boldsymbol{x}_2, \dots, \boldsymbol{x}_p\})$ into the m-neighborhood system for $m = 6, 18, 26$, if any pair of the adjacent vertices of $\mathbf{CH}(\{\boldsymbol{x}_1, \boldsymbol{x}_2, \dots, \boldsymbol{x}_p\})$ are m-neighboring to each other. Table 1 shows the classification results of all $\mathbf{CH}(\{\boldsymbol{x}_1, \boldsymbol{x}_2, \dots, \boldsymbol{x}_p\})$ with respect to both the dimensions and neighborhood systems.

In Table 1, we see that 3-dimensional primitives for the 26-neighborhood system are constructed whenever more than three 1-points do not lie on a plane, and that 2-dimensional primitives are constructed whenever more than two 1-points lie on a plane. In the case of the 18-neighborhood system, 3-dimensional

Table 1. All primitives of n-dimensional discrete polyhedra for the 6-, 18- and 26-neighborhood systems where $n = 0, 1, 2, 3$.

primitives are not constructed for the arrangements P4b, P4c, P4d and P5a because any pair of 1-points such that the Euclidean distance between them is $\sqrt{3}$ are not considered to be neighboring. In the case of the 6-neighborhood system, a 3-dimensional primitive is constructed only for the arrangement P8.

2.2   Formulations of Unit Discrete Polygons and Polyhedra

In this paper, we focus on the primitives of $n = 2, 3$. They are called unit discrete polygons and polyhedra for $n = 2, 3$, respectively.

Definition 1. *If the convex hull of p 1-points x_1, x_2, ..., x_p in $\mathbf{D}(\cdot)$ has two dimensions and any pair of adjacent vertices are m-neighboring to each other for $m = 6, 18, 26$, then the set of p 1-points is called an unit discrete polygon for m-neighborhood system and denoted by*

$$\mathbf{S}_m = \{x_1, x_2, \ldots, x_p\}.$$

Let $\mathcal{G}_m$ be the sets of all unit discrete polygons for each $m = 6, 18, 26$. We consequently obtain the following relations from Table 1:

$$\mathcal{G}_6 \subset \mathcal{G}_{18} \subset \mathcal{G}_{26}. \tag{1}$$

From Table 1, we also see that any unit discrete polyhedron is bounded by a set of unit discrete polygons for each $m = 6, 18, 26$ as any unit discrete polygon is surrounded by a set of one-dimensional primitives which are line segments. If such unit discrete polygons are called the faces of a unit discrete polyhedra, then the definition of unit discrete polyhedra is given as follows.

Definition 2. *If the convex hull of p 1-points $\boldsymbol{x}_1$, $\boldsymbol{x}_2$, ..., $\boldsymbol{x}_p$ in $\mathbf{D}(\cdot)$ has three dimensions and any pair of adjacent vertices are m-neighboring for $m = 6, 18, 26$, then a unit discrete polyhedron is defined by*

$$\mathbf{P}_m = \{\mathbf{S}_m^1, \mathbf{S}_m^2, \ldots, \mathbf{S}_m^q\} \tag{2}$$

where $\mathbf{S}_m^1$, $\mathbf{S}_m^2$, ..., $\mathbf{S}_m^q$ are unit discrete polygons which are the faces of $\mathbf{P}_m$.

We set each $\mathbf{S}_m^i = \{\boldsymbol{x}_1^i, \boldsymbol{x}_2^i, \ldots, \boldsymbol{x}_p^i\}$ for $i = 1, 2, \ldots, q$ to be oriented to the exterior of $\mathbf{P}_m$. Such orientation of $\mathbf{S}_m^i$ is represented by the order of points such that the order, $\boldsymbol{x}_1^i, \boldsymbol{x}_2^i, \ldots, \boldsymbol{x}_p^i$, is the counterclockwise if we see it from a viewpoint outside $\mathbf{P}_m$. Let $\mathcal{H}_m$ be the sets of all unit discrete polyhedra for each $m = 6, 18, 26$. Similarly to (1), we then obtain

$$\mathcal{H}_6 \subset \mathcal{H}_{18} \subset \mathcal{H}_{26}.$$

3   Set Operations

Our goal of this paper is to define the set of all polyhedra in $\mathbf{Z}^3$, which we call discrete polyhedra, and to represent any deformation of such discrete polyhedra by their boolean operations. Since a boolean operation is also used for the recursive definition of discrete polyhedra as shown in the next section, we first give the definition of boolean operations in this section.

Let $\mathcal{P}_m$ be the family of sets of oriented unit discrete polygons for m-neighborhood system where $m = 6, 18, 26$. We define set operations for $\mathcal{P}_m$ which will be a larger set than the set of discrete polyhedra. For any pair of finite sets $\mathbf{A}$ and $\mathbf{B}$ in $\mathcal{P}_m$, we define the addition operation using the notations of $\cup$ and $\setminus$ for the union and difference sets, such that

$$\mathbf{A} + \mathbf{B} = (\mathbf{A} \setminus \mathbf{X_A}(\mathbf{B})) \cup (\mathbf{B} \setminus \mathbf{X_B}(\mathbf{A})) \tag{3}$$

where

$$\mathbf{X_A}(\mathbf{B}) = \{\mathbf{S} \in \mathbf{A} \ : \ \mathbf{S} = \mathbf{T}^{-1} \text{ for any } \mathbf{T} \in \mathbf{B}\} \, ,$$
$$\mathbf{X_B}(\mathbf{A}) = \{\mathbf{T} \in \mathbf{B} \ : \ \mathbf{T} = \mathbf{S}^{-1} \text{ for any } \mathbf{S} \in \mathbf{A}\} \, .$$

The notation $\mathbf{S}^{-1}$ represents a unit discrete polygon whose orientation is opposite to that of $\mathbf{S}$, and the relation $\mathbf{S} = \mathbf{T}$ indicates that $\mathbf{S}$ is the equivalent oriented unit discrete polygon to $\mathbf{T}$.

If we set the empty set as the neutral element such that

$$\mathbf{A} + \emptyset = \emptyset + \mathbf{A} = \mathbf{A}$$

for any $\mathbf{A} \in \mathcal{P}_m$, then we obtain the inverse element $-\mathbf{A}$ such that

$$\mathbf{A} + (-\mathbf{A}) = (-\mathbf{A}) + \mathbf{A} = \emptyset$$

and thus $-\mathbf{A} = \{\mathbf{S}^{-1} \ : \ \mathbf{S} \in \mathbf{A}\}$. The orientation of every unit discrete polygon in $-\mathbf{A}$ is opposite to that in $\mathbf{A}$. Note that some elements in $\mathcal{P}_m$ have their unit discrete polygons whose orientations are mixed so that some of them are to the

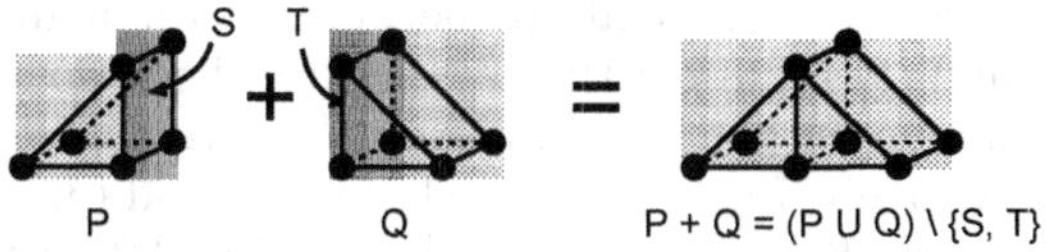

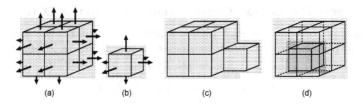

Fig. 1. An example of addition between two unit discrete polyhedra **P** and **Q** for the 26-neighborhood system.

exterior and the others are to the interior. From inverse elements, we define the subtraction of **B** from **A** such that

$$\mathbf{A} - \mathbf{B} = \mathbf{A} + (-\mathbf{B}) = (\mathbf{A} \setminus \mathbf{B}) \cup (-(\mathbf{B} \setminus \mathbf{A})) . \qquad (4)$$

Let us consider the addition of two unit discrete polyhedra **P** and **Q** in $\mathcal{P}_m$. Figure 1 illustrates an example of **P**+**Q** in the case of the 18- or 26-neighborhood system. After combining **P** and **Q** at their common faces of $\mathbf{S} \in \mathbf{X_P(Q)}$ and $\mathbf{T} \in \mathbf{X_Q(P)}$ such that $\mathbf{S} = \mathbf{T}^{-1}$, we exclude both **S** and **T** from the union of **P** and **Q** and obtain $\mathbf{P} + \mathbf{Q}$.

4   Discrete Polyhedra

4.1   Recursive Definition of Discrete Polyhedra

Similarly to the representation of unit discrete polyhedra given by (2), we have the boundary representation for discrete polyhedra which are given as sets of unit discrete polygons. By using the addition operation of (3), the set of discrete polyhedra for m-neighborhood system is defined from the finite set of unit discrete polyhedra for m-neighborhood system where $m = 6, 18, 26$. Assuming that each unit discrete polygon constructing a discrete polyhedron is oriented to the exterior such as (a) and (b) in Figure 2, we consider operations $\mathbf{A} + \mathbf{B}$ such as Figure 2 (c) and $\mathbf{A} - \mathbf{B}$ such as Figure 2 (d) but do not consider $\mathbf{A} - \mathbf{B}$ such as Figure 2 (c) and $\mathbf{A} + \mathbf{B}$ such as Figure 2 (d) for the construction of discrete polyhedra. To avoid such operation for constructing every discrete polyhedron, we use the function $\mathbf{W}(\mathbf{P}_m)$ for any addition of unit discrete polyhedra.

(a)   (b)   (c)   (d)

Fig. 2. If two sets of discrete polygons (a) **A** and (b) **B** in $\mathcal{P}_m$ are given, we consider the boolean operations $\mathbf{A} + \mathbf{B}$ such as (c) and $\mathbf{A} - \mathbf{B}$ such as (d) for construction of discrete polyhedra, but do not consider $\mathbf{A} - \mathbf{B}$ such as (c) and $\mathbf{A} + \mathbf{B}$ such as (d).

Table 2. Conceivable adjacent relations between two unit discrete polyhedra. Relations (a), (b) and (c) represent the adjacencies when two unit discrete polyhedra have the common vertex, edge and unit discrete polygons $\mathbf{S}$ and $\mathbf{T}$ such that $\mathbf{S} = \mathbf{T}^{-1}$, respectively. In the case of relation (d) and (e), two adjacent unit discrete polyhedra have the unit discrete polygons $\mathbf{S}$ and $\mathbf{T}$ at the joint, but $\mathbf{S}$ is not equivalent to $\mathbf{T}^{-1}$. All examples are for the 18- or 26-neighborhood system.

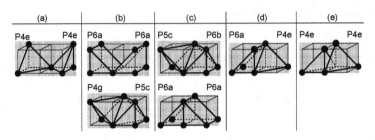

Definition 3. *Discrete polyhedra* $\mathbf{P}_m$ *are recursively constructed for each* $m = 6, 18, 26$ *as follows;*

1. *a unit discrete polyhedron becomes a discrete polyhedron* $\mathbf{P}_m$ *and we set*

$$\mathbf{W}(\mathbf{P}_m) = \{\mathbf{D}(\boldsymbol{x}) : \bigcup_{\mathbf{S} \in \mathbf{P}_m} \mathbf{S} \subseteq \mathbf{D}(\boldsymbol{x})\} ;$$

2. *if* $\mathbf{P}_m$ *and* $\mathbf{A}_m$ *are a discrete polyhedron and a unit discrete polyhedron respectively such that they satisfy the following conditions:*
   (a) $\mathbf{W}(\mathbf{P}_m) \cap \mathbf{W}(\mathbf{A}_m) = \emptyset$;
   (b) if there exist a pair of $\mathbf{S} \in \mathbf{P}_m$ *and* $\mathbf{T} \in \mathbf{A}_m$ *in* $\mathbf{D}(\boldsymbol{x}) \cap \mathbf{D}(\boldsymbol{y}) \neq \emptyset$ *where* $\mathbf{D}(\boldsymbol{x}) \in \mathbf{W}(\mathbf{P}_m)$ *and* $\mathbf{D}(\boldsymbol{y}) \in \mathbf{W}(\mathbf{A}_m)$, *then* $\mathbf{S} = \mathbf{T}^{-1}$,
   then $\mathbf{P}'_m = \mathbf{P}_m + \mathbf{A}_m$ *becomes a discrete polyhedron, and we set*

$$\mathbf{W}(\mathbf{P}'_m) = \mathbf{W}(\mathbf{P}_m) \cup \mathbf{W}(\mathbf{A}_m) .$$

If $\mathbf{A}_m$ is adjacent to $\mathbf{P}_m$, the addition of $\mathbf{A}_m$ to $\mathbf{P}_m$ is allowed only when their adjacent relation is one of (a), (b) and (c) in Table 2. It is not allowed when their adjacent relation is either (d) or (e) in Table 2. From Definition 3, we see that a discrete polyhedron $\mathbf{P}_m$ for $m = 6, 18, 26$ is constructed by combining unit discrete polyhedra $\mathbf{A}_m$s in all $\mathbf{D}(\boldsymbol{x}) \in \mathbf{W}(\mathbf{P}_m)$ one by one.

4.2   Discrete Polyhedron Construction from Volume Data

Let $\mathbf{V}$ be a set of volume data which is a finite subset of $\mathbf{Z}^3$. Setting all points in $\mathbf{V}$ to be 1-points, $\mathbf{Z}^3 \setminus \mathbf{V}$ becomes the set of all 0-points in $\mathbf{Z}^3$. Considering a discrete polyhedron $\mathbf{P}_m(\mathbf{V})$ constructed from any $\mathbf{V}$, we obtain

$$\mathbf{P}_m(\mathbf{V}) = \mathop{+}_{\mathbf{D}(\boldsymbol{x}) \in \mathbf{W}} \mathbf{P}_m(\mathbf{V} \cap \mathbf{D}(\boldsymbol{x})) \qquad (5)$$

where

$$\mathbf{W} = \{\mathbf{D}(\boldsymbol{x}) : \mathbf{D}(\boldsymbol{x}) \cap \mathbf{V} \neq \emptyset, \ \boldsymbol{x} \in \mathbf{Z}^3\} .$$

Each $\mathbf{P}_m(\mathbf{V} \cap \mathbf{D}(\boldsymbol{x}))$ is a 3-dimensional unit discrete polyhedron which is constructed with respect to 1-points of $\mathbf{V}$ in $\mathbf{D}(\boldsymbol{x}) \in \mathbf{W}$ by referring to Table 1.

Theorem 1. *For any given finite subset* $\mathbf{V}$ *of* $\mathbf{Z}^3$*, we can uniquely construct a discrete polyhedron* $\mathbf{P}_m(\mathbf{V})$ *for each* $m = 6, 18, 26$ *by* (5).

The proof is given in [8]. From theorem 1, we have the guarantee of the unique construction of $\mathbf{P}_m(\mathbf{V})$ for each $\mathbf{V}$ in a sequence. In other words, we obtain a unique sequence of $\mathbf{P}_m(\mathbf{V})$s corresponding to a sequence of $\mathbf{V}$s. This implies that the uniqueness of $\mathbf{P}_m(\mathbf{V})$ with respect to $\mathbf{V}$ is important for the polyhedral deformation description which is given in the next section.

5   Deformation of Polyhedral Objects

5.1   Deformation Description by Set Operations

Deformation of a discrete polyhedron $\mathbf{P}_m$ is mainly classified into two types of simple deformation. If $\mathbf{P}_m(t)$ and $\mathbf{P}_m(t + 1)$ are discrete polyhedra before and after deformation, respectively, then two types of deformation from $\mathbf{P}_m(t)$ to $\mathbf{P}_m(t+1)$ are described using the addition and subtraction operations such that

$$\mathbf{P}_m(t + 1) = \mathbf{P}_m(t) + \Delta \mathbf{P}_m , \tag{6}$$

$$\mathbf{P}_m(t + 1) = \mathbf{P}_m(t) - \Delta \mathbf{P}_m , \tag{7}$$

where $\Delta \mathbf{P}_m$ is a discrete polyhedron which is a difference between $\mathbf{P}_m(t)$ and $\mathbf{P}_m(t+1)$. Equations (6) and (7) are called expanding and shrinking, respectively.

5.2   Polyhedral Deformation from Sequential Volume Data

Any deformation of discrete polyhedra $\mathbf{P}(\mathbf{V}_t)$s constructed from a sequence of volume data $\mathbf{V}_t$s is described by a combination of expanding and shrinking operations (6) and (7). First, we consider two types of simple deformation of expanding and shrinking caused by adding a point $\boldsymbol{x}$ to $\mathbf{V}_t$ and removing $\boldsymbol{x}$ from $\mathbf{V}_t$, respectively.

By adding $\boldsymbol{x} \in \mathbf{Z}^3 \setminus \mathbf{V}_t$ to $\mathbf{V}_t$, $\mathbf{P}(\mathbf{V}_t)$ is expanded to $\mathbf{P}(\mathbf{V}_t \cup \{\boldsymbol{x}\})$ which is also uniquely determined by (5), such that

$$\mathbf{P}(\mathbf{V}_t \cup \{\boldsymbol{x}\}) = \mathbf{P}(\mathbf{V}_t) - \Delta \mathbf{P}_1 + \Delta \mathbf{P}_2 \tag{8}$$

where

$$\Delta \mathbf{P}_1 = \mathop{+}_{\mathbf{D}(\boldsymbol{y}) \in \mathbf{E}_{\boldsymbol{x}}} \mathbf{P}(\mathbf{V}_t \cap \mathbf{D}(\boldsymbol{y})) ,$$

$$\Delta \mathbf{P}_2 = \mathop{+}_{\mathbf{D}(\boldsymbol{y}) \in \mathbf{E}_{\boldsymbol{x}}} \mathbf{P}((\mathbf{V}_t \cup \{\boldsymbol{x}\}) \cap \mathbf{D}(\boldsymbol{y}))$$

for

$$\mathbf{E}_{\boldsymbol{x}} = \{\mathbf{D}(\boldsymbol{y}) \ : \ \boldsymbol{x} \in \mathbf{D}(\boldsymbol{y})\} .$$

Because the adding point $\boldsymbol{x}$ affects only the eight unit cubes in $\mathbf{E}_{\boldsymbol{x}}$, we only have to see the polyhedral change in $\mathbf{E}_{\boldsymbol{x}}$. In (8), we first subtract a unit discrete polyhedron $\Delta \mathbf{P}_1$ in $\mathbf{E}_{\boldsymbol{x}}$ from $\mathbf{P}(\mathbf{V}_t)$ and then add $\Delta \mathbf{P}_2$ as the replacement of

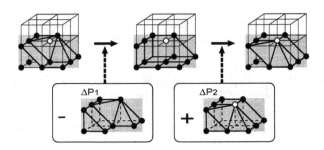

Fig. 3. An example of expanding $\mathbf{P}_{26}(\mathbf{V})$ by adding a white point in the figure.

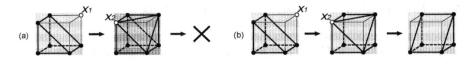

Fig. 4. Examples of expanding $\mathbf{P}_{18}(\mathbf{V})$ by adding a point x_1 and then subtracting a point x_2; (a) a deformation description based on (9) is not obtained at the subtraction stage and (b) a deformation description based on (8) is obtained at every stage.

$\Delta\mathbf{P}_1$. Figure 3 illustrates an example of expanding $\mathbf{P}_{26}(\mathbf{V}_t)$ by adding x to $\mathbf{V}_t$. The reason that we do not directly apply

$$\mathbf{P}(\mathbf{V}_t \cup \{x\}) = \mathbf{P}(\mathbf{V}_t) + \Delta\mathbf{P} \tag{9}$$

by setting

$$\Delta\mathbf{P} = \Delta\mathbf{P}_2 - \Delta\mathbf{P}_1$$

is because such operation collapses the unique decomposition of discrete polyhedra and may cause a problem of deformation description as shown in Figure 4. Figure 4 illustrates two different descriptions for polyhedral deformation such as (a) and (b) which correspond to (9) and (8) respectively. The changes of volume data are adding a point x_1 and then subtracting a point x_2 in this case. The figure shows that the description based on (9) may not give a convenient polyhedral decomposition in a sequence of changing volume data and may not enable us to obtain an expected discrete polyhedron at some stage of deformation. To avoid such problems, we need to consider decomposition of discrete polyhedra based on unit cubic regions $\mathbf{E}_x$ such as (8).

Similarly, an operation for shrinking $\mathbf{P}(\mathbf{V}_t)$ to $\mathbf{P}(\mathbf{V}_t \setminus \{x\})$ by removing x from $\mathbf{V}_t$ described by

$$\mathbf{P}(\mathbf{V}_t \setminus \{x\}) = \mathbf{P}(\mathbf{V}_t) - \Delta\mathbf{P}_1 + \Delta\mathbf{P}_3 \tag{10}$$

where

$$\Delta\mathbf{P}_3 = \underset{\mathbf{D}(y)\in\mathbf{E}_x}{+} \mathbf{P}((\mathbf{V}_t \setminus \{x\})\cap\mathbf{D}(y)) .$$

Given a sequence of volume data $\mathbf{V}_1, \mathbf{V}_2, \ldots$, we set $\Delta\mathbf{V}$ to be the difference between $\mathbf{V}_t$ and $\mathbf{V}_{t+1}$. If each of (8) or (10) is manipulated for every point in

$\Delta \mathbf{V}$, consequently we obtain $\mathbf{P}(\mathbf{V}_{t+1})$ from $\mathbf{P}(\mathbf{V}_t)$. Since deformation description based on (8) and (10) guarantees the unique polyhedral representation for each step of deformation from $\mathbf{P}(\mathbf{V}_t)$ to $\mathbf{P}(\mathbf{V}_{t+1})$, the result of $\mathbf{P}(\mathbf{V}_{t+1})$ does not depends on the order of choosing points from $\Delta \mathbf{V}$.

6   Conclusions

In this paper, we studied the algebraic framework for 3-dimensional polyhedral deformation in $\mathbf{Z}^3$. First, we showed that there exist the finite number of primitives of discrete polyhedra, which we call unit discrete polyhedra, in $\mathbf{Z}^3$. We also gave two set operations, addition and subtraction, for the family of sets of unit discrete polygons. By using the unit discrete polyhedra and the addition operations, we then presented the recursive definition of discrete polyhedra and also showed that such discrete polyhedron is uniquely obtained from a set of volume data. Finally, we represented deformation of discrete polyhedra by using the above two set operations, which we call expanding and shrinking of discrete polyhedra, and also showed that a sequence of discrete polyhedra can be uniquely obtained by a sequence of volume data.

References

1. Caselles, V., Kimmel, R., Sapiro, G. (1997): Geodesic active contours. International Journal of Computer Vision **22** **1** 61–79
2. Reinhardt, J. M., Wang, A. J., Weldon, T. P., Higgins, W. E. (2000): Cube-based segmentation of 4D cardiac image sequences. Computer Vision and Image Understanding **77** 251–262
3. Kong, T. Y., Rosenfeld, A. (1989): Digital topology: introduction and survey. Computer Vision, Graphics, and Image Processing **48** 357–393
4. Kenmochi, Y., Imiya, A. (2001): Extraction of topological features from sequential volume data. To appear in Proceedings of 4th International Workshop on Visual Form
5. Requicha, A. A. G. (1985): Boolean operations in solid modeling: boundary evaluation and merging algorithms. Proceedings of IEEE **73** **1** 30–44
6. Ghosh, P. K. (1991): An algebra of polygons through the notion of negative shapes. CVGIP: Image Understanding **54** **1** 119–144
7. Sugihara, K., Imai, T., Hataguchi, T. (1997): A proposal of an inversible Minkowski sum of figures (in Japanese). IEICE Transactions **J80-DII** **10** 2663–2670
8. Kenmochi, Y. (1998): Discrete combinatorial polyhedra: theory and application. PhD thesis, Chiba University

Inverse Quantization of Digital Binary Images for Resolution Conversion

Atsushi Imiya[1], Akihiko Ito[1], and Yukiko Kenmochi[2]

[1] Institute of Media and Information Technology, Chiba University, Japan
[2] School of Information Science, JAIST, Japan

Abstract. In this paper, we propose an inverse quantization method for planar binary images. The expansion and superresolution of digital binary images involve the same mathematical properties because, for the achievement of these processes, we are required to estimate the original boundary from digitized images which are expressed as a collection of pixels. We first estimate an area through which the original boundary curve should pass through. This area is an orthogonal polygon torus whose two boundary curves are orthogonal polygons. Second, applying curvature flow operation to an orthogonal polygon in this area, we estimate a smooth boundary.

1 Introduction

In this paper, we propose an inverse quantization method for planar binary digital images. If a shape is sampled and expressed as a digital shape, it is impossible to reconstruct high resolution boundary. Therefore, for the reconstruction of a shape in high resolution from digital shapes, we are required to solve an inverse problem which estimates the original boundary. The inverse quantization of digital terrain data for the recovery of a smooth terrain surface and series of isolevel counters on it are solved using variational problems. This is a surface reconstruction method common in computer vision and areal data processing[1, 2, 4]. The expansion and super-resolution of digital binary images are the same problem because, for the achievement of these process, we are required to construct a smooth boundary curve as an estimation of the original boundary from digitized images, which are expressed as a collection of pixels.

Spline curves and surfaces are used for the boundary expression of objects on a plane and in a space, respectively. Spline curves and surfaces are described as the solution of a variational problem for the fitting of smooth functions to a sequence of samples along a curve and an array of sample points on a surface. Therefore, splines are utilized for the estimation of the smooth boundary from a collection of samples [3–6]. The families of splines are attended by several authors in computer vision community for curve fitting [8], corner detection [9], shape recovery [2], and detection of discontinuities along the boundary [7]. The spline curves are also deeply attended in meteorology for the description of isolevel curves on the weather chart [4, 5]. Furthermore, a family of splines is recently

M. Kerckhove (Ed.): Scale-Space 2001, LNCS 2106, pp. 426–434, 2001.

studied in the context of wavelet theoretically and shape description practically for the application of shape expression for the data transmission through internet [10,11]. These applications partially go back to the application of splines in the computer vision for the data compression of boundary information.

We separate the process of the inverse quantization of digital shapes into two steps. Using morphological operation and curvature flow, we construct an algorithm for the estimation of a smooth boundary curve form an orthogonal polygon which is the boundary of a connected pixels. We first estimate an region in which the original boundary curve should pass through. This region is an orthogonal polygon torus whose two boundary curves are orthogonal polygons. Second, applying deformation operation based on the curvatures of points on a curve to an orthogonal polygon in this region, we estimate a smooth boundary for the original binary shape. For the deformation of digital polygonal curves, we define both local and global curvatures of polygonal curves. For the description of smooth boundary in each step of deformation we adopt B-splines. Once a smooth boundary is estimated, applying sampling again to the estimated shape, we can generate digital images in any resolutions. Therefore, as an application of our algorithm, we convert the resolution for binary images. Numerical examples show the performance of the proposed method.

2   Boundary Estimation

Setting x-y to be an orthogonal coordinate system on the Euclidean plane $\boldsymbol{R}^2$, we write a vector on $\boldsymbol{R}^2$ as $\boldsymbol{a} = (\alpha, \beta)^\top$, where $\boldsymbol{x}^\top$ is the transpose of vector $\boldsymbol{x}$. Points for which both coordinates are integers are called lattice points on $\boldsymbol{R}^2$ and the set of all lattice points is denoted by $\boldsymbol{Z}^2$. The 4- and 8- connected neighborhoods of the origin are expressed as $\boldsymbol{N}_4$ and $\boldsymbol{N}_8$, respectively. If point $\boldsymbol{x}$ is in the 4-and 8- connected region of point $\boldsymbol{y}$, a pair of points $\boldsymbol{x}$ and $\boldsymbol{y}$ are 4- and 8-connected, respectively.

Pixel $\mathbf{U}_{mn}$ is the unit square centered at $(m, n)^\top$. Setting $f(x, y)$ to be the gray value of a binary image defined on $\boldsymbol{R}^2$, let f_{mn} be the average of binary image $f(x, y)$ in $\mathbf{U}_{mn}$. For collection of vectors $\boldsymbol{F} = \{(m, n)^\top \mid f_{mn} = 1\}$, we define three sets,

$$\boldsymbol{A} = \{(x, y)^\top \mid f(x, y) = 1\}, \quad \boldsymbol{D} = \bigcup_{(m,n)^\top \in \boldsymbol{F}} \mathbf{U}_{mn}, \quad \boldsymbol{B} = \bigcup_{(m,n)^\top \in \Delta\boldsymbol{F}} \mathbf{U}_{mn} \quad (1)$$

for $\Delta\boldsymbol{F} = \{(\boldsymbol{F} \oplus \boldsymbol{N}_8) \setminus \boldsymbol{F}\} \bigcup \{\boldsymbol{F} \setminus (\boldsymbol{F} \ominus \boldsymbol{N}_8)\}$, where $\oplus$ and $\ominus$ are the Minkowski addition and subtraction, respectively, of two sets in a vector space. We assume that the boundary $\partial\boldsymbol{A}$ of the region $\boldsymbol{A}$ is a continuous smooth simple curve. Since we assume 4-connected boundary, the original boundary curve $\partial\boldsymbol{A}$ of an image is contained in the region $\boldsymbol{B}$, which is an orthogonal polygon curve of finite width.

Our problem is the reconstruction of boundary $\partial\boldsymbol{A}$ from a binary digital image $\boldsymbol{D}$. We adopt set $\boldsymbol{B}$ as the first estimation of the original boundary $\partial\boldsymbol{A}$.

Furthermore, as the second approximation of ∂A, we adopt the boundary of D. The boundary of set D is an orthogonal polygon curve $d(s)$ which lies in the finite closed set B. We assume that a set of point $\{p_\alpha\}_{\alpha=1}^n$ on curve $d(s)$ is ordered in the counterclockwise direction and points $p_{i\pm 1}$ and p_i are four connected

For the third approximation of ∂A, we construct a B-spline curve $p(s)$ of the order three, using ordered points $\{p_\alpha\}_{\alpha=1}^n$ along polygonal curve $d(s)$. This curve $p(s)$ passes through the area encircled by polygon torus P, which is the union of the convex hulls defined by four successive points p_i, p_{i+1}, p_{i+2}, and p_{i+4}, on ∂D, where $p_i = p_{n+i}$ for $i = 1, 2, \cdots, n$ [12]. This polygonal region P is contained in region B. Therefore, an estimation curve $p(s)$ might be closer to the original curve than orthogonal polygon curve $d(s)$.

The vertex angles of an orthogonal polygon are $\pi/2$ and $3\pi/2$ and the distance between each pair of control points is one. These configurations of points on a curve yield small smooth vibrations on the B-spline curve whose control points lie on an orthogonal polygon. If we deform polygonal boundary curve P using discrete curvature flow,

$$p_\alpha(t+1) - p_\alpha(t) = F(\theta_\alpha), \tag{2}$$

where θ_α is the discrete curvature of point p_α for the t-th iteration on a polygonal curve and $F(x)$ is a function, we can write a minimization criterion as

$$E(p(s), p_\alpha(t)) = \sum_{\alpha=1}^n |p(s_\alpha) - p_\alpha(t)|^2 + \lambda \int_0^S \left| \frac{d^2 p(s)}{ds^2} \right|^2_{s=t} dt. \tag{3}$$

3   Deformation of Polygonal Boundary Curve

The geometric configuration of sets P and B implies that, if we can generate a series of polygonal regions $P(t)$ such that

- $P(t+1) \subset P(t)$ for $t = 0, 1, 2, \cdots$, and $P(0) = P$;
- $\lim_{t\to\infty} |P(t)| = 0$, where $|P(t)|$ is the areal measure of polygonal set $P(t)$,

using the curvature of each point on a polygonal curve, we define an operation which approximately generates this sequence of polygonal curves.

From the vertices of polygonal curve $\{p_i\}_{\alpha=1}^n$, we define the vectors and their average

$$u_i^k(t) = \frac{1}{2k}\{(p_{i-k}(t) - p_i(t)) + (p_{i+k}(t) - p_i(t))\}, \quad v_i^n(t) = \frac{1}{n}\sum_{k=1}^n u_i^k(t), \tag{4}$$

for $k = 1, 2, \cdots, n$. Vector v_i^k expresses global configurations of points for $k \geq 1$, since vector v_i^k is defined from $(2k+1)$ successive points $\{p_\alpha\}_{\alpha=i-k}^{i+k}$ for point p_i.

The angle between vectors $(\boldsymbol{p}_{i-k} - \boldsymbol{p}_i)$ and $(\boldsymbol{p}_{i+k} - \boldsymbol{p}_i)$, and the average of these angles, for $k = 1, 2, \cdots, n$, are defined as

$$\theta_i^k = \cos^{-1}\left\{ \frac{(\boldsymbol{p}_{i-k} - \boldsymbol{p}_i)^\top (\boldsymbol{p}_{i+k} - \boldsymbol{p}_i)}{|\boldsymbol{p}_{i-k} - \boldsymbol{p}_i| \cdot |\boldsymbol{p}_{i+k} - \boldsymbol{p}_i|} \right\}, \quad \phi_i^n = \frac{1}{n}\sum_{k=1}^{n} \theta_i^k. \tag{5}$$

The angle θ_i^k expresses the local turn of a planar polygonal curve for $k = 1$. We call θ_i^k the vertex angle of the order k. The average of vertex angles describes global turns of a planar polygonal curve. We call ϕ_i^n the average vertex-angle of the order n. If the average vertex-angle ϕ_i^n is larger than a threshold τ, the polygonal boundary curve is not locally smooth. Conversely, if the average turn angle ϕ_i^n is smaller than a threshold τ, the polygonal boundary curve is locally smooth.

If a curve is not locally smooth at a point, we deform a vertex inward. Furthermore, if a curve is smooth globally, we deform vertex to enhance the global shape in a finite region. Based on these rules, we can describe the equation for the deformation of polygon as

$$\boldsymbol{p}_i(t+1) - \boldsymbol{p}_i(t) = \begin{cases} \alpha(t)\boldsymbol{u}_i^1(t), & \text{if } \phi_i^n > \tau, \\ \alpha(t)\boldsymbol{u}_i^1(t) - \beta(t)\boldsymbol{v}_i^n(t), & \text{otherwise.} \end{cases} \tag{6}$$

for a pair of monotonically decreasing positive functions $\alpha(t)$ and $\beta(t)$ such that $\lim_{t\to\infty} \alpha(t) = 0$ and $\lim_{t\to\infty} \beta(t) = 0$. These requirements for the coefficients of the recursive form might preserve the condition $\boldsymbol{p}_i(t+1) = \boldsymbol{p}_i(t)$ for large t. If this equality is satisfied, points on $\boldsymbol{P}(t)$ remain in a finite region along a finite polygonal curve.

For point $\overline{\boldsymbol{p}}_i$, which is defined as $\overline{\boldsymbol{p}}_i = \lim_{t\to\infty} \boldsymbol{p}_i(t)$, setting $\overline{\boldsymbol{P}} = \{\boldsymbol{p}_i\}_{i=1}^n$, the boundary $\partial \boldsymbol{A}$ of the support of the binary function $f(x, y)$ is estimated as the B-spline curve whose control points are elements of $\overline{\boldsymbol{P}}$. Here, we set $n = 3$, since the configuration of seven successive points determines the local shape of a curve expressed by B-spline polynomials of the order three.

One of the advantages of B-spline polynomials for the expression of curves is that B-spline polynomials approximate the original curve using few control points. Therefore, we derive an algorithm for the reduction of the number of control points $\{\overline{\boldsymbol{p}}_i\}_{i=1}^n$ to $\boldsymbol{P}_o = \{\boldsymbol{p}_j^o\}_{j\in I}$, where I is a subset of integers from 1 to n. Setting $\overline{\phi}_i^n$ to be the average vertex angle of polygonal curve $\overline{\boldsymbol{P}}$, for the generation of $\boldsymbol{P}_o$ from $\boldsymbol{P}$, we adopt point $\overline{\boldsymbol{p}}_i$ which satisfies one of the following conditions.

- The average vertex angle ϕ_i^n is larger than a predetermined threshold ϕ.
- If $\overline{\boldsymbol{p}}_i$ is an element of point set $\boldsymbol{P}_o$, then point $\boldsymbol{p}_{i+3}$ is an element and points $\boldsymbol{p}_{i+1}$ and $\boldsymbol{p}_{i+2}$ are not.

We set $n = 3$ for the computation of the average vertex angle, since we use B-spline polynomials of the order three.

4   Generation of High Resolution Images

The generation of a high-resolution image of $f(x, y)$ is mathematically achieved first by computing a binary set, applying sampling scheme to an expanded set of the support of $f(x, y)$, and second by reducing the length of the edges of pixels. Here, we define the resolution using the length of the pixels. For a set of point $\boldsymbol{F}$, denoting $\lambda \boldsymbol{F} = \{\lambda \boldsymbol{x} \mid \boldsymbol{x} \in \boldsymbol{F}, \lambda > 0\}$, this process is mathematically described as the computation of $\frac{1}{m} \boldsymbol{F}_m$, where $\boldsymbol{F}_m$ is a binary set computed from the binary image $f(mx, my)$. We derive an algorithm for the generation of high-generation digital images of $f(x, y)$ from set $\boldsymbol{F}$ which is obtained using the sample scheme with ordinary pixels.

The generation of a high-resolution digital image of $f(x, y)$ from set $\boldsymbol{F}$ is mainly achieved by estimating $m \partial \boldsymbol{A}$ from $\boldsymbol{F}$, since the boundary of $m \boldsymbol{F}$ is an orthogonal polygon. If an expanded set $m \partial \boldsymbol{A}$ is estimated, we can construct an approximation of set $m \boldsymbol{A}$ from set $m \partial \boldsymbol{A}$. Furthermore, set $m \partial \boldsymbol{A}$ enables us to generate an approximation of high-resolution images of $f(x, y)$ for an arbitrary resolution.

In the previous section, we proposed an algorithm for the estimation of boundary curve $\partial \boldsymbol{A}$ from digital set $\boldsymbol{F}$. Therefore, using the estimation $\overline{\boldsymbol{P}}$, we generate set $\frac{1}{m} \boldsymbol{F}_m$ according to the following steps.

1. Compute $\boldsymbol{P}$ from $\boldsymbol{F}$.
2. Compute the B-spline curve from $m \boldsymbol{P}$, and adopt its closure as the estimator of $m \partial \boldsymbol{A}$.
3. Apply the sampling scheme to the closure of the curve using unit pixels.
4. Reduce the size of pixels uniformly.

5   Numerical Examples

In figures 1, 2 and 3, we show examples for the generation of high-resolution images, from digital binary images using the algorithm derived in the previous sections. In each figure (a) shows the binary image obtained from (b) using the sampling scheme described in section 3. Figures (c) and (d) show the estimated boundary curve and the original boundary curve, respectively. In figure (e), the region in which the original boundary exists is shown. Points marked by label + in figure (f) express lattice points on the boundary of the support of the shape shown in figure (a). Points marked by + in figure (g) express the configurations of control points after deformation of the polygonal curve shown in (g). The curve in figure (h) is the estimated boundary curve after the reduction of control points. Points marked by + in figure (i) represent control points for the expanded images. These figures show that our algorithm accurately generates a high-resolution image from a given digital image.

Here, we set parameters $\tau = \pi/3$, $\phi = \pi/18$, and $T = 100$, where T is the maximum number of iterations for the flow computation. Furthermore, we set

	α	β	n_0	n_e
Figure 1	2	2	187	41
Figure 2	100/7	100/7	396	101
Figure 3	2/5	2/5	332	198

for $\alpha(t) = \alpha t^{-2}$ and $\beta(t) = \beta t^{-2}$, and n_0 and n_e are the numbers of initial control points and the reduced control points. In these examples, we could reduce the number of sample points.

6 Conclusions

In this paper, using a morphological operation and curvature flow, we constructed an algorithm for the estimation of a smooth boundary curve of the original image from an orthogonal polygon which is the boundary of connected pixels from a given digital images. Our algorithm first estimates an area through which the original boundary curve should pass. Second, applying the curvature flow operation to an isopolygon, our algorithm estimates a smooth boundary for the original binary shape. Using this estimation of the boundary curve, we can generate binary digital images for any resolution. Numerical examples conformed the performance of the proposed method.

References

1. Isomichi, Y.: Inverse-quantization method for digital signals and images: Point-approximation type, Trans. IECE, **63A**, 815-821, 1980.
2. Terzopoulos, D.: The computation of visible surface representations, IEEE, Trans, PAMI, **10**, 417-438, 1988.
3. Lu, F., and Milios, E.E.: Optimal spline fitting to plane shape, Signal Processing, **37** 129-140, 1994.
4. Wahba, G.: Surface fitting with scattered noisy data on Euclidean D-space and on the sphere, Rocky Mountain Journal of Mathematics, **14**, 281-299, 1984.
5. Wahba, G., and Johnson, D.R.: Partial spline models for the inclusion of tropopause and frontal boundary information in otherwise smooth two- and three- dimensional objective analysis, J. Atmospheric and oceanic technology, **3**, 714-725, 1986.
6. Chen, M.H., and Chin, R.T.: Partial smoothing spline for noisy boundary with corners, IEEE Trans. PAMI, **15**, 1208-1216, 1993.
7. Langridge, D. J.: Curve encoding and the detection of discontinuities, Computer Graphics and Image Processing, **20**, 58-71, 1982.
8. Paglieroni, D., and Jain, A.K.: Control point transformation for shape representation and measurement Computer Graphics and Image Processing, **42**, 87-111, 1988.
9. Medioni, G., and Yasumoto, Y.: Corner detection and curve representation using cubic B-spline, Computer Graphics and Image Processing, **39**, 267-278, 1987.
10. I. Daubechies, I., Guskov, I., and Sweldens, W.: Regularity of irregular subdivision, Constructive Approximation, **15**, 381-426, 1999.
11. Daubechies, I., Guskov, I., Schröder, P, and Sweldens, W.: Wavelets on irregular point sets, Phil. Trans. R. Soc. Lond. A, To be published.
12. Boehm, W. and Prautzsch, H.: *Numerical Methods*, Vieweg, Braunschweig, 1993.

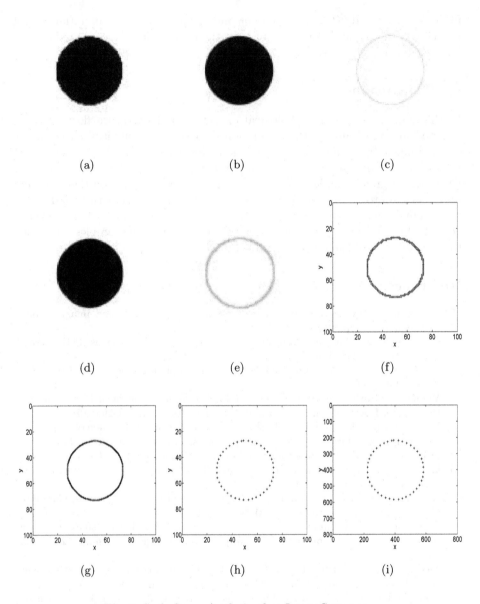

Fig. 1. Scale Space Analysis of an Image Sequence.

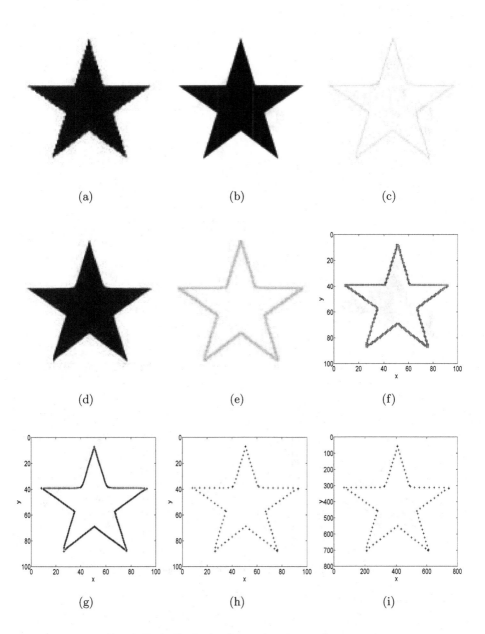

Fig. 2. Scale Space Analysis of an Image Sequence.

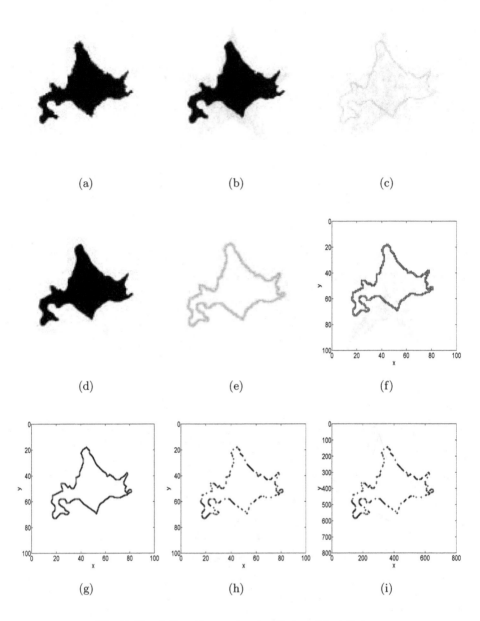

Fig. 3. Resolution Conversion for Geographical Data.

Author Index

Lecture Notes in Computer Science

For information about Vols. 1–2015
please contact your bookseller or Springer-Verlag